D1203367

Quest
for
Piety
and
Obedience

MINUTES

—OF THE—

General Council of the Brethren in Christ !

MET IN THE BRETHRENS' MEETING HOUSE, RINGGOLD, WASHINGTON CO., MD.,
MAY 18TH, 1881, AND ORGANIZED BY ELECTING MODERATORS AND
SECRETARIES.

ARTICLE 1ST. Will the Brethren allow members to attend boarding or high schools ?
ANSWER. By permission of the Church in District.

ARTICLE 2nd. Missionary report given and approved.

ARTICLE 3rd. What is the Standing Committee's authority or duty when called upon ?
ANSWER. Refered to Article 6th, Minutes of 1878.

ARTICLE 4th. On what points of the Gospel shall the Ministering Brethren be examined before the laying on of hands ?
ANSWER. Refered to Article 13th, Minutes of 1878.

ARTICLE 5th. Resolution of 1880 concerning a Periodical discussed.
ANSWER. Defered to some future Council.

ARTICLE 6th. How does the Church stand in regard to the publication of a Periodical ?
ANSWER. Fourteen Districts against, Nine in favor, Michigan, Southern Illinois and State of Kansas not reported.

ARTICLE 7th. How does the Church view the partaking of Intoxicating or Fermented Liquors as a beverage ?
ANSWER. That it is the sentiment of this Conference Meeting that the use of intoxicating or spirituous Liquors is a dangerous evil, sustained apparently by large monied interests, and we urge our people to abstain in every way from its use as a beverage, and earnestly urge our Brethren to use their influence against its use in every way consistent with the Word of God.

ARTICLE 8th. Is it not the duty of the Brethren and Sisters in the several districts to encourage and bear the expenses of holding protracted meetings ?
ANSWER. It is their duty.

ARTICLE 9th. Is it consistent with the Word of God to ask a Brother to make a public confession ?
ANSWER. The Brethren have always considered it so, and do yet.

ARTICLE 10th. Have the Brethren a right to engage in the board of trade ?
ANSWER. They have not.

ARTICLE 11th. *Resolved*—That the General Council consider whether it would not be expedient and for the general good of the Church, that the Council select and appoint Brethren to make a general visit throughout the Brotherhood, for the purpose of unity and oneness in the Church ?
ANSWER. General Council has appointed the following Brethren : Bro. Samuel Zook and Bro. Jesse Engle for the State of Kansas ; Bro. Henry Davidson, Bro. Levi Lukenbach and Bro. Joseph Hearshey, for the Western and Middle States ; Bro. Samuel Bucks, Henry Engle, and Jacob Hostetter, Sr. for the Eastern, Northern and Southern States ; Bro. Peter Rodes, Bro. Abraham Wenger, and Samuel Snyder for Ontario, Canada.

ARTICLE 12th. Bro. Jacob M. Engle was re-elected member of the Standing Committee for five years.

ARTICLE 13th. *Resolved*—That the Delegates from the several districts shall not leave until affairs are finally concluded.

ARTICLE 14th. Shall the three Brethren elected at the Council of 1880 to attend to the excursion arrangements with R. R. Co's. be continued?
ANSWER. Decided by rising vote they shall.

ARTICLE 15th. *Resolved*—That the decisions of the different Councils since 1871 be revised and printed, and Bro. Henry Davidson be appointed to carry out above resolution.

ARTICLE 16th. *Resolved*—That the next Annual Council will be held at Brubaker's Meeting House, Lancaster Co., Pa., commencing on the 3rd Wednesday of May, 1882. Nearest R. R. Stations—Mt. Joy on Penna. R. R. and Manheim on the Reading and Columbia R. R.

Blair, Steam Pr., Waynesboro, Pa.

This 1881 document is the first complete minute record of a General Council (Conference). Partial minutes for the period from 1871 to 1880 survive in four successive cumulative compilations of actions of Conference which the respective compiling committees chose to include with their work.

Quest
for
Piety
and
Obedience

The Story of the Brethren in Christ

Carlton O. Wittlinger

EVANGEL PRESS, NAPPANEE, INDIANA
1978

To my wife

Fay

whose understanding, encouragement

and research assistance

did so much to make

this book possible

Contents

Preface

My objective in this book is to tell the story of the Brethren in Christ without praise or blame. I know, of course, that complete objectivity is a will-of-the-wisp; no scholarly work proceeds without either explicit or implicit assumptions about its subject matter. On the other hand, reputable scholarship bears the obligation to strive for the truth and to delineate it from error and propaganda.

Two related points need to be made. First, my approach to the subject is that of an "insider." I grew up within the Brethren in Christ Church, served on various of its boards and committees, and soon will have taught for forty years in its educational institutions. This background inevitably gives me a perspective different from that of an observer looking at the group from the outside.

In the second place, I am by profession an historian. The historical methodology limits its practitioner to the use of historical records to establish facts and, insofar as possible, their interrelationships. Since the basic presuppositions of the Brethren in Christ assume transcendent realities beyond the reach of historical method, I cannot as an historian either affirm or deny these presuppositions but only describe them.

An explanation of word usage in the book title may be helpful. By "Piety" I refer to the definition of Christianity as a personal, heartfelt relationship with God through Jesus Christ. So defined, Christianity stresses primarily the experiential, subjective aspect of the Christian faith, an emphasis historically identified with the movement known as Pietism.

By "Obedience" I refer to the definition of Christianity as the outward expression through faithful discipleship of the inner experience of regeneration. So defined, Christianity stresses primarily the objective, ethical aspect of the Christian faith, an emphasis historically identified with the movement known as Anabaptism.

The founders of the Brethren in Christ believed that these two understandings of the primary meaning of Christianity could be synthesized. This book is the story of their successes and failures in quest of that synthesis.

Many people have helped to make the book possible. Dr. Cornelius Dyck and Dr. John C. Wenger of the Associated Mennonite Biblical Seminaries assisted me with Mennonite aspects of the work. Dr. Donald F. Durnbaugh of Bethany Theological Seminary gave similar assistance with the history of the Church of the Brethren (Dunkers). Mr. Edward Phelps of the University of Western Ontario helped me to establish the location of certain Brethren families settled in Ontario by 1880. Mr. William Meikle, a distinguished linguist, translated the major German documents cited, and verified the translation of German quotations. Mrs. Harriet Bicksler prepared the index.

The following read and criticized the preliminary manuscript: Bishop Ernest J. Swalm, Miss Miriam Bowers, Mr. Clarence W. Boyer, and Miss Dorothy Sherk. A dozen other Brethren in Christ church leaders read sections about which they had firsthand knowledge. Two faculty colleagues, Dr. E. Morris Sider and Dr. Norman A. Bert, reviewed the final draft. I am also indebted to those who previously researched in Brethren in Christ history, and especially to Dr. Owen H. Alderfer, Dr. Asa W. Climenhaga, Dr. H. Royce Saltzman, Dr. Martin H. Schrag, and Dr. E. Morris Sider.

Two other persons deserve special recognition. My wife, Fay, gave hundreds of hours in research assistance. My secretary, Miss Jane Wolverton, did specialized research, protected me from many compositional and substantive pitfalls, typed the final manuscript, and verified the citations.

Special thanks are due to Messiah College for a semester of sabbatical leave to begin the project and to the Brethren in Christ Publication Board for subsidizing some research and writing time. I also wish to thank the correspondents, interviewees, secretaries, Messiah College librarians, several members of the Old Order River Brethren and United Zion Churches, and all others who have been helpful.

None of those who contributed to the preparation of the book are responsible for any of its shortcomings. That responsibility is mine alone.

Carlton O. Wittlinger
Messiah College

Part One

The
First One Hundred Years

1780 — 1880

Theological Roots
Of the Brethren in Christ

The Brethren in Christ originated about 1780 along the Susquehanna River near the present town of Bainbridge in Lancaster County, Pennsylvania. At first known simply as "Brethren," the founders were rural people from the surrounding Pennsylvania-German community.* They gathered together in an environment of religious diversity and tolerance fostered by the policies of William Penn. At a time when religious freedom was rare in Europe and when established churches dominated most English colonies in America, Penn launched his "Holy Experiment" upon the principle of broad religious freedom. The "Great Law," enacted in 1682 by the first assembly of Pennsylvania freeholders, assured liberty of conscience to all who confessed and acknowledged one Almighty God.[1]

Although this act required religious tests for voting and office holding, most Europeans who settled in Lancaster County found few obstacles to the practice and proclamation of their respective faiths. Here English Quakers and Anglicans, Scotch-Irish Presbyterians, and various German groups including Lutherans, Reformed, Mennonites, and Dunkers lived and worshipped side by side.[2] In the late eighteenth century, a pietistic

*As indicated, the original name of the society was "Brethren." This term has always been used in the interpersonal relationships of members, and it occurs in later group names such as "River Brethren" and "Brethren in Christ." This study will refer freely to both the founders and their descendants as "Brethren," unless the context or some other reason requires the use of a later group name.

religious awakening created several new societies including the United Brethren in Christ, the Evangelical Association, and the Brethren in Christ. All three of these groups ministered to German-speaking peoples. The first two resembled the Methodists in spirit and organization and might have merged with them had it not been for the German language barrier.

The more formal Lancaster County churches—Anglican, Presbyterian, Lutheran, and Reformed—made little impact upon the early Brethren movement; their liturgies, polities, concepts of the church, and life-styles contrasted sharply with Brethren thought and practice. Nor is there evidence of direct Quaker influence, although common beliefs such as nonviolence, nonswearing of oaths, and conservative dress might suggest the possibility of such influence.[3] On the other hand Mennonites, Dunkers, and the emerging United Brethren in Christ influenced the Brethren and helped to form their theological roots which sprang principally from historic Christianity, Anabaptism, and Pietism.[4]

Historic Christianity

The early Brethren stood in the stream of historic Christianity mediated through the Protestant Reformation. Although they made no formal use of the pre-Reformation creeds of the church, they were in accord with much of the creedal substance. They had no reservations about doctrines such as the Trinity, the deity and humanity of Christ, the Atonement, and rewards and punishment in an afterlife. At the same time, they were children of the Reformation in its sharp break with the Catholic sacramental system. They would have agreed with Zwingli and Luther that salvation was by faith in Christ alone, that it required no priestly mediation, and that Scripture was the only authoritative basis for Christian belief and practice.

On certain crucial points, however, the Brethren did not concur with the theology of the Reformers. They rejected the doctrine of predestination and believed that Christ died for all mankind leaving each individual free to accept or reject His salvation. They also maintained that the church was a new society composed only of converted or regenerated persons gathered in a free covenant relationship with each other. In these respects the roots of Brethren theology went deeply into the so-called "Radical Reformation" of which the Anabaptists were such a conspicuous part. Some additional knowledge of Anabaptism is essential for an understanding of the development of the Brethren movement.

Anabaptism

Spiritual descendants of the Anabaptists began to enter Lancaster County in 1710.[5] The forebears of these immigrants had emerged in sixteenth-century Europe as advocates of the restitution of New Testament church life and of the complete separation of the church from the national or territorial state. They also believed that the German and Swiss reformers, Martin Luther, Ulrich Zwingli, and John Calvin, stopped short of the full truth of the Gospel by collaborating with secular magistrates in religious reform.[6]

Anabaptism, which appeared in many forms, cannot be encompassed by a simple, common definition. The name "Anabaptists" (rebaptizers) originated with their enemies, who capitalized upon the fact that imperial law since the reign of the Emperor Justinian in the sixth century made rebaptism a heresy punishable by death. To the charge that they were rebaptizers, the Anabaptists replied that baptism required responsible adult confession of faith so infants could not actually be "baptized." They also strongly believed that their convictions were grounded in Scripture, and therefore denied the charge of heresy leveled against them by their enemies.[7]

Both religious and secular authorities of the Reformation period tended to include as Anabaptists persons who often differed widely in some respects but who were united in rejecting the state-related territorial churches with their compulsory memberships based upon infant baptism. Such a loose classification scheme glossed over important distinctions between individuals and groups. Many persons, for example, categorized as Anabaptists repudiated the use of violence, but some endorsed the sword as a legitimate means to achieve their ends.[8]

This study is concerned with the peaceful, evangelical form of Anabaptism which first appeared in Switzerland in the early sixteenth century. Two of its principal leaders were Conrad Grebel and Felix Manz, both of whom applauded the early religious reforms of Zwingli in Zurich. When, however, Zwingli decided that the Zurich city council should control the pace of reform, that is, when he accepted the restraints of magisterial reformation, Grebel and Manz lost confidence in him. About this time

George Blaurock, a man of kindred spirit who shared their disillusionment with Zwingli, joined them. Faced by intense state and church pressures for religious conformity violating their convictions, these men reached the momentous decision to join together in a free church practicing the baptism of adult believers. In 1525 Grebel baptized Blaurock who then baptized the others.[9] This was the beginning of the "Swiss Brethren."

The influence of those early Swiss Anabaptists spread widely outside of Zurich. When Zwingli and the city council attacked them with violent persecution, their beliefs had already penetrated beyond the Swiss frontiers. Meanwhile, another Anabaptist movement with striking similarities emerged in the Netherlands. Here a Catholic priest named Menno Simons embraced Anabaptism and gave leadership to the adherents of his new-found faith.[10] Later generations of Menno's followers carried to the New World concepts of Anabaptism modified by two hundred years of fierce European persecution by Lutheran, Reformed, and Catholic churchmen and princes. These "Mennonites" were one channel by which Anabaptist theology entered the religious life of eighteenth-century Lancaster County.

As previously noted, the Anabaptists concurred with the magisterial reformers on many of the great doctrines of historic Christianity. They also strongly agreed with them on the doctrine of justification by faith. Dirk Philip of the Netherlands clearly stated the Anabaptist position:

> But although we as poor unprofitable servants desire to be diligent to do God's will by His grace, yet let no one think or imagine nor say of us that we seek our salvation in any other way than in the grace of God and in the merits of Christ alone. For we firmly believe and openly confess that we are saved by the grace of our Lord Jesus Christ, as the Apostle Peter confessed to the church of Jerusalem. Therefore we also . . . place our whole hope in the grace of God.[11]

In spite of many common theological bonds between the Anabaptists and the magisterial reformers, the two groups disagreed crucially on the doctrine of the church and the nature of the Christian life.[12]

In their church life the Anabaptists sought to reproduce primitive New Testament Christianity as revealed in the Scriptures. To them neither the Catholic *Corpus Christianum,* a unified Christian society under the spiritual leadership of the pope and the secular headship of the emperor, nor the national Reformation churches identified with territorial states and subject to magisterial control appeared to be scriptural. They insisted rather upon a church free from all political and territorial connections and composed of a gathered or voluntary membership based upon the principles of genuine repentance and regeneration, adult believer's baptism, and commitment to discipleship. In the words of one of their leaders:

> But they are the true congregation of Christ who are truly converted, who are born from above of God, who are of a regenerate mind by the operation of the Holy Spirit through the hearing of the divine Word, and have become the children of God, have entered into obedience to Him, and live unblamably in His holy commandments, and according to His holy will all their days, . . .[13]

This doctrine of the church placed the Anabaptists in direct oppostion to the Lutheran and Reformed church systems which retained the medieval concept of compulsory membership embracing entire populations from cradle to grave. These systems required the baptism of all infants (citizens) within the territory of a secular state.

The Anabaptists, furthermore, believed that members of the true church, although physically present in society, were spiritually separated from it in mind and heart; corporately and individually they aimed at nothing less than encompassing all aspects of their lives within what the Schleitheim Confession of 1527 referred to as "the perfection of Christ." For them inner regeneration and outer obedience were inseparably joined. If, they reasoned, Catholicism erred in seeming to stress works without faith, the magisterial reformers erred in seeming to stress faith without works. The characteristic Anabaptist connection of repentance and regeneration with obedience is expressed in this quotation: "He will not save you nor forgive your sins nor show you His mercy and grace except according to His Word; namely if you repent and if you believe, if you are born of Him, if you do what He has commanded and walk as he walks."[14] The Christian life viewed in this way is essentially obedient discipleship; all attitudes and conduct must be brought under the lordship of Christ, that is, be conformed to His teaching and example.

A conspicuous aspect of the Anabaptist understanding of discipleship was the application of the ethic of love and nonresistance to all human relationships. Within their own circles this meant the practice of true brotherhood; their loving concern for one another was not merely sentimental but practical in the actual sharing of possessions with those in need. In relating to the larger "worldly" society about them, they repudiated all manner of strife and violence, as well as the taking of human life by capital punishment or warefare.[15] Conrad Grebel wrote to Thomas Münster who endorsed violence:

> Moreover, the gospel and its adherents are not to be protected by the sword, nor are they thus to protect themselves . . . [they] must reach the fatherland of eternal rest, not by killing their bodily, but by mortifying their spiritual, enemies. Neither do they use worldly sword or war, since all killing has ceased with them . . . .[16]

Like all other aspects of their faith, the meaning of discipleship emerged from the Anabaptist understanding of the Scriptures, for they were confirmed biblicists. This characteristic of their movement is dramatically illustrated by the statement of Michael Sattler as he stood trial in 1527 on the eve of martyrdom for this faith:

> Whereas, then, we have not acted contrary to God and the gospel, you will find that neither I nor my brethren and sisters have offended in word or deed against any authority. Therefore, ministers of God [the judges], if you have neither heard nor read the Word of God, send for the most learned men and for the sacred books of the Bible in whatsoever language they may be and let them confer with us in the Word of God. If they prove to us with the Holy Scriptures that we err and are in the wrong, we will gladly desist and recant . . . .[17]

Later, responding to a question from one of his judges, Sattler added in words reminiscent of Luther's stand at the Diet of Worms: "We will continue in our faith in Christ so long as we have breath in us, unless we be dissuaded from it by the Scriptures."[18]

While regarding all Scripture as inspired and authoritative, the Anabaptists believed in progressive revelation. The Old Testament, in their view, was preparatory to God's fuller revelation of Himself in the New Testament. Upon this understanding of Scripture they grounded their rejection of participation in warfare and swearing of oaths, in both of which the Israelites engaged during the Old Testament period.[19]

Although they renounced the sword, the Anabaptists found it everywhere unsheathed against them. Noting that persecution and tribulation had been the lot of the New Testament church, their anguish under persecution confirmed their conviction that they stood in the true church tradition. References to the sufferings of Christians abound in their literature. Conrad Grebel wrote: "True Christian believers are sheep among wolves, sheep for the slaughter; they must be baptized in anguish and affliction, tribulation, persecution, suffering, and death; they must be tried with fire, . . ."[20] Many Anabaptists experienced martyrdom beginning with Felix Manz, who was drowned in Zurich in 1527.[21] Torture often preceded their executions. When Michael Sattler was put to death in 1527, the executioner cut out his tongue, mutilated his body with red-hot tongs, and then burned him to ashes.[22]

In spite of their sufferings, the early Anabaptists were passionately and aggressively missionary; they took the Great Commission with the utmost seriousness.[23] The violent hostility directed against them by the surrounding secular and religious societies was due partly to the tremendous impact of their witness which won large numbers of converts to their faith. One of their opponents, Sebastian Franck, acknowledged this in 1531.

> The Anabaptists spread so rapidly that their teachings soon covered, as it were, the land. They soon gained a large following, and baptized many thousands, drawing to themselves many sincere souls who had a zeal for God. . . . They increased so rapidly that the world feared an uprising by them, though I have learned that this fear had no justification whatsoever.[24]

Nearly two centuries of harsh persecution, internal division, and environmental accommodation caused later generations of Anabaptists to lose the missionary passion which characterized the founders of their movement. By the time the Mennonites emigrated from Europe to Lancaster County, Pennsylvania, the original Anabaptist vision had grown dim.[25] Their European sufferings and difficulties, however, did not completely sever their Anabaptist roots, and Anabaptism became an important influence in American Mennonitism.

Another group of European origin who, like the Mennonites, transmitted the Anabaptist influence to Lancaster County were the Dunkers.* They originated in 1708 in Schwarzenau, Wittgenstein, Germany, under the leadership of Alexander Mack.[26] Their faith combined

---

*The Dunkers, who significantly influenced the early Brethren movement, were also known by a variety of other names including "Brethren," "Dunkards," and "Taufers." In 1836 they adopted the name "Fraternity of German Baptists," which, in 1871, they changed to "German Baptist Brethren." The present society known as the "Church of the Brethren" is the largest of the groups descended from the Dunkers. See Donald F. Durnbaugh, ed., *The Church of the Brethren Past and Present* (Elgin, Ill.: Brethren Press, 1971). pp. 9-10.

elements of Anabaptism with Pietism which profoundly influenced the European religious scene in the seventeenth century.[27] Soon after they began, persecution, economic hardship, and internal division turned their attention toward the New World, and they emigrated en masse from their homeland to Pennsylvania in 1719.[28]

The Pietism which influenced the Dunkers reflected the post-Reformation resurgence of the experiential tradition in Christianity. In the midst of the doctrinal disputations and lack of Christian morality, characteristic of European life in the seventeenth century, the Pietists asserted that Christianity is essentially a personal, heartfelt relationship of the individual to God. Such a relationship, they believed, bore outward fruit in Christian love, resulting in a practical, applied Christianity. To produce this kind of religious experience, they stressed Bible study, prayer, and conventicles or gatherings of earnest Christians for mutual edification.[29]

The Dunkers were not the only Lancaster County settlers whose faith was leavened by European Pietism. Many Lutherans, Reformed, and Mennonites who made their way to Pennsylvania had also felt its influence to some degree. This historic exposure to Pietism created fertile soil for the revivalistic religious awakening which swept the German community in America in the late eighteenth century.

Although the Dunker founders had spiritual roots in Pietism, both the society which they formed and the writings of Alexander Mack reveal the impact which Anabaptism made upon them. Mack makes that influence clear in a statement referring to the sixteenth-century Anabaptists: "We are completely agreed with them as far as their doctrine is concerned, which does not teach anything in contradiction to the gospel."[30] In view of this strong endorsement of Anabaptism, the question arises as to why he and his followers did not join one of the existing Mennonite groups.

There are at least two answers to this question. In the first place, Mack, who was well acquainted with the Mennonites of his time, believed that they had fallen away from the faith of their forefathers. He wrote: ". . . they have deteriorated in doctrine and life, and have strayed far from the doctrine and life of the old Baptists [Anabaptists]. Many of them notice this and realize it themselves."[31] Furthermore, the Scriptures and church history had convinced the Dunkers that faithful observance of the ordinance of baptism required trine immersion, three separate acts each recognizing one person of the Trinity. Because of this conviction they could not conscientiously join the contemporary Mennonites who did not practice immersion. The dilemma faced by the Dunker founders when they desired trine immersion stands out clearly in this passage:

> They found in trustworthy histories that the early Christians during the first and second centuries were planted into the death by crucifixion of Jesus Christ, according to the commandment of Christ, through trine immersion in the water bath of holy baptism. They therefore diligently searched the New Testament, and found that everything agreed with this perfectly. They therefore had an ardent desire to be furthered through this means, practiced by Christ himself and commanded by Him, for the fulfillment of all righteousness, according to His saving counsel.
> This problem then presented itself. Who should perform this good work on them outwardly?[32]

The small fellowship of five men and three women were equal to the challenge posed by their convictions. They agreed to pray and fast in quest of a solution to the question of how Mack might secure baptism approved by "the church of Christ" so that he could validly baptize the others. In so doing "They were strengthened in this impasse by the words of Christ where He so faithfully speaks: 'For where two or three are gathered in my name, there am I in the midst of them.'" Accepting this statement as authority to act as the church of Christ, they drew lots among four of the men and selected one to baptize Mack, thus qualifying the latter to baptize the other seven. Then, in the early morning, they went out to the Eder River and proceeded with the baptismal service, after which "They were all immediately clothed inwardly with great joyfulness." To make sure that they would not be called by the name of any individual, a folly Saint Paul condemned in his first Corinthian letter, they covenanted never to reveal the identity of the first baptizer.[33]

Whether the Dunkers of 1708 were aware of the mutual baptism of the Swiss Brethren in 1525 is unknown. In any case they carried to Pennsylvania memories of their own mutual baptism in the Eder River. These baptismal memories may have inspired the action of the later group of Brethren along the Susquehanna River when they also faced the dilemma of how to secure baptism by trine immersion.[34]

Pietism

As previously noted a pietistic leaven was at work in Lancaster County in the eighteenth century, not only among the Dunkers who developed in part out of European Pietism but also among members of other religious societies. By the latter half of the century, this leaven helped to prepare the way for a tremendous surge of revivalistic Pietism among the German-speaking peoples in Pennsylvania and elsewhere.[35] In this movement the emerging United Brethren in Christ played a leading role which has special significance for the story of the Brethren.

Two men, Philip Otterbein and Martin Boehm, were the principal figures in the formation of the United Brethren in Christ. Coming from very different backgrounds but brought together on the basis of similar religious experiences and concerns, they cooperated across denominational lines to provide leadership for the spiritual awakening.

In 1752 Philip Otterbein responded to a call to serve as pastor of the German Reformed Church in Lancaster. His European background and education had already exposed him to Pietism with its concern for personal, practical Christianity. At Lancaster he had a profound religious transformation which made him a fervent exponent of an evangelical Christianity stressing the new birth as a personal, heartfelt experience.[36]

In the same decade Martin Boehm, a Mennonite minister who dreaded his preaching appointments because he felt the lack of a vital message to share with his people, experienced a dramatic conversion. This climaxed as he plowed a field and simultaneously prayed for aid to preach. Later, he described this experience as follows:

> While thus engaged in prayer . . . , the thought rose up in my mind, or as though one spoke to me, saying, "You pray for grace to teach others the way of salvation, and you have not prayed for your own salvation." This thought or word did not leave me. . . . I felt and saw myself a poor sinner. I was LOST. My agony became great. I was ploughing in the field, and kneeled down at each end of the furrow, to pray. . . . Midway in the field I could go no further, but sank behind the plough, crying, Lord save, I am lost!—and again the thought or voice said, "I am come to seek and to save that which is lost." In a moment a stream of joy was poured over me. I praised the Lord, and left the field, and told my companion what joy I felt.[37]

After this experience Boehm found that he no longer dreaded the approach of his preaching appointments; instead, he could hardly wait! "Like a dream, old things had passed away, and it seemed as if I had awoke to new life, new thoughts, new faith, new love. . . . This joy, this faith, this love, I wished to communicate to those around me, . . ."[38]

Boehm's testimony to his experience illustrates the nature of the spiritual awakening which he and Otterbein now promoted. This message stressed the new birth involving personal repentance, assurance of the forgiveness of sins, and holiness of life. The evangelists of the awakening endeavored to enlist pietistically converted Christians in the task of leading others into similar conversion experiences. Christian Newcomer, one of those evangelists, reveals in a remarkable journal the geographical scope and religious intensity of the awakening as Otterbein, Boehm, and others carried the evangelical message of the new birth far and wide.[39] Spectacular emotional manifestations characterized the movement. Newcomer describes such an occasion: "This morning at our Love-feast we had a real pentecost; some fell to the ground and laid as if lifeless, others cried for mercy, while some were shouting and praising God; no wonder some were amazed and confounded when they witnessed such demonstrations."[40]

The leaders of the awakening employed various techniques to spread their message. One was house-to-house meetings of persons who desired to fellowship in prayer and to cultivate the Christian life. These meetings, reminiscent of the devotional conventicles of European Pietism, broke through denominational barriers. People of different backgrounds including Mennonites, Lutherans, Reformed, and Dunkers participated in them.[41] Another technique took the form of "great meetings" at which masses of people from various religious backgrounds gathered to share spiritual fellowship and hear the messages of the evangelists.[42]

Otterbein and Boehm first met in a great meeting held about 1767 at the farm of Isaac Long near Landis Valley a few miles north of Lancaster. As Boehm preached, his sermon moved Otterbein deeply; the message revealed that they stood upon common spiritual ground. When the sermon ended and before Boehm could be seated, Otterbein arose, threw his arms around him, and exclaimed, *"Wir sind Brüder"* ("We are Brethren"). Deeply moved by this scene, some of those present "praised God aloud, but most of the congregation gave place to their feelings—weeping for joy."[43]

Although the United Brethren in Christ did not formally organize until the turn of the century, they regarded that dramatic occasion as the symbolic beginning of their movement, the central theme of which was a personal, heartfelt experience of the new birth.[44] The message of that experience was their special contribution to the religious life of Lancaster County.

The Brethren in Christ Roots

Religious toleration and the presence of peoples representing a wide variety of European religious backgrounds produced a heterogeneous religious community in eighteenth-century Lancaster County. Especially important for the story of the Brethren in Christ was the presence of societies with theologies and folkways deeply influenced by Anabaptism and, to a lesser degree, Pietism. Equally important was the revivalistic Pietism which swept Lancaster County in the latter part of the century. This latter movement produced several new indigenous groups stressing the crucial importance of a personal, heartfelt experience of the new birth.

The theological roots of the Brethren in Christ, nourished by historic Christianity mediated through the Protestant Reformation, go deeply into both Anabaptism and revivalistic Pietism. Finding themselves at the point of intersection of these two movements, the Brethren founders could neither sacrifice their understanding of the church and the nature of the Christian life derived from the former nor their conception of the new birth gained from the latter. These circumstances prevented them from making common cause with any other religious society and left them no alternative but to go their own way.

NOTES:

[1]Sylvester K. Stevens, *Pennsylvania: Birthplace of a Nation* (New York: Random House, 1964), p. 34.

[2]Ralph Wood, ed., *The Pennsylvania Germans* (Princeton, N. J.: Princeton University Press, 1942), chs. 3, 4; Walter M. Kollmorgen, "The Agricultural Stability of the Old Order Amish and Old Order Mennonites of Lancaster County, Pennsylvania," *American Journal of Sociology,* XLIX (November, 1943), 233.

[3]Owen H. Alderfer, "The Mind of the Brethren in Christ: A Synthesis of Revivalism and the Church Conceived as Total Community" (Ph. D. dissertation, Claremont Graduate School, 1964), pp. 25-27, analyzes the factors limiting the interaction of the Quakers with the German religious groups.

[4]There is no evidence of direct interaction between the Brethren and the Evangelical Association which organized early in the nineteenth century.

[5]Oscar Kuhns, *The German and Swiss Settlements of Pennsylvania: A Study of the So-Called Pennsylvania Dutch* (New York: Henry Holt and Company, 1901), p. 53.

[6]George Williams, *The Radical Reformation* (Philadelphia: Westminister Press, 1962), introd. and ch. 6.

[7]H. S. Bender, "Anabaptist," *The Mennonite Encyclopedia: A Comprehensive Reference Work on the Anabaptist-Mennonite Movement* (4 vols.; Scottdale, Pa.: Mennonite Publishing House, 1955-1959), I, 113-14.

[8]Harold S. Bender, "The Anabaptist Vision," in Guy F. Hershberger, ed., *The Recovery of the Anabaptist Vision* (Scottdale, Pa.: Herald Press, 1957), p. 35; N. van der Zijpp, "Münster Anabaptists," *Mennonite Encyclopedia*, III, 777-79.

[9]Hutterite Chronicle cited by George H. Williams and Angel M. Mergal, eds., *Spiritual and Anabaptist Writers: Documents Illustrative of the Radical Reformation* (Philadelphia: Westminster Press, 1957), pp. 44-45.

[10]Harold S. Bender, "The Anabaptist Vision," p. 31, and N. van der Zijpp, "The Early Dutch Anabaptists," p. 71, in Hershberger, *Anabaptist Vision;* Cornelius J. Dyck, ed., *An Introduction to Mennonite History* (Scottdale, Pa.: Herald Press, 1967), pp. 80-81.

[11]Quoted in John C. Wenger, "Grace and Discipleship in Anabaptism," *Mennonite Quarterly Review,* XXXV (January, 1961), 61.

[12]Scholars differ as to whether the Anabaptists' doctrine of the church or their concept of Christian discipleship was their central theological concept. See the essays of Franklin H. Littell and Harold S. Bender in Hershberger, *Anabaptist Vision.*

[13]*The Complete Writings of Menno Simons,* trans. from the Dutch by Leonard Verduin and ed. by John Christian Wenger (Scottdale, Pa.: Herald Press, 1956), p. 300.

[14]*Ibid.,* p. 92.

[15]J. Lawrence Burkholder, "The Anabaptist Vision of Discipleship," and J. Winfield Fretz, "Brotherhood and the Economic Ethic of the Anabaptists," in Hershberger, *Anabaptist Vision,* pp. 135-51, 194-201.

[16]Quoted in Williams & Mergal, *Spiritual and Anabaptist Writers,* p. 80. See also John C. Wenger, "The Schleitheim Confession of Faith," *Mennonite Quarterly Review,* XIX (October, 1945), 250-52.

[17]Quoted in Williams & Mergal, *Spiritual and Anabaptist Writers,* pp. 141-42.

[18]*Ibid.,* p. 142.

[19]John C. Wenger, "The Biblicism of the Anabaptists," in Hershberger, *Anabaptist Vision,* pp. 174-79. In other words, they perceived God's self-revelation as climaxing in Jesus Christ who called His disciples to love of enemy and renunciation of oaths.

[20]Quoted in Williams & Mergal, *Spiritual and Anabaptist Writers,* p. 80. See also "The Cross of the Saints" in *Writings of Menno Simons,* pp. 581-622.

[21]Christian Neff and H. S. Bender, "Felix Manz," *Mennonite Encyclopedia,* III, 473.

[22]"The Trial and Martyrdom of Michael Sattler," Williams & Mergal, *Spiritual and Anabaptist Writers,* p. 143.

[23]J. D. Graber, "Anabaptism Expressed in Missions and Social Service," in Hershberger, *Anabaptist Vision,* pp. 152-63.

[24]Quoted in John Horsch, *Mennonites in Europe* (Scottdale, Pa.: Mennonite Publishing House, 1942), p. 293.

[25]Ernst Crous, "Anabaptism, Pietism, Rationalism, and German Mennonites," in Hershberger, *Anabaptist Vision,* pp. 237-39; Dyck, *Mennonite History,* pp. 112, 291-92.

[26]Martin G. Brumbaugh, *A History of the German Baptist Brethren in Europe and America* (2nd ed.; Elgin, Ill.: Brethren Publishing House, 1910), p. 29.

[27]Donald F. Durnbaugh, "The Genius of the Brethren," *Brethren Life and Thought,* IV (Winter, 1959), 4-34. As this author shows, the degree to which Anabaptism and Pietism respectively influenced the German Baptist founders is currently a subject for scholarly debate.

[28]Donald F. Durnbaugh, "Brethren Beginnings: The Origins of the Church of the Brethren in Early Eighteenth-Century Europe" (Ph. D. dissertation, University of Pennsylvania, 1960), p. 136.

[29]F. Ernest Stoeffler, *The Rise of Evangelical Pietism* (Leiden: E. J. Brill, 1965), pp. 13-23; Philip Jacob Spener, *Pia Desideria,* trans. and ed. by Theodore G. Tappert (Philadelphia: Fortress Press, 1964), pp. 39-122; Cornelius Krahn, "Pietism," *Mennonite Encyclopedia,* IV, 176.

[30]Quoted in Donald F. Durnbaugh, comp. and trans., *European Origins of the Brethren: A Source Book on the Beginnings of the Church of the Brethren in the Early Eighteenth Century* (Elgin, Ill.: Brethren Press, 1958), p. 340. See also pp. 342-43, 358.

[31]*Ibid.,* 340.

[32]Alexander Mack, Jr., quoted in *Ibid.,* p. 121.

[33]*Ibid.,* pp. 121, 122. Mt. 18:20 is the Scripture cited. All biblical citations are from the King James Version.

[34]See Chapter II.

[35]This revivalistic Pietism emphasized a personal, heartfelt experience of the new birth.

[36]A. W. Drury, *History of the Church of the United Brethren in Christ* (Dayton, Ohio: Otterbein Press, 1924), pp. 54, 66.

[37]Quoted in Henry G. Spayth, *History of the Church of the United Brethren in Christ* (Circleville, Ohio: United Brethren in Christ, 1851), pp. 29-30.

[38]*Ibid.,* p. 30.

[39]*Christian Newcomer, His Life, Journal and Achievements,* ed. by Samuel S. Hough (Dayton, Ohio: Board of Administration, Church of the United Brethren in Christ, 1941).

[40]*Ibid.,* p. 100. See also pp. 61, 79-81.

[41]A Familiar Friend, "History of the River Brethren," *History of All the Religious Denominations in the United States* (Harrisburg, Pa.: John Winebrenner, 1848), p. 553. This is the most reliable secondary source for early Brethren in Christ history.

[42]Drury, *United Brethren,* pp. 88, 89; *Newcomer Journal,* pp. 4, 29, 61, 67.

[43]Spayth, *United Brethren,* p. 41.

[44] *Ibid.,* pp. 41-42.

II

How the Brethren Began

The Time and the Founders

Neither the founders of the Brethren in Christ nor their contemporaries recorded the date of that founding so the society cannot point back to an exact time of origin.[1] There is conclusive evidence that the group existed by 1788, for John Winger and Jacob Sider who carried the Brethren faith to Canada filed crown land petitions revealing that they arrived on the Canadian frontier in that year.[2]

In secondary accounts of the origin of the society, Jacob Engel is more prominent than any other person and more is known about him.[3] He was born on November 5, 1753, and married Veronica Schock at age twenty.[4] His father was Uhlrich Engel, a Swiss Mennonite, who arrived with his family at Philadelphia on the ship *Phoenix* in October 1754.[5] The Engels settled along the Susquehanna River in Donegal Township, Lancaster County, Pennsylvania, near the present town of Marietta.[6]

Jacob Engel died in 1833 and is buried in East Donegal Cemetery near Maytown, Pennsylvania. The English translation of the German inscription on his simple grave marker reads:

Here rests an old patriarch, whose labor in the work of God was with diligence. Now he is in his Father's land. Jacob Engel was his name. His name now is much better. He lived and died a true Christian, He brought his age to three months, seventy-nine years, five days. He now lives in eternal rest.[7]

Two questions about him are crucial. First, was he one of the Brethren founders? Second, was he actually born on November 5, 1753? Affirmative answers to these questions can establish an approximate date for the origin of the brotherhood.

The role of Jacob Engel as a founding father is assumed in all official Brethren literature which includes accounts of the origin of the society. Levi Lukenbach, a well-informed, nineteenth-century bishop, wrote the first such account including the following passage:

> Among the number of emigrants that landed in this country were two children . . . destined in after years to be mainly instrumental in founding the Church in this country. . . . Jacob Engle, the younger of those two, was apparently especially called of God for the work before him, namely, the building up of the cause of our Blessed Redeemer.[8]

In a later account of the origin, three of the ablest Brethren leaders, Henry K. Kreider, Eli M. Engle, and Samuel R. Smith, assigned Engel a leading founding role.[9] A tradition handed down through the generations of the Engle family reinforces this denominational acceptance of Jacob Engel as a founding father.[10]

All other secondary writers who name founders and early leaders include Jacob Engel among them. One author, who was a contemporary of both first and second generation Brethren, states: "Their first ministers were Jacob Engel, Hans Engle, C. Rupp, and others . . . . Soon after the formal organization of churches in Pennsylvania, Jacob Engel visited Canada, and at a later period, Ohio, to organize churches."[11]

Another account of the founding, published by John K. Miller in 1906, is of special interest. Unlike most secondary writers of Brethren history, Miller identified his sources. One was an elderly woman whose mother lived in the household of Ulrich Engel, brother of Jacob, and later transmitted Engel family history to her daughter. Another was the granddaughter of Jacob Engel, who reached young adulthood prior to her grandfather's death. Miller may be criticized for his acceptance of historical details related by these elderly women, but there is no reason to question their combined testimony on such a general question as the role of Engel in founding the society.[12]

Further evidence of the founding role of Engel is his name among eight Brethren leaders who endorsed an early manuscript confession of faith.[13] An intensive study of this confession dates its probable origin about 1780, eight years before John Winger and Jacob Sider carried the Brethren faith to Canada. Six of the eight signatures match six names on the Donegal Township tax lists of that period, and five of those men resided in the Township simultaneously during 1779-1782.[14] The Jacob Engel signature on this document indicates that he was a person of distinction in the early Brethren movement.

The data presented justify the conclusion that Jacob Engel was one of the Brethren founders. There is no hint of evidence to the contrary.

Because Engel was a founding father, the verification of his reported birth date is important in documenting the approximate time of the Brethren origin. Unfortunately, the only record of that date is in a secondary source of doubtful reliability. There are, however, several lines of evidence which converge to confirm the birth date as given.

In the first place, following the death of both parents, Jacob appeared on June 26, 1764, in the Lancaster County Orphans' Court which assigned Peter Witmore guardian of his person and estate.[15] Under the rules of that Court, minor children fourteen years of age and over had right of consent in the choice of their guardians. Although one of his brothers and two of his sisters exercised that right, Jacob did not. This proves that he was less than fourteen years of age on his day in court so he could not have been born prior to June 27, 1750.

Second, the Jacob Engel grave marker gives his life span as seventy-nine years, three months, and five days. His probated will proves his decease by March 12, 1833, which indicates that he could not have been born later than December 6, 1753.

Documentary sources thus restrict the birth date to the three and one-half year period between June 27, 1750, and December 6, 1753. Under these circumstances there is no reason to question November 5, 1753, as the actual date. Not only does it fall within the short proved period within which his birth occurred, but it yields a death date on February 10, 1833, approximately one month before the probation of his will. Also, the name of Jacob Engel appears on the Donegal Township tax rolls in 1775, and continues there until 1833. The first date corresponds with the presumed beginning of his legal majority and the second corresponds with the presumed time of his death.[16]

Since Jacob Engel did not reach his legal majority until late in 1774, there is little likelihood that he helped to found a new religious society before that time. This makes 1775 the earliest reasonable date for the origin of the Brethren. It is probable that the founding occurred later than 1775 after Engel became more mature.[17]

Jacob Engel gravestone in East Donegal Cemetery near Maytown, Pennsylvania.

Except for Jacob Engel, little is known about those early leaders who chose a course which led to the formation of a new religious society. Others who either shared in the founding or joined the group soon afterward were Samuel Bentzner, Benjamin Beÿer, John Engel (brother of Jacob), John Funk, John Greider, Stofel Hollinger, John Meÿer, Jacob Sider, Philip Stern, and John Winger.[18] A few of them had Mennonite backgrounds; these included Jacob and John Engel and John Greider.[19] John Winger may also have been a Mennonite.[20] The early Brethren were occasionally called "River Mennonites" because some of their first ministers had been connected with the Mennonites.[21]

No known sources reveal whether persons of church backgrounds other than Mennonite participated in the founding of the society.[22] Some former Dunkers joined the group prior to 1848, but these accessions may have occurred in the early nineteenth century.[23] If no Dunkers were among the founders, this poses an interesting problem. Although the Mennonites as well as the Dunkers stood in the tradition of Anabaptism, the Brethren showed a marked preference for practices of the Dunkers when these differed from those of the Mennonites. Like the Dunkers they selected church officials by elections rather than by lot, stressed the wearing of the beard, held love feasts in connection with communion services, had "visiting brethren" (deacons) canvass church members to ascertain their spiritual condition and attitudes toward fellow believers, referred to the disciplinary function of officials as "house keeping," and baptized by trine immersion.

Why the Brethren generally followed the practices of the Dunkers cannot be determined from present information. Possibly founders who had been Mennonites felt a need to break with some aspects of their Mennonite past, or the group may have been attracted by the underlying strain of Pietism which characterized the Dunkers from their beginning. Dunker services, especially the singing, reflected a certain emotional, heartfelt quality to which the Brethren may have responded.[24]

The Brethren and Revivalistic Pietism

All present living churches tracing their origins back to the Jacob Engel group—Brethren in Christ, Old Order River Brethren (Yorkers), United Zion, Calvary Holiness—place great emphasis upon personal, heartfelt Christian experience. The applicant for membership in any of these churches is expected to testify to being "saved," that is, to profess an experience of the new birth accompanied by assurance that his sins are forgiven. Such an experience occurs, or at least consummates, as a crisis at a given point in time so that the individual knows when he enters into the Christian life. This historic understanding of conversion is illustrated by the following passage:

> Some say they have salvation, but cannot tell the time and place where they got it. If you have it, you can tell when and where you got it. A definite time, at a definite place and you got a definite work. When a person has salvation he knows it . . . . If there is a doubt in your mind about your salvation, it is a good evidence that you are unsaved.[25]

This emphasis upon an experiential new birth for all who enter into the Christian life traces back to the eighteenth-century pietistic awakening in Lancaster County. The agreement of the early Brethren with the conversion emphasis of that movement is revealed by frequent source references to Jacob Engel and his colleagues as persons who professed heartfelt experiences of the new birth. Bishop Levi Lukenbach described them as pietistically converted persons.

> Although they were raised up among a peaceable, law-abiding and order-loving people, yet true evangelical religion was but very little known among them. But God's grace and His convicting spirit was [sic] at work, and finally those two persons, John and Jacob Engle, with others, were led to see themselves as sinners and sought and obtained pardon of their sins and their acceptance with Christ, . . .[26]

Other credible secondary sources concur with Lukenbach's condition that the experience of a heartfelt conversion was a crucial factor in the origin of the brotherhood.[27]

Early Brethren commitment to this pietistic understanding of the new birth found clear expression in the Eighteenth-Century Confession:

> Into . . . an open, poor sinner's heart the Lord Jesus will and can come, . . . to bestow comfort, peace, love and trust. Then the record of sins as well as the guilt of Adam is stricken out, he receives comfort and forgiveness of sins and eternal life. . . . So we confess that to be a new birth, revival of the mind, revival of the Holy Spirit.

Such a conversion, in the view of the Confession, is an indispensable prerequisite for the beginning of Christian discipleship and for baptism.

The evangelistic preaching of Martin Boehm, a Mennonite minister who later became a founder of the United Brethren in Christ, helped to make the Brethren founders aware of the doctrine and experience of the new birth.[28] His Mennonite heritage provided a point of contact with persons of Anabaptist background, and especially those of Mennonite faith. Since he preached in German, his revivalistic Pietism reached many Pennsylvania-Germans who may have been largely untouched by English-speaking evangelists.

Boehm's precise place in the events leading up to the founding of the Brethren is not clear. There is a United Brethren in Christ tradition that his role was administrative as well as inspirational. According to this tradition, Boehm became the leader or bishop of "flourishing congregations" (pietistic conventicles?) of awakened persons in Lancaster County. One of these was located along the Susquehanna River in the vicinity where the Brethren originated. With the passage of time, this congregation made up principally of Mennonites began to draw away from Boehm because of his liberal views on baptism and his widening relationships with persons of non-Mennonite views. Eventually, so the tradition goes, this Susquehanna River group became the "mother congregation" for the River Brethren.[29]

Although there is no supporting evidence that the Brethren originated as a secession of such a congregation from Boehm's administrative control or that they had ever been under his administrative supervision, the inference that he figured prominently in the circumstances surrounding their origin is correct. Some of the founders attended his meetings, endorsed his preaching, and may have professed the new birth under his ministry. Later, in his absence, they held prayer meetings and finally decided to form an organization patterned more closely on their understandings of the New Testament.[30]

This gradual, spontaneous emergence of the Brethren movement under Martin Boehm's influence is compatible with their founding as described by the most reliable early historian of the group.

> Between sixty and seventy years ago, awakened persons of Mennonites, Lutherans, German Reformed, Brethren or Taeufer, "whose hearts were closely joined together—had a common interest, not only in regard to the general cause of religion, but in each others [sic] individual edification," and they met in the capacity of a social devout band, from house to house, to make prayer and supplication for the continued influence of God's Spirit—out of these social circles, was organized the Religious Association, now [1840s] commonly known as the RIVER BRETHREN.[31]

However the founders may have differed with Boehm, they continued to share his pietistic warmth and his understanding of the new birth.

Why a New Religious Society?

Brethren belief in a personal conversion experience, coupled with their reservations about some views of Martin Boehm, its great exponent, foreshowed the development of their eclectic faith. This joined a pietistic understanding of the new birth as normative for all Christians with the deep commitment to scriptural obedience characteristic of Anabaptism.[32] Concern for obedience emerged clearly in their desire to practice the ordinances faithfully and fully.

The ordinance of baptism played a crucial role in the emergence of the society, for the founders were convinced that trine immersion was the baptismal mode prescribed by the Scriptures.[33] Having reached this conclusion, their question was not whether to obey but how. They had two possible alternatives—securing baptism by a minister of an existing religious society or taking the bold step of mutual baptism.

Viewed in historical perspective, the first alternative was unrealistic. In Lancaster County only the Dunkers baptized by trine immersion, and clergymen of other churches would have had to break the precedent of their respective faiths to administer it. The Dunkers, furthermore, regarded baptism as the rite of admission to their fellowship, and they also disagreed with the Brethren understanding of the ordinance.[34] In view of these circumstances, the Brethren founders were unduly optimistic if they hoped to find a Dunker minister who would baptize them.

There are various interesting but unverifiable traditions of their quest for trine immersion baptism. One relates that Jacob Engel and a companion named Witmer requested German Reformed minister Philip Otterbein to baptize them. Otterbein reportedly replied that he could not conscientiously do so because they had been previously baptized.[35]

A second tradition states that a Brethren delegation sought both baptism and church membership from Elder Christian Longenecker of the Dunker White Oak Church near Manheim. Longenecker at that time was having difficulty relating to his people. He asserted that his church was no longer based on the true foundations; it had the form but lacked life and spirit. In this context he advised the inquirers to start a church of their own and build it on the true foundations.[36]

After the meeting with Longenecker, so the tradition goes, the Brethren decided to start a church of their own. Because they still desired baptism by trine immersion, they requested it from a second Dunker, Elder George Miller, who is prominent in a third tradition recurring more frequently in the sources than either of the others.[37] This tradition gives no indication that those who spoke for the founders expressed interest in Dunker membership. They informed Elder Miller that they desired baptism but intended to stand alone and act for themselves. Miller replied that he had no authority to administer baptism if they did not intend to accept Dunker membership. When the delegation made another effort to persuade the Elder, he reportedly said, "If you want to begin something of your own you would better baptize yourselves."[38]

Some accounts of this tradition intimate that Miller reminded the delegation of the earlier scene at the Eder River in Germany where the founders of the Dunkers resolved a similar baptismal dilemma by mutual baptism.[39] In any case, the assumption that the Brethren founders agreed upon mutual baptism so dominates the sources as to leave little doubt of its authenticity.[40] The Eighteenth-Century Confession makes clear that it was by trine immersion, but all other details are vague. The number of persons participating varies in the sources from two to twelve.[41] There are reports of a group pledge to conceal forever the name of the first baptizer, possibly a man chosen by lot.[42] Surmises as to his identity include, in addition to Jacob Engel, men named Witmer, Rupp, and Shaeffer.[43]

Through this mutual baptism, the Brethren took the crucial step which launched a new religious society. Hints of the reasons why they could not affiliate with the Dunkers appear in the traditions of their attempts to secure baptism at the hands of elders of that group. It may seem ironical that two societies which agreed upon trine immersion as the New Testament mode of baptism found this ordinance such a serious obstacle to fellowship; however, the two groups differed basically on the meaning of baptism. The Dunkers, who stood aloof from the new birth as stressed by revivalistc Pietism, associated baptism and the remission of sins, although they did not espouse baptismal regeneration.[44] This position was irreconcilable with the Brethren view that baptism was an act of obedience by which the applicant testified to his experience of the new birth.[45] The point at issue was really a fundamental difference about the nature of the conversion experience. The Brethren could not make common cause with anyone who rejected the pietistic view of conversion as a personal, heartfelt experience occurring prior to baptism and of which baptism was merely a symbol.

Affiliation with the Mennonites, another theoretical option, was never a serious possibility, although the two groups agreed in many respects on the meaning of obedience. Both viewed baptism as an act of symbolic commitment to the Christian life, but they disagreed on the mode of the ordinance. The Mennonites baptized by pouring following the precedent of European Anabaptism. Commitment of the Brethren to trine immersion might have been sufficient to prevent their fellowship with the Mennonites.

More important than baptism, however, was the fact that the Mennonites, like the Dunkers, did not regard a personal, heartfelt experience of the new birth as normative for the beginning of the Christian life. When Martin Boehm testified to his Mennonite congregation of his conversion, he noted that some wept aloud and added:

"This caused considerable commotion in our Church, as well as among
the people generally. It was all new; none of us had heard or seen it before. A
new creation appeared to rise up before me, and around me. Now Scripture, before mysterious, and like a dead letter to me, was plain of interpretation, . . ."[46]

At the time of his conversion, Boehm knew of only one other person who,
in his judgment, had had a comparable experience.[47] Christian Newcomer,
a onetime Mennonite and an evangelistic associate of Boehm, asserts that
the Lancaster County Mennonites of their time did not accept the
piestistic teaching of the new birth.[48] Writings of Mennonite leaders of that
period confirm the accuracy of the observations of Boehm and Newcomer.[49] It is therefore clear that the Brethren could not agree with the
Mennonite understandings of either baptism or conversion.

A third possible option, identification with the emerging United
Brethren in Christ, also proved to be unacceptable. The United Brethren
movement was informal and unstructured at the time when the Brethren,
by their mutual baptism, assumed a separate group identity.[50] Since both
movements emphasized a heartfelt experience of the new birth, some
contemporary observers thought that they might eventually unite.[51]

These observers failed to perceive that different understandings of the
church and discipleship made such a union impossible. The United
Brethren considered church order and the ordinances to be much less
important than the pietistic conversion experience; furthermore, their
movement attracted persons of such different backgrounds that some
diversity in religious practices was inevitable. Philip Otterbein and Martin
Boehm, principal leaders of the early United Brethren, personally
represented the combination of German Reformed and Mennonite
elements in that movement, and representatives of other faiths such as
Dunkers, Mennonites, Presbyterians, and Lutherans rallied around them.
The result was a fellowship representing a wide variety of baptismal
traditions. The United Brethren, consequently, were willing to administer
baptism by sprinkling, pouring, or any form of immersion desired by the
applicant.[52] The following statement reveals their same broad approach to
other ordinances:

They believe also, that the ordinances, namely: baptism and the remem-
brance of the sufferings and death of Christ, are to be in use, and practised
by all Christian societies, but the manner of which ought always to be left to
the judgment of every individual. The example of washing the saints' feet is

left to the judgment of all to practise or not.[53]

This acceptance of individuality in the practice of the ordinances was completely foreign to the thought patterns of the Brethren. Because Jacob Engel and his associates did not find spiritual fulfillment until they followed their convictions in baptism by trine immersion, they could not accept the United Brethren in Christ position on baptism and the other ordinances.

The decision of the Brethren to launch their own religious society undoubtedly involved deep soul-searching. They eventually concluded that there was no other society within which they could combine their pietistic concept of the new birth with their understandings of the church and scriptural obedience. Bishop Levi Lukenbach, writing in the nineteenth century, portrays the spiritual wrestlings of the founders and the grounds upon which they finally decided to form a fellowship of their own. ". . . he [Jacob Engel] and his co-laborors [sic] met together in council, and, after deep meditation, and discarding all human creeds, and taking the unadulterated Word of the Lord as a guide, and seeking to follow the primitive teachings of Christ and His apostles, and adopting the New Testament as their rule of faith and practice, founded the Church in the United States of America."[54]

This passage summarizes the basic guidelines which the founders endeavored to follow as they struggled to define the implications of obedience to God's will. In the first place, they emphasized corporate rather than individual decision-making as they "met together in council." Second, they sought to by-pass religious creeds and go directly to the "unadulterated Word of the Lord" for guidance. Finally, they regarded the New Testament as the culmination of progressive biblical revelation and made it their "rule of faith and practice." Lukenbach states clearly what his generation of Brethren believed about the circumstances of their origin. His description corresponds with other data which illuminate their founding.

Group Names

The members of the new society referred to themselves simply as "Brethren," a name derived from scriptural passages such as: "Be not ye called Rabbi: for one is your Master, even Christ; and all ye are brethren."[55] With the passage of time, the United States branch of the movement became known as "River Brethren," although just when the members began to apply this name to themselves is unknown. The first documented use of it occurred in 1806, but in that instance the writer was not a member of the society.[56]

The name bears an obvious relationship to the Susquehanna River. Some writers have jumped to the conclusion that it originated from the mutual Brethren baptism which, they assume, took place in the Susquehanna.[57] There is no verifiable evidence that the first or any subsequent Brethren baptism occurred there. Jacob N. Martin (1847-1939) who lived near the site where the Brethren originated reported that the older brethren of his time always said that the first baptism took place in Conoy Creek.[58] If that baptism occurred near the junction of the two streams, the name of the larger could possibly have contributed "River" to the name.

Site of homestead acquired by Hans (John) Engel in 1770 at Stackstown, Pennsylvania, and sold by him to his brother Jacob Engel in 1786. Somewhere in Conoy Creek which flows through Stackstown on its way to the nearby Susquehanna River the first Brethren in Christ baptism occurred. The large house on the left was erected after the period when John and Jacob Engel owned the site. The small masonry house may have been on the premises when John Engel gained title to the property, although there is an unverifiable tradition that Jacob erected it.

The most plausible explanation of the River Brethren name is that it developed as a regional distinction within the movement. Members located elsewhere than at the founding site near the Susquehanna, referred to those who remained at that location as "the Brethren at the River," terminology which transposed readily into "River Brethren."[59] The following passage reveals that this name was used in the 1840s:

> Several societies in different parts of Lancaster County were simultaneously organized: one near *the Susquehanna river;* another on *Conestoga creek.* By way of *local* distinction, the latter were called the *Conestoga Brethren,* those on, or near Susquehanna, the *River Brethren,* an appellation by which the society is now generally known, to distinguish its members from the *German Baptists,* or *Brethren,* first organized in Europe.[60]

The preceding passage reveals at least one reason why a more definitive group name than the original "Brethren" became necessary. The name "Brethren" was also a common designation for the eighteenth-century Dunkers whom the Jacob Engel group resembled in many respects.[61] Since both societies had members in Lancaster County, similar names made the distinction between them difficult to discern. There is a hint in Dunker sources that before the River Brethren name came into general use the two groups were distinguished as "Old Brethren" (the Dunkers) and "New Brethren" (the Jacob Engel group).[62]

After the society in the United States accepted the River Brethren name, it was used until the Civil War. The military draft instituted by the Union Government then created the necessity for the Brethren to register in Washington as a nonresistant organization. After counseling about the matter, they decided to register as "Brethren in Christ."[63] The sources are silent about the reasons why they chose to substitute this name for the familiar "River Brethren."

In spite of the adoption of the name "Brethren in Christ," the group used "River Brethren" parenthetically for many years. As late as 1909, title pages of the minutes of General Conference carried the name "Brethren in Christ (River Brethren)."[64] Even when the older name fell into disuse within the society, it lingered among non-members. Writers tracing the religious heritage of the late President Dwight D. Eisenhower, for example, are prone to identify him with the "River Brethren" rather than the "Brethren in Christ."[65]

The Canadian branch of the brotherhood did not, except as a matter of historical reference, refer to themselves as "River Brethren."[66] This supports the previous conclusion that the name was not an original designation for the society in Pennsylvania. Had it been generally accepted there before 1788 John Winger and Jacob Sider would have identified themselves as "River Brethren" when they went to Canada.

While the Canadian members continued to think of themselves internally as "Brethren," they soon became popularly known as "Tunkers." This name of uncertain origin appears as early as 1793 in the Canadian Militia Act of that year.[67] One surmise is that it derived from the German *tunken* (to dip) and that it referred to the mode of baptism.[68] A Canadian observer who knew the group in the nineteenth century reported:

> The public, at least in Canada, knows them as Tunkers. To this there is seldom any objection either by ministers or laymen. So universal is the application of the name that very few outside of the society know they have any other name.[69]

This statement implies that the members themselves were aware of their Brethren name but that they were quite content to be known as "Tunkers."[70]

After the River Brethren in the United States officially adopted the name "Brethren in Christ," that designation was used to some extent in Canada.[71] This caused a Canadian church-name controversy extending over many years. In 1904 Canada Joint Council considered the question of incorporating the brotherhood in Canada with the Brethren in Christ in the United States under the laws of Pennsylvania. This led to a lengthy debate. Reluctance to relinquish the Tunker name was one reason why the council rejected incorporation with the United States Brethren.[72]

Another manifestation of Canadian reluctance to use the Brethren in Christ name surfaced in the General Conference of 1917. In 1879 the Canadian and United States brotherhoods had merged into one General Conference after which official literature appeared in the name of the "Brethren in Christ." Probably because of the desire to clarify their official status during World War I, the Canadian Brethren requested the Conference of 1917 to include the name "Tunker" on the title pages of church literature. Conference responded favorably and agreed to incorporate that name in the *General Conference Minutes* and *Evangelical Visitor*.[73] Thereafter the words "Known as 'Tunkers' in Canada" became a familiar feature of the official literature.

This conciliatory gesture of General Conference subdued the Tunker name controversy until the 1930s when unexpected circumstances again projected it into the foreground. At that time the Ontario Government became aware of uncertainty surrounding the official name of the Canadian Brethren and requested them to take immediate steps to adopt and register a name. Failure to do so would jeopardize the right of their ministers to receive legal credentials to solemnize marriages.[74]

The sudden need for clarification of the church polarized the Canadian membership into pro-Tunker and pro-Brethren in Christ factions. Black Creek District, where there was strong Tunker sentiment, petitioned Canada Joint Council to adopt the name "Tunker Church," to be accompanied in printed literature by the notation "associated with the 'Brethren in Christ' in U.S.A." The petitioners argued that this was necessary to safeguard the military exemption granted to the Tunkers by the Canadian Government. Their argument did not convince the council, and it postponed the action on the petition for one year while a committee studied the implications of the matter.[75]

When the committee reported, it recommended "Brethren in Christ" in preference to "Tunker" for the church name.[76] The report found the latter name to be vague, obsolete, and without scriptural support; furthermore, that name emphasized only the Brethren doctrine of baptism. The committee also pointed out that the Brethren in Christ name had clear scriptural authority, for the Apostle Paul addressed an epistle "To the saints and faithful brethren in Christ . . . at Colosse."[77] Finally, the committee supported its recommendation by emphasizing the mutual satisfaction with the administrative relationship of the Canadian and United States Brethren, which had been maintained for more than fifty years.[78]

These arguments convinced a large majority of the council, which adopted the report and made specific provisions for its legal implementation. The losing minority, however, was seriously estranged. By request of Bishop Bert Sherk of Black Creek District, moderator Ernest J. Swalm called a special meeting of members of that district present at the council. This meeting revealed that the supporters of the Tunker name were on the verge of secession from the brotherhood and that they might take the Bertie Church premises with them.[79]

A short time later long-standing tension between some Black Creek District members who found themselves on opposite sides of the name controversy became so intense that it broke out in arson with the burning of a barn. This startling incident sobered the secessionists who requested a reopening of the name question at a special session of Canada Joint

Council.[80] That council agreed upon "Brethren in Christ (Tunker)" as a compromise name and the crisis passed.[81]

Although this name remained officially on Canada Joint Council records for many years, the parenthetical "Tunker" gradually disappeared from the literature of the Canadian Brethren, but not without protest from some members.[82] Finally, the Canadian Conference of 1964 endorsed incorporation of the brotherhood in Canada as "The Canadian Conference of the Brethren in Christ Church."[83]

The moderator of that historic session of the Conference reported an almost unamimous vote in favor of the incorporation name.[84] All of the brotherhood were at last united as "Brethren in Christ."

NOTES:

[1]Almost no primary sources exist for the first century of the history of the Brethren in Christ. Secondary accounts of their origin did not appear until well into the nineteenth century.

[2]E. Morris Sider, "The Early Years of the Tunkers in Upper Canada," *Ontario History,* LI (Spring, 1959), 122, 124.

[3]The will of Jacob Engel (probated March 12, 1833) reveals that he retained the German "Engel" surname. A photostatic copy of the will is in the Archives of the Brethren in Christ Church, Messiah College, Grantham, Pennsylvania. This records depository is cited hereafter as "Church Archives."

[4]Jacob Engel personal statement in a family Bible. Quoted in Morris M. Engle, *The Engle History and Family Records of Dauphin and Lancaster Counties.* (Mt. Joy, Pa.: Bulletin Press, n.d.), p. 61.

[5]H. S. Bender, "A Swiss Mennonite Document of 1754 Bearing on the Background of the Origin of the Brethren in Christ Church," *Mennonite Quarterly Review,* XXXIV (October, 1960), 308-9; Qualification list of foreigners on board the *Phoenix,* photostatic copy in Church Archives.

[6]Uhlrich Engel and some members of his family are buried in a small graveyard on the original Engel homestead.

[7]The inscription is now partially illegible, but it can be read on an early twentieth-century photograph of the marker reproduced in John K. Miller, "The River Brethren," *The Pennsylvania-German,* VII (January, 1906), 18.

[8][Levi Lukenbach], "Brethren in Christ," *Origin, Confession of Faith and Church Government . . . of the Brethren in Christ . . . 1871-1881 Inclusive.* (Wooster, O.: "Democrat" Print, 1881), pp. 4-5. Volume cited hereafter as *"Church Government, 1881."*

[9]H. K. Kreider, Eli M. Engle, and S. R. Smith, "Brief History of the Brethren in Christ (River Brethren)," *Minutes of General Conferences of Brethren in Christ (River Brethren) from 1871-1904* . . . (Harrisburg, Pa.: 1904), pp. 312-13. Volume cited hereafter as *General Conference Index.*

[10]M. M. Engle, *Engle History,* p. 18; J. N. Engle, "Origin of the Brethren in Christ," in A. W. Climenhaga, *History of the Brethren in Christ Church* (Nappanee, Ind.: E. V. Publishing House, 1942), p. 345.

[11]Familiar Friend, "River Brethren," p. 553.

[12]J. K. Miller, "River Brethren," p. 22.

[13]Several copies and translations of this manuscript have been found among the Brethren in Christ and Old Order River Brethren. Titles and texts vary somewhat, but all clearly trace back to a common source. This study cites hereafter as "Eighteenth-Century Confession" a German-script version entitled "A Copy of the Confession of Faith of the Brethren," translated by William D. Meikle, a distinguished linguist of Harrisburg, Pennsylvania, (See Appendix A). There is no evidence that the Brethren as a whole officially adopted the Confession.

[14]Martin Schrag, "The Brethren in Christ Attitude Toward the 'World': A Historical Study of the Movement from Separation to an Increasing Acceptance of American Society" (Ph. D. dissertation, Temple University, 1967), pp. 308-9. In Appendixes A-C of this dissertation, Schrag discusses the Eighteenth-Century Confession, explores its dating, and presents two of its extant texts.

[15]Miscellaneous Book, 1763-1767, Lancaster County Register's Office, Lancaster, Pennsylvania, p. 85.

[16]Schrag, "Brethren Attitude Toward the World," p. 308.

[17]Secondary sources which give specific dates for the origin of the Brethren agree in placing it between 1776 and 1786. This concurrence in dating correlates positively with the time of origin established by the present writer.

[18]Signatures to the Eighteenth-Century Confession; Sider, "Tunkers in Upper Canada," p. 122; John Stehman, "Origin of the River Brethren," *Christian Family Companion,* III (April 23, 1867), 147. Stehman was a nephew of John Greider, one of the signers of the Eighteenth-Century Confession.

[19]Stehman, "River Brethren," 147.

[20]Schrag, "Brethren Attitude Toward the World," p. 14.

[21]Familiar Friend, "River Brethren," footnote, p. 553. This author states only that "some" of their first ministers had Mennonite connections; he does not assign a Mennonite origin to the group as a whole. Some writers cite an enigmatic passage in Mennonite Melchior Brenneman, *Auslegung der Wahren Taufe Jesu Christi, Nebst einer Vermahnung an Alte und Junge, Wie auch Eine Erklarung etlicher Schriftstellen* (Lancaster: George and Peter Albrecht, 1808), pp. 22-23, as support for the thesis of Mennonite origin of the Brethren. This passage is too obscure and involves too many critical problems to prove that thesis.

[22]The argument from source silence does not prove, of course, that no such persons shared in the Brethren founding. Indeed, Familiar Friend, "River Brethren," p. 553, hints at the possibility of such participation.

[23]Familiar Friend, "River Brethren," p. 553; Moses Miller, "The River Brethren," 1881 manuscript (photostatic copy) in Church Archives. Miller, a Dunker, names Jacob and Joseph Keefer, Henry Busor, Anna Brehm, Susanna Miller, and Catherine Risser as Dunkers who joined the Brethren. Since the first two were his cousins, the 1881 date of Miller's manuscript (He died in 1885 at age 65.) suggests the probability

that these particular six accessions occurred in the nineteenth century.

[24]This latter possibility was suggested to the present writer by a dialogue with a group of historians gathered for a Brethren Writers' Conference at Ashland Theological Seminary, April 19-20, 1974. These historians represented several different societies.

[25]Arthur Bossler, "The Old Time Regeneration," *Evangelical Visitor,* XIX (October 2, 1905), 6, periodical cited hereafter as *Visitor.* In recent times some church leaders among the Brethren in Christ recognize that conversion may be genuine even though the individual concerned cannot identify a definite time when it occurred.

[26]Lukenbach, *Church Government,* 1881, pp. 4-5.

[27]Familiar Friend, "River Brethren," p. 553; Abram H. Cassel, "Origin of the River Brethren," 1882 manuscript (photostatic copy) in Church Archives; "Church History," *Visitor,* I (December 1, 1887), 49-50. The present author has examined the credibility of this latter account in his "The Two Earliest Secondary Accounts of River Brethren Origin as Found in Our Denominational Literature," *Notes and Queries, in Brethren in Christ History* II (April, 1961), 5-10. This mimeographed quarterly is cited hereafter as *Notes and Queries.*

[28]See Chapter I for the conversion of Martin Boehm.

[29]J. Erb, *Die Geschaeftige Martha,* II (December 15, 1841), 93, translated by D. Snowberger, "Origin of the River Brethren," *Christian Family Companion,* III (February 5, 1967), 55; *Drury, United Brethren,* pp. 102-3. The Erb-Drury tradition of the origin of the Brethren does not stand up well under critical historical analysis, but space does not permit the inclusion of that analysis here. Both authors consistently refer to the group as "River Brethren," a designation commonly applied to the Brethren in the United States at the times when these authors wrote.

[30]Stehman, "River Brethren," 147; Cassel, "River Brethren."

[31]Familiar Friend, "River Brethren," p. 553. These "Brethren or Taeufer" were Dunkers.

[32]This combination of elements drawn from Pietism and Anabaptism is clearly evident in the Eighteenth-Century Confession.

[33]*Ibid.*

[34]These circumstances explain why any Dunker desiring to affliate with the Brethren at the time of their origin or later may have shared the common desire of the founders for a baptism satisfying their understanding of full obedience.

[35]J. K. Miller, "River Brethren," 17.

[36]*History of the Church of the Brethren of the Eastern District of Pennsylvania,* by the Committee appointed by District Conference (Lancaster, Pa.: New Era Printing Company, 1915), pp. 382-83.

[37]*Ibid.,* p. 383; Cassel, "River Brethren"; J. K. Miller, "River Brethren," 17-19; M. Miller, "River Brethren"; John M. Kimmel, Chronicles of the Brethren (Covington, Ohio: Printed for the Author by Little Printing Co., 1951), p. 57.

[38]M. Miller, "River Brethren." This author was the grandson of Dunker Elder George Miller. His account gives a measure of substance to the George Miller tradition. Furthermore, Moses Miller asserts that his grandfather was ordained a bishop (elder) in 1780. If that date is correct, it creates the presumption that any contact between him and the Jacob Engel group occurred after 1780, in which case the Brethren origin would also have occurred in or subsequent to that year.

[39]J. K. Miller, "River Brethren," 19; Kimmel, *Chronicles,* p. 57.

[40]Cassel, "River Brethren"; J. K. Miller, "River Brethren," 19; M. Miller, "River

Brethren,"; Kimmel, *Chronicles*, p. 57; "Church History," 49; J. N. Engle, "Brethren in Christ," p. 345.

[41]J. K. Miller, "River Brethren," 19; "Church History," 49; J. N. Engle, "Brethren in Christ," p. 345.

[42]"Church History," 49; J. K. Miller, "River Brethren," 19; Cassel, "River Brethren"; M. Miller, "River Brethren."

[43]J. K. Miller, "River Brethren," 19; J. N. Engle, "Brethren in Christ," p. 345; M. Miller, "River Brethren."

[44]Kimmel, *Chronicles*, pp. 73, 76; *Revised Minutes of the Annual Meetings of the German Baptist Brethren*, rev. by D. L. Miller, D. E. Price and Daniel Hays (Mount Morris, Ill.: Brethren Publishing House, 1889), pp. 18-19; M. Miller, "River Brethren"; Cyrus Bucher, "Brethren vs. River Brethren," *Primitive Christian*, I (August 8, 1876), 509; Christian Bucher, "Yes, Why This Contention?", *Primitive Christian* I (September 19, 1876), 605.

[45]The Brethren also disagreed with the Dunker view that Christ instituted a sacred supper to be shared by believers only as a prelude to the partaking of the bread and wine in the communion service.

[46]Quoted in Spayth, *United Brethren*, p. 30.

[47]*Ibid.*, p. 31.

[48]*Newcomer Journal*, p. 13.

[49]Schrag, "Brethren Attitude Toward the World," pp. 33-34.

[50]The leaders who founded the United Brethren in Christ met for the first time in a conference-like setting in 1789, but they did not consummate a denominational organization until 1800. William Hanby, "History of the United Brethren in Christ," *History of all the Religious Denominations in the United States* (Harrisburg, Pa.: John Winebrenner, 1848), p. 561.

[51]M. Miller, "River Brethren."

[52]Snowberger, "River Brethren," 55.

[53]Hanby, *Religious Denominations*, p. 562.

[54]Lukenbach, *Church Government*, 1881, p. 5.

[55]Familiar Friend, "River Brethren," p. 553. This is the only known theological explanation of the original name. The scriptural citation is Mt. 23:8.

[56]*Newcomer Journal*, p. 100. All titled copies of the Eighteenth-Century Confession refer to the group as "Brethren" rather than "River Brethren," which supports the thesis that the latter name came into use sometime after the founding period.

[57]Cassel, "River Brethren"; "Church History," p. 49.

[58]Told to Ernest J. Swalm by Jacob N. Martin. E. J. Swalm to C. O. Wittlinger, February 16, 1971.

[59]Kreider, *et. al.*, *General Conference Index*, pp. 313-14.

[60]Familiar Friend, "River Brethren," p. 553. Italics in original.

[61]See also, Kimmel, *Chronicles*, p. 57.

[62]Christian Bucher, "Yes, Why This Contention?", *Primitive Christian*, I (September 19, 1876), 605; Kimmel, *Chronicles*, p. 57.

[63]Kreider, *et. al.*, *General Conference Index*, p. 314; United States Department of Commerce, Bureau of the Census, *Religious Bodies: 1926. Volume II, Separate Denominations: Statistics, History, Doctrine, Organization and Work* (Washington: United States Government Printing Office, 1929), 291. Researchers have been unable to find any trace of that registration in the records of the Federal Government.

[64]*Minutes of General Conference of The Brethren in Christ (River Brethren) of U. S. A. and Canada convened at Abilene, Kansas May 18-21, 1909.* The General Conference (Council) was the highest ecclesiastical authority of the Brethren. Although "Conference" and "Council" are used synonomously in the annual printed minutes of this assembly, and the minute citations vary accordingly, the text of the present study consistently refers to the "General Conference" which is the present name of the body.

[65]Paul Hutchinson, "The President's Religious Faith," *Life,* XXVI (March 22, 1954), 151-52. This author knew of the name "Brethren in Christ," but he preferred to use "River Brethren." See also "Dwight Eisenhower's Bible-Based Legacy," a reprint from the *Bible Society Record* (July-August, 1969).

[66]Letters by Nelson Kitely of Fordwich, Ontario, in *Christian Family Companion and Gospel Visitor,* New Series, II (August 17, 1875), 525-26, and *Primitive Christian,* I (February 29, 1876), 140. In a later letter in *Primitive Christian,* I (July 18, 1876), 460, Kitely acknowledged the historical connection of the Brethren in Canada with the River Brethren in the United States. Somewhat inconsistently, he referred to the Canadian Brethren as "Dunkards" in his first letter and as "Tunkards" in his second.

[67]E. Morris Sider, "History of the Brethren in Christ (Tunker) Church in Canada" (M. A. thesis, University of Western Ontario, 1955), p. 18.

[68]*Ibid.,* p. 23.

[69]A. B. Scherck, "The Tunkers," *The United Empire Loyalists' Association of Canada, Annual Transactions,* VI (1909), 64.

[70]"Dunkards" and "Tunkards" appear occasionally in the Canadian sources as variants of "Tunkers." *Hymns and Psalms: Original and Modern* (Toronto: Printed for the Compilers, by Lovell and Gibson, 1862), p. iv. See also the letters of Nelson Kitely cited in note 66 of this chapter.

[71]*A Compilation of the Canadian Joint Council Minutes of the Brethren in Christ, (Tunker), Church from 1892 to 1941* (bound mimeographed volume), 1932, p. 93. Volume cited hereafter as *Canadian Joint Council Minutes.*

[72]*Ibid.,* 1904, p. 15. One Who Was There, "Canada Joint Council," *Visitor,* XVIII (October 15, 1904), 14; E. J. Swalm, "*My Beloved Brethren . . .*" *Personal Memoirs and Recollections of the Canadian Brethren in Christ Church* (Nappanee, Indiana: Evangel Press, 1969), p. 11.

[73]*General Conference Minutes,* 1917, Article 33, pp. 70-71.

[74]*Canadian Joint Council Minutes,* 1933, pp. 101-2.

[75]*Ibid.,* 1932, pp. 93-94.

[76]*Ibid.,* 1933, pp. 102. The committee apparently found no evidence that the society had either officially adopted or registered a name with the government.

[77]Col. 1:2.

[78]*Canadian Joint Council Minutes,* 1933, p. 102.

[79]Swalm, *Beloved Brethren,* pp. 11, 12; E. J. Swalm interview, March 3, 1971; John N. Hostetter interview, July 5, 1971. Both of the men interviewed were present in the meeting.

[80]Swalm, *Beloved Brethren,* p. 12.

[81]*Canadian Joint Council Minutes,* Special Session, October 13, 1933, pp. 105-6.

[82]Sider, "Brethren in Canada," p. 285.

[83]*Minutes of the Seventy-Third Annual Canadian Conference of the Brethren in Christ Church,* 1964, Article 6, p. 9.

[84]Swalm, *Beloved Brethren,* p. 12.

III

The Brethren World View

Those who start a new religious movement begin with an idea or cluster of ideas which reflect a particular view of the world and man's place in it. In the founding of the Brethren in Christ, four ideas were crucial: the authority of Scripture for faith and practice; a heartfelt conversion experience or new birth; the church as a visible community of converted adults; and a surrounding world hostile to the faith and life of that community. These ideas have been mentioned in previous chapters, but they must be perceived as an interrelated thought structure in order to understand the movement.

The Scriptures

In his sketch of the origin of the society, Levi Lukenbach noted the determination of the founders to reject all creeds and to stand upon the authority of Scripture, with special attention to the New Testament as the highest level of God's self-revelation.[1] This anti-creedalism, which was typical of Pietism, may be another example of Dunker influence upon the Brethren. One of the historians of the Dunkers wrote of their origin:

> Rejecting on the one hand the creed of man, and on the other hand the abandonment of ordinances, they turned to the Bible for guidance. From God's Word they learned that ordinances were vital and creed unnecessary. Adopting the Bible as their rule and guide they organized a church with no creed, and with all the ordinances as taught by Jesus and his followers, as recorded in the New Testament.[2]

There is no evidence that Jacob Engel and his associates consciously imitated the Dunkers, but the preceding statement indicates how the Brethren founders understood their own faith to be related to the Scriptures.

The biblical basis of the thought patterns of the brotherhood stands out in the Eighteenth-Century Confession. Although that document presents no formal doctrine of the Scriptures, it takes their authenticity and authority for granted.[3] The text includes a liberal sprinkling of biblical passages, and the eight leaders who signed the statement clearly believed that it encompassed the core of the biblical revelation.

Throughout the nineteenth century, the Brethren continued to avoid creedal statements and to emphasize the authority of Scripture.[4] Nothing resembling a creed appeared until 1881, and the short "Confession of Faith" published in that year did not really mark a break with their anti-creedal position. The author described it as merely "a synopsis of the doctrine of the Church as believed in and taught by the Brethren."[5] Its inclusion with the cumulative minutes of the General Conference shows, however, that its concepts were acceptable to the brotherhood.[6]

The Confession of 1881 states for the first time a doctrine of the Scriptures: "We believe that the Holy Bible, the Old and New Testament, is the Word of God, . . ." It then sketches briefly what the Brethren of that time believed to be the core of the biblical message. Characteristically, it coupled piety and obedience: ". . . by faith in our Savior, and true repentance, forgiveness of sin, and obedience to Christ and His commands, is the only true way that we may become and remain Christians." The remainder of the statement spells out the meaning of obedience. In many respects this document is a thumbnail sketch of the Eighteenth-Century Confession, which shows that the scriptural thought patterns of the group remained intact throughout the first one hundred years.

In view of their understanding of Scripture, the Brethren took the text seriously and sought to conform their lives to what seemed to them to be its obvious meaning. When Jesus told His disciples that they also "ought to wash one another's feet," the Brethren concluded that He meant the literal washing of feet. Again, when Paul exhorted Christians to greet one another with "a holy kiss," they took this as God's word to them and practiced the kiss as a fraternal greeting.

The inclination of the Brethren to interpret the Scriptures literally should not be mistaken for naivety. They were familiar, for example, with figures of speech. Christian Lesher, commenting in the mid-nineteenth century on the statement of Jesus that if an eye offends it should be plucked out, observed: "I would suppose no one to be so silly as to understand it in a natural way."[7] They also displayed exegetical resourcefulness when faced with seemingly contradictory passages such as Paul's various statements on the participation of women in the services of the church, or with the problem of reconciling the attitude of God toward war in the Old Testament with their nonresistant convictions based upon the New Testament.[8]

Sometimes, however, they by-passed the literal interpretation of what many readers of Scripture perceive to be clear and unambiguous passages, such as the teaching of Paul that those who preach the gospel should live by the gospel. In this instance they departed from their principle of giving the New Testament priority over the Old, for they strongly emphasized the passage from Isaiah: "Ho, everyone that thirsteth, come ye to the waters, and he that hath no money; come ye, buy, and eat; yea, come, buy wine and milk without money and without price." The latter passage, they believed, supported their understanding that the Gospel should be "free," that is, proclaimed without financial implications.[9]

Although the Brethren saw an overall unity in the Scriptures—God fashioning a holy and obedient people—they had a strong inclination to stress isolated or proof texts. On one occasion when General Conference debated life insurance, the ruling against it was supported by ten scriptural references, three from the Old Testament and seven from the New.[10] In another instance articles on sanctification approved by the Conference of 1887 included more than sixty biblical texts, mostly from the New Testament.[11] This concern for proof texts came forcefully to the foreground in a Pennsylvania State Council petition for a committee to furnish scriptural references to support doctrinal decisions of General Conference.[12] That petition also reflects the belief that the corporate brotherhood, as well as the individual, was bound by the Word of God.

Their insistence upon scriptural authority sometimes required the Brethren to question whether a time-honored position or practice had adequate biblical support. On one occasion a committee appointed by Conference to consider whether the prevailing system of a self-supporting ministry was in accord with the New Testament concluded that it was not and made recommendations to align practice with Scripture.[13] Subsequent history reveals, however, that the brotherhood was not easily persuaded to take scriptural exhortation for ministerial support seriously; in this instance their concept of obedience was qualified.

Another of their principles emphasized corporate rather than private interpretation of Scripture. They followed the precept that "in the multitude of counsellors there is safety."[14] When exegetical problems proved too difficult for local districts to solve, such questions normally passed to General Conference. This is illustrated by a petition for Conference to decide "whether the Second Definite Work Theme as taught in the Brotherhood, is entirely scriptural, and if not altogether scriptural, what part is, and should be taught?"[15]

In spite of the many changes which the Brethren made in belief and folkways during their history, they always maintained their commitment to a Bible-centered theology. Henry Davidson, speaking in the midst of ferment and controversy during the late nineteenth century, spoke the mind of the brotherhood when he commented:

> We do not want to stand in the way of the work of the Lord, but we want to accept the right even though we may have to give up some things that we formerly cherished as dear to us. Yet in no case can we give up the doctrine of the Bible.[16]

Advocates of change have been expected to demonstrate that proposed innovations represented more correct biblical interpretations than those ideas or practices which they would displace.

The Conversion Experience

In keeping with their pietistic background, the commitment of the Brethren to the concept of a heartfelt conversion was a crucial aspect of their world view. They believed that theological orthodoxy, church sacraments and ceremonies, Christian upbringing, moral behavior, and good intentions did not merit God's favor. Only as repentant sinners cast themselves upon the mercy of God who worked in them the miracle of regeneration or new birth could they join the ranks of the redeemed and share the fellowship of the church. One nineteenth-century leader, commenting upon the early Brethren movement, observed: ". . . we think it has not deviated from the old gospel land-marks upon which it was first established. Then they were a plain people, believing in genuine repentance and conversion and true spiritual worship, . . ."[17]

The Eighteenth-Century Confession strongly emphasizes the conversion experience. After a brief reference to God, the Confession proceeds immediately to Christ's redemptive work and explains how the sinner experiences its benefits. In the words of that document:

> He [Christ] reconciled God and offered a sacrifice that holds good forever, so that all who believe on Him shall not be lost, but shall have eternal life. This has all happened outside of ourselves, but to reveal this in us there appeared the healing Grace of God to convince us and to teach us that . . . we have by nature a heart averse from God, devious and sinful. If this is confessed and acknowledged, it works a regret and sorrow . . . in short, the Light reveals to us the Fall into which Adam and we all have fallen; and this causes a longing, a praying, a weeping, and a calling to the promised Savior . . . who died bleeding before such poor sinners. Into such an open, poor sinner's heart the Lord Jesus will and can come . . . to bestow comfort, peace, love and trust. . . . A poor sinner feels and experiences that; and there the living Faith has its beginning, . . . So we confess that to be a new birth, . . .

Other sources testify to the importance of this new birth which the "poor sinner feels and experiences." In the 1820s John Winger of Canada, writing to a young convert, rejoiced because of her conversion experience:

> It has given me great joy to hear of your conversion, beloved child, and sister in the Lord, be consoled, and encouraged, and allow yourself not to be made weak by the temptation of the enemy, as the experience of conversion is varied; for I understand in your letter that you have found peace, and comfort, and the substance of hope in your God, and wish you may remain virtuous and true to your God.[18]

Jacob Hershey of Lancaster County, who died in 1842, reported a time when "the bag wherein God had sealed my transgressions was rent in twain and all vanished, . . . I was endowed with such a power I cannot describe; it seemed like a baptism because the love of God was poured upon me, . . ."[19] In the 1840s William O. Baker first heard Brethren preaching in Wayne County, Ohio; he became aware of his need for salvation and, after considerable delay, experienced a spiritual transformation, when, he says: ". . . God exercised his great mercy toward me in the pardon of my sins."[20] Such accounts and present-day "experience meetings" of the Old Order River Brethren* reveal a conversion process

*The Old Order River Brethren (Yorkers) separated about the mid-nineteenth century from the River Brethren who later became the Brethren

which, although often complex and stressful, ultimately culminated in a decisive crisis.[21]

The typical conversion process began with an awareness of personal sinfulness—"conviction" the Brethren called it—and separation from God's favor. As the sinner considered the cost of yielding to God's will, the stress of the process became more acute. At some point the "seeker" began to obey, that is, to demonstrate genuine repentance by confessing personal sinfulness, making restitution for wrongs done to others, and changing behavior and relationships perceived to be displeasing to God. Finally, the thoroughly repentant sinner reached a crisis, exercised saving faith in Christ, and experienced assurance of forgiveness of sins.

Although the Brethren spoke freely of "works" of repentance, they did not believe in conversion by self-effort. In their view the Holy Spirit—"the good Spirit" in early Brethren language—was the active agent at every stage of the conversion process. This confidence in the ministry of the Spirit may help to explain why they did not develop conversion counseling until the late nineteenth century, when they became more open to the influence of mainline, evangelical Protestantism. In the earlier days the Brethren urged "seekers," persons convicted of their sinfulness, to "obey as the Lord might lead."[22] They were much opposed to what they considered to be shallow "only believe" conversion teaching.[23]

In spite of this strong emphasis upon the conversion experience, the Brethren were not revivalistic in the modern sense. They did not organize and preach with conversions as their primary goal, nor did they identify with the revivalistic practices of societies such as the United Brethren in Christ and the Evangelical Association. For their part, such churches did not consider the Brethren to be one of their number.[24] During the late nineteenth century, furthermore, the brotherhood still questioned revival methods which had a long prior history in other evangelical churches. In the 1870s General Conference discussed the legitimacy of protracted meetings, that is, revival meetings.[25] Ten years later it debated whether ministers were in order if they invited seekers to come forward in services.[26]

The commitment of the Brethren to pietistic conversion coupled with

in Christ. The former preserve much of the faith and folkways of the River Brethren movement prior to the separation and, thus, are an important source of information about the early Brethren in Christ. See Chapter VII for a discussion of the Old Order schism.

their rejection of revivalism may seem to be paradoxical. The explanation of this seeming paradox lies in their understandings of the church and the Christian life, which gave their concept of conversion special meaning. Their view of conversion may be illustrated from the closing verses of the Gospel of Matthew. This passage combines baptism, which the Brethren understood to symbolize a prior new birth, with the command to teach the "all things" which Christ commanded. In other words, piety (a salvation experience) and obedience (following Christ in the "all things") went hand in hand. Persons passing through the conversion process in Brethren settings characteristically perceived Brethren beliefs and life-style to embody the "all things" which Christ commanded. To be converted or born again, therefore, was not only to have a subjective salvation experience; it was also to accept the brotherhood understanding of the Christian life. As one member wrote:

> Those who are born into the kingdom of grace, and have been washed and cleansed by the blood of Christ, are born of God; and they will do the will of God. . . . The whole man will become changed within and without and become a new creature in Christ Jesus. . . . The people of God are a peculiar and separate people. They will come out from the world; . . .[27]

This writer clearly spoke out of the context of Brethren thought, for he added that persons "changed within and without" could no longer go to "places where mirth and levity are the ruling elements, such as birthday celebrations, wedding anniversaries, and surprise parties." Another member described her conversion:

> I felt as though I was in another world . . . old things had passed away and all things became new. I was now willing to be led by the Spirit. I was dressy before, now I wanted to be plain. When I began to change my dress my friends turned against me. . . . I thought a great deal of my friends; to leave them and go against them seemed very hard to me.
>
> I looked around me and wondered whether there was no other way to get to heaven than this narrow path; but there was no other way for me.[28]

This strong emphasis upon the fruits of conversion—"works" the Brethren frequently called them—sometimes produced a legalistic frame of mind. Since overt conduct stood out more conspicuously than inner attitudes, they could perceive correct outward forms more easily than changed hearts. The result was that some members became legalistic and failed to perceive clearly the full implications of the doctrine of salvation by grace.[29]

On the other hand, the preoccupation of the early Brethren with conduct speaks to something much more fundamental than legalism. They believed that faith and obedience were inseparably joined in the salvation experience, or, as asserted by James, that "faith, if it hath not works, is dead, . . ."[30] An article by Bishop William Baker developed the relation of faith and obedience. Taking "Faith Alone" as his subject, he distinguished between works repudiated by Paul and works endorsed by James. Paul, he stated, emphasized faith as the basis for Abraham's justification to show to his Jewish brethren that Abraham was not justified by the deeds of the law. James, on the other hand, emphasized works to show that if Abraham's faith had not been productive of obedience and a holy life, it would not have been imputed to him for righteousness.[31]

On these premises obedience was an integral part of the conversion experience. One did not exercise faith in Christ as Savior and then, at some future time, decide for or against obedience to Him as Lord. Rather, faith and obedience went hand in hand. In Baker's words:

> It is impossible to exercise that faith that will draw the blessings of God upon us if we are at enmity with our fellowmen or hold what we dishonestly took from them or live in any way in violation of God's moral law. People have prayed and seemingly cried mightily unto the Lord for days, trying to substitute prayer for confession and faith for honesty. Confession and restoration were first in order, without which no further progress could be made. "Obedience is better than sacrifice." No amount of praying, no amount of tears can take the place of these "works meet for repentance."[32]

This background is important for an understanding of the subject of works in the literature of the Brethren. They did not believe that they were saved by works but rather that they could not ignore their reckoning with obedience.[33] If, while seeking the salvation experience, they became aware of wrongs which they had committed, they assumed that those wrongs should be made right immediately. Seekers sometimes spent days and weeks going about their communities making amends for their wrongs. Some did not feel assured of peace with God until this process of restitution was completed. Others felt that they had much "work" to do after they testified to such assurance; only as they obeyed their understanding of God's leadings did they retain their assurance of a right relationship with Him. One young lady wrote of her conversion: "The love that I there received I cannot express, but I promised the Lord I would serve Him, it might go as it would. . . . I soon found that there is work for me to do, such as covering of the head, baptism, correcting wrongs."[34] Another testimony illustrates the deep concern for the works of obedience.

> I was not willing at all times to yield to God's Spirit. I would . . . sometimes think this or that will be just as good, but this would not do for me. I had to give up my will to God's will and everytime I would obey I was blessed. My hardest trial was to go to my parents and ask them . . . [to] forgive me all, whatsoever I have done amiss in their sight. I think it was two or three months before I was willing to go to them . . . but I got no pardon until I obeyed. . . .
>
> I had lots of work to do before I was pleasing in the sight of God.[35]

Not all Brethren felt entirely comfortable with a faith-obedience emphasis, which they perceived might compromise the doctrine of salvation by grace. Henry N. Engle lamented the time devoted by the brotherhood to the "dress question" while the "*simple Gospel of Savlation through the blood*" had, he felt, been only too meagerly proclaimed.[36] George Detwiler, who finished his active career as a teacher at the Messiah Bible School and Missionary Training Home, was distressed by what seemed to him to be general student ignorance of the doctrine of grace.

> Some things that have come to my notice more recently are puzzling me. This causes me to question whether it is really the teaching of the church that it is incumbent on sinners to make their peace with God. I have sometimes heard brethren (ministers) give that teaching, but I did not conclude that such is the teaching of the church. If however it is true that the church does teach so it explains to me how nearly all of the students that passed through my hands failed to answer, scripturally, and intelligently questions like these: "What did you have to do to obtain peace with God?" . . . Not a single one had learned that Jesus Christ made peace by the blood of the cross, that "He is our peace" or that "By faith we have peace with God through our Lord Jesus Christ."[37]

Descriptions of conversions in the late nineteenth century give the impression that these varied greatly in the degree to which they originated in a clear conception of the doctrine of grace as Detwiler understood it. Sources for their prior history are too limited to make clear how effectively the earlier Brethren integrated the doctrine of grace with their understanding of the relationship between conversion and obedience.

The Visible Church

The early Brethren perceived the church to be the visible people of God, the community of born again, obedient, disciplined, interdependent Christians in face-to-face fellowship. It was not a man-made institution created to produce either personal piety or the salvation of "souls," nor was it the total invisible community of those who had been born again. Salvation, they believed, was not only personal but corporate; the church as a visible community was to demonstrate the redemption of relationships; it should seek to be nothing less than an earthly microcosm of Christ's Kingdom.

This conception of the church as a visible community is prominent in the Eighteenth-Century Confession. After stressing the experience of personal salvation, the Confession proceeds to the life of the church. Jesus Christ is the pattern for His children who, because they love the One who bore them, love also those born by Him. The resulting fellowship of born-again ones is "a believing community through the unity of Spirit." This community should faithfully observe the ordinances of baptism, communion, and feet washing. Its members should have private meetings and opening and honestly share their Christian experiences with each other because "such new-born children are exposed to many temptations and when through filial revelation the craftiness of the devil is discovered, then one can talk open-heartedly with the other so that the body of Christ is renewed." These private meetings foreshadowed the "social" or "experience meeting" which loomed so large in the life of the Brethren.

The Confession also emphasizes the regulation of "the household of God," that is, the church. Because Christians are "bound through love to watch out for each other," nobody should do anything important—marry, change his residence, buy land—without brotherly advice. Matthew 18:15-20 is the basis for discipline within the fellowship, with excommunication from the brotherhood the ultimate remedy if a sinning member is unsubmissive when the group seeks to lead him or her to repentance and restored fellowship.

Elsewhere the Confession emphasizes the need for public meetings where the Word is preached to bring sinners to repentance. This reveals that the early Brethren joined their concern for the visible church with an awareness of the need for evangelism to expand the community of the converted. During their first one hundred years, however, they gave primary attention to being the church rather than to enlarging the church.

In the absence of revivalistic meetings and methods, the visible church grew through conversions which occurred in the customary Brethren services.[38] Members also carried their witness into community homes. One lady was convicted at an early age of her need for salvation while two members recounted their Christian experiences in her home.[39] A deacon in Manor-Pequea District reported the "Good News" that he visited in a home where the wife was "very heavy under conviction."[40]

Most Brethren converts prior to 1880 were adults.[41] Data on twenty-eight persons converted before 1870 show that their average age of conversion was twenty-three years. This relatively late age of conversion assured the maturity and stability needed to perform the duties of membership in the visible brotherhood community.[42] On the other hand, testimonies of dramatic adult conversions may have created the impression that a higher quality of Christian experience was the lot of individuals who "sowed their wild oats."[43] In any case, the brotherhood expected the conversion decision to involve a clear understanding that the seeker was renouncing "the world," which implied acceptance of the Brethren lifestyle.

Like most visions which come to fallible human beings, the Brethren understanding of the church had its limitations. By the mid-nineteenth century, three schisms rent the ranks of the group; brotherhood proved to be unequal to the task of reconciliation in these instances. Yet the conception of the church as a visible, earthly community in which God's will is done as perfectly as possible has been a beacon light in the history of the movement.

The Hostile World

Another important part of the faith of the Brethren was their perception of the world as a hostile force confronting the church. While the visible community of the converted sought to follow Christ fully, surrounding evil forces contrary to the spirit of this community were bent upon its destruction. These forces attacked through inner subjective appeals to the "flesh," through evil persons, and through the attitudes and organized structures of society. Thus, for the early Brethren "worldliness" had very serious connotations. They perceived its manifestations in a wide range of specific situations and took seriously the reference of the Eighteenth-Century Confession to "the craftiness of the devil." The many ways by which they sought to detect and resist worldliness resulted in a unique lifestyle.

Like all other beliefs of the Brethren, their doctrine of separation from the world—"nonconformity" they characteristically called it—rested upon their understanding of the Scriptures. The Confession of 1881 states: "We believe that the Scriptures teach that Christians should not be conformed to this world, but that they are a separate people, . . ."[44] Implications of this position appeared in the first "Rules of Church Government" published a few years later. These affirm that separation from the world is first shown by the daily walk and holy life of the Christian. In the words of this document:

> . . . separation should . . . be manifested by our holy lives, and this will lead us to put away, and to divest ourselves of, everything that is sinful, and to live pure lives in Christ Jesus, and to be "sanctified wholly," . . . Our apparel should be sanctified and made mete [sic] for the Master's use, as well as what we eat and drink.[45]

The document adds that the body, which is God's temple, should not be "prostituted and polluted by making it the resceptacle [sic] of that which is filthy and sickening, or that which intoxicates and destroys the reasoning powers." This latter statement shows the influence of the temperance movement; tobacco and alcohol were beginning to be classified with the pollutions of the world.[46]

In developing their doctrine of nonconformity, the Brethren gave much attention to personal appearance. Pride, they thought, embodied the essence of worldliness and was a deadly sin; humility, its opposite, was a primary virtue. They perceived personal appearance to be a domain where satanic pride and godly humility contended for dominion.

No description of the appearance of the founders exists. Their nineteenth-century descendants made their clothing from plain gray or black materials. Men wore long-tail coats and vests with erect collars, broad-fall trousers opening at the sides rather than in the middle, high-top boots or shoes, cape overcoats, and broad-brimmed hats. Women wore ankle-length dresses with long sleeves, heavily gathered skirts and aprons, separate capes (tippets) covering the bodice of the dress and extending in the back and front to a point below the waist, plain shoes, shawls, and cape bonnets. In response to the Pauline exhortation for women to cover their heads when praying or prophesying, they wore caps or "prayer veilings" of heavy white material tied under the chin. Both men and women parted their hair in the middle and combed it flat against the head. Women wore their hair long and rolled into a knot at the back of the head; men cut their hair square at the neck and wore full beards without the mustache.[47]

Portraits of three nineteenth-century Brethren in Christ. Top: Jacob Brechbill (1832-1902), Sarah Ober Brechbill (1839-1908), and (below) Henry Davidson (1823-1903). The latter was the first editor of the *Evangelical Visitor*. Note differences in the garb of the two men.

Brethren practices regarding the beard, mustache, and shingled hair for men closely paralleled those of the Dunkers and appear to have been influenced by many of the same considerations.[48] The latter group advocated the beard because, they said, it was according to nature, supported by scriptural teaching and example, and nonconformist when not trimmed or fashioned according to worldly styles. Shingling the hair, they felt, was also a violation of nonconformity. While they reluctantly conceded the mustache if a brother conscientiously felt that he should not shave at all, it was prohibited without the beard. Their objectives were to safeguard the group from worldly mustache styling and also to facilitate the kiss salutation.[49]

Closely related to their desire to remain separate from the world in hair and beard styling, was the Brethren concern for nonconformity in dress. Their logic in this matter was simple and direct. Converted men and women did not belong to the world system, so they should dress like pilgrims and strangers in it. An item in the first issue of the *Visitor* states: "Christians ought to be as peculiar for their modest apparel as worldlings are for ornamenting their persons."[50] A later writer comments: "Those who wear gay clothing or anything worn to seek glory from men, can not be humble followers of God. We are to be a separate people, zealous of good works, and living epistles known and read of all men."[51]

In the midst of a late nineteenth-century flurry of *Visitor* discussion about clothing, Editor Henry N. Engle penned one of the more thoughtful rationales for the Brethren position:

> What then does the Bible teach? First, there is the general and fundamental principal [*sic*] of separation from the world as expressed in 1 Jno. 2:15, 16; Rom. 12:2, and other passages.—"Love not the world, neither the things that are in the world; Be not conformed to this world." Second, we have the two specific passages in regard to dress, namely, 1 Tim. 2:9, 10 and 1 Pet. 3:3, 4.
>
> The direction here is to women only but all will admit that the *principle* is to be carried out by men, as well. These verses tell, in language that any child can understand, that women are not to adorn themselves outwardly with broidered or *curled (Syriac)* hair, or gold, or pearls, or costly array; but with a meek and quiet spirit and with good works.[52]

Engle emphasized the frustrations of denominations which had tried to keep people within the confines of certain rules and forms of dress. The reason was, he said, that pride is deeply rooted in the heart and may be present beneath a plain exterior. "Get the Lord enthroned within through the indwelling Holy Ghost, submitting to his teaching in the Word, and the dress question will be quickly settled."

Editor Engle also made clear that his support for modesty and plainness in appearance was not a defense of one special or set form of dress. He maintained that there were no scriptural injunctions for such a form. Specific statements in official Brethren documents concurred with this point of view until well into the twentieth century.[53] When General Conference of 1872 debated whether any given form of dress was scriptural, its decision was: "Nothing more than that it should not be in fashion with the world."[54] The first Rules of Church Government expressed this position more forcefully:

> Our apparel is therefore to be plain, not costly, but such as becometh those professing godliness. We have no express command in God's word as to what the cut of our clothing shall be, yet it does teach that we should not be conformed to this world.[55]

Although this was the official position on dress, group pressures for conformity to the traditional dress practices were very strong. General Conference of 1880 urged the brotherhood to retain plain apparel and later ruled that a brother conformed to the world in outward apparel and appearance could not be ordained to the ministry.[56] Local areas of the brotherhood, furthermore, pressed their members to adhere to traditional practices of nonconformity in appearance.[57] Canadian Jonas Winger probably expressed the dress convictions of the majority of members during the first one hundred years of the Brethren movement when he wrote:

> I have often said, we as Christians and as church members should strictly follow one and only one form of dress. And, oh! let us not deviate from that. . . . Now if any of us deviate from the simple and appropriate dress, that is customary among us as brethren and sisters, I think we are out of the way because we have an influence over others, and they look upon us as good men and women. . . . Oh! brethren and sisters, we might just as well say, Dress as you like, as to err in any form. How shall we keep house in the church if we don't keep strictly in one way.[58]

The efforts of the Brethren to safeguard themselves from the hostile world extended beyond plain dress to all artificial means of decorating the person. They took literally Paul's admonition to women to "adorn themselves in modest apparel, with shamefacedness and sobriety; not with broidered hair, or gold, or pearls, or costly array; But . . . with good works."[59] This exhortation, they believed, prohibited all jewelry including the wedding ring, artificial treatment of the hair, and expensive clothing for both men and women. Some members took the prohibition against gold so literally that they questioned its use in eyeglasses and watches.[60] Others, however, distinguished between the use of gold for adornment and its use for utilitarian purposes.[61]

Principles which determined Brethren definitions of worldliness in personal appearance often applied to other areas of their lives as well. Decoration of homes, barns, and conveyances tended to be questioned on the same grounds as decoration of the person. In the words of one member:

> . . . the true religion of Jesus Christ is a trimmer; it cleanses the heart first, it helps us to make wrongs right; it helps us to make strait paths for our feet; it takes pride out of the heart and the consequence is, it falls off from the outside of the body; it trims our houses, no more need for things to decorate the walls to please the eyes of the world . . . it tells us there is no need for those artificial lamps on that carriage, or those trimmings that hang almost into your face, . . .[62]

Another member observed: "If God allows me to build a fashionable barn or house he will also allow me to paint it with three or four different colors . . . [and] furnish it in the latest style; then have ourselves fixed and trimmed up also and . . . all would correspond."[63] He obviously saw no difference between appearing like the world personally or having a house "or whatever it may be" appear like the world. To this statement Editor Engle appended a note which stated succinctly the general principles which concerned the Brethren:

> We are glad for the brother's testimony. What has the soul which is truly begotten of God to do with the vain things of earth? Decency, cleanliness, and order go with the Christ-life, but superfluities and extravagance find no place with the consecrated soul.

Although the Brethren used biblical texts to support their position on nonconformity in appearance of persons, homes, barns and conveyances, they often felt the need to define worldliness in matters for which they had no specific texts. In this broad twilight zone, they consciously or unconsciously developed a special criterion—usefulness. Creature needs for food, clothing, housing, and transportation had to be met. The Brethren acknowledged the legitimacy of means useful to achieve these ends, but in employing such means they sought to avoid the encouragement of decorative inclinations. The result was that they sometimes identified aesthetic experience and even convenience with worldly conformity.

When seeking to apply their criterion of usefulness, the Brethren encountered problems of definition. Did "useful," for example, mean indispensable or merely convenient? The members of one district wondered whether sleeve holders were legitmately useful or worldly and, rather ambiguously, requested men "to abstain from all unnecessary display."[64] Another district, puzzled by changing window styles, decided that eight window panes were more consistent than a lesser number.[65] Carriage and wagon wheels were indispensable, but springs in conveyances raised questions. When United States Bishop Levi Lukenbach arrived at the Ontario Black Creek District for a love feast, the leaders there reportedly hesitated to admit him to communion because he came in a carriage or wagon with springs.[66]

Brethren concerns about nonconformist safeguards from the hostile world extended to aspects of their lives other than the appearance of persons and things. They disapproved of weddings conducted according to "the custom of the world."[67] Many believed musical instruments to be inconsistent with a nonconformist stand; Dayton District in Ohio denied ordination to an elected deacon because he had an organ in his home.[68] "Likenesses" or photographs troubled the Brethren, possibly because of the fear that they would nurture pride, but also because of the biblical injunction: "Thou shalt not make unto thee any graven image, or any likeness of any thing . . . ."[69]

Another concern about worldly conformity developed in connection with community relationships and activities. Some of these were regarded as being inherently worldly; others involved what the Brethren considered to be an "unequal yoke" with unbelievers.[70] The first category included picnics, excursions, fairs, exhibitions, theaters, dances, practically all forms of public entertainment, and recreation including sports and games.[71]

The Brethren strongly opposed membership in lodges and secret societies; such membership not only involved an unequal yoke but had other objectionable features. They could not even join agricultural organizations such as the Patrons of Husbandry (Grange) or Farmers' Alliances which generally had lodge connotations.[72] One member noted that something which requires "such strict secrecy and careful guarding that a man dare not tell his wife what they are doing, is, to put it at the mildest, very suspicious, . . ."[73] Another observed: "Why, the name of Christ dare not even be mentioned in the lodge! Query—Is such a place the place for a christian [sic]?"[74]

Their strong emphasis upon the hostile world also caused the Brethren to stand aloof from churches whose members and programs conformed to the patterns of prevailing culture. They recognized that Christians were not limited to their own circles.[75] On the other hand, they could not understand how other churches could condone costly edifices, questionable social activities, militarism, secret societies, musical instruments, and choirs, salaried ministers, and worldly conformity in appearance.[76] An editorial of the period articulated some of their deep feelings about such churches.

> The modern church service partakes largely of a performance . . . in which the entertainment idea largely predominates. The church is poor, and needs money to carry on her work so she soils her spotless robe by going into the amusement business, and when she undertakes to invite the worldling to repent and be converted he rightly wonders from what he is to be converted, since he meets the professor of religion . . . at the theater, at the dance, the circus, the horse race, card table, etc.[77]

The Brethren also felt estranged from other professing Christians who did not practice trine immersion, feet washing, and the prayer veiling.[78]

The preceding analysis makes clear why members of the brotherhood had few inter-church contacts. It also helps to explain why they leaned toward the principle of closed communion and why those among them who fraternized with other churches risked group disapproval.[79]

Although the Brethren strongly emphasized nonconformity to the hostile world, they understood that nonconformist church practices were no substitute for a right heart. As one of them observed:

> . . . the Lord wants a clean and perfect heart. I fear that I have only the form which the Church upholds, or in other words, my heart does not accord with my outward appearance. I often wish that when I speak for the cause of Christ, I might speak such words that originate in the heart; for when the love of God is shed abroad in our hearts, oh! what joy and happiness we can realize, . . .[80]

This belief in the right heart was joined with confidence in the corporate wisdom of the brotherhood to determine how that right heart should find expression in a right life. The resulting group definitions of Christian behavior had such wide-ranging implications that they amounted to a broad repudiation of contemporary life and culture. In a very real sense, the Brethren withdrew bodily as well as spiritually from society; they were a society unto themselves.[81]

Only a large measure of voluntary consensus permitted the brotherhood to maintain this sectarian detachment from the mainstream of social life. Several built-in strengths of their thought patterns contributed to this consensus. In the first place, they were a closely-knit, homogenous people, practically all of whom were engaged in agriculture; this gave them a common core of interest and experiences. They believed, furthermore, that their doctrine of nonconformity was an essential aspect of obedience; the Scriptures called them to walk in the narrow way of self-denial. Finally, their doctrine of the church predisposed them to be guided by definitions of worldliness determined by the brotherhood as a whole. In addition to these circumstances supporting voluntary consensus, group approval, frequently expressed in legislation, strongly reinforced compliance with nonconformist group norms.

In contrast to these supporting circumstances, other factors tended to modify the doctrine of nonconformity as the Brethren understood it. One of these was the difficulty of applying a general principle such as usefulness to specific practical situations. To rule falling-top buggies worldly, for example, and then, five years later, to accept them as legitimately useful raised questions about the credibility of the decision-making process.[82]

Another factor was the inexorable pressure of social change. The Brethren formulated many of their definitions of worldliness under specific social conditions. When those conditions changed so as to make a time-honored position or practice impracticable, the process of modifying it could be difficult and disruptive. This is illustrated by a problem which arose in the 1850s among the Dauphin County Brethren near Middletown, Pennsylvania. Here the membership had become too large for the customary house services so they decided to build a small, simple meetinghouse. This aroused so much opposition among members elsewhere in Pennsylvania that it finally resulted in the excommunication of the Dauphin County Brethren.[83]

A third factor was the age-old phenomenon of the generation gap which was also related to social change. Along with the acceleration of such change in the latter part of the nineteenth century, educational levels advanced. These circumstances tended to influence younger generations of Brethren more than their forebears. Also, members began to enter the brotherhood at earlier ages.[84] This combination of circumstances tended to create uncertainties about definitions of worldliness. One concerned member noted that "our young brethren and sisters . . . would like to reach over the line to get just a little of the world and still be on the Lord's side."[85] Another observed that "we see so many of our young brethren and sisters trying to drag their cross along. They give the evidence that they still want a little of the world . . . ."[86]

These countervailing influences gradually modified earlier definitions of worldliness. The formulation of those definitions by the Brethren must be understood, however, as a serious attempt to implement their world view which perceived the visible church to be in serious confrontation with the hostile world.

NOTES:

[1]Lukenbach, *Church Government,* 1881, p. 5.

[2]Brumbaugh, *German Baptist Brethren,* p. 33.

[3]The Confession was not a formal creed but rather a summary of the biblical understandings of the eight Brethren leaders who signed it. There is no proof that the brotherhood as a whole adopted the document as an offical statement of faith.

[4]Familiar Friend, "River Brethren," p. 554. A *"Compendium* of doctrine" (possibly the Eighteenth-Century Confession), which this author mentions, failed to gain the approval of a majority of the group.

[5]Lukenbach, *Church Government,* 1881, pp. 5-6.

[6]General Conference of 1906 authorized a small tract entitled: *Brethren in Christ. What We Believe and Why We Believe It.* The 1909 Conference approved a brief "Creed and Confession of faith and of the Non-Resistant Doctrine," which, however, was introduced as follows: "The Brethren in Christ have not accepted any historical creed or confession; but have certain recognized doctrines to which they adhere."

[7]Christian Lesher, *Christian Magazine,* transl. by Laban T. Brechbill (Chambersburg, Pa.: M. Kieffer & Co., 1849), p. 179. Lesher lived from 1775 to 1856.

[8]Later chapters will provide examples of this exegetical resourcefulness.

[9]H. Frances Davidson, *South and South Central Africa: A Record of Fifteen Years' Missionary Labors Among Primitive Peoples* (Elgin, Ill.: Printed for the Author by Brethren Publishing House, 1915), p. 19. The quotation is Is. 55:1.

[10]*General Conference Minutes,* 1905, Article 17, p. 14.

[11]"Sanctification," *Origin, Confession of Faith and Church Government . . . 1871-87 Inclusive.* Compiled and Revised for the Church (Abilene, Kas.: Daily Gazette Book and Job Print, 1887), pp. 55-64. Volume cited hereafter as *"Church Government, 1887."*

[12]*Pennsylvania State Council Minutes,* 1907, Article 4, pp. 5-6.

[13]*General Conference Minutes,* 1909, Article 15, pp. 24-30.

[14]Prov. 11:14.

[15]*General Conference Minutes,* 1909, Article 28, p. 46.

[16]*Visitor,* IX (April 1, 1896), 105.

[17][Henry Davidson], *Visitor,* I (January 1, 1888), 72.

[18]S. R., "An Old Letter," *Visitor,* I (January 1, 1888), 71.

[19]Jacob Hershey, *Confession of Jacob Hershey,* transl. by L. T. Brechbill, (n.p., n.d.), p. 13.

[20]W. O. Baker, "Reminiscences No. I," *Visitor,* I (August 1, 1887), 9.

[21]B. M., "A Few Words of Experience," *Visitor,* IV (April I, 1891), 107.

[22]George Detwiler, "Some Special Reminiscences," Asa W. Climenhaga Papers. Detwiler was not personally happy with an approach which provided no instruction as to how God saves sinners. Monroe Dourte, an elderly minister of Rapho District, Pennsylvania, reminiscing in 1975, told a group including the present writer that he received little conversion counseling when he became a "seeker" in his early life.

[23]J. H. Myers, "The Need of Contending for the Faith," *Visitor,* XXVI (January 8, 1912), 13.

[24]Schrag, "Brethren Attitude Toward the World," pp. 79-80.

[25]*Church Government,* 1887, p. 9.

[26]*General Conference Minutes,* 1882, Article 8. Chapter X traces the Brethren acceptance of revivalism.

[27]J. B. W., "Caution," *Visitor,* I (January 1, 1888), 76.

[28]Christy Ann Farmer, "My Experience," *Visitor,* II (June 1, 1889), 141.

[29][Henry Engle], "Modest Apparel," *Visitor,* XI (May 1, 1898), 175. See also George Detwiler, "Evangelical Visitor, Historical," MS in Asa W. Climenhaga Papers.

[30]Jas. 2:17.

[31]W. O. Baker, "Faith Alone," *Visitor,* III (September 1, 1890), 258.

[32]*Ibid.,* p. 259. See also D. Heise, "The Obedience of Faith Saves," *Visitor,* II (April 1, 1889), 98-99.

[33]A Brother, "Gospel Repentance," *Visitor,* I (August 1, 1887), 6-7; Jacob N. Engle, "Justified by Faith," *Visitor,* XV (July 1, 1901), 242.

[34]Mary E. Sheets, "Reading," *Visitor,* IV (April 1, 1891), 103.

[35]F. K., *Visitor,* III (September 15, 1890), 283.

[36][Henry Engle], "Modest Apparel," *Visitor,* XI (May 1, 1898), 175.

[37]George Detwiler, "Evangelical Visitor, Historical," Asa W. Climenhaga Papers.

[38]Jacob N. Martin to [Christian] Sider, March 1, 1924; Noah Zook, "Correspondence," *Visitor,* II (November 1, 1888), 25.

[39]Matilda Gingrich, "My Experience," *Visitor,* II (October 1, 1888), 13.

[40]Abram M. Hess Diary, January 27, 1883.

[41]Anthony Stoner, "I Am So Glad," *Visitor,* IV (February 1, 1891), 35; [Henry Davidson], "Our Young Men," *Visitor,* VI (June 15, 1893), 185.

[42]Schrag, "Brethren Attitude Toward the World," p. 92.

[43]E. J. Swalm, interview, March 3, 1971.

[44]*Church Government,* 1881, p. 6.

[45]*Church Government,* 1887, p. 53.

[46]See the latter part of Chapter X for the Brethren and the temperance movement.

[47]This description of early Brethren dress is from Climenhaga, *Brethren in Christ,* pp. 51, 306, from pictures and articles of dress in the Church Archives, and from contacts with the present Old Order River Brethren. See also C.S., "On the Brethren's Mode of Dressing," *Visitor,* IV (June 1, 1891), 166-67; Lizzie Dick, "Inconsistency," *Visitor,* III (November 1, 1890), 322; Laban T. Brechbill, *History of the Old Order River Brethren* (Published by Brechbill & Strickler, 1972), p. 21 AB.

[48]*General Conference Minutes,* 1888, Article 11; *Church Government,* 1887, p. 17; Henrich Klippert, "A View of the Past," *Visitor,* III (November 1, 1890), 323. See also South Dickinson District Council Minutes, September 20, 1894, Article 12; C. Stoner, "Points of Difference," *Visitor,* V (August 1, 1892), 231; J. E. Mishler, "The Cover and the Hair," *Visitor,* II (March 1, 1889), 82-83.

[49]*German Baptist Brethren Minutes,* p. 63.

[50]*Visitor,* I (August 1, 1887), 14.

[51]"Influence of Gay Dressing," *Visitor,* VI (May 15, 1893), 155.

[52][Henry Engle], "Modest Apparel," *Visitor,* XI (May 1, 1898), 175.

[53]See Chapter XV for the 1937 General Conference decision which finally endorsed specific church uniforms.

[54]*Church Government,* 1887, p. 9.

[55]*Ibid.,* pp. 53-54.

[56]*Ibid.,* p. 20; *General Council Minutes,* 1888, Article 15.

[57]North Dickinson District Council Minutes, October 10, 1882, Article 2; *ibid.,* October 6, 1885, Article 2.

[58]Jonas Winger, "Pride," *Visitor,* I (August 1, 1888), p. 186.

[59]I Tim. 2:9-10. See also I Pet. 3:3-4.

[60]A. J. Byers, *Visitor,* IV (May 1, 1891), 140; Adda G. Wolgemuth, "Wearing of Gold," *Visitor,* XII (December 15, 1899), 467.

[61][Henry Engle], *Visitor,* XI (October 15, 1898), 394.

[62]A. J. Byers, *Visitor,* IV (May 1, 1891), 140.

[63]Joseph O. Lehman, "Let Us Consider Our Ways," *Visitor,* X (June 1, 1897), 165.

[64]Markham District Council Minutes, January 27, 1888, Article 3.

[65]South Dickinson District Council Minutes, October 10, 1885, Article 1.

[66]M. L. Dohner interview, June 17, 1962.

[67]*Church Government,* 1887, p. 17; *General Conference Minutes,* 1890, p. 2.

[68]*Church Government,* 1887, p. 20; *General Conference Minutes,* 1883, Article 3; Dayton District Book of Record, August 17, 1895, Article 3.

[69]*Church Government,* 1887, pp. 7, 17; *General Council Minutes,* 1888, Article 14; *Rapho District Council Minutes,* February 8, 1917, Article 14. The scripture is Ex. 20:4.

[70]2 Cor. 6:14; D. Heise, "Serving Two Masters," *Visitor,* V (October 1, 1892, pp. 294-95. The problem of the "unequal yoke" is treated more directly in Chapter VI.

[71]*General Council Minutes,* 1888, Article 6; Dayton District Book of Record, November 29, 1879, Articles 2, 3; Markham District Council Minutes, January 29, 1904, Article 12; C. Stoner, "Points of Difference," *Visitor,* V (August 1, 1892), 230; J. B. W. "Caution," *Visitor,* I (January 1, 1888), 76.

[72]*Church Government,* 1887, pp. 10, 18-19, 20; Dickinson County Joint Council Minutes, March 15, 1890, Article 1.

[73]F. Elliott, "Secret Societies," *Visitor,* VI (May 1, 1893), 133.

[74]C. Stoner, "Points of Difference," *Visitor,* V (August 1, 1892), 231.

[75]Henry Davidson, "The Blessedness of Christian Union," *Visitor,* IX (February 15, 1895), 49-51; *Visitor,* IX (March 1, 1896), 65-67; *Visitor,* IX (March 15, 1896), 81-83; C. S., "Waterloo Notes," *Visitor,* II (July 1, 1889), 153; Familiar Friend, "River Brethren," p. 556; *General Conference Minutes* 1907, Article 18, p. 11.

[76]C. Stoner, "Peculiarity," *Visitor,* IV (February 1, 1891), 34 and "Points of Difference," *Visitor,* V (August 1, 1892), 230-31; F. Elliott, "Church Entertainments," *Visitor,* IX (November 15, 1896), 339-41; George Detwiler, "Worship," *Visitor,* XIII (August 15, 1900), 315.

[77]George Detwiler, "Worship," *Visitor,* XIII (August 15, 1900), 315.

[78]C. Stoner, "Peculiarity," *Visitor,* VI (February 1, 1891), 34, and "Points of Difference," *Visitor,* V (August 1, 1892), 230-31.

[79]Dayton District Book of Record, November 25, 1893, Articles 11, 12; Abram M. Hess Diary, February 23, 1895.

[80]P. G. H., "A Clean Heart," *Visitor,* I (June 1, 1888), 157.

[81]Chapter VII deals with other aspects of the Brethren doctrine of separation from the world.

[82]South Dickinson District Council Minutes, October 10, 1885, Article 5; Dickinson County Joint Council Minutes, March 15, 1890, Article 8.

[83]*Die Trennung der River-Bruder,* broadside in Church Archives. See the discussion of this schism in Chapter VII.

[84]Anthony Stoner, "I Am So Glad," *Visitor,* IV (February 1, 1891), 35.

[85]Lizzie Dick, "Inconsistency," *Visitor,* III (November 1, 1890), 322.

[86]Lizzie Paulus, "The Cross," *Visitor,* VII (August 1, 1894), 236-37.

Salvation and Ordinances

The Doctrine of Salvation

Regeneration or the new birth was a basic part of the doctrine of salvation as understood by the early Brethren. They believed that regeneration occurred in a pietistic or heartfelt conversion experience which marked the beginning of the Christian life.[1] The Brethren also believed that sanctification occurred simultaneously with regeneration and that this initial sanctifying experience marked the beginning of a process of sanctification or growth in perfection. They were confident that their doctrine of salvation offered the convert a life of spiritual fulfillment and ethical victory over sin.

Leaders of the Brethren dealt with the relationship between the instantaneous and progressive phases of sanctification. One bishop referred to the former as "a sanctifying act, or process." He explained: "This is nothing else than being born again, for as soon as we are born of God, we are holy, for nothing unholy can be born of God." In a later comment on Paul's reference to "perfecting holiness in the fear of God," the same writer noted that the only thing needed after the new birth to bring holiness to perfection was to live "'soberly, righteously, and godly in this present world.' "[2] An aged member commented: "We must first be obedient children and walk in true self-denial, and become willing to do all which is commanded. So doing sanctification will be sure to follow."[3] In other words, sanctification or holiness came to progressive fulfillment in the life of obedience.

A Canadian leader gathered together the various strands of early

Brethren thought on sanctification:

> When we are justified then are we sanctified, for the two necessarily go together, for if we are justified or born again and do not yield to the influence of the sanctifying power our new life will be of short duration, for it is impossible to remain in a justified state before God when we persistently disobey his commands and the influence of the Holy Spirit. But when we yield ourselves to the divine teachings of the Holy Spirit we do not only find it a continual work, but also a deeper work of grace.[4]

He goes on to speak of believers who, as they aspire to advance in holiness, become aware of their own weakness. Then, he says, "the answer comes quickly from high heavens, my grace is sufficient."

Like regeneration, therefore, sanctification was by grace and not by works, but grace and works were inseparably joined in both experiences. In this view of sanctification, the Brethren again demonstrated their conviction that they could never ignore their reckoning with obedience.

Although the Brethren strongly stressed the salvation experience, they did not expect it to occur until young adulthood. This posed the question of the spiritual state of children. The answer was that the benefits of the Atonement extended automatically to children before they were able to discern their sinfulness and need for salvation. Christian Lesher spoke to that point:

> Those minor children that . . . die in their ignorance will be saved through the merit of the crucifixion and blood of Jesus Christ. . . .
> I have said: the Lord Jesus has paid for the guilt of the original sin. . . . So long as the children do not know its origination, or that there is such a thing as a sin, or unknowingly drift after wrong things; because of their ignorance, their condition is not condemnable. When they begin to follow this drift of wrongness, and their conscience reveals to them that they have done something wrong, which is sin; it is then that their ignorance is past, and . . . innocency is lost.[5]

Lesher based his position upon Scriptures such as: "Even so by the righteousness of one the free gift . . . [came] upon all men unto justification of life" and "Jesus Christ the righteous . . . is the propitiation for our sins: and not for ours only, but also for the sins of the whole world."[6] The Ohio Brethren later supported essentially the same position as Lesher, although they cited other Scriptures.[7]

This trust in the Atonement for the salvation of children during their age of innocency does not imply that the Brethren had any reservations about free will. They believed emphatically that at the age of accountability each individual became personally responsible to respond to God's offer of salvation through Christ. Lesher argued in support of this personal responsibility.

> . . . in His word [God] . . . openly declares, the death of sinners He does not want. . . . In this time of grace, man has a free will to accept or reject this offered grace, he may open his heart or close it. Those that say, man does not have a free will, stand in jeopardy of falling into a terrible error. . . .
> . . . like an incautious man falls into a deep hole, and . . . [cannot] free himself, there . . . [comes] a good friend . . . [who drops] to him the end of a rope advising him to attach the rope to himself, that he may draw him out of the hole. Now would he not accept the offer to be drawn out of that hole, it would then be his fault that he must continue in that hole.[8]

The Brethren also stressed the consummation of salvation, which they believed would occur either at death or at the second coming of Christ. They looked forward hopefully to the possibility that their pilgrimage as strangers in a hostile world might end with Christ's return for his obedient disciples. A Pennsylvania bishop commented on 1 Thessalonians 4:16: "Not to be nailed to the cross! Not to call sinners to repentance! Not to pardon the penitent, but He will come and His reward with Him, to give every man according as his works shall be."[9] The Brethren placed much emphasis upon preparation for this climactic event.[10]

There is traditional evidence that millennial teaching produced controversial points of view in the brotherhood. By the early twentieth century, however, the group officially endorsed Premillennialism.[11]

Ordinances

The Brethren believed that faithful observance of the ordinances was one of the most important demonstrations of obedience. They understood ordinances to be symbolic practices prescribed for Christian believers. In deciding what practices to observe and how to observe them, they looked to Scripture, to the examples of Christ and the apostolic church, and, occasionally, to church history.[12]

Of the several ordinances observed, baptism was significant as one of the first evidences of obedience. One of the members, writing in the *Visitor*, states: "With the new born child of God, as soon as there is evidence of a new birth, there is also a work for that child to do; for works come by faith, and not faith by works, and according to the commission given to the apostles, first after believing comes baptism which is the answer of a good conscience toward God, . . ."[13]

This passage is another example of what the Brethren meant by "works." The term did not imply meritorious deeds but acts of obedience. While some members may have lacked discernment and become legalistic, the brotherhood did not consider baptism to be a good work conferring saving merit. It was, instead, in the words of the Eighteenth-Century Confession, "the outer sign for . . . newborn children." In the more familiar language of a later day, this meant that the new birth is "an inward work or regeneration wrought by the Spirit in the heart, of which water baptism is only a symbol or type."[14]

Brethren in Christ baptism, 1909. Black Creek District, Ontario. Asa Bearss officiating.

Baptism, in addition to symbolizing a new birth, was the visible sign of admission into the brotherhood. One leader commented: "By this *visible* birth we enter into relationship with the *visible* church."[15] For this reason General Conference long resisted the baptism of non-members.[16] In 1923, however, it modified that position. Thereafter applicants for baptism who gave "clear testimony of saving grace" could be baptized without accepting church membership if the district or bishop having oversight of the area consented. This change was made to bring converts under "the care of the church" and, hopefully, into church membership. There was growing concern that refusing baptism until acceptance of membership might encourage converts to look elsewhere for Christian fellowship.[17]

In administering baptism the Brethren insisted upon trine immersion—three separate dippings of the candidate face downward in the water. This mode, they believed, was supported by the Scriptures, by New Testament practice, and by early church history. The dipping under water was essential to their understanding that baptism symbolized union with Christ in his death, burial, and resurrection. Scriptural support for the three separate acts of immersion was the baptismal formula in the last chapter of Matthew's Gospel: "baptizing them in the name *of* the Father, *and of* the Son, *and of* the Holy Ghost."[18] They understood this passage to call for a separate baptismal act acknowledging each of the three persons of the Trinity.[19]

Uncertainty surrounds the rationale for the forward or face-downward immersion. One member suggested that the forward action was practical because "it is emblematic of a cleansing—of a spiritual washing."[20] A second explained it in keeping with the concern of the Brethren for obedience. "Christ in his suffering which he calls baptized . . . fell on his face . . . and . . . every act of submission and reverence toward God, manifested in the Bible is bowing forward, or falling on the face, which all goes to show that a backward movement (or immersion), is inconsistent and adverse to all usages, rules, or customs, and not founded in Holy writ."[21] Another biblical passage used to support forward immersion records the death of Jesus on the cross. "When Jesus had received the vinegar, he said, It is finished: and he bowed his head, and gave up the ghost." In view of His bowed head, the forward act of immersion appropriately symbolized baptism into His death.[22]

The Brethren emphasis upon careful observance of the ordinances raised questions about the administration of baptism. One of these involved membership applicants previously baptized by backward immersion;

General Conference decided that they must be rebaptized by trine immersion.[23] A more technical question arose when the applicant's former baptism had been by trine immersion. The answer to this question was typically Brethren. ". . . if the person was baptised by trine immersion on the evidence of pardon of sin and acceptance with God, and is satisfied with his or her baptism, he may be received as a member without being rebaptized."[24]

A difference between the Brethren understanding of baptism and that of the Dunkers underlies this decision. Applicants for Brethren membership, if previously baptized by trine immersion, could only have come from the Dunkers. The latter group did not make a heartfelt conversion experience a precondition for baptism so the Brethren did not automatically assume the validity of Dunker baptism administered by trine immersion.

On another occasion General Conference addressed itself to the question of a special baptismal formula. Although the conclusion was that the brotherhood had no such formula; Conference advised following "the practice of the old brethren . . . in accordance with the word of God."[25] This is one of many evidences that succeeding generations of Brethren had great respect for the judgment of their spiritual forebears. What the practice of "the old brethren" was may be inferred from the earliest recorded baptismal formula. " 'Upon the confession of your faith in the Son of God, which you have professed before God and many witnesses, thou art baptized in the name of the Father, and of the Son, and of the Holy Ghost.' "[26]

Like baptism, the Lord's Supper was an important ordinance of the Brethren, which marked the culmination of the love feast.[27] Their characteristic word for the ceremony was "communion"; its symbolism emphasized the church as the fellowship of believers separated from the world and rightly related to God, to each other, and to their fellowmen. They always communed in the evening, because Christ instituted the Supper in the evening, and they wished to follow His example as closely as possible.[28]

Preparation for communion stressed self-examination in obedience to the Pauline exhortation: "But let a man examine himself, and so let him eat of that bread, and drink of that cup. For he that eateth and drinketh unworthily, eateth and drinketh damnation to himself, not discerning the Lord's body."[29] A crucial aspect of self-examination was the mending of broken interpersonal relationships through penitence and confession. One member explained:

. . . if we are habitually indulging in any secret faults, known only to God and ourselves, we must confess to Him before our examination is thorough, or our reconciliation complete. And further, it is not only our duty to confess our faults which we committed against brethren and sisters, and against God, but it is equally encumbent on us to confess to men of the world, if we have wronged any.[30]

This passage covers the whole sweep of relationships—believer to God, believer to believer, and believer to worldling.

At its best, communion periodically reminded the Brethren of the need to keep their personal and corporate lives cleansed of hindrances to fellowship. Preaching, experience meetings, and the informal fellowship of the love feast had as their ideal goal the pure church gathered in brotherhood relationships around the table of the Lord.

Prior to the act of communion, the congregation sang and ministers prayed and commented on one of the biblical passages describing Christ's suffering and death. The act of communion then proceeded among the men and the women separately but simultaneously. Each communicant in turn held a flat strip of unleavened bread from which he or she broke a small piece after repeating to the next communicant the words of the ritual.[31] These were: "Beloved Brother [Sister], 'The bread which we break is the communion of the body of our Lord and Savior, Jesus Christ.' "[32] The fellow participant usually responded with a word or nod of agreement. After all were served they silently meditated while partaking of the bread. Following this the common communion cup was passed.[33] Before partaking the member holding the cup repeated to a fellow communicant the following statement: "Beloved Brother [Sister], The cup which we drink is the communion of the blood of our Lord and Savior, Jesus Christ.' " The salutation "Beloved Brother [Sister]" repeated twice during the service reminded each member of brotherhood relationships grounded in Christian love.

The early Brethren used fermented wine in communion, but this practice began to be questioned in the 1880s. Midway in that decade General Conference considered whether fermented or unfermented wine was preferable and recommended that the latter be used as much as possible thereafter.[34] Some members were unhappy with the ambiguity of the words "as much as possible." Two years later the issue of fermented wine came to Conference in a different form. "What shall be done with a brother . . . who publicly protests against the use of fermented wine at communion services neither will commune when it is used?" Conference recommended forbearance on the part of both the brother and the church.[35] While some members continued to be unhappy about the use of fermented wine, this ambiguous position of Conference allowed local areas of the brotherhood to deal with the matter at their discretion.[36] As late as 1921 the members of South Franklin District in Pennsylvania questioned why they communed with fermented wine and decided to use unfermented wine thereafter "if possible."[37]

Communion and feet-washing utensils in the Brethren in Christ Archives, Messiah College, Grantham, Pennsylvania. Top: common communion cups, wine goblet and pitcher, bread tray. Bottom: glass wine service, can to fill feet-washing vessels, feet-washing pail and tub.

Brethren understandings of the church and its relation to the world tended to orient many of them toward the position of closed communion. In their minds full fellowship with God was inseparable from full fellowship with each other. The latter required common understandings of faith and obedience, without which there was no basis for communion. A Canadian leader argued strongly for closed communion: "Inasmuch as we cannot commune with such a one who calls himself a brother and walks disorderly and who keeps not the traditions of the apostles, with just as little propriety can we commune with those who keep not all the commandments of the Lord, or with those who differ with us in faith and practice, even if they profess to be followers of the Lord."[38] The Canadian brotherhood strongly supported these sentiments.[39]

In 1907 this question came before General Conference through a request to have scriptural references supporting closed communion spread on the minutes. Conference considered the matter at length and decided "that the church, *as a whole,* has never really practiced what is generally termed as 'closed communion' but discourages promiscuous communion, . . ."[40] This implies that some areas of the brotherhood were less convinced than others of the validity of a rigid stand in favor of closed communion.

A related question, which gave the Brethren considerable concern, was whether Christ intended to institute a sacred meal as a prelude to the Lord's Supper. The Dunkers strongly endorsed the sacred meal, and the Brethren felt the need of a strong apologetic for their opposition to it. Jesse Engle devoted most of his treatise on the Lord's Supper to arguments against the sacred meal. Echoes of controversy between the two groups continued to sound into the twentieth century. A Brethren member who was related to Dunker minister George Bucher sent him a copy of the Jesse Engle pamphlet on baptism with the following note:

> By hearing . . . [your] discourse on Matt *26* I came under the impression that you are laboring under a delusion, toiling excessively to row your "ceremonial supper barge" against the Scriptural Stream.
> So please read this little work and compare it with the word of God.[41]

This critic later apologized to Bucher for manifesting a wrong attitude.[42]

Whenever the issue of the sacred supper arose, the Brethren steadfastly maintained the position of the Eighteenth-Century Confession that the bread and wine alone constituted the communion meal.[43] Although some wished to have the communion emblems present on the same table with the love feast supper, Conference opposed this.[44] The following minute record reflects the controversy: "Can not the general council devise some means to satisfy those members of Montgomery and Bucks Counties district [Pennsylvania], that want the supper and the bread and wine on the same table?" Conference named a committee to visit the Montgomery-Bucks brotherhood "for their mutual benefit, and [to] instruct them to adhere strictly" to the previous decision to keep the emblems off the supper table.[45]

Some support for the Montgomery-Bucks position continued thereafter, for the Jesse Engle treatise on the Lord's Supper gave rise to differences of opinion. The committee appointed by Conference to reconcile those differences concluded "that the memorial service of the bread and cup is the communion, and the full meal we eat is not sacred."[46] By adopting this report, Conference confirmed the historic stand of the Brethren against the sacred meal.

Feet washing was a third ordinance prominent in the life of the Brethren. To them the words of Jesus, "If I then your Lord and Master, have washed your feet; ye also ought to wash one another's feet," were a clear and unequivocal command to practice the literal washing of feet.[47] One of them observed: "There is probably no plainer language . . . made use of in the Bible than that found in John xiii . . . where our blessed Savior instituted that humble ordinance of feet washing."[48]

The founders concurred fully with this point of view; the Eighteenth-Century Confession reads: ". . . we see, believe and acknowledge that the Lord Jesus Christ at and during His communion meal, by washing His disciples feet, has established, practiced, and ordered it to be practiced, as a sign of true humility and abasement out of love and obedience to Jesus, our pattern."

So conceived, the ordinance appealed strongly to the Brethren who shunned pride, welcomed humility, and made obedience the guiding light of their faith and practices. A late nineteenth-century writer summarized their understanding of the practical implications of the ordinance:

Feet-washing . . . is a lesson of love of the purest type. It also teaches humility, and that we should esteem others better than ourselves. It also fosters a spirit of equality and of oneness among the children of God. It upsets and dethrones all selfish and domineering tendencies. It embraces and binds together in the inseparable bonds of love and true fellowship all the children of God.[49]

Like the Dunkers the early Brethren practiced double-mode feet washing; one member washed and another wiped the feet of several participants. By the late nineteenth century, various areas of the brotherhood were questioning this time-honored practice. In 1892 the brotherhood in Brown County, Kansas, requested General Conference to substitute the single mode by which one member both washed and wiped the feet of another.[50] Conference denied this request, but the denial did not end the desire for the change. Canada Joint Council voted that the double mode was not "according to Gospel," and advocates of the single mode pressed their point in Dayton District, Ohio.[51]

Under these circumstances Conference had to deal repeatedly with the question of feet washing. In 1908 it was asked to answer specifically "Yes" or "No" to the question of whether the double mode was scriptural. The context implies that some members doubted that the command to wash feet was obeyed by individuals who did not specifically perform the act of washing. It also implies that some districts were practicing the single mode regardless of Conference disapproval. In spite of these implications, Conference stood by past precedents and decided that the double mode ". . . covers the ground and is therefore scriptural, inasmuch as the scriptural rendering is, 'Wash one another's feet.' "[52]

This action indirectly strengthened the hand of advocates of the single mode by acknowledging that the phrase "wash one another's feet" was the point at issue. Opponents of the double mode could point to the minute record and argue that only the act of washing met the test of obedience. When Conference reconsidered the matter two years later, the single mode carried the day in the following resolution: "That General Conference . . . adopt the single mode of feet washing, to be practiced throughout the Brotherhood, with the provision that if the physical condition of the participant is such that will inconvenience him or her to participate in washing, that such brother or sister be relieved by another brother or sister, with a further provision that if no objections be raised and presented to General Conference within this Conference year, that this resolution shall stand and become the general practice for feet washing throughout the Brotherhood."[53]

Supporters of the traditional double mode insisted that the resolution was too drastic, but they could not muster the support needed to reconsider it. Because the action technically adopted the single mode for the ensuing year only, the question automatically came to General Conference the next year. In the interim, Pennsylvania State Council unanimously endorsed the single mode; this encouraged Conference to reaffirm its previous endorsement of that mode.[54] Since 1912 feet washing by the single mode has been the official policy, but the double mode died slowly in some parts of the brotherhood.

The Brethren observed the three ordinances described on the basis of specific commands of Christ. In addition they perpetuated two other practices—the prayer veiling for women and the salutation of the holy kiss—which, they believed, the New Testament Epistles commanded.

Their biblical support for the former was a portion of the first book of Corinthians, which reads in part:

> Every man praying or prophesying, having his head covered, dishonoureth his head. But every woman that prayeth or prophesieth with her head uncovered dishonoureth her head: for that is even all one as if she were shaven. For if the woman be not covered, let her also be shorn: but if it be a shame for a woman to be shorn or shaven, let her be covered.[55]

The prayer veiling was one of the few Brethren distinctives omitted in the Eighteenth-Century Confession, but early twentieth-century leaders believed that it had always been accepted by the brotherhood.[56] One of the first recorded General Conference rulings implies this; in 1872 General Conference took up the question: "Shall sisters wear the *usual* modest head covering when taken into the church?" Its firm answer was: "That they shall."[57] The 1887 Rules of Church Government also refer briefly to the veiling: "In worship, men shall have their heads uncovered, and women shall have their heads covered."[58] Four years later a statement of rationale and a firm directive for compliance with group expectations in the matter followed.

> . . . the church holds that . . . a woman professing godliness shall not appear in public nor in any way engage in praying or prophesying without having a plain and modest head-covering. This is not worn simply [as] a headdress but in reverence to the man as a token of subjection and a sign of authority. By complying with this requirement the woman has the authority to pray and prophesy both private and public; and no one shall be received into the church, or if in the church be entitled to all the privileges of the church, who is not willing to conform to this requirement.[59]

This passage summarizes the historic Brethren understanding of the prayer veiling. While it was required for private as well as public worship, the words "appear in public" suggest that women were not out of order if they laid if off while performing duties about the home. Questions arose about the practice of the veiling from time to time; General Conference had to deal with such questions three times in the 1870s[60] Women often associated the veiling with cross bearing or the "narrow way of self-denial," which helps to explain why conformity in wearing it could not simply be taken for granted.[61]

Spiritual prerogatives of women who participated in church life with veiled heads gave the brotherhood difficulty. The problem was the interpretation of "praying and prophesying" in Paul's first Corinthian letter. The Brethren doubted that this phrase authorized women to share equally with men in the activities of the church. They noted other Pauline passages which, they thought, sanctioned a patriarchial society. Paul wrote: "I suffer not a woman to teach, nor to usurp authority over the man, but to be in silence." And again: "Let your women keep silence in the churches: for it is not permitted unto them to speak; but they are commanded to be under obedience, as also saith the law. . . . for it is a shame for women to speak in the church."[62] These latter statements and the silence of the New Testament about the role of women in church offices led the Brethren to exclude them from official positions.[63]

The reconciliation of the Pauline admonition for women to keep silent in the churches with their prerogatives to pray and prophesy in worship posed a dilemma. General Conference sought to resolve this by ruling that "sisters shall not teach or preach in public meetings, but shall have full liberty to prophesy or speak of the wonderful works of God."[64] Conference did not make clear how to draw the line between teaching and preaching in contrast to prophesying. The practical effect of the ruling was to limit the role of women in the church to forms of inspirational expression such as prayer, song, and testimony.

While the Brethren officially limited the role of women in church life, some church leaders defended women's rights. Although these men did not discount the prayer veiling, they spoke in favor of greater freedom for women to exercise scriptural prerogatives. One leader, who concluded that Paul did not speak under inspiration when he admonished women to keep silent in the churches, wrote:

> Saint Paul according to his own admissions occasionally gave forth a sentiment "on his own hook" [and] the following must be one of them—"Let your women keep silence in the churches; . . ." Indeed, all that was written derogatory to the true position of woman by the apostle may be directly traced to the popular and all pervading sentiment of the times in which they lived. Yet it is astonishing to know that in these modern times right among us . . . are those that construe the above language of Paul to mean that our women . . . must keep their mouths shut as regards praying and prophesying in religious exercise. We don't think the Apostle meant any such thing, . . .[65]

Another churchman held that this Pauline admonition to women "was evidently for the Corinthians, and not applicable to other properly conducted Christian churches, either then or now."[66] These statements, of course, reflected minority opinion, but they are interesting examples of how some leaders did not hold that all New Testament passages were universally applicable as to time and place.[67]

Although the Eighteenth-Century Confession did not mention the prayer veiling, it referred indirectly to the kiss salutation, indicating that the practice was of early origin. The New Testament Epistles included several exhortations for believers to greet one another with "a holy kiss," and the Brethren took these seriously and literally.[68] They employed the salutation as a fraternal greeting and farewell, men with men and women with women, and also practiced it ritualistically on love feast occasions "as a token of filial love and union."[69] The following passage reveals its meaningful place in their church-world understanding:

> Let the world have her meaningless forms to herself. A cordial shake of the hand is pledge enough of the friendship of this world. Christian love and affection is [sic] always the same in its nature, . . . Christians should recognize one another by the use of the salutation on all occasions. Such a course will keep them under restraint and remind them of their consecration.[70]

The withholding of the salutation was a very serious matter. If a member withheld it at his own discretion from another, the resulting estrangement of brethren could be so serious as to require the attention of a district council or even General Conference.[71] On the other hand, if the group had to expel an individual, all other members were obligated to withhold the kiss from him or her. The Eighteenth-Century Confession stressed this disciplinary procedure, and General Conference reconfirmed it as late as 1906.[72]

Another practice endorsed by the Brethren was the anointing of the sick with oil and the offering of prayer for their physical healing. This differed from the ordinances and practices previously discussed, because the brotherhood held that it was a Christian privilege rather than an act of obedience binding upon all believers.[73] The principal scriptural basis for the anointing was the following passage from James:

> Is any sick among you? let him call for the elders of the church; and let them pray over him, anointing him with oil in the name of the Lord;

And the prayer of faith shall save the sick, and the Lord shall raise him up; and if he have committed sins, they shall be forgiven him.[74]

The 1887 Rules for Church Government provided guidance for the anointing ceremony and reflected the typical Brethren concern to follow scriptural injunctions literally.

The order shall be something like the following: It requires two brethren [James speaks of elders not elder], and when they meet at the house of the sick there shall be singing, exhortation and prayer by one or more as is thought best by those who are called, and if time will permit. The passage from James shall then be read as far as it relates to the subject, and brief comments made. Then the sick member is raised to a sitting position and the elder reaches forth his hand while the other brother pours the oil upon it which he then puts upon the head of the sick, and this shall be done three times, repeating the words of the apostle—"Thou art annointed [sic] in the name of the Lord unto the strengthening of thy faith, unto the comforting of thy conscience, and unto full assurance of the remission of thy sins;" or other words may be substituted covering the same grounds. Then prayer shall be offered for the sick.[75]

The columns of the *Visitor* reveal considerable Brethren interest in divine healing. Church leaders discussed its scriptural implications.[76] Others reported anointing services and testified to healings. Sarah McTaggart of Stayner, Ontario, gave one of the most striking testimonies. After many years of invalidism, she requested the prayers of the brotherhood at large. Soon she reported a radical transformation in her physical condition.[77] Some years later she reflected on this experience.

. . . after being an invalid for seventeen years, and bed-ridden for eight years, having spent great sums of money to no avail, and [been] given up as an incurable by the best physicians; then losing all confidence in man and giving up all medicine and medical means, trusting alone to God's almighty power, I was miraculously restored by prayer and faith. This was over five years ago. . . .[78]

Mrs. McTaggart's circumstances created "quite an excitement" in her community. Commenting on this situation, Editor Henry Davidson expressed the Brethren point of view about divine healing.

But while it no doubt seems strange to many, and some may be skeptical with regard to it; yet when we consider the promises of God and the power of Him who rules, why should we doubt? . . . If [God] . . . can save the sinner, why can he not much more heal the body of what ever disease we may have?[79]

Various testimonies of anointing and healings reveal that other Brethren felt that they had verified the truth of this presupposition.[80]

NOTES:

[1]Preceding chapters have dealt with the regeneration aspects of the Brethren doctrine of salvation. See especially "The Conversion Experience" in Chapter III.

[2]Charles Baker, "Santification, or Holiness, Reviewed," *Visitor,* VII (April 15, 1894), 115-17.

[3]An Aged Brother, "A Few Words on Sanctification," *Visitor,* V (December 1, 1892), 359.

[4]John Reichard, "Sanctification," *Visitor,* IV (March 1, 1891), 66. The Brethren were not sophisticated theologians. In the passage quoted "justified" and "born again" are synonyms.

[5]Lesher, *Christian Magazine,* pp. 86-89.

[6]*Ibid.,* p. 85. The Scriptures are Rom. 5:18 and 1 Jn. 2:1,2.

[7]*Ohio State Council Minutes,* March 17, 18, 1910, p. 2.

[8]Lesher, *Christian Magazine,* pp. 101-103.

[9]Jacob M. Engle, " 'Comfort One Another with These Words.'," *Visitor,* I (April 1, 1888), 122. See also W. O. Baker, "War," *Visitor,* X (February 1, 1897), 36.

[10]Charles Baker, "The Second Coming of Christ," *Visitor,* III (November, 1889), 20; Elias M. Smith, "The Second Coming of Christ and the Resurrection," *Visitor,* III (October 1, 1890), 289-91; J. R. Zook, "Second Coming of Christ," *Visitor,* XII (October 1, 1899), p. 364, is the first of a series of articles on this subject.

[11]*What We Believe,* 1906.

[12]See the later notes for this chapter, *passim.*

[13]D. E., "Baptism. When, How, and Why," *Visitor,* II (August 1, 1889), 163.

[14]*Ohio State Council Minutes,* 1913, p. 10.

[15]F. Elliott, "Born of Water," *Visitor,* X (August 1, 1897), 237.

[16]*General Conference Minutes,* 1905, Article 21, pp. 15-16.

[17]*Ibid.,* 1923, Article 27, p. 36.

[18]Italics added.

[19]William O. Baker, *A Treatise upon Christian Baptism* (Louisville, Ohio: W. O. Baker, Publisher, 1893). Baker's treatise became the official position of the Brethren by action of General Conference

[20]C. Stoner, "Points of Difference," *Visitor,* V (August 1, 1892), p. 231. The point seems to be that persons normally stoop forward to wash.

[21]D. E., "Baptism. When, How, and Why," *Visitor,* II (August 1, 1889), p. 163.

[22]Jn. 19:30; Rom. 6:3,4. William H. Boyer of Ohio stressed this passage. C. W. Boyer to C. O. Wittlinger, August 13, 1975.

[23]*Church Government,* 1887, p. 7.

[24]*Ibid.,* p. 12.

[25]*Ibid.,* p. 15.

[26]*Ibid.,* p. 44.

[27]See Chapter V for a description of the love feast.

[28]*Church Government,* 1881, p. 12.

[29]1 Cor. 11:28, 29.

[30]C. Stoner, "Self-Examination," *Visitor,* V (September 15, 1892), 273. See also S. E. Graybill, "'But Let a Man Examine Himself'," *Visitor,* III (October 15, 1890), 305.

[31]"Extracts from Private Letters," *Visitor,* X (July 15, 1897), 224. The unleavened communion bread symbolized Christ as the believer's Passover. See Jesse Engle, *A Treatise on the Lord's Supper,* (Louisville, Ohio: W. O. Baker, Publisher, 1893), p. 25. Engle's treatise became the official position of the Brethren by action of General Conference.

[32]*Church Government,* 1887, p. 51. This source is the first to give the words of the communion ritual.

[33]William Baker, a physician, was concerned about the sanitary implications of the common cup. See his "Religion and Sanitation," *Visitor,* VI (July 15, 1893), 209.

[34]*General Conference Minutes,* 1885, Article 4.

[35]*Ibid.,* 1887, Article 5.

[36]C. Stoner, "Following Other Churches," *Visitor,* IV (July 15, 1891), 211; "Extracts From Private Letters," *Visitor,* X (July 15, 1897), 224.

[37]South Franklin District Council Minutes, February 10, 1921.

[38]Charles Baker, "Communion," *Visitor,* VI (November 1, 1893), 324.

[39]Asa Bearss, " 'Close Communion,' " *Visitor,* II (March 1, 1889), 85; Charles Baker, "Communion," *Visitor,* VI (November 1, 1893), 324; *Canadian Joint Council Minutes,* September 13, 1906, p. 19, and Resolution B, p. 18. See also *ibid.,* September 14, 1894, p. 2.

[40]*General Conference Minutes,* 1907, Article 18, p. 11. Italics added. See also Familiar Friend, "River Brethren," p. 556.

[41]This pamphlet was in the possession of William P. Bucher of Quarryville, Pennsylvania, in April 1963.

[42]J. R. Brubaker to George Bucher, January 23, 1914, photostatic copy in Church Archives.

[43]Jacob M. Engle, "Early Customs of the Church," *Visitor,* II (October 1, 1888), 9; Samuel Baker, "Early Customs of the Church in Canada," *Visitor,* II (November 1, 1888), 26; Benjamin Shupe, "Customs of the Love-Feasts in Waterloo, Ontario," *Visitor,* II (December 1, 1888), 40.

[44]*Church Government,* 1887, p. 16.

[45]*Ibid.,* p. 24.

[46]*General Conference Minutes,* 1890, p. 3.

[47]Jn. 13:14.

[48]D. Heise, *Visitor,* IV (January 15, 1891), 17.

[49]Charles Baker, "Feet-washing," *Visitor,* VI (January 1, 1894), 5. For a detailed treatment of feet washing, see William O. Baker, *A Treatise on the Washing of the*

Saints' Feet (Louisville, Ohio: W. O. Baker, Publisher, 1893), which became the official position of the Brethren by action of General Conference.

[50]*General Conference Minutes,* 1892, p. 2.

[51]*Canadian Joint Council Minutes,* September 17, 1896, p. 5; Dayton District Book of Record, 1878-1902, March 17, 1900, Articles 3, 4.

[52]*General Conference Minutes,* 1895, p. 2; *ibid.,* 1897, Article XIII, p. 6; *ibid.,* 1909, Article 40, p. 50.

[53]*Ibid.,* 1911, Article 29, p. 54.

[54]*Pennsylvania State Council Minutes,* 1912, Article 2, p. 4; *General Conference Minutes,* 1912, Article 24, p. 106.

[55]1 Cor. 11:4-6.

[56]*General Conference Index,* p. 281.

[57]*Church Government,* 1887, p. 8. Italics added.

[58]*Ibid.,* 1887, p. 54.

[59]*Origin, Confession of Faith and Church Government, . . . of the Brethren in Christ, . . . 1871-1901 Inclusive* (Abilene, Kas.: News Book and Job Print, 1901), p. 89. Cited hereafter as *Church Government,* 1901.

[60]1872, 1873, 1878. See also the diary of a general-church visitor appointed by General Conference in 1885. This diary is in the back of a copy of *Church Government,* 1887.

[61]M. L., "A Duty for Sisters," *Visitor,* I (November 1, 1887), 46; Sarah McTaggart, "The Power of Covering of the Head," *Visitor,* (October 1, 1888), 5; Alice J. Linebaugh, "The Experience of a Young Sister," *Visitor,* IV (September 15, 1891), 282-83; Lydia Otewalt, "Writing for the Visitor," *Visitor,* V (February 15, 1892), 57.

[62]1 Tim. 2:11, 12; 1 Cor. 14:34, 35.

[63]Charles Baker was one prominent leader who believed that the office of deaconess was justified. "Teaching," *Visitor,* VII (February 15, 1895), 55.

[64]*Church Government,* 1887, p. 18. The Conference action cited Joel 2:28, 29 in support of this decision.

[65]A. Bearss, "Women's Rights," *Visitor,* VII (December 15, 1895), 356.

[66]S. E. Graybill, "Prophesying," *Visitor,* II (February 1, 1889), 66.

[67]When the Brethren became corporately involved in missions, they began to ordain women for missionary service. These ordinations, however, did not confer ministerial prerogatives such as performing marriages, baptizing, burying the dead, and presiding over councils.

[68]Rom. 16:16; 1 Cor. 16:20; 2 Cor. 13:12; 1 Thess. 5:26. 1 Pet. 5:14 is similar except that "kiss of charity" is substituted for "holy kiss."

[69]Scherck, "The Tunkers," p. 67; *Church Government,* 1887, p. 51.

[70]S. E. G., "The Salutation," *Visitor,* I (October 1, 1887), 23.

[71]*General Conference Minutes, 1887, Article 5.*

[72]*Ibid.,* 1906, Article 16, p. 12.

[73]*Church Government,* 1887, p. 17.

[74]Jas. 5:14, 15. Other supporting passages were Mt. 8:16; Mk. 16:18; Ps. 103:3; Is. 53:4, 5. *What We Believe,* 1906.

[75]*Church Government,* 1887, p. 50.

[76]John Reichard, "Anointing the Sick," *Visitor,* III (February 1, 1890), 45, 46; T. A. Long, *Visitor,* IV (January 1, 1891), 6, 7; Charles Baker, "Anointing," *Visitor,* XII (January 1, 1899), 5-7.

[77]Sarah McTaggart, "How I was Raised from a Bed of Affliction," *Visitor* III (May 15, 1890), 156-58.

[78]Sarah M'Taggart, "To the Afflicted," *Visitor,* VII (September 15, 1895), 277.

[79][Henry Davidson], "A Remarkable Case of Divine Healing," *Visitor,* III (May 15, 1890), 152.

[80]C. A. Myers, "The Blessing Promised For Obedience," *Visitor,* II (February 1, 1889), 66; Fannie Steinbraker, "Soul and Body Healed," *Visitor,* V (December 1, 1892), 363; T. A. Long, "Testimony to Healing," *Visitor,* XI (September 1, 1898), 326-27.

Services and Polity

Services

The Brethren in Christ began as a "house church," holding services—worship, love feast, communion, harvest praise, and council—in homes and barns. As members migrated to new localities, they carried this house-church concept with them, and it was a distinctive feature of their movement for seventy-five years.

In the services the congregation divided into two face-to-face groups, men on one side and women on the other, with the ministers or "ministering brethren" in a central location.[1] This arrangement permitted a personalized, family-like setting in which members shared spiritual experiences, listened to the exposition of the Scriptures, practiced the ordinances, and prayed and counseled together.

To describe them in modern terms, the Brethren were preoccupied with group dynamics rather than with "churchly" atmosphere. For them the "church" was the visible people of God assembled in Christ's name in loving face-to-face fellowship to gain the inspiration, spiritual enlightenment, and mutual support needed for the endeavor to perfect obedience in their personal and corporate living.[2] To implement this theology of the church, any space in a home or farm building large enough for the group to gather was as appropriate as any other.

The founders developed their house-church customs for convenience and as a conscious expression of their doctrine of the church; their disapproval of many aspects of the mainline Protestant churches may have reinforced any reservations which they had about the use of special buildings for worship. In any case, a problem arose when the numbers of worshipers began to outgrow homestead facilities in the mid-nineteenth century. Many of the members of that period, especially in Lancaster County, did not favor the use of buildings designed specifically for religious assemblies. In spite of opposition, however, the mid-1800s witnessed the beginning of the transition of their services to "meeting houses," as they called their first church buildings.[3]

Exterior of the Ringgold "Meeting House," one of the oldest in the brotherhood, erected at Ringgold, Maryland, in 1871. Men entered by the left door and women by the right.

These first meetinghouses were plain frame or brick rectangular structures with pew dividers to separate the seating for men and women. Those who planned the buildings had no interest in architectural design or artistry to create atmosphere. For all practical purposes the house church simply moved into larger quarters. Ministers officiated behind a table on floor level in the center of one of the longer sides of the rectangular room. Part of the worshipers sat face-to-face with the ministers, but tiers of pews facing the ministers from their left and right perpetuated the brotherhood circle concept. Later, more sophisticated and less discerning generations would christen these side tiers the "amen corners."[4] There were, of course, local variations of the typical meetinghouse arrangements. In at least some meetinghouses in Franklin County, Pennsylvania, for example, the deacons and the wives of both ministers and deacons sat facing the rear of the assembly room.[5]

Congregational singing unaccompanied by an instrument played a significant role in the early worship of the Brethren. An articulate leader stated the function of their singing:

> Singing is, indeed an important factor in our worship. It is soul-cheering and uplifting to every traveler on the narrow way from earth to heaven. It is more pleasing to the Lord than the most charming music that ever was produced by any harp, or musical instrument; but it must be in accordance with the word of God.[6]

The Brethren had clearly defined views about the meaning of singing "in accordance with the Word of God," and these excluded instruments. One of their favorite tests was: "I will sing with the spirit, and I will sing with the understanding also."[7] The Scriptures coupled this text with a similar statement on prayer, which led the Brethren to apply the same considerations to both activities. This eliminated musical instruments; prayer obviously required no mechanical aids. Furthermore, Christ and the apostles engaged in both prayer and singing, but the New Testament was silent on instrumental music. One member summarized the thought of the brotherhood on the use of instruments:

> . . . the complete transformation and simplification of worship under the Gospel, the removal of nearly every vestige of material observance, the spiritual character of the Gospel, the mention of singing in the upper room, in the jail at Phillipi, in Ephesians and in James' Epistle, and the utter silence of the New Testament on instrumental music in worship and its incompatibility with our text [1 Cor. 14:15], are evidence that the use of such instruments is not a part of Christian worship. But singing is placed on the same basis as prayer and is of the same spiritual character.[8]

Another leader who found no New Testament support for instrumental music concluded: "The human voice cultivated in the fear of God and used to his glory is of divine origin. The instrument is of man's invention or origin." He added that the instrument is effective for "the enthusing of the flesh" while the voice is able "to enthuse the spirit . . . ."[9]

These men spoke the mind of the early Brethren, for General Conference ruled that members could not consistently use musical instruments nor teach music as an occupation.[10] If a member erred in this respect, Conference directed that he be admonished and readmonished in love and forbearance.[11] This widespread opposition to musical instruments effectively excluded their use in group assemblies, but districts varied in their attitudes toward instruments in homes. One area of the brotherhood denied ordination to an elected deacon who allowed an organ in his home, but other areas took a more lenient view of home organs.[12]

Few members ventured to oppose publicly the rejection of musical instruments, although one had the courage to do so. Pointing out in the *Visitor* that harps were prominent in the heavenly visions of Revelation, he observed: "Reader, what will you do if you are so fortunate as to get near enough to hear the voice of harpers harping with the harps of God? Will you . . . get angry and refuse to go in?"[13] To this challenge Editor George Detwiler appended a note acknowledging that there are two sides to a question and that one side is not always wholly wrong nor the other wholly right. Until the mid-twentieth century, however, the brotherhood as a whole could discern no adequate reason to question the rejection of musical instruments in worship services.[14]

Choir music in worship, the Brethren believed, was as improper as musical instruments.[15] One of their leaders summarized objections to choir music. In the first place, only a select group participated in the singing so it could not be heartfelt and congregational in the spirit of Ephesians 5:19—"singing and making melody in your heart to the Lord." Also, repetitive words and phrases in choruses and anthems seemed to be "vain repetitions" which, if forbidden by Scripture in prayer, were equally unacceptable in song. Finally, he associated choir music with "worldly" churches which, from the Brethren perspective, failed to require proper scriptural standards of regeneration and nonconformity for those who did the singing.[16] This writer summarized his view of church music as follows:

He that will sing praises acceptable unto the Lord "must sing with the spirit." The only music that penetrates through the roof of the church, and that reaches heaven, and enters into the ears of the Lord of Sabaoth, is that of converted people "singing with grace in your hearts to the Lord." . . . All other music is an abomination unto Him with whom we have to do.[17]

Since this concept of church music stressed spiritual sincerity and gave no place to aesthetic quality and artistry, the early members had little incentive to cultivate singing ability. By the late nineteenth century, however, singing schools appeared among them, indicating the gradual development of interest in improving their music.[18]

From a present-day point of view, the song services of the early Brethren were unique.[19] They sang meter hymns without notes, slowly and in unison. For many years they considered part singing "dividing the voices" a worldly practice. Rapho District in Pennsylvania objected to it as late as 1915.[20]

Because of the scarcity of hymnals in the early days, the custom of "lining" the hymns developed. A leader recited a line or two of the text in a singsong manner, and the congregation responded by singing the lined material to a given tune. Various hymns could be sung to a number of tunes. Sometimes the members of the congregation did not know what tune was intended, and they began a variety of tunes simultaneously with the hymn gradually perishing in the confusion. This kind of experience helped one member to form her concept of heavenly bliss:

> Praise the Lord! when we get over yonder there will be all new singing; not part of one tune and part of another to the same verse, then a break-down followed by bad feelings . . . .
> But will it not be a happy day? There will be no one to find fault with the singing.[21]

The Brethren conducted their services almost entirely in German until well into the nineteenth century.[22] As they gradually made increased use of English in daily life, they also introduced it into their worship. In 1862 the Canadian Brethren published in English the first hymnal of the society, with the express purpose of assisting the brotherhood to make the transition from German to English in worship services.[23]

This change from German to English in the worship service proceeded slowly. Hymnals published from 1874 to 1906 included songs in both languages, but the German songs disappeared after the latter date.[24] The same gradual shift occurred in the spoken parts of the service. When, for example, the congregation at Fordwich, Ontario, chose their first resident ministers in 1875, they selected John Reichard to preach in German and

Nelson Kiteley to preach in English.[25] Lancaster County ministers preached in both languages when the first three districts of the brotherhood organized in the 1880s.[26]

One of the most prominent parts of the early worship service was the "social," or "experience" meeting. The Eighteenth-Century Confession perceived this meeting to be an important contribution to Christian growth and emphasized that through it ". . . love grows and faith, and confidence is strengthened, because such children [believers] are exposed to many temptations and when through filial revelation the craftiness of the devil is discovered, then one can talk open-heartedly with the other so that the body of Christ is renewed, . . ." In other words, the church was a family fellowship characterized by openness in interpersonal relationships and by the free sharing of spiritual experiences.[27]

The Old Order River Brethren perpetuate an early form of the experience meeting. When a member wishes to speak, he or she lines a short passage from a hymn which is then sung by the congregation. The thought or sentiment of the hymn usually becomes the introduction to what the speaker wishes to say. This may be an account of the speaker's conversion or of subsequent experiences in the Christian life. Usually the participant speaks at some length; statements from five to fifteen minutes are common. The tone of the presentations is often serious, with speakers emphasizing the temptations and conflicts of the Christian walk. Many comment freely on their defeats and limitations and express the desire to be more faithful and obedient. Others share burdens for family or friends or relate recent experiences which have caused them joy or sorrow.

The early Brethren held their worship services bi-weekly or at longer intervals, for travel was difficult and slow. Members from a distance would arrive before Sunday, thus providing opportunity for a Saturday evening prayer meeting. Similar meetings attended by smaller groups of local members might be held during the afternoon or evening of the open Sundays.[28] Prior to the erection of meetinghouses, Sunday services rotated among the homes of members.[29] Later, when a district had several meethinghouses, the services rotated among them from Sunday to Sunday.

Since the Brethren had a multiple ministry, several ministers participated in each service. In 1873 a Lancaster County member reported a meeting in which five ministers shared. One opened the meeting, a second read the text on the talents and preached "rather long," a third "very satisfactory," a fourth "a little," and a fifth "very affective" [sic] and closed the meeting.[30]

Long experience meetings usually preceded such preaching, suggesting that the Brethren of that day were obviously not time conscious. One who attended reports a service at which the experience meeting lasted until nine o'clock (he does not say when it began) followed by preaching until noon.[31] Assuming an hour for the experience meeting, the total service continued for at least four hours. This lengthy period included songs, prayers, and Bible readings, as well as preaching and the relating of Christian experiences.

Interior of the Ringgold "Meeting House" which is being restored as an historical memorial by the Brethren in Christ Allegheny Conference. Note the long, floor-level preaching table, the coal-oil lamps, the original stove, and the rocking chair for the comfort of an aged or infirm member.

Services, of course, grew shorter with the passage of time. Early in the twentieth century, the California Brethren were distressed by long meetings and raised the question: "Could not our Sunday morning services be shortened without hindering the cause?" To this the council gave the somewhat equivocal reply: "As the Lord may direct."[32] Direction presumably came from some source, for services in California and elsewhere grew shorter as the tempo of life quickened with the passage of time.

In the early days the entire congregation always knelt during prayers, including the final prayers which closed the service. After General Conference of 1871 approved the use of the benediction, the practice of closing with the congregation standing gradually replaced the kneeling prayers of earlier days.[33]

An annual harvest-praise service characteristically celebrated the harvest in late summer or early fall. As a farming people the Brethren were sensitive to the fruitfulness of the land; they considered crops to be bounties from God. Their understanding of this special service is revealed in the following passage:

> As the summer rolls along we are all, and particularly so as an agricultural people, the recipients of bountiful blessings, to a greater or less degree, from Him who saith, "Every beast of the forest is mine, and the cattle upon a thousand hills." . . . Should we not therefore, in recognition of these blessings spend a half day or several of them in meeting . . . and pour out our praises in song, prayer or speaking, and have our teachers gather from the Word of life special teachings for these occasions.[34]

The most important service was the love feast held at least twice a year in the spring and the fall.[35] On this occasion Brethren fellowship and brotherhood culminated symbolically and practically. Members from other districts often traveled long distances, sometimes hundreds of miles, to enjoy and contribute to love-feast occasions.[36]

A typical "feast" began on Friday evening or Saturday morning and continued until Sunday noon. Both members and non-members shared fellowship meals at the place of meeting. On Saturday evening large crowds of community non-members often assembled with the Brethren for the pre-communion supper.[37] In Canada a nineteenth-century observer noted that the menu included lamb, lamb soup, potatoes, bread, butter and sauce.[38] Lamb was also a part of early Lancaster County love-feast suppers, which may suggest a trace of Passover symbolism.[39]

The day services were preparatory for the evening feet washing and communion. In these preparatory services members shared experiences and heard expositions of the fourth chapter of Ephesians and the eleventh chapter of Paul's first letter to the Corinthians. These traditional love-feast passages spoke directly to concerns about church order, unity, and obedience. Ministering brethren placed much emphasis upon preparation for coming to the Table of the Lord. Members were exhorted to examine themselves and to make any confessions required to bring their lives into conformity with God's will.

The high point of the love feast was the Saturday communion. When the evening fellowship meal ended, the non-members took back seats while the feet-washing service proceeded around the tables. Here, too, the communicants received the bread and wine, after which the women cleared the tables and washed the dishes.[40]

With the growth of the Brethren and their erection of meetinghouses, basements provided space for the fellowship meals, and the assembly rooms accommodated the feet-washing and communion services. Special pews in some of the assembly rooms preserved the table arrangement for communion. Every second and third pew had adjustable backs hinged at the ends. For the Saturday evening service, the second pew converted into a table, and the back of the third pew reversed so that persons seated on it faced the table. White tablecloths added additional realism to the atmosphere for communion.

Polity[41]

Officials of the Brethren were of three categories—bishops (also known as elders or overseers), ministers and deacons.[42] All acquired their offices by plurality elections in the respective districts in which they resided. Some members thought that the choice of their officials by lot would be more scriptural, presumably in the light of passages such as Proverbs 18:18 and Acts 1:26. General Conference, however, steadfastly resisted pressure to endorse selection by lot unless the vote in a given instance resulted in a tie.[43] Church officials held their offices for life on condition of good behavior.[44]

The bishop was responsible for the administrative supervision of his district. Other districts lacking resident bishops might call upon him for service on their behalf.[45] Within his district he presided at public services and functions—worship, love feast, council, reception and expulsion of members, baptism, elections for church officers, and marriages.[46]

The primary duty of the minister was to preach. In the absence of the bishop, or by his advice or consent of the church, he might temporarily perform some or all of the bishop's duties.[47]

Deacons provided for the needs of the poor and infirm of the district, cared for financial matters, made the arrangements for feet-washing, communion, and baptismal services, and assisted the bishop in his supervision of the district.[48] At least once a year, they conducted a general visitation of the district membership to evaluate the spiritual progress of the members and to determine their attitudes toward the brotherhood.[49] Because of this function, they were often called "visiting brethren." Their visits made important contributions to church unity. One district council record included the laconic entry: "Church visits! What are they for? Answer: To maintain peace and unity in the church."[50]

The annual deacon visitation occurred prior to a meeting of the district council so that the findings of the visit could be reported to the district membership.[51] After a visitation in the Conestoga region of Lancaster County, one deacon noted that they had found "All the members with a desire . . . to work on in the good work and . . . [wishing] that they could live nearer to God."[52] A later California visitation reported "a feeling of unity, harmony and good courage" among the membership.[53] Visiting brethren were sometimes less optimistic about their findings. In one instance the grievances and disunion reported were so serious that the district council petitioned General Conference for assistance.[54]

The Brethren took very seriously the choice of church officers. Before a vote was taken, council members listened to the reading of 2 Timothy 3:1-13, which described qualifications for church leaders. Then a bishop (or bishops) conducted the election by ballot, or by individual voice vote to tellers including at least one bishop. In the event of a tie, the outcome was determined by lot. After the election, the bishop, in the presence of other members, examined the person elected with regard to his character and to his soundness in faith and doctrine. Ordination could then follow immediately or be postponed to some future time. One or more bishops from other districts always presided at a district election for a bishop.[55]

Districts evolved gradually as the basic administrative units of the brotherhood. Under the 1887 Rules of Church Government, as few as twelve members could petition the General Conference for district organization. A fully organized district included at least one bishop, one or more ministers, and one or more deacons.[56] A bishop could be non-resident at the discretion of the district council.

The Brethren placed much emphasis upon council meetings for which they found biblical grounds in Proverbs 11:14: "Where no counsel is, the people fall: but in the multitude of counsellors there is safety."[57] The district functioned through a district council which was organized on the "congregational" principle, meaning that all members in good standing could participate.[58] In the words of one writer:

> At this meeting all members meet on an equal basis, excepting, of course, the difference which talent and experience makes. The government of the districts being democratic . . . each member has an equal say in all questions in hand and should therefore be present and . . . be heard by speaking and voting in an intelligent manner.[59]

Part of what this writer meant by "talent and experience" was the fact that in the councils of the brotherhood, the membership held the elderly and officials in high regard and esteemed bishops "worthy of double honor."[60] In practice this could mean that a council would defer to the convictions or wishes of the bishop or the older members even when others preferred a different course of action.

The assumption that each member had "an equal say" in the district council requires some qualification with regard to women. Although they often appear to have voted on an equal basis with men, the Pauline statement that women should "keep silence in the churches" probably acted as a psychological restraint upon their participation in discussion. As late as 1905, for example, one district council questioned whether women could consistently vote in council since they could not consistently speak in the church.[61]

The district council met in regular session at least once a year, and the bishop could call it into special session to meet emergency needs. Questions about the work of the district or the behavior of any of its members came within the council's jurisdiction.[62] Such district matters could range from the question of serving beef at a fall love feast to the disciplining or expulsion of members.[63] The district council also elected delegates to General Conference and prepared items for the consideration of that body.[64]

Much district council business was routine, but serious or controversial issues could electrify the atmosphere and provoke vigorous discussion. One participant in the 1880s reported that they had a very good council until the marriage question came up, and then a good deal of confusion and heaviness prevailed.[65]

Not all council debate was relevant and not all of it reflected brotherly love. In the 1890s one writer advised: "In reference to our speaking, we should speak intelligently and to the point, remembering Charlotte Bronte's prayer which was as follows: 'So long as I have nothing to say, God give me grace to keep silent.'" The same writer says of brotherly love:

> O, that in every conference meeting this might be the ruling element! . . . What do we gain when we lose brotherly love, even though we do carry our point? Too often it is only *our* point after all. Better sacrifice any cause we may be upholding than brotherly love.[66]

In spite of the human limitations of the district councils, they expressed the concept of the visible church and were one of the major influences which shaped the life of the brotherhood.

Larger administrative units known as state or joint councils appeared soon after the close of the first one hundred years of Brethren history. They eventually became channels through which the district councils sent matters of business to General Conference.[67]

Two separate General Councils (Conferences) holding authority over the district councils met annually in Canada and the United States respectively.[68] These were the forerunners of the present unified General Conference.

In 1878 the Brethren in the United States named a committee of three "to bring about a closer union with the Canadian brethren in general council."[69] The outcome of this successful merger effort consummated in 1879 and was recorded as follows: "Decided: That the brethren of general council of the United States having offered union, and the council of the brethren in Canada having accepted, the union is hereby considered complete and hereafter there shall be but one general council.—(Unanimously carried.)"[70] This is the first Conference decision which the minutes note was made with unanimous consent.

Like other Brethren gatherings, General Conference assembled in homes or farm buildings. In the early days one room sometimes sufficed to accommodate all who attended.[71] The first such assembly known to have been held in a meetinghouse was the Conference of 1880, at Markham, Ontario, following the merger of the Canadian and United States Brethren in 1879.[72]

General Conference of 1929 held in Henry Schneider's new barn at Merrill, Michigan.

Early General Conferences were simple and informal; if they kept written minutes, these have not survived.[73] The United States General Conference recorded official minutes beginning in 1871. These show that two years later it began to organize formally by appointing moderators and secretaries, the choices to be made from among the bishops by plurality vote of delegates only.[74] No records of the Canadian General Conference prior to its merger with the United States General Conference survive.

Bishops, ministers, and deacons were members of General Conference in addition to delegates chosen by the district councils. Although voting was restricted to the groups named, all Brethren in good standing could attend and participate in the deliberations. From time to time there was restlessness about the heavy influence of church officials in General Conference, but attempts to limit decision-making to the votes of elected delegates always failed.[75]

Items for General Conference consideration came principally from the districts. These matters were usually questions of doctrine, practice, or government which had more than local significance, or which were too complex for the district councils to decide without assistance. Examples of questions considered in the 1870s are:

> Is it right for members to marry such as are not members of the church? (1871)
> Is it scriptural to have any given form of dress? (1872)
> May a brother serve in the ministry, who is so much involved that he is not able to pay his debts? (1875)
> Is it consistent for members to use tobacco in any form? (1877)
> Will it be tolerated for sisters to neglect wearing the covering of the head? (1878)

These examples reveal that General Conference formulated membership standards and assisted the districts in the instruction and disciplining of members. In this manner the total brotherhood participated in the crucial role of defining obedience and promoting unity in doctrine and practice at all administrative levels.

The early Brethren held General Conference in high esteem, but compliance with its more controversial rulings could not be taken for granted. This explains why subjects such as the wearing of the prayer veiling and the use of tobacco came repeatedly to the Conference floor. In the early twentieth century, Conference expressed despair because many of its rulings were "more or less ignored throughout the Brotherhood."[76] In response to a petition questioning some previous decisions, it ordered submission to thirteen rulings made between 1871 and 1903, as well as to a section in the By-Laws of 1904.[77] Such data indicate that the history of the Brethren cannot be correctly understood by assuming that a declaration of position by the Conference meant that the entire brotherhood faithfully supported that decision.

Just as deacon visitations sought to promote district unity, occasional churchwide visitations sponsored by General Conference had the same end in view. For reasons that are not clear, the mid-1880s was a time of special concern for Brethren unity, and Conference of 1885 considered the following item: "Brethren from several districts pray General council to appoint suitable brethren to visit the brotherhood in their families, and inquire into their standing as regards unity and oneness." The Conference responded by appointing six brethren to make this visitation and provided for the payment of their expenses.[78]

One of these visitors in Pennsylvania kept a diary which provides insight into both the nature of the visitation and the conscientious, methodical efforts of the men who made it.[79] They began in Blair County on August 15, 1885, and ended in York County in December of that year. During this period of approximately four months, they made hundreds of home visits and held or shared in many services. Excerpts from their findings are interesting and enlightening:

> Found the Brotherhood in unity & oneness, with but few Exceptions . . . there seems to be a disposition among the Brothers & Sisters to keep the unity of the Spirit, but as to the oneness, we found some diversity of opinion; such as pronounsing [sic] the Benediction, rising to sing a doxology, and the covering of the Head among some of the Sisters, . . . (Martinsburg-Woodbury area)
>
> . . . here we met the Brotherhood in good order & in unity desiring to hold to the doctrine of the Brethren as . . . recorded in the Minutes (Lykens Valley)
>
> . . . in this district we find divers opinions on various subjects but still are endeadvouring to keep the unity of the spirit in our opinion . . . . (Cumberland County area)
>
> Thus far the Brethren seem to be united with the decisions of general council but have considerable trouble among themselves, some missunderstanding [sic]. (Franklin County area)
>
> . . . we find the Brethren willing to submit to decisions of council but find some fault with some of the decisions, and have much trouble among themselves. This district is in need of an Elder who . . . [possesses] much wisdom. (Montgomery and Bucks Counties)

This visitation summary pictures the Brethren striving earnestly to keep the districts in step with General Conference. The tone of the diary, on the whole, is optimistic and the document makes clear that divergent local views were often held in check by the willingness of individuals and localities to submit to the guidance of Conference as the ultimate expression of brotherhood consensus.

Discipline played a significant role in a group so concerned with being a pure church characterized by brotherly love and unity of doctrine and practice.[80] All members shared responsibility for building the church upon these principles. That is why they placed so much emphasis on the eighteenth chapter of Matthew and why a section of it was included in their membership vows.

Prior to taking the vows, the applicant for church fellowship was examined by the membership. First, he gave a personal testimony of conversion, which was to embody "a consciousness of the pardon of . . . sins through the atoning blood of Christ, peace with God and harmony with the doctrine of the Bible as taught by the Church,"[81] After hearing that testimony the members met privately to discuss the individual's qualifications to become one of their number. This procedure dramatized the fact that the applicant was seeking membership in a visible community which corporately judged his sincerity of purpose and the quality of his Christian life. Implicit in the reception process was the assumption of responsibility by the group for the spiritual well-being and conduct of each of its members.

The four membership vows taken by the approved applicant reveal a great deal about the content of early Brethren thought.[82] Two focused upon evangelical conversion, nonconformity, and fidelity to the church; two others sought to ensure the mutuality of responsiblity for the healing of relationships between brethren. The first recorded text of the vows follows:

> Do you believe in an Almighty, Triune God, Father, Son and Holy Ghost and in Jesus Christ (the Son) as the Savior of a lost and ruined world, and that he brought a soulsaving gospel from Heaven?
>
> And inasmuch as you have received the pardon of your sins, you have heretofore but do you now publicly renounce the world, the devil and your own corrupt nature; do you promise allegiance to God, and fidelity to the church?
>
> And do you promise that if your brother or sister should trespass against you that you will go and tell him (or her) his faults between him and you alone, as taught in Math. 18 . . .?
>
> And inasmuch as we are all fallible, if you should trespass against a brother (or sister) and he should come and tell you of your fault (according to Math. 18), are you willing to receive it?[83]

The mutual asking and granting of forgiveness embodied in the last two vows—willingness "to tell and be told" in Old Order River Brethren vocabulary—was the approved procedure to restore fellowship and heal broken relationships between estranged members. If it proved ineffective, the offended member could enlist the assistance of one or more neutral members. When even this failed to accomplish reconciliation, the church as a whole was to consider the matter.[84] In other words, the Brethren believed that the power to "bind" and "loose" in a disciplinary sense resided ultimately in the total brotherhood.[85]

This involvement of increasing numbers of persons in the effort to restore broken relationships was often a dynamic process. When an offended member requested neutral members to render assistance, they might find him or her to be wholly or partially responsible for the problem. In one instance the assisting members found both parties in a dispute to be at fault in different degrees. The estranged brethren responded positively to this judgment of their spiritual peers, "made things right and melted down in warm tears and . . . [agreed] to not say any more about it."[86]

When neutral members could not effect reconciliation between disputants, the matter came before a council of the total district brotherhood. Such a council sought to reconcile two Kansas brethren, with the following outcome:

> It was resolved that the church heartily accept the offer of Bro. S. Zook that he is willing, and does acknowledge his failings and promises that by the help of God he will try to do the best he can for the church and the glory of God: and further be it resolved that Bro. Gish as well as all other brethren who have been grieved will accept in good faith Bro. Samuel Zook's offer and we all heartily forgive one another and will endeavour in good faith to forgive all the past and work together for the glory of God and the prosperity of the Church.[87]

The Brethren believed that broken relationships compromised the corporate witness of the people of God. For this reason estranged members who were reconciled through mutual forgiveness often asked forgiveness of the church as a whole. In one such instance two Lancaster County men "made confession and . . . [begged] pardon of the church" where they may have been an offence to any one by not being careful enough in their dealings with each other.[88]

Those who read the official documents of the Brethren, such as the membership vows, may fail to distinguish between ideals and realities. The attempt to heal relationships often involved a complex process, and long-standing tensions between individuals, families, and groups were not unknown. There was also the possibility of applying punitively a process designed to bring about loving reconciliation. Those who read the account of the excommunication of Matthias Brinser and his followers, for example, may suspect that somehow, perhaps on both sides of the issue, members were less sensitive to the spirit of their membership vows than they might have been.[89]

Many disciplinary problems did not involve direct controversies between individuals but arose because a member departed from the accepted group standards of attitude and conduct. The Brethren believed deeply that God required a pure church, that is, a community in which obedience as defined by the group was practiced by every member. They often used the analogy of housekeeping to describe the process of keeping proper order and spirit in the church. A Kansas district, for example, had before it the insistent request of its bishop, Joseph Fike, "to be relieved from housekeeping in the Church in Kansas."[90] Again, a council inquired: "How will the brethren keep house with regard to the use of . . . [tobacco]?"[91]

An individual's departure from clearly defined standards of conduct often became quickly apparent, in which case the church officials under the direction of the bishop became responsible to initiate corrective procedures. The eighteenth chapter of Matthew provided the guidelines for these procedures which sought to win the wayward member to repentance and confession and thus to right relationship with God and the brotherhood. The first step was to counsel and admonish the offender with "due diligence in love and forbearance."[92]

When counsel and admonition were insufficient, discipline took various forms depending upon the nature of the offense. One of the most common forms was public confession to the local church. The Brethren placed much emphasis upon personal humility and willingness to submit to the judgment of the brotherhood as a whole. They expected that members who professed to repent of waywardness would willingly demonstrate sincerity of purpose by humbling themselves in the presence of their spiritual peers. One district council decided that a member should confess that he did wrong in seeking public office and serving as a clerk on the fair grounds.[93] Another council, one of whose members went to saloons and played pool, requested him to make a public confession of wrongdoing and directed the deacons to so inform him.[94]

Discipline might end with the requirement of public confession, but it could assume other forms. The Brethren frequently disciplined an erring member by withdrawing communion privileges; in 1885 General Conference made members whose privileges were withdrawn ineligible for district letters of recommendation.[95] When an official's conduct was in question, he faced the prospect of possible suspension from office.[96]

The ultimate form of discipline was excommunication after all other means failed to bring the wayward member back into harmony with the brotherhood. At its best excommunication did not imply spiritual abandonment of the transgressor. One official disciplinary statement specifically cautioned that "diligence should be given that the expression used in expelling members do [es] not taint after enmity, prejudice or anything that would show . . . [that] the Church organization would not be concerned about the spiritual welfare of the member expelled."[97] When excommunication did occur, the brotherhood discontinued all spiritual fellowship with the excommunicant. General Conference, for example, ruled emphatically against members greeting an excommunicated person with the holy kiss.[98]

District councils frequently became involved in matters of discipline, although the extent and manner in which they did so may have varied from district to district. Council actions such as the following sought to sharpen general sensitivity to brotherhood norms of conduct:

> Complaint that pride is coming into the church. —Admitted; and brethren and sisters are admonished to withstand and be circumspect.[99]

> The subject of "pride in the church" was considered at length. The church is earnestly admonished to adhere strictly to the doctrine of simplicity and humility. The brethren by a large majority (rising) manifested their disposition to hold to the above sentiments and doctrines.[100]

> Voting at Political Elections by members considered inconsistent, and persons doing so should be admonished.[101]

On the other hand, council actions frequently dealt with the discipline of specific members. In the late nineteenth century one council had before it "Some very . . . sad cases." One woman had fallen back into the world and another was working with other churches.[102] A council in a different locality decided that a member should have a month's time "in which to make full reconciliation with those Brethren with whom the . . . [grievances] exist and failing to do so he will be disowned by the Brethren."[103] A third council informed a married woman that the church could not tolerate separation of husband and wife and advised her to be reconciled with her husband and live together with him as man and wife. Unless she complied with these conditions, she could not be a member of the church.[104]

Disciplinary activities of the district councils eventually aroused concern lest some members be judged unfairly by their local peers. In response to this sentiment, General Conference created a Standing

Committee to hear appeals "made by such persons as think they have been unfairly judged by a former district council." This committee had full power to investigate and decide in person or to appoint another committee nearer the place of trouble to care for the matter.[105] Later, responding to the question of whether a local district had power to overrule or dictate to the Standing Committee, General Conference made the authority of the committee very clear by the simple, unequivocal answer—"They have not."[106] At a later date a General Executive Board became responsible to assist in settling district problems, and the Standing Committee became unnecessary.[107]

The simple church program of the Brethren created few financial problems during their first one hundred years. Church officials received no salary for administrative or ministerial service, although they sometimes were reimbursed for actual travel expenses incurred on assignments. They could, of course, accept freewill gifts or offerings.

Regular worship and special services involved little additional expense. Donated farm produce fed both members and their horses. Hymnbooks were a minor expense offset in whole or part by the sale of books when the Brethren began to publish their own hymnals. Even the erection of meetinghouses made little change in financing, for donated labor helped with both construction and upkeep.

By the 1880s at least some districts handled their modest finances through regularly organized treasuries. Both the North Dickinson and South Dickinson Kansas Brethren had treasuries by the early part of that decade. They replenished them by a graduated church tax. Each landowner paid a small percentage on his property valuation; in 1883 it was one dollar per thousand.[108]

The early Brethren occasionally became involved with financial projects of the church as a whole. If a member suffered a large material loss beyond the capacity of his district to cover, the total brotherhood might assist him.[109] In 1884 General Conference agreed to raise $3000 in voluntary contributions to assist poor Russian Mennonite families to emigrate to America.[110] This ambitious fund-raising project failed to achieve its goal, and Conference ultimately abandoned it.[111]

Financial changes were at hand as the group entered the latter part of the nineteenth century. In 1871 Conference created a general missionary fund to be raised by voluntary contributions collected by the deacons of the various districts.[112] Later the donation of a sum of money for relief of the poor marked the beginning of a general church "Poor Fund."[113]

In 1884 the North Dickinson Brethren discussed whether the collection of money for church and benevolent purposes was right and decided that it was.[114] This decision symbolized that the Brethren would have to make significant changes in the financial aspects of their church life as they moved into their first period of transition. General church enterprises such as missions and institutions would call for increasing financial contributions from the total brotherhood. At the same time, local church needs such as Sunday school literature and offerings for evangelists would require funds.

As early as 1908 the Ohio Brethren discussed increased financial support for ministers as a necessary condition for more effective ministerial service. One Ohio district even went so far as to propose freeing as many ministers as possible from earning livelihoods in order that they might devote all of their time and energy in the interests of "the Kingdom."[115] This proposal, however, was far in advance of its time.

In this same period tithing or systematic giving became a subject for debate. Some members were committed to the principle by 1902, and *Visitor* Editor Detwiler urged all to accept it.[116] Tithing, however, had opponents as well as advocates. In one instance a strong pro-tithing article in the *Visitor* was followed on the same page by another entitled "Tithing—Not Gospel."[117]

These changing financial needs and attitudes show that by the turn of the century the Brethren were engaged in serious reappraisal of the relatively simple financial arrangements which had characterized their first one hundred years.

NOTES:

[1]This meeting arrangement is still perpetuated by the Old Order River Brethren who hold their services in houses and barns.

[2]Mt. 18:19, 20.

[3]Chapter VII deals with the transition to meetinghouses in the 1850s. See also Enos H. Hess, "The Sunday School," *Visitor*, XIX (March 15, 1905), 6.

[4]The Brethren in Christ Allegheny Conference has partially restored and plans to preserve as a historical site the Ringgold Meetinghouse at Ringgold, Maryland, one

of the oldest houses of worship in the brotherhood.

[5]Certified by Harvey B. Musser who grew up in the Franklin County area.

[6]Charles Baker, "Music in Church," *Visitor,* XI (March 1, 1898), 83.

[7]1 Cor. 14:15.

[8]F. Elliott, "On Singing," *Visitor,* V (March 1, 1892), 68.

[9]T. A. Long, "Singing and Music," *Visitor,* V(February 15, 1892), 51.

[10]*Church Government,* 1887, pp. 9, 20.

[11]*General Conference Minutes,* 1883, Article 3.

[12]Dayton District Book of Record, November 30, 1878, Article 1; *ibid.,* August 17, 1895, Article 3; Herbert Royce Saltzman, "A Historical Study of the Function of Music among the Brethren in Christ" (D. M. A. dissertation, University of Southern California, 1964), pp. 69-70.

[13]D. W. Gingrich, "Musical Instruments," *Visitor,* XIV (May 1, 1901), 164.

[14]*General Conference Minutes,* 1937, Article 5, p. 12.

[15]Choirs were practically unknown among the Brethren in Christ until well into the twentieth century.

[16]Charles Baker, "Music in Church," *Visitor,* XI (March 1, 1898), 82-83.

[17]*Ibid.,* 83.

[18]*General Conference Minutes,* 1883, Article 8; Markham District Council Minutes, December 29, 1900, Article 5.

[19]Saltzman, "Music among the Brethren," pp. 76-77 describes the early song services.

[20]Rapho District Council Minutes, February 11, 1915, Article 18, p. 104.

[21]Sarah Wismer, "Time and Eternity," *Visitor,* XI (May 1, 1898), 170.

[22]Familiar Friend, "River Brethren," p. 556.

[23]*Hymns and Psalms: Original and Modern,* Preface, p. iv.

[24]Saltzman, "Music among the Brethren," pp. 312-15.

[25]Nelson Kiteley, "Letter from Ontario," *Primitive Christian,* I (February 29, 1876), 140.

[26]Abram M. Hess Diary, March 18, 1883.

[27]Early Brethren group dynamics reveal something in common with the many movements—house churches, communes, Faith at Work, Alcoholics Anonymous, etc.—which seek to replace the depersonalization and facades of modern life with a new sense of community and integrity.

[28][W. O. Baker], "Reminiscences No. 2" *Visitor,* I (October 1, 1887), 22.

[29]*Ibid.*

[30]Abram M. Hess Diary, August 24, 1873.

[31]*Ibid.,* May 21, 1874.

[32]Upland Church Council Minutes, September 21, 1909, Article 7.

[33]*Church Government,* 1887, p. 7.

[34]"Harvest Meetings," *Visitor,* VII (August 15, 1894), 256. See also J. F. K., "Harvest Meeting," *Visitor,* VII (September 15, 1894), 283.

[35]Scherck, "The Tunkers," 66.

[36][W. O. Baker], "Reminiscences No. 2," *Visitor,* I (October 1, 1887), 22; Nelson Kiteley, "Letter from Ontario," *Primitive Christian,* I (February 29, 1876), 140.

[37]Scherck, "The Tunkers," 66.

[38]*Ibid.*

[39]Jacob M. Engle, "Early Customs of the Church," *Visitor*, II (October 1, 1888), 9.

[40]*Ibid.*

[41]For a study of Brethren in Christ polity, see Paul L. Snyder, "A History of the Polity of the Brethren in Christ Church," (S. T. M. thesis, Lutheran Theological Seminary at Gettysburg, Pa., 1965).

[42]*Church Government*, 1881, p. 6. To avoid confusion, the present study consistently refers to the chief administrative officer as bishop, except in quoted passages where original terminology is retained.

[43]*Church Government*, 1887, p. 12; *General Conference Minutes*, 1882, Article 9; Familiar Friend, "River Brethren," p. 554.

[44]*Church Government*, 1881, p. 7.

[45]"Election of Elder," *Visitor*, VIII (April 15, 1895), 125.

[46]*Church Government*, 1881, p. 7; Familiar Friend, "River Brethren," p. 554; *General Conference Minutes*, 1883, Article 11; Markham District Council Minutes, March 3, 1886, Article 2; *General Conference Index*, p. 253.

[47]*Church Government*, 1881, p. 7.

[48]*Ibid.*, pp., 7, 8; *General Conference Index*, p. 253.

[49]*Church Government*, 1881, p. 7.

[50][Kansas] District Council Minutes, February, 1883, Article 6. This council item may refer to church-wide visits sponsored by General Conference.

[51]*General Conference Index*, p. 253.

[52]Abram M. Hess Diary, February 8, 1883.

[53]Upland Church Council Minutes, March 31, 1914.

[54]*General Conference Minutes*, 1915, Article 20, p. 71.

[55]*Church Government*, 1887, pp. 44-45 and footnote, p. 46. There appears to have been no general policy prior to 1878 for the pre-ordination examination of church officials. See *ibid.*, 1887, p. 17.

[56]*Ibid.*, p. 46.

[57]*Ibid.*

[58]*Ibid.*; *General Conference Index*, p. 253.

[59]"About District Councils," *Visitor*, VII (February 1, 1894), 44.

[60]*Church Government*, 1881, p. 7.

[61]Markham District Council Minutes, February 24, 1905, Article 1. Dayton District also wrestled with the question of women's participation in the councils. Dayton District Book of Record, March 15, 1902, Article 9.

[62]*Church Government*, 1887, pp. 46-47.

[63]Dayton District Book of Record, July 28, 1888, Article 3; *ibid.*, March 30, 1889, Article 2; *ibid.*, November 25, 1893, Article 11, 12.

[64]*Church Government*, 1887, pp. 46-47.

[65]Abram M. Hess Diary, February 19, 1883.

[66]"About District Councils," *Visitor*, VII (February 1, 1894), 44.

[67]These units are not mentioned in *Church Government*, 1887. Kansas had a joint council by 1888 and Canada had one by 1892. They had become commonplace by the close of the century. See *Church Government*, 1901, p. 44.

[68]Familiar Friend, "River Brethren," p. 556.

[69]*Church Government*, 1887, p. 17.

[70]*Ibid.*, p. 18.

[71][Henry Davidson], "Our Annual Conference," *Visitor,* V (April 1, 1892), 104; Familiar Friend, "River Brethren," p. 556.

[72]*Church Government,* 1887, p. 20.

[73][Henry Davidson], "Our Annual Conference," *Visitor,* V (April 1, 1892), 104; Familiar Friend, "River Brethren," p. 553.

[74]*Church Government,* 1887, pp. 10-11.

[75]*General Conference Minutes,* 1885, Article 5; *ibid.,* 1886, Article 11; *ibid.,* 1893, p. 2.

[76]*Ibid.,* 1906, Article 14, pp. 10-11.

[77]*Ibid.*

[78]*General Conference Minutes,* 1885, Article 15.

[79]This unsigned manuscript is in the back of a copy of *Church Government,* 1881.

[80]Christian Lesher was the first known Brethren leader to write at length on church discipline, and his exposition of Mt. 18 probably reflects the thought of the early church fathers. He regarded "disagreement and disunion" as the most dangerous of all sins that may arise in the church. See his "How to Keep Order in God's House," translated from the German and reprinted in three successive issues of the *Visitor* beginning with XVII (June 1, 1904), pp. 14-16. Lesher's writings reveal considerable scholarship. He may also have had creative mechanical skills, for the Smithsonian Institution in Washington, D. C., has an innovative early nineteenth-century plow which, according to tradition, he developed.

[81]*Church Government,* 1887, p. 42.

[82]For the first known publication of these vows, see *ibid.,* pp. 43-44.

[83]*Ibid.*

[84]Mt. 18:17.

[85]Mt. 18:18-20.

[86]Abram M. Hess Diary, January 21, 1873.

[87]South Dickinson District Council Minutes, Special Council, September 14, 1892.

[88]Abram M. Hess Diary, March 18, 1883.

[89]See the account of Brinser's excommunication in Chapter VII, and see also the section on "Group Names" in Chapter II.

[90]South Dickinson District Council Minutes, September 15, 1892, Article 2.

[91]North Dickinson District Council Minutes, September 29, 1887, Article 2.

[92]*Church Government,* 1887, pp. 16-17; *General Conference Index,* p. 274; *General Conference Minutes,* 1883, Article 3.

[93]South Dickinson District Council Minutes, September 24, 1887, Article 12.

[94]Dayton District Book of Record, March 18, 1899, Article 11.

[95]*General Conference Minutes,* 1885, Articles 7, 8.

[96]Dickinson County Council Minutes, Special Council, February 3, 1891; Dayton District Book of Record, August 17, 1895, Article 3.

[97]*General Conference Index,* p. 274.

[98]*General Conference Minutes,* 1882, Article 3.

[99][Kansas] District Council Minutes, October 10, 1882, Article 2.

[100]North Dickinson District Council Minutes, October 6, 1885, Article 2.

[101]Black Creek District Council Minutes, December 30, 1887, Article 7. In such an instance, the council may have had an individual (or individuals) in view.

[102]Abram M. Hess Diary, February 23, 1895.

[103]Black Creek District Council Minutes, February 12, 1886, Afternoon Session.

[104]Dayton District Book of Record, March 30, 1889, Article 2.

[105]*Church Government,* 1887, p. 16.

[106]*General Conference Minutes,* 1885, Article 9.

[107]*General Conference Index,* pp. 255-56. After its creation, Pennsylvania State Council elected the General Executive Board until the incorporation of the Brethren in Christ in 1904 with headquarters in Pennsylvania. General Conference Minutes, 1905, Article 13, p. 11.

[108][Kansas] District Council Minutes, October 2, 1883, Article 2.

[109]See Chapter VI.

[110]*General Conference Minutes,* 1884, Article 12. See also Markham District Council Minutes, January 30, 1885, Article 2.

[111]*General Conference Minutes,* 1893, p. 2.

[112]*Church Government,* 1887, p. 8.

[113]*General Conference Minutes,* 1898, Article 7, pp. 4-5; *ibid.,* 1902, Article 34, p. 23. This Fund had a varied career until 1913 when Conference created a Beneficiary Poor Fund Board. That Board survived only a short time, but Conference eventually replaced it with the Beneficiary Board which, as the Board of Benevolence, still is an active agency of the Brethren in Christ.

[114][Kansas] District Council Minutes, September 30, 1884, Article 4.

[115]*Ohio State Council Minutes,* March 20, 21, 1908, Article 5, p. 2. See also *ibid.,* March 18, 19, 1909, p. 3.

[116][George Detwiler], *Visitor,* XVI (January 1, 1902), 14-15.

[117]Jacob N. Engle, "Tithing," *Visitor,* XXI (January 1, 1907), 4-5; H. B. Musser, "Tithing—Not Gospel," *Visitor,* XXI (January 1, 1907), 5.

The Brethren and Society

The original world view of the Brethren in Christ was that of a visible church of born-again believers confronting a hostile world. This world view had broad social implications; the Brethren perceived social structures such as government, economic arrangements, and cultural life as embodying elements of "worldliness" against which they had to be on guard. The result was that they gave much attention to the question of how they should relate to society. Their answers to this question were primarily attempts to implement their doctrine of nonconformity to the world.[1]

War and Other Coercive Processes

The commitment of the Brethren to biblical nonresistance separated them from mainline Protestantism and identified them with that small group of religious societies known as the Historic Peace Churches. Together with the Quakers, Mennonites, and Dunkers, they understood the Scriptures to forbid Christians to engage in military service or to take human life under any circumstances. In support of this position, they cited especially the Sermon on the Mount, "the Gospel Statutes" one leader called them, from which the Eighteenth-Century Confession deduced that it was "completely forbidden to bear the sword for revenge or defence."[2]

While their case for nonresistance rested heavily upon the Sermon on the Mount, it drew additional support from other parts of the New Testament, from church history, and from the practical realities of war. A mid-nineteenth-century observer noted that the Brethren opposed war in all its features as being "at variance with the peace-breathing precepts of

the Saviour, contrary to the teachings of the apostles, and . . .
[incompatible] with the practise of primitive Christians."[3] Some writers
also expressed dismay about the grim realities of war; one spoke of "the
gigantic criminality it is committing and entailing upon humanity, . . ."[4]
He asserted: "If Christ would have declared one thousand more beatitudes
against this gigantic evil, He would not have made our duty any plainer or
more easy to understand."[5]

The nonresistant position of the brotherhood was consistent with their
church-world view which stressed the doctrine of two kingdoms, that is,
the kingdom of heaven, of which the visible church sought to be a microcosm, and the kingdom of the world. They noted that Jesus had said: "My
kingdom is not of this world; if my kingdom were of this world then would
my servants fight, that I should not be delivered to the Jews; but now is my
kingdom not from hence."[6] To those who asked what Christians should do
if invaders were to ravish their country, a Pennsylvania spokesman replied:

If this is our country we should defend it to our hearts content; but hear
what the apostle says about the Hebrew Brethren, . . . "For ye had
compassion of me in my bonds, and took joyfully the spoiling of your goods,
(Why?) knowing in yourselves that ye have in heaven a better and enduring
substance." The great trouble with the professed people of God is that they
have their citizenship too much here in this world, and their claim and
attachment to the upper world is not as strong as it should be; and because of
this the reasoning is not of Christ, but of the world.[7]

This passage reveals the strong commitment of the Brethren to the
primacy of their heavenly citizenship. They could not understand how
Christians could relate to the corporate, war-making structures of the
present world and perform acts contrary to New Testament principles of
heavenly citizenship. As one of them wonderingly observed: "When one
man kills another it is called murder, [but] when one thousand men kill
another thousand it is called war."[8]

Nonresistance posed an exegetical problem for the Brethren because in
the Old Testament God condoned and even commanded wars. While they
seldom dealt directly with the complexities of this problem, their
acceptance of the New Testament as ultimate authority resolved it to their
satisfaction. One of them wrote:

In the Old Testament . . . [God's people] are commanded, urged and helped
to destroy their enemies with the sword and in some cases to show no mercy

to women or children. They were told to love their neighbor and hate their enemy. But in the opening chapter of the Gospel Statutes, . . . Christ says: "Blessed are the merciful, . . . Blessed are the peacemakers. . . ." In striking contrast to the Mosaic precept quoted, He says: "But I say unto you, Love your enemies, bless them that curse you, do good to them that hate you, and pray for them that despitefully use you, and persecute you."[9]

Elsewhere this writer commented on the militaristic spirit of some of the Psalms: "The Psalms . . . as far as they agree with the Gospel are all right, but many do not, as they breathe a Spirit of war and bloodshed, quite incompatible with the Sermon on the Mount."[10] In other words, the New Testament superseded the Old whenever the two value systems seemed to conflict.

In rejecting war and practicing nonresistance, the Brethren had no illusions that society as a whole would accept their position and bring about a reign of peace in the world. Such peace awaited the second coming of Christ, as an Ohio leader noted:

If all were Christians in deed and truth there would be no need of any remedy; for all the Scripture truths already quoted would be crystalized into deeds of love and all violence would cease from the earth. When Christ comes in the clouds of heaven and gathers His elect together and assumes his millenial [sic] reign, then the art of war will be learned no more.[11]

Although world peace awaited Christ's return, the Brethren believed that Christians were called to live at peace with all men in this present age. For them the Kingdom had come regardless of the motivations and behavior of the larger society around them. This explains why they practiced nonresistance, condemned war as sinful, advocated peace, and rejoiced at any evidence of progress in the peaceful settlement of international disputes. William Baker even advocated an international court of arbitration.[12]

This nonresistant faith caused the brotherhood to reject participation in activities through which government exercised the internal police power. Members could not consistently serve on juries or in the police force, both of which they conceived to be coercive in nature and which could result in the taking of human life.[13]

The Brethren also held that going to law was contrary to the gospel; it involved the use of coercion to secure personal rights.[14] They noted that the Apostle Paul condemned lawsuits between brethren and that Jesus taught His followers to acquiesce in loss of personal property if they were sued in court.[15] One writer commented on the latter point from the Sermon on the Mount:

> This is not the principle of self-defense or fighting for one's rights, but rather that of taking wrong and suffering ourselves to be defrauded, . . . In trying to defend our cause and maintain our rights, it is very easy to get over zealous and overstep the mark, so that someone else is wronged or defrauded. . . . Thus it is always best to take wrong and avoid being a wrong-doer.[16]

These sentiments were more than an individual point of view. General Conference of 1899 was asked: "Has a church member the privilege under the Gospel . . . to go to law?" The answer was a simple, unqualified "No."[17]

The word "nonresistance" suggests negative connotations, and although the Brethren tended to stress these, some of them recognized nonresistance as a positive way of life. A Canadian leader expressed this insight:

> . . . let us who hold nonresistant principles remember that it means more than refusing to do military service. They have a positive as well as a negative side. "If thy enemy hunger, feed him; if he thirst, give him drink; if naked, clothe him. . . ." We have seen nonresistant people sometimes who were very combative in their families, their neighborhoods, and their church whenever their wishes were crossed or others did not see fit to repeat their shibboleths. While hurting no one's body they often deeply wound their souls.[18]

One of the earliest rulings of General Conference illustrates efforts to apply nonresistance positively in practical life situations. The question was whether members could foreclose mortgages and sell property by sheriff sale. Conference replied "No," thus expressing brotherhood disapproval of the coercive process to secure financial redress.[19] A member succinctly summarized the implications of the positive approach to nonresistance in the presence of violence and injustice: ". . . we can give glory to God in the highest and advance by precept and example peace on earth and . . . good will toward men."[20]

The Brethren in both Canada and the United States faced the problem of gaining government recognition for their nonresistant faith. In the Militia Act of 1793, the Legislative Assembly of Upper Canada granted exemption from service to Mennonites, Quakers, and Tunkers, although those exempted had to pay a fine or commutation tax. Persons applying for the benefits of the act had to prove membership in one of the three groups named in it.[21]

This proof-of-membership provision created problems for Tunker youth who normally did not join the church until marriage or a relatively mature age. In 1810, in response to a Mennonite and Tunker petition on behalf of their young people, the Legislative Assembly extended the exemption privileges to minor children of the petitioners.[22]

These early Militia Acts set a pattern followed throughout the nineteenth century. Later petitions from the nonresistant groups reveal that the commutation taxes were burdensome, since as rural, farming people, Brethren families were large and their incomes small. In spite of financial hardships, however, the brotherhood in Canada stood by the nonresistant faith.[23]

Nothing is known about the response of the brotherhood to militarism in the United States during the American Revolution and under the later state militia acts. The Eighteenth-Century Confession strongly supports the inference that members objected to military involvement during that period, and, like the Tunkers, they may have paid commutation fines in lieu of militia service.

The Civil War forced the United States Brethren to face the test of their nonresistant convictions when the Union Government drafted troops. Isaac Trump of Illinois and Jacob Ulery of Ohio were among the draftees; both registered as conscientious objectors.[24] Others in Pennsylvania also did so, but their names are unknown.[25] Ulery and some of the Pennsylvania men paid commutation fines.[26]

If these limited data are typical, United States men of draft age stood by their nonresistant faith. Their consciences permitted them to pay commutation fines, although in Ohio, at least, the money went into a "Military Fund."[27] Speaking for the brotherhood in Pennsylvania, Jacob S. Engle informed Thaddeus Stevens, a Pennsylvania representative in the national House of Representatives, that payment of the fines was as far as they could conscientiously go. They could accept neither military service nor the option of hiring substitutes to perform it.[28]

Government and Politics

The Brethren believed that non-involvement in government and politics was a necessary corollary of their refusal to bear arms or share in other coercive processes of society. Reactions of public officials who ruled on requests for exemption from military service confirmed this conclusion. When, during the Civil War, Isaac Trump and another non-Brethren man appealed for conscientious-objector status, the judge approved Trump because he had never voted and refused the other man because he had regularly done so.[29] The Canadian brotherhood understood their exemption from military service to be conditioned upon non-participation in political affairs.[30]

Such considerations led the Brethren to perceive a sharp distinction between government with ultimate recourse to the sword and the church with ultimate recourse to suffering love. Government and politics, they believed, belonged to the kingdom of the world; their call as the people of God was to demonstrate on earth the meaning of the kingdom of heaven.[31]

They also had another practical reason for their non-involvement in politics. Political participation, they thought, would cause them to become "unequally yoked" with unbelievers. One of them stated this concern forcefully when he deplored "joining with the unbelieving crowd of boisterous politicians on election day to vote with a party composed of all shades of society—unbelievers, swearers, and drunkards."[32]

Wide use of the civil oath in governmental processes may have been another deterrent to Brethren participation in political processes. Christ's injunction to "swear not at all" was a guideline for the brotherhood, but the political structures of society did not take this biblical precept seriously.[33]

Not all members of the group believed in complete non-involvement in political life, and this issue appeared on the agenda of General Conference from time to time. Conference condemned electioneering and attendance at political elections generally.[34] It did not, however, disapprove of voting if the issues involved were "not political." Election of a school board director fell into that category. An Ohio member had served as a director as early as 1848, and General Conference of 1882 specifically exempted school board elections from the category of "political elections" disapproved two years earlier.[35]

The Brethren response to the temperance movement caused them to face the issue of voting on the prohibition question. When the matter reached General Conference, that body defined prohibition as a moral rather than a political question and committed the issue of voting on it "to the conscientious consideration of each brother" but forbade any encouragement of the liquor traffic.[36] Later, when facing dissatisfaction with this ruling, Conference rejected the protest and reaffirmed its support for

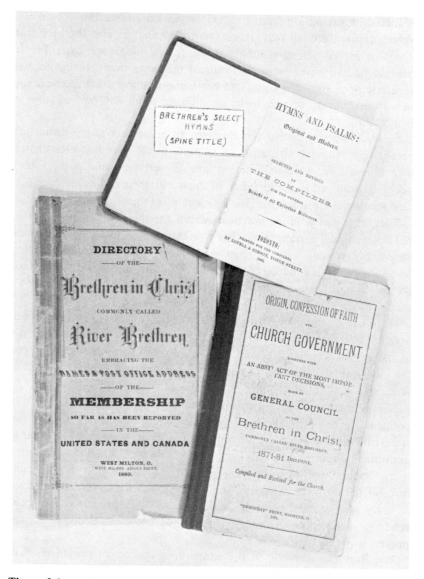

Three of the earliest pieces of official Brethren in Christ literature. Top: the first
Brethren hymnal, *Brethren's Select Hymns,* published in Toronto by the Canadian
brotherhood in 1862. Bottom, left to right: first membership directory (1880) of
Brethren households; first cumulative compilation of important General Council
(Conference) decisions for the period from 1871 to 1880.

the resolution.[37]

Public office holding became a specific issue in the General Conference of 1894. The question was typically brief. "Is it allowable for Brethren to hold public offices?" The decision was affirmative "under the restrictions of the church." Conference than named a committee of five to clarify these restrictions, and the committee reported as follows:

Inasmuch as we believe that there is great danger in opening the door for Brethren to hold public offices indiscriminately; and inasmuch as the church is located under different governments, therefore we would submit the matter to the careful and discriminate consideration of the several districts, and since we, the committee, cannot point out the various offices which Brethren might hold under the different forms of government where they are located, we would advise that Brethren should not allow themselves to be used in public offices for fear of becoming involved in political strife, which is contrary to the faith of the church on conscientious scruples.[38]

This action reflects ambiguity in the late nineteenth-century attitude of the Brethren toward involvement in public life. Whatever their theory, they did not in practice follow an all-or-none principle. A study of that period reveals that members here and there held local office in fields such as public education and town government. Rarely, however, did this participation involve significant departure from the brotherhood commitment to avoid "political" involvement.[39] One safeguard was "the careful and discriminate consideration of the several districts" as envisioned by the preceding committee report, and there is evidence that districts took this responsibility seriously. Dayton District in Ohio required confession in council of members who attended public or general elections.[40] The Kansas Brethren insisted upon a confession of wrongdoing from a member who sought political office.[41]

Economics

The early Brethren defined worldliness in many areas of their lives, but they rarely saw any danger of it entering into their principal vocation, agriculture. This attitude permitted them to adapt flexibly to agricultural innovations and thus gave indirect sanction to the aggressive pursuit of material gain. A spokesman for a later generation perceived a resulting paradox:

In matters of farming we, as farmers, seem much more liberal than we do in our religious affairs. Our aim in farming is to grow maximum crops at minimum cost. If a self-binder, mower, cultivator, etc., serves our main purpose, we get the new implement and do not give the question of right or wrong much thought.[42]

Several factors combined to separate vocational pursuits from worldliness as the Brethren defined it. In the first place, they tended to apply the principle of usefulness when they sought to identify worldliness. Was the function of an article of dress useful or decorative? How could several colors of paint on a house be more useful than one? Humility, they believed, yielded to pride, the essence of worldliness, when anything primarily decorative was condoned.

The application of this rule of usefulness to vocation and work produced a unique outcome. If a new tool or innovative procedure yielded greater returns, it obviously was more useful than the old tool or traditional procedure which it replaced. There was no reason, therefore, why members should not devote their diligent attention to increased agricultural productivity. Work was essential and therefore good.

In the second place, the confinement of Brethren activities primarily to religious services and agriculture promoted material endeavor. Because they avoided community gatherings, shunned most general reading matter, and condemned sports and games as worldly, work was one of the few activities which they could fully approve. Under these circumstances it naturally absorbed much of their time and energy.

A third factor encouraging the Brethren to be diligent in vocation was their belief that financial success was evidence of capacity for leadership roles in the brotherhood. If a man could not manage his farm in an efficient, businesslike way, they reasoned, he could not manage and lead effectively in the affairs of the church. Furthermore, their church-world understanding led them to feel that careless individual financing brought reproach upon the group as a whole and hindered the corporate witness. When a member who failed to seek or heed the counsel of his spiritual peers in business matters fell into financial difficulty, he became subject to church discipline.

The importance attached to vocational success stands out in the instance of a minister who got into serious financial difficulty. His district required him to "make before the Church and the world an humble and penitent confession" and silenced him in his ministry. The district council also appointed representatives to accompany him to his creditors whom he could not satisfy and offer "conditions of peace."[43] Three years later, after he "fully acknowledged and asked pardon for his mistake in his venture in business matters which brought upon himself and family, and also upon the church, a great burden and much distress," he finally received unanimous pardon and reinstatement in his ministerial office.[44] Vivid object lessons of this kind strengthened the impressions that financial success was highly desirable and that failure to obtain it disgraced both the individual and the church.

These several factors gave the life of the early Brethren a practical, materialistic bent. Their descendants, although rarely persons of large wealth, tended to place a high rating upon economic values. Rhoda E. Lee, foreign mission enthusiast, found this distressing. In a paper read to the General Conference in 1895 at Stayner, Ontario, she said:

> In some localities in our country the words River Brethren are but another name for prosperity, and I speak it to our shame that in the 190 [sic] years of our church's existence she has never sent a foreign missionary to the field. It is a marvel to many that a church professing separation and whose members possess such a large amount of property has not done so.[45]

Rhoda Lee was not the only voice warning of the dangers of materialism. Another member pressed this issue upon the conscience of the brotherhood:

> Is it true that we are separate, when we are like the world on our farms, pushing the world from early sunrise till late at night so that we cannot see to work any more? (Jesus said, Are there not twelve hours in a day?) How is it when we go to sell our produce, especially in the sale of small market products? Is it truly said of us that we ask the highest prices and then when we should lay by for the Lord's work give so sparingly?[46]

In Kansas some members were concerned lest economic distinctions should creep into the church and undermine the fellowship. The first entry in the council records of the Kansas Brethren (1882) reads: "There . . . [were] some complaints offered stating that the rich brethren have not the sympathy and mercy for the poor members which they should have." The council action was: "Complaint sustained."[47] Such illustrations show that the brotherhood was not entirely indifferent to the perils of materialism.

There is other evidence which demonstrates the refusal of many members to be fettered by materialism. This was the impressive record of dedication and sacrifice made by men who left their farms and families, sometimes for long periods and often at their own expense, to serve the church and preach the gospel.[48] Noah Zook was one of these. A visitor to the Zook home in the 1880s found that the husband and father had been away four months in missionary work and possibly would be away several months more. The visitor, evidently deeply moved, commented:

> Bro. Noah Zook is not as fortunate as I and many others are in the church. He has a large family, eight children and some of them small. Bro. Noah, when at home, works hard and struggles under disadvantages to make an honest living for himself and family. It is true they own 160 acres of land, but there is an incumbrance on it of $2500; . . . they are living in a very small house—a small kitchen covered with shed roof and not plastered and a small room, perhaps 10 x 12 feet and two bedrooms just large enough for one bed each, no cellar, no upstairs. Now I felt a pity for them, I thought of my own comfortable house; many brethren live in large, comfortable houses, and this our Bro. who is out and we believe is useful in the hands of God for good has to feel that his family is deprived of these comforts, which even many of those have to whom he is breaking the bread of life.[49]

This sacrificial, non-material phase of the life of the Brethren coexisted, somewhat paradoxically, with the tendency toward practical materialism. The group seems to have taken for granted both the minority of Noah Zooks who made great material sacrifices and the majority of members who lived in material comfort and security. In modern terminology the brotherhood had a double standard of commitment to Christian service.

While members could farm without restraint, the brotherhood gave guidance to those who wished to borrow money. General Conference instructed members not to make debts which they had no reasonable way of paying. As a safeguard they were to accept the advice of the church in all important financial matters.[50] The Eighteen-Century Confession based the receiving and giving of financial and other counsel upon the doctrine of the church whose members ". . . are bound through love to watch out for each other . . . that nobody in important affairs should do anything without brotherly advice, such as marry, or change his dwelling, buy land, or whatever important may occur." The Kansas Brethren had a standing committee to give financial advice.[51]

Once a man had obligated himself financially, the brotherhood held him strictly responsible to meet his obligations. He could not, for example, take advantage of bankruptcy laws, which, in the view of General Conference, defrauded creditors.[52]

Church supervision extended also to the investment and lending of money. Members were not to engage in speculative activities except with the knowledge and approval of their respective districts.[53] In at least one district, the council forbade them to buy bank stock.[54] General Conference approved mortgage loans but restricted interest on investments of any kind to the legal rate; anything more was regarded as extortion. These financial guidelines show that the Brethren wished members to understand and practice obedience in financial affairs and, in so doing, to safeguard the reputation of the brotherhood.

Insurance was another issue to which the Brethren gave much time and thought. Many of them perceived the principle of insurance as a concession to the spirit of the world. This was due both to their fear of the unequal yoke in insurance company relationships and to their feeling that protective hedging on "acts of God" was unchristian.

One of the first manifestations of the latter concern involved the use of lightning rods, to which there was strong opposition. General Conference ruled the rods inconsistent, and this stood as official policy for nearly forty years.[55] Then, although by "virtue of the tenets and teachings of the Church," Conference could not encourage their use, it referred the matter to the individual conscience with the exhortation that ". . . those who cannot conscientiously use them shall bear and forbear with those who use them and those who use them shall exercise love and forbearance with those who cannot conscientiously use them."[56]

Like lightning rods, life insurance was disapproved by Conference.[57] Also, like lightning rods, Conference finally made such insurance a matter of individual conscience, but in this instance seventy-five years of controversy intervened.[58]

The Brethren, in their characteristic way, assembled scriptural passages to support their opposition to life insurance.[59] Although the implications of some passages are obscure, two basic concerns stand out in the others. One group of passages implied that life insurance repudiated trust in God's providential care for His people. Jesus had enjoined His followers to take no thought for the morrow because their heavenly father knew their needs and would supply them. His followers also had the Pauline assurance: "But my God shall supply all your need according to his riches in glory by Christ Jesus."

A second group of passages emphasized nonconformity; the children of God were "a peculiar people." Since life insurance was a part of the financial structures of the world, the Brethren concluded that holding it would compromise their church-world understanding. The purchase of commercial insurance policies would create an unequal yoke with unbelievers.

Fire insurance met with more favor in the brotherhood than life insurance, but many members could not support its purchase from regular commercial companies. Instead, they created non-profit fire relief agencies of their own, in Canada and in the United States respectively. The former also provided coverage for the small group of members in western New York and later extended its services to the members in Michigan.[60]

The Canadian Brethren formed their Fire Relief in 1880.[61] They intended to restrict participation in it to members of the brotherhood, but some non-member children, widows, and widowers gained admission.[62] This agency limited its risks strictly to fire and made assessments from time to time based upon the property valuations of the insurees. It did not insure meetinghouses; that is, they were not valued and assessed for losses, but if one burned, all members insured in the program were assessed to finance the rebuilding.[63]

Canada Joint Council exercised direct control over the Fire Relief, which made it a church agency rather than a mutual insurance company. The actual administration of the Fire Relief is none too clear. District Councils concerned themselves from time to time with insurance matters and passed actions which Canada Joint Council could not ignore.[64] In 1895, for example, Black Creek District ruled out steam works as a risk. This action led Canada Joint Council into a discussion "bearing on the general unity of the Church" and ultimately to the decision that Black Creek and Markham Districts should appoint a committee "to adjust the matter so as to have unity."[65] This rather unusual approach to policy making indicates that the council was more concerned with the attitudes and unity of the brotherhood than with the precise technicalities of the making of policy.

The Canadian Fire Relief had a very good financial record during its first twenty-five years, due in part to careful management by its treasurer, Peter M. Climenhaga of Black Creek District.[66] It made twelve assessments which netted $6,948.35 and paid nineteen claims amounting to $6,878.79. Administrative costs were negligible due to the Brethren practice of donating their time for service to the brotherhood.[67]

Problems of various kinds beset the Fire Relief after 1904. Revised rules soon required further revision, officials connected with the program occasionally failed to understand their duties, and assessments sometimes fell into arrears. Some aspect of the Fire Relief came before Canada Joint Council annually from 1908 to 1915. By the latter year the council decided that, in spite of the wishes of 110 members to continue the program, it would have to end. The resolution to discontinue the Fire Relief fixed January 1, 1916 as the date of termination.[68]

Canada Joint Council of 1916 faced a deficit for the last two fire losses and appealed for the payment of all back assessments on the ground of "honesty and honor." The full payment of such assessments would have met the deficit, but the council authorized a general church assessment to cover the balance outstanding as of January 1, 1917.[69] With the termination of the Canadian Fire Relief, many members exercised their option to join the fire insurance program known as Mennonite Aid.[70]

The United States Fire Relief began about 1870 when General Conference named three men to launch the undertaking. Prior to this time some members were insuring in outside companies. This aroused concern as did most activities which required membership involvement in the structures of society.

In its early years this Fire Relief did not receive the support which its promoters felt was its due. The reasons for this are not clear. Some members, of course, opposed all insurance on principle. Others may have preferred outside companies, possibly because they thought that such companies were stronger financially or gave better protection.[71] The somewhat tenuous relationship of the Fire Relief to the General Conference may also have been a deterrent to some who otherwise would have purchased its insurance.[72]

Unlike its Canadian counterpart, the United States Fire Relief was a self-governing mutual company. It is not mentioned in the General Conference records from 1871 to 1906, which indicates that it was not subject to church control as was its Canadian counterpart. In the latter year, however, Conference authorized its incorporation in Pennsylvania as the Brethren in Christ Fire Relief.[73]

The company did business under the approved name, but it did not incorporate. This aroused uneasiness in the brotherhood. Elkhart District in Indiana petitioned General Conference of 1914 to negotiate the incorporation of the company and to bring it under the auspices of the Church, but Conference rejected this petition.[74] Another petition in that same year requested a change of company name to avoid the possibility that the church might become legally involved in disputed claims. Conference replied that it had no jurisdiction in the matter and therefore could not act.[75] Although Conference carefully refrained from any attempt to dominate the Brethren in Christ Fire Relief, the company took the initiative and changed its name to the Brethren's Mutual Fire Aid.[76]

Rules of the organization permitted only members of the brotherhood and their wives to belong.[77] Building assessments were three-fourths of valuation. In case of a loss, the company paid up to the full amount of the assessment. The company also took risks on building contents, livestock, and even automobiles, although responsibility for the latter was limited to fifty per cent of valuation. Coverage extended to damage from lightning as well as fire, later the company extended it to include storm.[78]

The company prospered. After an investigation General Conference pronounced it "safe financially and morally" and recommended it to all districts of the brotherhood.[79]

This Brethren's Mutual Fire Aid continued without incorporation until 1930 when it was examined for the first time by the Pennsylvania Insurance Commission. The examiners found $4,205,098 of insurance in force and recommended immediate incorporation.[80] This was done under the name "The Brethren's Mutual Fire Insurance Company," with headquarters at Mount Joy, Pennsylvania.[81]

The examination of its records and procedures revealed to the company that the insurance business was entering an era of increased complexity and regulation. In addition to recommending immediate incorporation, the Insurance Commission proposed the bonding of the treasurer and a major increase in records and paper work. Minutes of the company during the 1930s reveal a growing struggle to comply with new insurance regulations both within and without the Commonwealth.[82]

Due to these and other circumstances, it decided to discontinue business and to transfer policies in force in Pennsylvania and Ohio to another Pennsylvania mutual fire insurance company. Business ceased as of September 1, 1939, and the Lancaster Court of Common Pleas dissolved the company on January 8, 1943.[83]

These ventures of the Brethren into fire relief were in keeping with their understanding of brotherhood. They felt and endeavored to assume mutual responsibility for each other's welfare and needs. One of the promoters of fire relief, who clearly saw its brotherhood implications, wrote:

> I think it is the duty of the church to mutually aid each other in the losses sustained, . . . I think it is a duty that belongs to us, because the scripture says, "Bear ye one another's burdens." And I think . . . [there] is no better way to bear one another's burdens in this matter of loss by fire than just this

arrangement, for you know charity begins at home. I will say then to the members . . . in other fire aids, think over this and see if you are doing right.[84]

Fire relief was but one manifestation of the Brethren concern to practice brotherhood through mutual aid. Whenever practicable local areas or districts provided for the special needs of their members. An Ohio district contributed from time to time to an elderly member's support, a Pennsylvania district financed repair of a wooden leg, and an Ontario district decided that a female member without a home should "make home from place to place among the Brethren."[85] Sometimes a district assumed responsibility for needs in more distant places, as did Dayton District, Ohio, in sending $12.00 to the "poor Brethren in Virginia" in 1883.[86]

Church units larger than districts also occasionally concerned themselves with problems of the needy in the brotherhood. Canada Joint Council made provision in 1894 to raise $12.00 yearly for house rent for an elderly brother and sister and, the following year, forgave a member a note for $825.00 and interest which the Canadian Mission Board held against him.[87] To cover this amount the council urged the brotherhood to give more liberally to the cause of missions.

Even General Conference occasionally addressed its attention to individual needs. When the mission in Columbus, Ohio, petitioned for the relief of an elderly minister with an indebtedness of $642.00, Conference directed that the amount be raised by voluntary contribution throughout the church within sixty days.[88] In these various ways the Brethren demonstrated their commitment to the Pauline assertion about the church: "And whether one member suffer, all the members suffer with it."[89]

Marriage and Divorce

The Brethren perceived marriage to have important implications for the life and well-being of the brotherhood, and they sought to regulate it by both counsel and legislation. The Eighteenth-Century Confession stated that brotherly counsel should be sought by those contemplating marriage. One district provided courtship guidelines; it informed younger members that keeping "promiscuous company" with persons outside of the church was inconsistent. It also urged them to conduct their courtships in the daytime rather than at night. These district minutes read: "Young brethren and sisters have the mutual encouragement and sanction of the church if they should choose to make their *special* visits in the daytime, since the church believes it to be a more consistent time, for the christian [*sic*] than at night."[90]

The marriage question came to the foreground repeatedly in General Conference. One of the questions raised most often was whether members might marry non-members.[91] An 1843 General Conference in Lancaster County formulated the policy which governed this matter for several decades. That policy indicating the desire of the Brethren to remain flexible on the question while providing safeguards for the integrity of their group life was as follows:

> That when a member wishes to marry out of the church, he or she shall make it known to the brother who is to unite them in marriage. Said brother is to council with two or three other brethren, who shall visit the person who is not a member; and if the person is not a despiser of God or of the church, or profligate, or light minded, but virtuous . . . a lover of the truth or penitent, then he may join them in marriage.[92]

Repeated requests for reconsideration of this decision indicate serious differences of opinion about it. Some of the questions related to the possibility of members marrying unconverted persons. General Conference, however, was reluctant to depart from the broad position of 1843 which permitted each situation to be judged on its own merits.[93] Not until the early twentieth century did Conference become more specific in a decision to "discourage the marriage of brethren and sisters with persons who are unconverted, since it is inconsistent with the Word of God." Four scriptural passages supported this decision.[94]

Biblical marriage was understood by the Brethren to be a lifelong commitment. A remarriage while the former spouse was living constituted adultery. This sin of adultery was a continuing sin as long as the former spouse lived.[95] On this premise they could not countenance a member's marriage to a divorced person whose former husband or wife still lived, nor could they accept into membership a remarried person whose former partner still lived.[96] On at least one occasion, however, even General Conference recognized the complexities surrounding a divorce situation and kept the way open for the district to receive the parties in question into the church. In this instance Conference sought to guard against setting a precedent by ruling that it was "a special case."[97]

In spite of the firm stand of General Conference on this question, the districts varied in the degree to which they enforced the regulations. Some districts firmly disciplined members involved in divorce and remarriage situations, but other districts were more lenient.[98]

Conference finally sought to come to grips with these irregularities. It reaffirmed former decisions with the amendment that "all thoroughly converted applicants for Church membership, who have been living in adultery, and discontinue their co-habitation, whether divorced or not, shall be eligible to be admitted to Church membership." This meant that a remarried person who had a living former spouse, or one married to a divorced person whose former spouse was still living, could qualify for church membership if the two parties agreed to discontinue sexual relationships as husband and wife.[99] In spite of the growing complexity of marital relationships in a changing society, Conference maintained essentially this position on divorce and remarriage until the 1960s.[100]

In the early twentieth century, concerns about marriage and divorce caused the Brethren to make one of their rare contacts with government. At that time General Conference sent a memorial to President Theodore Roosevelt commending him for his concern about the laxity and lack of uniformity of state laws regulating marriage and divorce.[101]

Intellectual and Cultural Interests

Preoccupation of the Brethren with work and worship during their early history precluded their serious interest in the intellectual and aesthetic aspects of the society around them. Even after the mid-nineteenth century, when accelerating social and economic changes were transforming that society, those changes had little direct effect upon the brotherhood. The social detachment reflected in their records suggests that many Brethren did not even read newspapers.

This social isolation developed in part out of their circumstances as a rural people in an age when communication was difficult and slow; it may have been accentuated by their German language. Many of their comtemporaries, who were less earnest in religious pursuits, shared this social detachment to a considerable degree. The Brethren, however, consciously reinforced isolating circumstances by relegating many of the structures or arrangements of society to the realm of the world. Culture as a conscious cultivation of the intellectual and aesthetic phases of life was not for them.

While rural isolation and religious conviction thus combined to cut them off from cultural influences, their separation from other religious societies closed even that channel through which those influences might have flowed into their life. Their very limited interdenominational contacts were principally with Mennonites and Dunkers who also had reservations about many aspects of culture.[102]

Brethren disapproval of formal education beyond the elementary level also delayed their acceptance of cultural pursuits. As a people deeply committed to the Scriptures and work, they had practical reasons to encourage literacy. If they were to obey the Bible, they had to read it; if they were to manage farms, they had to write and calculate. Most of them saw no need for learning more than these basic skills. They were also suspicious that advanced education might open the door for worldliness to come among them.

In the midst of this prevailing anti-intellectualism, a few nineteenth-century members of the brotherhood were exceptions to the rule. Some pioneered in advanced education.[103] Others such as Christian Lesher, Henry Davidson, Henry N. Engle, and Eli Engle developed their intellectual capacities to impressive levels by self-education.

Such intellectualism as there was expressed itself primarily through religious pursuits, but here and there individual minds ranged further afield. H. Frances Davidson completed liberal arts degrees.[104] As a physician William Baker was, of course, familiar with the medical science of his day. In addition he read in a multi-volume work on the history of civilization and attended a literary club which conducted studies of mythology and evolution.[105] Eli M. Engle was sufficiently familiar with the Renaissance to distinguish precisely between different pronunciations of the term.[106]

Although some individuals were receptive to culture broadly defined, the Brethren as a whole tended to resist it. One district forbade members to attend debating schools.[107] Another ruled against their attendance at theatrical performances "which make unreal things seem real," including dramatic presentations in schools and churches.[108]

This objection to the unreal element in dramatics helps to explain Brethren opposition to novels which, like dramatics, were imaginative. In addition the Brethren reacted to what they considered to be the immoral and evil content of fictitious writings.[109] Their serious objection to the novel is expressed in the following comments:

> Novels are the devil's guide books to hell and are used by the infernal
> spirits to fascinate men and women and more especially the young, and lead

them into sin and give them a hell-born inspiration for sin and crime. One should detest and shun novels and those story papers as they [sic], would vipers. Every book and paper containing fictitious and immoral matter should be destroyed or branded with a skull and cross bones, . . .[110]

Not all members rejected fictional literature completely. Some of them accepted works with a religious message, such as John Bunyan's *Pilgrim's Progress.*[111] The daughter of one influential bishop read Jules Verne's *Trip Around the Moon* and Harriet Beecher Stowe's *Uncle Tom's Cabin.*[112] These exceptions illustrate a point made several times previously in this study. Strong assertions of what appear to be positions of the brotherhood may require qualification; there were often dissenters, sometimes in significant numbers, to those positions.

Aesthetic interests also had little place in the life of the early brotherhood. Two factors especially inhibited their development. One was the belief that anything decorative or refined fostered pride and wordliness. The other was the way in which the Brethren attached virtue to work; the drive of a practical materialism tended to smother the aesthetic impulse. Both of these factors appear in the following passage:

I have been thinking . . . that some of the sisters, with a great many others that do not profess to be as separate from the world as we believe and have it taught us, are still spending some of their valuable time in things that are no particular benefit to any one, but a temptation to others. I have seen in travelling, birds in cages, and an abundance of house plants which all need their proper care and perhaps other things neglected which are of more importance. I sometimes think a little more time might in many instances be bestowed in our kitchens tiding [sic] up things a little or having our food prepared in a good appetizing and nourishing way, . . .[113]

Henry Davidson's recommendation of *Vick's Floral Guide,* which he described as "A beautiful book devoted to vegetables and flowers," provides another interesting example of the working of the Brethren mind. After naming the book he made no further reference to flowers or floral beauty. Instead, he directed the reader's attention to the practical and profitable aspects of gardening, with a bit of moralizing added for good measure. ". . . a good garden is to the family a great help toward a comfortable living, and the labor attending it is more healthful exercise than lawn tennis, or base ball [sic], and is besides healthful exercise, a labor of profit, while these plays for amusement are only invented to kill time and give very little return of any benefit to those engaged in them, and often result in much harm."[114]

Davidson's reference to "plays" for amusement, which are invented to kill time, opens another window into the thought patterns of the brotherhood. Typical members regarded the Christian pilgrimage as an extremely serious matter. Everything the Christian did should serve some definite religious or vocational end; whatever failed to do so should be shunned as part of the vain things of the world. The Brethren noted that Paul in his letter to the Ephesians classified foolish talking and jesting in a catalog of sins including fornication, filthiness, and covetousness, and that he also urged his readers to redeem the time for the days were evil.[115]

Any activity, therefore, which did not produce some tangible or practical good they considered to be displeasing to God. In the words of one convert; "Laughing, jesting and all foolish conversation . . . became very sinful to me, and I could then realize the true meaning of those words, 'The friendship of the world, is enmity with God' . . ."[116] Other young converts felt that obedience required them to discontinue participation in the sports and games of the schoolyard.[117] One district decided that members should not attend surprise parties, go on excursion trips, or go out with hunting groups "for pleasure or jolification [sic]."[118] All such activities, in addition to being non-productive, militated against the seriousness of purpose and demeanor which, in the view of the Brethren, should characterize the Christian pilgrim.

The seriousness so characteristic of their early history stands out clearly in a controversy about an article entitled "Cheerfulness," which appeared in an early issue of the *Visitor*. The author touched a very sensitive nerve as she wrote:

> It is a sad mistake that persons are religious in proportion as they are sad and melancholy. There are professed Christians who talk and act as if it was a sin to be happy and enjoy life . . . is it any wonder we fail to win people, and especially young people for Christ, when they receive the impression from Christians themselves, that in order to live a Christian life, they must give up all that makes life pleasant and desirable?
>
> . . . .
>
> There is vastly more Christianity in a smile than there is in a frown, and there is more true Christianity in a good hearty laugh than there is in a groan. . . . We should not be giddy and vain, but . . . nothing can be more natural than for a happy person to laugh, . . .[119]

In the next issue of the *Visitor*, the editor expressed regret that

"Cheerfulness" had found its way into the paper. He did not doubt the good intention of the author, but added: "While the title is good, and we think the Christian, of all others, has the greatest reason to be cheerful, yet the tone of the article would rather incline to levity and have a tendency to take away the sanctity that should attend the Christian religion."[120]

Soon a rebuttal article appeared under the title "Be Sober." Speaking from the historic tradition of the group, this writer maintained that a Christian should not laugh heartily or outright, though many "through the weakness of the flesh do so." She came firmly to grips with the thesis of "Cheerfulness":

> I am not afraid to say, "there is more Christianity in a smile than there is in a frown," but I would not dare to say, "there is more Christianity in a good hearty laugh than there is in a groan." We can read of where our Savior groaned and where he wept, but we cannot read of where he laughed. Were I to select all the passages in the New Testament, contrary to mirth and laughter, it would require a great deal of space.[121]

The author of "Cheerfulness" stood her ground and answered her critics by pointing out that the Bible spoke of "a time to weep and a time to laugh." She also asserted that there were many other scriptural references to laughter and that each context revealed whether the reference was to "the sinful injurious laughter of wickedness" or to "the pure innocent laughter which harms no one."[122] There can be no doubt, however, that her original article sounded an unfamiliar note in Brethren circles. One of their leaders made this clear in the following passage:

> Our old fathers and mothers in the church were a deeply serious people, among the world it was reckoned as one of their noted characteristics. In my acquaintance with Eld. Peter Cober, Bro. Jacob Heise and other well known brethren, while I have often seen them smile, I seldom saw them laugh, and that but slightly. Their time was too precious to spend in mirth and foolish laughter.[123]

The intense seriousness of the early Brethren, which was a part of their church-world understanding, integrated readily with their practices of worship and work. Anything falling outside of these areas was at best useless and at worst sinful. Pilgrims on the heavenly pathway had no need for earthly amusement, mirth, and merriment, which could only lead them astray. Anything done "to kill time" furthermore, seemed nonsensical to the Brethren, for they were a rural people persuaded of the virtue of work.

In view of the complexities of these beliefs and feelings, the repudiation of intellectual and aesthetic elements of culture by the early brotherhood is quite understandable. Even their criticism of the mainline Protestant churches was in part a reaction to the cultural expressions of those churches with educated ministers, decorative and expensive edifices, and sophisticated music perceived by the Brethren as worldly substitutes for the simplicity and separation of the gospel. They could not see how advanced intellectual pursuits or the cultivation of aesthetic sensitivities had anything to offer serious pilgrims on the narrow, self-denying way to heaven. Nor could they see how either intellectualism or aestheticism met their rule of usefulness applied to work; culture did not help to prepare a nourishing meal, strip tobacco, nor plow corn.

NOTES:

[1]This chapter expands upon the doctrine of nonconformity introduced in the last section of Chapter III.

[2]F. Elliott, "War," *Visitor*, VIII (January 15, 1895), 17.

[3]Familiar Friend, "River Brethren," p. 554.

[4]Geo. S. Grim, "The Support and Continuance of War," *Visitor* XII (April 15, 1899), 145. See also W. O. Baker, "War," *Visitor*, X (January 15, 1897), 18, 19.

[5]Geo. S. Grim, "War vs. Christianity," *Visitor*, VII (June 1, 1894), 167.

[6]J. H. B., "War, a Great Evil," *Visitor*, IV (July 1, 1891), 195; W. O. Baker, "War," *Visitor*, X (February 1, 1897), 35.

[7]T. A. Long, "Be Ready to Answer," *Visitor*, I (June 1, 1888), 149.

[8]J. H. B., "War, a Great Evil," *Visitor*, IV (July 1, 1891), 195-96. See also W. O. Baker, "War," *Visitor*, X (February 1, 1897), 34-35, and Geo. S. Grim, "The Support and Continuance of War," *Visitor*, XII (April 15, 1899), 145.

[9]F. Elliott, "War," *Visitor*, VIII (January 15, 1895), 17-18.

[10]F. Elliott, "On Singing," *Visitor*, V (March 1, 1892), 69.

[11]W. O. Baker, "War," *Visitor*, X (February 1, 1897), 36.

[12]F. Elliott, "War," *Visitor*, VIII (January 15, 1895), 18; W. O. Baker, "War," *Visitor*, X (February 1, 1897), 36.

[13]*Church Government*, 1887, p. 9; *General Conference Minutes*, 1913, Article 32, p. 55.

[14]*General Council Minutes*, 1899, Article 5, pp. 4-5.

[15]1 Cor. 6:1-8; Mt. 5:40.

[16]J. G. Cassel, "Thoughts on 1st Corinthians," *Visitor*, XIV (January 1, 1901), 2.

[17]*General Conference Minutes,* 1899, Article 5, pp. 4-5. Ironically, the next General Conference found itself in the awkward position of condoning a lawsuit in defense of a property bequest to the Des Moines Mission in Iowa. Considerable mystery surrounds the origin and circumstances of this case which was won on appeal by the plaintiffs contesting the will of the donor, and which left the brotherhood with an indebtedness of approximately $2600.00. See *General Conference Minutes,* 1900, pp. 8-9; *ibid.,* 1903, Article 22, pp. 14-15; *Pennsylvania State Council Minutes,* 1902, Article 2, pp. 4-5; [George Detwiler], *Visitor,* XVI (August 15, 1902), p. 314; *ibid.,* XVII (May 15, 1903), 13.

[18]F. Elliott, "War," *Visitor,* VIII (January 15, 1895), 18.

[19]*Church Government,* 1887, p. 9.

[20]F. Elliott, "War," *Visitor* VIII (January 15, 1895), 18.

[21]Sider, "Brethren in Canada," p. 157.

[22]*Ibid.,* pp. 158-60.

[23]*Ibid.,* pp. 160-69.

[24]E. J. Swalm, *Nonresistance Under Test* (Nappanee, Ind.: E. V. Publishing House 1938), p. 21; Jacob Ulery commutation fine receipts, Church Archives.

[25]Schrag, "Brethren Attitude Toward the World," Appendix C.

[26]*Ibid.;* Ulery commutation fine receipts.

[27]Ulery commutation fine receipt, September 8, 1863.

[28]Jacob S. Engle to Thaddeus Stevens, January 4, 1864, printed in Schrag, "Brethren Attitude Toward the World," p. 323.

[29]Swalm, *Nonresistance,* p. 22.

[30]Asa Bearss and Wellington Duxbury, *Origin and History of the Tunker Church in Canada As Gathered from Authentic and Reliable Sources* (Ridgeway, Printed by M. V. Disher, 1918), p. 7; *Canadian Joint Council Minutes,* September 11, 1913, Article 2, p. 31.

[31]D. Heise, "Serving Two Masters," *Visitor,* V (October 1, 1892), 294-95.

[32]*Ibid.,* p. 294.

[33]Eighteenth-Century Confession; C. Stoner, "Points of Difference," *Visitor,* V (August 1, 1892), p. 231.

[34]*Church Government,* 1887, pp. 9, 20.

[35]W. O. Baker, "Reminiscences No. 1," *Visitor,* I (August 1, 1887), 9; *General Conference Minutes,* 1882, Article 7.

[36]*General Council Minutes,* 1889, Article 10.

[37]*Ibid.,* 1893, p. 2.

[38]*Ibid.,* 1894, p. 2.

[39]Schrag, "Brethren Attitude Toward the World," pp. 177-78.

[40]Dayton District Book of Record, August 6, 1881, Article 3.

[41]South Dickinson District Council Minutes, September 24, 1887, Article 12.

[42]Enos H. Hess, "The Sunday-School," *Visitor,* XIX (March 15, 1905), p. 16.

[43]Dickinson County Joint Council Minutes, February 3, 1891.

[44]Kansas Joint Council Minutes, March 23, 24, 1894, Article 4.

[45]Rhoda E. Lee, "Foreign Missions," *Visitor,* VIII (July 1, 1895), 194.

[46]John H. Myers, "Separation," *Visitor,* X (September 15, 1897), 315.

[47]North Dickinson District Council Minutes, October 10, 1882, Article 1.

[48]Davidson, *South and Central Africa,* pp. 19, 20.

[49]Isaac Shockey, "An Appeal," *Visitor,* II (February 1, 1889), 76.

[50]*Church Government,* 1887, p. 10.

[51]Dickinson County Joint Council Minutes, March 13, 1886, Article 1.

[52]*Church Government,* 1887, p. 15.

[53]*Ibid.,* p. 10.

[54]South Dickinson County District Minutes, February 19, 1891, Article 3.

[55]*Church Government,* 1887, p. 10.

[56]*General Conference Minutes,* 1912, Article 45, p. 115.

[57]*Church Government,* 1887, p. 15.

[58]*General Conference Minutes,* 1951, Article XIX, pp. 37-38.

[59]*Ibid.,* 1905, Article 17, p. 14. The passages are Mt. 6:31-34; Lk. 14:26-34; Rom. 12:10, 17; Phil. 4:19; Col. 3:3; 1 Pet. 2:9; 2 Pet. 2:3; Deut. 14:2; Jer. 17:5-8; Mal. 3:10.

[60]*Canadian Joint Council Minutes,* 1893, p. 2; *ibid.,* 1897, p. 6.

[61]P. M. Climenhaga, "The Brethren's Fire Relief in Canada," *Visitor,* XVIII (May 15, 1904), 13.

[62]*Canadian Joint Council Minutes,* 1905, p. 16; *ibid.,* 1912, p. 28; *ibid.,* 1912, p. 30.

[63]*Ibid.,* 1897, p. 6.

[64]*Ibid.,* 1895, p. 4.

[65]*Ibid.*

[66]*Ibid.,* 1905, p. 16; *ibid.,* 1906, p. 17; P. M. Climenhaga, "The Brethren's Fire Relief in Canada," *Visitor,* XVIII (May 15, 1904), 13.

[67]P. M. Climenhaga, "The Brethren's Fire Relief in Canada," *Visitor,* XVIII (May 15, 1904), 13.

[68]*Canadian Joint Council Minutes,* 1915, p. 37.

[69]*Ibid.,* 1916, p. 39.

[70]Sider, "Brethren in Canada," p. 225.

[71]H. B. Musser, "A Plea for the Fire Relief," *Visitor,* VI (October 1, 1893), 300. Musser dates the beginning of the Fire Relief in the early 1870s. If it began subsequent to 1871, however, the General Council minutes which start with that year should record the appointment of the committee to launch it. They do not, which implies that the organization began before 1871.

[72]*General Conference Minutes,* 1914, Article 43, p. 64.

[73]*Ibid.,* 1906, Article 17, p. 13.

[74]*Ibid.,* 1914, Article 43, p. 64.

[75]*Ibid.,* Article 44, p. 65.

[76]*Rules Governing the Brethren's Mutual Fire Aid* (Mount Joy, Pa.: n.d.), Asa. W. Climenhaga Papers; *General Conference Minutes,* 1916, Article 34, p. 72.

[77]No original rules of the Brethren's Fire Relief survive, but it may be inferred that its membership requirements were similar to those given here.

[78]*Rules Governing the Brethren's Mutual Fire Aid;* Pennsylvania Insurance Commission Examiner's Report (copy), Minute Book of the Brethren's Mutual Fire Insurance Company. Photostats of this document and those cited in notes 80-83 are in the Church Archives.

[79]*General Conference Minutes,* 1916, Article XXXIV, p. 72.

[80]Pennsylvania Insurance Commission Examiner's Report.

[81]Memorandum of Agreement between the Brethren's Mutual Fire Insurance Company and the Lititz Agricultural Mutual Fire Insurance Company, August 31, 1939.

[82]Minutes of the Brethren's Mutual Fire Insurance Company, March 26, 1930; October 2, December 4, 1933; January 27, 1937; July 14, 1939.

[83]Memorandum of Agreement between The Brethren's Mutual Fire Insurance Company and the Lititz Agricultural Mutual Fire Insurance Company, August 31, 1939; Copy of The Final Account of the Officers and Directors of Brethren's Mutual Fire Insurance Company—in Liquidation.

[84]H. B. Musser, "A Plea for the Fire Relief," *Visitor*, VI (October 1, 1893), 300.

[85]Dayton District Book of Record, November 26, 1887, Article 3; *ibid.*, March 29, 1890, Article 4; Rapho District Council Minutes, April 27, 1905, Article 5; Markham District Council Minutes, July 8, 1899, Article 4.

[86]Dayton District Book of Record, August 4, 1883, Article 7.

[87]*Canadian Joint Council Minutes,* September 14, 1894, p. 3; *ibid.*, September 12, 1895, p. 3.

[88]*Church Government,* 1887, p. 36.

[89]1 Cor. 12:26.

[90]North Dickinson District Council Minutes, October 10, 1882, Article 5.

[91]*Church Government,* 1887, pp. 7, 11.

[92]*Ibid.*, p. 11. This restates an 1843 policy for which no original minute record exists.

[93]*Ibid.*, pp. 11, 16.

[94]*General Conference Minutes,* 1906, Article 29, p. 18. The scriptural passages are Gen. 6:1-3; Amos 3:3; 1 Cor. 7:39; 2 Cor. 6:14-18.

[95]*Church Government,* 1887, p. 8; A Brother, "Adultery Considered," *Visitor*, III (November 1889), 25; D. B. K., "Divorcement," *Visitor*, IV (September 15, 1891), 277-78.

[96]*Church Government,* 1887, pp. 8, 15.

[97]*General Conference Minutes,* 1895, p. 3. No details are known about it.

[98]*Ibid.*, 1914, Article 25, p. 55.

[99]*Ibid.*, 1914, Article 25, p. 55; *ibid.*, Article 32, p. 59.

[100]*Ibid.*, 1951, Article 22, p. 46; *ibid.*, 1952, Article 28, p. 52. See Chapter XX for the position on divorce after 1974.

[101]*General Conference Minutes,* 1905, Article 16, p. 12.

[102]George Detwiler, "A Brief Biographical Statement," Asa W. Climenhaga Papers; Jacob N. Martin to Bro. Sider, March 1, 1924, Asa W. Climenhaga Papers; D. Heise, "Love-Feasts," *Visitor*, I (October 1, 1887), 25.

[103]See Chapter XIII.

[104]*Ibid.*

[105]William O. Baker Diaries, January 22, 1901, and January 4, 1907.

[106]About 1933 the present writer heard the aged Eli Engle refer to the Renaissance in an address at Messiah (Bible) College, Grantham, Pennsylvania.

[107]South Dickinson District Council Minutes, February 18, 1892, Article 4.

[108]Markham District Council Minutes, January 29, 1904, Article 12.

[109]"Novel-Killed," *Visitor*, I (March 1, 1888), 107-8; J. G. C., "A Flood of Poisonous Literature," *Visitor*, IV (April 1, 1891), 108; F. Elliott, "Novel Reading," *Visitor*, VI (June 1, 1893), 161-62.

[110]"Novels," *Visitor*, XIV (February 15, 1901), 73.

[111]F., "Reading," *Visitor*, I (October 1, 1887), 30; F. Elliott, "Novel Reading," *Visitor*, VI (June 1, 1893), 161; Anna M. Sider, "Change of Raiment," *Visitor*, VI (July 15, 1893), 211.

[112]Lillian Baker's Diary, April 29, 1900, and March 25, 1901, Church Archives.

[113]C. S., "Are We Sufficiently Careful?" *Visitor,* III (May 1, 1890), 144.

[114][Henry Davidson], *Visitor,* V (February 15, 1892), 57.

[115]Eph. 5:3-5, 16; Markham District Council Minutes, January 29, 1904, Article 12.

[116]Sister Susanna Martin, "Words of Encouragement," *Visitor,* I (March 1, 1888), 107. See also Charles Cocklin, "Let Us Be Careful," *Visitor,* IV (July 1, 1891), 195.

[117]J. B. Musser, "Honesty the Best Policy," *Visitor,* III (July 1, 1890), 194; Lizzie Book, "A Testimony," *Visitor,* XI (July 15, 1898), 266.

[118]Dayton District Book of Record, November 30, 1878, Article 2; *ibid.,* November 29, 1879, Articles 1, 3.

[119]Sallie Kniesly, "Cheerfulness," *Visitor,* I (July 1, 1888), 164.

[120][H. Davidson], *Visitor,* I (August 1, 1888), 184.

[121]Sarah McTaggart, "Be Sober," *Visitor,* I (September 1, 1888), 194.

[122]Sallie Kniesly, "An Explanation," *Visitor,* II (November 1, 1888), 23.

[123]F. Elliott, "Some Thoughts," *Visitor,* VII (February 1, 1894), 34.

VII

Geographical
Expansion and Schisms

Expansion to 1880

Two striking characteristics of the early Brethren in Christ movement were its wide geographical expansion and its slow numerical growth. Soon after the group organized near Bainbridge, Pennsylvania, the membership expanded northward to Elizabethtown, Mount Joy, and Manheim, southeastward between the Susquehanna River and Lancaster City, and southward into York County. At an early date families also migrated to Ontario, Canada, to other counties in Pennsylvania, and westward across the Appalachian Mountains.

The leadership of the Brethren during those early decades of expansion is obscure. According to tradition Jacob Engel was the first overseer or bishop, and Jacob Strickler succeeded him in the 1830s. John Gish, traditional successor to Strickler, may have served jointly with Jacob Hostetter.[1]

Whatever the early leadership arrangements were, they had become inadequate by 1873. During that year the society decided to elect three bishops, one for each of the Donegal, Rapho, and Conestoga regions.[2] In the spring of 1874, Jacob Hostetter ordained Jacob Graybill bishop of the Conestoga members, thus laying the foundation for Manor-Pequea District.[3] At about the same time, according to tradition, Jacob M. Engle and Benjamin Shelley became bishops of the Donegal and Rapho memberships respectively.[4]

This ordination of three bishops with specific territorial jurisdictions marked the origin of the three original Brethren in Christ districts in

Lancaster County. Donegal District comprised a triangular area formed by Marietta, Elizabethtown, and Mount Joy, plus the members in York County. Rapho District included the region between Mount Joy and Manheim, and Manor-Pequea District the territory south of Lancaster City.[5]

While the brotherhood expanded in Lancaster and York Counties, members were also migrating to other parts of Pennsylvania. By the mid-

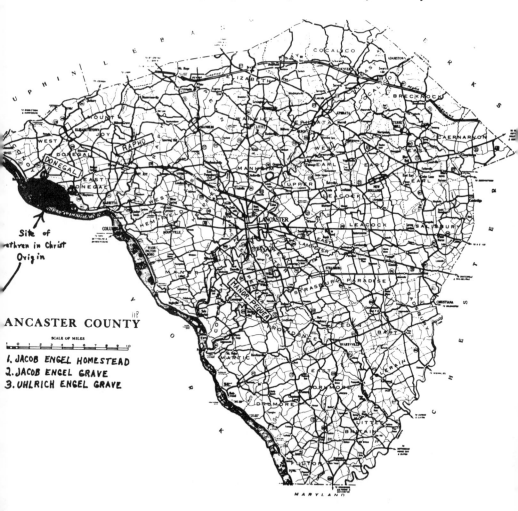

Site of
rethren in Christ
Origin

ANCASTER COUNTY

SCALE OF MILES

1. JACOB ENGEL HOMESTEAD
2. JACOB ENGEL GRAVE
3. UHLRICH ENGEL GRAVE

Site of origin of the Brethren in Christ, together with locations of their three districts which subsequently developed in Lancaster County, Pennsylvania.

nineteenth century, they had reached Bucks, Dauphin, Franklin, Westmoreland and several other counties.[6] Thirty years later they were in eighteen counties, with Lancaster, Franklin, and Blair having the largest memberships, and with Cumberland, Dauphin, Lebanon, Montgomery and Perry having significant numbers. Each of ten additional counties had fewer numbers. One group of families had crossed the southern boundary of Pennsylvania to settle near Ringgold, Maryland.[7] By 1880, therefore, the society had spread over the approximate area of the present-day Pennsylvania brotherhood.

Migration of the Brethren to out-of-state regions proceeded simultaneously with their expansion in Pennsylvania. John Winger and Jacob Sider emigrated to Ontario, Canada, in 1788. The reasons for their leaving the United States are not clear. One surmise is that the British flag offered greater security to persons of nonresistant faith than did the flag of a new nation born in violent revolution.[8] If this is the reason Winger and Sider went to Canada, it fails to explain why more Brethren did not promptly take up residence on British soil. Another and more plausible explanation is that members who settled in Canada were responding to the opportunity to secure Southern Ontario land on favorable terms, just as other members went westward in the United States to acquire land on the frontier.[9]

By 1880 Brethren families had settled in nine Southern Ontario counties and in Erie County, New York, just across the Niagara River. Their principal Ontario membership was in York County north of Toronto, where the development of Markham District was well under way. The second largest membership concentration was in Welland County, where it formed Black Creek District. A third cluster of families in Waterloo and Huron Counties comprised the Waterloo-Howick District.

At that time only a few families were in Haldimand County which would be included in the Wainfleet District when it later emerged out of the western part of Black Creek District. A small group of families had also located in Simcoe County on the southern shore of Georgian Bay where Nottawa District would eventually detach itself from Markham District.

While expanding in Pennsylvania and Canada, the Brethren also joined the westward movement across the Appalachian Mountains. By 1880 they had two fairly large membership concentrations in Ohio, one in a tier of counties stretching from Mansfield to Canton and the other in the Dayton-Springfield area. Another group of considerable size was in northwestern

Illinois, with a few families scattered in the eastern part of the state. Small groups were also present in northern and eastern Indiana, central Iowa, and southern Michigan. Some families who had found their way to Kansas in the 1870s were joined there in 1879 by a large colony which originated in Pennsylvania and Maryland.[10]

The principal reason for the restless migrations of the Brethren prior to 1880 was their quest for a better economic life. While the American frontier had only entered Lancaster County in 1710, it passed rapidly westward. Much of the best land of that county was already taken up by the time the group organized as a religious society about seventy years later.[11]

After the frontier passed through any good farming country, land prices tended to rise, and the area could not absorb a continuous increase of farmers. Large landowners could subdivide their estates among their sons, but there was a point beyond which farm division was not economically feasible. Farm tenancy offered limited opportunities for some families to accumulate capital for land purchase. Other options were farming inferior land or moving to different areas where good farms were available at favorable prices.[12]

Together with many of their neighbors, a considerable number of Lancaster County Brethren chose the last alternative. Near and far they sought for the desired farms, and this process was repeated elsewhere wherever clusters of their families settled and the difficulties of farm acquisition increased.

The tendency of the Brethren to migrate as groups of families or to follow each other into areas of promising economic opportunity permitted them to continue the practice of their faith. As they organized their church life in new communities, they bore witness to that faith in the presence of their neighbors. Early church extension was thus more of a result rather than a cause of Brethren migration.

The wide geographical expansion of the Brethren during their first one hundred years may create a misleading impression of their numerical growth. Although no accurate statistics of communicant membership exist, 2,000 is a rough approximation of their number by 1880.[13]

This small numerical increase of the brotherhood is not impressive compared with the rapid growth of a contemporary religious society such as the United Brethren in Christ, but the situation must be understood in the light of the nature of the Brethren movement. For persons not born and nurtured within the group, acceptance of their beliefs and life-style was not an easy decision. From the point of view of the Brethren themselves, success was not measured by the number of communicants. They were preoccupied with the goal of a pure church in which the community of the converted sought to perfect obedience in visible fellowship with each other and in sharply defined tension with the surrounding world.

Schisms

By the mid-nineteenth century schism had three times rent the ranks of the United States Brethren. The groups which went their separate ways were the Wengerites, the Yorkers, and the Brinsers.

Obscurity surrounds the Wengerite crisis which is known only through conflicting oral tradition. It occurred in Southern Ohio between approximately 1828 and 1841. The name "Wengerites" lends credence to the report that John Wenger led the dissenters, although the group eventually called themselves "Brethren in Christ" long before the Brethren in Christ of the present study adopted that name.[14] While the traditional sources offer no common explanation for the schism, they concur in picturing the dissenting group as more progressive or liberal than the parent body.

These dissenters from the River Brethren, together with others who joined them, presently split into "Wengerite" and "Swankite" factions, each retaining the name "Brethren in Christ." The latter more progressive group united in 1861 with a group of like-minded persons in Armstrong County, Pennsylvania.[15] In the early 1950s a surviving remnant of that union, attracted by the Brethren in Christ name adopted by the United States River Brethren in the 1860s, sought out Bishop Henry S. Miller of the Center, Clinton, and Lycoming District in Pennsylvania to explore possible historical connections between the respective societies as well as posible future relationships.[16] Representatives of the two groups subsequently fraternized with each other and discussed the possibility of merger, but their respective faiths and sentiments did not provide an adequate basis for it.[17]

The paths of one of these groups of Brethren in Christ and those who are the subjects of this study also crossed significantly at one point in the nineteenth century. In the 1890s Charles Good, who appears to have been a Wengerite, attended the General Conference of 1893 at Franklin Corners, Illinois. Good was deeply interested in mission work in his home community of Des Moines, Iowa. He was of advanced age and his denomination was unable or unwilling to undertake sponsorship of a mission there. Following Good's appearance at Conference, Bishops Isaac Trump, Henry Davidson, Samuel Zook, and others visited Des Moines to evaluate his program. Later, John R. Zook went there and took over administration of the Charles Good mission. That act marked the beginning of the present Brethren in Christ church work in Des Moines.[18]

The second of the three River Brethren divisions resulted in a society known originally as "Yorkers" or "Yorker Brethren," because their first leaders and members resided principally in York County, Pennsylvania.[19] Tradition suggests that their first bishop was Jacob Strickler, Jr., successor in York County to his father, River Brethren Bishop Jacob Strickler.[20] Difficulties among the River Brethren in nearby Franklin County later produced a group known as "Hooverites" after their leader, Christian Hoover, who made common cause with the Yorkers.[21] At the present time the spiritual descendants of the Yorkers identify themselves as "Old Order River Brethren." They live principally in York, Lancaster, and Franklin Counties, Pennsylvania, with a few in Ohio and Iowa. Schisms eventually divided them into several groups, three of which have merged in recent years.

Relatively little is known about the circumstances which led to the separation of the Yorkers, but all traditions agree that they represent a conservative reaction to change taking place among the River Brethren. Approximately 125 years later the Old Order River Brethren still strive to perpetuate the basic faith and life-style of their spiritual forebears. Their plain dress, beards, house and barn services, metered hymnody, double-mode feet washing, experience meetings, and other practices provide insights into Brethren in Christ life before late nineteenth-century innovations transformed their movement. For the most part, the Old Order groups have steadfastly resisted these innovations such as revivalism, organized mission enterprises, the Sunday school, and Wesleyan holiness.[22]

Some secondary sources assign the date of 1843 to the Yorker schism, but this date has no support other than its appearance in early twentieth-century Brethren in Christ literature.[23] There is better support for another tradition placing the separation of the Yorkers in the 1850s and relating it to the third River Brethren schism which created the group known first as "Brinsers," or "United Zion's Children" and later as the "United Zion Church."[24]

Of the three schisms which rent the ranks of the River Brethren, most is known about the one which produced the Brinsers. Matthias Brinser, the principal figure in this schism, was a colorful River Brethren bishop in Dauphin County, Pennsylvania. He joined the Brethren at an early age and was later ordained to the ministry in which he exercised long and vigorously. His presence was much in demand for funerals and weddings as well as for regular preaching appointments; on one occasion he preached by request in the courthouse in Harrisburg.[25] A contemporary wrote of him: "He looks like an old prophet—some fiery Tishbite—brimful of Scripture, and terribly eloquent, especially when he stands on Mount Ebal."[26]

Sketch of the Brinser Meetinghouse erected in the 1850s between Middletown, Pennsylvania, and the Susquehanna River. This drawing was done about 1900 by Matthias Brinser's grandson, H. S. Brinser, who attended services in the meetinghouse during his boyhood.

The immediate cause of the schism was the decision of Matthias Brinser and his Dauphin County followers to build a small meetinghouse near Middletown, Pennsylvania. An increasing Brethren membership in that locality was outgrowing the capacity of homes to accommodate the worship services.

This was not, as the resulting controversy might suggest, the first use of a meetinghouse by members of the brotherhood. There is a United Brethren in Christ tradition of that society joining in 1843 with River Brethren and Dunkers to erect a union meetinghouse at Hummelstown, Pennsylvania, and another tradition of River Brethren participating with three other groups to build a union church in Southern Ohio about 1850.[27] Even if both traditions are in error, there is convincing proof that the Brethren of Wayne County, Ohio, held monthly meetings as early as 1850 in a union meetinghouse known as Paradise Church.[28]

Perhaps Brinser knew that some of the Brethren elsewhere had set a precedent for houses of worship. On the other hand, he was an aggressive leader who may not have been greatly concerned about objections to what he and his supporters felt needed to be done.

The meetinghouse which divided the River Brethren was an unpretentious, single-story frame structure with vertical clapboarding.[29] In the words of one who attended there as a boy:

> The house would hardly have been taken for a school house by a passing stranger, for it was far below the general appearance of that kind of building. Being in a corner of a field, hard by the public road, a stranger would have been apt to regard it as an implement shed.[30]

Simple as this meetinghouse was, it aroused a storm of opposition especially among the Lancaster County Brethren. According to tradition, the council which debated the building project convened during a day of very heavy rain, and the resulting psychological atmosphere was not conducive to the reconciliation of serious differences. Debate reportedly continued until two o'clock in the morning. At that time Brinser hurriedly departed, declaring that he did so to avoid being cut off by swollen streams, but his opponents interpreted his abrupt departure as defiance of the council.[31] They accordingly formulated the following strong statement of admonition:

> The peace of God and the love of Jesus we wish you, dear brethren, with a hearty greeting. We, the undersigned brethren, have taken counsel together

concerning the projected building of a meeting-house in your vicinity and have unanimously agreed to request you to leave it uncompleted, for we believe that such a building will open a door to great harm and will cause heavy suffering to many brethren; therefore we ask you, in hearty love, to receive our dear advice.[32]

There is no way to determine the meaning of "great harm" and "heavy suffering" referred to in this document signed by twenty-six men. Whatever these expressions meant, however, the Brinser group declined to heed the admonition, and pushed their project to completion. The result was that the meetinghouse controversy reached a climax in the summer of 1855 with the River Brethren excommunication of Matthias Brinser and all of his supporters. The decree of excommunication reads:

This communication shows you, Matthias Brinser, that a unanimous decision was reached to the effect that the counsel, which was made at Jacob Engle's, shall be carried out on you; it says: "If he does not listen to the congregation, consider him as a heathen and tax-collector." [Matthew 18:17] And you have not listened, therefore you can no longer be a Brother until you conform, and the congregation is separated from you and the brethren who hold with you; and it has been decided that the congregation has failed, that it has not followed the counsel in the beginning, as you have not listened.[33]

Traditional sources tie the Yorker and Brinser schisms together by suggesting that the delay in disciplinary action between the admonition to Brinser in 1853 and his excommunication in 1855 alienated the Yorkers. One source reports that Bishop Levi Lukenbach, counseled Brinser that he could eventually have his meetinghouse if he would only be patient and wait. The conservative Yorkers, sensing this "liberal" point of view and finding it completely unacceptable, severed relationships with the parent body.[34] Even if this historical linkage of the two schisms is correct, it does not eliminate the possibility of other causal factors in the rupture between the River Brethren and the Yorkers.

Whatever the relationship between the two schisms, Brinser's excommunication seems to have fixed a point of no return for his group. Referring to that action, he reportedly remarked: " 'Sie Fressen einmal . . . [was] sie now kutzen'." ("They will sometime eat what they now vomit").[35] He could not, of course, have foreseen how soon this prophecy would be fulfilled. Within the next decade River Brethren meetinghouses appeared at Woodbury, Pennsylvania, and near Canton, Ohio. Early in the 1870s the Franklin County Brethren began to build them, and they soon became commonplace even in Lancaster County.

Faced with the fact of excommunication, the Brinsers had either to abandon the meetinghouse or to accept the finality of their shattered fellowship with the River Brethren. In a council at the home of Matthias Brinser, they chose the latter alternative. Someone at the council is said to have remarked that they were "'all children of Zion'," and this became the inspiration for the name "United Zion's Children."[36]

The Brethren in Christ have not lived comfortably with the memory of the Brinser schism. As early as 1876 they made a gesture toward reunion, as indicated by the following General Conference action:

> Whether the matter in reference to the reunion of the church with the part of or division known as Brenser [sic] Brethren was carried out according to the decision of the council of last year (1876) in Ohio. Decided: that it was carried out to . . . [the] satisfaction of the brethren.[37]

Another merger effort began indirectly in 1917 when the United Zion's Children petitioned the General Conference for the privilege of publishing news of their fellowship in the *Evangelical Visitor*.[38] This led eventually to the creation of a committee representing both societies, which drew attention to various reasons why closer relationships between the two groups would be "an enhancement of Christ's Kingdom on earth."[39] That committee was active until 1924 when, in the absence of a report from the United Zion section, General Conference deferred indefinitely the quest for closer relations.[40] There the matter rested for more than a decade, although by 1930 the two groups had developed "a very beautiful spirit of cooperation" in foreign mission work.[41]

This merger possibility seemingly would not die. In 1935 General Conference approved representation of the United Zion's Children in both Pennsylvania State Council and General Conference.[42] Two years later Conference authorized a new committee to revive the merger efforts discontinued in 1924.[43] Then began a long, earnest effort to find the way back to ecclesiastical unity.

For the next thirty years the two groups cooperated in the development of closer relationships. These included mutual exchange of the respective church papers, *Zion's Herald* and *Evangelical Visitor,* annual joint fellowship meetings, exchange of members by letters of transfer, United Zion representation on Brethren in Christ boards, and various other interrelationships.[44]

By 1955, the centennial year of the schism, the two bodies had reached the point of a significant "associated relationship."[45] Some Brethren members believed, however, that their group should go further by asking forgiveness for the excommunication of Matthias Brinser and his followers. Consequently, Clarence W. Boyer, acting by special privilege of Conference, introduced a resolution which "humbly" asked the United Zion Church to forgive the Brethren in Christ "for the unwise and unjust action of the church council of 1855."[46]

Most members of General Conference were not yet prepared to ask forgiveness for an act committed by their forebears. No one knew much about the circumstances surrounding that act; both sides could have been at fault in the dispute. United Zion representatives present in the Conference, furthermore, stated that they did not believe a request for forgiveness was required by their group. Conference accordingly tabled the resolution.[47]

There the matter rested until 1967. By that time General Conference had concluded that the merger issue should be brought to decision and that a request for United Zion forgiveness should be included with a definite proposal for organic union. It therefore prepared a proposal to the United Zion Church, which included the following passage:

> As your sister denomination, we humbly admit to the failure of our efforts to reestablish the two churches as one in the complete sense of the term. This is apparent in our lack of humility in approach and our delayed request for forgiveness. We do now humbly request your forgiveness and crave your indulgence to forget the past.
>
> We sincerely and officially invite you to give consideration to begin negotiations at any time you wish, toward becoming one organized fellowship.[48]

The United Zion Church replied the next year as follows:

> Whereas, it is unchristian not to forgive our erring fellow man and especially so when confession of wrong and forgiveness is requested. Whereas the members of 1967 General Conference of the Brethren in Christ Church have humbly craved our forgiveness. Be it therefore resolved, that we the members of the 1968 General Conference of the United Zion Church do freely and sincerely forgive them of their share in causing the division of the two churches in 1855.[49]

The letter added that the United Zion Church did not desire to begin negotiations for merger at that time but hoped for a continuance of "the fellowship with the Brethren in Christ Church we have enjoyed in the past years."

Since those crucial years of decision, informal fellowship between the two churches and cooperation in missions and Christian higher education have continued. The United Zion Church is represented on the Brethren in Christ Board of Missions and the Messiah College Board of Trustees.

NOTES:

[1]Climenhaga, *Brethren in Christ,* pp. 56, 60, 61.

[2]Abram M. Hess Diary, November 9, 1873.

[3]*Ibid.*, February 8 and May 21, 1874.

[4]Climenhaga, *Brethren in Christ,* p. 63.

[5]Lancaster County townships provided the nomenclature for these district names.

[6]Familiar Friend, "River Brethren," p. 553.

[7]See Appendix B for a distribution by counties of Brethren in Christ households in the United States and Canada in 1880. Except as otherwise indicated, the remainder of this section is based upon the membership directory used in compiling that data.

[8]Sider, "Brethren in Canada," p. 10.

[9]*Ibid.*, p. 11.

[10]See Chapter VIII for an account of this colony.

[11]James T. Lemon, *The Best Poor Man's Country: A Georgraphical Study of Early Southeastern Pennsylvania* (Baltimore and London: Johns Hopkins Press, 1972), ch. 3.

[12]*Ibid.*

[13]The earliest membership directory (1880) lists 864 Brethren households in the United States and Canada. In view of known omissions from the list, this total may have been considerably higher. Using this higher figure as a base, and arbitrarily assuming two to three communicant members per household, the total membership in 1880 could easily have been 2,000.

[14]Jasper A. Huffman, ed., *History of the Mennonite Brethren in Christ Church* (New Carlisle, Ohio: Bethel Publishing Company, 1920), p. 83; Ohmer U. Herr, "Historical Sketches of the Brethren in Christ Church of Southern Ohio (unpublished paper, 1926), pp. 1-2. Church Archives; Schrag, "Brethren Attitude Toward the World," p. 329.

[15]Huffman, *Mennonite Brethren in Christ,* pp. 84-86; J. Carl Wolgemuth, The Story of the Brethren in Christ in Western Pennsylvania (unpublished paper, Messiah College, 1953), chs. 3, 4. *Origin, Constitution, and Article of Faith of the Brethren in Christ* (Pittsburgh: W. S. Haven, 1866), Church Archives. The Swankites were followers of John Swank.

[16]Henry N. Miller to J. Carl Wolgemuth, May 7, 1953, Church Archives.

[17]*General Conference Minutes,* 1952, Article 36, p. 96; *ibid.,* 1953, Article 36, p. 45.

[18]C. Nysewander, *Visitor,* XXXII (December 1, 1919), 8-9.

[19]*General Conference Index,* pp. 313-14; Department of Commerce, Bureau of the Census, *Religious Bodies, 1916; Part II, Separate Denominations: History, Description and Statistics* (Washington: Government Printing Office, 1919), p. 180.

[20]Laban T. Brechbill, *History of the Old Order River Brethren,* ed. by Myron Dietz (Brechbill & Strickler, 1972), pp. 35-36.

[21]Daniel M. Hawbaker interview, July 1962. Hawbaker was an elderly Old Order River Brethren bishop in Franklin County, Pennsylvania.

[22]The present writer has had fifteen years of contact with the Old Order River Brethren.

[23]*General Conference Index,* pp. 313-14.

[24]J. K. Miller, "River Brethren," 22.

[25]H. S. Brinser, "Bishop Brinser and the Brinser Meeting-House," *The Pennsylvania-German,* II (January, 1901), 25, 27. The author was a grandson of Matthias Brinser.

[26]C. H. Balsbaugh, "Genesis and Exodus," *Primitive Christian,* I (May 16, 1876), 316. Balsbaugh knew Matthias Brinser from childhood.

[27]Phares B. Gibble, *History of the East Pennsylvania Conference of the Church of the United Brethren in Christ* (Dayton, Ohio: East Pennsylvania Conference Church of the United Brethren in Christ, 1951), p. 226; Ohmer U. Herr, "Historical Sketches of the Brethren in Christ Church of Southern Ohio" (unpublished paper, 1926), Church Archives.

[28]W. O. Baker, "Reminiscences No. 1," *Visitor,* I (August 1, 1887), 9.

[29]Brinser, "Brinser Meeting-House," 25, 28. This article includes a picture of the meetinghouse as drawn from memory by the author.

[30]*Ibid.,* 28.

[31]J. K. Miller, "River Brethren," 20-21; Moses L. Dohner interview, June 15, 1962. Bishop Dohner received the Brinser information from his mother, the daughter of Levi Lukenbach, Bishop of Center, Clinton, and Lycoming Districts in Pennsylvania.

[32]*Die Trennung der River-Brüder.* An English translation of this German broadside appeared in the Middletown (Pa.) *Journal* and also in another unidentified newspaper. The broadside apparently originated with Matthias Brinser for the latter newspaper includes the following notation: "Der originelle Brief in welchem dieses abgefasst wurde, ist noch zu sehen bei Matthias Brinser, in Dauphin County, Pa."

[33]*Ibid.*

[34]J. K. Miller, "River Brethren," 21; Moses L. Dohner interview June 15, 1962. There was no doubt in Bishop Dohner's mind that the two schisms were directly related. His view received strong support from J. Lester Myers, Bishop of Montgomery District, Franklin County, Pennsylvania. Myers knew the Old Order of his area and their traditions of origin. He emphatically endorsed to the present writer the linkage of the Brinser and Yorker schisms. Worthy of note also is the fact that Familiar Friend, "River Brethren," made no mention of the Yorkers when he published in 1848. If, as some think, they originated as early as 1843, he might reasonably have been expected to have mentioned them.

[35]Brinser, "Brinser Meeting-House," 28.

[36]*A Compilation of the More Important Decisions from the General Conference*

Minutes of the United Zion's Children, 1893-1940 (n.p., n.d.), p. 2. This group, which numbered 931 in March, 1975, is located principally in Lebanon, Dauphin, and Lancaster Counties.

[37]General Council Minutes, 1877, Article 9, typescript with the Asa W. Climenhaga Papers. The typescript gives no indication of the location of the original minute record. Since all printed compilations of the Council (Conference) Minutes prior to 1881 omit some articles, this typescript article is credible.

[38]*General Conference Minutes,* 1917, Article 40, p. 83.

[39]*Ibid.*, 1922, Article 5, p. 7.

[40]*Ibid.*, 1924, Article 4, p. 9. General Conference did, however, retain its merger committee.

[41]*Ibid.*, 1930, Article 17, p. 36.

[42]*Ibid.*, 1935, Article 45, p. 72.

[43]*Ibid.*, 1937, Article 18, pp. 33-34.

[44]*Ibid.*, 1937-1954, *passim.*

[45]*Ibid.*, 1955, Article 26, p. 47.

[46]Manuscript copy of the preamble and resolutions in the Church Archives.

[47]*Ibid.* The present writer was a member of the General Conference of 1955.

[48]*General Conference Minutes,* 1967, Article number missing, p. 60.

[49]*Ibid.*, 1968, Article XII, p. 29.

Part Two

The
First Period of Transition

1880 — 1910

VIII

The Continued Advance
Of the Brethren Frontier

Many changes occurred in the life of the Brethren in Christ during the years from 1880 to 1910. These three decades marked the first of two major periods of transition in their history. During those decades the Brethren remained primarily a rural people responsive to the agricultural revolution with its emphasis upon mechanization and increased capital investment. They were not, however, very directly affected by revolutionary developments in industry, transportation, communication, and urbanization characteristic of that time.

The most observable changes were in their faith and religious practices, both of which were modified by influences from conservative, evangelical Protestantism. By 1910 their response to those influences was beginning to modify their sect psychology and move them toward the greater openness of a denomination. This shift of emphasis significantly altered their doctrines of the church and the world. Beginning with a survey of the continued advance of the Brethren frontier, the next six chapters analyze the changes made by the brotherhood from 1880 to 1910 and evaluate the impact of those changes upon their movement.

Migrations and Mission Journeys

The Brethren increased numerically from an estimated 2,000 in 1880 to approximately 4,000 in 1910.[1] While they grew slowly numerically, they continued to expand widely geographically. This expansion resulted primarily from the redistribution of existing members rather than from the accession of new members.

By the turn of the century, some significant changes had occurred in Canada. Nottawa District with Charles Baker as its first bishop had emerged out of Markham District.[2] The small cluster of Brethren families in western Black Creek District was increasing; this area would eventually become a part of Wainfleet District with John Sider as the first bishop.[3] Early in the century Canadian Government offers of virtually free land lured Brethren from Ontario, as well as from the United States, to the western prairies near Kindersley, Saskatchewan.[4]

By the summer of 1907 the vanguard of these migrating to Saskatchewan were at their destination, living in tents and busily erecting sod and frame houses against the onslaught of winter.[5] Their minister, Isaac Baker, commissioned for his task by Nottawa District, immediately upon arrival began Sunday services in a tent.[6] Baker's wife was the only woman in the party.[7] They had come, as one of the group said, " 'To take advantage of the reasonable offer of the Government, and to cause this part of God's earth to shine for Him'."[8]

In the eastern United States, the Brethren engaged in a few minor settlement and mission enterprises outside of Pennsylvania. By the early 1880s some had located in the vicinity of Chambers' Valley, Virginia.[9] About the same time a few were also in North Carolina.[10] Shortly after the turn of the century, the latter conducted four mission Sunday schools near Culberson, North Carolina, and were interested in beginning an orphanage for the children of the "poor mountain whites."[11]

Other minor Brethren ministries outside of Pennsylvania during this period touched New Jersey, Massachusetts and Virginia. Ministering brethren visited Atlantic City, New Jersey, to baptize and receive into church fellowship an elderly man whose parents had been members of the brotherhood.[12] Canadian Fred Elliott conducted a missionary effort in Massachusetts but left no report of its outcome.[13] Finally, Bertha Boulter, an isolated member who had been converted at the Philadelphia Mission, made a valiant attempt to launch a Brethren work at Wachapreague, Virginia, on the eastern shore of the Maryland and Virginia penninsula.[14]

A major population shift of the United States Brethren occurred during this period as members migrated to Kansas where good land was available. By the 1870s a few families had moved there, among them the Jacob F. Eisenhowers, grandparents of Dwight D. Eisenhower.[15] In 1878 General Conference named Joseph Hershey and Henry Lesher as "missionary brethren" to visit these scattered Kansas families.[16]

About that time a large group of Pennsylvania and Maryland members, which was forming to colonize in Kansas, asked General Conference for permission to choose a bishop to accompany them. When their request was granted, they selected Bishop Jesse Engle of Cumberland County, Pennsylvania.[17] This inclusion of a bishop permitted the prospective colony to migrate as an organized church body.

The interest that produced this colony had been building for some time as reports from the scattered Brethren in Kansas drifted back to Pennsylvania. Three strong supporters of the colony migration, John M. Sheets, Benjamin J. Brubaker, and Jacob Shelley, had made a prior trip "to spy out the land." They happened to be in Kansas during a prosperous year and returned favorably impressed. Much discussion followed among persons interested in relocating there but who realized the serious implications of moving families many hundreds of miles to a new and less-developed community.[18]

By the spring of 1879, those who had decided to join the colony were ready for the great adventure. On Tuesday, March 25, 1879, about 300 strong, they poured into the Pennsylvania Railroad Station in Harrisburg from many places in south-central Pennsylvania and northern Maryland. Here the party, ranging in age from twenty-one days to forty-five years, boarded a special train section comprised of eight passenger coaches and three baggage cars.[19]

For people who, in most cases, had never been far from home, the trip west was a fascinating experience. When they passed through Indiana in bright spring weather, some were so impressed with the countryside that they briefly considered settling there.[20] Instead they pressed on and arrived in Abilene, Kansas, in two groups on March 27 and 28, 1879. Here they offered praise and thanksgiving to God and spread out to take up farms and erect new homes.[21] Many other eastern and midwestern families followed the main colony to Kansas. Within twenty years the Kansas Brethren had organized nine districts with a total membership approximately one-third as large as that of Pennsylvania.[22]

Kansas in turn became the principal jumping-off point for the further westward movement of the Brethren, as well as for wide-ranging mission efforts west of the Mississippi River. Members of that state were active at one time or another, either as settlers or missionaries, in Arizona, California, Minnesota, Missouri, Nebraska, Oklahoma, Oregon, and Texas.[23] Some of them were interested in mission work in Mexico.[24] Not all of the persons who engaged in these or other western ventures were from Kansas. The Ohio Brethren, for example, contemplated a Colorado colony for which they purchased 520 acres of land with an option on a total of 4,000 acres.[25] Today there are Brethren in Christ congregations in only five of the states mentioned—Oklahoma, California, Oregon, Colorado, and Texas.[26]

The Oklahoma work began in Custer County near the present town of Thomas. Here the Brethren settlers, some of whom had arrived by 1893, experienced frontier hardships. David Book, a Kansas minister who held services in Oklahoma that year, encouraged persons who wished to correspond with the settlers to enclose stamped return envelopes, as they did not have "the conveniences of life" and needed "many little things."[27] As late as 1899 their homes were mostly dugouts, that is, excavations into hillsides. Because of the smallness of these primitive homes, they were inadequate for public worship services, and the pioneers were struggling to raise money for a small house of worship then under construction.[28]

Brush-arbor tabernacle erected for evangelistic services at Leedy, Oklahoma, in 1909. Evangelist Bert Sherk from Black Creek District, Ontario, is the third man from the right.

From the beginning the Kansas brotherhood endeavored to minister to the spiritual needs of the Oklahoma pioneers. In 1895 General Conference discussed the need for a resident ministry in Oklahoma and referred the matter to the Kansas Church.[29] Two years later Samuel Zook visited the Oklahoma Brethren and presided over a ministerial election which resulted in the choice David Eyster, who was immediately examined and ordained.[30] Later, Kansas State Council authorized the organization of the Oklahoma membership into a separate district, and David Eyster was ordained bishop in 1907.[31]

While the Oklahoma pioneers endured frontier privations, other Kansas Brethren were settling in the more hospitable environments of the Pacific coast, especially California. As early as 1890 several Kansas Brethren planned to locate there.[32] Among them was the Noah G. Hershey family, whom the Kansas Church approved to make the move together with "such others who wish to accompany him."[33] By the spring of the following year, the Noah Hershey and John Engle families had settled in the vicinity of North Cucamonga, California.[34] Other Kansas families soon followed.[35]

Not all of the early Brethren who settled in California emigrated from Kansas. One of the first to locate in that state was Anna Rhodes, daughter of Bishop Peter Rhodes of the Clarence Center District in New York State. Miss Rhodes was a nurse, perhaps the first representative of the brotherhood in that calling, who practiced in Los Angeles and vicinity.[36] Other Brethren who settled in California emigrated from an Arizona settlement, among them the Christian C. Burkholder family who settled in North Ontario.[37]

Soon after his arrival Christian Burkholder was in charge of the "California Mission" under the supervision of the Kansas Church, and there was talk of organizing a regular California District.[38] In 1904 General Conference referred to the Kansas Church a petition to organize such a district.[39] Acting on this authority Bishop Jacob N. Engle of Kansas went to California and organized the California Church at Upland. The choice for bishop fell upon Christian Burkholder, with Joseph B. Leaman as minister and Jacob Haldeman as deacon.[40]

One other Kansas venture was an attempt to launch a mission in St. Louis, Missouri, in 1904. While this produced no permanent church work, it is of considerable interest. Benjamin Gish was the moving force. Inspired by the location of the World's Fair in St. Louis, he sought the support of anyone who would listen to his plea for help with a mission project.[41] He hoped Brethren members would "not allow the enemy to use the World's Fair as a scare. Daniel and his three brethren stood firm and undefiled of the king's meat and drink, and the Lord could do wonders, make kings tremble and nations fear."[42]

When no one would join him in this undertaking, Gish went anyway. With a combination of faith and courage, he contracted for a tent sixty feet in diameter, which he was unable to erect alone, and waited for help to come. He well knew, he said, "that Satan understands his business. . . . he gets all deviltry and devices of sin and wickedness in operation, . . . and sounds the alarm, that 'in the time of the World's Fair, St. Louis, Mo., is no place or time to do gospel mission work'."[43] He added:

> You members who never have been away from the church circle cannot comprehend it. As above stated, if left alone here I will be classed among the swarmers or fanatics, and the great work which might have been done will be a failure, and the powers of darkness rejoice over it. Therefore, for the sake of Christ, the church, and humanity, heed the Macedonian cry "Come over and help us."[44]

Help came at last. Avery and Mary Long of Pennsylvania felt "definite leadings" and joined Gish in his work. They did not "expect to resort to bells, timbrels, blowing of trumpets or any such thing to draw the people," but hoped "to reach many with . . . [their] voices in song, prayer and preaching the word, . . ." They also hoped that the brotherhood would supply them with thousands of copies of the *Visitor* and tracts suitable for distribution.[45] Unlike Gish, who hesitated to attempt mission work on the World's Fair ground itself, Long went there boldly distributing tracts and searching for a suitable preaching site.[46]

In spite of the dedicated efforts of the little mission band, their hopes for a permanent work were unfulfilled. A storm destroyed their tent, and they could find no other satisfactory hall in which to continue the work.[47]

Before leaving the city the workers spent some time visiting existing city missions.[48] They were fascinated by a Christian Jewish Mission where they shared in both indoor-hall and street meetings. A Baptist Mission gave them an unusual introduction to "skid-row" work. This mission had permission to hold services in a large saloon and beer garden, provided they did not enter the place until after midnight.

Long was deeply shocked by the signs and slogans: "Drunkards made to order." "All who enter here leave hope behind." "This place has changed hands—gone from bad to worse." Although believing that their lives might be endangered, the mission party entered. Later, Long described this experience:

> Well, I will say that when we entered and saw into the interior I began singing . . . , "The pearl that worldlings covet is not the pearl for me." And as we walked through the bar-room to the beer garden we sang the entire hymn. It seemed for a few moments to stop the men of which I supposed there were from 150 to 200, but soon they went on in their revelry, sitting around the beer tables, some drinking, others talking, while a few were smoking, and others attentive to every song, prayer, testimony, and exhortation given. While on the whole it would seem like casting pearls before swine, yet we can say, before the meeting closed six or seven were not ashamed to come . . . and have us pray for them. One old man with gray hair said, "from this night on I will serve the Lord."
> The second Saturday night . . . seventeen men came forward and knelt in prayer. The scene was the most awful I ever saw, but I believe those services will never be forgotten by some of those men.[49]

The missionaries also visited a number of opium dens, distributing tracts and preaching Christ, but their hopes of establishing a permanent work failed to materialize.[50]

The migrations and mission travels of western members were extremely important aspects of the history of the Brethren during their first period of transition. Those who participated were among the most courageous and adaptable of the membership. Their ventures into and through newly developing areas of Canada and the United States exposed them to new climates, new peoples, and perhaps most important, new ideas. These experiences helped them to achieve a degree of openness and a capacity for change not shared in the same degree by large numbers of members in the older, established church communities, especially in Pennsylvania. It was no mere coincidence that almost all of the major innovations accepted by the Brethren between 1880 and 1910 were nurtured on the periphery of the brotherhood.

Kansas, where the Brethren only arrived in strength in 1879, is the most striking illustration of the innovative spirit. Here the foreign and city mission enterprises of the brotherhood began, experiments with tent and caravan evangelism occurred, second-work holiness received its major impetus, and the *Visitor* found a supportive home after it moved from Michigan to Abilene. In addition, the Kansas Church played vigorous roles in the Sunday school and protracted meeting movements, and cooperated in a non-Brethren orphanage near Hillsboro.

The openness of the midwesterners in Kansas and elsewhere to new approaches in church life went hand-in-hand with their loyalty to traditional Brethren values. Wherever they went as settlers or missionaries, they perceived themselves to be emissaries of the Brethren faith. They thus led the way in the attempt to blend historic attitudes and practices of the Brethren with the innovations in their church life which began in the late nineteenth century.

This blending process was exemplified in the life of Bishop Samuel Zook, a highly regarded Kansas leader and, briefly, editor of the *Visitor*. Zook greatly respected the early leaders and heritage of the brotherhood but was open to new ideas and methods. In the fall of 1892 he and some companions made an extensive mission tour from Kansas to the West Coast. Typically, his purpose was "to hunt up scattered members and brethren's children, and to preach the Gospel when opportunity will afford." In Denver, Colorado, he attended "a Gospel meeting" and reported:

> . . . an evangelist named Jennings, an Englishman, spoke to the people. At first I was not so favorably impressed, but after a while he seemed to have the whole house pinned down to an almost breathless attention, not by eloquent language but by an earnest, straight-forward Gospel. "He spake as one having authority." The meeting had been held previously and a number had come out on the Lord's side and that evening five more were added to the number, . . . The evangelist is by no means an educated man; he used very common language, just what common people need, but he spake as though he meant what he said.[51]

This comment illustrates a subtle change taking place in the attitudes of some of the Brethren. In their early history the group tended to emphasize their differences from other religious societies; now at least some of them were beginning to stress similarities. Once Zook got over his first unfavorable impression of the English evangelist, he evidently felt quite at home with both his message and his methods.

At the same time, Bishop Zook was very loyal to the Brethren. When he arrived at Salt Lake City, he reported that the journey had impressed him with the need for suitable tracts to distribute. He had some from a tract society but added ". . . why not have some that fully express the Gospel truths as believed and practised by . . . the brethren? When will the church awake to a sense of this duty?"[52]

In Salt Lake City the Zook group attended a Sunday morning service in a mission conducted by "an old time Methodist." Here they were so warmly and courteously received that Zook wrote:

> Surely in this respect they showed us a good example which we ought to imitate.
>
> Let us not forget, brethren and sisters, that the true Spirit of Christ is winning and not repulsive. If we want to win souls to Christ we must show to them a spirit of loveliness, and thus win them over to Christ.[53]

Once again the Brethren leader acknowledged instruction from "outsiders."

During the afternoon Zook had another experience quite at variance with the traditions of the Brethren who opposed the use of musical instruments and choirs in worship. He attended a service in the Mormon Tabernacle and described some of his impressions:

> At the time for services the great organ began its music and afterward was joined by the choir of trained singers, and also by times by the congregation. Among the hymns sung, which were generally announced by one of the elders, was the well-known hymn, "Oh thou in whose presence my soul takes delight." It was sung to the old familiar tune which we sing among us. To say I enjoyed it is putting it mildly.[54]

Many Brethren of that period would have dwelt upon the "worldliness" of the scene and upon Mormon heresies, but Bishop Zook found this experience with organ music and a trained choir exhilarating.

Along the route of their journey the missionary party found acquaintances. In the State of Washington, Zook preached and conducted prayer meetings with the members of several Musser families. Apparently none held membership with the Brethren and some made no Christian profession; however, of a "Sister" Frances Risser, mother of one of the Musser wives, the bishop wrote: "Tho not received into the church as yet, we could recognize her as a sister."[55] From Washington he moved into Oregon where he found four Brethren and preached in two Sunday services which, to his knowledge, were "the first meetings held by the Brethren in the state of Oregon."[56]

Arriving in San Francisco on Saturday evening, Zook and his associates attended various services the next day. One was a Salvation Army meeting, the first that the Bishop had witnessed. He noted that the service seemed strange, but then commented:

> Yet I felt that these people were doing a work for the Lord for which I want

to give them credit. While in their meetings listening to the testimonies of those who confessed they had been drunkards and were lifted out of the gutter, I felt to say, let the work go on. I thought of the disciples who, when they saw a man, who went not with them, casting out devils in Christ's name, forbade him. But Jesus said they should not forbid him.[57]

Not all services which he attended in San Francisco impressed Zook as favorably as this, but he obviously was growing in appreciation for Christian work under non-Brethren auspices.

Proceeding from San Francisco to Los Angeles, he missed seeing "Sister" Anna Rhodes, who was away on a nursing assignment. In this instance his Brethren loyalties were in evidence, for he was glad to hear that Miss Rhodes, "though isolated from the church, has the reputation of being an earnest and consistent Christian and worthily represents the church by her Christian walk and conduct."[58] In Los Angeles he attended "a holiness mission meeting, where we found a common but earnest people engaged in the work of the Lord. . . . I can truly say that our hearts were very much drawn out towards them."[59]

The missionaries returned home from California by way of Arizona where Bishop Zook presided over a council of the small Brethren mission community. This council organized a church with twenty-two members, two resident ministers, and a deacon. The little church then shared a love feast about which Zook reported: ". . . we had a precious season, the first of the kind ever held in the far west. All seemed to enjoy the occasion. The ordinances were celebrated in the evening."[60]

This Arizona interlude is important because it reveals Samuel Zook back in his familiar, traditional role of providing forceful administrative leadership for the Brethren. The long mission journey which preceded it, however, revealed that he was a man in whom old and new values of the Brethren coexisted.

This capacity to synthesize old and new values was not a western monopoly. It appeared in individuals elsewhere in the brotherhood as a state of mind independent of geographical location. Canadians like Asa Bearss, Fred Elliott, and George Detwiler, and Pennsylvanians like Avery Long, John H. Myers, Samuel R. Smith, and Enos H. Hess were warm supporters of many of the innovations which entered the brotherhood between 1880 and 1910. The history of the first period of transition, nevertheless, reveals the deep influence of the restless migrations and the missionary travels of the men and women on the frontiers of the brotherhood. Their activities played a crucial role in initiating innovations and, through men like Samuel Zook, helped to point the Brethren in Christ toward the possible synthesis of old and new values.

Confrontation with Russellism

In the late nineteenth century, Russellism, also known as Millennial Dawnism, made inroads among the brotherhood in both Kansas and Ohio. This movement, named after its founder, Charles Taze Russell, was the forerunner of the present-day Jehovah's Witnesses.[61]

As early as 1891 the tenets of Russellism agitated the Kansas Brethren, who condemned them in council and referred the problem to General Conference.[62] The latter pronounced these views "contrary to sound Gospel principles . . . pernicious and misleading" and directed that no one holding them should be ordained to church office.[63] Ten years later this issue was still alive in Kansas, and Russellite influence appears to have gained ground among the Brethren there, for they now requested General Conference to appoint an "impartial" committee to reconsider the 1891 action. Conference refused to reopen the question.[64]

Henry N. Engle, prominent Kansas leader and successor to Henry Davidson as editor of the *Visitor,* was one of those attracted by the views of Charles T. Russell. Just when he began to drift into the stream of Russellism is not clear, but it appears to have been sometime after he became editor that a neighbor introduced him to Russell's first book, *Food for Thinking Christians.*[65]

As Engle became increasingly committed to Russellite thought, he began to propagate it.[66] By the late summer and fall of 1898, his writings in the *Visitor* reveal traces of the shift in his theology.[67] When the leaders of the Brethren became aware of his position, General Conference of 1899 asked for and received his resignation. His request for a hearing to defend Russellite views was refused, but Conference voted an expression of appreciation for his "faithful service" and awarded him an honorarium of $150.[68] He was also permitted to continue for a time as office manager of the paper.[69]

The small Sippo Valley Church in Wayne County, Ohio, also struggled against the infiltration of Russellism. Here the senior minister in charge was Anthony Stoner, serving under the supervision of Bishop Jacob Hershey of the Canton District. Stoner was an able man and an influential speaker. Under his ministry the Sippo Church attracted new interest.[70] The two associate ministers were Lewis Berg and a young man, William Myers.

Early in the 1890s Stoner's preaching began to undergo a subtle change. He had imbibed Russellite doctrine, and for two years he taught it little by little from the Sippo pulpit. Often he raised questions without answering them and urged his listeners to go home and think about what the answers might be. As he gained support from some of the members, he became bolder and plainer in presenting his divergent views.[71]

When Bishop Hershey learned of these developments, he called a council meeting to deal with the situation. The dramatic climax of that council is reported by Lewis Berg's son:

> Bishop Hershey in his final decision said, "I will allow you Bro. Stoner three months to make your decision as to what you follow, C. T. Russell or the Brethren in Christ teaching." Elder Stoner replied, "I need no time for decision. My mind is decided what I will do." He rose up and walked out. Being a man of influence, the members thought highly of him and forty out of forty seven walked out after him, my father [Lewis Berg] included. Elder Stoner then turned back and opened the church door and said to the remaining seven, "Good bye for ever." And it proved so for only one returned.[72]

This schism left the junior minister, William Myers—"Willie" as he came to be known in church life—with the difficult task of serving the few remaining members. As the next day was Sunday, he had the painful duty of conducting the morning worship service. In his words:

> "Nobody knows the sorrow I felt as I stood in the Sippo pulpit that morning and, looking out the window, saw twenty-eight of the congregation drive past to a home one mile east of the church where they organized another congregation. My heartache was the heaviest as I beheld my own dear wife among the number, as well as two of my fellow ministers who had preceded me in the ministry."[73]

Later, William Myers became known as the Jeremiah of the Brethren in Christ Church because of his tender heart and weeping ministry, characteristics which perhaps developed out of his own great sorrow. His wife, whom he affectionately called "Emmy," although always hospitable to his friends, never swerved from her Russellite commitment to the day of her death.[74] Discouragement almost overwhelmed him at times as he ministered in Sunday services to a half-dozen people and in mid-week prayer meetings to one married couple.[75]

Myers had some bright spots along his lonely way. One Monday morning he went to the home of a faithful couple named Doubledee to say that he guessed they would have to close the church. There the following dialogue occurred:

> Sister Doubledee said, "Why?" "Because," said Brother Myers, "no one is coming to the service any more." To this Sister Doubledee replied, "I thought my husband and I were there yesterday." Brother Myers said, "Oh, yes, you were, and I sure appreciate it, but we can't carry on this way." Sister Doubledee said, "Willie Myers, as long as you are in the pulpit to preach, my husband and I will be there to hear you if we are able."[76]

Elsewhere Myers told of many years of prayer meetings shared by another couple, the Ezra Mohlers, and himself; ". . . even with three and God we had glorious times. Sister Mohler in it all sometimes was so happy that she would clap her hands . . . [until] one would think they would almost blister. God bless their dust."[77]

After many years the Sippo Valley Church began to recover. One of the happiest moments for William Myers in that recovery was the return of his former ministerial associate, Lewis Berg. For fourteen years after he followed Anthony Stoner out of the Sippo council, Berg worshipped and ministered nearby with "The Church of the First Born," the group of former Brethren who now endorsed Russellism. He became a personal friend of Charles Russell and served as a delegate to Russellite conventions in Pittsburgh and Canada.[78]

About 1908 Anthony Stoner made a sermon comment which jolted Lewis Berg and started his re-evaluation of Russelite doctrine. Stoner said: "'As of today I will no longer preach or teach the incarnation or Deity of Jesus Christ.'" When Berg requested clarification, Stoner simply reiterated his position. Concluding that such teaching could not be reconciled with Scripture, Lewis Berg did the unusual; he forsook Russellism.[79]

For some time after this decision, he visited area churches seeking a new church home. One Sunday morning as he drove past the Sippo Valley Church, William Myers saw him through the window, hurried out, and invited him to the service. At first Berg held back saying, "'No, I cannot face the people; having been absent fourteen years.'" But Myers pressed him to come in just for Sunday school, and he finally yielded. Both the teacher and assistant happened to be absent. When the superintendent asked the class to name someone to teach, a half dozen voices cried, "'Let Lewis Berg teach.'"[80]

Shaken by this sudden turn of events, Berg later confessed to wishing that he could have disappeared, but he finally accepted the invitation and taught. When he returned home, his wife said, "'That is where you belong'." A short time later he requested and received reinstatement to full fellowship with the Brethren. Eventually, he regained his ministerial privileges and preached for many more years.[81]

There is a final touching incident in this story. One Sunday in the 1920s Lewis Berg preached in the Valley Chapel Church near Canton. As he looked out over the congregation, he saw in a front pew the last person he expected to see—Anthony Stoner, now aged and ill. As Berg preached fervently from Jeremiah 8:22—"Is there no balm in Gilead; is there no physician there? why then is not the health of the daughter of my people recovered?"—Stoner wept much.[82] When the two former comrades met after the service, Lewis Berg greeted his old friend and asked, "'How is it with you, Bro. Stoner?'" To which he replied, "'I am not well in body or soul'." Again he wept and left the service, the last, so far as is known, which he ever attended.[83]

Russellism made its major impact upon the Brethren in Christ in the Midwest. Pennsylvania State Council, however, voiced alarm about its possible drift eastward and directed the bishops of the state to arrange a concerted teaching effort to counteract it.[84] This alertness in the East may have been a factor in confining the influence of Russellism to a limited area of the midwestern brotherhood.

NOTES:

[1]Alderfer, "Mind of the Brethren," pp. 132-33.

[2]*Directory of the Church of the Brethren in Christ for the Year 1899*, (n.p., n.d.), p. 62.

[3]Wainfleet District Council Minutes, 1913-14.

[4]*General Conference Minutes*, 1913, Article 38, p. 57-58; Sider, "Brethren in Canada," p. 107.

[5][George Detwiler], *Visitor*, XXI (August 1, 1907), 2.

[6]*General Conference Minutes*, 1913, Article 38, p. 58.

[7][George Detwiler], *Visitor,* XXI (August 1, 1907), 2.

[8]Quoted in Climenhaga, *Brethren in Christ,* p. 123.

[9]*General Conference Minutes,* 1883, Article 1.

[10]*General Council Minutes,* 1886, Article 15.

[11]A. J. Tomilson, "Account of Mission Work in N. C.," *Visitor,* XVI (July 1, 1902), 255; Abbie Cbess (*sic*), "A Plea for Culberson, N. C.," *Visitor,* XVI (July 1, 1902), p. 255.

[12]David Engle, Sr., "A Call from Atlantic City, New Jersey," *Visitor,* V (May 15, 1892), 156.

[13]F. Elliott, "Our Church Paper," *Visitor,* IV (January 15, 1891), 31.

[14]Bertha Boulter, "A Letter to the Brotherhood," *Visitor,* XVIII (March 15, 1904), 13-14; Enos H. Hess, "The Virginia Mission Work," *Visitor,* XVIII (November 15, 1904), 6.

[15]*Church Government,* 1887, pp. 15, 18; Jesse Lady, "The Trip of the Colony of the Brethren in Christ Church from Harrisburg, Pa. to Abilene Kans. . . . March 25-28, 1879," (unpublished manuscript, n. d.), p. 1, Asa W. Climenhaga Papers.

[16]*Church Government,* 1887, pp. 15, 18.

[17]*Ibid.,* p. 18.

[18]Lady, "Colony of Brethren," pp. 1-2.

[19]*Ibid.,* pp. 3-4; "Westward Ho! A Colony of Lancaster County People En Route for Kansas," *Marietta* [Pa.] *Times,* March 29, 1879.

[20]Lady, "Colony of Brethren," p. 6.

[21]*Ibid.,* p. 7.

[22]*Brethren in Christ Directory, 1899, pp. 88-105.*

[23]South Dickinson District Council Minutes, September 15, 1892, Article 3; Jacob N. Engle and Noah G. Hershey, "Visit to California," *Visitor,* III (May 15, 1890), 155-56; [Samuel Zook], *Visitor,* XII (August 1, 1899), 294; Jacob F. Eisenhower, "An Open Letter," *Visitor,* IV (January 1, 1891), 13; Joseph Fike, *Visitor,* III (January 15, 1890), 32; Alice E. and W. H. Elliott, "From Oregon," *Visitor,* III (June 15, 1890), 186; [Henry Engle], *Visitor,* XII (January 1, 1899), 14.

[24][Henry Engle], *Visitor,* XI (July 1, 1898), 254; [George Detwiler], *Visitor,* XIII (February 1, 1900), 54.

[25][George Detwiler], "Another Colonization Project," *Visitor,* XXII (March 16, 1908), 2.

[26]The Texas and Colorado works are of recent origin and have no historical roots in the period under consideration.

[27]David Book, Sr., "A Visit to Oklahoma Territory," *Visitor,* VI (August 1, 1893), 235.

[28]Samuel Zook, Eld., "An Appeal," *Visitor,* XII (February 1, 1899), 55.

[29]*General Council Minutes,* 1895, pp. 2, 4.

[30]Samuel Zook, "Visit to Oklahoma," *Visitor,* X (July 15, 1897), 227.

[31][George Detwiler], *Visitor,* XXI (May 1, 1907), 3.

[32]J.H.E., "Chapman, Kan., May 2, 1890," *Visitor,* III (May 15, 1890), 154.

[33]Kansas Joint Council Minutes, May 10, 1890.

[34]J. H. Byer, Jr., "A Visit to Southern California," *Visitor,* IV (March 1, 1891), 74; J. M. Engle, "The Visitor," *Visitor,* IV (May 15, 1891), 92.

[35]R. E. Hershey, "Moving Westward," *Visitor,* IV (October 1, 1891), 300.

[36]Jacob N. Engle and Noah G. Hershey, "Visit to California," *Visitor,* III (May 15, 1890), 156; Samuel Zook, "A Western Mission Tour," *Visitor,* VI (February 15, 1893), 59.

[37][George Detwiler], *Visitor,* XVI (March 1, 1902), 94.

[38]*General Conference Minutes,* 1902, Article 24, p. 18; *ibid.,* 1904, Article 30, p. 19.

[39]*Ibid.,* 1904, Article 30, p. 19.

[40]*Ibid.,* 1905, Article 8, p. 9.

[41]Benjamin Gish, "The St. Louis Mission," *Visitor,* XVIII (July 1, 1904), 2.

[42]Benjamin Gish, "Regarding the St. Louis Mission," *Visitor,* XVIII (September 1, 1904), 14.

[43]B. Gish, "A Letter from Brother Gish," *Visitor,* XVIII (September 15, 1904), 13.

[44]*Ibid.*

[45]T. A. and Mary J. Long, "Work in St. Louis, Mo., to Begin," *Visitor,* XVIII (October 1, 1904), 9.

[46]T. A. Long, "From St. Louis," *Visitor,* XVIII (November 1, 1904), 13. By this time Mrs. Gish had also joined the party.

[47]Benj. Gish, "A Letter from Brother Gish," *Visitor,* XVIII (December 1, 1904), 7.

[48]This is an example of how the Brethren were opening themselves to "outside" influences.

[49]T. A. Long, "The St. Louis Mission," *Visitor,* XVIII (December 1, 1904), 13.

[50]*Ibid.*

[51]Samuel Zook, "A Western Mission Tour," *Visitor,* V (December 15, 1892), 378.

[52]*Ibid.*

[53]*Ibid.,* VI (January 1, 1893), 10-11.

[54]*Ibid.,* 11.

[55]*Ibid.,* VI (January 15, 1893), 28.

[56]*Ibid.,* VI (February 1, 1893), 42. There is no known link between these early Oregon Brethren and the later development of an organized church work in that state.

[57]*Ibid.,* 43.

[58]*Ibid.,* VI (February 15, 1893), 59.

[59]*Ibid.*

[60]*Ibid.,* VI (March 1, 1893), 75.

[61]Winthrop S. Hudson, *Religion in America,* (New York: Charles Scribner's Sons, 1965), pp. 347-50.

[62]Kansas Joint Council Minutes, March 13, 14, 1891.

[63]*General Conference Minutes,* 1891, Article 1.

[64]*Ibid.,* 1901, Article 20, p. 11.

[65]Naomi Engle to Carlton O. Wittlinger, September 11, 1960. Miss Engle was the daughter of Henry Engle.

[66]*Ibid.*

[67][Henry Engle], "Transition Period—Church to Kingdom," *Visitor,* XI (August 1, 1898), 295; *Visitor,* XI (September 1, 1898), 335; "Why Carry the Gospel," *Visitor,* XI (September 15, 1898), 355; *Visitor,* XI (October 15, 1898), 394.

[68]*General Conference Minutes,* 1899, Articles 16 and 17, pp. 9-10.

[69]*Ibid.,* Article 17, pp. 9-10; [Samuel Zook], "Salutatory," *Visitor,* XII (June 1, 1899), 214.

[70]W. J. Myers, "History of the Sippo Valley Church," manuscript notes, ch. 4, Church Archives.

[71]*Ibid.,* ch. 5.

[72]Marion L. Berg, manuscript notes compiled April, 1973, Church Archives.

[73]William J. Myers, as told to E. J. Swalm, "The Russellism Crisis at the Sippo Church," *Notes and Queries*, VII (October 1966), 27.

[74]*Ibid.*

[75]W. J. Myers, "Sippo Valley Church," ch. 7.

[76]Myers and Swalm, "Russellism Crisis," 28.

[77]W. J. Myers, "Sippo Valley Church," ch. 7.

[78]Marion L. Berg manuscript notes.

[79]*Ibid.*

[80]*Ibid.*

[81]*Ibid.*

[82]*Ibid.*

[83]*Ibid.*

[84]*Pennsylvania State Council Minutes,* 1908, Article 7, pp. 6-8.

IX

The Early Mission Movement

The Brethren in Christ made no corporate or general church efforts to win converts to their faith until the late nineteenth century. This does not indicate that they lacked interest in evangelism and missions, but rather that such interest expressed itself through individuals acting on their own initiative. Traditions tell of leaders who traveled widely, nurturing the expanding brotherhood and preaching the Brethren understanding of the gospel in many communities of the United States and Canada. H. Frances Davidson penned a classic account of that period:

> Previous to that time [late nineteenth century] the old fathers of the church had made many missionary journeys through the United States and Canada for the advancement of Christ's Kingdom and in the interests of the faith they so dearly loved. These journeys were made without remuneration and often with great discomfort and sacrifice of time and money. The precept that the Gospel was free, "without money and without price," seemed so instilled into their hearts that some of them, no doubt, would have felt pained for people to think that they expected money for their services. So while the laity were busy with their own temporal duties, these heralds of the Cross would often leave their little farms in care of their wives and of help, hired at their own expense, and devote weeks and months to evangelistic work, expecting what? Nothing but their food and sometimes sufficient to pay their car fare, if they went by train. But it often happened in those early days that the entire expense of whatever sort was borne by themselves. They looked for no reward on earth save the consciousness that they were about their Master's business and seeking to extend His Kingdom on earth.[1]

Some members who later advocated corporate mission projects tended to overlook the phase of their history described by Miss Davidson. They assumed that the mission spirit first manifested itself in the late nineteenth century.[2]

Avery Long, annoyed by this lack of historical perspective, reminded these members—many of them relatively young people—that the widespread migrations of the Brethren had created settlements which became bases from which itinerant evangelists conducted visitations and preaching ministries in the surrounding communities. He had great respect for the dedication and sacrifice of those early missionaries and wrote feelingly that ". . . some of our dear, old brethren walked and rode on horseback hundreds of miles, visiting and preaching the word of God."[3]

Long further stated that, many years before he wrote, a few members conceived the idea of a mission to Germany. Three of them—John Engle, John Gish, and David Schlagenweit—volunteered to go. These men made the journey, presumably at their own expense, but found that Germany felt no need for missionaries and that there were few open doors for gospel work in that country.[4]

Rural Missions

By the 1870s the Brethren were beginning to develop a sense of corporate responsibility for carrying out the Great Commission. General Conference of 1871 responded to this new mission spirit by creating a general mission fund to be collected by the deacons throughout the brotherhood.[5] The next year Conference established a board of missions, with a member in each district, to take charge of "the spread of the gospel in localities heretofore unacquainted with the doctrine as taught by the church."[6] These two actions envisioned a loosely organized program of itinerant evangelism with funds to pay the expenses of ministers who conducted preaching missions outside of organized church districts. Opportunities for these missions would arise primarily through scattered Brethren families settled in localities where their faith was new to their neighbors.

Exponents of this modest mission program soon realized the need to clarify and strengthen it. In 1874 General Conference passed several resolutions to give it more substance. One designated as missionaries those ministers sent out on special assignments to preach the gospel in new communities. A second provided for the appointment of ten or twelve such minister-missionaries annually, "subject to call" for mission service. A third created a small Board of Missions and authorized it to receive calls from all sections where missionary labor was desired.[7] The board could assign missionaries to fields of labor, although General Conference was also free to make assignments.[8] This appointment of a Board of Missions directly accountable as a unit to General Conference was an important change of concept from the former board consisting of a member from each district, with each member acting independently of all the others.

As a result of Conference actions from 1871-1874, the Brethren found themselves with a corporate mission program involving funds, administrative organization, and field personnel. Friends of missions contemplated the situation with high hopes, but such hopes were not well-founded. Within little more than a decade, Conference had to admit that the program was floundering.

The crisis in this first corporate mission effort came dramatically to the foreground in the General Conference of 1886 in which the members confronted the question: "Do the Brethren carry into effect the commission of Matthew xxviii . . .?" Acknowledging that they did not do so, Conference took action: "*Resolved,* That the Brethren exert themselves to furnish men and means, to carry out the commission."[9]

The reasons for the breakdown of the mission program after fifteen years of effort are fairly clear. In the first place, the Brethren were not accustomed to general church projects which required continual financial support. The idea that all members were personally responsible to help finance mission activities, of which many of them were only dimly aware, did not easily gain acceptance.

In the second place, regional differences tended to sap the vitality of the mission program. Members of the older, established churches in the heartland of the brotherhood, who tended to be absorbed in the familiar routines of church life, were often unenthusiastic about missions championed by newer churches elsewhere. Since many of the older churches were also wealthier, their coolness toward the itinerant mission program was a crucial factor in the failure of efforts to fund it.[10]

Finally, the annual appointment of a group of regular ministers— "brethren subject to call"—to conduct brief preaching ministries of a mission nature had serious limitations. Not only were ministers unevenly qualified to preach the Brethren faith in new localities, but the pressures of home duties often affected both the time when they could serve and the length of periods of service. Problems due to absence from families, farms, and home ministries were very real. When to these problems was added the possibility that the missionaries might have to finance traveling expenses from their own pockets, they labored under severe handicaps.[11] Effective follow-up of initial mission efforts often proved to be impossible.

With the passage of time, leaders began to recognize these weaknesses of the mission program. They saw especially that a change of attitude toward missionary support was essential for effective church outreach. One of them summarized the problems:

> The Church has not yet adopted a proper system by which to make her work a success; and much of the labor done by her ministers has consequently been lost. I have often heard our ministers complain for this—that after they had made a visit to certain places and labored for a while, probably as long as their circumstances at home would admit . . . they were obligated to leave the work and return to provide for their families, which is just and right. For it becomes our duty first to provide for our own house (I Tim. 5:8); and if the Church does not provide the necessary means for her minister when he is laboring for the Church, he must necessarily provide for himself and his own as best as he can, and leave the work in the hands of the Church, and those who are calling for the bread of life, to care for themselves. Right here . . . the responsibility falls upon the Church, and not upon her minister, as some suppose.[12]

This passage shows that at least some Brethren were ready to reappraise their historic concept that the gospel was free. They were beginning to see that its effective proclamation would create expenses which a few individuals alone could not pay.

In 1886, frustrated by lack of mission funds and the difficulties of depending upon "Brethren subject to call," General Conference abolished that program.[13] In doing so it provided no alternative and seemed uncertain about its next mission move. This inaction, of course, did not prevent the Board of Missions from continuing to encourage preaching ministries of a mission nature if men and means were available for them.

The following year Conference was ready for a new effort to stimulate responsibility for more liberal and systematic giving for missions. It accordingly took action: "*Decided:*—That the deacons throughout the whole church be instructed to make a personal appeal to each member of their respective districts, for some contribution to the mission work of the church at least once a year."[14] This approach differed from earlier efforts to raise mission funds by being directed specifically toward each member who, hopefully, would respond at least once a year.

This same Conference reacted enthusiastically to the prospect of a mission to the American Indians. Brethren who had visited the Indian Territory described the need for mission work there. Conference voted "That we heartily support an attempt in that direction" and named a committee to determine the locality and means for such a venture, but nothing came of it.[15] This outcome may have been influenced by the fact that some hoped-for government funds for work among the Indians were not available.[16]

While General Conference was seeking means and methods for mission work, *Visitor* correspondents championed the cause and offered suggestions. Some were keenly aware of the shortcomings of past efforts. One of them pointed out: "To send a ministering brother or two, here and there, into new fields and unfrequented places, who can stay but a very short time and then leave again for an indefinite period, looks like an indifferent or unsystematic way of 'fishing'."[17]

This writer proposed a mission colonization plan subsidized by the church, which, he thought, would both spread the gospel and improve the economic lot of the colonists. His analogy was the beehive:

> When a colony [of bees] gets numerous enough to afford it, the queen and a part of the workers separate from the rest, by coming out and clustering on some convenient bush or shrub; as much as to say to the "bee-man," "We can be spared from the old home, and here we are at your disposal. If you can use us *profitably,* point out where we are to labor."

This imaginative member suggested that five families, including a minister, who were willing to sell out and move, should each receive a colonization bounty from the brotherhood. He saw great opportunities for such colonies in the South and West and thought that a new colony might be launched each year without burdening the church financially any more than it was by the present ineffective methods.

Other writers strongly emphasized the need to provide better financial support for missionaries. One wrote:

> Our convictions have ever been that so long as we can reasonably . . . [dispense] with salaried mission workers, we should absolutely do so; but the reason it has become necessary in many of the modern church organizations . . . is simply because of the slothfulness and indifference of the laymembers

of such bodies towards the Gospel cause—being manifest either in their unwillingness, or *neglect*, to administer of their substance to those whose wants must also, by some means, be supplied.

. . . .

It is beyond doubt that the faithful evangelist meets with trying seasons, when currency will have a more effectual working on the discouraged mind, than the many "God bless you's"; and in consequence of the same, we might have the "God bless you's" returned upon our own heads.[18]

In spite of the problems encountered, missions represented a vision whose time for fulfillment had come. Further difficulties would have to be surmounted, but within a decade the Brethren would be involved in several new forms of corporate mission effort—"traveling missionaries," regionally organized mission programs, city missions, and overseas missions.

The traveling missionary program began in 1888. After debating how to facilitate mission work, General Conference elected two ministers as traveling missionaries for a year, to be responsible to the Board of Missions. The action included an imaginative provision. "Said brethren shall be supplied substitutes to take charge of their affairs at their homes, if the district in which they live so direct."[19] Conference was becoming increasingly aware that long-term mission service implied a direct brotherhood financial responsibility for those involved in mission work.

General Conference chose Noah Zook of Kansas and Avery Long of Pennsylvania as the first two traveling missionaries. Their projected ministry differed in two important respects from that of the former "brethren subject to call." Home districts were to examine and ordain them specifically for the mission task, and they were to devote their entire time to it, as much as possible.[20]

In appointing Zook and Long, Conference did not specify their field of labor other than it was to be outside of any organized church work. The missionaries eventually chose Michigan and planned to begin a ministry there in the fall of 1888.[21] Zook, who was to be separated from his wife and eight children for six months, described his departure:

. . . after having made all necessary arrangements to leave my home and family . . . I accordingly . . . bade farewell to loved ones and committed them to the keeping of a loving Father, and also myself to the keeping as well as guidance of Him who has all power in heaven and on earth. Although I never left my family as I did this time scarcely knowing whither I was going or when I should return, yet the Lord wonderfully sustained me in the sacrifice that I was called upon to make, and . . . I can say thus far the Lord has helped and He is to-day my strength and shield.[22]

To Zook's disappointment, Long was unable to join him in Michigan at the time agreed upon, having been delayed by family afflictions and duties.[23] Undismayed, the former launched the mission alone, assisted occasionally during the two-month period prior to Long's arrival by other Brethren ministers.[24]

During that fascinating journey, the missionaries made their contacts with new communities through Brethren families scattered here and there with no organized church life. Their declared purpose was "to establish the doctrine of Christ and the apostles as believed and taught by the Brethren."[25] This meant the preaching of heartfelt conversion coupled with the Brethren concept of obedience. Hearer response varied; Zook reported that at times he was "very much encouraged in the work" while at other times his courage fell to "a pretty low ebb."[26]

One high point of the mission was a reception service in Eaton County for five membership applicants. The service was typically Brethren, and Zook administered baptism by trine immersion in the dead of winter. Eleven members then communed in "a glorious season of feasting on the love of Jesus." Zook further noted: "The example of washing the saints' feet was quite a curiosity to many of the spectators and many smiled at the practice, but this did not disturb our peace for we were conscious of doing as Jesus bade his disciples to do . . . ."[27]

When Avery Long finally arrived, the missionaries concentrated much time and effort in the vicinity of Carland. Here they encountered opposition from a group which opposed all church organization, repudiated the ordinances, and denounced anything that Christ taught which seemed to pertain to church government. Through preaching and visitation, Zook and Long confronted these critics with the Brethren understanding of the Scriptures. Following one of the missionaries' services, a leader of the opposing group announced that he would preach. Zook reported:

We staid to hear him, and he talked and read the Bible for two hours; and we said amen to all that was Bible and to what was not we said no. He hardly knew what to make of us since he could bring out nothing upon which to establish a quarrel. And we were so glad that we could say that we were not the followers of any man, having no man's name attached to our brotherhood.[28]

The debate continued the next day. In the presence of a house full of witnesses, Zook and Long proposed that if their opponent could "show anywhere by authority of God's word when all church ordinances were done away . . [they] would begin to preach that doctrine from that day on." When he failed to meet this challenge to their satisfaction, they declared him vanquished and humbly prayed that the Lord would show him and his followers the error of their ways.[29]

Following this debate, and perhaps because of it, the Carland mission gained momentum. The missionaries reported some "powerful Holy Ghost meetings," and they were gratified by "sister help," three Brethren women from Ohio, of whom they observed:

> We are much pleased to see the willingness of these sisters to work for the Lord, and are free to admit that they have already done more work in [the] way of encouraging the sisters, who have come out on the Lord's side to go on and forward in the ways of self-denial, than we possibly could have done. We are of the opinion that no effectual work can be done in such places without sister help, for the Lord does wonderfully use these humble sisters to reach the hearts of both men and women.[30]

This generous tribute to "sister help" likely influenced a proposal by *Visitor* Editor Henry Davidson that the brotherhood recognize women as a special class of mission workers. In his judgment they were more effective than men in many ways.[31]

The mission at Carland reached its climax early in 1899. Surrounding communities sent in numerous calls for the missionaries. In one reception service eighteen applicants presented themselves for membership and others applied later. Again, applicants submitted to the rigors of winter baptism. The missionaries did make one concession to the temperature by delaying the laying on of hands, usually done while the applicant knelt in the water, until all of those baptized were gathered together indoors.

Before leaving the Carland area, Zook and Long held an election for deacons and installed Henry Schneider and Charles G. Baker in this office.[32] Baker had professed conversion under the ministry of the missionaries.[33]

This first traveling missionary experiment enlarged the vision of the brotherhood and produced an outpouring of financial support for the missionaries and their families. More members seemed to realize that the Brethren concept of a free gospel required reappraisal.[34] General Conference was so encouraged by the outcomes of the venture that it sponsored similar projects from time to time.[35]

Soon, however, old and familiar difficulties brought the mission program to a new impasse, which was faced by the Conference of 1890. Two problems were the judicious selection of fields of labor and the finding of willing and qualified workers.[36] Various churchmen took the floor to deplore the "painful lethargy" of the Brethren in mission work, and it is perhaps significant that all of them named in the minutes—William Baker, Isaac Trump, Jesse Engle, and Henry Davidson—were midwesterners. The concentration of Brethren membership and wealth was in Pennsylvania where at that time there was no strong enthusiasm for missions.

Conference refused to despair in the face of these difficulties and urged the general church "to support nobly the ministry in their efforts to disseminate the gospel." It appointed a committee of twelve, representative of the brotherhood in the United States, to assist the Board of Missions in locating fields of labor and qualified workers.[37] The obvious purpose of this agency, which came to be known as the Working Missionary Committee (or Board), was to bridge the gap between the various regional memberships and the general mission program. Pennsylvania and Ohio had three members each, Kansas two, and New York, Indiana, Illinois, and Iowa one each.[38]

This committee had broad prerogatives to promote and administer the mission program. It could select fields and personnel and promote special efforts to raise funds needed for the work. Although its decisions required approval of both the Board of Missions (now the General Mission Board) and General Conference, the committee clearly understood that it was to assume the leading role in the mission effort.[39] In 1893, for example, it requested each district and each Sunday school to provide a mission service and to receive a mission offering.[40]

During the 1890s the mission program moved slowly forward along the itinerant mission paths marked out in the two preceding decades of trial and error. Perennial problems of personnel, methods, and funds continued to provoke criticism and debate. At the same time, however, mission interests and energies of the brotherhood were flowing into new channels and especially into organized regional mission programs.

The Canadian Brethren were the first to promote a regional mission program. Before their union with the United States Brethren in 1879, they had their own mission fund. After the union the Canadian and United States mission funds merged in a common treasury in the latter country.[41] The intent seems to have been to merge the mission programs as well as the funds.

These arrangements almost immediately proved to be unsatisfactory. In 1883 the Canadian Brethren petitioned for a restoration of their own mission fund, but Conference postponed action indefinitely.[42] The following year the Canadians asked for both their own mission treasury and mission board on the grounds that a sum of money had been bequeathed to the brotherhood in Canada for mission work in that country. This bequest strengthened their case, and Conference yielded on condition that mission work in Canada be conducted according to the plan adopted by the Brethren in the United States.[43]

The bequest for Canadian mission work was $5,000 from the estate of Samuel Dix, a member of the Markham District. Known as the Dix Fund, the principal was invested and the income used for mission work in Canada for many years until the main portion of the principal was lost in 1919 by the bankruptcy of the Standard Reliance Corporation in which it had been invested.[44]

Formation of the Canadian Mission Board occurred soon after its authorization by General Conference in 1884. It functioned under the supervision of the General Conference in much the same way as did the United States Mission Board. When, for example, Conference of 1886 considered the question of supplying Mosa and Brook Missions in Canada with regular preaching, the decision was to grant the supply at the option of the Canadian Mission Board.[45] In that same year Conference requested Jacob Eyer, treasurer of the Canadian mission fund, to report on the state of its treasury; subsequent submission and approval of these Canadian reports became routine.[46]

The Canadian Board of Missions was responsible to Canada Joint Council as well as to General Conference; when the council began to keep records in 1892, its first minute dealt with plans for mission work. This action does not mean that Conference no longer felt a responsibility for Canadian mission matters, for in accepting the Canadian mission report of 1894, it urged "that more effectual work be done during this conference year."[47]

Early Canadian mission work relied upon itinerant minister-missionaries, as did the United States mission program, and faced similar problems. The following Black Creek District Council record in 1887 reveals the slow development of general mission concern in Canada: "After a lengthy discussion concerning mission work, it was the feeling of this meeting that the Brethren as a Society are not alive to the importance of the work as they should be, and the subject should be agitated with a view to the society becoming more active in the matter."[48]

In the United States the Kansas Brethren pioneered regional mission work. Their plan, which was implemented in the spring of 1888, provided a committee of three to solict the local membership for funds and to send out minister-missionaries in response to calls for missionary service.[49]

The Kansas brotherhood hoped that this regional mission effort would "secure better results than . . . the system (or lack of system) formerly in vogue."[50] Although the quotation suggests disillusionment with the past mission program of General Conference, the same writer reports the enthusiasm and expectancy of the Brethren as they ordained and sent Noah Zook on his traveling missionary assignment. They evidently perceived their regional program as a supplement to rather than a substitute for mission activity by General Conference.

One of the innovative aspects of the Kansas mission work was tent evangelism. In 1892 Jacob Eisenhower, one of the first Brethren advocates of gospel tent work, proposed to the North Dickinson District Council the purchase of a tent and a plan for its operation.[51] His vision was fulfilled almost immediately when Kansas Joint Council named a committee which, at a cost of $239.50, secured a tent with a seating capacity of 500.[52]

The following June the first tent meeting in the brotherhood began in Abilene with Noah and Mary Zook, Katie Hershey, Susan Hoffman, and John K. Forney as the staff of workers. For nearly five months the tent moved from one central Kansas community to another, operating almost continuously with a total cost of only $128.85. This cost resulted primarily from transportation of equipment and personnel; most food for the staff came from communities where the tent located. The workers made no formal requests for offerings in their meetings, thus conforming to the Brethren ideal that the gospel should be free.[53] Personal contributions provided approximately one-half of the operating expenses, and the Kansas mission program underwrote the remainder.[54] A similar campaign followed the next year.[55]

This tent program absorbed the full time of the workers. They held afternoon and evening meetings and conducted extensive home visitations, talking and praying with people and distributing religious literature. In the services Zook took the lead "handling the 'sword of the Spirit' fearlessly, while the sisters . . . [did] their part faithfully in singing, praying, testifying and calling to sinners to accept salvation."[56] Occasionally, the sisters held a meeting for women only.[57]

These first Brethren tent campaigns produced a modest number of professed conversions, and a few church accessions.[58] The workers were prepared to receive into church fellowship all who gave evidence of having been born of God and a willingness to take "the plain old Bible way," including plainness in dress.[59] Zook observed that they might have had many more converts, or at least "joiners," if they had moved out on "the modern and more popular way."[60] Since the tent frequently located near groups of Brethren, some additional converts may have eventually joined the brotherhood.

Many non-Kansas Brethren developed interest in tent evangelism as a result of Zook's accounts of his campaigns and their observations of the tent in use at General Conference of 1894, which met at the Bethel Church in Kansas.[61] Kansas initiative thus helped to prepare the brotherhood for this new form of evangelistic outreach destined to play an important role in their twentieth-century mission enterprises.

A few years after the beginning of Kansas tent work, the mission concern of that area broke into a new channel—caravan evangelism. A corps of workers, Jacob H. Eshelman, Abraham L. Eisenhower, Annie Eisenhower, and Barbara Hershey traveled from town to town in a "Gospel Wagon" equipped with living quarters and serving as a base to offer the "free gospel" in a street ministry.[62] The following excerpt from a worker's report reveals the nature of this unique campaign:

> Arrived at Herington, a town of 1,500 inhabitants with eight churches. . . . We began meeting on the street, Friday night, with song, prayer and the Word, the Holy Ghost witnessing to the truth. Conviction was manifest upon the people. On Saturday at 3 p. m. we addressed a large and attentive audience, with demonstration of the Spirit and with power. The meetings are growing in interest and are well attended in spite of the opera only a stone's cast away. A dead ministry, dead church, and sin in high places, as well as secret sin, all receive rebuke and warning. We hope to be able to set before this people a standard of righteousness, that will draw the people to Christ.[63]

Like the preceding tent campaigns, caravan evangelism aimed at the proclamation of the gospel without any organized provision for follow-up or the bringing of converts into the Brethren fellowship.

This surge of regional mission activity in Kansas impressed the brotherhood. In 1893 General Conference urged each state with a sufficiently large membership to organize itself into a home mission district as Kansas had done.[64] Ohio soon responded to this appeal and joined Canada and Kansas in regionally administered mission work.[65]

City Missions

Prior to 1894 mission work sponsored by General Conference, as well as by regional areas of the brotherhood, relied upon itinerant evangelism which often made effective follow-up difficult or impossible. An alternative mission approach, the stationing of full-time workers in a specific location, received its first test in the city of Chicago.

Several factors contributed to the choice of this city. Chicago was the dominating metropolis and rail junction for the midwestern United States, and the Brethren of that area were in the forefront of the missionary movement of the brotherhood. In the second place, several Brethren who had located in Chicago had no place of worship.[66] Finally, B. A. Hadsell, a Church of the Brethren (Dunker) member, who manufactured plain clothing in that city, was so eager to have a Brethren in Christ minister locate there that he offered him a partnership in his business.[67]

One of the first serious expressions of interest in a mission in Chicago came from Noah Zook. He had visited Hadsell and other residents of the city to review prospects for mission work there and saw great opportunity for it, although he noted that it would be expensive.[68]

In 1890 General Conference recognized the mission possibilities of Chicago by voting unanimously to begin a work there.[69] Making the decision proved easier than implementing it. The Brethren were not of one mind about a venture which posed such serious problems of personnel and finance.[70] Three succeeding General Conferences endorsed the project, but the summer of 1894 arrived before regular services began in the first mission hall at 6028 Peoria Street.[71]

The four members of the first mission staff were brought together under unusual circumstances. Abram L. Myers, the minister in charge, who had previously done some individual mission work in Chicago, left his family in Freeport, Illinois, and took up residence in the city in 1894.[72] Benjamin Brubaker and wife, Brethren members resident in the city, assisted him as they could within the limitations imposed by the husband's employment.[73] Due to a fascinating combination of circumstances, Sarah H. Bert of Kansas was also in Chicago at the time of Myers' arrival. She testified that she had felt definitely called to the city after a deeply moving spiritual experience in the Bethel Church in May of 1894, but she did not know what was in store for her in the city.

Miss Bert later recounted what happened as she waited in Chicago for some clue to the meaning of her sense of calling:

> One day, a letter came from Bro. J. Meyers [sic] of Freeport, Illinois, stating that the Lord had laid upon his heart the burden of Mission work in Chicago, and that he would soon arrive to look up a location for a Mission to be started. Immediately, the Holy Spirit took me back to the Sunday evening, when from my burdened heart for his cause and precious souls, I cried. I didn't know that there and then I had been taken captive by the Lord. In His mercy and kindness, He showed me that it was He who lead [sic] me forth when I understood not, and had He shown it to me then, I would have said, "No, this I cannot do."[74]

Sarah Bert, co-founder of the first Brethren in Christ city mission (Chicago) in 1894.

Other Chicago Mission workers would come and go, but for more than fifty years Sarah Bert continued at her post as missionary to the great metropolis.

This early city mission program included a preaching ministry, home visitation, and a Sunday school which, at the end of the first year, enrolled approximately 125 pupils. Miss Bert also organized a sewing class of girls and a few boys, which became a feeder to the Sunday school.[75]

September 15, 1895, was a landmark in the history of the Mission, for five converts united with the Brethren and were baptized in Lake Michigan. John W. Hoover, then mission pastor, reported:

> On the 15th of September we received five precious souls into the church. We met together . . . at the hall for worship and to read the Scripture to those that had made application for baptism. The 18th chapter of Matt. and the fourth chapter of Ephesians were read and commented upon, after which they were requested to give their experience, which was very satisfactory to all present. Bro. and Sister Misekelter, Bro. and Sister Dodson and Sister Hall were the five who joined with us. The services were solemn and I think a good impression was made. At 1:30 p.m. we met at the hall to sing and praise God, and to go to the Lake for baptism. We . . . marched to the street car, about 40 in number, and thence to Lake Michigan, at the foot of 68th street, where we met for prayer and singing on the beach, and for the baptism. Here those five were baptised in the name of the Father, and of the Son and of the Holy Ghost . . . .
>
> Those who were baptized were all heads of families, and it made such . . . an effect upon the children that some of them requested baptism also.[76]

A few weeks later the mission group held their first love feast. Sarah Bert reported that the interest was good and that "Some expressed a desire to be with us . . . we hope and trust the time may not be far distant when they shall be of the number."[77] These membership accessions so soon after the launching of the mission demonstrated that at least some city dwellers could be reached by the message of the Brethren.

The Chicago Mission began in the midst of a great national depression, and the workers immediately encountered stark material and physical human needs such as few Brethren had ever seen. Prior to launching the work, Abram Myers warned the brotherhood of these realities:

> Dear brethren and sisters, I can hardly write upon this important subject when I think of the vile outcasts of that wonderful city, the many thousands who have not sufficient clothing to show themselves, and often not anything

to fill the stomach, going along the streets and allies [sic] picking rotten vegetables out of the refuse boxes—no warm room to shelter them from the stormy blast, no soft pillow to rest their weary, aching heads, and, above all, no one to bring to them the comforting words and to point them to the Lamb of God that taketh away the sin of the world.[78]

Myers emphasized that "a person going there with a close hand and pocket can accomplish very little good, and is not filling the mission that Christ designed that we as a church should fill."[79]

From this beginning in Chicago, the Brethren went on to launch a succession of missions in other cities. Some of the earliest of these were Philadelphia, Buffalo, San Francisco, and Dayton.[80]

The Chicago Mission began under the auspices of the General Mission Board and its auxiliary, the Working Missionary Committee.[81] This dual administrative structure proved cumbersome in dealing with the many new problems of city mission work. It lacked Canadian representation, furthermore, and the Canadian Brethren were actively interested in city mission work in Buffalo and Toronto. For those reasons, General Conference of 1904 replaced the old administrative structure with a new Home Mission Board of twelve men representing both the United States and Canada.[82] Three years later women gained representation on this board and retained it through 1918.[83]

In placing Canadians on the Home Mission Board, Conference may have contemplated the possibility of the termination of the Canadian Mission Board. When that agency did not dissolve immediately, some persons challenged Canadian participation in the work of the new joint Home Mission Board. Conference replied, however, that there was no reason why the Canadian members should not serve on the Home Mission Board with entire freedom.[84]

By 1919 the Canadian Brethren were beginning to feel that their local mission interests could best be served by merging them with those of the United States Brethren, thus bringing all home mission work under the jurisdiction of the Home Mission Board.[85] Canada Joint Council accordingly placed Canadian mission activities directly under the supervision of that board, and General Conference ratified the action.[86] Until its merger with the Board for World Missions in 1966, the Home Mission Board thereafter continued to administer all mission and evangelistic work for which the brotherhood as a whole was responsible in the United States and Canada.[87]

Overseas Missions

The Brethren did not permit the difficulties encountered in beginning home missions to deter them from launching overseas missions. Foreign mission interest was a natural outgrowth of their increasing concern to proclaim the gospel to the unconverted. While this concern had previously focused on rural areas and the unchurched masses of the cities, it now expanded to distant lands where missionaries were few.

One of the immediate forces impelling the Brethren toward foreign mission work was their contact with four other societies—the World's Gospel Union, the Hepzibah Faith Missionary Society, the Central American Mission, and the Christian and Missionary Alliance—all of which strongly emphasized missions abroad.[88] Young men and women from Brethren circles came into contact with these groups in various ways and from them absorbed a passion for foreign mission work. In June of 1898, for example, nine of these young people were at Tabor, Iowa, headquarters of the Hepzibah Faith Missionary Association, "tarrying with the Lord" and absorbing the missionary zeal which was a special characteristic of the Hepzibah movement.[89]

As various members began to advocate foreign missions, the brotherhood had to listen to their earnest pleas. Some who agreed with them on the need for such work thought that the limited membership and financial resources of the Brethren precluded it. Among the foreign mission enthusiasts, however, were those who felt so keenly the inactivity of the group in this field that they were prepared, if necessary, to sever their membership connections on this account.[90]

In the midst of this ferment, several members prepared to enter mission service abroad on an independent basis or under non-Brethren mission boards.[91] Hettie Fernbaugh, a member of the Abilene Church in Kansas, was the first to leave. She sailed for Morocco, North Africa, on December 19, 1894, as a volunteer under the World's Gospel Union.[92] The Kansas Brethren counseled to decide whether she could remain a member under these circumstances but agreed to permit her to do so.[93] Miss Fernbaugh was not primarily an active missionary but a housekeeper for missionary families, thus freeing others for mission work among the Muslims. During her years in Morocco, she remained steadfastly loyal to the Brethren in matters such as plain dress and the prayer veiling.[94]

Others followed Hettie Fernbaugh into foreign mission service without specific Brethren endorsement. David Zook, son of Noah Zook, and his wife left America in 1896 as faith missionaries to India.[95] David, however, remained in good membership standing with the Brethren as shown by a minute of Kansas Joint Council: "It was decided that while we do not recognize Bro. David Zook as officially representing the Brethren in Christ as a foreign missionary, we hold him in loving confidence as a Brother in Christ, and wish him God speed in his work abroad."[96]

Quite a number of Brethren eventually followed Hettie Fernbaugh and David Zook into foreign mission service without official assignment by the Brethren. By the close of the century, there were eight of these.[97] In the meantime, the pressure for a mission abroad under direct Brethren auspices increased until it became irresistible.

In 1894 General Conference, which met at the Bethel Church in Kansas, took the first formal step toward a foreign mission venture. It did so largely as a result of the endeavors of two persons, Rhoda E. Lee and Jacob E. Stauffer.

Rhoda Lee, a recent convert of the Brethren. became deeply interested in foreign missions through the preaching of Albert Nathan, a Christian Jew and missionary. He conducted meetings in Abilene under the auspices of the World's Gospel Union and strongly emphasized evangelism and mission work. Under the inspiration of his preaching, Mrs. Lee prepared a paper on foreign missions.[98] On the last day of Conference she was granted permission to read her paper to the assembly.[99]

This well-organized presentation dealt with the needs of the heathen, the gospel call to evangelize, and some of the responses which Christians had made to that call. The paper closed with the following ringing appeal:

> Oh may I dare to hope that a missionary fund may be started and a systematic method of foreign work be organized, and that each of us will practice economy and self-denial to swell the fund? "The King's business requires haste," and may God speed the time when I "hear a rumor from the Lord that an ambassador is sent among the heathen."

To the great disappointment of some present, Conference took no active steps to launch a foreign mission, but rather tabled the matter indefinitely. Later in the same day, however, Jacob Stauffer arose and placed a five dollar bill on the Conference table, stating that the money was for foreign mission work.[100] This was too good an opportunity for Rhoda Lee to miss! She seized a hat and passed it through the audience to receive an offering for foreign missions. Jacob Eshelman was the first to put a five dollar bill into the hat. "The conference members and other were . . . spell bound and no one had any remarks to make."[101]

This unexpected and dramatic sequence of events forced General Conference to take action. Here was money for foreign missions; it could not be ignored. Conference accordingly responded with the following action: "On motion it was decided to organize a Foreign Mission Fund and appoint a treasurer. Brother Jacob E. Stauffer, of Newton, Harvey County, Kansas, was duly appointed."[102] By the close of Conference, the treasurer had thirty-five dollars in hand.[103]

The work of Rhoda Lee was not done. A few months later she wrote an article for the *Visitor*. Observing that there was a great deal of recent debate on the foreign mission question, she spoke out sharply as follows: "We hear a great deal of talk about obedience now, but most of us simmer it down to obeying a few church rules and keeping the ordinances, with an occasional testimony in meeting, and expect a blessing; while the greater commands, to 'go into all the world and preach the Gospel,' to be self-denying and to 'give freely,' pass, for the most part, unheeded."[104]

Mrs. Lee, by thus coupling the concept of obedience with response to the Great Commission, placed those members opposed or indifferent to foreign mission work on the defensive. She continued to press this advantage in the *Visitor* and in another paper which she prepared for the General Conference of 1895.

The influence of Rhoda Lee over two successive General Conferences is remarkable in view of the inclination of the Brethren to restrict women's role in church life. Yet even the official minutes of 1895 recognized that influence by noting: "A paper on foreign mission work by Rhoda E. Lee was read setting forth the necessity of, and urging the brethren to, a more active work in that direction."[105] This is something of an understatement, for her paper probed mercilessly into the conscience and lethargy of the church on the foreign mission question. In her words:

> Where does He give a greater command than, "Go ye therefore into all the world and preach the Gospel to every creature?" Brethren, we profess to love the Lord Jesus, and talk much of obedience; is it not time for us this year, this day, this *hour* to begin some definite work for spreading the Gospel?
>
> We have had our feelings touched often by the appeals of the heathen, have shed a few tears about them, and perhaps eased our consciences by stepping into some other church and dropping a few cents into the foreign missionary collection, and decline again into carelessness. On the 23rd of last September a collection for foreign missions was taken up. Some of our best

givers refused to subscribe, preferring to place their money where it could soonest be used for the salvation of souls, instead of putting it away for the "moths and rust to corrupt." There were others who contributed to the fund hoping for results. And what are the results? Months have passed and no steps taken for the work. How long, O Lord, how long must this be so? If we let this Conference pass without doing some definite work for foreign missions, we are not true to our trust.[106]

The paper pointed out what Mrs. Lee saw as the inconsistency of having four or five ministers for one congregation while millions of people in heathen lands were without a single witness for Christ. She appealed prayerfully to the brotherhood, and especially to those in authority, to cast aside procrastination and "to be up and about the 'King's business'." She also indicated that foreign mission concern, if not given an approved outlet within the brotherhood, would break forth into other channels. This was a sharp arrow for her bow, and she used it to good advantage:

> Already has one of our band set the noble example and soon, in darkest Africa, will be telling the story of redemption. God bless Hettie Fernbaugh and may she be an inspiration to "go forth weeping bearing precious seed" that we may "come again rejoicing, bringing our sheaves with us."[107]

Conference recessed with Mrs Lee's impassioned plea ringing in their ears. When it reconvened the foreign mission question came immediately to the foreground. This resulted in the appointment of a foreign mission board of three members—Peter Steckley of Ontario, Benjamin F. Hoover of Ohio, and Jacob Stauffer of Kansas—for a term of five years and subject "to the advice and control of General Conference."[108]

When General Conference met in 1896, the foreign mission fund had increased to $419.60. With this encouragement Conference enlarged the Foreign Mission Board from three to twelve members charged with the duty of soliciting foreign mission funds in their respective districts. It also created an Operating Foreign Mission Board of three to receive applications from persons who felt called of the Lord to foreign service and to examine such applicants prior to their recognition as foreign missionaries. The action specified that all applicants must be fully consecrated to God and "That the Lord shall do the calling and provide for the going."[109]

In spite of this action, months passed without applicants for foreign service. In January of 1897 the Operating Foreign Mission Board, over the signature of Samuel Zook, published an urgent appeal for workers:

> We would call attention to the fact that the committee appointed at last Conference is ready to act on the Foreign Mission work, but up to this time they have received no applications. Why is it? Does the Lord not speak to some hearts? Or is it because the Church is not praying the Lord of the Harvest to send laborers into His harvest? The field is white. The harvest is ready. Who will go forth in the name of the Master, filled with the Holy Ghost, ready to lay his or her life down for the cause of Christ's Salvation to the Heathen?[110]

Left to right: H. Frances Davidson and Adda G. Engle who launched the first Brethren in Christ mission (Macha) in Northern Rhodesia (now Zambia) in 1906.

Zook encouraged continued giving to the foreign mission treasury, and reported that a choice of field had not yet been made. He noted that South Africa, South America, and Central America had been mentioned and assumed that God would indicate the field when somebody was willing to go.

At the time of this appeal, Frances Davidson, daughter of Henry Davidson, was teaching at McPherson College in Kansas. Years later she explained the impact of the appeal upon her:

> The day that "The Appeal" appeared in the *Visitor,* it was read like other matter and nothing further was thought of it; but the day following the Lord came to me, as it were, in the midst of the class work, in the midst of other plans for the future, and swept away my books, reserving only the Bible. In reality He showed me Christ lifted up for a lost world. He filled me with an unutterable love for every soul who had not heard of Him, and with a passionate longing to go to the worst parts of the earth, away from civilization, away from other mission bodies, and spend the rest of my life in telling the story of the Cross.[111]

Miss Davidson immediately sought release from her teaching appointment and notified the Operating Foreign Mission Board that she was called to service and ready to go at once, if they deemed this advisable. The Board accepted her but made clear that she was the only applicant. Soon, however, she learned that Jesse Engle and his wife were also seriously considering foreign work.[112]

While still a young man, Jesse Engle had felt called to carry the gospel to unevangelized lands. The Brethren had no foreign work at that time, and other factors may also have inhibited his response. Now, at fifty-nine years of age, he volunteered to go.[113]

Miss Davidson did not profess a call to a specific field but only to the place where the need was greatest. When she learned that Jesse Engle felt called to Africa, this determined her choice of field.[114]

General Conference of 1897 accordingly approved Jesse and Elizabeth Engle, Frances Davidson, and Alice Heise, another Kansas member who offered herself, as foreign missionaries. The Foreign Mission Board wished to add another man to the party as an assistant to Jesse Engle but none could be found. Jeremiah I. Long declined an invitation to be that man, preferring to go to Japan with Leonard B. Worcester of the Hepzibah Faith Missionary Association.[115] Barbara Hershey joined the group shortly before their final farewell service at Harrisburg, Pennsylvania. All five missionaries were from Kansas.[116]

The missionary party sailed from New York to Liverpool, England, and from there to Cape Town, South Africa, where they arrived on December 26, 1897. After much prayerful consideration, and with the personal encouragement and assistance of Cecil Rhodes, promoter of British Empire interests in Africa, they launched their mission in the Matopo Hills near Bulawayo, Southern Rhodesia. The native people were the Matabele, a branch of the Zulu tribe of Southeast Africa.[117]

The missionaries bore the inconveniences of their primitive surroundings with fortitude and struggled to master the native language. As soon as they completed crude housing to replace their tent dwelling, they began a school. By deed and word they sought continually to communicate their understanding of the gospel. Although their ministry seemed to make little impact upon adult Africans, some of the young people soon responded to it, and in August 1899, Jesse Engle baptized the first converts—nine boys and one girl—in an African stream.[118]

Frances Davidson felt that her sense of calling was not completely fulfilled as the mission program expanded in Southern Rhodesia; she still longed to penetrate further into the interior. In 1906, therefore, two intrepid women, she and Adda Engle, who had joined the Matopo Mission staff, assisted only by two native Christian young men, pushed nearly 500 miles northward from Bulawayo across the Zambezi River to found Macha Mission in Northern Rhodesia.[119] Within the short span of eight years, the missionaries had laid the foundations for the Brethren in Christ mission program in the present nations of Rhodesia and Zambia.[120]

Jesse Engle, pioneer leader of the founders of Matopo Mission, did not live to see much of the fruit of his dedication and labors. In the spring of 1900, after less than three years of service, he died and became the first assignee of the Foreign Mission Board to lay down his life on the field. Shortly before his death, he wrote of his concerns for the work and his relation to it in words which express the spirit of many missionary successors at home and abroad:

> "I wish the Lord would raise up some brother of middle age who is well established in grace, and blessed with business talent, as well as for spiritual work. Such a brother, who has the foreign work at heart would prove invaluable in connection with the Mission if it is to become, and shall be carried on, in the self-supporting principle. As for myself it would be a very small matter to decide to spend the short remnant of my life in Africa were it the Lord's will, but rather incline to the thought that after a few years more

we will think of coming home, . . . The matter, however is entirely with the Lord; my coming to Africa was no half-concluded step. There was not much ceremony about it, but enough of clearness in the call to move me forward with an unconditional surrender even unto death; so now I have nothing to choose or dictate. The Lord will doubtless consummate all things well."[121]

Jesse Engle, leader of the founders of the first Brethren in Christ overseas mission (Matopo) in Southern Rhodesia (now Rhodesia) in 1898. This informal photograph of Engle and the donkey team against the background of the early Matopo Mission huts is the only known surviving picture of this missionary pioneer.

The growing surge of Brethren foreign mission interest soon focused attention on the possibilities of a work in India. In 1903 General Conference authorized the Operating Foreign Mission Board "to proceed with establishing a Mission in India, to be under the auspices of the church, and supervised by consecrated workers, two at least to be man and wife."[122] The next year when Conference created a new Foreign Mission

Board of seven members, it authorized the board "to take immediate steps toward establishing a Mission in India."[123]

Volunteers for India were ready to go at their own expense. They were Amos and Katie Musser of the Airhill District in Pennsylvania, Henry and Anna Angeney of Philadelphia, and Maggie Landis also of Philadelphia.[124] The Examining Board cleared their credentials, and General Conference confirmed them as foreign mission workers.[125] Following Conference the missionaries speeded their arrangements for departure, but ship delays forced postponement of their plans until December 1904.[126]

While waiting for their sailing date, they toured the Pennsylvania churches. Although all of the party were Pennsylvanians, few churches in that state, other than the Philadelphia Brethren, rallied strongly with financial support. From his office in Harrisburg, the editor of the *Visitor* observed that the mission giving of Canada and the Western States gave proof of a mission interest that, he was sorry to say, needed "to be brought to birth yet in this State."[127] The older, established churches of the brotherhood were still relatively unconcerned about mission work.

The missionary party arrived in Bombay on January 6, 1905, and eventually took up residence in Arrah near the border between India and Nepal. While engaged in language study, they conducted Sunday preaching services and Sunday school for persons who understood English.[128] By October of 1905 they had baptized three converts—a Brahman and a Muslim father and daughter.[129]

About a year later the Angeneys became estranged from the Brethren in Christ, tendered their resignations, and joined another society known as the "'Burning Bush'," They justified their withdrawal by the text in Revelation: "Come out of her, my people, that ye be not partakers of her sins, and that ye receive not of her plagues."[130] This was a severe blow to the India mission cause, and General Conference of 1906 directed the Foreign Mission Board to seek an able leader to take charge of the work there.[131]

Following the withdrawal of the Angeneys, the Mussers and Maggie Landis resolutely continued their mission efforts in spite of India's heat, the dangers of famine, bubonic plague, and affliction with smallpox. Moving to Lucknow, they began an industrial school in which Musser instructed boys in the manufacture of furniture and the repair of simple mechanical equipment. In addition to Sunday services, the missionaries engaged in visitation, ministered to the sick, needy, and widows, and conducted Bible classes.[132] Sometime later they sponsored a school for women and children of the poorer class. This program included reading, writing, spelling, mathematics, singing, and Bible stories.[133]

In October, 1907, the missionaries conducted another baptism. The candidates were a Hindu high caste Brahman and the daughter of Mr. Sen, a Bengali Christian associate of the missionary group.[134] As reported to General Conference of 1908, the mission community numbered ten, and by the next year it had increased to fifteen.[135] These statistics were not impressive in themselves, and the brotherhood in the homeland could not readily understand the tremendous difficulties of making Christian converts in a society such as the missionaries encountered in India.

The report of the Foreign Mission Board to the General Conference of 1909 indicated that the India mission work had met neither the expectations of the board nor of the Brethren generally. Results did not seem commensurate with expenditures so the board vetoed the development of an industrial mission station and requested the staff to reduce costs. The board also appealed urgently for "a competent and able manager" to take charge of the work in India.[136]

Raising funds for India missions proved to be a difficult task. Two factors hindered the Foreign Mission Board in its fund raising efforts. One was the momentum already built up for giving to the work in Africa.[137] As the first Brethren mission overseas, Africa naturally attracted special attention. Its founders, led by such a well-known churchman as Jesse Engle, all came from Kansas, which at that time had a large membership and great missionary zeal. As the missionary staff in Africa expanded, it added personal links to areas of the church other than Kansas. Supplementing these supportive influences was an imposing report of church accession statistics and mission progress furnished to the success-oriented brotherhood in the homeland.

India had none of these advantages. The first five missionaries to that country were all from Pennsylvania where the missionary spirit was slow to develop, and they included no recognized churchman comparable to Jesse Engle. The India workers found themselves in a culture totally different from that of Africa. A rigid caste system in India confronted the Christian witness with hostility. When to these circumstances was added the withdrawal of the Angeneys from church membership and the limited statistical evidence of progress, the contrast between the two fields was striking and unfavorable to the work in India.

A second factor hindering fund-raising was the presence in India of several present or former Brethren members engaged in mission work not sponsored by the Foreign Mission Board. These unofficial mission efforts, which began in the 1890s, built up sources of support within the brotherhood before General Conference approved a mission to India.[138] The result was competition between unofficial and official India mission programs for the limited financial resources of the Brethren.

Some years before the first official Brethren venture in India, the diversion of funds to missions, other than those officially sponsored in Africa by the Foreign Mission Board, was already causing concern in various quarters.[139] That situation was part of the price the brotherhood paid for its slowness in sponsoring overseas missions to absorb the energies of the first group of young foreign mission enthusiasts. They were determined to go, and they went without anyone being able to foresee that within a few years they might be an obstacle to the launching of a Brethren mission in India.

The first foreign mission deputation, Jacob N. Engle and John M. Sheets, visited the India field between the Conferences of 1909 and 1910. In general they reported favorably on the work, which was to concentrate thereafter on village visitation until a promising permanent location could be secured.[140] There is a tradition that the oral report of the deputation to General Conference of 1910 was less optimistic, and that this led John N. Hoover to make an urgent plea: "'Brethren, we are losing our hold on India'!" He went on to ask whether God was calling anyone present to the work in that country, and Effie Rohrer of Ohio dated her call to India from that meeting.[141]

The India missionaries returned home in 1912.[142] Their efforts did not establish a permanent mission station, but they blazed a trail and helped the brotherhood to gain experience in mission work in that country. That experience revealed the need for stronger leadership on the field, for a permanent mission station able to cope with problems created by the caste system which ostracized converts to Christianity, and for more adequate financial support.

The three young people who would eventually comprise the second party of workers sent to India were to be instrumental in meeting these needs. They were Effie Rohrer of Ohio; Henry L. Smith, son of Bishop and Mrs. Samuel Smith of Pennsylvania; and Katie Burkholder, daughter of Bishop and Mrs. Christian Burkholder of California.

At the General Conference of 1911, the Foreign Mission Board recognized Effie Rohrer as a prospective missionary to India but requested her to wait until a married couple also qualified to go.[143] Henry and Katie

Burkholder Smith became this couple. Following their engagement they had presented themselves to the Foreign Mission Board, expecting to be sent to Africa. While separated by a continent, each came independently to the conclusion that God was calling to service in India. Still assuming that the other was called to Africa, each wrote a letter breaking their engagement. These letters passed each other in the mails, and this confirmed the senders' sense of mutual calling to India.[144]

Following the Smith-Burkholder marriage, the Foreign Mission Board recognized them as prospective missionaries to India and, mindful of past financial difficulties, announced to the brotherhood that "Another attempt is to be made to establish a work in India, providing sufficient funds will be obtained in this special fund to meet the need of the undertaking."[145]

The mission board felt that if $2,000 could be raised by the mission party before their departure for India, the initial test of "sufficient funds" for the undertaking would be met. When the missionaries exceeded this goal by several hundred dollars, it was clear that their enterprise had

The missionaries who established the first permanent Brethren in Christ mission work in India (North Bhagalpur District) in 1914. Left to right: Henry L. Smith, Katie Burkholder Smith, Effie Rohrer.

strong constituency backing. They accordingly sailed from San Francisco and reached Calcutta in the fall of 1913.[146]

Soon after their arrival in India, the missionaries spent a month observing the facilities and methods of the Mennonite Mission in the Central Provinces and the Church of the Brethren Mission in Bombay Presidency, after which they began to search in earnest for their own field of labor.[147] Smith made a three-day tour of the territory which the Amos Musser party had considered. He found one promising location but turned away from it because the nearest missionary was not sympathetic to a Brethren in Christ mission in that region.

Bishop Mahlon C. Lapp of the Mennonite Mission then accompanied Smith into Bihar Province, a part of India bounded on the north by Nepal.[148] The two men finally decided upon a location in the North Bhagalpur District, a great open plain between the Ganges River on the south and the Nepal border on the north. Smith judged the field to be about the size of Lancaster or Lebanon County in Pennsylvania. It was densely populated, some parts having over nine hundred people to the square mile. As Smith looked across the countryside, he was deeply moved:

> Truly it was the "Land which I will shew thee" and in its beauty and noble reach it was "A far stretching land." As our eyes gazed over this vast expanse of territory, with its Million Souls, in faith I could see the "Uplifted Standard" and the "High Way" which shall be there. Even the coarse, the guttural and harsh cries and banterings of the rabble I could hear thru Him transformed into the "Songs" which the Holy ear of Isaiah tingled with as his prophetic soul rainbowed the future to this our day.[149]

When the missionary party moved to their chosen field, they had only makeshift living quarters. Their first home was a mud-walled house in the village of Saur eight miles south-east of Saharsa railroad junction. Some months later they moved twelve miles north-east of Saur to Madhipura and took up residence in a dilapidated building which had been used as a stable for goats and cows.[150] Undaunted by these privations the little group pressed forward under the capable leadership of Henry Smith to lay the foundations for the present Brethren in Christ mission work in India.[151] Their view of the situation in those early days in India is well expressed in the following quotation: "We have before us most wonderful opportunities for a grand work for the Lord."[152]

The buoyant optimism of the Henry Smith statement reflects the zeal and dedication of many early missionaries. Those who heard and read such statements were often unaware of the human price paid by the mission pioneers and by many who later followed them into mission work at home and abroad. There is pathos in this situation, for those same hearers and readers often had more than enough financial resources to reduce that price. The following communication from Henry Smith is a case in point:

> This [losses and delays in the transmission of funds during wartime] is a severe strain upon us, especially when we have scarely enough to live on when the money comes regularly. We sincerely trust we shall be relieved of this undue strain and worry. It has cost us up to the present no less than One Hundred and Fifty Dollars because of Sickness of my dear wife. Most of this cost is due to the first sickness which if properly cared for would have saved us all the subsequent expenses. But though I have repeatedly written to both you and brother Climenhaga, I have up to the present received no single word from either authorizing me to use any or a certain portion [of money sent to the field] for giving her proper care in her sickness. I fear . . . she must linger on in a state which may mean her death in the next year. . . . If the Board will come forward and really authorize her using Seventy Five or one Hundred Dollars for rest and treatment of a proper kind we can under Providence raise her up to health and for real Service. But until the Board actually takes action, I am powerless to do anything.[153]

This particular crisis had a happy ending; the wife recovered her health to resume her missionary role.

This incident demonstrates two things in addition to the complications which World War I caused for mission work overseas. It reveals that the Foreign Mission Board had to learn by experience how to work with missionaries assigned thousands of miles away in the midst of cultures and health hazards which board members only dimly understood. It also illustrates that the Brethren held high expectations for their missionaries and often gave them verbal accolades but only limited and inadequate financial support.

The Foreign Mission Board was not directly responsible for this difficult situation. Its members were servants of a people who at times tended to measure progress in head counts and dollar statistics. Although the board constantly pled for increased financial support, it had to work with what it could get rather than with what it needed. Many early and later missionaries, therefore, were a part of the sacrificial minority of the brotherhood who by "blood, toil, tears, and sweat" built the reputation of the Brethren in Christ as a missionary-minded church.

Effects of Missions

One outcome of the mission program was a new spiritual dynamic resulting from the discovery that response to the imperative of the Great Commission was a crucial aspect of corporate obedience. It is a striking fact that, for one hundred years, a group dedicated to the principle of scriptural obedience practiced it so selectively; they saw its corporate implications for their church order and life-style more clearly than for preaching the gospel to the whole world. The impact of the mission movement required them to consider how to balance the historic concern for being the church with a new degree of concern for extending the church. Evangelism, formerly an individual effort, now became the responsibility of all, and the process by which it did so released a flood of spiritual vitality into the Brethren movement.

A second effect of missions was the beginning of a significant shift in the Brethren understanding of spiritual calling. Historically, they had emphasized the corporate or group call to service, and they would continue to depend upon it for many years to choose ministers and personnel to carry out Conference and council assignments. Missions, however, created a new class of Christian workers, those identified by a personal, subjective sense of calling, which the brotherhood came to recognize as a call from God to a special task or field of service.

A third result of the mission movement was the creation of opportunities for full-time careers in Christian service. Although unsalaried, and often largely dependent upon personal financial resources or those of their families, missionaries gradually gained recognition as church workers for whose basic needs—food, clothing, shelter, and medical care—the brotherhood was responsible. Women, as well as men, found career opportunities in missions at home and abroad. This was the first time in the history of the Brethren movement that the talents of women could be employed directly and fully in the life of the church.

Finally, missions encouraged the Brethren to reevaluate some of their historic beliefs and practices. The first Kansas tent campaigns, for example, opened channels of communication between the staff and other evangelical Christians who attended and sometimes participated in the meetings. Such intermingling created a setting in which some Brethren began to modify their historic tendency to stress differences between themselves and others and to stress similarities instead.

The ministry of Noah Zook demonstrates this changing perspective. As a traveling missionary in 1888, he indicated that his purpose was "to establish the doctrine of Christ and the apostles as believed and practiced by the Brethren."[154] Five years later, as a pioneer tent campaigner, he wrote: "May the Lord help us all as co-workers with Him that we may forget all names and all sectarian feelings and work for one common end: the salvation of souls and the glory of God."[155] This shows that, although the messages and general tone of Zook's tent campaigns were basically Brethren, he was beginning to think in new categories. The "salvation of souls" (individualized, experiential conversions), he now perceived to be an end in itself, with the earlier conversion-obedience synthesis of the Brethren receding somewhat into the background.

In the ministry of John Zook, the growing distinction between conversion and obedience—acceptance of Brethren beliefs and life-style—also appears. Probably his contacts with non-Brethren groups, such as the Iowa State Holiness Association, influenced his point of view. One who heard him preach in Des Moines, Iowa, shortly before his death in 1919, reported that when he invited sinners to come forward, Zook said: "I'm not inviting [you] to come forward to join church, but that you may be soundly converted, and then choose your church home."[156] Such a conversion invitation, so sharply separated from the Brethren understanding of obedience, would have been incomprehensible to the brotherhood during their first one hundred years.

City mission work also challenged some historic positions of the Brethren. Their theology and practices formulated in a rural setting had to face the test of an unfamiliar urban environment. Workers at the Chicago Mission soon experienced the practical difficulties of mission singing without instrumental music. They discovered the reluctance of urban converts to comply with the practice of plain dress, and, when the city walled off the lake front at their baptismal site, they, with "great reluctance," installed a baptistry in the mission. All of these circumstances caused ripples of criticism among the Brethren and came to the attention of General Conference.[157] City mission work clearly would not permit the brotherhood to take all tradition-hallowed positions for granted.

Like home mission work, overseas missions raised questions which the Brethren had not previously faced. Amos Musser in India, for example, wondered how to reconcile the traditional concept of the prayer veiling with the sari or cultural headdress of the women of India and presented the following question to the Foreign Mission Board:

> "Shall, or must we teach these people to wear the same covering as our sisters wear? . . . These women have a better covering than our sisters, and it is more according to the Gospel than the one the brethren have selected."[158]

The Board replied that only General Conference could "grant any changes from the present form so general in use, . . ." Somewhat ambiguously it then offered the following counsel:

> . . . there seems to be no impropriety in adopting some uniform form in India, if fully as modest and becoming as our present accepted form, providing there are good reasons for such changes. However, it should be wisely, carefully and prayerfully considered, to avoid rash and hurtful conclusions, which would prove detrimental in the future.[159]

To be on the safe side, the board skillfully made the brotherhood an indirect party to this counsel by spreading the correspondence with Musser on the minutes of General Conference. The result was that the sari of India became the accepted prayer veiling for women converts, although the early missionaries to India continued to wear the traditional prayer veiling.[160]

Soon the Foreign Mission Board had before it the much more complex question of polygamy in the culture of Africa. The problem was what to do about converts with polygamous relationships "when they give clear evidence of conversion." The board concluded that they should be admitted to church membership under certain conditions, as follows:

> *Resolved,* That the workers of South Africa be authorized to receive into church fellowship and administer the rite of baptism to all who give clear and convincing evidence of salvation; [sic] although living in polygamy, providing, matrimonial relation was contracted and completed while in ignorance of Scriptural teachings on this subject. However, such members shall have no right or privilege to act in any official capacity in the church.[161]

By supporting the Foreign Mission Board in these instances, the brotherhood demonstrated that it was at least making an effort to grapple with the realities of proclaiming the Brethren message in cultures differing radically from that of the homeland.

Judged by modern sociological and anthropological insights, the early missionaries were not adequately prepared to translate the gospel into forms adaptable to the cities and to the cultures of Africa and India. They often attempted to reproduce in the mission settings models of their faith and life-style as formulated in rural North America. On the other hand, the mission movement forced the Brethren in Christ, both at home and abroad, to reappraise their value system and, in the process, to open their movement to possibilities for change.

NOTES:

[1]Davidson, *South and Central Africa,* pp. 19-20.

[2]G. Clifford Cress, "Prayer and Missions," *Visitor,* XXV (July 24, 1911), 1.

[3]T. A. Long, "The Mission Spirit," *Visitor,* XXIV (June 13, 1910), 7. Others shared Long's view that criticism of the early Brethren for a lack of missionary zeal was unfair. See *Visitor,* XXV (August 21, 1911), 2.

[4]T. A. Long, "The Mission Spirit," *Visitor,* XXIV (June 13, 1910), 7.

[5]*Church Government,* 1887, p. 8.

[6]*Ibid.,* p. 9.

[7]*Ibid.,* pp. 12-13.

[8]*Ibid.,* p. 18.

[9]*General Council Minutes,* 1886, Article 10.

[10][Henry Davidson], "Notes on the Work of Conference," *Visitor,* III (June 15, 1890), 184-85.

[11]D. Heise, "Our Mission Work," *Visitor,* I (January 1, 1888), 67-68.

[12]*Ibid.,* 67.

[13]*General Council Minutes,* 1886, Article 20.

[14]*Ibid.,* 1887, Article 13.

[15]*Ibid.,* Article 9.

[16]*Ibid.,* 1888, Article 20.

[17]C. Stoner, "Gospel Missions," *Visitor,* I (March 1, 1888), 97.

[18]H. N. Engle, "Help," *Visitor,* II (December 1, 1888), 36.

[19]*General Council Minutes,* 1888, Article 13.

[20]*Ibid.;* John H. Engle, "Notes from Kansas," *Visitor,* I (September 1, 1888), 201; [Henry Davidson], "Mission Workers," *Visitor,* I (September 1, 1888), 200.

[21][Henry Davidson], "Mission Workers," *Visitor,* I (September 1, 1888),200.

[22]Noah Zook, "Correspondence," *Visitor,* II (November 1, 1888), 25.

[23]Noah Zook, "Mission Report," *Visitor,* II (January 1, 1889), 58.

[24]Noah Zook, "To the Readers of the Visitor, Greetings:," *Visitor,* II (December 1, 1888), 41.

[25]*Ibid.*

[26]*Ibid.*

[27]Noah Zook, "Mission Report," *Visitor,* II (January 1, 1889), 57-58.

[28]*Ibid.,* II (February 1, 1889), 74.

[29]*Ibid.*

[30]Zook and Long, "Mission Report," *Visitor,* II (March 1, 1889), 92-93.

[31][Henry Davidson], "Notes on the Work of Conference," *Visitor,* III (June 15, 1890), 184-85. Davidson was one of the principal supporters of the early mission work.

[32]Zook and Long, "Mission Report," *Visitor,* II (April 1, 1889), 106-7. This Henry Schneider was the father of the late Henry Schneider, former Bishop of the Michigan District, who died in 1970.

[33]Charles G [C?] Baker, "A Letter," *Visitor,* II (March 1, 1889), 92.

[34][Henry Davidson], "Our Evangelists," *Visitor,* II (October 1, 1888), 8-9; J. H. Eshelman, "Missionaries," *Visitor,* 13-14; Isaac Shockey, "An Appeal," *Visitor,* II (February 1, 1889), 76.

[35]*General Council Minutes,* 1889, Articles 16, 21; *General Conference Minutes,* 1890, p. 4; *ibid.,* 1893, pp. 2, 3; *ibid.,* 1894, p. 4.

[36]"General Conference," *Visitor,* III (June 1, 1890), 161.

[37]*General Conference Minutes,* 1890, pp. 3, 4. Canada was not represented on this committee because the Brethren in Canada had their own mission board.

[38]*Ibid.,* p. 4.

[39][Henry Davidson], "Notes on the Work of Conference," *Visitor,* III (June 15, 1890), 184; "Meeting of the Missionary Committee," *Visitor,* III (December 15, 1890), 378-79.

[40]D. Heise, Samuel Zook, "An Appeal," *Visitor,* VI (April 1, 1893), 106.

[41]*Church Government,* 1887, p. 21.

[42]*General Conference Minutes,* 1883, Article 13.

[43]*Ibid.,* 1884, Article 4.

[44]Sider, "Brethren in Canada," pp. 128-29.

[45]*General Council Minutes,* 1886, Article 4.

[46]*Ibid.,* 1886, Article 8. See the General Conference minutes of succeeding years beginning in 1888.

[47]*Canadian Joint Council Minutes,* September 28, 1892, p. 1; *General Conference Minutes,* 1894, p. 3.

[48]Black Creek District Council Minutes, 1887.

[49]John H. Engle, "Notes from Kansas," *Visitor,* I (September 1, 1888), 201.

[50]*Ibid.*

[51]J. F. Eisenhour [*sic*], "Mission Work in Kansas and the West," *Visitor,* V (March 15, 1892), 89.

[52][Henry Davidson], *Visitor,* V (November 1, 1892), 328.

[53]J. G. Cassel, "Gospel Tent," *Visitor,* VII (June 15, 1894), 187.

[54]*Visitor,* VI (July 1, 1893), 200; J. K. Forney, "Statement of Expenses and Donations for the Gospel Tent," *Visitor,* VI (November 15, 1893), 345.

[55]See the *Visitor* reports from June 15 to November 1, 1894.

[56]J. G. Cassel, "Gospel Tent Work," *Visitor,* VI (September 15, 1893), 279.

[57]Noah Zook, "Gospel Tent," *Visitor,* VII (August 15, 1894), 249.

58*Ibid.*, VI (August 1, 1893), 326; *ibid.*, (October 1, 1893), 296; *ibid.*, (November 15, 1893), 328-29; *ibid.*, VII (July 1, 1894), 202; *ibid.*, (November 1, 1894), 330.

59Noah Zook, "Gospel Tent," *Visitor,* VII (July 15, 1894), 224.

60*Ibid.*, VII (November 1, 1894), 330.

61J. G. Cassel, "Gospel Tent," *Visitor,* VII (June 1, 1894), 187.

62[Henry Engle], "Gospel Wagon," *Visitor,* X (July 15, 1897), 226.

63Workers, "Gospel Wagon," *Visitor,* X (August 1, 1897), 2.

64*General Conference Minutes,* 1893, p. 3.

65[Henry Davidson], *Visitor,* VII (September 15, 1894), 280.

66*General Conference Minutes,* 1893, p. 3; [Henry Davidson], "General Conference," *Visitor,* VI (June 1, 1893), 168.

67Noah Zook, "Correspondence," *Visitor,* II (November 1, 1888), 25; [Henry Davidson], "Minister Wanted," *Visitor,* III (October 15, 1890), 313.

68Noah Zook, "Correspondence," *Visitor,* II (November 1, 1888), 25.

69*General Conference Minutes,* 1890, p. 3.

70*Ibid.*, 1892, p. 2; A. L. Myers, "Obedience," *Visitor,* VI (May 1, 1894), 134-35.

71A. L. Myers, "The Chicago Mission," *Visitor,* VII (August 1, 1894), 234.

72A. L. Myers, "A Report of Mission Work," *Visitor,* IV (December 15, 1891), 381; A. L. Myers, "The Chicago Mission," *Visitor,* VII (August 1, 1894), 234.

73A. L. Myers, "The Chicago Mission," *Visitor,* VII (August 1, 1894), 298.

74Sarah H. Bert to Miss E. Winger, November 8, 1916. Printed in *Sunday School Herald,* XII (July 18, 1948), 227.

75*Ibid.*, 227-28.

76J. W. Hoover, "Chicago Mission," *Visitor,* VIII (October 1, 1895), 298.

77Sarah Bert, "Chicago Mission," *Visitor,* VIII (November 15, 1895), 345.

78A. L. Myers, "Obedience," *Visitor,* VII (May 1, 1894), 135.

79*Ibid.*

80C. N. Hostetter, Jr., "Rural and City Missions of the Brethren in Christ," *Visitor,* L (August 28 and 29, 1937), 47. Cited hereafter as *Visitor, Fiftieth Anniversary.*

81*General Conference Minutes,* 1894, p. 4.

82*Ibid.*, 1904, Article 37, p. 21. See also *General Conference Index,* p. 258.

83*General Conference Minutes,* 1907, Article 29, p. 20.

84*Ibid.*, 1905, Article 32, p. 25.

85*Canadian Joint Council Minutes,* September 11, 1919, pp. 45-46.

86*Ibid.*, September 9, 1920, p. 48; *General Conference Minutes,* 1921, Article 37, p. 49.

87In 1958 the name of the Home Mission Board was changed to Board for Home Missions and Extension.

88For a study of these four groups and their interaction with the Brethren, see: Schrag, "Brethren Attitude Toward the World," pp. 335-55.

89G. C. and Sara Cress, "Hearts Set for the Field," *Visitor,* XI (June 1, 1898), 2l6.

90Davidson, *South and Central Africa,* p. 20.

91*Ibid.*

92Wilma Wenger Musser, "Hettie L. Fernbaugh, Missionary Pioneer," *Notes and Queries,* VI (July 1965), 16.

93Elizabeth E. Zook, "Extension of Mission Work in Kansas," *Visitor,* XXXIV (August 1, 1921), 10.

[94][Henry Engle], *Visitor,* XI (January 1, 1898), 14; Musser, "Hettie L. Fernbaugh," 17, 18.

[95]D. W. Zook, "Enroute for India," *Visitor,* IX (February 1, 1896), 37-38.

[96]Kansas Joint Council Minutes, March 5 and 6, 1896, p. 3.

[97]Eber and Amanda Witter Zook, Jeremiah I. Long, Fannie L. Hoffman, Elmina Hoffman, Barbara Hershey, and J. G. and Susan Cassel. Beginning in January of 1898, the *Visitor* lists Brethren in foreign mission service, including those under church auspices and those independent of church control.

[98]J. K. Forney, "A Reminiscence," *Visitor, Fiftieth Anniversary,* p. 31; Carlton O. Wittlinger, "Rhoda E. Lee, Missionary Enthusiast," *Notes and Queries,* II (July 1961), 11-13.

[99]Davidson, *South and Central Africa,* p. 20. The text of Mrs. Lee's paper is in the *Visitor,* VII (June 1, 1894), 162-63.

[100]Davidson, *South and Central Africa,* pp. 20-21.

[101][J. K. Forney] quoted in Wittlinger, "Rhoda E. Lee, Missionary Enthusiast," 13.

[102]*General Conference Minutes,* 1894, p. 4.

[103]Minutes of the Board of Foreign Missions of the Brethern [*sic*] in Christ Church, p. 1, Christian N. Hostetter Papers, Church Archives.

[104]Rhoda E. Lee, "Home and Foreign Missions," *Visitor,* VII (August 15, 1894), 242.

[105]*General Council Minutes,* 1895, p. 2.

[106]Rhoda E. Lee, "Foreign Missions," *Visitor,* VIII (July 1, 1895), 193-94.

[107]*Ibid.,* 194.

[108]*General Council Minutes,* 1895, p. 2.

[109]*Ibid.,* 1896, p. 3; Davidson, *South and Central Africa,* p. 21.

[110]Samuel Zook, "An Appeal," *Visitor,* X (January 15, 1897), 25.

[111]Davidson, *South and Central Africa,* p. 23.

[112]*Ibid.,* pp. 24-25.

[113]*Ibid.,* p. 25.

[114]*Ibid.,* pp. 25-26.

[115]Jeremiah I. Long interview, August 16, 1962.

[116]*General Conference Minutes,* 1897, pp. 6-7. Davidson, *South and Central Africa,* pp. 27-28.

[117]Davidson, *South and Central Africa,* pp. 29-45. Barbara Hershey left the party at Cape Town to work at Johannesburg with a non-Brethren mission.

[118]*Ibid.,* pp. 53-93.

[119]*Ibid.,* pp. 237-76.

[120]Miss Davidson's book is the best account of the early years of this program. Anna R. Engle, John A. Climenhaga, and Leoda A. Buckwalter, *There Is No Difference: God Works in Africa and India* (Nappanee, Ind.: E. V. Publishing House, 1950) is a survey of the first fifty years of Brethren in Christ missions in Africa and India.

[121]Jesse Engle quoted by Detwiler, *Visitor,* XIII (June 1, 1900), 214-15.

[122]*General Conference Minutes,* 1903, Article 33, p. 21.

[123]*Ibid.,* 1904, Article 51, p. 34; *General Conference Index,* p. 257.

[124]*General Conference Minutes,* 1904, Article 55, p. 35; Engle, *et. al., There Is No Difference,* p. 231.

[125]*General Conference Minutes,* 1904, Article 55, p. 35.

[126]Amos L. Musser, "'Go Ye into All the World,'" *Visitor,* XIX (January 16, 1905), 15.

[127]Henry Angeney, "The India Missionaries," *Visitor,* XIX (February 15, 1905), 14; [George Detwiler] *Visitor,* XIX (February 1, 1905), 3.

[128]Henry S. Angeney, "The India Missionaries," *Visitor,* XIX (February 15, 1905), 14; Henry S. Angeney, "A Letter from India," *Visitor,* XIX (September 1, 1905), 15.

[129]Henry Angeney, "From the India Missionaries," *Visitor* XIX (November 1, 1905), 15, Amos L. Musser, "A Letter from India," *Visitor,* XIX (December 1, 1905), 14.

[130][George Detwiler], *Visitor,* XIX (December 15, 1905), 3, and *Ibid.,* XX (February 1, 1906), 3. One reason for the dissatisfaction of the Angeneys was their objection to Amos Musser's desire to launch an industrial school as a means for reaching the people of India.

[131]*General Conference Minutes,* 1906, Article 55, p. 38.

[132]*Ibid.,* 1908, Article 51, p. 71. Maggie K. Landis, "A Letter from India," *Visitor,* XXI (May 1, 1907), 14-15; Amos L. Musser, "Lucknow, India," *Visitor,* XXI (December 16, 1907), 5.

[133]Amos and Katie Musser, "Indian Correspondence," *Visitor,* XXIII (July 1, 1909), 5.

[134]Amos L. Musser, "Lucknow, India," *Visitor,* XXI (December 16, 1907), 5.

[135]*General Conference Minutes,* 1908, Article 51, p. 71; *ibid.,* 1909, Article 81, p. 97.

[136]*Ibid.,* 1909, Article 83, pp. 105-6.

[137]P. M. Climenhaga, "Foreign Mission Fund," *Visitor,* XIX (April 15, 1905), 12.

[138]D. W. Zook, "India Correspondence," *Visitor,* XXIX (July 12, 1915), 19.

[139]"Addresses of Missionaries" and accompanying editorial, *Visitor,* XVI (August 1, 1902), p. 294; *General Conference Minutes,* 1902, Article 33, p. 22; *Pennsylvania State Council Minutes,* 1901, Article 1, pp. 4-5; *ibid.,* 1902, Article 1, p. 4.

[140]*General Conference Minutes, 1910, Article 61, pp. 104-5.*

[141]*Engle, et. al., There Is No Difference,* p. 232.

[142]*General Conference Minutes,* 1912, Article 23, p. 105; ibid., 1913, Article 16, p. 46.

[143]*General Conference Minutes,* 1911, Article 28, p. 53; Buckwalter, *et. al., There Is No Difference,* p. 233.

[144]Engle, *et. al, There Is No Difference,* p. 234.

[145]P. M. Climenhaga, "Foreign Mission Funds Report for January and February, 1913," *Visitor,* XXVII (March 24, 1913), 142.

[146]*General Conference Minutes,* 1914, Article 22, pp. 44-45.

[147]*Ibid.,* Effie Rohrer, "A Letter from India," *Visitor,* XXVIII (March 23, 1914), 13.

[148]Amos D. M. Dick certified that Bishop Lapp's first name was "Mahlon."

[149]*General Conference Minutes,* 1914, Article 22, p. 47.

[150]*Ibid.,* 1915, Article 11, p. 50.

[151]In addition to Smith's leadership in pioneering the location of Brethren mission work in India, he skillfully promoted the cause through the *Evangelical Visitor* and his reports to the General Conference.

[152]*General Conference Minutes,* 1914, Article 22, p. 49.

[153]Henry L. Smith to C. N. Hostetter, May 20, 1917, Christian N. Hostetter Papers.

[154]Noah Zook, "To the Readers of the Visitor, Greetings:," *Visitor,* II (December 1, 1888), 41.

[155]Noah Zook, "Gospel Tent," *Visitor,* VI (September 1, 1893), 264.

[156]C. Nysewander, *Visitor,* XXXII (December 1, 1919), 9.

[157]*General Conference Minutes,* 1903, Articles 42, 43, pp. 24-25; *ibid.,* 1905, Article 32, p. 25; *ibid.,* 1915, Article 36, p. 79.

[158]*Ibid.*, 1906, Article 55, p. 39.

[159]*Ibid.*, p. 40.

[160]Mrs. Amos D. M. Dick, interview, July 14, 1975.

[161]*General Conference Minutes,* 1911, Article 28, p. 52.

X

Local Church Outreach

The Protracted Meeting

The Brethren in Christ adopted new techniques for local church outreach during the period when they also launched their early mission enterprises. One technique was the protracted meeting, a series of daily or periodic services designed to produce the spiritual awakening of unconverted persons, as well as the spiritual growth of the converted. Later generations referred to such services as "revivals." These meetings characterized the Brethren movement until recent times and, with considerable modification, still play a significant role in the life of many congregations.

Prior to their use of the protracted meeting, the Brethren occasionally held series of evangelistically oriented prayer services. This was in response to special and unpredictable manifestations of spiritual concern on the part of the unconverted in their communities. Such meetings continued as long as the concern lasted.[1] The difference between them and the later protracted meetings is obvious. While the former capitalized upon spontaneous manifestations of spiritual interest, the latter assumed that such interest could be produced through specially planned services.

One series of spontaneous prayer meetings broke out in the Donegal District before protracted meetings became commonplace there. Noah Myers, a minister in Franklin County, Pennsylvania, preached in the Conoy meetinghouse in Lancaster County. He stayed over for community visitation, and Jacob Martin of the Donegal District accompanied him. Interest grew as they went from home to home, and they began to hold meetings several times weekly; these continued for seven weeks with many professed conversions.[2]

The planned protracted meeting began to appear in Brethren circles about 1870. Such a basic change in methods of evangelism soon came to the attention of General Conference, which debated the question: "Is it according to scripture to hold protracted meetings?" The discussion may have been long and serious, but the answer was short and unequivocal: "It is."[3] A decade later Conference went further by declaring that the districts of the brotherhood were duty bound to encourage and finance such meetings.[4]

With this positive official encouragement, the protracted meeting slowly gained momentum, especially in Canada and the midwestern United States, although not without opposition. In Pennsylvania the districts responded with characteristic caution to this new practice.[5]

The introduction of protracted meetings provoked considerable controversy. While some Brethren strongly defended such meetings, others objected seriously to them. Critics may have had difficulty disassociating the protracted meeting from its use by the so-called "worldly" evangelical churches. Some members were especially skeptical of revivalistic methods which they identified with "too much excitement, confusion, and wild fire."[6] Others feared that conversions professed in protracted meetings would lack genuine depth and quality; they noted that converts often discontinued their professions of faith when the close of the meetings removed the special stimuli to which they had responded.[7] One leader expressed his misgivings about the quality of conversions in the new evangelistic setting:

> I think of our fathers and mothers in the church years ago, . . . They were not prayed through at the altar at once, coming forward and bowing on one knee. No, but they were in penitence and confession till God did send forth judgment unto victory. Yes, they did not repeat a confession after the preacher, but in a hallelujah they knew that God, for Christ's sake, had forgiven them, . . .[8]

Another feared that shallow evangelistic procedures would separate conversion from obedience, and leave the convert basically unchanged in life-style. He stated:

> The preparatory work of the convert is very often unduly hastened by an overzealous or inexperienced evangelist. . . . Apparently many who claim to

be a branch in the "true vine," seem as though they were never cut loose from the world, . . .[9]

An incident in Waterloo District, Ontario, illustrates how serious the opposition to protracted meetings could become. Here a proposal to build a meetinghouse languished for twenty years because one of the ministers refused to sign a statement that it would never be used for more than three consecutive evening meetings unless all of the officials agreed.[10]

In spite of misgivings about the protracted meeting, it came into the life of the brotherhood "little by little."[11] Its advocates found biblical support for it in scriptural passages such as Paul's statement to the Corinthians: "'I ceased not to warn every one day and night with tears'."[12] These advocates, furthermore, linked the protracted meeting to the growing Brethren concern to minister more effectively to the unconverted. In the words of one of them:

I long to see the time come, when all the members may feel it their duty, to labor more extensively for the cause of Christ—to promote religious revivals, for the salvation of souls . . . . In order that this desired work of grace may be brought about, and revivals promoted, we must adopt special means; the meetings must be multiplied; the ordinary Sabbath services . . . have not generally the desired effect . . . special meetings are required.[13]

The success of some early protracted meetings in producing converts helped to create favorable sentiment for such endeavors. Morrison Cove District, which was in the forefront of Brethren revivalism in Pennsylvania, held a six-week meeting in which fifty-one persons professed conversion, of whom twenty-seven united with the brotherhood.[14] About the same time protracted meetings at Pelham and Markham, Ontario, produced marked results. Some of the twenty-five persons who "came out" at Pelham were "hard skeptics," while half of the twenty who responded at Markham were mature individuals from forty to eighty years of age.[15] In spite of criticism of the protracted meeting, planned revivalism got numerical results and enlarged the brotherhood.

Gradual acceptance of the protracted meeting forced the Brethren to wrestle with questions of an appropriate methodology for it. A Canadian evangelist expressed this concern in connection with a meeting which he held in Nottawa District, Ontario. He wrote:

We tried to avoid all the extravagances of the modern revival, having too often seen the deplorable results of using too much man power and resorting to all kinds of expedients to get people up from their seats. Many will rise from the excitement of the moment and when the meetings are over their religion is gone too. Yet on the other hand we felt bound by the word of God to give at each meeting an earnest, pressing invitation to sinners to come to Christ and confess it by rising.[16]

Rising in a service to make known the desire to live a Christian life was in accord with historic precedent in the life of the Brethren. Once they began to hold protracted meetings, however, they confronted various unfamiliar practices associated with the revival movement in evangelical Protestantism.

Especially controversial was the invitation for seekers to come forward for counsel and prayer. In some non-Brethren circles this "altar service" created an emotional atmosphere repugnant to many of the brotherhood. Furthermore, designation of the front of the meetinghouse as a special place to approach God had no precedent among them. They believed that true repentance and personal faith were the only conditions for the salvation experience and that the place where this experience culminated was completely irrelevant.

These reservations about the use of the revival invitation reached General Conference in 1872. Here those advocating it carried the day, for Conference ruled that inviting seekers to come forward was consistent with the Word of God "if in Christian order, but that no *special* bench shall be set out for the seekers."[17] This ruling shows that the "mourner's bench" was not yet at home among the Brethren.

Aversion to the altar service declined slowly within the brotherhood. By the 1890s this service was being used by the Kansas churches.[18] The following minute reveals, however, that Kansas Joint Council was not fully at ease with it:

The conference discussed at some length the use of the church altar. It was the sentiment of the remarks that although there is no merit in the altar as such it is not an unsuitable place to seek and worship the Father, and that in truth the altar is wherever the individual meets his God. It was unanimously agreed to lay no restrictions upon the use of the altar service, but that those who are in charge are urged to use their best judgment and submit to the Spirit's guidance in every instance.[19]

Other areas of the brotherhood were accommodating themselves to the invitation and altar service by the turn of the century.[20] An interesting situation developed in a meeting held by George Detwiler in the Bertie

Church in 1899. Here penitents came forward spontaneously without being invited to do so.[21] A few years later Peter Stover of the Philadelphia Mission reported that penitents had the privilege to come forward and kneel for prayer with the service leaders, but he carefully assured the brotherhood that the mission had no mourner's bench.[22]

Stover's statement about the mourner's bench reveals that it was still a sensitive issue at that time.[23] Opposition to it gradually declined, although there is no record that General Conference rescinded the 1872 ban on its use.

Another innovation which accompanied the protracted meeting was the revival specialist, the minister who gave large amounts of time to an evangelistic ministry throughout the brotherhood. Local district ministers conducted some of the first protracted meetings.[24] Soon, however, districts began to call outside ministers such as Jacob Martin, Noah Zook, John W. Hoover, Avery Long, George Detwiler, and John Zook to provide ministerial leadership for their meetings. The fervency and homiletical ability of these men elevated them in the awareness of the Brethren, and for decades the evangelist was one of the most honored and respected figures in the brotherhood. Sometimes an evangelist's wife regularly accompanied him; Noah and Mary Zook were one of the first and most prominent of these husband-wife evangelistic teams.[25]

As these specialists emerged, they assumed primary roles in local evangelistic enterprises. This is illustrated by meetings which John W. Hoover held in Stark County, Ohio.[26] He arrived at Valley Chapel on a Sunday morning, where he became acquainted with "good, warm Brethren and sisters." His report continues:

> . . . I felt that the good Lord had visited them and they all seemed anxious to see the Lord do a work there. So we all agreed to open fire at once on the enemy of souls. . . . After about two weeks hard labor, the ice began to break, the strong cords that Satan has to bind the souls of men broke loose and to the praise of God some eight or ten were out as seekers at one time, and it seemed that we all got revived. Old and young cried to God for mercy. . . . But we kept on having meetings at 10:00 A.M. and 7:00 P.M. and I visited around between times as much as convenient, . . .

Twenty-five or more seekers came forward in this meeting. The evangelist baptized a number of them before he left to hold a similar series of services at the nearby Sippo Church. Some of the Valley Chapel converts followed him to Sippo "to help along the meetings," which were interspersed with baptisms of converts from both places, all administered by Hoover.

At the close of the final night service, a young woman convert wept because she thought that Hoover's early morning departure would prevent him from baptizing her. He found a prompt solution to her problem: "... we concluded to baptize her that evening, and at once received her and went to the water and baptized her, and as Philip did, went on our way rejoicing." This evening baptism may well have been a "first" among the Brethren.

As time passed, local evangelistic efforts were concentrated primarily in annual protracted meetings with outside evangelists. Some Brethren saw disadvantages in this trend. One who felt deeply about the situation wrote:

> ... I fear our people have got from one extreme to the other, perhaps equally wrong. ... With us ... to-day we have nearly ceased to look for conversions unless we have special services and get some "big gun," or more properly speaking, some noted preacher, from a distance to take charge of the work. This very thing is working untold mischief in our church ....
> What are the main body of our ministers called *for*, if it is *not* to lead sinners to Christ? ...
>
> This present way of doing things is having a *depressing* effect on the main body of the ministry, yea, a *deadening* effect. Once [you] get the idea into your head rightly that you are no use, it won't be long till it is only *too true*.[27]

This writer, anticipating criticism for his stand, sought to make clear that he was and always had been in favor of protracted meetings "on right lines."

The tide of sentiment was running against those who shared such concerns. A few years later General Conference named a "Lookout Committee" to identify men qualified for evangelistic work and to recommend them to the Examining Committee for approval and appointment to the evangelistic office. Conference recommended persons so appointed "to the hearty sympathy and material support of the brotherhood." Districts did not have to confine themselves to the approved slate of evangelists but were encouraged to do so whenever feasible.[28]

Creation of the office of evangelist and the availablility of slates of approved evangelists further united the protracted meeting with evangelistic specialists. Districts scheduled protracted meetings annually or semi-annually and called outside evangelists to give them leadership.

These arrangements led the Brethren to begin to think of "revivals" in terms of calendar dates just as they thought of love feasts. As a result, by the early twentieth century they had formed the standardized patterns of revivalism which characterized their movement for the next half century.

The Sunday School

Along with the protracted meeting, the Brethren in Christ borrowed the Sunday school from contemporary Protestantism and made it their second major technique for local church outreach. Black Creek District in Ontario operated a Sunday school in the 1880s and probably a decade or more earlier.[29] In 1876 General Conference had to decide whether a small group of members in Columbus, Ohio, could have a Sunday school in their

Asa and Nancy Bearss. The former pioneered Sunday school work among the nineteenth-century Brethren in Christ in Canada, a contribution memorialized by the General Conference of 1963.

church. They could, the Conference ruled, "provided they hold control of it," a reservation intended to forestall any drift toward a union school.[30]

In spite of this favorable Conference ruling, critics continued to oppose the Sunday school. Some opposition may have reflected attitudes formulated in an earlier period when the brotherhood did not stress the evangelism of children nor their spiritual nurture outside of the home.[31] There were also specific objections to the innovation. It was not a New Testament institution, and the Brethren fathers had not recognized it.[32] One of its supporters replied to these objections as follows:

> The principles of Christianity never change, but the proper applications of those principles change to best meet the environment under which we are placed. . . . In the early history of our church the most feasible place for worship was in the house or barn of the members. To-day very few would maintain that the church building does not serve a useful purpose in our religious life.[33]

Other opponents of the Sunday school feared that it would encourage pride and worldliness, open doors to unsound doctrines and questionable social practices, or compromise the quality of Bible instruction.[34] The Sunday school was new and untried among them. Their fears were not lessened by its popularity among "wordly" churches nor by the programs and picnics which the Sunday schools of those churches promoted.

On the other hand, advocates of the Sunday school perceived it as an opportunity for spiritual progress. They pled earnestly for the evangelization and spiritual nuture of children and youth. To those who believed the Sunday school to be evil, they replied that the crucial question was how it was used; employed with proper safeguards it could accomplish much good.[35] The cause of the Sunday school, furthermore, was supported by a very practical consideration; if the Brethren did not provide Sunday schools of their own, members would drift into the schools of others.[36]

The Sunday school controversy climaxed on the floor of General Conference in 1885. This time the question did not involve a specific school as in 1876 but had broad policy implications: "Should Sabbath schools be encouraged among the brethren?" Champions of the Sunday school convinced the Conference which ruled affirmatively, on condition that such schools should be "properly conducted by the brethren, and nothing but God's word be admitted . . . to teach from, and no picnics or celebrations [be] allowed."[37]

This policy decision of 1885 did not sweep away all opposition to

Sunday schools, for one of the most powerful apologies for them was published as late as 1905.[38] The decision did, however, pave the way for the advance of the Sunday school movement, and the number of schools increased across the brotherhood during the latter part of the century.[39]

The Kansas Brethren were particularly active in this enterprise; five schools operated in Dickinson County in 1888, with opposition rapidly waning.[40] When George Detwiler of Sherkston, Ontario, visited Kansas in 1894, he observed: ". . . in no other state is the church so alive to the importance of Sunday school work as in Kansas; and consequently we find special attention given to it in the councils of the church, and . . . a regular plan of organization."[41]

As the Brethren expanded Sunday school work, controversy developed about the use of Sunday school literature or "helps." The Conference decision of 1885, which encouraged the Sunday school movement, restricted the curriculum to the Bible itself. This restriction indicated concern to safeguard the brotherhood from questionable doctrine and teaching. Lesson helps were also in disfavor on the grounds that they might decrease Bible reading and that the money spent for them could be put to better use.[42]

Teaching helps did not lack defenders.[43] Although there is no record that General Conference rescinded the ruling limiting instruction to the Bible, *Visitor* Editor Davidson felt free by 1890 to recommend the helps issued by the Mennonite Publishing Company at Elkhart, Indiana. "We think the lessons are well explained," he wrote.[44] A short time later he stressed the Bible as the basis of instruction but pointed out that helps could assist the youthful mind to grasp the truth. Since the brotherhood did not provide its own helps, he still believed that the Mennonite materials were the best available.[45]

The use of helps originating outside of the brotherhood posed the problem of teaching that which might be objectionable to a group so sensitive to the need to safeguard its faith. By 1903 General Conference had before it a petition to publish Sunday school literature under the auspices of the church. This request was deferred indefinitely as was a similar request in 1907.[46] John H. Engle of Kansas, however, prepared a column of International Sunday School Lesson helps for the *Visitor,* which continued for several years.[47]

The following year the Mennonite Book and Tract Society of Scottdale, Pennsylvania, offered to provide the Brethren with Sunday school literature.[48] This offer included quarterlies with Brethren in Christ imprint and pre-publication editorial privileges, and two take-home papers, *Words of Cheer* and *Beams of Light,* including one page of Brethren copy in each issue. Conference accepted this offer and named George Detwiler to edit the new literature.[49] That decision began a Mennonite-Brethren in Christ Sunday school relationship which continued to the mid-century.

Early Brethren Sunday schools usually began in May and continued into the fall, although some operated throughout the year.[50] The following passage describes a typical school:

> The average attendance is fifty. Seven firm members of the church are employed as teachers, and one superintendent. The New Testament is used as the basis of our studies. No Lesson Helps have as yet been adopted. The teachers go over the lessons to their respective classes and then the superintendent reviews the lesson before the whole school. Our school is supported by members . . . who are favorable to Sunday-school, and it is controlled by the church alone.[51]

The sources provide a few other glimpses into the activities of the early Sunday schools. Scripture memorization had an important role in the pedagogy of that day. In the Bertie Sunday school, a number of the smaller scholars were quite active in Scripture memorization; one learned 275 verses and two others learned over 200 each.[52]

This Bertie school had already initiated what would become a common procedure in Brethren Sunday schools—the giving of gifts on some appropriate occasion. During the closing exercises in mid-November, "the children were made glad with suitable presents, after having listened to some earnest and appropriate addresses by several of the brethren present." The Philadelphia Mission Sunday school, begun in 1897, also gave gifts to the young scholars. A correspondent reported the children's response: "The many smiling faces I shall never forget, many of them being quite poor children."[53]

Not all Brethren approved of gifts to Sunday school scholars. As late as 1914 a request came to the General Conference for "a clear, intelligent, and Scriptural expression whether it is consistent to present Sunday School scholars with Christmas gifts," but Conference refused to take a stand on the question and tabled the petition.[54]

Certain other activities now commonplace in Brethren Sunday schools aroused much disfavor in the nineteenth century. General Conference, in approving Sunday school work in 1885, banned picnics and celebrations. Not all areas of the brotherhood, however, saw dangers in picnics. The

Brethren of Upland, California, for example, had annual picnics from the beginning of their Sunday school early in the twentieth century.[55]

Many Brethren members also objected to what they called "child exhibition" in recitations and programs. These activities, they thought, fostered the child's love of praise and engendered egotism. A selected article, "The Dangers of Child Exhibition," printed with strong editorial approval in the *Visitor*, illustrates this concern:

> "The custom of training children to 'show off' their singing and recitation and other little accomplishments is to be deplored. A tiny creature, beautifully dressed, standing up to 'speak' before an audience is a questionable spectacle. They may enjoy it, and parents too, but at what cost? Self-consciousness, vanity, and aggressiveness drive modesty out of a child's heart, while the elders are laying up for themselves a stock of annoyance for the future."[56]

As a result of such objections, child recitations and programs had little or no place in early Brethren Sunday schools. In 1906 *Visitor* Editor Detwiler wrote: "So far as we know the Sunday-schools of the Brotherhood are free from the practice of 'Child-Exhibition,' which prevails so largely in many of the other schools."[57]

Most teachers in the early Brethren Sunday schools had no formal pedagogical training. Their effectiveness depended upon natural ability developed by whatever means of self-improvement were available to them.

Some pioneer Sunday school leaders among the Brethren saw the need for pedagogical improvement. One of them, J. Myers Bosler, advocated libraries, teachers' meetings, and teachers who, in addition to being well versed in the Scriptures, were "well read in history and anecdotes, and abreast the times with missionary work."[58] He then struck a surprisingly modern pedagogical note:

> A written sermon is no more disgusting than a recital from the helps. Gem memory verses, questions, reproduction in writing, are a few of many means by which a recitation may be enlivened. . . . In Sabbath Schools the object method of teaching truth and principle to the premature reader is very much needed to draw the mind and affections and impress the very susceptible and tender hearts. The pictorial, the blackboard, and the real object methods certainly can be thus used so as to meet the demands of the laws of mind and heart.

Having begun Sunday school work, the Brethren soon adopted a related institution—the Sunday school convention. The first such convention met at the Bethel Church in Kansas preceding Kansas Joint Council in 1893. Little is known about it, but one who attended wrote: "... we were forcibly impressed with the importance of Sunday School work and the benefits derived from it if under proper control."[59] The Kansas Brethren held another convention the next year, and the following topics reflect the varied facets of Sunday school interest at that time:

> The International Sunday School Lesson Series
> Lesson-helps, their use and abuse
> Are our old members benefitted by the Sunday School?
> How may the Sunday-School be made a means to a more thorough Bible knowledge?
> What dangers are we liable to in Sunday School work?
> Superintendents, (a) their qualifications, (b) their duties?[60]

Presentations of these topics apparently varied in quality, for Editor Davidson reported: "How well they were handled we will not undertake to say; but upon the whole we think that the Sunday School conference was profitable to those who were present . . . ."[61] Such conventions became annual events in the life of the Kansas Brethren; other areas of the brotherhood were slower to introduce them.[62] In 1911 a Sunday school meeting held in conjunction with General Conference began a tradition continued until recent times.[63]

This church-wide meeting was only one of several signs that the Sunday school was coming of age among the Brethren in the early twentieth century. Another sign was the appointment of the first General Sunday School Board.[64] As conceived by General Conference, the board had three objectives—Information, Education, and Inspiration.[65] The next year Conference directed each state or provincial council to appoint a Sunday school secretary, and later it authorized the preparation of a Sunday school teacher's training course.[66] Acting under this authorization, John A. Climenhaga and Enos N. Engle produced the *Teacher's Training Course of the Brethren in Christ.*[67]

John H. Engle—"Sunday School John"—of Kansas summarized the state of the Sunday school movement in an address to the General Conference of 1906.[68] Defining the Sunday school as "'The Bible-studying and Bible-teaching service of the church'," he was honored to plead its cause before Conference. Happily, in his view, it no longer required arguments in its defense, although a few congregations still failed to perceive its benefits.

The ringing challenge of Engle's closing remarks suggest the conclusion toward which the brotherhood was gradually moving. "We have, in the Sunday-school, a great opportunity, a great obligation. Let us embrace our heritage!"[69] In time the Brethren reached consensus with him, and the Sunday school appeared wherever they had organized church life.

Effects of the New Methods of Local Outreach

Few Brethren could have forseen the ways in which new methods of local church outreach would alter their faith and life-style.[70] One consequence of the protracted meeting and Sunday school was a lessening of their religious exclusiveness. During their first one hundred years, they perceived other churches as a part of the "world" and had little to do with them. Now, as they found interests in common with evangelical Protestantism, they began to associate with other evangelicals in revival and Sunday school activities.[71] These relationships exposed them to new views and life-styles and facilitated a slow process of acculturation which made them less sensitive to their differences with other churches. Sectarianism gradually gave ground to denominationalism.

A second result of the new outreach methods was the encouragement of individuality at the expense of community. At first the Brethren sought to make these methods conform to their own faith and life-style, but this ultimately proved to be unrealistic. The models of evangelism and child nurture offered by evangelical Protestantism were so dynamic and influential that they gradually determined the conditions for their inclusion in the life of the brotherhood. With the passage of time, protracted meetings and Sunday schools of the brotherhood, became less and less distinguishable in purpose and procedures from those of other evangelical groups. Even such a loyal churchman as Henry Davidson wrote:

> ... the work of the Sunday School is not intended to simply obtain members for any one church. The teaching is on a different plan and it is generally non-sectarian, but largely evangelical, and this evidently should be the proper course.[72]

Davidson's statement strikingly illustrates how the thought of the group was being conditioned to accept the Sunday school on its own terms as a means for promoting non-sectarian, individualized Christianity.

Expressed differently, the new outreach mentality emphasized personal Christian experience at the expense of the historic Brethren understanding of obedience. The shift was from preoccupation with the church as the visible people of God, with emphasis on Brethren beliefs and life-style, to individual Christian experience and evangelism.

A closely related aspect of the new outreach mentality was the tendency to introduce a time interval between conversion and commitment to obedience. The 1881 Confession of Faith declared that "by faith in our Savior, and true repentance, forgiveness of sin, *and obedience to Christ and His commands,* is the only true way that we may become and remain *Christians* [italics added]."[73] In contrast, an official tract published in 1906 asserted that "eternal life is a free gift and must be appropriated by faith; that obedience and good works are only evidence of faith."[74]

At first thought, the differences between these two statements appear minimal and, in a sense, they were. The more discerning Brethren leaders in 1881 would probably have agreed with both of them. There was, nevertheless, a subtle, underlying difference of emphasis developing. The 1906 tract marked progress toward the view that conversion professed under Brethren ministries need not imply commitment to the Brethren faith and life-style. In other words, conversion and obedience could be increasingly separated in time, in contrast with the earlier view that seekers for salvation could not delay their reckoning with obedience as understood by the brotherhood.

This trend toward the separation of conversion from obedience developed slowly and almost imperceptibly. This was partly because evangelists such as Noah and John Zook, who were loyal to the brotherhood and highly respected, continued to define conversion in a generally traditional way but with a somewhat different perspective. John Zook, for example, set forth his views as follows:

Joining church will never save us. Laying off your pride will never say you. . . . Being baptized will not redeem us. Partaking of the eucharist and washing the saints' feet will not remove sin nor cleanse our hearts. Agonizing and confessing will not bring real peace and joy—it is GRACE applied by a living faith. . . . Repentance, confession, giving up of pride, etc., are only prerequisites to a living faith.

Baptism, the eucharist, the washing of the saints' feet etc., are requisite to manifest our love and obedience to God—or in other words, they are only evidences of our love and faith.[75]

Thus, without repudiating the historic Brethren faith, Zook gave conversion a "new look." His message stressed the doctrine of salvation by grace as a personal subjective experience set in sharp contrast to the "prerequisites" and "evidences" identified with it.[76]

The earlier Brethren had been accustomed to a doctrine of conversion which, while theologically compatible with Zook's position, did not draw such sharp distinctions between prerequisites for salvation, the actual experience of God's grace, and evidences for the validity of that experience. Zook unintentionally posed a question of great importance for the Brethren: Could the salvation experience occur, for example, in the absence of some "prerequisites," such as giving up pride as understood by the Brethren, and was it valid if it did not produce some "evidences" such as feet washing? In other words, Zook's message challenged by implication both the traditional perspective of the conversion experience and the historic life-style of the Brethren.

At the time Zook wrote, some other leaders, such as George Detwiler, thoroughly agreed with his doctrine of grace. The latter, who united with the Brethren in 1874 and entered the ministry in the early 1880s, had always been a "grace" preacher. He was concerned lest the Brethren concept of obedience be corrupted into a doctrine of salvation by works. On one occasion he asserted; "It is as important that believers maintain the same attitude towards modern Galatianism where pure faith in salvation is mixed with our own works, usually designated obedience, as towards worldliness for both are equally fatal to the life of the Spirit."[77]

Other leaders were less open theologically than Detwiler to the growing preoccupation with the individualized experience of grace and its potential detachment from their historic understanding of obedience. They were uneasy lest these circumstances undermine confidence in Brethren distinctives and militate against their commitment to be the visible church.

One sign of this uneasiness was the reaction of Canada Joint Council to the rumor that Noah Zook was communing with and administering communion to persons of other denominations. The council requested the Home Mission Board to investigate this rumor and discipline Zook if it proved to be true.[78]

Another sign was a statement by Charles Baker, one of the principal supporters of the historic faith. In discussing "Thoughts on How Our Youth May be Won for the Church," Baker expressed both optimism and concern. He disagreed firmly with the idea that choosing a church home was a matter of secondary importance, and went on to say:

We are glad that our Brotherhood has thus far tried to adhere to the "principles" of God's house. They are God-given "principles," and it behooves all officials to impress their hearers with the thought that God demands of all His children to obey Him. . . . If it were not necessary for God's children to adhere to all the ordinances of God's house, why did the Saviour tell his disciples to teach their followers to "observe all things" whatsoever He had commanded them? . . . Why all this, if it made no difference with what body of Christian believers we were identified.[79]

Canada Joint Council and Charles Baker did not oppose either the Sunday school or protracted meetings. The intention was rather to counteract what seemed to be a possible compromise of the historic faith of the brotherhood. What they and many of their contemporaries failed to realize, however, was the way in which the new methods of church outreach were helping to transform Brethren life and thought so as to move the group position closer to contemporary evangelical Protestantism.

A third consequence of the new outreach emphases was the shortening of the conversion experience. During the first one hundred years of the Brethren movement, adult conversions typically involved long periods of spiritual unrest and search often extending for weeks, months, or even years before the seeker felt assured of peace with God. While the individual was in this state of unrest, the Brethren encouraged him to obey God but gave him little specific counsel or guidance about how to experience conversion.[80]

The protracted meeting proceeded on different premises. Persons spiritually awakened in a meeting ideally experienced the new birth promptly. This expectation became more sharply defined as the protracted meeting movement advanced. In its early stages, awakened persons sometimes "sought" continually throughout the meeting; Henry K. Kreider, later bishop of Dauphin-Lebanon District in Pennsylvania, "went forward" every night for six weeks before he felt assured of his salvation.[81] With the passage of time, evangelistic specialists became skillful in guiding seekers more rapidly towards the kinds of experiences considered to be normative. John Zook published a guidance manual for evangelists entitled *A Guide for Instructors to Instruct Penitents; Seekers of Holiness and Empowerment and Divine Healing.*[82] Theoretically, immediate conversion was within the reach of all who made the appropriate responses described by Bishop Zook.

A fourth outcome of the new methods of outreach was the projection of child nurture and evangelism into the forefront of concerns of the Brethren. This was in marked contrast to their first one hundred years when they regarded decisions to profess Christ and join the church as acts for mature adults who could understand the full implications of such decisions.[83]

The following account of profession of faith by an eleven-year-old Ohio boy, Levi Herr, reveals that child conversions were unusual as late as the 1870s:

> It was a rare occurrence in those days for children to begin their Christian life so young. As he was small for his age, it caused a surprise in the assembly when he arose and gave this testimony:
> "Brethren and sisters, pray for me. I feel like serving my Lord." His brave stand and determination won the admiration and confidence of all present.[84]

By the turn of the century, child conversions were commonplace; many seekers in protracted meetings were children and youth. John Hoover reported a meeting at Valley Chapel in which "Several young boys took courage to stand up to speak for the Master."[85] Later, when evangelist John Zook came to this church, about twenty children testified that they had "given their hearts to Jesus."[86] Children's testimonies of conversion also began to appear in the *Visitor,* and many child converts entered into church fellowship at ages which would have been unthinkable some decades earlier.[87]

As the Brethren turned seriously to child nurture and evangelism, they accentuated the process by which the protracted meeting was shortening the conversion experience. Children responded more readily than adults to the appeal to "give their hearts to Jesus," and they professed Christian faith simply and easily, as illustrated by the following testimony:

> I am a little girl ten years old. I was converted over a year ago, and was baptized July 1, 1906. I love Jesus. I love his service. I want to become more and more like him. I am so happy because I know I am his child.[88]

A side effect of child conversions was the "repeat convert." In early Brethren history the person who, after much deliberation, made his commitment to God and the Brethren, tended to stand firmly by that commitment. "Backsliding"—ceasing to make a profession of faith—was much less common than it later became. The protracted meeting, which provided annual or semi-annual exposure to earnest evangelistic preaching, frequently had an unsettling effect upon children, as well as some adults. The result was that many persons presented themselves repeatedly as candidates for conversion.

Some critics blamed the phenomenon of convert instability on questionable evangelistic methods. One leader, himself an evangelist, deplored resorting to all kinds of methods to secure salvation decisions.[89] A Pennsylvania district objected to putting congregations to the test on "extreme points" such as readiness for death or the coming of Christ.[90]

While the methodologies which produced the intense atmosphere of protracted meetings varied with different evangelists, annual ministries directed toward decisions injected a new emotional element into Brethren life. This, often coupled with lack of clear teaching and pastoral shepherding between meetings, helped to produce the perennial seeker who became a conspicuous figure in those meetings.

A fifth result of church outreach was the transition of Brethren music from the traditional, sober, metered hymnody to wide use of gospel songs and choruses. From 1874 to 1902 successive issues of *Spiritual Hymns* continued the early traditions, but the sounds of musical change were being heard across the brotherhood. The child-centered Sunday school was awakening interest in music with special appeal to children. An Ohio speaker noted:

> New hymns to learn should possess the spirit of joy, life and hope. Gloomy, melancholy ones are almost always out of place. . . . When children are permitted to choose the songs and in Sunday-school this is advisable to induce them to sing—they always select those full of life, vim and vigor. For the music and words most express the strenuous, active and joyful life of boys and girls.[91]

Simultaneously, the protracted meeting fostered an interest in music which sought to make the services "jubilant and victorious for the Christian, but penetrating and scrutinizing for the sinner."[92]

Sentiment for musical reform culminated in the new 1906 hymnal which, although retaining the traditional title *Spiritual Hymns,* marked a radical break with the past.[93] Only 112 selections, nineteen per cent of the total, came from the previous hymnal; only 120 selections, or twenty-five per cent of the entire hymnbook could be classified as standard hymns.[94]

Among the new songs were some of inferior poetical and musical quality, such as the following:

Are Your Windows Open?	Keep Moving On the Way
Be It Mine To Plant a Flower	The Evergreen Mountains of Life

Better Farther On	The Handwriting On The Wall
Father's Letters	The Shelf Behind The Door
I Am On the Gospel Highway	Why Not Catch The Sunbeams[95]

In spite of some of its limitations, the 1906 Brethren hymnal expressed the new forces and ferment at work in the life of the Brethren. Protracted meetings, Sunday schools, missions, and Wesleyan holiness were uniting to create new attitudes and a new emotional tone in striking contrast to the former sober, restrained life-style. The spontaneity and enthusiasm of the gospel song now appealed strongly to many of them, so the new hymnal featured songs such as: "Heavenly Sunlight," "O Happy Day," and "Feasting With My Lord."[96] Similar songs stressing praise, peace, love, joy, assurance, and fellowship abound in the book. The subjectivity or experiential emphasis of the new songs, combined with the simplicity of the music, gave them strong appeal to a significant cross-section of the Brethren moved by buoyant attitudes and feelings. The new individualism would not be denied musical expression.

Publication of the 1906 *Spiritual Hymns* occurred in the midst of an intense discussion about Brethren music, a discussion involving both musical quality and the question of whether notes should accompany the texts.[97] One leader protested against "the deluge of modern, wishy-washy, vapid trash that passed for hymns and devotional songs" and against picturing the Christian life "like a fascinating panorama of birds, fruit, flowers and music instead of the narrow thorny path of self denial and suffering with our master by walking in his steps." He added: "There is such a sensuous attraction in good singing especially in some of the lively high-flying tunes of the day that we need to search our hearts . . . and see if the spirit of true devotion can keep up to the rattling pace of the tune."[98]

Brethren hymnals prior to the 1906 *Spiritual Hymns* had no notes. When some music reformers began to advocate notes, persons willing to accept them divided on whether they should be shaped or round.[99] Others would have no part of notes in any form. One frustrated member wrote:

Oh, it makes me feel sad to think we have brethren in our common church who want notes to sing by. Oh, the church is drifting. . . .

My feeling is to print more of the good old books we have, and let well enough alone and save labor and expense. Fill all the earth with our old-fashioned books; they are so dear to me.

My prayer is for the church to remain humble. . . . My feeling is, the notes do not belong to our profession.[100]

When notes finally gained a foothold in the 1906 hymnal, they were round.

In view of considerable entrenched traditionalism in Brethren music, the radical shift of emphasis in the 1906 hymnal may seem surprising. The explanation for this shift lies in the personnel of the hymnal committee, and the manner in which it functioned. Two of its members, John Zook and Samuel Smith, played the leading roles and were largely responsible for the final selections of texts and tunes from a list prepared by the former. As a leading evangelist and exponent of Wesleyan holiness, Zook thus became the channel through which the new emotional climate fostered by the Sunday school, protracted meetings, and holiness teaching found its way to the forefront in the music of the Brethren.[101]

The selections for the 1906 hymnal attracted repeated criticism.[102] Judged by present musical standards it marked a "severe and abrupt alteration of Brethren in Christ hymnody which saw the Church abandon a rich poetic and musical heritage in favor of songs considerably impoverished in quality."[103] On the other hand, it must be regarded as an expression of music welcomed by many people passing through a period of spiritual transition with strong emotional overtones.

Finally, new methods of local church outreach helped to edge the Brethren into the mainstream of the temperance movement. The International Sunday School Lessons systematically emphasized temperance, and protracted meetings gave temperance evangelists opportunities to link beverage alcohol and tobacco with sin and worldliness.

Temperance teaching was relatively new to the Brethren.[104] Like their eighteen- and nineteenth-century contemporaries, few of them had developed scruples against the moderate use of alcohol. Many kept hard cider and various wines—grape, dandelion, and raspberry—in their cellars.[105]

On one occasion in the late nineteenth century a group of five male members traveled by team and wagon to a love feast a considerable distance from their homes. In those days hotels with facilities to water horses were located at intervals along the highways. The water was free, but custom decreed that the hotels should be patronized in return for accommodation of the horses. At the first watering stop four of the five each had a glass of whiskey; the fifth took lemonade. This ritual was repeated until the one who took lemonade noticed that his companions were, in his words, getting "boozy." He thereupon emphatically reminded them that they were on their way to a love feast and that it was not right from them to act so giddy and light-minded. After this exhortation all drank lemonade![106]

Tobacco, like beverage alcohol, was commonly used by the early Brethren. When they built meetinghouses in the latter part of the nineteenth century, they equipped many of them with spittoons for the convenience of tobacco users.[107] Many Pennsylvania members raised cigar tobacco, and they would have seen nothing inconsistent in the conduct of a deacon who stripped tobacco all day and went to experience meeting in the evening.[108] Some women members used tobacco in clay and corncob pipes.[109]

Temperance was arousing lively controversy among the Brethren by the late nineteenth century. In 1885 one district considered whether a minister could consistently take an intoxicating drink at a hotel bar or accept a drink from anyone and ruled that he could not.[110] Later, this district decided that a minister could not consistently preach "a full-gospel" and use tobacco.[111] In 1888 another district discussed whether a member who habitually used tobacco could be ordained to the ministry.[112] From a third district came the following report:

> *Glorious victories!* The meetings in these parts I must confess are accompanied with grand results, . . . Oh, I am so glad to state that we have the terrible convictions of brethren chewing tobacco brought to the front. One of the ministering brethren here who had been a tobacco user for eighteen long years became convinced of the sinfulness and quit the habit, . . . The brethren here are in earnest to get rid of the habit and we predict in a short time the entire brotherhood in these parts will have cleaned out the last vestige of the same.[113]

This temperance ferment at the grassroots level had its counterpart at General Conference which, in the 1870s and 1880s, put the brotherhood solidly on record in support of the temperance cause. The tobacco question came to the foreground first. In answer to the question, "Are brethren permitted to traffic or speculate in tobacco?", Conference of 1872 said simply, "No."[114] The intent of this action as it related to "traffic" in tobacco is uncertain. Members obviously could not become tobacco merchants without defying General Conference, but it is unlikely that "traffic" included the cultivation of tobacco.

Five years later Conference ruled on the use of tobacco stating "That it is not consistent and that it is acknowledged an evil, especially among the ministering brethren. And those using it are heartily warned by the council to abstain from its use."[115] Soon Conference linked the cultivation of tobacco with its use and held both to be inconsistent with the Pauline principle: "If meat make my brother to offend, I will eat no flesh while the world standeth."[116]

In 1888 the question of beverage alcohol reached General Conference, which ruled against it as follows: "That it is the sentiment of this . . . Meeting that the use of intoxicating or spirituous Liquors is a dangerous evil, sustained apparently by large monied interests, and we urge our people to abstain in every way from its use as a beverage, and earnestly urge our Brethren to use their influence against its use in every way consistent with the Word of God."[117] Some years later Conference decided that members might vote at the polls against the liquor traffic.[118]

These earliest temperance rulings of General Conference were contemporary with the beginnings of the protracted meeting and Sunday school among the Brethren. This suggests that the group would have shifted toward the temperance position without these innovations in local church outreach. As the new outreach methodologies increased in influence, however, they provided channels through which the temperance message flowed to all localities and age groups of the brotherhood. As a result, the use of tobacco and beverage alcohol declined more rapidly than it might otherwise have done, although the growing of tobacco continued well into the twentieth century.

NOTES:

[1]Moses L. Dohner, cited in Alderfer, "Mind of the Brethren," p. 106.

[2]Jacob N. Martin to Bro. Sider, March 1, 1924, Asa W. Climenhaga Papers.

[3]Church Government, 1887, p. 9.

[4]General Conference Minutes, 1881, Article 8.

[5]Jacob N. Martin to Bro. Sider, March 1, 1924; Visitor, 1887-1889, passim.

[6]Samuel Baker, "Protracted Meetings," Visitor, I (February 1, 1888), 85.

[7]F. Elliott, "Thoughts on Revival Meetings," Visitor, VIII (October 1, 1895), 294.

[8]J. H. Myers, "The Need of Contending for the Faith," Visitor, XXVI (January 8, 1912), 13.

[9]Charles Baker, "The True Vine," Visitor, XXVI (April 1, 1912), 7.

[10]George Detwiler, "Reminiscences."

[11]T. A. Long to Christian Sider, January 31, 1924; Jacob N. Martin to Bro. Sider, March 1, 1924, Asa W. Climenhaga Papers.

[12]Samuel Baker, "Protracted Meetings," *Visitor*, I (February 1, 1888), 85.

[13]*Ibid.*

[14]A Brother, "Correspondence," *Visitor*, I (May 1, 1888), 137.

[15][Henry Davidson], *Visitor*, I (April 1, 1888), 121, and (May 1, 1888), 136. See also J. W. Hoover, "Evangelistic Work," *Visitor*, III (February 1, 1890), 43, for a report of protracted meetings in Ohio.

[16]F. Elliott, "A Series of Meetings," *Visitor*, III (March 1, 1890), 74.

[17]*General Conference Minutes*, 1882, Article 8.

[18][Henry Davidson], *Visitor*, IX (February 1, 1896), 40.

[19]Kansas Joint Council Minutes, March 10, 11, 1898, p. 3.

[20]Noah Zook, "On Our Mission," *Visitor*, X (April 15, 1897), 122.

[21]Detwiler, "Reminiscences."

[22]Peter Stover, "Blessed are the Peacemakers," *Visitor*, XVII (January 1, 1903), 10.

[23]See also Detwiler, "Reminiscences."

[24]Jacob N. Martin to Bro. Sider, March 1, 1924; Monroe Dourte, cited by Owen Alderfer, "Mind of the Brethren," p. 137.

[25]Mary Zook to [Sider], Asa W. Climenhaga Papers.

[26]J. W. Hoover, "Evangelistic Work," *Visitor*, III (February 1, 1890), 43, 48.

[27]F. Elliott, "Revival Meetings," *Visitor*, XXI (January 1, 1907), 7.

[28]*General Conference Minutes*, 1903, Article 18, pp. 13-14.

[29]A long-standing tradition that Asa Bearss of the Black Creek District pioneered the first Brethren Sunday School in 1863 is incorrect, for he did not join the brotherhood until 1867. Carlton O. Wittlinger, "The Sunday School Movement in the Brethren in Christ Church in the Nineteenth Century," *Notes and Queries*, III (April-June, 1962), 8-9; Nancy Bearss obituary, *Visitor*, XXXII (August 26, 1918), 21.

[30]*Church Government*, 1881, pp. 14-15.

[31]Anthony Stoner, "I Am So Glad," *Visitor*, IV (February 1, 1891), 35-36.

[32]A Friend of S. S., "Sunday Schools — Their Influence," *Visitor*, III (February 1, 1890), 45.

[33]Enos H. Hess, "The Sunday-School," *Visitor*, XIX (March 15, 1905), 16.

[34]*Ibid.; General Conference Minutes*, 1885, Article 11; [Henry Davidson], *Visitor*, III (July 15, 1890), 216-17.

[35]A Friend of S. S., "Sunday Schools — Their Influence," *Visitor*, III (February 1, 1890), 44-45; Thomas Lewis, "Sunday Schools," *Visitor*, III (March 15, 1890), 89; [Henry Davidson], *Visitor*, III (July 15, 1890), 216-17; Charles Baker, "Sabbath Schools," *Visitor*, V (February 15, 1892), 51; Enos H. Hess, "The Sunday School," *Visitor*, XIX (March 15, 1905), 16.

[36]Bro. Zook, "On Our Mission," *Visitor*, X (February 1, 1897), 42.

[37]*General Conference Minutes*, 1885, Article 11.

[38]Enos H. Hess, "The Sunday School," *Visitor*, XIX (March 15, 1905), 2-3, 16.

[39]Geo. Detwiler, "Report of Sabbath School," *Visitor*, I (January 1, 1888), 75; John H. Engle, "Notes from Kansas," *Visitor*, I (September 1, 1888), 201; [Henry Davidson], *Visitor*, III (January 15, 1890), 24, and (July 15, 1890), 216; Sm. Whistler, *Visitor*, V (March 15, 1892), 92; L. B. Heise, "Markham, Ont.," *Visitor*, VII (June 1, 1894), 175; S. G. Engle, "An Appeal from Philadelphia, Pennsylvania," *Visitor*, IX (February 1, 1898), 57.

[40]John H. Engle, "Notes from Kansas," *Visitor*, I (September 1, 1888), 201.

[41]Geo. Detwiler, "Some Impressions," *Visitor*, VII (March 15, 1894), 87.

[42]*Visitor,* II (December 1, 1888), 46; J. D. K., "Concerning Sabbath Schools," *Visitor,* V (May 1, 1892), 131-32.

[43]Thomas Lewis, "Sunday Schools," *Visitor,* III (March 15, 1890), 89; [Henry Davidson], "Sunday School Supplies," *Visitor,* V (April 15, 1892), 120; J. Myers Bosler, "The Sabbath School," *Visitor,* XII (September 1, 1899), 327.

[44][Henry Davidson], *Visitor,* III (August 15, 1890), 249.

[45][Henry Davidson], "Sunday School Supplies," *Visitor,* V (April 15, 1892), 120.

[46]*General Conference Minutes,* 1903, Article 19, p. 13; *ibid.,* 1907, Article 16, p. 11.

[47]For the objectives of this column see [George Detwiler], *Visitor,* XX (March 1, 1906), 2; J. H. Engle, "The Sunday School," *Visitor,* XX (March 1, 1906), 11.

[48]*General Conference Minutes,* 1908, Article 39, p. 25.

[49]*Ibid.,* 1909, Article 21, pp. 38-40.

[50]Geo. Detweiler [*sic*], "Report of Sabbath-School," *Visitor,* I (January 1, 1888), 75; J. D. K., "Concerning Sabbath Schools, *Visitor,* V (May 1, 1892), 131; L. B. Heise, "Markham, Ont." *Visitor,* VII (June 1, 1894), 175.

[51]L. B. Heise, "Markham, Ont." *Visitor,* VII (June 1, 1894), 175.

[52]Geo. Detweiler [*sic*], "Report of Sabbath-School," *Visitor,* I (January 1, 1888), 75.

[53]S. G. Engle, "An Appeal from Philadelphia, Pennsylvania," *Visitor,* I (February 1, 1898), 57.

[54]*General Conference Minutes,* 1914, Article 34, p. 61.

[55]Upland Church Council Minutes, March 11, 1905, Article 5, p. 4; *ibid.,* March 20, 1906, Article 2, p. 7; *ibid.,* March 19, 1907, Article 5, p. 10.

[56]"The Dangers of Child Exhibition," *Visitor,* XX (June 15, 1906), 7.

[57][Henry Davidson], *Visitor,* XX (June 15, 1906), 2.

[58]J. Myers Bosler, "The Sabbath School," *Visitor,* XII (September 1, 1899), 327.

[59][Henry Davidson], *Visitor,* VI (April 1, 1893), 105.

[60]*Ibid.,* VII (April 1, 1894), 104.

[61]*Ibid.*

[62]*General Conference Minutes,* 1917, Article 20, p. 63.

[63]*Ibid.,* 1911, pp. 3-5.

[64]*Ibid.,* 1909, Article 36, p. 48.

[65]*Ibid.,* Article 37, pp. 48-49.

[66]*Ibid.,* 1910, Article 6, p. 10; *ibid.,* 1915, Article 13, p. 55.

[67]No publication data given.

[68]John H. Engle became an active leader in the interdenominational Sunday-school movement.

[69]*Visitor,* XX (June 1, 1906), 11, 16. Editor Detwiler identifies John H. Engle as the author of this address.

[70]Brethren missions and the impact of Wesleyan holiness accentuated the changes discussed in this section.

[71][George Detwiler], *Visitor,* XXVIII (November 30, 1914), 2-3; *ibid.,* XXVIII (December 28, 1914), 4-5; *ibid.,* XXIX (February 22, 1915), 4; North Dickinson District Council Minutes, September 20, 1892, Article 5. Martin Schrag, "Brethren Attitude Toward the World," p. 203, describes the interdenominational Sunday-school activities of some of the Kansas brethren.

[72][Henry Davidson], "Sunday School Supplies," *Visitor,* V (April 15, 1892), 120.

[73]*Church Government,* 1881, p. 6.

[74]*What We Believe,* 1906.

[75]J. R. Zook, "The Work and Responsibility of a Minister," *Visitor,* XXIII (June 15, 1909), 6-7.

[76]See the section "Effects of Missions" in Chapter IX for additional information about the preaching emphases of John and Noah Zook.

[77][George Detwiler], "Dangers That Christians Need to Guard Against," *Visitor,* XXIX (March 8, 1915), 3.

[78]*Canadian Joint Council Minutes,* September 13, 1906, Resolution B, p. 18.

[79]Charles Baker, "Thoughts on How Our Youth May Be Won for the Church," *Visitor,* XXV (February 20, 1911), 7.

[80]George Detwiler, "A Brief Biographical Statement," Asa W. Climenhaga Papers.

[81]Henry K. Kreider, as told to E. J. Swalm. E. J. Swalm interview, July 15, 1972.

[82]No publication data given.

[83]I. W. Musser and John A. Climenhaga cited by Schrag, "Brethren Attitude Toward the World," pp. 224-25.

[84]Iva C. Herr, *Gleanings from the Christian Life of One made Perfect in Love,* . . . (Dayton, Ohio: Bethel Publishing Company, n.d.), p. 12.

[85]J. W. Hoover, "Evangelists Work," *Visitor,* III (February 1, 1890), 43.

[86]Aaron Bechtel, "Meetings at Valley Chapel, Ohio," *Visitor,* XVII (March 2, 1903), 12.

[87]L. M. Pyke, "From A Young Sister," *Visitor,* I (April 1, 1888), 126; Annie J. Stoner, "From a Young Sister," *Visitor,* I (May 1, 1888), 143; "Children's Testimonies" *Visitor,* XX (October 15, 1906), 11.

[88]Lela Cassel, "Children's Testimonies," *Visitor,* XX (October 15, 1906), 11.

[89]F. Elliott, "A Series of Meetings," *Visitor,* III (March 1, 1890), 74.

[90]Rapho District Council Minutes, February 10, 1916, p. 121.

[91]"What Can We Do to Make the Sunday-School Hour Brighter," *Visitor,* XXII (May 1, 1908), 7.

[92]Saltzman, "Music Among the Brethren," p. 246.

[93]*Spiritual Hymns of Brethren in Christ. Compiled, Published, and Edited By The Hymnal Committee, Appointed by General Conference of 1906 of the Brethren in Christ,* (n.p., n.d.) This hymnal was actually released to the church in 1909.

[94]Saltzman, "Music Among the Brethren," p. 168.

[95]*Ibid.,* p. 168. Saltzman, commenting on such selections, writes: "The texts are doggerel and the tunes paltry."

[96]*Spiritual Hymns,* 1906, Nos. 208, 181, and 186.

[97]S. R. Smith, "The Hymn Book Question," *Visitor,* XV (May 15, 1901), 183.

[98]F. Elliott, "Hymn Books and Singing," *Visitor,* XIV (April 15, 1901), 159.

[99]S. R. Smith, "Church Hymnal Committee Notice," *Visitor,* XXII (March 2, 1908), 3.

[100]Catherine Cleverstone, "A Sister's Concern for the Church," *Visitor,* XXII (March 2, 1908), 9.

[101]Saltzman, "Music Among the Brethren," p. 170.

[102]*Ibid.,* p. 166.

[103]*Ibid.,* p. 168.

[104]Anthony Stoner, "I Am So Glad," *Visitor,* IV (February 1, 1891), 36; S. C. Heisey, *Visitor,* IV (February 15, 1891), 60; Jacob E. Stauffer, "Sanctification," *Visitor,* I (March 1, 1888), 105; E. J. Swalm to C. O. Wittlinger, June 14, 1973.

[105]E. J. Swalm to C. O. Wittlinger, June 14, 1973.

[106]Charles Baker, as told to E. J. Swalm. E. J. Swalm to C. O. Wittlinger, June 14, 1973.

[107]Some of these spittoons are in the Church Archives.

[108]Abram M. Hess Diary, November 27, 1873.

[109]E. J. Swalm to C. O. Wittlinger, June 14, 1973; Amos D. M. Dick interview, May 24, 1977.

[110]Markham District Council Minutes, January 30, 1885, Article 10.

[111]*Ibid.*, January 29, 1909, Article 10.

[112]Kansas Joint Council Minutes, March 17, 1888, Article 8.

[113]T. A. Long, "South Western Ohio," *Visitor,* I (January 1, 1888), 73.

[114]*Church Government,* 1887, p. 8.

[115]*Ibid.*, p. 15.

[116]I Cor. 8:13.

[117]*General Council Minutes,* 1881, Article 7.

[118]See the section on "Government and Politics" in Chapter VI. The Kansas Brethren became especially active in the prohibition movement and, in 1917, named two trustees to serve in the Anti-Saloon League of Kansas. *Kansas Joint Council Minutes,* 1917, Article 18.

XI

Awakening Interest
In Wesleyan Holiness

Early Wesleyan Influences

The Wesleyan doctrine of Christian perfection or entire santification as an experience of the Christian life entered into subsequent to regeneration, began to influence the Brethren in Christ in the latter part of the nineteenth century. While its most conspicuous impact was made upon the Kansas churches in the 1890s, there is evidence of its presence within the brotherhood prior to that time.

The growing openness of the Brethren to evangelical Protestantism facilitated contacts with other societies emphasizing sanctification as a second work of grace. These contacts created a context within which members of the brotherhood could evaluate that doctrine as interpreted by the American Holiness Movement. Such societies included the Free Methodists, the Salvation Army, the Hepzibah Faith Missionary Association and others.[1]

Traces of perfectionism appeared in the literature of the brotherhood in the 1870s and 1880s.[2] Their 1874 hymnal included fifty hymns by Charles Wesley.[3] Most of these dealt with familiar Brethren themes—repentance, surrender, the new birth, heaven, and others—but a few had perfectionist overtones. One example, "Perfect Heart the Redeemers Throne," concludes with the following stanzas:

> A heart in every thought renew'd
>   And full of love divine;
> Perfect, and right, and pure, and good,
>   A copy, Lord, of thine.

227

> Thy holy nature, Lord, impart;
> Come quickly from above,
> Write thy new name upon my heart,
> Thy new, best name of love.[4]

The Brethren evidently perceived such hymn texts to be compatible with their understanding that regeneration and sanctification occurred simultaneously in the conversion experience. Until their encounter with spokesmen of the American Holiness Movement, they could sing a hymn of this type without an awareness that the sentiments of the text offered a potential challenge to their historic faith.

Like early Brethren hymnody, the *Evangelical Visitor* included material originating in Wesleyan circles. In 1887, the paper's first year, Editor Henry Davidson published Wesley's definition of Christian perfection:

"By Christian perfection, I mean (1) loving God with all your heart. Do you object to this? I mean (2) a heart and life devoted to God. Do you desire less? I mean (3) regaining the whole image of God. What objection to this? I mean (4) having all the mind that was in Christ. Is this going too far? I mean (5) walking uniformly as Christ walked. And this surely no Christian will object to. If any one means anything more or anything else by perfection, I have no concern about it."[5]

Although perfectionism was becoming an issue among the Brethren by that time, Davidson never became a vocal supporter of it. It is unlikely that either he or his readers perceived anything innovative in Wesley's sentiments.

Considerable additional material in the early *Visitor* originated with holiness writers and holiness periodicals.[6] While not all of these articles dealt specifically with perfectionism, they suggest some awareness of literature originating in holiness circles.

A letter by a midwestern minister, Lewis W. Shaeffer, reveals that by the late 1870s an occasional individual was becoming aware of the implications of the doctrine of Wesleyan holiness. Shaeffer concurred with the traditional Brethren view that sanctification began in justification, but held that it consummated later at a specific time. He explained his position to a young convert:

Yes, to be Sanctified, is to be cleansed and set apart for Holy and divine purposes, But we must be Justified before we are Sanctified, for, we are

Justified by faith in the Son of God, and then we are cleansed by being washed by his Blood, so then we are Sanctified allready [sic] in degree, But not Holy Sanctified, untill [sic] we are with Paul, crusified [sic] unto the world, and the world unto us.[7]

One example of a holiness-type Christian experience dates back to the mid-1850s. The person was Elizabeth Lukenbach, daughter of Bishop Levi Lukenbach. Her experience, as reported by her son, was as follows:

In 1855, before my mother was married . . . while she and her parents were living in Center County, Penna., following her baptism the congregation had returned to the place of service where dinner was to be served, when my mother got blessed, began praising the Lord, and testifying in such a way that even though the call to dinner had been made, the folks did not respond and go to the tables. Complaint was made to him as Bishop [Levi Lukenbach] because the meal was being delayed, and request made that he tell his daughter to be quiet. He responded by saying, "Let her go, she just got the Holy Ghost." About the year 1905 or 1906, when many were being sanctified at the Highland Church in Miami County, Ohio, I heard my mother say that these experiences were just like hers back there in Pennsylvania when she was baptized.[8]

The data presented in this section suggest that perfectionist influences, although not entirely absent from Brethren circles before the late 1880s, had made little impact upon the brotherhood as a whole. Beginning in 1886, however, the group became increasingly aware of the implications of the doctrine of sanctification as understood and promoted by the American Holiness Movement.[9]

Factors Predisposing the Brethren to Respond Favorably to Perfectionism

Several factors combined to prepare many Brethren to respond favorably to the new holiness message. One was their historic pietistic emphasis upon Christian experience involving a heartfelt conversion or new birth. To an experientially oriented people, the idea of advancing in the Christian life by sanctification as a second spiritual crisis was not as difficult to comprehend as it would have been for others nurtured in less experiential religious traditions.

A second factor making the holiness message attractive was the

Brethren goal of perfecting obedience in their daily walk; in attitude and life-style, they sought to conform as closely as possible to Christ's teaching and example. Many of them, however, apparently strove to practice obedience as defined by brotherhood expectations without achieving a satisfying sense of success and spiritual fulfillment. What they perceived themselves to be fell far short of the Christ-like ideal which they sought to attain.[10]

To these individuals borne down by a sense of defeat, the message that perfection was not achieved through a gradual process accompanied by an unfulfilled spiritual yearning came as a welcome relief. The offer of instantaneous sanctification promising immediate heart perfection, spiritual fullfiment, and the empowerment of the Spirit for full obedience spoke to some deep need of many in the brotherhood.

A third factor attracting the Brethren to perfectionism was the nonconformity theme running through the American Holiness Movement. The Hepzibah Faith Missionary Association, for example, through which second-work holiness came to the Kansas Brethren, stated its opposition to secret orders, oath-bound obligations, pride in dress and declared: "We have NO COMPROMISE to make with the devil on any line but expect to cry out against sin."[11] Noah Zook, who visited the headquarters of this group at Tabor, Iowa, reported them to be:

> . . . a very plain, self denying people, both as to their way of living and also to their dress, discarding all useless ornaments and evil habits. But above all they seem to have much of the true spirit of humility and are powerful in prayer. . . . May the Lord bless these dear people in the work of the Lord. May they ever be led by the Holy Spirit is our humble prayer.[12]

This awareness that many holiness people shared important aspects of their nonconformist views made the Brethren more open and sympathetic to the message of perfectionism.

These factors, which helped to prepare many Brethren for the second-work holiness message, did not prepare all. Perfectionism, in fact, became highly controversial with strong, respected leaders taking opposite sides. This raises the question as to whether most Brethren lived in a state of spiritual frustration before the brotherhood became aware of the concept of second-work sanctification.

While some undoubtedly did experience a spiritual need, the evidence suggests that others found a satisfying experience of the so-called "deeper

Christian life" through their historic understanding of salvation—sanctification beginning simultaneously with regeneration[13] and continuing thereafter as a process. A perceptive traveler from Kansas to Pennsylvania in 1907 noted a number of significant changes, including holiness, transforming the brotherhood and wrote:

> The fact that clearer light is shining on our pathway casts no reflection upon our fathers. They lived as clean lives as we do, perhaps cleaner, although they did not grapple with the same doctrinal questions as we do now, or at least not in the same way. Each generation has its own problems to solve.[14]

The 1887 General Conference Article on Sanctification

In 1886 the doctrine of sanctification suddenly became a General Conference issue. Why it did so at precisely that time is unknown. Evidently there was need to clarify the doctrinal position of the brotherhood, for General Conference appointed a committee of five "to set forth the sentiment of the church on sanctification."[15] The next Conference approved a lengthy report from the committee, which was later published under the title "Sanctification."[16]

This article stops far short of full endorsement of perfectionism as a second definite work of grace, but it has identifiable Wesleyan overtones. In the following passage the beginning of sanctification is linked with justification in the traditional Brethren way:

> . . . holiness is essential to our admission into heaven; so we conclude that a measure of holiness must accompany justification, or the simply justified person will fail of heaven. . . . This we deem sufficient to show the beginning of sanctification.

The article further holds that converts differ widely in the degree of sanctification experienced at the time of justification:

> There is perhaps as much difference in young converts, as in new born babes. Some are born into vigorous life, others have but a feeble existence. But all are born, hence have a being. This difference results not from their justification, for all are equally justified, that is, their sins are all forgiven, but from the measure of sanctification they obtain with justification, and this is commensurate with the degree of consciousness of their fallen, sinful state, their hatred of sin and consecration to God.

On these premises the completion of sanctification at the time of justification is theoretically possible, but the article assumes it to be improbable and places strong emphasis upon a later awakening to a spiritual need unknown at the time of conversion:

> That sanctification is rarely completed with conversion is a common experience. The great body of justified persons do not claim to be wholly sanctified; they still feel a proneness to sin. . . .[17]
>
> In the ardor of our first love, these remains of "inbred sin" are in the background, but afterwards make themselves felt again. Nothing is more common in an experience meeting than to hear an experience of this kind: "When I was converted I thought that I was entirely delivered; but since, I have discovered that . . . I am still inclined to the things of the world and have sharp contentions with the flesh."
>
> We hear more of shortcoming than of progress in the divine life. Among the saints it was not so.

The article then cites Job, David, Paul, Peter, and John on the experiences of the saints whose lives demonstrated spiritual victory and obedience. It asserts that believers whose spiritual state differs from that of the saints are either backslidden in heart or lacking "something" which they never had.

The something lacking is sanctification in its fullness. To prove this the article cites a series of New Testament passages interpreted as descriptions of persons regenerated but not wholly sanctified.[18] On the basis of this distinction, the text generalizes: "Sanctification, in its fulness, is the completion of a process begun in regeneration and may be completed as soon as a clear knowledge of its necessity is obtained and a perfect consecration effected."[19]

This passage marks a break with the earlier understanding of the Brethren that sanctification occurred simultaneously with justification and continued thereafter as "a deeper work of grace." After 1887 they officially held that sanctification could and should be completed as soon as the conditions of "clear knowledge" and "perfect consecration" were met.

The article then explains that both man and God have something to do with the consummation of entire sanctification. It affirms that:

> Man's part consists in consecration, in submitting his will to the will of God, in resisting the devil, striving against sin, rendering obedience to God, exercising a living faith, praying fervently and trusting. All this can only be

performed through God's help. To God belongs the cleansing, liberating, dedicating, and out-pouring of the Spirit and sealing, . . .

Man's part in the acquisition of holiness "is generally gradual, not necessarily prolonged; . . ." God's part, the application of the atoning blood of Christ, is instantaneous. Finally, the article summarizes the results of being "wholly sanctified" under two headings as follows:

> 1st. What it does not do: It does not materially effect [sic] the knowledge or judgment of the individual. It does not remove the infirmities that cling to the flesh. It does not eradicate the passions, but restores them to their lawful uses. It does not exempt from temptation, nor from apostacy [sic]. It does not bring absolute perfection, neither angelic nor Adamic.
>
> 2d. What it does: Its effects are not mainly in the outer life; as conversion changes the whole tenor of the life, and produces a pure morality. It mainly affects the inner life: The entire man must become submissive to the will of God, hence it produces true humility. It perfects the love of God in the soul.[20]

This 1887 article on sanctification moved the Brethren in the direction of perfectionism. In some respects its position was closer to original Wesleyanism than to the American Holiness Movement which stressed a second definite work of grace so sharply as to neglect emphasis on process in sanctification. The Brethren attention to process, for example, accorded with the Wesleyan principle that "It [sanctification] is constantly both preceded and followed by a gradual work."[21]

The official shift of General Conference toward moderate accommodation to perfectionism was in advance of the thought and experience of members at the grassroots level. *Visitor* testimonies rarely sound a Wesleyan note for several years following 1887, and articles generally expound the traditional Brethren view of sanctification.[22]

On the other hand, the leaven of perfectionism was at work. This is illustrated by an incident related by Moses Dohner about his grandfather, Levi Lukenbach. Dohner wrote:

> When I was a lad, about the year 1887, I recall him sitting in repose on the porch, while five young sisters were seated on the edge of the porch nearby discussing the subject of sanctification. Finally they turned to him and one of the number . . . asked if such an experience is possible for us today. With a smile, in his gentle but very positive manner, he replied: "Ja, von mier glay genung sin." ("Yes, when we are little enough.").[23]

Occasional *Visitor* articles like the following also reveal a moderate perfectionism:

> It is an evident fact that we cannot serve him in holiness unless we are holy, and we cannot possibly be holy unless we are sanctified, and we cannot be sanctified unless we are justified, all in its proper order. But one may ask, how long must I be justified until I can be sanctified? That depends upon the surroundings and teachings. It may be so closely connected that we are hardly able to make a point and yet, there may be a period between. But a person cannot stand very long in justification without sanctification.[24]

In summary, elements of Wesleyan perfectionsim began to penetrate the theology of the Brethren in the latter part of the 1880s. The 1887 General Conference article on sanctification was a moderate accommodation to perfectionism. It had some earmarks of original Wesleyanism, suggesting that it was influenced by John Wesley's *Plain Account of Christian Perfection*.

This Conference statement of 1887 was sufficiently broad to allow for different interpretations of sanctification in Christian experience. It therefore provided a framework within which traditional Brethren theology could coexist with newer theology incorporating varying degrees of perfectionist thought.

Second-work Holiness Among the Kansas Brethren

By 1910 the Kansas Brethren found themselves in circumstances which eventually helped to pave the way for a major shift in the General Conference position on sanctification as formulated in 1887. These resulted from strong influences exerted by some of the radical holiness societies active in Kansas in the 1890s and the following decade.

Articles in the *Visitor* reveal that teaching stressing the principle of sanctification as a second definite work of grace was circulating in Brethren communities in Kansas by the early 1890s.[25] In 1892 an article presented the disciples of Christ as converted men awaiting "the 'second blessing'—the Pentecostal experience which should come to them in fifty days."[26] Its author took an uncompromising stand for a more radical holiness position than the Brethren had embraced in 1887. He wrote: "Every Christian ought to have a day of conversion and a day of sanctification as clearly and definitely as a day of birth and a day of marriage."[27]

This author did not use the expression "second definite work of grace," but it clearly represented his position. He thus foreshadowed the issue around which one of the most divisive controversies in Brethren history developed. Missing from his presentation was any reference to the 1887 view that sanctification began in justification, that a process ensued between justification and entire sanctification, and that there was no one stereotyped pattern of experience by which believers reached the position of the "wholly sanctified."

The Kansas Brethren probably did not widely hold sharply defined second-work views as early as 1892. Two years later, however, holiness doctrine was causing them sufficient concern to make it an issue in a district council which admonished its members as follows: "Since the Doctrine of Holiness is at par with all other vital gospel doctrines, it should be both preached, believed, and enjoyed: but brethren should be careful not to be carried away by one special doctrinal question, however weighty."[28] Within a few years this special doctrinal question forced itself to the forefront in the life of the Kansas brotherhood.

One of the first dramatic manifestations of the new movement occurred in 1895 at the Bethel Church near Detroit, Kansas. An eyewitness, Katie Bollinger, concluded that "there was definitely a moving of the Spirit of God among the church at Bethel." She continued:

> As for myself, my hunger for God was inexpressible. . . . As I stood to my feet and tried to give expression, I saw God's great hands. There He was, He was holding in His right hand a pitcher of water, in the other hand He held a funnel, and from this pitcher he was pouring water into this funnel. The water overflowed and all came down on me. . . . I fell helplessly backward and I shouted the praises of God. No one present had ever witnessed such a scene. I myself did not understand what had happened.[29]

Another member of the Bethel congregation soon gave a similar testimony, but such experiences lacked theological definition. Mrs. Bollinger stated that the term "second work of grace" was not yet in use among the Bethel people. She recalled someone referring to the experience by saying, "Now this person has 'that' too."[30]

The following year the new holiness emphasis made a strong impact upon the Zion Church near Bethel. This was due to the influence of David

W. Zook, son of Noah Zook, who had recently spent considerable time among people of the Hepzibah Faith Missionary Association at Tabor, Iowa.

The Hepzibah group stressed "thorough and evangelical repentance, and faith in the Lord for the remission of sins and in the definite work of sanctification and baptism of the Holy Ghost."[31] Their statement of faith read: "We believe in SANCTIFICATION as a definite work of grace. That means a REAL DEATH to CARNALITY."[32]

David Zook evidently became aware of the Hepzibah group through his father who, in the course of his evangelistic campaigning, met Leonard B. Worcester, one of their principal leaders.[33] During his time at Tabor, the younger Zook married a non-Brethren in Christ.[34] Later, the young couple, brimming with enthusiasm for evangelism, missions, and holiness, volunteered for faith mission work in India under the general auspices of the Hepzibah Association. En route to their assignment, they stopped for ten days in Kansas with Zook's parents, and the son had an opportunity to hold meetings in the Zion Church.[35] According to his report, many responded enthusiastically to the holiness message. He wrote:

> While there [at the Zion Church] the Lord wonderfully manifested his power. Many were convicted of their need of the second definite work of grace in our hearts. Many were at the altar and sought to have everything taken away that would hinder them in receiving the baptism of the Holy Ghost. . . . Praise the name of our God forever![36]

This is the first known instance of the use of the expression "second definite work of grace" within the context of a Brethren service.[37] Concerning the Zion meeting, David Zook's brother, Eber, wrote: "Truths were brought into prominence that were scarcely ever alluded to by our ministry, viz., entire sanctification, cleansing from the carnal nature, consecration without any reserve, . . ."[38] These "Truths" expressed the meaning of sanctification as a second definite work of grace.

David Zook was only one of a number of Brethren young people who went to Tabor, Iowa, for fellowship and study with the Hepzibath Faith Missionary Association. Those from Kansas included Jeremiah Long and his sister; G. Clifford Cress and Sara Zook Cress; Eber Zook and Amanda Witter Zook; and Rhoda Zook.[39] Other young people went to Tabor from as far away as Pennsylvania. About 1898 Josiah Martin of Elizabethtown and Eliab Wenger of Chambersburg were there.[40] In addition to these young people, Jacob M. Zook and wife of Kansas had charge of the Tabor orphanage work for a time, and Emma Herr, also of Kansas, taught in the Tabor school program from 1902-1929.[41] Some of these individuals eventually resigned their memberships with the Brethren, but the group as a whole became a channel through which the doctrine of sanctification as a second definite work of grace flowed into Brethren life, especially in Kansas.

This holiness influence increased through interaction between ministers of the Kansas Brethren and Tabor leaders. Noah Zook, Daniel D. Steckley, and Samuel Zook, all Kansas ministers, visited Tabor.[42]

Tabor ministers also visited and preached among the Brethren. George Weaver (also Weavers), founder of the Hepzibah Faith Missionary Association, preached not only in Kansas but in Brethren services as far east as Pennsylvania. At the Messiah Home a Pennsylvania minister, John Myers, without hesitation or formal introduction, greeted him with the holy kiss.[43] After Weaver preached at the Philadelphia Mission, a hearer wrote:

"I think it was the best sermon I ever heard. It is a green spot to which I expect to return from time to time for pasture and be satisfied. The Holy Ghost is working out His own way with many of our people. I am so glad that we are getting away from a religion that burdens our lives, and causes continual lameness."[44]

It is clear that George Weaver, strong advocate of second-work holiness, made a favorable impression upon many Brethren.

Weaver's close associate, Leonard Worcester, spontaneously joined in a Noah Zook tent campaign at Junction City, Iowa, in 1894. Worcester reported the effects of his own preaching as follows: "'Some leaped, some shouted, some wept, some laughed, others danced for joy'."[45] Zook observed: "This man and his wife seemed to be filled with the Holy Spirit,...."[46]

Several years later Worcester held meetings in various Brethren churches in Kansas prior to his departure for mission work in Japan. When he left for that country, Brethren member Jeremiah Long accompanied him, having declined an invitation to become the second man in the Jesse Engle mission party.[47] Some Kansas Brethren held Worcester in high esteem, as revealed by an incident when he was en route to the West Coast on an earlier mission trip to Japan. Worcester reported that he spent a profitable day visiting two Brethren in Christ ministers and added: "They bid us God-speed on our mission.... As we separated several of the brethren gave us the holy kiss."[48]

Communication through the printed page supplemented these personal contacts between the Tabor people and the Brethren. *Sent of God*, a Hepzibah paper, found its way into Brethren homes, and some of its articles appeared as reprints in the *Visitor*.[49]

The Hepzibah Faith Missionary Association played the predominant role in introducing the Kansas Brethren to sanctification as a second definite work of grace, but another Kansas holiness society also had considerable influence upon them. That group, variously known as the "Iowa Fire-Baptized Holiness Association," "Fire Brand," and "World's Missionary Association," had its headquarters at Shenandoah, Iowa.[50] Benjamin H. Irwin, a leading spokesman for the group, held meetings among the Brethren at Bethel, Zion, Abilene, and Belle Springs testifying to the "definite experiences of baptism by the Holy Ghost and Fire."[51] Clifford and Sara Cress, who became missionaries to Africa, professed sanctification in Irwin's meetings.[52] Early the next year Irwin was in Chambersburg, Pennsylvania, preaching sanctification. Although only a few Franklin County Brethren went to hear him, some of them responded enthusiastically to his message.[53]

Holiness as preached by the ministers of the Fire Baptized Holiness Association included a so-called "fire baptism," a work of grace subsequent to second-work sanctification and baptism with the Holy Spirit. Exponents of this position defended it on the basis of the statement of John the Baptist: "... he shall baptize you with the Holy Ghost, and with fire."[54]

Henry Engle, second editor of the *Visitor*, who fought a running battle with the fire-baptism enthusiasts, recorded the following impression of the experiential phenomenon in question:

> Fire baptism is nowhere in the Word defined to be a burning sensation in the system, or the seeing, literally, of a white, fiery flame; and, yet more, this distinct and apart from the baptism of the Holy Ghost. That individuals have had these manifestiations and demonstrations in the flesh, we have no reason to doubt. . . . But when it goes to insisting, as some do, that individuals shall seek after these *manifestations* and that *such a sensation only* is *the* baptism of fire referred to in the Gospels, we feel to take our place definitely as against a movement which will lead into the dire fanaticism.[55]

The efforts of Editor Engle and other Brethren leaders in the Midwest, including John Zook of Iowa, to counteract the fire-baptism movement did not prevent it from producing a stir among the Kansas Brethren.[56] Added to the emotional but relatively more stable holiness message of the Hepzibah movement, it created the image of Kansas "wildfire" which aroused anxiety and opposition to holiness in other areas of the brotherhood.[57] One *Visitor* correspondent wrote: "'It makes my heart sad to see the Kansas people running after this wild fanaticism.'"[58] Another noted: "'Who would have ever thought that our own beloved people would run into such excentricities [sic]?'"[59]

The agitation of the fire-baptism movement came dramatically to the foreground in the summer of 1899. Editor Engle reported with "sadness of heart" a week's meeting of the Fire Baptized Association in Dickinson County. Benjamin Irwin and associate G. M. Henson shared with others in leadership of the service. Engle described the tumultuous climax of the meeting:

> The preaching was to a great extent made up of hard sayings against other churches and especially against the Brethren. The proceedings so aroused the community that the meeting was finally broken up by a mob, cutting down the tent in which the meeting was held, . . . The scene is said by those who saw it to have been of the most disgraceful nature . . . we certainly are not in sympathy with such unlawful proceedings. B. H. Irwin had left the day previous, which [sic] was the man the mob was looking for, and not finding him they took Henson, the next leader, and violently threw him into a water tank close by, which was repeated several times.[60]

The serious difficulties encountered by the Kansas Brethren as they were confronted by the holiness messages of the Hepzibah Faith Missionary Association and the Fire Baptized Holiness Association did not cause them to reject the basic concept of entire sanctification as an experience subsequent to justification.

Not all members, of course, who accepted this doctrine yielded to the extremism which often surrounded its presentation. Noah Zook, who moved among all kinds of holiness people and became a leading holiness spokesman, seems to have held himself aloof from most of the eccentricities, arrogance, and radical positions characteristic of many holiness enthusiasts. Again, as noted above, Henry Engle strove to defend his view of the biblical truth of the holiness position from the extremism of many of its advocates.[61]

The efforts of these and other stable, discriminating leaders such as Bishop Samuel Zook, helped the Kansas Brethren survive the turmoil and

membership losses brought about by their exposure to the radical phase of
the perfectionist movement. The stresses which they experienced, however,
were heavy. Henry Davidson was perplexed by the situation. Near the
close of his *Visitor* editorship, he surveyed the Kansas scene from his
editorial office in Abilene and penned the following thoughts: "We are well
aware that there is just now an apparent breaking away from the old
landmarks, and the introduction of something new. Whether these things
will tend to glorify God, we do not know."[62]

By the turn of the century, the main sweep of the radical holiness crisis
in Kansas had passed. George Detwiler, who went from Canada to Abilene
to work in the office of the *Visitor,* reported his positive impressions of the
spirit of Kansas Joint Council of 1900. "Considering the very critical
situation which has prevailed in the State for the last few years we could
not but rejoice for the charity and evident good feeling existing, and we are
persuaded that, while the defection which has taken place and which is
certainly much to be regretted, is keenly felt, yet the church looks forward
hopefully . . . that the broken ranks may be closed up again, and that she
may again go forth to victory."[63]

Second-work holiness doctrine spread from Kansas into other parts of
the brotherhood. The extremism and "wild-fire" which had been so
disruptive in that state were largely confined to the Midwest, but they
tended to arouse prejudice against perfectionism elsewhere.[64]

Printed page and spoken word combined to promote the new holiness
emphasis. When Henry Engle assumed the editorship of the *Visitor* in
1896, he converted the paper into a holiness journal.[65] Noah Zook, one of
the most active and widely-traveled of the holiness evangelists, preached
the message wherever he had opportunity. His widow wrote: "Husband
was specially called to stir up the church on the line of Holiness . . . ."[66]

John Zook, who also preached the doctrine widely and promoted it
through the *Visitor,* published a paperback exposition of it under the title,
*Holiness and Empowerment Both Defined: How to Obtain Them, How to
Retain Them.* Although avoiding the expression "second definite work of
grace," Zook's pamphlet endorsed the essence of that concept. The
preface states: "I launch this treatise in the name of Jesus, believing it will
prove a help and blessing to many a soul who is seeking the experience of
Holiness and the anointing of the Holy Spirit; . . ."[67] That his primary
concern was for a second definite work is clear from the following passage:

Entire sanctification and power is [*sic*] INSTANTANEOUS. It came "suddenly" on the one hundred and twenty on the day of Pentecost, and on the young converts of Samaria, who were saved by faith and baptized by Philip, and received the laying on of hands by the Apostles, Peter and John. It also came suddenly on Cornelius while Peter was preaching. Our part of the work may be slow and gradual, and often entirely too much so in yielding ourselves fully to God, and in exercising unfaltering faith in the promises; but the moment we have met the condition, the blessing is ours; . . .[68]

Noah and Mary Zook. The former, one of the influential early Brethren in Christ evangelists, preached the message of second-work sanctification throughout the brotherhood.

Another holiness evangelist, Daniel Steckley, carried the message of entire sanctification to Canada. Steckley, who had been raised near Gormley, Ontario, later moved to Ramona, Kansas, where he became a

convert to the second-work holiness position.[69] When he returned to
Gormley for General Conference of 1898, he remained there to conduct a
series of holiness meetings. A hearer wrote:

> O, I thank God that the church is being awakened to see where they are
> standing. There are a great many of the Brethren and Sisters reaching out
> for the baptism of the Holy Ghost, which they acknowledge that they have
> not in possession. But Praise the Lord! There are a number that have
> received the Holy Ghost and others are getting the light.[70]

Various other evangelists shared in the holiness ministry. Among them
were Joseph Leaman of California and John Myers of Pennsylvania.[71] As
previously noted, non-Brethren holiness preachers such as George Weaver
and Benjamin Irwin also ministered in Brethren services.

By the early twentieth century, converts to second-work perfectionism
were scattered throughout the brotherhood. Many Brethren, however,
were cautious about accepting the holiness message and others were
openly critical of the second-work doctrine. Pennsylvania offered considerable resistance to it, although here and there individuals testified to
holiness experiences.[72]

The 1910 Redefinition of Sanctification

For several reasons second-work holiness teaching was highly controversial among the Brethren. It marked a radical departure from their
previous biblical understanding of sanctification begun simultaneously
with regeneration. It also went significantly beyond the moderate and
broad statement on sanctification approved by General Conference in
1887. As a result, many conscientious members perceived the second-work
position as basically unscriptural. The perplexities and reservations of the
anti-perfectionists stand out in expressions such as the following:

> There is a holiness taught which sets up a certain experience as an end rather
> than a beginning to an end. It has the spirit of intolerance in it. You must
> come just "that way" or you will be a subject for prayer . . . . This kind leads
> to fanaticism. It leads to ignoring the plain manifestations of self.[73]

> . . . when the transgressor is enlightened and comes as a penitent sinner to
> God, he has his actual, committed sins blotted out and is then just as free
> from sin as though he had never sinned. But the tendency to sin within us is

not taken away. Neither is it taken away by a second experience as some claim. If . . . [it] were taken away, there would be no possibility for us to sin any more.[74]

I do not understand Bro. J. R. Zook's way of printing things. It seems according to his way there must be two spirits, the one converts, and is not able to do the rest,—the other more powerful . . . [is] able to do the rest. I always thought that sanctification starts with repentance.[75]

In addition to their biblical concerns, many Brethren were repelled by the eccentricities and extremism of the holiness movement. Some perfectionists opposed the eating of pork.[76] Others conspicuously displayed holiness insignia on hats, harnesses, and buggies.[77] Still others encouraged volatile emotionalism and judged harshly those who differed with them, as illustrated by the following letter:

Dear Bro. This Fire-baptized Movement is the Pentecostal line Hallelujah which has the dynamite of God in it that shakes heaven, earth, and hell. . . . We are having glorious times out here. There are only a few in number but they are clean and purified by the precious blood of Jesus and we have shouting, dancing and singing in our camp every service and the devil is wonderfully enraged . . . . The spirit of God is driven out of the churches in the R. [River] Brethren church out here they have had the light and they separated us from their company and then and there they drove away the spirit of God and now they are the habitation of Devils and God will pronounce Judgement on the R. Brethren if they will not repent of their evil deeds.[78]

Holiness enthusiasm manifested by vocal and physical demonstrations distressed many Brethren accustomed to the serious, subdued atmosphere of their tradtional services. One critic of such enthusiasm wrote:

There is much said about sanctification which word we find in the Bible, and I am glad for it, and would not say a word against it, no never, but the way it is *practiced*. Sanctification is not noisy. A hymn speaks of holy quietness.
"O the quietness, holy quietness," etc., but often it is forgotten and things become pretty noisy.[79]

Reports of holiness enthusiasm in Kansas aroused concern as far away as Africa. Disturbed by concern for the Kansas Brethren, Jesse Engle wrote: "May they all be faithful and may they not be carried away with wild enthusiasm, but be planted calmly on the solid rock, . . ."[80]

Another aspect of the holiness movement which disturbed many Brethren was the possibility that it would exalt private religious opinion above the corporate mind of the brother. Some perfectionists concluded that Brethren distinctives such as plain clothing, conservative hair-styling, and the prayer veiling were a hindrance to the sanctified. As one of them wrote from Kansas:

> I would like to know how things are . . . now, are souls getting out in the light or are they still on the old church form. I praise God that he saved me from wearing long hair . . . parted in the middle in order to make me look humble. I praise him for heart humility and heart purity I am also delivered of caps and capes. hallelujah! . . . I am glad that we don't have to preach these things which are outward, we want to know that the heart work is done.[81]

Such sentiments were unacceptable to many Brethren who advocated holiness, as well as to many who opposed it. Mary Zook, wife of Noah Zook, herself a staunch perfectionist, sought through the *Visitor* to counteract holiness teaching which undermined respect for the Brethren position on plainness in appearance.[82] Another member who had been warned about Kansas "wild-fire" before moving there concluded that holiness could reinforce Brethren distinctives. She reported:

> We found fire among the brethren and sisters, but praise God! the Holy Spirit is connected with the fire; and these two elements, taking hold of a person, they will thoroughly cleanse and purify from all dross. We saw a great change had taken place when we were in the brethren's houses. No sham pillow-cases; no pictures for ornaments [sic] sake; no foolish talking or jesting; no tobacco; no trimming of children's clothing. That fire and spirit have made a visible mark, . . .[83]

Their questions and reservations about the holiness movement show that some Brethren perceived second-work holiness as a challenge to their faith and life-style; other perceived it as a spiritual advance. A polarization of factions for and against perfectionism was thus inevitable. In 1898 General Conference debated the question: "Is a second definite work of grace necessary for securing eternal Salvation?" The discussion revealed wide diversity of feelings, opinions, and experiences, for Conference ruled that "the different elements be kept under control by largeness of love, and much forbearance, according to Eph. 4:1, 2, 3, 31, 32."[84]

Keeping the different elements under control proved to be no easy task. The next year (1899) the sanctification question again came to Conference.

Its phrasing implies that the anti-perfectionists were endeavoring to stem the holiness tide. The minute record reads: "Is it the teaching of Christ and the Apostles, that those who have been born again, according to John 3:3 . . . [and] thus became a branch in the vine, Jn. 15:5, must seek a second definite work of Grace to be sanctified?"[85]

The question came to the floor on Wednesday afternoon and, after considerable discussion, was held over for further attention on Thursday morning. Appropriately, reading from the fourth chapter of Ephesians began this session. Then followed a lengthy discussion including presentation of "a number of views," after which Conference—unanimously, according to the minutes—decided that the statement on sanctification adopted in 1887 adequately answered the question.

It is clear from this action that the conservatives and moderates on the sanctification issue were still in the majority, but the long debate indicates that the perfectionists, who acquiesced with the final decision, were growing restless with the 1887 statement. On the other hand, those who supported the historic Brethren position were uneasy about the display of growing perfectionist influence. Within the same year, Canada Joint Council expressed this uneasiness by emphatically stating the historic position of the Brethren—the believer receives a clean heart in regeneration "When the blood of Jesus Christ is applied which cleanseth from all sin."[86]

In 1903 Kansas projected the second-work issue onto the floor of General Conference. Some Kansas perfectionists were teaching that the second work of grace fully and finally destroyed or eradicated the sin nature. This implied that entire sanctification rendered the believer incapable of sinning. The Kansas brotherhood wished to know whether ministers who taught "the doctrine of a 'Second Work' commonly known as the 'Total Eradication Doctrine'" should be tolerated.[87] Once again Conference decided that the 1887 statement on sanctification adequately covered the concerns of the petition, thus avoiding official commitment on the total eradication question.

The following year General Conference had before it another petition for a revision of the 1887 article. This was referred to a committee of seven bishops who reported that they "did not find sufficient reason for remodeling the Article of Sanctification as previously accepted and published," and their report was approved.[88] Although unwilling to change the 1887 article on sanctification, this Conference conceded a related point by recognizing scriptural authority for ministers to lay hands on Christian believers for the anointing of the Holy Ghost.[89]

After these 1904 decisions there was a five-year lull before the holiness question returned to the Conference floor. Meanwhile, second-work teaching continued to circulate in the brotherhood. This caused one of the Pennsylvania districts to petition in 1909 for a definitive official statement as to whether such teaching was entirely scriptural.[90]

Redefining the Doctrine of Sanctification

General Conference had now reached the point where it could no longer sidestep modification of the 1887 statement on sanctification. It according-ly named William Baker, John Zook, Millard G. Engle, Enos Hess, and Samuel Smith a committee to "delineate the article on Sanctification as accepted by the Church, and define the different terms and themes as taught in advocating a Second Definite Work, with scriptural qualifications." Their report set the stage for a major confrontation between the perfectionists and anti-perfectionists in the Conference of 1910.

Prior to open debate on this report, Conference granted a petition to form the bishops present into a committee to examine it.[91] This implied that the issue was too sensitive to handle in open Conference session, an inference supported by the fact that the bishops continued in private session until one o'clock in the morning.[92] When the report came from the committee of bishops, it was a lengthy article covering sixteen of the 106 pages of the Conference minutes.[93]

An examination of the document reveals that it was a compromise, which probably explains why it came to the floor claiming unanimous approval by the committee of bishops and why, subsequently, it passed the Conference as a whole without opposition. At least one bishop, Charles Baker, found it unacceptable, although he refrained from opposing or voting against it on the floor.[94]

In general the article moved the brotherhood considerably closer to the position of sanctification as a second work of grace. Advocates of that view received recognition in the following passage:

> Sanctification as obtained in justification is a cleansing away of the guilt of our committed sins and places the old man or carnal mind in the background leading up to where entire sanctification can be consummated.

> Perfect holiness or entire sanctification removes the old man, carnal mind, the principle of sin. Entire sanctification is obtained by a living appropriating faith in the atonement of our Lord Jesus Christ preceded by entire submission and consecration to the will of God.[95]

On the other hand, the article recognized the concerns of the anti-perfectionists by specifically rejecting the terminology "second definite work of grace."

> Whereas, the term "Second Definite Work of Grace" has led to the abuse of the conditions of the developments of grace resulting in a subverting of the truth to the extent of wresting God's word; therefore be it
> *Resolved,* That the term "Second definite Work" be modified and substituted by GRACE OF CLEANSING COMPLETED.

After approving the article, Conference ordered it "to be a standard of teaching on the lines of Justification, Sanctification, Holiness, etc." Although somewhat ambiguous and a partial compromise, the article tipped the balance toward the new perfectionist forces by endorsing the eradication principle, that is, the removal by entire sanctification of "the old man, carnal mind, the principle of sin."

This 1910 statement on sanctification remained the official position of the brotherhood until the 1930s. In the interim the conflict between the factions supporting and opposing the second definite work of grace concept continued, with the perfectionist forces finally gaining the ascendancy.[96]

Effects of Second-work Holiness

Second-work holiness was one of the most important of the innovations which penetrated the life of the Brethren in the late nineteenth century. Although its effects cannot be completely isolated from those of various other changes, perfectionism had a number of identifiable consequences.

In the first place, many Brethren found through the experience of second-work holiness a sense of spiritual fulfillment and dynamic which seemingly had eluded them within the context of the historic Brethren theology of sanctification. Whether their previous spiritual frustration was due to inherent limitations of that theology or to ineffective presentation of it, the new message of perfection had a powerful appeal for many leaders

and laity alike. Only on this premise can the eager response to that
message be explained.

A second consequence of the introduction of perfectionism was
accentuation of the pietistic or experiential aspect of the Brethren faith.
Holiness as a second work of grace made a personalized, individual
experience the basis for professing that God had performed a special
sanctifying act subsequent to regeneration. This profession did not readily
lend itself to verification by the brotherhood, as did the initial conversion
experience.

This increasing experiential orientation of the Brethren movement
encouraged a shift toward the concept of the personal, inner "call" to
some special form of Christian service, especially missions. During their
earlier history, the Brethren believed that God called primarily through
the corporate mind of His people, the church, who acted in the spirit of
Acts, chapter thirteen, where the Holy Spirit said to the church: "Separate
me Barnabas and Saul for the work whereunto I have called them." By
the late nineteenth century, however, they were moving toward the
position that the call of the Holy Spirit was personal and experiential; the
church should send those who testified to inner calls. Not infrequently the
individual who professed a call related it to an experience of consecration
and sanctification.

The experiential holiness emphasis upon consecration and calling, and
the fact that many early perfectionists enthusiastically supported missions,
might suggest that the emergence of second-work holiness caused the
development of Brethren interest in a corporate mission program. This
conclusion is open to question for several reasons. General Conference
began to lay the foundations for a mission program fifteen years before it
became involved with the Wesleyan view of sanctification. When the
sanctification issue arose, furthermore, some of the principal supporters of
evangelism and missions—Charles Baker, Henry Davidson, Avery Long,
Frances Davidson and George Detwiler—were either outspoken opponents of perfectionism or noncommital in response to it. Finally, some
other churches which launched mission enterprises in the late nineteenth
century never endorsed perfectionism; the Brethren commitment to
corporate missions was in step with a broader surge of mission interest not
directly traceable to perfectionism.

A third result of the impact of the holiness movement was prolonged
controversy and tension in Brethren life. Sincere supporters of perfectionism confronted equally sincere opponents of it. Neither the 1887 nor

the 1910 statement of General Conference on sanctification laid the issue to rest. Both statements sought to unify the brotherhood, but as *Visitor* George Detwiler wrote some years later: "In the light of what has developed since [1910], how mistaken the fathers were when they adopted that committee report on sanctification with the thought that it would serve to unify the church on that question so as to forestall any future trouble on that account."[97]

A fourth outcome of perfectionism was the division of the Brethren membership into two categories—the saved and the sanctified. This had wide and perplexing ramifications. Editor Detwiler, who noted that a non-Brethren minister expressed pleasure at meeting "'a number of sanctified River Brethren'" at a camp meeting, observed:

> The inference is that "sanctified River Brethren" are so rare that they merit special attention when they appear somewhere. How is it, brethren? Who is qualified to be a judge of another's standing in grace? ... We trust, however, that the grace of sanctification, in experience and practice, heart and life, among our brethren is not so rare an article as the above testimony would indicate.[98]

Detwiler was obviously troubled by the tendency toward a two-fold membership categorization unfamiliar to the historic Brethren faith.

Many members found this division of members distressing because it seemed to them to lower the standard of God's work of grace in regeneration. Much that its advocates claimed for sanctification as a second work of grace the traditionalists understood to be an essential part of regeneration accompanied by simultaneous sanctification and its perfection through the process of obedience.[99]

This membership categorization also tended to foster judgmental attitudes on the part of both perfectionists and anti-perfectionists, thus straining the ties of brotherhood. The Conservatives were critical of some perfectonists who appeared to disparage church forms and church order. One woman wrote:

> Sanctification don't [*sic*] teach me to lay off my covering neither will it you. ... did we not testify that the Lord led us to lay off fashionable attire, and adopt modest apparel and a covering? ... This new teaching takes this away, it is not needed any more; we need no covering; we can have a plain hat, yes, a plain dress with perhaps plain puffed-up sleeves, and quite a number of plain little things and still be a Christian. Now mind, if the heart is thoroughly sanctified these things will all be put away ... .[100]

Another anti-perfectionist lamented the tendency of holiness advocates to "join hands with all classes of Christian believers, regardless of faith and practice." His conviction was that intimate spiritual fellowship required basic agreement on the proper observance of the ordinances and other aspects of the historic Brethren understanding of obedience.[101]

On the other hand, perfectionists sometimes criticized those who did not profess their level of spiritual attainment or who disagreed with their position. A correspondent wrote to *Visitor* Editor Henry Engle: "Have you ever noticed that the called-out ones sometimes get a little harsh and intolerant toward those who are not led exactly on the same lines as they are . . . ?"[102] Later, possibly with this query in mind, Engle printed a warning against egotism and intolerance on the part of those who "have been cleansed and sanctified . . . ."[103]

A response to a *Visitor* question asking whether "Saved but not sanctified" was a scriptural concept provides another example of the reaction of some perfectionists to those who differed with them. To this question a young perfectionist replied:

> When first I noticed the above expression in the "Visitor" number of Jan. 24th. I was astonished that there should still exist among us such amazing spiritual ignorance as to make it necessary to even ask is such expression scriptural? However, we believe that there was a good motive in raising the question, and we wish heartily to say, Yes, it is scriptural, . . .[104]

There were more replies rejecting the scriptural validity of the statement, "Saved but not sanctified," than supporting it, showing that traditional Brethren thought was still much in evidence as late as 1916.[105]

A fifth consequence of second-work holiness was the confusion of many members due to lack of uniformity in the teaching of holiness doctrine, a phenomenon which persisted for many decades. This problem was especially marked in Kansas, which experienced a flood of radical holiness teaching in the 1890s. Although the Kansas situation was not duplicated elsewhere, problems frequently arose in connection with what was a relatively complex theological concept. A perceptive observer, who rejoiced at the progress of holiness, wrote:

> . . . our rejoicing is with some trembling, for there seems to be such a confusion of teaching. . . . I have the impression that it would take a pretty well advanced Christian to pick out the truth from among so much that is plainly contradictory. The testimony of the church on this vital Scriptural

doctrine is certainly far from being of one accord; and herein lies a real danger to the future harmonious progress in church and missionary activities.[106]

Confusing teaching, frequently accompanied by strong emotional overtones, often produced unstable Christian experience. As revivalism produced the "repeat convert," who sought the conversion experience again and again, so holiness teaching produced the "repeat perfectionist," who sought repeatedly to be sanctified.

A sixth effect of perfectionism was the movement of the brotherhood toward more open relationships with other holiness churches. As revivalism and the Sunday school created bridges between the brotherhood and conservative evangelical Protestantism, so holiness now led members into closer contact with that segment of Protestantism identified with the second-work holiness message. They began to attend interdenominational holiness meetings.[107] In other words, holiness opened the brotherhood in greater measure to the acculturating influences of perfectionist Protestantism around them.

A seventh result of second-work holiness was the potential development of an individualism which posed a threat to the long-standing devotion of the Brethren to the church as a visible brotherhood community through which, they believed, the Holy Spirit acted to guide the individual in the practice of obedience. On the premise that the Holy Spirit created instantaneous perfection of heart in the individual, there appeared to be less need for brotherhood guidance in defining the meaning of the Christian life. If part of the people of God were unsanctified, the member who professed perfection had less reason to rely upon the counsel of the church when he or she was confident of the inner experiential guidance of the Holy Spirit.

Stated differently, personal inspiration could take precedence over the corporate mind of the church, as illustrated by a comment from a member in California:

I never thought that after I was sanctified I must die also to the things which I have been called upon to die to. I have had to die to my church-form (which no doubt many will think is of the devil); but, dear one, if you knew how I clung to it . . . . I used to say that though every one else would lay it [plain dress] off, I would still cling to it. But remember that *I* said this, not the Holy Spirit.[108]

To this testimony Editor Samuel Zook, a moderate perfectionist, spoke the longstanding conviction of the brotherhood about divine guidance.

> We feel sorry for our sister . . . because we fear that she is on dangerous ground. . . . Is the plain modest way of dressing which our sisters have adopted indeed a church form [?] . . . When you cut loose from the plain teaching of God's Word and *accept your own revelations* [italics added] you are adrift and you know not where you will land. . . . Sisters, do not cover up sin with a plain garb; but when your hearts are pure and your lives right the world will respect your modest apparel.[109]

Another illustration of how perfectionism could accentuate individualism was a statement in a General Conference debate on the sanctification question. Amid the tenseness created on the floor by this issue, an influential leader and strong champion of second-work holiness declared that only those who had such experiences ought to speak on the subject. As might have been expected, this called forth a sharply phrased rebuttal from an equally strong churchman who served as spokesman for the anti-perfectionist point of view.[110]

These illustrations were a warning that the Brethren would have difficulty integrating perfectionist individualism with their historic doctrine of the visible church, which assumed that the individual should accept the spiritual guidance of the group. On the other hand, a changing society was forcing them to reappraise their value system generally, and too rigid adherence to the past would merely pose another set of problems. The following 1904 statement strikingly illustrates their dilemma:

> We have come to the parting of the ways, in the history of our church. In the last six years there has been much breaking up of old ties, discarding of old customs, preaching new doctrines, throwing doors open to fanatics, and firebrands, and reaping from their sowing a harvest of dissension, separation and sorrow. In the wildness of their enthusiasm and their *professed* fulness of the spirit, many have publicly derided and thrown away, as man made expedients, those safeguards, and advisory rulings of Conference that were formerly obeyed *without* question. It is needless to add that the above spirit is as contagious as smallpox and about as disfiguring to those who catch it. When individual experiences are exalted above the Word of God, when an individual's feeling, or leading as they [*sic*] call it, runs directly counter to the multitude of counselors it is certainly not a path of *safety*, but of *anarchy*.
>
> Again on the other hand there can be a stern and rigid observance of rules and customs, a correct tithing of mint, anise, and cummin, . . . the latter

class (in part) often seem blind to the needs of the days we live in, and expect the same old methods to succeed under *entirely altered* circumstances. This is not always wisdom; . . .[111]

As this passage suggests, the Brethren of the early twentieth century found themselves in the midst of a momentous era of transition. Their exposure to Wesleyanism as interpreted by the American Holiness Movement, was a major factor in producing confrontation between values cherished for more than a hundred years and new ideas presented by the evangelical and perfectionist Protestantism of the late nineteenth and early twentieth centuries.

NOTES:

[1]Alderfer, "Mind of the Brethren," pp. 156-59; Schrag, "Brethren Attitude Toward the World," pp. 263-64. The American Holiness Movement, which was interdenominational, sought to recover and promote the doctrine of Wesleyan perfectionism.

[2]The term "perfectionism" will be used freely hereafter to designate an instantaneous experience of sanctification subsequent to regeneration.

[3]Saltzman, "Music Among the Brethren," p. 324.

[4]*A Collection of Spiritual Hymns, Adapted to the Various Kinds of Christian Worship, and Especially Designed for the Use of the Brethren in Christ, Known As "River Brethren"* (Lancaster, Pa., 1874), p. 203.

[5]*Visitor*, I (November 1, 1887), 46.

[6]Alderfer, "Mind of the Brethren," pp. 127-28.

[7]L. W. Shaeffer to Ambrose Miller, July 8, 1878, Church Archives.

[8]M. L. Dohner to C. O. Wittlinger, July 4, 1962.

[9]Later sections of the chapter will analyze the growing interest in perfectionism after 1886.

[10]P. G. H., "A Clean Heart," *Visitor*, I (June 1, 1888), 157; C. D. Erb, "Experience," *Visitor*, X (November 15, 1897), 381; J. G. Cassel, "Some Impressions," *Visitor*, XXI (March 15, 1907), 8; *Church Government*, 1887, p. 60.

[11]From the Association's statement of faith quoted in Schrag, "Brethren Attitude Toward the World," p. 344.

[12]Noah Zook, "Home Again," *Visitor*, VIII (April 1, 1895), 106.

[13]S. E. G., "Heart Purity," *Visitor*, I (January 1, 1888), 71; John Reichard, "Sanctification," *Visitor*, IV (March 1, 1891), 65-66; S. B. Kokanour, "What Sanctification Is," *Visitor*, VI (October 1, 1893), 295.

[14]J. G. Cassel, "Some Impressions," *Visitor*, XXI (March 15, 1907), 8.

[15]*General Council Minutes,* 1886, Article 12. See also [Henry Davidson], *Visitor,* I (January 1, 1888), 72.

[16]*General Conference Minutes,* 1887, Article 3. The full text of the report is in *Church Government,* 1887, pp. 55-64.

[17]Here the article cites a verse from the hymn "Come Thou Fount of Every Blessing," which includes the words "Prone to wander, Lord I feel it, prone to leave the God I love."

[18]1 Cor. 3:1-3; 2 Cor. 7:1; 1 Jn. 17:17.

[19]The article cites 2 Cor. 7:1; 1 Jn. 1:7; 1 Thess. 5:23; Eph. 1:13; Acts 2:4, and affirms that "Paul, Peter, John, Stephen, Zacharias, Elizabeth, etc., were all filled with the Holy Ghost."

[20]Here the article cites 1 Jn. 2:5 and 4:17-18; Ps. 37:37; Rom. 6:6, 22 and 8:21.

[21]Rev. John Wesley, *Plain Account of Christian Perfection* (Christian Witness Co.: Chicago and Boston, n.d.), p. 104.

[22]*Visitor,* 1887-1894, *passim.*

[23]M. L. Dohner to C. O. Wittlinger, July 4, 1962.

[24]A. L. Myers, "Holiness Viz. Sanctification," *Visitor,* IV (May 15, 1891), 146.

[25]Daniel Fike, "Jesus' Last Sermon," *Visitor,* V (October 1, 1892), 292; R. J. Finley, "Cornelius a Christian," *Visitor,* V (November 1, 1892), 324; S. B. Kokanour, "What Sanctification Is," *Visitor,* VI (October 15, 1893), 295.

[26]Daniel Fike, "Jesus' Last Sermon," *Visitor,* V (October 1, 1892), 292.

[27]*Ibid.,* p. 293.

[28]North Dickinson District Council Minutes, September 18, 1894, Article 6.

[29]Katie Bollinger quoted by Alderfer, "Mind of the Brethren," p. 161.

[30]*Ibid.*

[31]Noah Zook, "On Our Mission," *Visitor,* IX (May 1, 1896), 138.

[32]Quoted in Schrag, "Brethren Attitude Toward the World," p. 344.

[33]Schrag, *ibid.,* pp. 346-51.

[34]Jeremiah I. Long interview, August 16, 1962.

[35]D. W. Zook, "Enroute for India," *Visitor,* IX (February 1, 1896), 37-38.

[36]*Ibid.,* p. 38.

[37]Alderfer, "Mind of the Brethren," p. 162.

[38]Eber Zook, "My Call," *Visitor,* IX (November 1, 1896), 325.

[39]Jeremiah I. Long interview, August 16, 1962; G. C. and Sara Cress, "Hearts Set for the Field," *Visitor,* XI (June 1, 1898), 216; Noah and Mary Zook, "On Our Mission," *Visitor,* XI (July 15, 1898), 277-78; D. D. Steckley, "Notes by the Way," *Visitor,* XI (August 15, 1898), 317; Rhoda M. Zook, "Experience," *Visitor,* XII (February 1, 1899), 45.

[40]Noah and Mary Zook, "On Our Mission," *Visitor,* XI (March 15, 1898), 116; Eliab N. Wenger, "Testimony," *Visitor,* XII (March 15, 1899), 110.

[41]Noah and Mary Zook, "On Our Mission," *Visitor,* XI (July 15, 1898), 277; Emma Herr interview, October 2, 1960.

[42]D. D. Steckley, "Notes by the Way," *Visitor,* XI (August 15, 1898), 317-18. Samuel Zook, "Iowa" *Visitor,* IX (November 1, 1896), 329.

[43]John H. Myers, "Here and There," *Visitor,* XII (April 1, 1899), 136-37.

[44]*Visitor,* XII (March 15, 1899), 114.

[45]Quoted in Schrag, "Brethren Attitude Toward the World," p. 346, footnote.

[46]Noah Zook, "Gospel Tent," *Visitor,* VII (August 15, 1894), 248-49. Zook does not name Worcester but Schrag, "Brethren Attitude Toward the World," p. 346, identifies him from Worcester's account of the incident in *Sent of God,* a Hepzibah Faith Missionary Association paper.

[47]Jeremiah I. Long interview, August 16, 1962.

[48]Quoted in Schrag, "Brethren Attitude Toward the World," p. 347.

[49]D. W. Zook, "Abiding in Christ," *Visitor,* XI (August 1, 1898), 286; Jesse Haldeman cited by Alderfer, "Mind of the Brethren," p. 164-65.

[50]Jeremiah I. Long interview, August 16, 1962; Noah Zook, "Home Again," *Visitor,* VIII (April 1, 1895), 106; [Henry Engle], "Searching Meetings," *Visitor,* XI (August 1, 1898), 294. A recent writer characterizes this group as one of the most radical of those issuing from the National Holiness Association. See Vinson Synan, *The Holiness-Pentecostal Movement in the United States* (Grand Rapids, Mich.: William B. Eerdmans Publishing Co., 1971), pp. 61-67.

[51][Henry Engle], "Dickinson County, Kansas," *Visitor,* X (May 15, 1897), 153.

[52]G. C. and Sara Cress, "Hearts Set for the Field," *Visitor,* XI (June 1, 1898), 216.

[53]Annie S. Lehman, "Experience," *Visitor,* XI (January 1, 1898), 11; J. O. Lehman, "Sanctifying Power," *Visitor,* XI (January 1, 1898), 10; Amos O. Musser, "Christian Experience," *Visitor,* XI (April 1, 1898), 131.

[54]Mt. 3:11; Lk. 3:16.

[55][Henry Engle], "Fiery Experiences," *Visitor,* XI (July 15, 1898), 275.

[56]*Ibid.*; "Baptized with Fire," *Visitor,* X (November 1, 1897), 366-67; J. R. Zook, "Fire Baptism," *Visitor,* XII (May 1, 1899). 163-64. Irwin eventually advocated several successive fire baptisms identifying them by names such as "dynamite," "lyddite," and "oxidite," Synan, *Holiness-Pentecostal Movement,* p. 66.

[57]William Boyer, born 1871 who lived in the Dayton, Ohio, area, cited by Alderfer, "Mind of the Brethren," p. 168; Jeremiah I. Long interview, August 16, 1962.

[58][Henry Engle], "Religious Fanaticism," *Visitor,* XII (May 1, 1899), 176.

[59]*Ibid.*

[60][Henry Engle], *Visitor,* XII (September 1, 1899), 334-45.

[61]See his editorials previously cited.

[62][Henry Davidson], *Visitor,* IX (April 1, 1896), 104-5.

[63][George Detwiler], *Visitor,* XIII (March 15, 1900), 114-15.

[64]Abraham M. Engle, "A Visitor to the East," *Visitor,* XVIII (March 1, 1904), 13-14.

[65]Alderfer, "Mind of the Brethren," p. 165.

[66]Mary Zook, Tabor, Iowa, to [?] Sider, February 3, 1924, Asa W. Climenhaga Papers.

[67]The materials in this booklet first appeared in 1919 as a series of articles in the *Visitor.*

[68]Zook, *Holiness and Empowerment,* pp. 23-24.

[69]Alice A. Heise, "Gormley Church News," *Visitor,* XI (August 1, 1898), 295.

[70]*Ibid.,* 295-96.

[71]Alderfer, "Mind of the Brethren," p. 166; John H. Myers and Wife, "A Voice from the Field," *Visitor,* XI (March 15, 1898), 116.

[72]Alderfer, "Mind of the Brethren," pp. 165-71, 183-84.

[73]"Extracts from Private Letters," *Visitor,* X (November 15, 1897), 381.

[74]Charles Baker, "Sin," *Visitor,* XII (May 15, 1899), 186.

[75]John Keefer, *Visitor,* XIX (March 1, 1905), 3.

[76]Noah Zook, "On Our Missions," *Visitor,* IX (May 1, 1896), 138; Eliab N. Wenger, "Testimony," *Visitor,* XII (March 15, 1899), 110.

[77][Henry Engle], *Visitor,* XII (August 1, 1899), 294.

[78]Letter (name deleted), Moonlight, Kansas, to Harry N. Lehman *et. al.,* February 13, 1900, typescript among Asa W. Climenhaga Papers. Punctuation as in the original source.

[79]R. K., "Carefulness Enjoined," *Visitor,* XII (November 15, 1899), 427.

[80]Quoted by Alderfer, "Mind of the Brethren," p. 190.

[81]Letter (name deleted), Moonlight, Kansas, to Harry N. Lehman *et. al.,* February 13, 1900. Punctuation as in original source.

[82]Mary Zook, "Warning," *Visitor,* XVI (March 15, 1902), 104-5. See also [Samuel Zook], *Visitor,* XII (June 15, 1899), 235.

[83]Sarah Dohner, "Testimony," *Visitor,* XI (March 1, 1898), 86.

[84]*General Conference Minutes,* 1898, Article 9. A few months later Canada Joint Council emphatically repudiated the second-work doctrine. *Canadian Joint Council Minutes,* 1898, p. 7.

[85]*General Conference Minutes, 1899, Article 7, p. 5.*

[86]*Canadian Joint Council Minutes,* 1899, p. 8.

[87]*General Conference Minutes,* 1903, Article 21, pp. 13-14.

[88]*Ibid.,* 1904, Articles 32, 53, pp. 19-20, 34.

[89]*Ibid.,* Article 34, p. 20.

[90]Dauphin and Lebanon District Council Minutes, February 25, 1909; *Pennsylvania State Council Minutes,* 1909, Article 3, pp. 4-5.

[91]*General Conference Minutes,* 1910, Article 9, pp. 11-12.

[92]Alderfer, "Mind of the Brethren," p. 198.

[93]*General Conference Minutes,* 1910, pp. 11-27.

[94]E. J. Swalm to C. O. Wittlinger, August 18, 1972. Baker told Swalm that he consented to the report in committee on condition that certain changes would be made in it before it came to the floor. Although some of those changes were omitted, he chose not to voice his opposition in open Conference.

[95]The article cites Acts 2:4; Eph. 1:13 and 4:24, 25; 1 Thess. 5:23; 1 John 1:7.

[96]See Chapter XIV.

[97][George Detwiler], "Another Year,—Some Visitor History," *Visitor,* XXX (December 25, 1916), 2-5. See Chapter XIV for the continuing controversy after 1910.

[98][George Detwiler], "Are They a Rarity?," *Visitor,* XX (September 15, 1906), 2.

[99]John Reichard, "Sanctification," *Visitor,* IV (March 1, 1891), 66.

[100]R. K., "Carefulness Enjoined," *Visitor,* XII (November 15, 1899), 427.

[101]Charles Baker, "Sin," *Visitor,* XII (May 15, 1899), 186.

[102]"Extracts from Private Letters," *Visitor,* X (June 1, 1897), 170.

[103]*Visitor,* X (July 1, 1897), 193.

[104]V. L. Stump, "Saved But Not Sanctified," *Visitor,* XXX (March 20, 1916), 7.

[105]For another writer's comments on the tendency of both the perfectionists and anti-perfectionists to become judgmental, see John Bock, "On Sanctification," *Visitor,* XIX (March 1, 1905), 8.

[106]J. G. Cassel, "Some Impressions," *Visitor,* XXI (March 15, 1907), 8.

[107]Noah Zook, "A Voice from the Field," *Visitor,* VII (December 15, 1894), 378; [Henry Engle], *Visitor,* XI (January 1, 1898), 14.

[108]Mary A. Stoner, "Delight in the Lord," *Visitor,* XII (June 1, 1899), 203.

[109][Samuel Zook], *Visitor,* XII (June 15, 1899), 235.

[110]E. J. Swalm, who was present at that Conference, described the debate to the present writer.

[111]Fred Elliott, "Bible Training School," *Visitor,* XVIII (February 15, 1904), 4. Elliott's assertion that Conference rulings were "formerly obeyed without question" requires considerable qualification.

XII

Institutional Beginnings: Publication and Benevolence

Publication

The Brethren in Christ communicated with each other during their first century by personal contact and letter. District memberships met frequently in worship services, councils, and love feasts, with members from other districts often sharing in the latter service. Annual General Conferences brought together representatives from the entire brotherhood and occasionally sponsored church-wide visitations conducted by leaders who visited members in their homes and also conducted services to foster fellowship and unity.

By the 1870s some members questioned the adequacy of these traditional methods of communication. Denominational periodicals were then becoming a conspicuous feature of American Protestantism. Progressive individuals among the Brethren began to think of some type of periodical as a means to unify the widely separated brotherhood and promote its distinctive faith and life-style.

The idea of a church periodical, however, aroused strong opposition. Some critics saw no need for more than open Bibles and ministering brethren to propagate their faith.[1] Others believed that such periodicals were potential sources of false teaching.[2]

The movement for a church periodical had its strength on the geographical periphery of the brotherhood. In 1874 Michigan members petitioned General Conference to approve a church paper, but that body postponed the question for a year.[3] The succeeding Conference duly considered the matter "in love and harmony" but again postponed a decision because of fear that "the brethren were not ready to choose the best."[4]

For several years the periodical question languished.[5] In 1880 Conference again took up the matter and requested district councils to vote on three resolutions for initiating a periodical. The first proposed: "That there be published, under the control of general council, a weekly church paper devoted to religious intelligence and to the maintenance of the doctrine of the Bible as understood and taught by the church of the brethren in Christ."[6] The other two resolutions outlined the structure and functions of a publication board to supervise the proposed periodical.

These resolutions were defeated in the district voting; nine districts supported and fourteen opposed them.[7] Faced with these results General Conference of 1881 deferred the periodical question indefinitely.[8]

Six years passed before the Michigan Brethren revived the question in the Conference of 1887. Perhaps it is significant that this Conference met in Kansas where the more conservative eastern districts of the brotherhood were less strongly represented. In any case, Conference endorsed the three periodical resolutions of 1880 and decided to publish a church paper on a trial basis.[9]

When the committee appointed to take charge of the paper named an editor, he was one of their own number, Henry Davidson of White Pigeon, Michigan. Davidson, a bishop and influential leader, had been a principal figure in the long, hard struggle for the periodical.

Several guidelines governed the new publication. The first specified that General Conference would own and completely control it through a publication committee to which the editor was accountable.[10] The second guideline stated that the periodical must be financed entirely by subscriptions and contributions; it could not accept advertising.[11]

This restraint on advertising created a passing stir in 1891. The editor, who urgently needed a typewriter which he could not afford, sought to secure the needed funds by advertising the Odell Typewriter Company of Chicago. Negative reaction was so swift and decisive that the advertisement survived only one appearance. Editor Davidson was greatly disappointed. He could see no disadvantage in advertising "any article of merit," but he yielded to those who objected to every form of advertising.[12]

A third crucial guideline was a concession to those grieved by Conference approval of the publication. This made continuation of the *Visitor* conditional on a favorable referendum at the end of four years. The referendum would be by "congregational vote," meaning that all members present at the referendum Conference could participate. The Conference, furthermore, would convene in the area of the brotherhood most opposed to the paper, which was Eastern Pennsylvania.[13]

Perhaps the most significant factor in bringing the *Visitor* to birth was the editorship of Henry Davidson. He had little formal education for such an assignment but, in the words of a daughter, "'Father was a great reader and because of that seemed to be a better educated man than he really was'."[14] To compensate for some of his own limitations, Davidson turned to his daughter, Frances, one of the best-educated Brethren members of that period. She later related how her father gave her manuscripts unfit for publication, with the suggestion that she should try to salvage something from them. Miss Davidson slyly observed that some contributors may have had considerably difficulty recognizing what they had written.[15]

Editor Davidson assumed his responsibilities with some trepidation. This was expressed in his first editorial.

> In accepting the position of Editor, . . . we are well aware of the arduous duty and great responsibility resting upon us. It is therefore not without some fear and a consciousness of our own inability to do justice to the work before us, and to meet the approbation of the church that we enter upon it. . . we may not *always* meet the approbation of all; but, though we may err, the error will not be of the heart, and we hope our brethren will be ready to correct and to forgive.[16]

In spite of his acknowledged limitations, Davidson stated clearly that he would think and act for himself in his new role. "While we shall select with care, we shall feel it our duty to decide fearlessly and impartially what to publish and what not to publish."[17] This proved to be easier said than done; later he deplored the limitations imposed upon an editor who is "made to feel that he is the servant and is expected to do the bidding of others."[18]

After his appointment Davidson wasted no time, and the first issue of the paper appeared under date of August 1, 1887, as the *Evangelical Visitor,* with the following publication objectives: "Devoted to the Spread of Evangelical Truths and the Unity of the Church." The masthead enlarged upon this by stating that the paper appeared in the interests of the Brethren in Christ Church "for the exposition of Evangelical Truths and the promotion of true practical piety among all classes." In his first editorial, Davidson made clear what this meant: "It would be impossible for us in our inexperience to lay down or form any special rules to guide us in the publication of this paper in the future; but this we will say that the

Evangelical Visitor.

A RELIGIOUS MONTHLY JOURNAL.

Published in the interest of the Church of
the Brethren in Christ for the exposition of
Evangelical Truths and the promotion of true
practical piety among all classes, at one dollar
a year, or fifty cents for six months. Speci-
men copies free.

August 1, 1887.

☞ Entered at the Post Office at Elkhart, as
second class mail matter.

ALL COMMUNICATIONS for the "Visitor" should be written with pen and ink
and only on one side of the paper.

OUR FIRST NUMBER.—This number of
the Visitor is sent free to you as a sample
copy of what we desire to do; yet we acknowledge that from our lack of experience and from the want of more material
to select from, it is not what we would desire it to be. But look it over carefully,
and, if you think such a paper with the
improvements that we trust we shall be
able to make, from time to time, will suit
you, SUBSCRIBE for it. It will be published monthly at one dollar a year, commencing with the first of October.

THE PRICE OF OUR PAPER.—It may
be thought by some that the subscription
price to the EVANGELICAL VISITOR is too
high since it is only a monthly; but, in
consultation with the publishers, we learn
that it cannot be published for much less,
and then too it is not an individual enterprise, but is the property of the Church,
and under the control of the Church.

If there should be a surplus after paying for material and labor it will remain
the property of the Church and may become a fund for the purchase ultimately of
a press. It will, however, take a liberal
support to make it self-sustaining, and we
hope the Church will in every locality
take the necessary interest, so as to make
it self-sustaining. Send in your subscriptions early and liberally. A good church
paper should be in the hands of every
member of the Church, and now, since
we have one of our own, let us support it,
even if it should be at the expense of
some luxury of doubtful benefit.

TO THE BROTHERHOOD.—We proba-
bly owe an apology for referring again to
the subject of our subscription to the
VISITOR, but we wish to be rightly understood.

We would say then we expect to have
in every locality some person to solicit
subscriptions. Do not wait however until
you are asked to subscribe, but send us
your name at once, so that we may know
how many copies to have printed; and if
not in time, we will have to correct our
list and that takes time and labor. Send
all communications for publication to the
VISITOR with your full name signed, not
necessarily for publication, but so that we
may know who is the author. All business letters and all money orders or drafts
should be made payable to Henry Davidson, White Pigeon, Michigan. Always
sign your full name with Post Office,
County and State plainly written, so that
no mistake need occur in sending out
papers.

WE HOPE that the churches throughout the brotherhood will not forget to act
on the suggestion of our last General
Conference in regard to the means for the
support of our mission work. Make the
gift liberal and make it early. Take the
apostle's advice "Let every one of you lay
by him in store as God has prospered
him." Remember, "The Lord loveth a
cheerful giver."

NOTICE.—The committee appointed by
last General Conference to publish the decision of Conference since 1870, request
the different districts to report at once the
number of copies they desire for their use
as they are ready to go to press, and are
only waiting to know how many copies
to print.

CHURCH NEWS.

LOVE FEAST IN ELKHART DISTRICT.
—The love-feast in Elkhart Co., Indiana,
took place on the fourth and fifth of June,
in the Brethren's Meeting-house located
sixteen miles south of the town of Elkhart.
And we might mention here that it is the
place where our next Annual Conference is
to be held.

Services were to begin at eleven A. M.
on the fourth.

And promptly at the appointed time all
were very comfortably seated, and the

house was soon filled with songs of praise,
followed by the reading of Scriptures, exhortations, and prayer.

The time was then devoted to experience and many were the glorious testimonies which fell upon our ears during
that afternoon. Among others we heard
those witness for Jesus, who had, but a
couple weeks previous, united with the
Church and been baptized, and were for
the first time about to partake of the emblems of the broken body and shed
blood of our blessed Redeemer. It does
our souls good to hear others tell of their
enjoyments in the Christian life, and especially those who have but recently joined
the army of God.

Early in the evening supper was served
for all who desired to partake of it.

The evening was then spent, as is the
custom among the Brethren, in the reading
of Scripture, exhortation, administering
the bread and wine and the ordinance of
feet-washing. On Sabbath morning the
weather being quite unfavorable, some
were prevented from going to the church,
but the Lord was there and we had a good
meeting.

The ministering brethren gave excellent instruction from the word of God
which seemed to be appreciated by the
interest manifested by those present.

After the meeting closed we returned to
our homes feeling much revived, and a determination to be more zealous in the
service of our Master.   E.

THE BRETHREN CONFERENCE.

[In the absence of any special report for
the VISITOR, of our Conference proceed-
ings held in Dickinson Co., Kansas, in
May last, and for which we have been
waiting for some time, we give below report from one of the Abilene papers, published at the time, but unfortunately we
are unable to state from what paper it was
taken.—Ed.]

"The Brethren in Christ" — commonly
known as the "River Brethren,"—held
their last General Conference a few miles
south of town, at the home of Cyrus
Lenhert, on Wednesday, Thursday and
Friday, May 18, 19 and 20.

This meeting is composed largely of
representatives from various parts of the
Church, which is confined to the United
States and Canada. For a week before
the appointed time, visitors and delegates

BIBLE, *its doctrine and its Evangelical truths* shall constitute the basis of our publications."[19]

At first thought, the lack of specific reference to the distinctive faith of the brotherhood seems surprising. What must be kept in mind, however, was the assumption that the Brethren faith embodied the "doctrine" and "Evangelical truths" of the Bible. Davidson stated this succinctly in an editorial seeking to secure more material for publication. Noting that accounts of Christian experience were in good supply, he appealed for "articles on doctrinal points" and added:

> We have a faith and doctrine of which we need not be ashamed, and we have a doctrine that cannot be successfully contradicted. Lately we read an article in one of our exchanges on the design of baptism with which we could not fully agree. The subject is one of too grave a nature to be treated in any other way than to try to bring out the Gospel design. Then again there is . . . the Communion . . . also that despised and neglected ordinance of washing the saints' feet, and many other points believed in and practiced by our people which would be profitable subjects on which to write, . . .[20]

Only a man with common sense, fortitude, and spiritual dedication could have coped with the many problems that arose during the early years of the *Visitor.* Henry Davidson proved to be such a man. He was, furthermore, a loyal churchman deeply committed to the Brethren but ready to consider new ideas and methods which he believed would vitalize and promote their faith.

For five years Davidson published the *Visitor* from his home in White Pigeon, Michigan. In 1891 he sold his Michigan farm and moved the publication office to Abilene, Kansas.[21] One reason for this change was his desire to locate the office in the midst of a large membership of Brethren friendly to the enterprise, who would "sustain the paper morally as well as financially." Davidson, furthermore, was dreaming of the day when the *Visitor* would have its own press and a large open field for the spread of religious literature. Kansas, he felt, was such a place.[22]

In his desire for a denominational press, Editor Davidson was far ahead of his day.[23] Soon, however, the *Visitor* did have its own type and typesetter. A few years after the editorial office moved Davidson advertised readiness to handle job printing with the press work done by contract.[24]

As the time for the four-year referendum approached, friends of the paper rallied to its support. Jacob Eisenhower of Kansas wrote that he had abandoned neutrality on the issue and strongly supported the *Visitor*. He now realized what the periodical meant to those deprived of regular contact with Brethren services. In his words:

> ... I had the privilege to sit among the brethren every Sunday and oftener, and did not starve for the gospel of Jesus. Oh brother, I feel for those that have not the gospel, and I hope the Lord will not suffer it, that the brethren shall look at the VISITOR as an evil, and put it aside; for my part if I would help to do so, I would feel as though I would take the bread from my own children.[25]

Joseph Hershey of Ohio had also shifted from opposition to support. He now saw that the paper was "a comfort to many and especially to those living away from church privileges" and that it met the need for a church paper to scatter abroad "the doctrine of the Bible, as believed in, and taught by the church."[26]

Hershey's concern for those whose location restricted their church fellowship was echoed from California where the vanguard of a Brethren community had arrived. John M. Engle spoke on their behalf:

> O how cheering it is to read the letters of our dear brethren and sisters, telling their experiences, and of their progress in the most holy faith, bound together into one brotherhood by the bonds of love, from one end of our land to the other. I feel it a duty to put in a plea for the VISITOR in behalf of those here on the Pacific coast, isolated from the brethren.[27]

Some supporters of the *Visitor* approached the issue of its continuance more methodically. Avery Long of Pennsylvania perceived seven advantages of the paper.[28] Anthony Stoner of Ohio gave various arguments on its behalf and closed with a bit of scare psychology. There was, he thought, evidence that the hindering of an official church paper might tempt an individual to launch a private publication in its place.[29]

By March of 1891 friends of the *Visitor* were deluging Editor Davidson with testimonials and arguments favoring its continuance.[30] Although surprised and gratified by this outpouring of support, he decided early in April to cease publishing such materials. With the crucial four-year referendum only a few weeks away and "the matter . . . now clearly before the church for consideration," he evidently felt constrained to curtail the use of the paper to perpetuate its own life.[31]

The time for the referendum arrived at last. General Conference of 1891 convened in the Mastersonville meetinghouse in Lancaster County,

Pennsylvania, "an Eastern location which placed the [periodical] issue in the very heart of the opposition."[32]

When the question came to the floor, a lively debate took place with strong expressions from both sides. At a critical point in this debate, Daniel Brubaker, a Pennsylvania conservative from Lebanon County, made an unexpected and forceful plea for the *Visitor*. An observer credited Brubaker's speech with the creation of a more favorable sentiment for the paper.[33]

This occasion was a dramatic moment in the life of the brotherhood. Since the vote was "congregational," women as well as men voted. Years later Eli M. Engle, who had defended the *Visitor*, wrote: "With joy . . . I remember that a little old sister (Anna Engle) in her 80th year stood in favor of its continuation."[34] There is an unverifiable tradition that Moderator Martin Oberholser granted the last minute of debate time to Sarah Dohner of Orrstown, Pennsylvania. She, according to the tradition, expressed appreciation for the *Visitor* on behalf of her invalid father who was unable to attend church services.[35]

The voting proceeded in an atmosphere of hushed suspense. Davidson observed: "During the progress of the voting, the interest in the large audience was great, and as the work progressed, the fears and hopes of the friends, as well as of those opposed alternately arose and fell, yet silence prevailed and resignation to the decision, whatever it might be, was no doubt the firm resolve of all present."[36] According to one account, John Musser and his wife of Pennsylvania arrived on the Conference floor a few minutes before the balloting ceased. Both promptly voted "yes" for continuation of the paper. Their votes, the reporter of the incident believed, determined the outcome, for the final tally revealed a very small majority in favor of the *Visitor*.[37]

Whether the votes of the Mussers saved the *Visitor* is uncertain. Eli Engle thought that it had a nine-vote margin, and there was general agreement that the vote was very close.[38] Editor Davidson noted the goodwill which characterized both winning and losing factions:

We were very much gratified to notice the Christian forbearance and spirit of resignation that was manifested. Not a word was spoken in our hearing that seemed like exultation by the friends of the measure, nor a word of dissatisfaction by those opposed, but a general acquiescence to the decision.[39]

Davidson believed that the decision of 1891 assured the periodical a more prosperous future, but he underestimated the significance of such a close vote. Within a few years, in fact, the *Visitor* was in serious difficulty. Some of the eastern Brethren were critical of the paper's western location.[40] Perhaps more serious, however, was the fact that the project was not meeting expenses, and the brotherhood took a dim view of financial insolvency of either person or institution.[41]

The financial crisis could have been resolved had all subscriptions been paid. Some subscribers, however, could not pay; others, in spite of repeated efforts to collect from them, would not pay.[42]

Faced with this emergency, Davidson devised an experimental fund-raising technique; he added a detachable cover with advertisements solicited from the businessmen of Abilene. Again criticism descended upon him.[43] Offsetting it was the additional revenue from the advertising and the fact that he had dramatized a need and illustrated a possible way to meet it. He accordingly looked forward to the Conference of 1896 hoping that it would devise a plan to make the paper self-supporting.[44]

Once again a General Conference debated the *Visitor* in Pennsylvania where opposition to it was most intense. The decision "to exonerate" the Board of Publication and appoint a new board indicates that serious criticism of the paper was expressed on the floor.[45] This action implies that the editor received the main thrust of criticism, an inference supported by the termination of his editorship effective October 1, 1896.[46]

Conference also considered the question of relocating the *Visitor*. Brethren regionalism was clearly evident in this debate; Pennsylvania, Iowa, Ohio, and Kansas all desired the publication office. As might have been predicted from the location of the Conference, Pennsylvania had the votes to carry the day.[47]

To replace Editor Davidson the Publication Board chose Henry Engle of Kansas.[48] He was an able man already known to the readers of the *Visitor* through his writings.[49] Engle offered to serve without salary and trust the Lord and friends of the paper for his support.[50] Due to the precarious finances of the publication and the new editor's inability to move his family to Pennsylvania immediately, the Publication Board decided to produce the paper indefinitely in Abilene.[51]

The editorial transition went smoothly. Davidson's final editorial reveals the pain he felt in severing his journalistic roots. Although there are intimations that he was hurt by the abruptness of the termination of his editorship, he had kind words to say about both the Publication Board and his successor. Of the latter he wrote:

He is one of our best writers and has contributed largely to the columns of the VISITOR in the past. We trust you will accord to him the same courtesy that you have to us in the past, and under the new arrangement may the VISITOR prosper and do good work for the Master and may it always be a true exponent of the doctrine of the Bible as believed in and taught by the peculiar people which it represents.[52]

Under the editorship of Henry Engle, the *Visitor* continued its strong support for Brethren missions and evangelism. It also became a vigorous advocate of second-work holiness and thus threw its weight on the positive side of the holiness debate agitating the brotherhood.[53] This was forshadowed in a passage from Engle's first editorial:

We are aware that there will be minds of wide extremes to deal with. There are those who have sacrificed all by an unreserved consecration, opposed to which are minds steeped in formality and wordliness. There are those whose highest ambitions seem to be a final salvation when they die, opposed to which are such who live under present assurance in hope of the promised Kingdom of God.[54]

Although a warm supporter of perfectionism, Editor Engle was outspokenly critical of what he considered to be the excesses of the American Holiness Movement. He strongly opposed, for example, both emotional extremism and "eradicationism."[55]

The new editor was less inclined than his predecessor to stress Brethren distinctives, as he frankly acknowledged in the following statement:

We confess that we are not very churchy; . . . That a vigorous conflict at present exists in the realm of churchism, between the various elements either distinctly discarding or positively upholding and contending for sectism, no one who is in an attitude to feel the religious pulse will pretend to deny. . . . we need be careful least [*sic*] Christendom as a whole, and the various branches of the nominal system in particular, in their zeal for "the faith once delivered to the saints," be found fighting against the purpose and plan of God in these closing scenes of the Gospel dispensation, . . .[56]

Later he noted: "As long as any organized body lays restrictions and binds with cords the liberty of thought and freedom to act out candid convictions of right[s] of its members, so long will turmoils exist and new reformatory eruptions take place; . . . "[57] These citations are from his 1899 editorials and may reflect his drift into the thought patterns of Russellism, a drift which led to his forced resignation as editor in June, 1899.[58]

Conference next appointed Samuel Zook of Kansas as editor, and once again the public editorial transition was smooth and gracious.[59] Engle continued to serve as office manager until October, 1899, when George Detwiler from Sherkston, Ontario, arrived to take his place.[60]

Samuel Zook had accepted the editorship to meet the emergency created by the resignation of Henry Engle and to nurture the confidence of the brotherhood in the *Visitor*. In him the historic faith of the Brethren and the innovations which they accepted in the late nineteenth century were better synthesized than in many other members. The following passage from his pen reflects the spirit which pervaded his year of editorial service:

> It was our privilege to become one with our dear Brethren when young in years and have had a personal acquaintance with many of our old Fathers in Israel and we know of what we speak when we say that we learned to know them as a sincere and zealous people of God, and have never had any doubt but that their faith and teaching was according to sound doctrine. The disposition on the part of some at this time is to speak lightly of them . . . in such a way that casts a reflection upon them; saying, they walked in all the light they had, but intimating that they did not have the light as they should have had, and that now a clearer light has dawned upon us. This reflection has a tendency to destroy confidence and to speak lightly, and gives rise to a spirit that ignores the work of the church, and gives encouragement to factions that spring up among us, and go out on an independent line. That the Brotherhood did . . . need to be aroused on some important questions, and issues at stake, is no question, but we would say let us beware of causing division.[61]

Zook then illustrated his concerns by reference to missions and holiness. Although he supported both, he emphasized that they must be handled with care lest they nurture divisiveness.

In view of the expressed desire of Samuel Zook to retire from the editorship as soon as possible, General Conference of 1900 named George Detwiler to succeed him. Conference also voted to continue the *Visitor* another year in Abilene, in spite of the long postponement of the decision to relocate it in Pennsylvania.[62] Since the new editor had spent some months as manager of the publication office, this new transition in the editorship was a simple matter.

The nineteen-year period of editorial service by George Detwiler reflects the high esteem in which he was held by the brotherhood. This long term was also a tribute to his good judgment and skillful church statesmanship, for he faced two important and quite different difficulties. In the first place, he was skeptical of the historic Brethren concept of obedience, perceiving it to be a potential compromise of the doctrine of salvation by faith. Too many Brethren, he thought, tended to stress doing things rather than trusting Christ for salvation.[63] The central theme of his ministry and editorship appears in an excerpt from one of his articles:

> The blood of Christ is *precious* because it is the only means of our redemption. Not the blood of bulls and goats could make atonement. It took the precious blood of Christ. Our peace is made by the blood of His cross, and redemption, even the forgiveness of sins is ours through it. Even this *precious blood* is the foundation of eternal joys, . . .[64]

This strong emphasis upon salvation by grace was not necessarily incompatible with the historic Brethren synthesis of faith and obedience.[65] Detwiler merely saw more clearly than many of his contemporaries the perils of legalism to which many Brethren stressing obedience exposed themselves. He was inclined, however, to move so forcefully in the opposite direction that he could have been interpreted as discounting obedience.

On the other hand, Editor Detwiler faced quite a different peril because he rejected second-work holiness. For this reason he risked the opposition of the growing perfectionist wing of the Brethren movement.[66]

Early in Detwilers' editorship the long-delayed relocation of the *Visitor* in Pennsylvania took place. General Conference of 1902 ordered this move by overruling the recommendation of the Publication Board that the office be continued in Abilene for another five years. Evidently the opposition to relocation made a strong stand, for the recommendation of the Publication Board "was considered at great length" before it was set aside.[67] This defeat of the recommendation left a residue of dissatifaction. Later, a church leader from the Midwest charged that "Our church paper . . . [had been] published in Abilene, Kansas, well cared for and flourishing, but the East came by force of vote at Belle Springs Conference without good reasons and took it to Harrisburg, Pa."[68] Regional rivalries evidently operated strongly in Brethren circles in the early twentieth century.

In January of 1903 Detwiler announced that the editorial office had moved to Harrisburg and occupied space in the place of business of Samuel Smith.[69] The office remained in Harrisburg until Vernon Stump succeeded George Detwiler in the editorship in 1919. This automatically relocated the editorial office in Nappanee, Indiana, the new editor's place of residence.[70]

Effects of a Church Periodical

The publication of a church periodical had important effects upon the Brethren in Christ. One was the creation of a new and effective medium of communication to unify the members of a small religious society scattered widely in the United States and Canada and, beginning in the late nineteenth century, several foreign countires. News of church life, sharing of personal testimonies and needs, promotion of common beliefs, and the publicizing of brotherhood enterprises all helped to strengthen the sense of brotherhood and community.

A second consequence of the *Visitor* was the expansion of the religious and intellectual horizons of a people unaccustomed to much reading. The *Visitor* published materials from other religious publications as well as numerous articles by Brethren authors. This selected material demonstrated that non-Brethren writers could have something worthwhile to say, and thus it helped to counteract the provincial-mindedness of a rural people preoccupied with their own faith and life-style.

A third effect of the church periodical was the facilitation of change within the brotherhood. A new venture in itself, the *Visitor* promoted other changes such as evangelism, missions, and the Sunday school. How the periodical related to change at any given time depended largely upon the perspectives of the editor. During the first period of transition in Brethren history, each of the men who occupied the editorial office—Henry Davidson, Henry Engle, Samuel Zook, and George Detwiler—had his own view of the validity of the historic Brethren faith and the new influences bearing upon it, and each made his own distinctive contribution to the life of the Brethren.

Finally, the *Visitor* illustrated the practical advantages of education. Many persons who wrote for the paper, as well as those who read it, could perceive the advantages of writing skills. The more discriminating readers may also have noted that articles by some writers—those formally or self-educated—could be identified by the qualities of thought and insight displayed by their authors. In addition, the paper actively promoted education by giving editorial support to the pre-service training of missionaries and to the founding of a church school.

Benevolence

Two factors combined to lead the Brethren into a program of benevolent institutions. One was their sense of responsibility to aid each other in time of personal or family need; the other was their growing evangelistic and social concern.

An interest in benevolent enterprises broke out spontaneously across the brotherhood in the late nineteenth century. As early as 1879, General Conference granted the Kansas Brethren permission to purchase a tract of land for the benefit of poor widows and orphans, but the project did not materialize.[71] By the 1890s, however, some of the members in Kansas were active in the work of a non-denominational orphanage known as the "Industrial School and Hygiene Home for Friendless Persons" near Hillsboro, Kansas. It was begun by Amanda Dohner of Franklin County, Pennsylvania, with the strong support of Tobias and Susanna Martin of Mercersburg in the same state.[72]

Late in the decade of the 1890s, John and Caty Ann Myers launched benevolent institutions in Lancaster, Pennsylvania.[73] These ventures, the Ishi Faith Home for orphans and the Ebenezer Faith Home for the aged, were shortlived.[74]

By the turn of the century, Brethren members were promoting two midwestern orphanages in Oklahoma and Illinois. In Oklahoma Abraham and Anna Eisenhower founded the "Jabbok Faith Orphanage and Missionary Training Home" at Thomas in 1899.[75] Ten years later the Eisenhowers gave their farm of 150 acres and the orphanage facilities as an annuity to the Brethren in Christ Church, which continued to conduct the orphanage program until 1924.[76]

The Illinois orphanage sponsored by Brethren members began in 1900 near the town of Morrison. Abram G. and Rosa A. Zook, responding to what they felt to be a call from God, made their thirteen-room home and small farm available for a children's home.[77] Organized on May 27, 1900, they and their supporters at first referred to themselves as the "Zion Faith Home Association," but two days later the group reconvened and changed the name to "Mt Carmel Faith Missionary Training Home and Orphanage."[78] Workers at the Chicago Mission, who felt an urgent need for an appropriate country place to which they could send homeless children, gave this venture special encouragement.[79] In 1912 General Conference accepted the Mt. Carmel Orphanage as an official Brethren in

Christ institution, which it remained until its program terminated in 1968.[80]

None of these benevolent enterprises had consequences as far-reaching as the institutions which developed among the Pennsylvania Brethren in the districts surrounding Harrisburg. Here the idea of a home for the elderly and orphans originated in 1895. In January of that year, two women members were visiting in the Hummelstown vicinity; without forethought the conversation turned to the possibility of starting a benevolent home. Because of their mutual interest in the matter, the women, at least one of whom appears to have been from Mechanicsburg, decided to bring it before the Cumberland District Council scheduled to convene at the Mechanicsburg Church in February.[81]

A few weeks prior to the council Katie Breneman of Mechanicsburg, acting on behalf of the Hummelstown visitors, requested the visiting deacon brethren to place on the council agenda the question of starting a home. They did so but the press of others matters prevented its consideration. The council then decided to call a special meeting "to consider a plan or devise ways for the establishment of a home for the homeless among the Bretheren [sic]."[82] Under the caption "A Home for the Poor," an invitation to consider launching such an insititution went out to the entire Brethren membership in Pennsylvania.[83]

When the special council convened in April of 1895, Bishop Jacob M. Engle of Lancaster County presided. After considerable discussion of various proposals and sites, the assembly unanimously approved the following resolutions:

> Resolved,—That it is the sense of this meeting that a home for the aged, the afflicted and the poor, including all ages, regardless of sex, for the Brethren in Christ Church and as the Lord may direct is a to be desired end.
>
> Resolved,—That it is the sense of this meeting that Harrisburg or a farm in the vicinity of Harrisburg offers advantages superior to any other place.[84]

An institution to serve the aged, afflicted, and poor of both sexes and all ages was a daring and ambitious enterprise for rural people with no experience in such undertakings. They began immediately, however, to implement their vision by naming from the districts surrounding Harrisburg a committee of eight to select a site for the home and another committee of five to solicit subscriptions and donations for its purchase.[85]

Both committees encountered difficulties. The committee of eight could not reach unanimous agreement on a site. A majority of the group favored a location at 1175 Bailey Street, Harrisburg, on the crest of a hill overlooking the downtown area and the State Capitol grounds. The committee, therefore, named two if its members to negotiate for purchase with Josiah Brandt of Philadelphia, owner of the Bailey Street property. They secured from Mr. Brandt a sixty-day option to purchase the property for the sum of $9,000.[86]

In the meantime the soliciting committee failed to meet its goal for contributions. The special April council at Mechanicsburg had made acquisition of a site conditional upon cash receipts and pledges necessary to acquire it, so the solicitors strove to meet the deadline of the sixty-day purchase option.[87] When these efforts failed, the project appeared to be in jeopardy.[88]

Supporters of the home, meanwhile, would not accept defeat. Acting on their personal initiative without formal church authority, they began to explore the possibilities of establishing a benevolent home on a non-sectarian basis, but with rules and regulations formulated according to the principles and faith of the Brethren in Christ.[89]

This group held a preliminary meeting in February at the Bailey Street residence of Henry Garman. John Myers, who served as temporary chairman, announced the purpose of the meeting to be the establishment of "a permanent place of worship, as well as for Sunday School and a Home for the needy, aged, feeble and friendless and a department for Rescue work."[90]

The group then elected temporary officers, all of whom were residents of Harrisburg. Their colleagues in the venture were men and women from Dauphin, Lebanon, Lancaster, and Cumberland Counties. Presumably most of the group were Brethren in Christ.[91] Samuel Smith, one of the officers, was not, however, for he with his wife and three daughters accepted Brethren membershp at the first love feast held at the home.[92]

Meanwhile, circumstances had opened the way to launch the enterprise at 1175 Bailey Street on the site previously considered for purchase by the committee named at the special council at Mechanicsburg. John and Caty Ann Myers were instrumental in gaining access to this property. Having visited widely in Harrisburg, they were deeply concerned about the need to do something for the homeless of the city and to correlate what was done with a teaching and preaching ministry. When they learned that the northern half of the Brandt building at 1175 Bailey Street was available for occupancy, they rented it for thirteen months at fifteen dollars per month.[93]

The group interested in beginning a home then assumed responsibility for the rental contract negotiated by John Myers, and a committee of eleven men and women launched a campaign to solicit "money, clothing, household goods and furnishing of every description, provisions, etc." With the contributions received, they equipped their half of the building and dedicated it on March 1, 1896, as the "Messiah Rescue and Benevolent Home of Harrisburg, Pennsylvania."[94] John and Caty Ann Myers offered to serve without salary as steward and matron until others could be found to take their places.[95]

These were very modest beginnings in plant development and staff recruitment for the kind of institution envisioned, but its promoters labored to strengthen both the organizational structure and legal base. They appointed a permanent Board of Managers, various standing committees, a physician, and adopted a Constitution and By-Laws which became the basis for eventual legal incorporation.[96] On April 15, 1896, the Court of Dauphin County chartered the institution as "The Messiah Rescue and Benevolent Home."[97]

The home admitted four classes of members: primary, secondary, life, and rescue. Primary members were persons homeless and destitute, including children. Secondary members paid fifty-dollar admission fee and a regular monthly installment decided by the Board of Managers. Life members paid a $1,000 admission fee and an additional annuity as decided by the board. Rescue members were destitute men and women "fallen and degraded in morals," and deserted children. They differed from primary members only because their admission came under the jurisdiction of a Rescue Committee empowered to act in instances where the persons involved required immediate assistance. An Investigating Committee methodically processed all other applications for admission.[98]

The home accepted as its first member a non-Brethren woman thirty-three years of age, who had been ill for thirteen years. She had no financial resources and was dependent for her support upon a brother and sister who were themselves in destitute circumstances.[99] By the beginning of July, the number of members had increased to six. Three were children and three were adults. Of the latter one was an invalid, one a cripple, and one an aged woman of eighty years.[100]

While arranging facilities and admitting members, those responsible for the home simultaneously developed a program of Christian worship, witness, and nurture. They immediately began Sunday services and week-day prayer meetings.[101] Following dedication of the building, they conducted a protracted meeting and organized a Sunday school.[102] The precise date of their first love feast is not known, but Avery Long, the second steward, reported in July that it was well attended and "a real feast to our souls."[103]

The home was technically non-sectarian, but the Brethren in Christ provided the models for its religious program. This was the clear intention of those who launched the project. In October, 1897, the Board of Managers formalized this intent by granting the Brethren in Christ a ninety-nine year privilege of worship at the home.[104]

Even as the institution began, its founders recognized the basic inadequacy of their physical facilities. The rented building was about thirty-five years old. Although originally well constructed, time and neglect had taken their toll, and some parts of the structure were deteriorating.[105] For this reason the Board of Managers began almost immediately to seek for a new building site.[106]

While this search proceeded, the way opened for the home to rent the remaining southern portion of the building for fifteen dollars a month. Samuel Smith left an interesting account of how this development occurred. The southern part of the property, Smith noted, had been occupied by "what was called a 'club'." He continued:

> . . . the nature of the work that was carried on there was not generally known, since their meetings were held behind locked doors; suffice to say that guests from different parts of the country, as well as of the city of Harrisburg, Pa., assembled there, who required kegs and cases of beer and bottled champagne almost daily; and while there were evening prayer-meetings each day, as well as Sabbath meetings held by the Home workers, the reader can easily form an idea of the contrast between the two kinds of meetings which were daily conducted by the tenants of the one building; and seldom is the power of the Spirit more manifested than in this case, since while the workers of the Home and those who met there for worship, kindly and in a Christ-like manner conducted themselves towards the club frequenters, and offered many prayers in their behalf, that in about six weeks after the Home had practically begun operations, the club people relinquished their claims to the buildings, and reported to the rent agent that the place was getting too "religiously hot for them;" [sic] and quietly moved away.[107]

Occupancy of the entire building on a rental basis did not, of course, adequately meet the needs which had prompted the Board of Managers to seek a new building location. They had viewed various sites which proved to be either unsatisfactory or unavailable.[108] Under these circumstances they reopened negotiations to purchase the rented building, and eventually secured it for $10,000. Contributions provided $5,000 in cash for the purchase, and a mortgage secured the additional $5,000.[109]

Ownership of the building caused much discussion as to whether it should be replaced or merely repaired and remodeled. In 1897 an all-Pennsylvania council decided in favor of replacement. This was done at a cost of approximately $5,000, thus doubling the indebtedness.[110]

The new facility was a three-story frame structure with a steam heating system and twenty-eight rooms for residents and attendants. It had two complete indoor bathrooms as well as "an outside retreat." The chapel, which was illuminated with electricity, had a seating capacity of approximately 300.[111]

On November 4, 1897, the dedication of the new building as the "Messiah Rescue and Benevolent Home" and as a place of worship for the Brethren in Christ of Harrisburg took place. Jesse Engle, en route to mission work in Africa, preached the dedicatory sermon on the theme: "Where is the house that God built?" Twenty-one ministers were present.[112]

Improved physical facilities resolved some of the pressing problems of the home but others remained. The task of harmonizing relationships between persons of diverse backgrounds, age, and sex proved to be very difficult.[113] One of the most trying aspects of the situation was the presence of young children in the same quarters with adults ranging in age up to 100 years. These circumstances hindered the children's phase of the work until the erection of a separate children's building.[114]

Barbara Kern of Indianapolis, Indiana, furnished the financial impetus for such a building by offering $3,000 to construct it, an amount later increased to $3,525. Herself an orphan, Miss Kern acted from a sense of appreciation for the kind care given to her sister by a member of the Brethren in Christ Church.[115] When completed the new children's quarters erected south of the home was a substantial brick structure with two main stories and a finished attic.[116] It was dedicated as "Messiah Home Orphanage" on May 19, 1901.[117] The dedicatory statement read:

> Before we separate we will, in the fear of God, . . . set apart and dedicate to God this house . . . for the use of destitute and homeless children, . . . Here may they be cared for. Here may they receive physical, intellectual, moral

and spiritual instruction, and may this Home never be prostituted to the teaching of unsound or questionable doctrine, but may it ever be kept by the power and grace of God; . . .[118]

A city environment posed problems for the orphanage work. Public school attendance had an unwholesome effect upon the children's morals and discipline. In an effort to counteract this, the orphanage established its own private school with Mary Hoffman as teacher.[119]

The Messiah Home Orphanage family in 1905. Miss Barbara Kern, financial benefactress of the orphanage, second from left in top row.

Those interested in the orphanage eventually decided that it should be moved to a country site where the children could receive household and industrial training in a setting free from the problems of urban life.[120] In 1913 a location committee chose a small farm of twenty-eight acres in York County along the Yellow Breeches Creek near the town of Grantham.[121] In the summer of the following year, the children above six years of age moved to the new facility known as "Messiah Orphanage." The younger children remained at the Messiah Rescue and Benevolent Home in a department known as the "Nursery Messiah Orphanage" until June 1915, at which time they were also transferred to the York County location.[122]

To provide for the educational needs of the children, the orphanage erected a school on land leased from the Messiah Bible School and Missionary Training Home. Mary Hoffman, who had taught the orphanage children in Harrisburg, gave her full time to their instruction in Grantham.[123]

In 1925 the Messiah Orphanage moved to Florin (now Mount Joy), Pennsylvania, where it has remained.[124] At the present time it carries on a professionally directed program as Messiah Children's Home, a name adopted in 1954.[125]

Although many regarded the Messiah Home and Orphanage as a Brethren in Christ institution from the beginning, it operated for several years merely as a project of a group of individuals, most of whom were Brethren memebers.[126] Under its by-laws, the only religious requirement for service on the Board of Managers was membership in "some orthodox association who believe in and practice the teachings of our Lord and Saviour Jesus Christ as laid down in the four fold gospel."[127] When General Conference assumed title to the home, about seventy percent of the residents were members of other denominations.[128]

The non-sectarian beginning of the Home was not an obstacle to its later transfer to the Brethren in Christ Church, but there was strong opposition to this transfer on other grounds. In 1899 when General Conference considered accepting the home, some members feared that it would become a financial encumbrance upon the brotherhood. Friends of the home, after defeating a motion to continue the previous incorporation, finally carried the day with a strong vote favoring transfer.[129]

On March 30, 1900, the Board of Managers conveyed to five trustees appointed by General Conference the title deed with all "right, title, claim and interest as vested in the Messiah Rescue and Benevolent Home organization."[130]

In 1936 the home relocated in a new three-story brick structure at 2001 Paxton Street, Harrisburg.[131] Usage gradually substituted the name "Messiah Home" for the original name, a change officially confirmed by General Conference in 1964.[132] At the time of this writing (1976) the institution is in the process of relocating near Mechanicsburg, Pennsylvania, as "Messiah Village."

Effects of Benevolent Enterprises

These early benevolent enterprises did not disrupt traditional attitudes of the Brethren as much as did some of the other changes made by the group in that period, but they had some significant consequences. One was increased missionary interest and its identification with social concern for the aged, orphaned, and morally fallen. The men and women who pioneered these benevolent undertakings saw them as opportunities both to evangelize and to minister to basic human needs for shelter, food, and love.

A second effect of the benevolent activities was the development of Brethren in Christ congregations associated with some of them. In Harrisburg a new congregation emerged as a result of the founding of the Messiah Rescue and Benevolent Home. Concerning the influence of the Mount Carmel Orphanage, an observer noted:

> The Home is located near the Franklin Corners Church. The Home and Church are inseparable. One is a part of the other. We are reminded of a statement made by our sainted Bishop Isaac Trump in the early years of the work when he said, "This Home is the saving of the church in Northern Illinois."[133]

A third consequence of benevolent enterprises was encouragement for the Brethren to modify their characteristic separation from Christians of other backgrounds. The orphanage in which some members participated at Hillsboro, Kansas, was non-denominational. The Messiah Rescue and Benevolent Home was non-sectarian in its origin, with by-laws providing for the cooperation of persons from different evangelical denominations.

Finally, the care of charity residents by benevolent institutions of the Brethren helped to modify the traditional brotherhood detachment from the social and economic structures of society. Had a private agency not assumed financial responsibility for this care, some of the persons involved, such as homeless children, would have become public charges. This fact suggested the possibility that benevolent institutions might qualify for public assistance for at least part of the costs of caring for indigent persons. Soon after its founding the Messiah Rescue and Benevolent Home inquired whether Pennsylvania would provide some financial assistance, but the state government was unwilling to grant funds to this new and unproved enterprise.[134]

The Ishi Faith Home in Lancaster, Pennsylvania, was the first benevolent project of the Brethren to receive public assistance. That home secured some of its children from the Lancaster County Alms Home. When the County Board of Poor Directors of the latter institution offered one dollar and seventy-five cents per week toward the care of two female infants, the personnel of the home hesitated. This hesitation was not due to the public source of the funds but to the fact that an assured measure of monthly income seemed to compromise the principle of "faith work" to which those sponsoring the institution were committed. They agreed, however, that they could accept the monthly payments as a "donation." This led the County Board of Poor Directors to make the shrewd observation that the staff of the home had no reason to object if the "donations" were not always forthcoming.[135] Clearly, the Brethren saw no conflict between their doctrine of separation from the world and the acceptance of public funds for benevolent purposes.

Public assistance soon became a regular source of income for the Mount Carmel Orphanage. Prior to the depression of the 1930s, the institution received a total allowance of thirty dollars per month from Whiteside County, Illinois. Later, when depression conditions threatened closure of the orphanage, the county increased this monthly allowance to ten dollars per child.[136]

NOTES:

[1]Joseph Hershey, "For Peace and Unity," *Visitor,* IV (February 1, 1891), 40; Anthony Stoner, "'Look Before you Leap': An Open Letter to the Brotherhood," *Visitor,* IV

(March 15, 1891), 91.

[2][Henry Davidson], "The Annual Conference," *Visitor,* IV (June, 1891), 168; J. M. Engle, "The Visitor," *Visitor,* IV (March 15, 1891), 92.

[3]*Church Government,* 1887, p. 13.

[4]*Ibid.,* p. 14.

[5]In 1876 General Conference postponed the periodical issue for the third time.

[6]*Church Government,* 1887, p. 21.

[7]*General Council Minutes,* 1881, Article 6. Three additional districts failed to report.

[8]*Ibid.,* Article 5.

[9]*General Conference Minutes,* 1887, Article 7.

[10]This committee was soon referred to as the Publication Board. *General Conference Minutes,* 1890, p. 4.

[11][Henry Davidson], *Visitor,* I (June 1, 1888), 152; *ibid.,* III (January 1, 1890), 9.

[12]*Ibid.,* IV (January 15, 1891), 25.

[13][Henry Davidson], "The Annual Conference," *Visitor,* IV (June 1, 1891), 168; Eli M. Engle, "Personal Reminiscences of the Introduction of the Evangelical Visitor," *Visitor, Fiftieth Anniversary,* p. 29.

[14]Quoted by Fannie Davidson in "Our First Editor," *Visitor, Fiftieth Anniversary,* p. 17.

[15]Told by Frances Davidson to Naomi Brubaker Brechbill. Naomi Brubaker Brechbill interview, February 25, 1973.

[16][Henry Davidson], "Salutatory," *Visitor,* I (August 1, 1887), 1.

[17]*Ibid.*

[18][Henry Davidson], "The Editor's Difficulty," *Visitor,* III (December 1, 1890), 360. See also [Henry Davidson] *Visitor,* IX (September 15, 1896), 280.

[19][Henry Davidson], "Salutatory," *Visitor,* I (August 1, 1887), 1.

[20][Henry Davidson], *Visitor,* I (August 1, 1888), 184. See also his "Why Not One Church Only?," *Visitor,* IV (November 1, 1891), 328.

[21]Henry Davidson, "Farm for Sale," *Visitor,* II (March 1, 1889), 88.

[22][Henry Davidson], *Visitor,* IV (July 1, 1891), 200.

[23]The Brethren acquired their own press in 1920 when the Publication Board purchased the Murray Printing Plant at Nappanee, Indiana. *General Conference Minutes,* 1920, Article 24, p. 36; *ibid.,* 1921, Article 35, p. 40.

[24][Henry Davidson], "Corrections," *Visitor,* V (July 15, 1892), 216; *Visitor,* V (August 1, 1892), 232.

[25]Jacob F. Eisenhower, "An Open Letter," *Visitor,* IV (January 1, 1891), 13.

[26]Joseph Hershey, "For Peace and Unity," *Visitor,* IV (February 1, 1891), 40.

[27]J. M. Engle, "The Visitor," *Visitor,* IV (March 15, 1891), 40.

[28]T. A. Long, "The Visitor," *Visitor,* IV (April 1, 1891), 106.

[29]Anthony Stoner, "'Look Before You Leap': An Open Letter to the Brotherhood," *Visitor,* IV (March 15, 1891), 91.

[30]Five such articles appeared in the issue of March 15, 1891.

[31][Henry Davidson], *Visitor,* IV (April 1, 1891), 104.

[32]Eli M. Engle, "Personal Reminiscences," *Visitor, Fiftieth Anniversary,* p. 29.

[33]*Ibid.*

[34]*Ibid.*

[35]P. J. Wiebe, "Early Recollections," *Visitor, Fiftieth Anniversary,* p. 27.

[36][Henry Davidson], "The Annual Conference," *Visitor*, IV (June 1, 1891), 168.

[37]J. K. Forney, "A Reminiscence," *Visitor, Fiftieth Anniversary*, p. 30.

[38]Eli M. Engle, "Personal Reminiscences" *Visitor, Fiftieth Anniversary*, p. 29; [Henry Davidson], "The Annual Conference," *Visitor*, IV (June 1, 1891), 168.

[39][Henry Davidson], "The Annual Conference," *Visitor*, IV (June 1, 1891), 168.

[40][Henry Davidson], *Visitor*, IX (April 1, 1896), 105.

[41]*Ibid.*, IX (January 15, 1896), 24.

[42]*Ibid.*

[43]*Ibid.*

[44]*Ibid.*

[45]*General Conference Minutes*, 1896, p. 2.

[46]*Ibid.*

[47]*Ibid.*

[48]*Ibid.*

[49][Henry Davidson], *Visitor*, IX (October 1, 1896), 297.

[50]Samuel Zook, "Notice," *Visitor*, IX (September 15, 1896), 280.

[51]*Ibid.*

[52][Henry Davidson], *Visitor*, IX (October 1, 1896), 297.

[53][Henry Engle], "Holiness unto the Lord," *Visitor*, XI (May 15, 1898), 181.

[54][Henry Engle], "Salutatory," *Visitor*, IX (October 15, 1896), 305.

[55]See the following sampling of his editorials: "Fiery Experiences," *Visitor*, XI (July 15, 1898), 275; "Religious Fanaticism," *Visitor*, XII (May 1, 1899), 175; "Holiness unto the Lord," *Visitor*, XII (May 15, 1899), 194-95.

[56][Henry Engle], "The Relation of the Church to the Course of This Age," *Visitor*, XII (January 1, 1899), 15.

[57][Henry Engle], "Religious Unrest," *Visitor*, XII (February 1, 1899), 55.

[58]See Chapter VIII for Engle's adoption of Russellism.

[59][Henry Engle], "Valedictory," *Visitor*,XII (June 1, 1899), 214.

[60][Samuel Zook], *Visitor*, XII (October 15, 1899), 394.

[61][Samuel Zook], "Conference Forecast," *Visitor*, XIII (May 1, 1900), 174.

[62]*General Conference Minutes*, 1900, p. 14.

[63]Detwiler, "Evangelical Visitor," Asa W. Climenhaga Papers.

[64][George Detwiler], "Redeemed," *Visitor*, XIII (July 15, 1900), 261.

[65]See Chapter III.

[66]Detwiler, "Evangelical Visitor."

[67]*General Conference Minutes*, 1902, Article 41, p. 25.

[68]J. R. Zook, "A Voice for Righteousness and Success," *Visitor*, XXI (August 15, 1907), 6.

[69][George Detwiler], "Our New Location," *Visitor*, XVII (January 1, 1903), pp. 2-3.

[70]Masthead, *Evangelical Visitor*, XXXII (January 13, 1919), 8.

[71]*Church Government*, 1887, p. 19. Elder Jesse Engle of Kansas got into serious financial difficulty by personally investing heavily in Dickinson County land for an orphans' home. See D. Heise, "A Proposition," *Visitor*, IV (January 1, 1891), 11; Jesse Engle "Correction," *Visitor*, IV (February 1, 1891), 41.

[72]*Prospectus of the Industrial School and Hygiene Home for Friendless Persons* (Marietta, Pa.: Urie B. Engle, printer, 1893), pref. and pp. 1-5; [Henry Davidson], *Visitor*, VII (September 15, 1894), 280; E. Adella Engle, "Work Among the Orphans,"

Visitor, XII (August 1, 1899), 296; John H. Myers, "Pleasant Recollections," *Visitor,* XXI (September 16, 1907), 6.

[73]They previously shared in the founding of the Messiah Rescue and Benevolent Home in Harrisburg, Pennsylvania.

[74]C. A. Myers, "What Shall the Women Do?" *Visitor,* XII (March 1, 1899), 85; C. A. Myers, "Ebenezer Faith Home," *Visitor,* XIII (February 15, 1900), 78; Ishi Workers, "Concerning the Ishi Faith Home," *Visitor,* XV (May 15, 1901), 197.

[75]"History of Jabbok Bible School," *Visitor, Fiftieth Anniversary, p. 58.*

[76]*General Conference Minutes,* 1909, Article 43, pp. 51-53; *ibid.,* 1924, Article 39, pp. 49-50; *ibid.,* 1925, Article 32, pp. 51-52. The annuity payment to the Eisenhowers was $500 per annum.

[77]"Mt. Carmel Home," *Visitor, Fiftieth Anniversary, p. 45.*

[78]Records of Mt. Carmel Faith Missionary Home and Orphanage, May 27 and 29th, 1900, Church Archives.

[79]*Ibid.,* January 13, 1909.

[80]*General Conference Minutes,* 1912, Article 71, p. 182; *ibid.,* 1968, Article 24, p. 102.

[81]*History of the Messiah Rescue and Benevolent Home and Messiah Home Orphanage to January 1st,* 1902, compiled by S. R. Smith, Secretary (Harrisburg, Pa.: Central Printing and Publishing House, 1902), pp. 13-14. Cited hereafter as *Messiah Home and Orphanage.*

[82]*Ibid.,* p. 14.

[83]"A Home for the Poor," *Visitor,* VIII (April 1, 1895), 109. See also the citations in the preceding note.

[84]Amos Z. Myers, "A Home for the Homeless," *Visitor,* VIII (May 1, 1895), 140; typescript of the minutes of this meeting, Asa W. Climenhaga Papers.

[85]*Messiah Home and Orphanage,* pp. 14-15.

[86]*Ibid.,* 15-16.

[87]Amos Z. Myers, "The Proposed Home in Harrisburg," *Visitor,* VIII (September 1, 1895), 265.

[88]*Messiah Home and Orphanage,* p. 16.

[89]*Ibid.,* pp. 16-17.

[90]Record of Minutes of Messiah Rescue and Benevolent Home of Harrisburg, Pa., February 12, 1896, cited hereafter as M.R. & B.H. Minutes; *Messiah Home and Orphanage,* pp. 16-17.

[91]M.R. & B.H. Minutes, February 12, 1896; *Messiah Home and Orphanage,* pp. 16-17.

[92]T. A. Long, "From the Harrisburg Home," *Visitor,* IX (July 15, 1896), 219.

[93]C. A. Myers, "The Home Begun," *Visitor,* IX (April 15, 1896), 121; M.R. & B.H. Minutes, February 12, 1896; *Messiah Home and Orphanage,* p. 18.

[94]M. R. & B. H. Minutes, February 12, 1896; *Messiah Home and Orphanage,* p. 18.

[95]*Messiah Home and Orphanage,* pp. 17-20.

[96]M.R. & B.H. Minutes, March 3 and 10, 1896.

[97]*Constitution and By-Laws of the Messiah Rescue and Benevolent Home, Harrisburg, Pa., Chartered April 15, 1896,* Constitution, Article 1.

[98]*Ibid.,* By-Laws, Article 6.

[99]M.R. & B.H. Minutes, March 28, 1896.

[100]T. A. Long, "From the Harrisburg Home," *Visitor,* IX (July 15, 1896), 219.

[101]*Messiah Home and Orphanage*, p. 22.

[102]M.R. & B.H. Minutes, March 3 and April 14, 1896.

[103]T. A. Long, "From the Harrisburg Home," *Visitor*, IX (July 15, 1896), 219.

[104]M.R. & B.H. Minutes, October 28, 1897.

[105]*Messiah Home and Orphanage*, p. 21.

[106]M.R. & B.H. Minutes, April 14 and 21, 1896.

[107]*Messiah Home and Orphanage*, pp. 22-23.

[108]M.R. & B.H. Minutes, April 21, 1896.

[109]*Messiah Home and Orphanage*, pp. 24-25.

[110]*Ibid.*, pp. 27, 31. By 1901 the Home had cleared this indebtedness.

[111]*Ibid.*, pp. 51-52.

[112]*Middletown Press*, November 13, 1897, cited in *Visitor*, X (December 15, 1897), 430.

[113]*Messiah Home and Orphanage*, pp. 45-46.

[114]*Ibid.*, p. 41.

[115]*Ibid.*, p. 34; A. B. Musser, "Report of Orphan Home," *Visitor*, February 1, 1901, 56; Ada G. Engle, "Dedication of Orphanage at Harrisburg, Pa.," *Visitor*, XV (July 1, 1901), 257. Miss Kern was present at the dedication.

[116]*Messiah Home and Orphanage*, p. 52.

[117]*Ibid.*, p. 34-35; Ada G. Engle, "Dedication of Orphanage at Harrisburg, Pa." *Visitor*, XV (July 1, 1901), 257.

[118]*Messiah Home and Orphanage*, pp. 34-35.

[119]*General Conference Minutes*, 1906, Article 54, p. 29.

[120]*Ibid.*, 1915, Article 16, p. 58.

[121]*Ibid.*, 1914, Article 17, p. 20. The orphanage building erected on this site is now owned by Messiah College and is known as "Treona."

[122]*Ibid.*, 1915, Article 16, pp. 59-60; *ibid.*, Article 43, p. 85; *ibid.*, 1916, Article 58, pp. 89-90.

[123]*Ibid.*, 1915, Article 7, p. 20. This explains the origin of the "Schoolhouse," a small, brown, block building on the present campus of Messiah College.

[124]*Ibid.*, 1925, Article 33, p. 57.

[125]*Ibid.*, 1954, p. 21.

[126]*Messiah Home and Orphanage*, p. 32.

[127]*Constitution and By-Laws of the Messiah Rescue and Benevolent Home, Harrisburg, Pa., Chartered April 15, 1896*, By-Laws, Article 3.

[128]*Messiah Home and Orphanage*, p. 32.

[129]*General Conference Minutes*, 1899, Articles 13 and 33.

[130]*Messiah Home and Orphanage*, p. 33.

[131]"Messiah Rescue and Benevolent Home," *Visitor, Fiftieth Anniversary*, pp. 43-44.

[132]*General Conference Minutes*, 1964, Article 22, p. 86.

[133]"Mt. Carmel Home," *Visitor, Fiftieth Anniversary*, p. 45.

[134]M.R. & B.H. Minutes, December 8, 1896. See also *ibid.*, December 15, 1898.

[135]"Spiritual and business work of the Ishi Faith Home," April 26, 1899, typescript among Asa W. Climenhaga Papers.

[136]"Mt. Carmel Home," *Visitor, Fiftieth Anniversary*, p. 45.

XIII

Institutional Beginnings:
Education

Awakening Interest in Advanced Education

The Brethren in Christ saw no need for more than elementary education during their first one hundred years. Their preoccupation with worship and work made advanced learning irrelevant, and their perception of change as a threat to their faith led them to suspect such learning as a "worldly" influence.[1] When individual members here and there began to desire advanced education, they faced the indifference and disapproval of the brotherhood. To keep these desires under supervision, General Conference of 1881 ruled that members could attend high or boarding schools only by permission of their respective districts.[2]

Some areas of the brotherhood were more ready than others to respond sympathetically to interest in education. One Kansas district, for example, granted a young man's request for permission to qualify for public school teaching.[3] On the other hand, church members joined parents and relatives in opposing another young man in Pennsylvania who wished to attend normal school. Although he persevered—"tugged and toiled"—and completed the course, he wrestled with inner feelings of uncertainty about being in God's will and finally concluded that he was "not created to grapple with these foolish things."[4]

The opposition of the Brethren to education gradually declined in the midst of the ferment which characterized their movement as it underwent transition from 1880 to 1910. Several factors contributed to their awareness of the need for more than elementary education. One was rising educational expectations in society generally. At the same time the

Brethren were also generating internal pressures for change. When they accepted Sunday schools, a church periodical, and corporate mission work, discerning members saw that such enterprises required knowledge and skills which few of them could hope to acquire without formal education.

The wholesome attitude of the few young men and women who braved opposition and entered high schools and colleges was another factor which caused the Brethren to take a more positive view of advanced education. Since these young people generally remained loyal to the brotherhood while acquiring education, they demonstrated that educational pursuits did not necessarily undermine faith.

William Baker, influential nineteenth-century leader in Northern Ohio, was the first professionally educated member. He read medicine under the tutelage of an uncle and later attended lectures at Jefferson Medical College, Philadelphia, and Western Reserve, Cleveland. His medical practice began in 1855 about the time that he united with the brotherhood.[5]

Traditional evidence suggests that a few other leaders in Baker's generation had respect for advanced education. Levi Lukenbach studied German, English, and Latin.[6] Charles Baker came to Canada from Germany where education was highly regarded. Although too young to have progressed far with formal schooling before his family emigrated from their homeland, his *Visitor* articles and the impressions of one who knew him well indicate that he was a relatively learned man compared with most of his nineteenth-century Brethren contemporaries.[7]

Beginning in the 1880s a number of younger members acquired advanced education. These included John Zook, noted holiness evangelist, Frances Davidson, pioneer missionary to Africa, Clara and Mary Hoffman, Edna Booser, and Enos Hess, all of whom served on the faculty of the Messiah Bible School and Missionary Training Home, and Peter J. Wiebe who helped to found four Brethren schools.[8] With the exception of Zook, all eventually completed baccalaureate programs; Davidson, Clara Hoffman, Hess, and Wiebe also earned Masters' degrees.[9] In addition Samuel Smith had earned a Master's degree in accountancy from Columbia College prior to his acceptance of Brethren membership in the 1890s.[10]

While these courageous educational pioneers pressed forward, the mission movement gradually awakened other members to the values of education. George Detwiler was in the forefront of those who stressed the educational needs of foreign missionaries. In 1904 he commented:

Whether there should be an educational test in the examination of candidates who feel called to the foreign field, has not come up yet for consideration, but we think the church cannot wisely continue to ignore it much longer. . . . We think those who have had opportunity to study the question are able to speak with some authority, and the testimony of such is that in studying the language, those who know the grammar of their own language have large advantage . . . . Those who go forth as ambassadors of the Christ will find that there is more required than to tell one's experience.[11]

As editor of the *Visitor,* Detwiler later received letters noting that missionaries should have knowledge of common diseases and should be trained in nursing the sick, obstetrics, and general hygiene "in addition to an acquaintance with Bible Truth and some practical training in actual work in soul winning, . . ."[12] Other prominent churchmen such as John Zook also argued forcefully for the educational preparation of mission workers for both home and foreign fields.[13]

Messiah Bible School and Missionary Training Home

The growing awareness that education was important for the proclamation of their faith led some Brethren to become advocates of a denominational Bible school and missionary training home. By the early twentieth century, young men and women were seeking this type of training in institutions such as the Hepzibah Faith Missionary Training Home in Tabor, Iowa, the Christian and Missionary Alliance School in Nyack, New York, the Moody Bible Institute in Chicago, and the Toronto Bible Training School in Ontario.[14]

These circumstances aroused concern lest the teaching at such institutions undermine commitment to the distinctives of the Brethren faith. A member of the General Foreign Mission Board wrote:

We . . . discover that those who attend other institutions for special preparation . . . frequently have partaken of some particular doctrine that is not in accord with our belief or teaching and thus embarrass both them and the church. . . . The injuries we have thus suffered I need not relate, for you are all too well acquainted with the facts.[15]

Perhaps the writer had in mind individuals such as David Zook who attended the Hepzibah Faith Missionary Training Home, married a non-Brethren woman, went as a faith missionary to India, and eventually withdrew his membership from the Brethren.[16]

Many members, however, were unconvinced that the Brethren needed their own school to safeguard and promote their faith. The result was formation of pro- and anti-school factions engaged in a controversy which surged through a decade in the life of the brotherhood.

The anti-school group represented a variety of concerns. Typical Brethren opposition to change from time-honored tradition was in evidence. One member wrote: "O, I love the foundation of the Brethren—let us adhere to it. O, how it hurts me that the Bible school . . . and other things are invented and brought into the church. Woe unto you, inventors of things!"[17] Another member, who opposed such traditionalism, observed: "I sometimes think there is too much of this spirit among us,—well our forefathers were good honest Christian men, and they believed thus and so, . . . on this and that line, and why should we depart from it."[18]

Some opponents of a church school questioned the biblical authority for founding an educational institution. Bishop Charles Baker of Ontario, a school supporter, believed this to be a basic issue in the controversy. He acknowledged the New Testament silence about schools but argued from both Old and New Testament passages that the Scriptures indirectly supported them.[19]

Practical considerations also encouraged opposition to a school. Another Canadian leader, Fred Elliott, forcefully articulated these. In his view the group lacked the membership, money, and personnel to provide a first-class institution and "a school that was not first-class would be a failure from the start."[20] He also foresaw the division of the church on the issue of second-work sanctification as an insurmountable obstacle to the effective cooperation of the two factions in a school project. In his words:

Can the radical [second-work holiness] and conservative [traditional Brethren view of sanctification] ideas be taught together? Never. If the radical theories alone are taught, what loyal member would want his boy or girl to attend it? If the conservative element controlled it, the radical element would go to Tabor or elsewhere as before, and still claim recognition of the church.[21]

Elliott's solution for the educational dilemma facing the church was to encourage members to attend selected existing schools. The Toronto Bible Training School in Canada and Church of the Brethren (Dunker) schools in the United States were, he thought, adequate for the Brethren needs. He pointed out that Frances Davidson, who earned college degrees from and taught for a time at a Church of the Brethren college, was not harmed by her educational experiences.[22].

Some members were unimpressed with this proposed solution of the educational dilemma.[23] An 1897 petition from Des Moines, Iowa, requested General Conference "to consider the propriety of establishing a World's Missionary Training Home, for the benefit of those who are called of God to do missionary work." Conference postponed the question for a year and then postponed it indefinitely.[24]

After a lapse of several years, the school question again came before General Conference, this time from Northern Ohio.[25] Conference then appointed a committee to consider the advisability of starting a school.[26] In 1905 the committee, noting that a majority of the districts opposed the project, advised against it. Noting, however, "the evident misleading teachings and influence to which our younger members especially are subjected," the committee recommended Bible study sessions in meetinghouses throughout the various districts of the brotherhood. Brethren members certified by the Examining Board would provide the instruction. Conference accepted these proposals.[27]

This decision against establishing a Brethren school did not dispose of the issue. As the 1906 General Conference approached, Editor Detwiler noted:

> All reforms meet with more or less . . . opposition before they are adopted, whether in church or State. But sooner or later, if there is worth in them, they will be adopted. The above remarks, we believe, will also, in the end, be true of the Missionary Training Home and Bible School question. The matter has been before conference in some shape or form several times and has, as might be expected, met with defeat. Yet the question, like Hamlet's ghost, "will not down." . . . One correspondent expresses the fear that if the church continues to refuse to recognize the imperative need, and continues to ignore it, the matter will possibly be taken up independent of the church and cause a condition of things not the most desirable.[28]

Detwiler's concluding observation raised the specter of a church-related school outside of Brethren control. This did not, however, deter the anti-school faction from continuing their opposition. Reader response to Detwiler's comments revealed wide differences of opinion about the school matter, and he concluded that there would be "need of large charity and much benevolence so that love may not be too much strained."[29]

Events transpiring in Ohio, meanwhile, brought the school question back to General Conference in 1906. Ohio State Council met in March of that year. Samuel Smith of Pennsylvania was present and received the courtesy of council membership normally extended to visiting church leaders. At that time he enjoyed special status in the brotherhood because of his visibility in the office of General Conference Secretary.[30]

Smith's presence at this particular Ohio State Council appears to have been planned with a special purpose. He carried with him a detailed proposal for launching a school subject to Brethren control. Whether he released the proposal in Ohio because he believed that Pennsylvania State Council would reject it or because he felt that it would carry more weight coming to Conference from the Midwest is unknown. Whatever his motives, the Ohio officials granted him a sympathetic hearing, and Ohio State Council unanimously approved the submission of his plan to General Conference.[31]

Basic to this so-called "Ohio proposition" was Smith's proposal ". . . that this Council pray General Conference of 1906 to recognize any efforts that individual members, if any, may be disposed to make toward establishing such an institution and give it moral support, the institution and its promotor or promotors [sic] to be amenable to General Conference only and not to any single district or person wherever it might be located, . . ."[32] This proposal sought to clear the way for an individual or group to start a school and also to make sure that it would not be controlled by any segment of the brotherhood. Other resolutions specified that the institution should be self-supporting and subject to the supervision of an executive board of loyal members of the Brethren appointed by General Conference.

There are no existing records of the General Conference debates on the Ohio proposition. The minutes state only that Conference considered and debated the advisability of establishing "a Training Home and Bible School," but the resulting vote of two to one in favor of a school was a significant victory for the friends of advanced education.[33] This vote committed the brotherhood to undertake a school project corporately but provided no means to implement the decision.

General Conference of 1907 addressed itself to the task of implementation. It considered three petitions as "to how, when and where the work shall be undertaken" and referred the matter to a committee instructed to report back to the current session.[34]

The committee's report recommended appointment of a representative board of seven men to be known as "The Bible School Incorporating

Board, or Board of Managers." This board was to take immediate steps to formulate plans for organizing and conducting a church school. These plans were to include qualifications of teachers, curriculum, methods to solicit funds both to launch and sustain the project, and investigation of a suitable location available by purchase, rental, or bequest.[35]

Conference then authorized the Incorporating Board to proceed as soon as the sum of $10,000 was donated or subscribed but instructed it not to enter into any contract for the purchase of property or anything else that would involve the church in a financial obligation. Other resolutions authorized the board to choose a school name and to secure a charter guaranteeing that "the method of conducting, teaching, etc., would remain in harmony with the faith of the Brethren."

A committee request that General Conference express itself about the location of the school encountered vigorous opposition. Bowing to this pressure, Conference named a committee of five to decide the location. When that committee announced its preference for Pennsylvania, Conference rejected the recommendation and directed the Incorporating Board to choose the location.

This 1907 flurry of debate over the location of the school was the opening skirmish in a major struggle between Pennsylvania and the Midwest. Educationally minded churchmen across the brotherhood had united in support of a Brethren school; they now divided on the question of its location.

Soon after the close of the 1907 Conference the Incorporating Board decided to name the institution "Messiah Bible School and Missionary Training Home" and to locate it at or in the vicinity of Harrisburg, Pennsylvania.[36] At that time the board visualized its curriculum and program as follows:

> The study of the Bible in all its various departments. A preparatory course for those who are not versed in language and other literature to properly study the Bible. The Missionary Training Department shall be used only for those who contemplate doing Home and Foreign Mission work and who must first be recommended by the Home District, examined by either the Home or Foreign Mission Board, and the Examining Committee . . . nothing shall be introduced into the school that cannot stand side by side with God's Word outside of the necessities of life, eliminating games of every kind, societies that are in any form tainted with secrecy, thus making a school where even the most fastidious need have no fear to send their sons and daughters. The school must be self-supporting; . . .

The name of the institution emphasized a combination of theoretical and applied studies. "Messiah Bible School" stressed the theoretical (Bible, language, etc.) and "Missionary Training Home" the practical (daily mission work). Some articulate advocates of a school had made a strong point of locating it where opportunities for city mission work abounded.[37] Both home and foreign mission interest, furthermore, were growing in the brotherhood, and "Missionary" capitalized upon that interest. "Messiah" likely was suggested by the prior naming of the "Messiah Rescue and Benevolent Home" and the "Messiah Home Orphanage."

Those who favored a midwestern location sharply criticized the decision to place the school in Pennsylvania, and Bishop John Zook was their spokesman. He had long cherished the hope of locating it at Des Moines, Iowa. Charles Good, benefactor of Brethren mission work there, be-

Original "campus" of Messiah Bible School and Missionary Training Home at 46 North 12th Street, Harrisburg, Pennsylvania. Prior to 1910 this building was the residence of Samuel R. Smith, first president of the school.

queathed a plot of land to the Brethren in Christ Church as a site for a missionary training home.[38] Failure to comply with the terms of this bequest led to litigation and loss of title, an outcome which Zook attributed to the resistance of the East to a school in Iowa.[39]

When the Incorporating Board announced in July, 1907, that the school would open in Pennsylvania, the decision was a stunning blow to Bishop Zook. With the next General Conference months away, the only forum for voicing his frustration was the *Visitor*. George Detwiler's sense of fair play overruled his editorial misgivings when he decided to print one of the most scathing articles to appear during his editorship.[40]

Zook began by challenging the bishops who were present at General Conference of 1907, and who, as directed by that body, had chosen the Incorporating Board. Their assignment called for the appointment of a representative group of seven. How, he asked, could a board including only one member west of Ohio meet that criterion? Noting that Indiana, Illinois, Iowa, Oklahoma, and California were unrepresented, he saw this as evidence of unfair eastern influence and asked indignantly: ". . . is it right? Is it fair? Is it equality? I imagine I hear a multitudinous response with the voice of a Niagara, 'No'."

He then charged that the minutes of General Conference of 1907 did not correctly reflect the implications of the vote against locating the school in Pennsylvania. Zook maintained that Conference rejected the Pennsylvania location because of floor arguments favoring points west of that state. In his view the minutes should have read: " 'Conference refused to endorse said recommendation by virtue of arguments in favor of points west of the Alleghenies.' "

Bishop Zook also used the westward movement of the Brethren, which he expected to continue, as an argument against placing the school in the East. To locate it at an extreme point such as Harrisburg would, he thought, "at once provoke a strong agitation for a school in the West. I know it will come, because I have heard such remarks already. . . . And with what fairness could it be refused?"

In closing his article Zook dwelt upon what he called the "Baneful Effect of Piling All Church Institutions on a Heap." Here he gave classical expression to the typical concerns of western Brethren about the concentration of ecclesiastical and institutional power in Pennsylvania. Such "piling" of institutions, he wrote:

. . . destroys the general interest of the brotherhood. It malforms the character of the church. It collects too many of our strong personalities which should be distributed throughout the brotherhood into one place, and thus reduces and curtails the much needed influences of such personalities. It centralizes control too much, and thus throws many strong and useful men into disuse—working some to death, while others, equally good, are rusting out. It destroys confidence and co-operation. It is only reasonable that the moral influences of our church intitutions should be distributed throughout the brotherhood.

This article fell like a bombshell upon the school project. Editor Detwiler explained why he published it, asserted that he should not have done so without the knowledge of the Incorporating Board, and asked forgiveness.[41] Fred Elliott seized upon the article to support his previous warning against the premature founding of a denominational school: "O, brethren, this won't do; to push this project on in the face of such disunion would be a suicidal policy."[42] John Myers disagreed; noting that the question had been thoroughly discussed in Conference, he urged immediate action while calling upon the church to "pray for the committee and stand by them with our means so that they can push the work forward." Myers also administered a subtle rebuke to John Zook, holiness evangelist.

What a pity to delay what is so important. The King's business requires haste.
"Let brotherly love continue." How can it under such circumstances? In this way we not only hinder the church work but show to the public how much we are sanctified, or perhaps I should say how little.[43]

Zook's article was especially critical of the Incorporating Board. None of its members felt the attack more keenly than Samuel Smith. As General Conference Secretary, he had been responsible for the accuracy of the 1907 minutes criticized by Zook, and his residence was in the locality proposed for the school. He apparently read the passionate Zook statement as a personal attack upon himself, for he promptly resigned from the Incorporating Board.[44] These tensions cast a shadow over the new venture into which the Brethren were painfully feeling their way, but reconciling forces were at work. In 1908, after reporting to Conference, the members of the Incorporating Board resigned, citing "certain conditions" which disqualified them for further service. Conference accepted the resignations, approved with amendments the curriculum proposals of the board, and endorsed the decision to locate the school in the vicinity of Harrisburg. It then authorized the bishops present to choose a new enlarged Incorporating Board. The original board members were declared eligible for re-election because the "certain conditions" cited in support of their resignations, although involving "some mistakes," had been satisfactorily adjusted.[45]

The election board of bishops promptly reappointed all members of the original Incorporating Board, plus Bishops John Zook of Iowa and Christian Burkholder of California. Zook now had the western representation he desired, but Pennsylvania already had the school![46]

Finally, and no doubt with much relief, Conference authorized a statement of reconciliation spread on the minutes and published in the *Visitor.* "'The misunderstandings caused by an article published in the *VISITOR* of August 15, 1907, relative to the Bible School and Missionary Training Home has [*sic*] been amicably adjusted and relegated to oblivion and the church is unanimous in the project of the Bible School and Missionary Training Home, and that it shall be a united effort.'"[47]

This closing of the breach between the advocates of a school cleared the way for the Incorporating Board to press forward with the enterprises. By 1909 it had completed the tedious task of incorporation and was wrestling with the problem of a suitable location in Harrisburg or vicinity. Conference continued to be cooperative by appointing Boards of Managers and Trustees.[48]

These signs of progress toward the launching of a school were somewhat misleading. Only a small proportion of the required $10,000 was in hand or pledged.[49] The brotherhood as a whole was not excited about the prospect of a school, or at least not sufficiently to provide adequate financial support for it. Traditional opposition to advanced education, furthermore, was deeply entrenched and gave ground slowly under the pressure of the convinced, dedicated, and sacrificial minority of men and women who believed that a school was essential for the well-being of the life of the Brethren. Some members of this minority had their moments of despair. Samuel Smith, for example, commented wearily in a report to General Conference of 1909:

> In listening to the criticisms and evident dissatisfaction, which sometimes is [*sic*] expressed concerning this undertaking, it was a serious question with me whether it was advisable to continue the effort under such adverse

conditions and the serious question with me is, what would the ultimate outcome be if the work is undertaken under such conditions and since my convictions are, that the Church has waited too long to undertake something of the kind as prescribed in these efforts, yet I feel for my individual part, that I would rather not continue in an antagonistic position against those who are not favorable to the undertaking, and yet on several occasions were instrumental in placing us in our position.[50]

Dissatisfaction with the school project received impetus from new issues which arose from time to time. Discussion of a curriculum precipitated questions to which few members had given thought.[51] One church leader found the original curriculum proposals astonishing. He had "all along been simple enough" to think that only a Bible school and missionary training home was intended, but when he read the curriculum, he had to smile at his own simplicity and ignorance, and observed:

> For what reason we are to send young people hundreds of miles from home, and at great expense, to engage in secular studies which they could learn more cheaply and effectively in their nearest High School, is more than I can fathom. I may be counted dense, if I fail to find the connection between Bible study and Trigonometry, Geometry, Caesar or Virgil, and the History of the United States.[52]

In addition to these subjects, the proposed curriculum included German, Greek, English, algebra, and physiology.[53] Peter Wiebe forcefully defended non-biblical studies. He associated language study, for example, with linquistic skills needed by missionaries who must master a new language and also stressed the importance of these skills for correct biblical understanding. In reinforcing the latter point, he quoted a statement attributed to Philip Melanchthon, associate of Martin Luther. "'Scripture cannot be understood theologically unless it is understood grammatically'."[54]

Another proposal which provoked debate was the qualification of teachers. The men supporting the school project believed that its faculty should hold at least normal school certificates, that is, they should be legally certified teachers. Conference modified this somewhat by specifying that a teacher's qualifications should "be equal to" the normal school certificate.[55]

Charles Baker defended normal school training. He noted that the original Incorporating Board had projected two departments for the proposed school, "one a secular, and the other an ecclesiastical part." That board also had acknowledged that some church members without normal school certificates might be better qualified to teach the Bible and Brethren doctrine than those with certificates, but the board members had unanimously agreed that certificates were "absolutely necessary" for those who taught other subjects. They reasoned:

> . . . this school is not only to be started and conducted for the children of the Brethren, but it is to be open to all classes of students regardless of their religious principles, providing they submit to the rules of the school. Therefore, . . . unless we had a teacher . . . , who held a certificate required by the law of the country in which the school is located, we could not expect any students from outside sources to attend our school. No parent would care about sending their [sic] sons, or daughters, to a school where the teacher engaged did not hold a lawful certificate.[56]

This was an interesting position; because those striving for an institution to safeguard their own faith consciously planned it to draw patronage from those of other faiths.

While debates about curriculum and teacher qualifications proceeded, the Messiah Bible School and Missionary Training Home struggled toward birth. By the fall of 1909, the institution had gained a location in uptown Harrisburg. This was the residence of Samuel Smith at forty-six North Twelfth Street, a property valued at $8,100, which he offered to donate for school purposes in return for minor financial considerations.[57]

Encouraged by this proposal, Editor Detwiler sought to rally financial support for a final drive to launch the institution. He frankly admitted that committed friends of the school constituted a small minority of the brotherhood, that another group was "indifferently favorable" and would make only small contributions from twenty-five cents to ten dollars, and that a third group opposed the project. Then he pressed the following appeal:

> We are aware that many good brethren are doubtful whether the Lord is in this move, and be it far from us to misjudge or censure any one for whatever attitude they [sic] may take. On the other hand there are equally excellent members who seem to realize that the church has come to a time when, if it is to go forward successfully in its missionary enterprises, at home and in foreign lands, and if the many intelligent young people of the church shall be retained the change from the old to the new, however

revolutionary, must be made, and failing this the consequences may be disastrous to the forward progress of the church.

Now brethren, whoever you may be, what will be your answer to this appeal?[58]

As often happened with Brethren enterprises, a small group of men and women were prepared to make almost any sacrifice for the cause. They had in hand at the close of 1909 less than one-third of the needed $10,000.[59] General Conference of 1910 designated that sum to be a Founder's Fund of which the income only could be used for real estate, improvements and repairs. Conference further ruled that a strenuous two-month effort should be made to raise an additional $10,000 for an operating fund.[60] Mystery surrounds the final, frantic efforts to meet these financial requirements. There is a credible oral tradition that Enos Hess came forward at the eleventh hour with an offer of cash and donated services sufficient to assure the opening of the school for the 1910-1911 year.[61]

Student group of the Messiah Bible School and Missionary Training Home, 1910-1911. Standing, left to right: Samuel Smith (Jr.) with daughter Elizabeth; Henry L. Smith; Ira J. Zercher. The latter was the first registrant when the school opened in the fall of 1910. Kneeling, left to right: unidentified; Irvin O. Musser.

In the fall of 1910, the first faculty and staff assembled. It included Samuel Smith, president, Enos Hess, vice president and secretary; Peter Wiebe, steward; Daniel V. Heise, treasurer; Mary Keefer, matron; Mary Hoffman, and George Detwiler.[62] Later, Henry Smith and John Climenhaga joined the group. Three of the teaching faculty served full-time and three part-time. Several made significant sacrifices to share in the project; their individual earning power exceeded the amount paid to all teachers combined.[63]

Registration for the first of three terms fell on September 26, 1910, at which time a small group of prospective students gathered expectantly outside the former Samuel Smith residence. According to tradition, Ira J. Zercher, who had been denied a high school education until he became of age, entered to become the first registrant. The total enrollment for the year was thirty-seven. Tuition for those enrolled in the first term was free.[64]

The curriculum was quite extensive, considering the size of student body and faculty. Students without high school background could elect either the Bible School Preparatory Course or the Preparatory Course. The latter was comparable to an academic high school program of today; in the second annual catalog, it was entitled "College Preparatory Course." For students who had completed high school, there were four options—Bible Course, Missionary Training Course, Scientific Course, and Pedagogical Course.[65]

Messiah Bible School and Missionary Training Home thus made a modest beginning in pursuit of its objectives, which were: "To educate men and women for home and foreign mission or evangelistic work; for the dissemination of a knowledge of the Bible, and Christian spiritual training according to the faith and discipline of the Brethren in Christ; and to give men and women an opportunity of preparing themselves in secular studies for future occupations, especially for religious work."[66] These objectives demonstrate both the strong religious and vocational emphases of the institution at the time of its founding.

The charter statement emphasized the school's adherence to the faith and discipline of the Brethren in Christ, thus identifying it as a denominational institution. By another charter provision General Conference was authorized to elect the trustees and ratify the constitution and by-laws under which they functioned, thus assuring the brotherhood full legal control.[67]

The immediate introduction of a winter Bible conference brought before the students an imposing array of Brethren leaders as speakers and attendants, which enhanced both the religious emphasis and church-relatedness of the program.[68] Annual Bible conferences became a long-standing tradition of the campus.

Although Brethren in Christ in origin and purpose, the school always welcomed students from other backgrounds. President Samuel Smith expressed the intent of the founders when be wrote: "This is an institution to which Christian people of all denominations can look with comfort."[69]

The first-year attendance exceeded "the most sanguine expectations" of the Board of Managers and prospects were bright for an immediate increase. This made relocation of the school an urgent necessity. In December of 1910 the Boards of Managers and Trustees decided to move the campus to Grantham, Pennsylvania. The offer of an unknown donor (probably Samuel Smith) to provide $2,000 to purchase five acres of land along the Reading Railroad on the site of the present Messiah College influenced the decision.[70]

Building plans went rapidly forward, and the 1911 fall term began at Grantham. The four-story brick building now known as "Old Main" was not quite completed, and temporary community quarters served for classrooms and women's housing.[71] Bishop John Zook, who had fought so hard to locate the school west of Pennsylvania, displayed a magnanimous spirit in preaching the dedicatory sermon at the new location.[72]

In announcing the first term at Grantham, President Smith set forth a capsule educational philosophy which has continued to be a guiding light for the institution through its history. The school, he observed, is: "An Institution where the word of God is held up as the main standard of teaching and all secular branches of study are held up and taught as rays emanating from the great center—God."[73]

Soon the academic program expanded into a four-year academy and, in 1920, into the first junior college in Pennsylvania. This curricular growth required a charter amendment in 1924, changing the name to "Messiah Bible College."[74]

By 1951 further academic and financial growth led to state authorization for the institution to confer degrees, necessitating another charter amendment changing the name to the present "Messiah College."[74] Accreditation by the Middle States Association of Colleges and Secondary Schools followed in 1963.[75]

Messiah College merged in 1965 with Upland College, its regionally accredited sister institution in Southern California, thus consolidating the program of higher education within the Brethren in Christ Church.[76] In

1972 General Conference transferred legal control of the merged institutions to a self-perpetuating Board of Trustees. Since that time the church and college have cultivated their relationship under a covenant of mutual understandings and responsibilities.[77]

The Midwest Bible School Project

The blunt assertion of John Zook that the location of a Brethren school in Pennsylvania would provoke agitation for a school in the West was prophetic. Five years after Messiah Bible School and Missionary Training Home opened its doors in Harrisburg General Conference received a Des Moines, Iowa, petition for another school in the Midwest.

The Des Moines petitioners cited the fact that attendance at school in Pennsylvania was inconvenient and expensive for midwestern young people. A number of these youth attended non-Brethren schools, which "sad experience has proved detrimental." The petition further alleged an "original understanding that the West should also, in course of time, have a school under the supervision of the church." Conference accordingly appointed a committee to study the concerns of the petitioners.[78]

During the following year the committee explored sentiment relating to the Des Moines petition and received reaction ranging from strong opposition to enthusiastic support.[79] Pennsylvania considered the idea impractical, but its council action suggested an uneasy conscience, for it recognized that ". . . our western brethren have stood by in the launching, supporting and patronizing of the Messiah Bible School and Missionary Training Home."[80] Like Pennsylvania, Ohio was unfavorable.[81] Both of these areas could be served adequately by the existing school at Grantham.

On the other hand, the Upland District Council in California voted unanimously in support of the Des Moines proposal.[82] Attendance of their youth at Grantham three thousand miles away seemed prohibitive to the California Brethren. For awhile, nevertheless, they had loyally contributed funds to the Pennsylvania school.[83]

The subsequent history of this abortive Midwest Bible School project was deeply disappointing from the viewpoint of its supporters. Discerning western leaders realized that a church school located in Pennsylvania placed the outlying areas of the brotherhood at a serious disadvantage financially and otherwise. They were aware that attendance at non-Brethren schools in their region could lead their youth away from the brotherhood, and some may have foreseen that school attendance at Grantham would draw many young people permanently to the East.

Faced with these problems, the Brethren of the Midwest made various financial proposals. They also suggested specific cities—Abilene, Chicago, Des Moines—as possible sites for a second Brethren school. At one point they urged the merging in Indiana of Messiah Bible School with a new Midwest Bible School. Even after Beulah College was operating in California, a Kansas committee promoted the idea of a merger of Messiah and Beulah with a new school in the Midwest.[84]

Faced with this unceasing pressure, General Conference struggled with the complexities of the situation. Practical leaders saw the dangers of over-extending Brethren programs—missions, homes, orphanages, and schools—but the educational concerns of the Midwest were obviously real. Conference vacillated, approved and disapproved; it set up investigating committees, postponed actions, called for further studies, and sometimes appeared to go simultaneously in opposite directions. The dilemma which it faced was strikingly illustrated by two successive preambles in a 1920 committee report.

> Whereas, the launching of said project might interfere with the best interest of the school already in operation; and
> Whereas, undue delay to establish a school in the middle west might seriously imperil the spiritual welfare and usefulness of our young people; . . .[85]

In 1917, when General Conference appeared ready to support the movement for a Midwest school, it created an interim student traveling fund to facilitate attendance at Messiah Bible School by young people outside of Pennsylvania. Conference then named one committee to manage this fund and another to have custody of the fund for the Midwest Bible School.

The sudden death of Bishop John Zook, while he was conducting a service in the Highland Church pulpit, removed the most vigorous advocate of a school in the Midwest, but his death did not end the movement.[86] Kansas thereafter became the main focus of attention. In 1922 Conference approved a Kansas school project as soon as the sum of $25,000 was pledged for a cash fund and twice this amount for an endowment fund. The next year the solicitation committee had $83,000 in hand or pledged, which more than met the specified conditions.

At this point events took a strange turn. Kansas State Council took up the school matter in the spring of 1924, but, as the following minutes show, a motion to launch a school passed by a narrow margin.

> Upon the question of the proposed Mid-West Bible School, a motion was made to go forward without delay.
> After considerable discussion the motion carried with 25 for and 21 against.[87]

This evidence that the Kansas Brethren themselves were seriously divided about locating a school in their midst undercut the movement. The joint committees involved with the project of a Midwest Bible School counseled further delay by General Conference citing, among other reasons, "a division of sentiment among those most interested." The committees also recommended an increase of the student traveling fund "so that no child may be prevented from attending our Church School because of traveling expense."[88]

Until 1927 General Conference temporized with the Midwest school issue and then tabled it indefinitely. Although it never again received serious consideration, the idea of a school in the Midwest was still on record in the Kansas State Council minutes at the mid-century.[89]

A side effect of the controversy about a Midwest Bible School was impetus for the creation of a General Education Board. By 1922 Beulah College and Bible Training School was operating in California, although it was not yet recognized as a general church institution. The prospect of injecting a third school into the life of such a small denomination caused concern to the exisiting schools, as well as to church leaders; a need for an agency concerned primarily with school problems was apparent.

A recommendation to create this agency came to the General Conference of 1922 from the managers and trustees of Messiah Bible School: "With the School problem as it presents itself to us at present, we believe that the time has come to have a General Educational Board, who should be responsible for a proper co-relation [sic] of the educational work now in progress or to be inaugurated by the Church, . . ."[90] At this same Conference one of the committees working on the question of a Midwest Bible School recommended that such a board should have supervision of all schools of the brotherhood.[91]

Words such as "correlate" and "supervision" fell short of an agency empowered to exercise effective control over the beginning and development of Brethren schools. When General Conference created the new board, it had authority only "to see to the proper correlation of the educational activities of the Church and to institute and foster such methods as will propagate and perpetuate the educational work to the highest interests of the Church."[92] With two schools already operating and competing for the patronage of the Midwest, this broad, ambiguous statement was as far as Conference felt able to go in defining the legal jurisdiction of the General Education Board.[93]

Conference also charged the new agency to harmonize the work and operations of the various schools as much as possible with the beliefs of the Brethren and to guard against false teachings and harmful worldly tendencies.[94] In discharging this responsiblity the board prepared a statement of faith to which teachers in the schools were to subscribe. The statement strongly emphasized regeneration, sanctification, and the Brethren understanding of "Gospel commandments" such as baptism, the holy kiss, feet washing, the prayer veiling, and nonconformity.[95]

Beulah College and Bible School

In 1916 the California Brethren had voted unanimously for a Midwest Bible School, but within a few years they embarked upon an educational venture of their own. Their principal reason for this was a strong sense of need to bring Christian influence to bear upon the education of their children.[96] Few of these young people became church members during the decade from 1910-1920; their parents tended to attribute this to the influence of the public schools.[97]

As previously noted, Bishop Christian Burkholder had helped to launch the Pennsylvania school, but it was too far away to meet the needs of Californians concerned about the educational welfare of their children.[98] In 1917, therefore, they decided to launch their own school and named a committee to explore the possibilities for doing so.[99]

Another cluster of Brethren families near Tulare in the San Joaquin Valley launched a similar survey.[100] At a joint meeting of the two groups, the Tulare members reported $1,600 in sight and several tracts of land available for purchase at reasonable figures.[101]

The question of whether the school would locate at Upland or Tulare may have been one of the "various hindrances" which slowed the realization of the project.[102] In the spring of 1919, with the location problem still unsolved, the Pacific Coast District Council voted twenty-nine to six in favor of a school and directed the Upland and Tulare congregations to vote separately at a later date on the choice of a site.[103] That vote put the school temporarily in Upland.[104] The next year the council confirmed seven trustees, adopted a charter, decided that the first year's tuition should be free, and invited suggestions for a name.[105]

An offer from the Upland congregation to make their church building available for school purposes influenced the decision to locate temporarily in that community on the northwest corner of Third Avenue and F Street, "a quiet, secluded spot."[106] In spite of this action, rivalry between the Upland and Tulare members for the permanent location of the school continued until 1922 when the former group finally triumphed.[107]

After considering various names for the institution, the founders selected "Beulah College and Bible Training School." This name expressed their Christian ideals and invoked biblical images of the Holy Land, as well as the country of peace and joy in *Pilgrim's Progress."* "Dwelling in Beulah Land" served as an unofficial school song.[108]

Christian Burkholder became the first president and Peter Wiebe, possibly the best educated of the California Brethren at that time, the first dean. Nine additonal men and women served on the faculty and staff. Of these Wiebe, Henry Smith and Mary Hoffman had previously shared in launching Messiah Bible School. Miss Hoffman headed the grammar school department, for Beulah's founders envisioned a program from the elementary grades through college.

The educational dream of the West Coast Brethren came true in September 1920, when Beulah College and Bible Training School opened its doors and enrolled twenty-six students, with others expected later.[109] Its educational objectives were:

> . . . to give young men and women opportunity to secure a good secular, as well as religious, education, without exposing them to the false teachings and errors all too prevalent in many educational institutions of today. We aim not only to educate our young people, but also to have them converted—to get them filled with the Holy Ghost, established in the divine life, and rightly prepared for Christian service.[110]

The California brotherhood strongly supported missions, and this concern was expressed in the additonal statement: "A special feature at this school shall be to prepare workers for Home and Foreign Mission work. Do you have a call . . . ? If so, come to this school; we shall do what we can to give you the needed preparation."[111] The charter statement of objectives closely resembled that of Messiah Bible School.[112]

Like its sister institution in the East, Beulah College and Bible Training School welcomed students from outside of the brotherhood. Its early literature announced that "students of other denominations, or those of no denominational affiliation, are made just as welcome, and are placed on the same footing as others, so long as they comply with the rules . . . ."[113]

The first curriculum included a four-year academic or college preparatory course, two and four-year Bible courses, and a four-year college course.[114] An elementary school program launched simultaneously lasted only two years. Lack of adequate enrollment and other factors revealed that elementary courses were not feasible.[115]

Agitation for the relocation of the school elsewhere in Upland began almost immediately after it opened in the Upland Church. Although possible educational use had been considered in constructing the church, the building had limitations which became more apparent with increasing enrollments and an expanding program. As early as 1925 the trustees requested authority to relocate.[116] Attention centered from time to time on various possible sites until finally, in 1935, the Pacific Coast District Council voted overwhelmingly to buy the Alpine Resort at 792 West Arrow Highway.[117] This property, including three buildings and land "beautifully and thickly studded with trees which . . . [gave] the touches of a typical college park campus," became the new home of Beulah College.[118]

Another important development in the early history of the school was its recognition as a general church institution. During the first year of the program, the Upland Church Council considered the question: "Whereas, the Bible School has been launched and has been so far successful, has not the time arrived that it should be presented to General Conference for acceptance or rejection?"[119] A few weeks later the Pacific Coast District Council voted for the presentation.[120]

General Conference of 1921, however, limited itself to "a strong sentiment of sympathy . . . toward the splendid effort of the Church in California, . . ."[121] The stated reason for not accepting the California school at that time was "deference to the right of the Mid-west to be recognized in their privilege of establishing a school prior to such acceptance, . . ."[122]

Several years later the Pacific Coast District Council instructed its General Conference delegates to revive the question of general church recognition of Beulah College "if they feel it advisable."[123] The delegates evidently made some approach to Conference, for the General Education Board recommended that a representative of Beulah College be permitted to give a verbal report of the past year and that contributions to a traveling fund for students attending Beulah College be permissible.[124]

General Conference granted recognition to the California school in 1926, but the action was financially ambiguous. On the one hand, it made the church in California responsible for the financial obligations of Beulah College; on the other it granted Beulah equality with Messiah "in regard to solicitation."[125] When the Conference of 1927 cleared this ambiguity, the two colleges stood in the same official relationship to the denomination.[126]

Beulah College changed its name to Upland College in 1949.[127] A decade later it achieved regional accreditation by the Western College Association.[128] In 1965 it merged with Messiah College on the latter's campus at Grantham, Pennsylvania.[129]

Jabbok Bible School

Jabbok Faith Missionary Home and Orphanage at Thomas, Oklahoma, closed in 1924, although children then in residence received care as long as necessary.[130] This phasing out of the orphanage program occurred in the midst of agitation for a Midwest Bible School.

After the decision to terminate the orphanage, the Oklahoma Brethren decided to utilize its facilities for a school. In the summer of 1925, they hired teachers and made other arrangements to begin the program in September.[131] The charter of Jabbok Faith Missionary Home and Orphanage was broad enough to provide legal authority for a school program. General Conference had no voice in the venture.[132]

The two Brethren congregations in Oklahoma, Bethany and Red Star, with a combined membership of about 150, provided a narrow resource base for such an ambitious undertaking. In addition to generous donations of labor, supplies, and money, however, the school enjoyed the advantage of income from the former orphanage farm and dairy.[133]

Like the two church schools which preceded it, Jabbok reflected the concern to educate children under the influence of the Brethren faith and to prepare them for Christian service. Its announced purposes were:

... to give our young people as good an education as can be obtained in any school. . . . to give them a thorough training in the doctrines of the Bible, so that they may be prepared for mission work at home and in the foreign field. Above all . . . to get the students converted, filled with the Holy Spirit, and established in the divine life.[134]

Bishop David Eyster was one of the principal figures in the founding and nurturing of the Oklahoma school, and Peter Wiebe left Beulah College to become its first president.[135]

Sixty students enrolled during the first year, with the number equally divided beteen the high and elementary school departments.[136] For those of high school standing, the early curriculum provided options of a four-year academic or college preparatory course and a two-year English Bible course.[137]

In 1926 Jabbok Bible School requested official General Conference recognition, a move prejudicial to prospects for a Midwest Bible School in Kansas.[138] Although embarrassed by this situation, Conference found the request difficult to deny because it was about to extend official recognition to Beulah College begun under similar circumstances. To have recognized Beulah while rejecting Jabbok would have been an affront to the Oklahoma Church.

Faced with this dilemma, Conference accepted Jabbok with a reproof and reservations: "Resolved, that Conference overlook this lack of regard for proper authority and grant the present organization to continue for another year provided the work does not exceed the 12th grade, to the end that Kansas have one more year to determine what action it will take in respect to the organization of a Mid-west Bible School."[139] Conference made clear at the same time that Jabbok itself, in conjunction with the Oklahoma Church, must assume financial responsibility for the undertaking; support by the church as a whole should be "a matter of good will and faith." Teachers employed were to subscribe to the articles of faith adopted by the preceding Conference.[140]

This qualified acceptance of their school by General Conference was not satisfactory to the Oklahoma Brethren. The next year they petitioned for "an equal basis of recognition with the other Church schools." The supporting argument stressed that operation of a school was the only feasible means to continue to hold legal title to the property under terms of the charter, since the orphanage program had been terminated. Conference then yielded and authorized the school to continue to offer "standard High School Work," but once again affirmed that the Oklahoma Church must assume the financial obligations.[141]

These financial restrictions on Jabbok proved to be temporary. Under pressure from the Oklahoma Church, General Conference soon ruled that the school need not confine its financial solicitation to Oklahoma so long as it limited itself to pre-college work.[142]

The collapse of the Kansas phase of the Midwest Bible School project helped to pave the way for this broader recognition of Jabbok. Conference, however, was uneasy about the multiplying of educations institutions. Finding itself with three recognized schools, two begun without previous authorization, that body ruled that no section or district could begin either primary or secondary school work without the "inspection and approval of the Education Board and confirmation of General Conference."[143]

Like any school competing with the public school system, Jabbok soon found that state accreditation was essential for continuation of its program. By the close of the decade, public school officials visited the campus by invitation from time to time and pointed out changes required for accreditation. Trustees and faculty labored diligently to meet these requirements, which included termination of the elementary school.[144] By the summer of 1930, Jabbok had met all state requirements and was an accredited high school.[145]

Jabbok Bible School continued its educational ministry through three decades terminating with the 1955-1956 academic year. Then, because of student and faculty limitations, it recessed for the year 1956-57, while the Jabbok Board of Trustees and the Board for Schools and Colleges sought to determine the best course of action for the future.[146] When those boards concluded that student and faculty potential did not justify renewed operations, Conference confirmed the permanent closing of the school and directed the transfer of its student records to Messiah College.[147]

Ontario Bible School

By the late 1920s the Canadian Brethren were also interested in launching a school. The General Education Board does not appear to have discouraged this interest in spite of the fact that three schools approved by General Conference were already operating in the United States.[148]

In 1929 Canada Joint Council debated a so-called "request" from that board to consider launching a Bible school in Canada and named a

committee to investigate the matter.[149] When the committee found that
Ontario law made adequate provision for private educational institutions,
the council named Clarence Fretz to canvass the brotherhood and explore
prospects for students and finances. He was also to inquire about a
program of studies which would attract interest.[150] A petition from the
Saskatchewan Brethren asking for permission to begin a Bible school in
Western Canada made prompt action by the brotherhood in Ontario
imperative.[151]

Fretz found a "very favorable" attitude toward the school project. His
survey made in depression times revealed, however, that the financial
capacity of the Ontario Brethren to support a school was more limited
than had been anticipated.

In view of these circumstances, Canada Joint Council tabled the
question for one year but agreed to petition General Conference for
permission to begin a school when deemed advisable by the Canadian
Church.[152] The council also authorized each district to hold a six-week
Bible course with the privilege of teaching "whatever secular subjects
would be beneficial to the students."[153]

The petition from Canada Joint Council stressed several points unique
to the Canadian situation. It emphasized that difficulties frequently arose
in passing through the immigration office at the United States border, that
the value of the Canadian dollar was often below par in the United States,
and that the Ontario Department of Education did not give equivalent
credit for work taken in United States schools. In addition the petition
included the following assurance; "The Canadian Church is prepared to
meet the present need in a measure at least, and on an inexpensive
basis."[154]

To this petition the General Education Board appended a statement that
the project should only be launched when the Canadian Brethren were
able to meet the financial obligations in full, both for the present and
the immediate future. Conference granted the petition with this
qualification.[155]

The scene next shifted to the Springvale Church in Wainfleet District. In
January 1932, the Springvale Brethren, acting upon the previous
authorization for each district to hold a six-week Bible course, launched a
school in their church building. One of the enrollees, who seemed to sense
that history was being made, commented: "At last we were ready. With
almost awe in our hearts we walked in and took our places for Chapel"
which opened with the singing of "that good hymn, 'We Gather on this

Joyful Day.' ''[156]

Peter Wiebe, sharing in his fourth founding of a church school, Edward Gilmore, and John Nigh comprised the faculty. Nine regular and two special students enrolled.[157]

When Canada Joint Council met in 1932, it took over the Bible school project by naming a representative committee to launch another three- or four-month Bible term.[158] That committee decided to continue with the Springvale location and announced this decision in a small pamphlet entitled *A Short Bible Term under the auspices of The Brethren in Christ in Ontario.* The pamphlet stated that the school's purpose was ". . . to disseminate a knowledge of the Bible in order that our young people may be prepared for Christian work both at home and in the foreign field; and to give them such preparation as they may need for their life's work." Bible history, Bible doctrine, English, and vocal music constituted the main course, with electives in mathematics, history, and Christian service available upon sufficient demand.[159]

Faculty who served in that first Bible School under the official auspices of the Canadian Brethren as a whole were Peter Wiebe, principal and teacher of high school subjects, Stella Heise, music, and Alvin Winger, Bible. Ten full-time and five part-time students enrolled.[160]

In 1934 the school moved to the Markham District where Clara Wideman made her large commodious house available for educational purposes.[161] Here it remained until 1938 while Canada Joint Council wrestled with the problem of a permanent location. Various districts vied with each other to gain the school, but the availability of the vacant Belmont Club House property on the Niagara River between Fort Erie and Niagara Falls gave Black Creek District the prize.[162] The Ontario Bible School, as it was then known, moved into its new home in the fall of 1938.[163]

By the 1939-40 school year, the institution offered high school and Bible as four-year programs, and a two-year commercial course. That year the Ontario Department of Education sent inspectors to the campus and, on the basis of their report, granted the school full, four-year accreditation.[164]

In the 1940s Ontario Bible School added Grade Thirteen to its curriculum, and in 1950 it became Niagara Christian College in keeping with Ontario educational policy which provides for the recognition of private high schools as "colleges." The new name emphasized the location in the Niagara River area and, by inclusion of the term "Christian," indicated that what was now primarily an academic high school retained a distinctive Christian value system linking it with its Bible school past.[165]

Niagara Christian College currently shares its campus with the annual summer Holiness Camp Meeting of the Brethren in Christ Canadian Conference.[166] The development of buildings and other facilities proceeds with the needs of both programs in view.

Effects of the Church Schools

The church schools exerted an important influence upon the life of the Brethren in Christ. While the impact of these institutions cannot be completely isolated from other factors, some effects of church-related education are apparent.

One of the most obvious was the shift of the attitude of the brotherhood toward a more positive view of education. From indifference and hostility to advanced learning, group sentiment shifted to general appreciation for its value. The number of educated members gradually increased as dozens and then hundreds of young people passed through the church schools, to be followed eventually by successive generations. Since many of those who attended these institutions remained loyal to the brotherhood, they helped to convince the indifferent and fearful of the value of education.

Another effect of the schools was their contribution to the unity of the brotherhood. As young people came together from different parts of the church, they discovered and evaluated regional differences in attitudes and practices. They often intermarried across regional lines, with resulting minimization of differences in geographical backgrounds. Church-controlled education thus helped to undermine regional provincialism and to build awareness of the brotherhood as a whole.

A third effect of the schools was the creation of unique centers for teaching the Brethren faith, as well as for evangelism and the recruitment of personnel for the enterprises of the church. Many students remembered their school years as the time when they made important spiritual and Christian service decisions. As time passed, increasing numbers of home and foreign missionaries, ministers, and faculty and staff members of the schools themselves had studied on one or more of the campuses, and laymen alumni abounded in local church programs.

A fourth outcome of educational institutions was new dynamic and flexibility within the Brethren movement. Traditionalism, a powerful historical influence, gave ground before an advancing rationalism. Young men and women nurtured in school environments were less ready to believe what they were told and more inclined to question and think for themselves. The brotherhood, consequently, had to respond to the growing demand for evidence to support belief; it also had to open itself to the possibility of changes reflecting the new mentality nurtured by educational experience.

A fifth result of the church schools was geographical redistribution of the Brethren membership. Many young people from the Midwest who attended Messiah College or Beulah College found the East or West so attractive that they failed to return to their home communities. Although other social and economic influences contributed to the decline of Brethren membership in the Midwest, the church schools played a significant role in this change.

Finally, the founding of schools and, to a lesser extent, other institutions introduced regional tensions into the life of the Brethren. Young people from districts located near a school could attend more easily than those residing in districts hundreds or even thousands of miles away. Institutions tended, furthermore, to attract leaders to staff them and families seeking their services. For these reasons, various regions of the brotherhood perceived institutions as prizes to be sought and won. The resulting struggle for regional advantage has been a prominent aspect of the story of the Brethren in Christ.

NOTES:

[1]The text of this chapter uses the terms "advanced education," and "advanced learning" broadly to include all formal schooling above the elementary level.

[2]*General Conference Minutes*, 1881, Article 1.

[3]North Dickinson District Council Minutes, February 19, 1889, Article 9.

[4]J. O. Lehman, "Divine Guidance," *Visitor*, IX (July 15, 1896), 227.

[5]William O. Baker obituary, *Visitor*, XXX (December 25, 1916), 21; W. O. Baker, "Reminiscences No. 1. My Recollections of the Early Wayne Co. Church," *Visitor*, I (August 1, 1887), 9.

[6]Levi Lukenbach obituary, *Visitor*, IX (February 1, 1896), 48.

[7]E. J. Swalm interview, March 3, 1971.

[8]Schrag, "Brethren Attitude Toward the World," pp. 282-84, mentions several additional individuals who pursued advanced education.

[9]*Ibid.* The educational histories and degrees of most of the persons named are in the early catalogues of the Messiah Bible School and Missionary Training Home. See the years 1912-13, 1925-26.

[10]Columbia College was in Poughkeepsie, N. Y. Smith's diploma is in the custody of Messiah College.

[11][George Detwiler], *Visitor,* XVIII (August 1, 1904), 3.

[12][George Detwiler], "Editorial Notes," *Visitor,* XX (March 15, 1906), 1.

[13]J. R. Zook, "The Needs of the Church," *Visitor,* XVI (May 15, 1902), 182.

[14]A Worker, "Our Great Need," *Visitor,* XVII (December 15, 1903), 5-6; I. J. Ransom, " 'Rightly Dividing the Word of Truth,' and How to Prepare for It," *Visitor,* XX (April 16, 1906), 8.

[15]J. R. Zook, "The Needs of the Church," *Visitor,* XVI (May 15, 1902), 182-83.

[16]*Visitor,* XVI (September 1, 1902), 334.

[17]Levi W. Mumaw, Jr., "My Conversion," *Visitor,* XXI (May 15, 1907), 5.

[18]A Brother, "A Few Thoughts on Our Coming Conference," *Visitor,* XX (April 16, 1906), 15.

[19]Charles Baker, "Bible Training School," *Visitor,* XXI (February 15, 1907), 4.

[20]F. Elliott, "The Bible Training School," *Visitor,* XVIII (February 15, 1904), 4.

[21]*Ibid.*

[22]*Ibid.*

[23]F. Elliott, "Here and There," *Visitor,* XVIII (April 1, 1904), 5.

[24]*General Conference Minutes,* 1897, Article 6, p. 5; *ibid.,* 1898, Article 9, p. 5.

[25]*Ohio State Council Minutes,* March 18, 19, 1904, Article 4, p. 2.

[26]*General Conference Minutes,* 1904, Articles 19, 35, pp. 16, 20.

[27]*Ibid.,* 1905, Article 7, p. 9.

[28][George Detwiler], "Editorial Notes," *Visitor,* XX (March 15, 1906), 1.

[29]*Ibid.,* (April 2, 1906), 3.

[30]S. R. Smith, "Notice," *Visitor,* XX (April 2, 1906), 3.

[31]*Ohio State Council Minutes,* March 16, 17, 1906, Articles, 7, 9, pp. 5-7. [T. A. Long], "From Bro. T. A. Long," *Visitor,* XX (June 15, 1906), 15; J. H. E., "Additional Notes of the Recently Held General Conference," *Visitor,* XX (June 15, 1906), 5.

[32]*Ohio State Council Minutes,* March 16, 17, 1906, Article 7, p. 6.

[33]J. H. E. "Additional Notes of the Recently Held General Conference," *Visitor,* XX (June 15, 1906), 5.

[34]*General Conference Minutes,* 1907, Article 25, p. 12.

[35]*Ibid.,* Article 25, p. 13.

[36]S. R. Smith, "The Bible School and Training Home," *Visitor,* XXI (July 1, 1907), 4, 10. Smith, who was secretary of the Bible School Incorporating Board, later told his personal secretary, Amos D. M. Dick, that he refrained from voting on the location question. Amos D. M. Dick interview, September 20, 1975.

[37]Harvey Frey, "Concerning a Training School," *Visitor,* XIV (May 1, 1901), 164-65; J. R. Zook, "The Needs of the Church," *Visitor,* XVI (May 15, 1902), 182-83.

[38]*General Conference Minutes,* 1900, Article 5, p. 10.

[39]J. R. Zook, "A Voice for Righteousness and Success," *Visitor,* XXI (August 15, 1907), 5.

⁴⁰*Ibid.*, 4-6.

⁴¹[George Detwiler], *Visitor,* XXI (September 2, 1907), 2.

⁴²F. Elliott, "The Bible School Again," *Visitor,* XXI (November 1, 1907), 6.

⁴³John H. Myers, "A Plea for Brotherly Love," *Visitor,* XXI (October 1, 1907), 8.

⁴⁴S. R. Smith, *Visitor,* XXI (September 2, 1907), 3; [George Detwiler], *Visitor,* XXI (September 2, 1907), 2.

⁴⁵*General Conference Minutes,* 1908, Article 8, pp. 11-14.

⁴⁶*Ibid.*, Zook later implied that his support for the Pennsylvania location had been gained by assurance that the Midwest could have a school of its own in due time. *General Conference Minutes,* 1915, Article 25, p. 75.

⁴⁷*General Conference Minutes,* 1908, Article 8, pp. 13-14; J. N. Engle and J. N. Hoover, *Visitor,* XXII (June 15, 1908), 3.

⁴⁸*General Conference Minutes,* 1909, Articles 17, 19, pp. 36, 37.

⁴⁹[George Detwiler], "What of the Bible School?" *Visitor,* XXIII (October 18, 1909), 2.

⁵⁰*General Conference Minutes,* 1909, Article 16, pp. 35-36.

⁵¹No known copy of this document exists, but its general scope is preserved in brief excerpts in the minutes and in debates about it in the *Visitor.*

⁵²F. Elliott, "The Bible School Again," *Visitor,* XXI (November 1, 1907), 6.

⁵³P. J. Wiebe, "Education," *Visitor,* XXIII (August 23, 1909), 7; *General Conference Minutes,* 1908, Article 8, p. 12.

⁵⁴P. J. Wiebe, "Education," *Visitor,* XXIII (August 23, 1909), 7.

⁵⁵*General Conference Minutes,* 1908, Article 8, p. 12.

⁵⁶Charles Baker, "Different Thoughts Considered," *Visitor,* XXII (August 15, 1908), 6.

⁵⁷[George Detwiler], "What of the Bible School," *Visitor,* XXIII (October 18, 1909), 2; *General Conference Minutes,* 1910, Article 13, pp. 31-32.

⁵⁸[George Detwiler], "What of the Bible School," *Visitor,* XXIII (October 18, 1909), 2-3.

⁵⁹[George Detwiler], "Bible School Subscriptions," *Visitor,* XXIII (December 27, 1909), 3.

⁶⁰*General Conference Minutes,* 1910, Articles 12, 13, pp. 29-32.

⁶¹Mrs. Virgie Kraybill interview, October 3, 1974. Mrs. Kraybill was a student during part of the first school year.

⁶²*Messiah Bible School and Missionary Training Home Bulletin,* I (September, 1910), 3.

⁶³*General Conference Minutes,* 1911, Article 11, p. 20.

⁶⁴*Ibid.*, p. 19; [George Detwiler], "The Messiah Bible School," *Visitor,* XXIV (October 3, 1910), 3. John E. Zercher, "Roots and Faith," *Visitor,* LXXXVII (May 10, 1974), 3.

⁶⁵*Messiah Bible School and Missionary Training Home Bulletin,* I (September, 1910), 5-9.

⁶⁶"Charter," *Second Annual Catalogue of Messiah Bible School and Missionary Training Home,* 1911-1912, p. 7.

⁶⁷*Ibid.*, p. 8.

⁶⁸*General Conference Minutes,* 1911, Article 11, p. 19.

⁶⁹S. R. Smith, "The Messiah Bible School," *Visitor,* XXV (September 4, 1911), 3.

⁷⁰*General Conference Minutes,* 1911, Article 12, p. 22; Amos D. M. Dick interview, August 20, 1975. Smith's new residence and place of business were then in Grantham.

[71]*General Conference Minutes,* 1912, Article 10, pp. 48-50.

[72]"Dedication, Messiah Bible School and Missionary Training Home, Grantham, Cumberland Co., Pa., January 6-7, 1912," program in Church Archives.

[73]S. R. Smith, "The Messiah Bible School," *Visitor,* XXV (September 4, 1911), 3.

[74]*A Report by Messiah College to the Commission on Institutions of Higher Education of the Middle States Association of Colleges and Secondary Schools,* August 1972, pp. 5-7.

[75]*Ibid.,* p. 7.

[76]*Ibid.,* p. 7; *General Conference Minutes,* 1966, Article 23, p. 83.

[77]*General Conference Minutes,* 1972, Article 19, pp. 98-103.

[78]*Ibid.,* 1915, Article 25, p. 75; This petition is the only known intimation of an "orginal understanding" between the East and West.

[79]*Ibid.,* 1916, Article 18, p. 32.

[80]*Pennsylvania State Council Minutes,* April 6, 1916, Article 4, p. 5.

[81]*Ohio State Council Minutes,* March 16, 17, 1916, Article 8, p. 9.

[82]Upland Church Council Minutes, March 21, 1916, Article 7, p. 44.

[83]*Ibid.,* September 19, 1911, Article 4, p. 27; *ibid.,* March 20, 1917, Article 4, p. 46; General Conference Minutes, 1908, Article 8, p. 13.

[84]General Conference Minutes, Article 26, p. 38; *ibid.,* Article 9, p. 12; *Pacific Coast District Council Minutes,* March 28, 1924, Article 6, p. 25.

[85]*General Conference Minutes,* 1920, Article 19, p. 28.

[86]Mazy Dohner, "Called to His Reward from the Pulpit," *Visitor,* XXXII (December 1, 1919), 3.

[87]*Kansas State Council Minutes,* April 2, and 3, 1924, Article 19.

[88]*General Conference Minutes,* 1924, Articles 8, 9.

[89]Kansas State Council Minutes, April 7, 1949, Article 16.

[90]*General Conference Minutes,* 1922, Article 39, p. 44.

[91]*Ibid.,* Article 8, p. 11.

[92]*Ibid.,* 1923, Article 9, p. 9.

[93]*Ibid.,* "Education" gradually replaced "Educational" in the name of this board.

[94]*Ibid.*

[95]*Ibid.,* 1925, Article 14, pp. 27-28.

[96]Viola Burkholder, "Pacific Coast Extensions," *Visitor,* XXXV (April 10, 1922), 13; Upland Church Council Minutes, September 18, 1917, Article 3, p. 48.

[97]E. Morris Sider, *A Vision for Service: A History of Upland College,* (Nappanee, Ind.: Evangel Press, 1976), p. 19.

[98]In 1918 California decided not to support the Messiah Bible School traveling fund created by General Conference because the distance to Grantham was too great. Upland Church Council Minutes, September 17, 1918, Article 11, p. 53.

[99]*Ibid.,* September 18, 1917, Article 3, p. 48.

[100]*Second Annual Catalogue, Beulah College and Bible School,* 1921-1922, p. 5, cited hereafter as *Beulah Catalogue.*

[101]Upland Church Council Minutes, March 19, 1918, Article 4, p. 50.

[102]*Beulah Catalogue,* 1921-1922, p. 5.

[103]*Pacific Coast District Council Minutes,* April 19, 1919, Article 3, pp. 1-2.

[104]*Ibid.,* March 25, 1920, Article 6, p. 5.

[105]*Ibid.,* Articles 6-10, pp. 5-6.

[106]Upland Church Council Minutes, March 2, 1920, Article 17, p. 58; *Beulah Catalogue,* 1921-1922, p. 5.

[107]Upland Church Council Minutes, February 22, 1921, Article 5, p. 94; *Pacific Coast Council Minutes,* March 4, 1921, Article 3, p. 7; *ibid.,* March 10, 1922, Article 14, p. 13.

[108]Sider, *Upland College,* p. 30.

[109]P. J. Wiebe, "Beulah Bible School," *Visitor,* XXXIII, (September 20, 1920), p. 2.

[110]*Beulah Catalogue,* 1921-1922, p. 13.

[111]*Ibid.,* p. 14.

[112]Sider, *Upland College,* p. 25.

[113]*Beulah Catalogue,* 1921-1922, p. 10.

[114]*Ibid.,* pp. 7-9.

[115]Sider, *Upland College,* pp. 35-36.

[116]*Pacific Coast District Council Minutes,* March 13, 1925, Article 7, p. 9.

[117]*Ibid.,* Special Session, January 24, 1935, pp. 4-9. *Beulah College Bulletin; Catalogue Number, 1936-1937,* title page.

[118]"At Beulah College," *Visitor,* XLVIII (March 4, 1935), 78.

[119]Upland Church Council Minutes, February 22, 1921, Article 4, pp. 62-63.

[120]*Pacific Coast District Council Minutes,* March 4, 1921, Article 2, p. 7.

[121][Vernon Stump], "Editorial," *Visitor,* XXXIV (July 4, 1921), 1.

[122]*General Conference Minutes,* 1926, Article 17, p. 32.

[123]*Pacific Coast District Council Minutes,* March 13, 1925, Article 6, p. 9.

[124]*General Conference Minutes,* 1925, Article 14, p. 27.

[125]*Ibid.,* 1926, Article 17, p. 33.

[126]*Ibid.,* 1927, Article 23, pp. 41-42.

[127]*Ibid.,* 1950 Article 41, p. 134. The former name caused some people unfamiliar with the institution to assume that it was a women's college.

[128]*Ibid.,* 1959, Article 31, p. 115.

[129]*Ibid.,* 1966, Article 23, p. 83. For the background of this merger, see Sider, *Upland College,* Chapter 14.

[130]See Chapter XII for a discussion of this orphanage.

[131]"History," *Third Annual Catalog of Jabbok Bible School, 1927,* pp. 8-9, cited hereafter as *Jabbok Catalog.*

[132]"Charter," *ibid.,* p. 7.

[133]Charles F. Eshelman, "History of Education of the Brethren in Christ Church," (Ed. D. dissertation, Cornell University, 1952), p. 389.

[134]"Character and Purpose," *Jabbok Catalog,* 1927, p. 9.

[135]"Faculty," *Jabbok Catalog,* 1927, p. 5.

[136]Eshelman, "Brethren in Christ Education," p. 391.

[137]"Course of Study," *Jabbok Catalog,* 1927, pp. 12-13.

[138]*General Conference Minutes,* 1926, Article 17, pp. 31-32.

[139]*Ibid.,* p. 32.

[140]For the article of faith proposed by the Education Board as a standard of Brethren orthodoxy, see *ibid.,* 1925, Article 14, pp. 27-28.

[141]*Ibid.,* 1927, Article 30, p. 47.

[142]*Ibid.,* 1929, Article 51, p. 67.

[143]*Ibid.,* 1928, Article 16, p. 33.

¹⁴⁴*Ibid.*, 1929, Article 43, pp. 55-56; *Jabbok Catalog,* 1929-30, p. 7.

¹⁴⁵*Jabbok Catalog,* 1930-31, p. 6.

¹⁴⁶The Board for Schools and Colleges became the successor to the General Education Board in 1949.

¹⁴⁷*General Conference Minutes,* 1956, Article 32, p. 106; *ibid.*, 1958, Article 30, p. 125.

¹⁴⁸*Canadian Joint Council Minutes,* September 12, 1929, p. 76.

¹⁴⁹*Ibid.*

¹⁵⁰*Ibid.*, September 11, 1930, p. 79.

¹⁵¹*Ibid.*, pp. 79-80. For a sketch of the Saskatchewan Bible School movement, see Sider, "Brethren in Canada," pp. 234-36.

¹⁵²*Canadian Joint Council Minutes,* September 19, 1931, p. 85.

¹⁵³*Ibid.*

¹⁵⁴*General Conference Minutes,* 1932, Article 26, p. 46.

¹⁵⁵*Ibid.*

¹⁵⁶Lily G. Winger, "The Opening of Bible School at Springvale, Ontario," *Visitor,* XLV, (February 1, 1932), 42.

¹⁵⁷*Ibid.*

¹⁵⁸*Canadian Joint Council Minutes,* 1932, Article 9, p. 92.

¹⁵⁹Pamphlet in Church Archives (n.p., 1933).

¹⁶⁰*Canadian Joint Council Minutes,* September 14, 1933, pp. 96-97.

¹⁶¹*Ibid.*, September 14, 1934, p. 109.

¹⁶²*Ibid.*, September 12, 1935, p. 121; *ibid.*, September 10, 1936, p. 140; *ibid.*, September 8, 9, 1937, p. 153; *ibid.*, May 10, 1938, p. 68; *ibid.*, September 14, 15, 1938, pp. 173, 180-81, 183.

¹⁶³*Fourth Annual Catalogue of the Ontario Bible School,* 1935-1936, title page. The present writer joined the faculty in the fall of 1938 and assisted with the adjustment of the school to its new quarters.

¹⁶⁴*Canadian Joint Council Minutes,* September 11, 12, 1940, pp. 214-15.

¹⁶⁵*Annual Minutes of the Ontario Joint Council . . . of the Brethren in Christ Church,* September 3, 1949, p. 81; *ibid.*, 1950, p. 95, cited hereafter as *Ontario Joint Council Minutes;* Dorothy Sherk to C. O. Wittlinger, February 20, 1976; Stuart W. Cooke to C. O. Wittlinger, February 25, 1976.

¹⁶⁶*Ontario Joint Council Minutes, September 4, 1948, p. 69; ibid.*, September 3, 1949, p. 81.

Part Three

The
Period of Adjustment

1910 — 1950

XIV

The Triumph of
Second-Work Holiness

Stress and uncertainty characterized the life of the Brethren in Christ during the period from 1910 to 1950. The innovations which they made during the preceding period of transition created tensions with their historic faith and life-style and posed problems which challenged their capacities for adjustment.

Accelerating social change complicated their efforts to bridge gaps between old and new. Increasing numbers of members were leaving the farm for vocational careers in industry, business, and the professions. This movement weakened the base of common rural experience which had been a stabilizing influence even during the transitional years from 1880 to 1910, and it also exposed the brotherhood to the "world" in a new way.

In the midst of the ferment and change after 1910, the Brethren did not self-consciously seek a new group identity. Rather, they pragmatically endeavored to adjust the interrelationships of old and new practices and values. The underlying assumption was that both their historic positions and their recent innovations had relevance as the brotherhood moved forward in the twentieth century.

The perspective of history makes clear that the problems involved in this period of adjustment were much greater than many of those involved in it realized. The next five chapters analyze the life of the Brethren from 1910 to the mid-century as they sought to cope both with past changes and with new problems arising from a changing social environment.

Continued Controversy About Sanctification

The year 1910 marked a milestone in the progress of second-work holiness among the Brethren. In that year General Conference adopted a statement on sanctification embodying much of the substance of perfectionism as advocated by the American Holiness Movement. In one important respect, however, the action was a compromise. It specifically repudiated the term "second definite work of grace" to describe the sanctification experience and substituted "grace of cleansing completed."[1]

This compromise attempted to narrow the gap between perfectionists and supporters of the historic view that sanctification occurred simultaneously with regeneration and continued thereafter as a process. Conference hoped that the 1910 article would put an end to nearly two decades of agitation about the sanctification issue, but the hope proved to be false.[2]

As long as George Detwiler edited the *Visitor* (1900-1918), both the perfectionists and the anti-perfectionists shared the forum of its pages. Only two months after the Conference of 1910, Bishop Charles Baker of Ontario expressed concern about the teaching of total eradication which, he thought, implied that the sanctified Christian no longer had inner propensities to sin. On the contrary, he argued, all Christians carry about with them a "fallible nature . . . and this fallible nature we all have need to watch."[3] He labeled eradicationism "a pernicious doctrine" and prayed that the whole brotherhood would rise in unison against it. The editorial staff concurred with Baker's rejections of total eradication, believing that neither the 1887 nor the 1910 Conference statement on sanctification upheld it.[4]

Some years later, in "Thoughts on Carnality," Baker took strong exception to the teaching that all converted persons are carnal, lacking "clean" hearts and the indwelling of the Holy Ghost. This article was, in fact, an exposition of the historic Brethren view of sanctification.[5] Since the forthrightness and forcefulness of his position invited perfectionist reaction, the editors appended a precautionary note:

> There . . . [likely] are those who have a different view of the subject treated in the above article. And since it is somewhat of a mooted question as to what Carnality is . . . it might be well to have the matter discussed in subsequent articles in order that a more unified position could be secured by the Brotherhood.[6]

These challenges to the perfectionist view of sanctification did not elicit critical replies. One who judges the years from 1910 to 1915 only by the columns of the *Visitor* might conclude that the controversial phase of the sanctification issue had passed. Articles on the subject were moderate in tone and, on the whole, supported the historic Brethren position more than the newer second-work emphasis.[7]

One of the factors reducing the tensions of the preceding years was the decline of the holiness extremism or "wild fire" which seriously agitated parts of the brotherhood at the turn of the century. The operation of this factor is illustrated by the mellowed attitude of Fred Elliott, who had previously been an outspoken opponent of second-work holiness. In 1913 he wrote two articles dealing with depth and maturity in the Christian life, which were more compatible with perfectionism.[8] When perfectionists, who had been offended by his earlier opposition, now questioned his consistency and integrity, he was perplexed. He assumed that, like Saul of Tarsus, when he preached what he once opposed, others would glorify God in him also.

Elliott humbly apologized, nevertheless, for any unkind or harsh words which he had written in the past on this or any other subject and added: "I am afflicted with the gift of sarcasm, and it has sometimes slipped out of its muzzle and run off my pen." Then he offered the following explanation for the changed spirit of his writings:

> . . . what I opposed was not so much the *doctrine* of "Christian Perfection" as the extravagant, exaggerated manner in which it was presented to the people. I freely admit it that it excited my, shall I say, "*righteous* indignation," to hear conversion or the 'New Birth' that brings "Eternal Life" into dead souls, so cruelly *minimised* and what they called "Second Work" magnified so utterly beyond its *real* proportions. That was at the time of the "fire" agitation in our church and I am safe to say if some of our preachers and people could see verbatim copies of the sermons and testimonies delivered in that feverish time by *themselves,* they would, to say the least, feel *astounded.* The fact that perhaps nearly all have modified their positions to a saner, more tenable and Scriptural ground than they then occupied is proof positive of their former error.[9]

This articulate leader had not made a radical shift from the traditional Brethren view of sanctification. He still emphatically rejected the term "second work of grace" as unscriptural and misleading, but he endorsed a "second rest" entered into subsequent to the "rest" of justification by faith. In his words: "Walking with Him [after conversion] in implicit and continuous obedience and full surrender would bring us quickly into the 'Second Rest,' a found rest and a 'short cut to Canaan," instead of a long desert journey."[10] After a later visit to Pennsylvania, he again expressed his changed attitude toward perfectionism. In the course of that visit, he said, it was:

> . . . an agreeable surprise to hear so many testimonies of deeper experiences of divine grace and consciousness of the "Divine Presence" in their daily life. There was none of that wild, radical form of expression that repels rather than convinces the reverent thoughtful hearer, but a calm tender recital of God's leading up to higher ground. This is, to my mind, the happy medium between cold formality on the one hand and blatant radicalism on the other.[11]

While Elliott may not have been typical of many Brethren members who initially rejected the new holiness emphasis, his mellowed attitude and his observation that persons on both sides of the question had moved toward more balanced positions suggest that stablilizing influences were at work. The spirit of brotherhood was asserting itself in spite of major differences of opinion. This helps to explain why the Brethren avoided a major schism under the pressure of later holiness controversy which created severe strain, especially in certain localities.

One of the most serious local crises developed at the Merrington Church in Saskatchewan. Here Bishop Isaac Baker resolutely opposed the movement of the brotherhood toward perfectionism, a trend accelerated by the 1910 General Conference statement on sanctification. From the point of view of Baker and his supporters, that statement was not sound doctrine. Another part of the Merrington congregation, however, sided with General Conference against their bishop.[12]

Into this potentially explosive situation came evangelist Joseph Leaman, preaching a second definite work of grace. His ministry divided the congregation into factions so seriously estranged that the possibility of their working harmoniously together became increasing remote. General Conference labored strenuously to reconcile the differences, but when this prolonged controversy ended, Bishop Baker and some other Merrington members had been lost to the brotherhood.[13]

Like the Merrington Church, Miami District in Southern Ohio experienced stresses as the historic Brethren doctrine of sanctification confronted the advancing tide of perfectionism. Here both the local ministry and the laity divided on the sanctification issue. The resulting disunity was complicated by visiting ministers and evangelists who presented a confusing variety of teachings about justification and sanctification. In response to a Miami District petition, General Conference sought to encourage greater unity of teaching in this doctrinal area and committed itself "to discourage emotionalism, sensationalism, and open personal condemnation, and [to] foster forbearance, unity and love."[14]

Christian perfection also caused grassroots unrest in Ontario. Markham District lamented lack of unity on the doctrine of sanctification and debated inconclusively whether any Scripture proved that Christians should testify to being sanctified. Wainfleet District was concerned about local opposition to the 1910 Conference statement on that doctrine.[15]

Later, in the 1920s and 1930s, another period of holiness controversy swept the Kansas churches, especially in the North Dickinson District. As a result, some members of the more radical faction left the brotherhood, part of them returning after the tensions subsided.[16]

Perfectionist Control of the *Visitor*

In 1916 the holiness controversy erupted anew in the columns of the *Visitor*. Editor Detwiler, who had personally avoided perfectionist criticism for several years after 1910, triggered the debate by raising the following provocative question:

> Saved but not sanctified is an expression which we hear more or less frequently these days, and we have often been impressed to hold it up with a question mark. We have heard individuals testify in this way, saying, "I am saved but not sanctified." Is it scriptural? We would be pleased to have [some] of our ministers, or lay members, for that matter, discuss this question, so that our readers may have reliable instruction in this matter.[17]

Detwiler's venturesome questioning may have been prompted by an article on consecration appearing in the same issue of the paper. Its author was Orville Ulery, who along with Vernon L. Stump, Lafayette Shoalts, and Henry Landis among others, represented the second generation of perfectionists. Ulery's article stressed "the absolute necessity of a complete and thorough consecration being wrought in every soul seeking to enter the sanctified, victorious, more abundant life so clearly portrayed in all the apostolic writings, . . ." He obviously intended to distinguish between persons "saved" and those "sanctified."

Responses to Editor Detwiler's query soon arrived in his office. Within two months he had four articles in hand. Noting that the question of sanctification was a live one, and that the church was not in full agreement on it, he published three of the articles as "a creditable symposium of the subject."[18] One of the writers was Vernon Stump who would soon succeed Detwiler in the editorship of the *Visitor* and whose ardent perfectionism foreshadowed things to come.[19]

In a succeeding issue of the *Visitor*, Orville Ulery responded to the symposium articles. In "A Harmonizing Voice," he expressed concern lest the controversy should threaten "the vital truths of God's word on this important question." Since only Vernon Stump had argued unequivocally for perfectionism, Ulery accepted the Stump position as correct and sought to show wherein the other two writers disagreed with it. The result was a vigorous defense of sanctification as a second work of grace.[20]

Several months after the appearance of Ulery's article, Detwiler published three additional responses to his query about the expression "saved but not sanctified."[21] All of these argued that it was unscriptural. This shows that the historic Brethren view of sanctification, although confronted by a new and zealous generation of opponents, still had vitality.

Following this exchange of views, the debate about sanctification temporarily subsided in the *Visitor*. Ulery reopend the question in the fall of 1917 with "A Scripture Study." Acknowledging that the presentation from "one classed as very radical" might be unpopular with some, he presented the following theses:

1. We do not know of one clear scriptural command for sinners to sanctify themselves, or a single promise that they may be sanctified, without first being saved from their sins. The command to sinners is always to repent, confess, and forsake their sins.

The call and command to sanctify was always given to God's people,...

2. Neither do we know of a single promise that sinners may receive the Holy Ghost.

3. Neither have we ever heard sinners under conviction . . . pray for the Lord to sanctify, . . .[22]

Ulery disclaimed intent to raise the issue of one or two works of grace, but his personal commitment to the latter was apparent. He seems to have reached the conclusion that the Holy Spirit indwelt only those who had a separate experience of sanctification subsequent to justification, a position which he later vigorously championed.[23]

Views such as those of Stump and Ulery reveal concern to promote a sharply defined doctrine of second-work holiness after a period during which the historic Brethren doctrine of sanctification and a moderate perfectionism coexisted in fairly stable truce. The second generation of holiness supporters, furthermore, were about to take charge of the *Visitor* as a conscious medium for the dissemination of their understanding of sanctification.

The appointment of Orville Ulery to the Publication Board in 1916, and to its chairmanship the following year, set the stage for perfectionist influence of the church paper.[24] There was little chance that Editor Detwiler, advocate of the historic doctrine of sanctification, and Chairman Ulery, champion of second-work holiness, could coexist indefinitely in their respective offices. The fact that Vernon Stump, a gifted young man whose holiness views coincided with those of Ulery, was available for the *Visitor* editorship encouraged the perfectionists to raise the issue of Detwiler's removal.

The showdown for control of the periodical came in the General Conference of 1918 to which the Publication Board brought the following recommendation: "Whereas, the Publication Board has deemed it advisable for the future welfare of the Evangelical Visitor to shift the editorial mantle to younger shoulders, we therefore recommend that Eld. V. L. Stump, Nappanee, Ind., be named as editor and the former editor continue in active management of the Publication, until such time within this Conference year as may be agreed."[25]

This recommendation implied that the advanced aged of the editor was incompatible with the future welfare of the *Visitor,* but Detwiler asserted that the real issue was his position on sanctification. He also stated that the same Conference which adopted the Publication Board recommendation passed another unrecorded resolution charging that his editorial policy "was not in harmony with what the church stood for, which called for change of editors, . . ."[26] Later he explained: "The reason given in open Conference was that I failed to measure up to what the church had adopted on the line of holiness, and [this] should have been so stated in Conference minutes instead of attributing it [removal from the editorship] to my advanced age, . . ."[27]

In his final editorial Detwiler thanked General Conference for a unanimous vote of appreciation for his service—"faithful and untiring" according to the minute record. He frankly confessed, however, that he could not reconcile this vote of appreciation with the unrecorded resolution charging that the testimony of the paper had not been in harmony with the stand of the brotherhood.[28] In the same editorial he graciously transferred the editorship to his "worthy successor," Vernon Stump, who began service in January, 1919.

The new editor forthwith converted the paper into a holiness journal. His masthead was more doctrinally oriented than that of his predecessor.[29] It announced that the paper was:

> Committed to the teaching of Justification, Sanctification, The Second Coming of Christ, Divine Healing, and all sacred ordinances and truth pertaining to the Christian life.
> It is an earnest advocate of gospel missions, at home and abroad and stands ready to espouse every good thing in Christ Jesus.[30]

Previously cited articles of Editor Stump make clear that the "Sanctification" mentioned in the masthead was a second work of grace.

Soon the editor took other steps to bring the perfectionist view of holiness to the foreground. In September of his first year, he began a series of articles by Bishop John Zook on "Holiness and Empowerment," in which the great evangelist set forth his mature views on the subject.[31] The next spring Solomon G. Engle followed Zook with another series on "Holiness."[32]

The *Visitor,* which Editor Detwiler had kept open to contributions from both the advocates and the opponents of second-work holiness, was now clearly devoted to the promotion of perfectionism. This marked the end of an era during which the Brethren believed that vigorous presentation of differing points of view in the church periodical furthered truth and unity.

The Triumph of Second-work Theology

The desire of the perfectionists to move the brotherhood toward commitment to the theology of a second work of grace came closer to fulfillment in the 1930s. During the early years of that decade, the *Visitor* offered a steady stream of perfectionist articles.[33] This provided background for an attempt to amend the 1910 article on sanctification.

In 1935 Clark County District in Southern Ohio, which was under the oversight of Bishop Orville Ulery, began the effort to strike "grace of cleansing completed" from the 1910 statement and to substitute "second definite work of grace" as the "only complete and scriptural expression" to describe sanctification. Supporters of this position argued that the 1910 wording was illogical because the article "clearly and definitely . . . [taught] Sanctification as an experience to be sought, apart from and subsequent to, Justification or the New Birth."[34]

Ohio-Kentucky State Council, to which Clark County District addressed its request for revision of the 1910 article, prepared a proposal for General Conference, including the following passage: "This perfection of Holiness, or Entire Sanctification, obtained by an act of living, appropriating faith, subsequent to regeneration, as outlined herein, is only realized as a definite experience, theologically known as a "Second Definite Work of Grace.'"[35]

This passage proved to be too strong for General Conference to accept as the anti-perfectionists rallied against it.[36] Although agreeing to eliminate both "grace of cleansing completed" and negative reference to "second definite work" from the 1910 article, Conference refused to substitute "second definite work of grace" to describe the sanctification experience.[37]

The result of this 1935 debate on sanctification was principally a victory for the perfectionists who succeeded in removing official stigma from the expression "second definite work," which the 1910 article had criticized as leading to "the abuse of the conditions of the developments of grace resulting in a subverting of the truth . . . ." On the other hand, the anti-perfectionists could take some comfort from the fact that Conference refused to give second-work terminology official endorsement in the literature of the brotherhood. The dissatisfaction of the perfectionists with this compromise is revealed by a subsequent Michigan State Council action endorsing the Ohio-Kentucky definition of sanctification as a second definite work of grace.[38]

The sanctification controversy again came to the foreground in the work of the committee appointed by General Conference of 1935 to revise the consititution and by-laws of the church. In its first proposal for a doctrinal statement on sanctification, this "Revision Committee" formulated the following basic concepts:

> First, initially, Sanctification has its beginning in justification. . . .
> Second, experimentally, Sanctification is an experience to be attained instantaneously and subsequent to the new birth, . . .

Third, progressively, Sanctification is a process by which the believer is daily cleansed from the defilement of a sinful world, . . .

Fourth, finally, Sanctification is a state of absolute perfection to be realized only through glorification.[39]

Missing was specific second-work terminology, although the second concept described what was essentially a second work of grace.

When this proposal came to General Conference, it encountered strong opposition from the perfectionists. This was due in part to differences of opinion within the Revision Committee itself. Although muted in the committee sessions, these differences surfaced outside of those sessions among some of the principal perfectionist leaders, who perceived the statement to be too weak and indecisive about a second work of grace. In the vigorous discussion of the proposed article at the Conference of 1936, one of those leaders characterized it as " 'nothing but a hodge-podge and a compromise'."[40] Such reactions made clear to the Revision Committee that its work on the sanctification issue was unfinished; it accordingly rewrote parts of the material.

Although the actual text of the revised statement embodied much of the original substance, the semantic changes were significant. The statement that ". . . Sanctification has its beginning in justification" disappeared along with reference to the completion of sanctification in glorification. These changes tended to mute emphasis upon "process" and to increase emphasis upon the "instantaneous" aspect of the holiness experience.[41]

Another change of wording dealt with the period after the experience of instantaneous sanctification. The initial proposal of 1936 asserted that sanctification was followed by "a process by which the believer is daily cleansed from the defilement of a sinful world." Again, out of deference to the perfectionists who feared too much leeway for "process" in holiness, this passage was changed in the 1936 revision to "is now kept clean from the defilement of a sinful world."[42]

When General Conference adopted the revised statement on sanctification, the cause of second-work holiness triumphed officially among the Brethren. Although the term "second work of grace" did not appear in the statement, its essence was embodied in the definition of sanctification as an experience "obtained instantaneously and subsequent to the new birth."

By 1937, therefore, the Brethren doctrine of sanctification had lost its flexibility and become a matter of precise definition. Advocates of second-work terminology could use that language freely after 1935 when the

Conference action of that year removed the stigma attached to it in the previous statement of 1910. On the other hand, defenders of the original Brethren understanding of sanctification had to face the fact that the doctrinal statement of 1937 repudiated their position and endorsed the essence of perfectionism.

The Holiness Camps

The holiness camps emerged in the Brethren movement while preaching, writing, and legislation pushed perfectionism to its legislative triumph in the 1930s. In some respects tent meetings and Bible conferences were forerunners of the holiness camps, but the latter were unique in making holiness doctrine and experience the unifying emphasis of the services and related activities. These were not merely camp meetings but "holiness" camp meetings.

The first camp developed from a series of annual evangelistic services begun in the 1930s on the outskirts of the small town of Roxbury, located in northern Franklin County, Pennsylvania. These meetings caused a religious awakening among the Franklin County Brethren, as well as among many non-Brethren in and around Roxbury.

This was but one of a number of such awakenings in which the Brethren were involved about that time. The late 1920s witnessed a surge of response to the evangelistic ministries of Alvin C. Burkholder, William F. Lewis, Cletus Naylor, and Lafayette Shoalts in and around Dallas Center, Iowa.[43] Another major awakening occurred in the 1930s around Saxton, Pennsylvania, under the preaching of Roscoe Ebersole, Harry Fink, Herman Miller and others.[44]

What became Roxbury Holiness Camp began unexpectedly in the summer of 1933 when the Mowersville-Greenspring District called J. Lester Myers to hold a tent meeting in the vicinity of the town of Roxbury.[45] The William Rosenberry family residing there felt that the community greatly needed an evangelistic ministry and strongly urged the Mowersville-Greenspring Brethren to provide it.[46] While searching for a site, the tent-location party noticed and examined an abandoned dance hall on the outskirts of town. This building impressed them favorably, and Myers remarked, "Brethren, this is the place." When they contacted the owner, Milton Gabler, he readily consented to their use of the building for evangelistic purposes.[47]

In this old dance hall Myers began one of the most unusual ministries of his career. Nearly three decades later he stated that he had never held a meeting in which there was such a manifest hunger for holiness experience. Crowds estimated to number at times as many as one thousand people packed the building and stood at the open windows. Sources differ as to the number of listeners who responded to the altar calls of the evangelist.[48]

Annual evangelistic campaigns continued in the dance hall through 1935, in which year Henry W. Landis of Des Moines, Iowa, ministered for seven weeks. His first message was: "'When the People Were Prepared, The Lord Came Down.'" Holiness teaching and the need to receive the baptism of the Holy Spirit were the central emphases of the services. Prayer and fasting occupied a prominent place in the campaign, which also included Saturday evening street meetings in Roxbury.[49] Again large crowds came and approximately 300 responded to the altar calls. In some instances whole families professed salvation or the experience of sanctification.[50] Walls which once echoed to the noise and merriment of dancers now resounded to fervent preaching, earnest praying, singing, weeping, and shouts of religious ecstacy.

These circumstances created strong sentiment to hold a holiness camp meeting in the summer of 1936. In 1935, moving with this tide of enthusiasm, the North Franklin District named a camp meeting committee of five under the chairmanship of Samuel Z. Bert.[51] A member of the original committee later described the situation as many perceived it in that pioneer period:

> Roxbury was new . . . . It was not . . . to try to do what some other camps had done, or to be like other groups . . . but rather it was thrust upon us. There was nothing else to be done. God had moved! Things had happened! The opportunity was . . . before us! People would pray and fast and meet! It would have been outright . . . ignoring of a flaming opportunity had the camp not been permitted to continue, in fact, nothing could have stopped it.[52]

Although the committee of 1935 faced many practical problems, it gave birth to the first Roxbury holiness camp, a ten-day meeting preceded by evening evangelistic services. In the process of planning the camp, the committee had to answer questions, such as:

> If a camp? [sic] then how long? How many sessions daily? Will there be people in attendance throughout the day? If so, how shall we feed them and

where shall we lodge them? Finances—from where will they come? Shall we charge for board and lodging? It all looked like a large step to take.[53]

By present-day standards the available facilities were limited. They consisted of the old dance hall seating approximately 450 to 500 and surrounded on two sides by dense brush, a small kitchen annex which had once served as a refreshment stand, a good well, and adequate parking space. Low spacious windows in the hall provided for overflow attendance.[54]

In spite of the limitations, the committee went boldly forward with their plans. In July they announced a "Program of the Services by the Brethren in Christ for the Promotion of Holiness" to be held in Gabler's Air Park at Roxbury. The Bible teachers were Orville Ulery, Ray I. Witter, and Lester Myers; Henry Landis returned to serve as evangelist. Youth and children's meetings were held, and such meetings have played a continuing role in the history of the camp. The committee also began other Roxbury traditions by setting aside periods of time for the promotion of home and foreign missions and by providing board and lodging on the free-will offering plan. A unique feature of the first camp was a series of messages on "Bible Ordinances" by Lester Myers, which may suggest an original intent to stress a wider range of Brethren doctrines than holiness.[55]

Like the preceding evangelistic campaigns, the first camp meeting stimulated great interest and enthusiasm. Emotional demonstrations were commonplace, being regarded by many as evidence of visitations of the Holy Spirit.[56]

Word and rumors of the camp spread far and wide.[57] In distant Indiana such a staunch perfectionist as Vernon Stump, editor of the *Visitor,* was deeply concerned by the rumors. In an attempt to get an objective view of the situation, he had an observer on the ground "to give the facts as he saw them" and that observer reported:

"Roxbury could be made a great blessing if meetings were properly sponsored, and conducted."

"The Church needs a great Camp Meeting, where there can be the development of spiritual life and experience among our people."

"The saddest thing to us was the fact that all about the place there seemed to be multitudes of unsaved souls who were wondering what it was all about, while a small group of professors held a religious feast."[58]

Editor Stump deplored "the indiscretions of these Meetings" and the manifestations of "a zeal without knowledge." He felt that the work of the Lord had greatly suffered in Roxbury and the surrounding community, but he urged the Brethren to avoid prejudice against the camp-meeting movement which, he believed, had great potential for good.[59]

Much of the negative reaction to the first Roxbury camp was the result of circumstances which developed after it officially closed. Some two dozen or more persons, mostly young, remained on the grounds to pray, fast, and wait for the fulfillment of their visions of what God was about to do at Roxbury.[60] These unauthorized activities embarrassed the North Franklin District, which disavowed them and apologized to community churches for critical statements made by those who tarried on the camp grounds.[61]

Special attention centered on the ministry of the camp evangelist, Henry Landis. Reports circulated attributing rash statements to him, including criticisms of boards and institutions of General Conference. Some months after the camp closed, he published an expression of regret that he had

Second and third generation exponents of second-work sanctification. Left to right: Charlie B. Byers, Luke L. Keefer, Lafayette Shoalts, Marshall A. Winger, Moses L. Dohner, Charles Nye, and Henry W. Landis. Photograph taken at tabernacle entrance, Roxbury Holiness Camp, Roxbury, Pennsylvania.

been misunderstood and asked forgiveness for not making his attitudes and teachings clearer.[62]

These early difficulties did not deter the supporters of the camp from pressing forward with future camps and with the gradual development of better facilities to accommodate the attendants. In the early Roxbury meetings, the sponsors rented the grounds at a daily rate; later they leased them for an annual fee of $100.[63] As long as the camp operated on a rental basis, investment in major improvements was impracticable.

Eli Engle of Mount Joy, Pennsylvania, was the first to urge purchase of the site. His reasons were:

> . . . that this place could be outstanding for God, and the natural conveniences of the grounds made it very suitable. He expressed the belief that this camp should be the means of saving souls from sin and leading them on to a deeper experience of holiness.[64]

Engle's desire was realized in 1941 when the camp meeting committee purchased the facilities with fifteen acres of land for $3,250.

The camp of that year included a service to dedicate the grounds. Orville Ulery preached the dedicatory sermon with allusion to the Old Testament Feast of Tabernacles during which the Israelites left their houses for a week and "lived in booths or tabernacles for the sole purpose of honoring and praising God." The camp executive committee and the trustees then pledged fidelity to the following principles which indicate what the holiness camp movement meant to its supporters at that time:

> 1. The Camp located at Roxbury, Penna., shall be known as the "Brethren in Christ Holiness Camp Meeting grounds."
>
> 2. The object and purpose of the Camp shall be for the promotion of Scriptural Holiness, both from a doctrinal standpoint and instruction for holy living. The Biblical doctrines of Justification from committed sins and the Sanctification of our natures, as definite experiences shall be clearly taught.
>
> 3. The grounds shall be kept clean in this that it shall not be used for any gathering that is not for spiritual welfare.
>
> 4. The Camp shall be carried on by the freewill offering plan, and shall be kept free from any drastic measure to raise funds, but rather by prayer and faith.
>
> 5. The pulpit and management shall be kept free from any teaching or influence that would run counter to a clear and definite experience of

sanctification and a holy life, and shall not be given to any one whose
teachings and practices would not be conducive to promote the principles
and doctrines of the Brethren in Christ Church.[65]

Soon after Roxbury Camp acquired possession of the dance hall with its
surrounding grove, the holiness camp meeting seed sown there began to
spring up in other parts of the church. This had been the prayerful
expectation of Orville Ulery, who expressed the hope that Roxbury would
lead to the "pioneering of similar camps throughout the Brotherhood,
ministering to the spiritual unity and upbuilding of the Brethren in
Christ.[66]

Canada was the first to pick up the torch. With the Canadian Tent
Board assuming major responsibility, the Canadian Brethren held their
first holiness camp in the summer of 1941 on the campus of the Ontario
Bible School at Fort Erie, Ontario.[67]

Then the camp meeting movement spread westward. In 1944 the three
districts in Southern Ohio launched an annual camp in a grove donated by
Mr. and Mrs. Harvey Hoke near West Milton, Ohio. This camp for the
"spreading of Scriptural Holiness and obtaining of the experience of
holiness, and the Salvation of sinners" was the beginning of the present
Memorial Holiness Camp.[68] Kansas was the next area of the brotherhood
to adopt the camp meeting. The Brethren there held their first camp in
1949 on the grounds of the Belle Springs Church.[69] In 1964 the movement
reached the West Coast when the Pacific Conference conducted a camp on
the Upland College campus.[70]

These developments brought holiness camp meetings within the reach of
most Brethren except those in Saskatchewan and Florida, where distance
from the camps made attendance difficult. Circumstances soon changed
the Florida situation, as members from Canada and the United States
began to vacation and establish winter homes in that state. By 1963 these
circumstances paved the way for the establishment of Camp Freedom, a
winter holiness camp at St. Petersburg, Florida.[71]

Effects of the Holiness Camps

The holiness camp movement has been a major influence in the life of
the Brethren in Christ. Generalizations about the movement are difficult,
however, because each camp developed its own identity as a result of its
location and the backgrounds of those who regularly attended it.

One outcome of the camps was increased emphasis upon second-work sanctification among both Brethren members and non-members attracted to the services. At the same time, the camps helped to shape the sanctification experience into a typical pattern with successive steps facilitated by counsel, song, prayer, and emotional expressions at camp altars. Counselors exhorted seekers to examine their lives for evidence of sins which, if discovered, were to be confessed and put "under the Blood"; no one whose life was not free from known sins was a candidate for sanctification. When the seeker testified to freedom from past sins, the next step was to "die out," which meant to surrender wholly and unreservedly to God for all time. The final step was the exercise of faith for the "infilling" or "baptism" with the Holy Spirit.

The sanctification experience might be highly emotional or relatively subdued, depending upon the personality of the seeker and the atmosphere created by those who led and shared in the altar service. It also tended to reinforce some Brethren attitudes and doctrines, especially the doctrine of nonconformity. A participant in the 1935 Roxbury holiness revival reported: "Many of the young ladies had to remove their jewelry, such as watches, bracelets, rings and beauty pins, before they could get through to victory." Other seekers gave up alcohol and tobacco.[72]

Another result of the camp meetings was numerous spiritual decisions—professions of conversion, sanctification, healing, and calls to the special fields of Christian service. Men like John Rosenberry and Harry Hock, for example, who played important evangelistic and pastoral roles in the life of the brotherhood, pointed back to Roxbury Camp as the place where they experienced profound spiritual changes in their lives.

A third influence of the camps was an accentuation of the subjectivism and emotionalism which were the legacy of previous acceptance of protracted meetings and awakening interest in second-work holiness. Time and camp leadership have gradually moderated some of the emotional extremism of the early camp meetings, but the tendency to perceive emotional demonstration as a manifestation of the presence of the Holy Spirit is a continuing aspect of the camp-meeting movement. This is illustrated by a passage from the first report from Camp Freedom to the Atlantic Regional Conference: "His Spirit was manifest through joy, tears, shouts and seekers."[73]

A fourth outcome of the camps was provision for large numbers of Brethren and others to meet and fellowship together and thus to learn to know and understand each other better. Even when members differed seriously about some issues in church life, their common interest in holiness often forged a bond of goodwill and understanding which neutralized or minimized other differences. During the 1950s the denomination was to experience considerable stress as changes took place which radically altered the Brethren movement. The judgment of church leaders that the holiness camps played a significant role in holding the Brethren together is perceptive.[74]

A fifth result of the camp-meeting movement was a tendency toward subtle polarization of the brotherhood, which was the converse of the unifying influence previously noted. This polarization developed in part as a reaction to the subjectivism and emotionalism which characterized the movement. Some Brethren members perceived aspects of the camp atmosphere to be spiritually unfulfilling or even damaging. This perception led them to question the holiness message and either to identify with the historic Brethren doctrine of sanctification or to turn to other theological definitions of the path to spiritual fulfillment and maturity.

Recent years have witnessed a trend to broaden the camp meeting base so as to counteract the tendency toward brotherhood polarization. The objective is to continue a clear emphasis upon the doctrine of second-work holiness while, at the same time, recognizing that Christian experience cannot be confined to a single, rigid mold.

NOTES:

[1]See Chapter XI for a discussion of the 1910 statement on sanctification.

[2][George Detwiler], "Another Year,—Some Visitor History," *Visitor*, XXX (December 25, 1916), 4.

[3]Charles Baker, "Inbred Sin," *Visitor*, XXIV (July 25, 1910), 7.

[4]Editors, "Inbred Sin," *Visitor*, XXIV (August 22, 1910), 1. For the 1887 statement on sanctification, see Chapter XI.

[5]Charles Baker, "Thoughts on Carnality," *Visitor*, XXVIII (April 6, 1914), 6-11.

[6]*Ibid.*, pp. 11-12. William Baker, Samuel Smith, and Enos Hess, in addition to Detwiler, made up the editorial staff.

[7]"Sanctification," *Visitor*, XXV (July 10, 1911), 13 (selected by W. S. Hinkle); J. O. Lehman, "Thoughts on Sanctification," *Visitor*, XXV (November 27, 1911), 9-10; Lewis Berg, "Some Thoughts on Sanctification," *Visitor*, XXVI (April 1, 1912), 9-10; continued in two succeeding issues; Catherine Booth, "Address on Holiness," *Visitor*,

XXVI (August 12, 1912), 1 (selected). See also Charles Baker's articles previously cited.

[8]F. Elliott, "Enlargement of the Heart," *Visitor,* XXVII (January 27, 1913), 6; F. Elliott, "The Two Rests," *Visitor,* XXVII (March 10, 1913), 10.

[9]F. Elliott, "An Open Letter," *Visitor,* XXVII (June 2, 1913), 10.

[10]*Ibid.,* 10-11.

[11]F. Elliott, "A Visit in Pennsylvania," *Visitor,* XXXI (September 24, 1917), 8.

[12]*General Conference Minutes,* 1913, Article 38, 39, pp. 57-59.

[13]*Ibid.,* p. 59; *ibid.,* 1914, Article 14, p. 17; *ibid.,* 1915, Article 6, p. 18; *ibid.,* 1917, Article 27, pp. 68-69; *ibid.,* 1918, Article 8, p. 12; Sider, "Brethren in Canada," p. 116. Baker published his side of the case in *Misrepresentation and Error Exposed* (n.p., n.d.).

[14]*General Conference Minutes,* 1915, Article 20, pp. 71-72.

[15]Markham District Council Minutes, January 31, 1919, Article 17; ibid., December 29, 1923, Article 11; *Canadian Joint Council Minutes,* September 13, 1923, Article 15, p. 55.

[16]Kenneth B. Hoover interview, August 29, 1976.

[17][George Detwiler], *Visitor,* XXX (January 24, 1916), 5.

[18]*Ibid.,* (March 20, 1916), 3-4. See in the same issue the articles by V. L. Stump, F. Elliott, and P. J. Wiebe. The first was perfectionist, the second anti-perfectionist, and the third in between.

[19]V. L. Stump, "Saved But Not Sanctified," *Visitor,* XXX (March 20, 1916), 7.

[20]Orville B. Ulery, "A Harmonizing Voice," *Visitor,* XXX (April 3, 1916), 12.

[21]Lewis Berg, "A Few Thoughts on The Question of Being Saved and Not Sanctified," *Visitor,* XXX (July 10, 1916), 10; Charles Baker, "Saved but Not Sanctified," *Visitor,* XXX (July 10, 1916), 14; Albert T. Hopkins, "Saved and Sanctified," *Visitor,* XXX (July 10, 1916), 19.

[22]O. B. Ulery, "A Scripture Study," *Visitor,* XXXI (October 8, 1917), 9.

[23]In a Bible Conference in the 1930s, the present writer heard Bishop Ulery emphatically state his view that the Holy Spirit is "with" the justified, regenerated believer and "within" the sanctified Christian.

[24]*General Conference Minutes,* 1916, Article 3, p. 6; *ibid.,* 1917, Article 3, p. 5.

[25]*Ibid.,* 1918, Article 41, p. 43.

[26][George Detwiler], "Editorial," *Visitor,* XXXII (December 16 & 30, 1918), 3. Detwiler specifically stated that the Conference minutes omitted this resolution of censure.

[27]George Detwiler, "Evangelical Visitor," Asa W. Climenhaga Papers.

[28][George Detwiler], *Visitor,* XXXII (December 16 & 30, 1918), 3.

[29]For the Detwiler masthead, see *ibid.,* p. 2.

[30]*Visitor,* XXXII (January 13, 1919), 8.

[31]J. R. Zook, "Holiness and Empowerment," *Visitor,* XXXII (September 8, 1919), 4-5.

[32]S. G. Engle, "Holiness," *Visitor,* XXXIII (March 8 and 22, 1920), 4.

[33]See, for example, W. H. Boyer, "Heart Purity and Cleansing from All Sin," *Visitor,* XLIV (June 21, 1931), 198; L. Shoalts, "Keeping Sanctified," *Visitor,* XLV (April 11, 1932), 117; [V. L. Stump], "Sanctified—But How Far?" *Visitor,* XLVI (March 27, 1933), 99; R. I. Witter, "Carnal Mindedness," *Visitor,* XLVII (January 15, 1934), 19.

[34]*Ohio-Kentucky Joint Council Minutes,* March 14-16, 1935, Article 20, pp. 25-26. The Clark County petition was directed at the 1910 article as then published in the

Constitution and By-Laws of the Brethren in Christ Church, Revised 1924 (n.p., n.d.), p. 110.

[35]*Ohio-Kentucky Joint Council Minutes*, March 14-16, 1935, Article 20, p. 27.

[36]Alderfer, "Mind of the Brethren," pp. 250-51.

[37]*General Conference Minutes*, 1935, Article 44, p. 72.

[38]*Michigan State Council Minutes*, October 19, 1936, Article 8, p. 8.

[39]*Constitution-Doctrine, By-Laws and Rituals, Tentative Unapproved Edition.* Report of Revision Committee According to Articles V, VI, VII, Pages 10-13, General Conference Minutes of 1935 (n.p., n.d.) p. 13.

[40]E. J. Swalm to C. O. Wittlinger, September 17, 1973. Swalm was assistant chairman of the Revision Committee. This and other critical comments were made to him or in his presence.

[41]*Ibid.*; C. W. Boyer to C. O. Wittlinger, August 4, 1973. Boyer, a member of the Revision Committee, argues that the revised statement included all of the substance of the original article except reference to the completion of sanctification in glorification. The present writer believes, however, that this view does not adequately account for the change in semantic tone when the two articles are placed in juxtaposition.

[42]For the sanctification statement approved in 1937, see *Constitution-Doctrine, By-Laws and Rituals of the Brethren in Christ Church*, Adopted . . . June 4, 1937, (Nappanee, Indiana; E. V. Publishing House, n. d.), pp. 15-16.

[43]C. B. Byers, "Camp Meetings—Their Birth and Development in the Brethren in Christ Church (Roxbury in Particular)," (unpublished paper in Church Archives), p. 2. Byers was a member of the first Roxbury camp meeting committee appointed in 1935, and he has been officially associated with that camp ever since.

[44]*Ibid.*, pp. 2-3; E. Morris Sider, *Fire in the Mountains* (Mechanicsburg, Pa.: W. and M. Printing Press, 1976), is an account of the Saxton revivals.

[45]Some sources give 1932 for the date of this first meeting, but the evidence is conclusive for 1933. See "Mowersville—Greenspring, Dist., Pa." *Visitor*, XLVI (September 25, 1933), 313.

[46]"Memoir by Frances (mother) Rosenberry of Altoona, Penna.," *Roxbury Holiness Camp. 25th Anniversary, Roxbury, Pennsylvania*, 1935-1960, compiled by Order of the Board of Directors (n.p., n.d.), p. 42. Brochure cited hereafter as *Roxbury, 25th Anniversary.*

[47]J. Lester Myers, "I Preached in the Dance Hall," taped address (1960), Church Archives.

[48]*Ibid.*, "Mowersville-Greenspring, Dist., Pa." *Visitor*, XLVI (September 25, 1933), 313.

[49]*Roxbury, 25th Anniversary*, p. 13.

[50]M. E. W., "Gleanings from the Roxbury Revival," *Visitor*, XLVII (November 11, 1935), 361.

[51]The road beside the dance hall was the dividing line between the Mowersville-Greenspring and North Franklin Districts, with the site actually within the jurisdiction of the latter. The Mowersville-Greenspring evangelistic meetings from 1932-1935 were, therefore, by mutual agreement technically held in North Franklin District.

[52]Byers, "Camp Meetings," p. 5.

[53]*Roxbury, 25th Anniversary*, p. 17.

[54]"Mowersville-Greenspring Dist., Pa." *Visitor*, XLVI (September 24, 1933), 313; *Roxbury, 25th Anniversary*, p. 11.

[55]*Visitor,* XLIX (July 20, 1936), p. 229; P. W. McBeth, "At Roxbury," *Visitor,* XLIX (September 25, 1936), 315.

[56]Amos D. M. Dick interview, June 11, 1973.

[57]Luke L. Keefer, "Holiness in My Life and Roxbury," taped address (1960), Church Archives.

[58][V. L. Stump], "Let Brotherly Love Continue," *Visitor,* L (January 4, 1937), 3.

[59]*Ibid.*

[60]Byers, "Camp Meetings," p. 3.

[61]"Church Notice," *Visitor,* XLIX (November 9, 1936), 371.

[62]H. W. Landis, "To Whom It May Concern," *Visitor,* XLIX (December 21, 1936), 417.

[63]A. C. Zook, "The Brethren in Christ Holiness Camp Meeting at Roxbury, Penna.," *Visitor,* LIV (September 22, 1941), 297.

[64]*Ibid.*

[65]*Ibid.*

[66]O. B. Ulery, "A Retrospect," *Visitor,* XLIX (September 28, 1936), 315.

[67]*Canadian Joint Council Minutes,* September 10, 11, 1941, Article 3, pp. 239-40.

[68]*Ohio-Kentucky Joint Council Minutes,* March 9-11, 1944, pp. 26-29; *ibid.,* March 14-16, 1946, Article 11, p. 14.

[69]*Kansas State Council Minutes,* April 8, 1948, Article 8, p. 7.

[70]*Pacific Conference Minutes,* March 6-8, 1964, Article 5, p. 14; *ibid.,* March 5-7, 1965, Article 10, p. 24.

[71]*Atlantic Conference Minutes,* 1963, Article 6, pp. 9-10.

[72]M. E. W., "Gleanings from the Roxbury Revival," *Visitor,* XLVIII (November 11, 1935), 361.

[73]*Atlantic Conference Minutes,* 1964, Article 20, p. 30.

[74]Esther Dourte, "Roxbury Holiness Camp: Its History and Influence on the Brethren in Christ Church," *Notes and Queries,* XI (January, 1970), pp. 8-9.

XV

Nonconformity Under Stress

Several factors combined to make the doctrine of nonconformity a subject for debate among the Brethren in Christ after 1910. One was the impact of the preceding period of transition which raised many questions about their traditional beliefs and practices. Another was the changing life-style of society, which had increasing influence upon the brotherhood as many members left the farm and became involved in industry, business, and the professions. A third factor was the increasing zeal of the brotherhood for evangelism and missions.

After the Brethren accepted corporate responsibility for the Great Commission, they were eager to see numerous conversions and church membership accessions. Although still seriously concerned about a "pure" church, they now had a deepening interest in a "growing" church. This interest focused attention upon the reasons for their slow numerical growth, a fact which became more apparent after 1926 when they started to publish annual membership statistics.[1]

Thoughtful members began to wonder about the implications of this slow growth; they were perplexed because a group, which professed to be so scriptural, remained so small. Since their doctrine of nonconformity tended to restrict membership, they began to reflect upon that doctrine from new perspectives.[2]

George Detwiler, in his characteristic questioning way, drew attention to the large number of young people rejecting membership in their parents' church. He had before him a letter from one of them, now an adult, eulogizing his Brethren parents and the Christian heritage which they gave him. Detwiler asked:

How is it that this Christian man, and he is only one of many, is not a member of the church of which his godly parents were faithful members? We notice that others of what are known as plain churches are asking the same question and are trying to get an answer from the parties themselves. . . . Is the church at fault in some way in that it fails to gather in . . . [its] own children? Who will answer?[3]

Answers came quickly and they revealed divergent points of view about the practice of nonconformity. One who replied saw rigid standards of plain dress as a principal reason for the rejection of church membership by Brethren youth. ". . . you can't compel young people to adopt dress that was the style of a century ago, when they can wear something that is just as plain and more comfortable."[4] Another writer agreed that plain dress was a problem but attributed this to the unwillingness of youth to obey God, and added: ". . . should we as a church . . . founded . . . on the true foundation, the Bible, deviate from it to get some unwilling-to-obey . . . men and women to join the church?"[5] A third respondent saw evidence of need for more unprejudiced and reasoned teaching of the Scriptures. "'We are living in an age when we *must* appeal to men from the standpoint of reason, . . . To say that you must be separate from the world . . . does not satisfy the candid mind'."[6]

This flurry of discussion about the doctrine of nonconformity reflected a basic question: Should nonconformist patterns of the past be carefully adhered to, or should they be adapted to new conditions resulting from social change? Although not new to the Brethren in Christ, this problem now took on larger dimensions because of the rapid acceleration of social change.

To many in the brotherhood, the old nonconformist landmarks seemed threatened, and they rallied vigorously against the forces of change. Others were open to consider the possible merits of modifying time-honored customs. The result was a continuing debate and a process of adjustment during which tradition and change each had times of triumph and times of defeat.

Adjustments to New Technology

Unlike some churches with a strong nonconformist emphasis, the Brethren accepted the automobile without a major crisis. It did, however, create some regional problems, as in Rapho District where a member had to confess publicly that he transgressed in not heeding advice and admonition against buying an automobile.[7] This issue never became church-wide, however, and even Rapho District soon legitimized automobile ownership.[8] In accepting this modern form of conveyance, the brotherhood acted on the principle that it was not inherently good or bad; the issue was how it was used.[9]

New communication technology—radio, motion picture, and television—also aroused nonconformist concerns among the Brethren. Some members perceived these media as channels through which the "world" entered homes where, at least in some instances, even newspapers had previously been questioned.[10] Of the three devices, the radio encountered the least resistance, but there was some grassroots uneasiness about it. The writer recalls, for example, a moment of family consternation during his boyhood when, in the presence of the bishop of Black Creek District, he innocently announced that an uncle was constructing a crystal radio set. Although some local uncertainties about the radio persisted for a time, it soon became an accepted part of many Brethren homes.

Unlike the radio, the Brethren regarded the early motion picture as a menace and classified it with games of chance, the dance, the theater, horse-racing and "all other vain amusements."[11] *Visitor* Editor Detwiler forcefully expressed their point of view about the motion picture industry in deploring the sacrifice of the nation's youth to this "juggernaut of destruction." He thought that "Satan never started any scheme that . . . [would fill] hell more rapidly than this craze."[12] As early as 1914 rumors of a few members viewing films with religious content caused one churchman to make the following protest:

> And where would Christ go? . . . Would he go to the theatre or the moving picture? I would say no. And even the devil goes so far as to make merchandise of Christ and puts the life of Christ on films, and then they show them in some church and that is the way the devil gets the Christian to go to see those pictures, and I am ashamed to say, I heard even some of our plain sisters went to see them. I think it is just a bait from the devil to get Christians to go to moving picture shows . . . .[13]

These strong reactions against the motion picture must be understood against the background of previous Brethren history. The early brotherhood had rejected photography, believing that it encouraged worldliness and violated the Old Testament injunction against the making of "likenesses."[14] As late as 1912 this attitude toward taking photographs was still strongly held, for General Conference refused to admit pictures of foreign mission stations and workers into the *Visitor*.[15] The popularity of the new commercial films with their violence and eroticism strongly reinfored the existing predisposition to reject photography itself as inherently questionable.[16]

As society increasingly employed photography for educational purposes, the Brethren had great difficulty drawing a distinction between its use and misuse. General Conference gradually and laboriously worked its way through this problem. Noting that the New Testament was silent on the question of images and likenesses, and that the Old Testament passages referring to them were, in fact, directed against idolatrous worship, the Conference of 1921 reached the following conclusion:

> Photographs have special value in bringing to us life like views and a comprehensive knowledge of our various mission fields and other church activities which could not otherwise be secured, this same principle applying to countless usages of pictures and photographs. For purpose of identification, our foreign missionaries and visitors to the foreign mission fields are required to have their photographs attached to their passports.
>
> It would therefore be unwise to renounce every use of photographs and rigidly require all to entirely abstain from their use.

Conference was moving cautiously, however, for it added that photography was largely "a worldly pastime" which often absorbed money better spent in spreading the gospel. It also admonished members to be conscientious and consistent in the use of photographs.[17]

This Conference action legitimized photographs and their use in denominational literature; however, the photography issue took a new turn in the 1940s. By that time equipment for slide- and motion-picture projection was readily available to the general public. Missionaries returning from their fields of service overseas were eager to present visual descriptions of their work. This aroused a great deal of positive interest but also serious questioning.[18] If such pictures were to be shown, how should they be approved or censored and where should they be viewed? There was much objection to showing them in church buildings on the grounds that this made improper use of "the sanctuaries of God."[19]

In facing the issue of projected pictures, General Conference acknowledged their value, although noting a tendency for even professing Christians "to become infected with a desire for pictures for social entertainment, which are silly, humorous and witty, which cannot . . .

promote virtues of Godliness." To safeguard against this danger, Conference ruled that all pictures shown by missionaries should be censored by both the Executive Committee on the mission field and the Foreign Mission Board. Church buildings, Brethren or otherwise, were not to be used for these showings.[20]

This restriction proved difficult to enforce. Within a few years Pennsylvania State Council petitioned for clarification of the picture-projection policy. The council noted that visual teaching was proving its value in the religious education field, with implications for Sunday schools and young people's groups, and also that more missionaries were bringing pictures from the fields. Audiences were viewing these pictures in places adjacent to Brethren churches and sometimes even in the churches themselves.[21] General Conference referred this petition to the General Executive and Foreign Mission Boards, with opportunity for church leaders to offer personal suggestions for a new statement of policy.[22]

The joint committee report reflected considerable diversity of thought on projected pictures. One of its preambles summarized the underlying concerns: ". . . it is apparent that extreme caution must be exercised lest we follow the trend toward that which is merely entertaining and exciting, and thereby lose our close contact with God and our testimony against the modern picture show and the world, and destroy the sanctity of the sanctuary."[23]

Conference then adopted recommendations limiting projected pictures to actual scenes of mission and relief work, created a Previewing Committee with representation from the church boards most directly concerned, and established local district option on the showing of projected pictures.[24]

These arrangements proved to be inadequate for the advancing program of Christian education in the local churches. In 1954 the Previewing Committee and the Board of Christian Education jointly asked General Conference to approve the use of projected pictures in religious education without limiting their content to actual scenes of Brethren mission and relief work. This report also proposed that any church board or committee might approve and recommend pictures for projection, subject to whatever censorship local districts might see fit to provide.[25]

By adopting the joint report, Conference recognized that picture projection was now widely accepted for the promotion of church work and for Christian education generally, although not all districts were ready to admit it into church buildings.[26] This action did not, however, give any encouragement for attendance at public motion picture theaters, but forces at work would eventually qualify the earlier view that such theaters were inherently worldly. Having approved the principle of picture projection, the Brethren could not as easily oppose attendance at the showing of selected films in public theaters. The advent of television, furthermore, gave the problem of picture projection a whole new dimension.

Television sets were appearing in an increasing number of Brethren homes by the mid-century, and their influence upon the family, especially children, was a matter of deep concern to the brotherhood. A television study submitted to General Conference noted that "a large percentage of the present programs center around the strictly entertainment area, featuring horror and mystery dramas, cheap movie film, entertainment of the 'skidrow' type, humor and jokes which have been described as 'livery stable humor,' most obnoxious and filthy, and, . . . it would be shocking if our people would frequent the places where this variety of entertainment prevails; . . ."

As adopted by Conference, the report appealed to government authorities controlling television to require all programs "to be clean, and of moral and spiritual value" and urged members to voice this concern to broadcasting companies. It also directed overseers and ministers to teach the members of their congregations that prayer and due consideration should precede any decisions to bring television sets into homes, that if sets were brought in, much discretion should be used in selecting programs, and that special supervision should be given to children's viewing.[27]

This action reflects a different Brethren approach to an issue about which they felt deeply and yet differed considerably among themselves. Past General Conferences had often legislated sweeping prohibitions of behavior, such as that against the use of photography, only to have the brotherhood repudiate the restrictions by slow and painful degrees. In this instance, however, the brotherhood recognized the force of social change and accepted the necessity for members to learn to use wisely, if at all, a new medium of communication which could be put to an undesirable use.

Nonconformity in Personal Appearance

The questions which new forms of technology posed for the Brethren were less difficult than those arising from influences challenging their emphasis on plainness in dress and appearance. One of these influences was the general social revolution in women's fashions after the first world war, which gradually altered the appearance of women, many of whom shortened their skirts, cut their hair, and patronized the new cosmetics industry. A second was the expanding program of missions and evangelism bringing members into contact with persons and groups with different life-styles. Another was the increasing number of members engaged in business and professions such as nursing and teaching, pursuits which raised new questions about the practice of nonconformity in personal appearance. A fourth influence was the church schools where, in spite of strong emphasis upon Brethren distinctives, intellectual interests combined with the presence of some non-Brethren students created an atmosphere which increasingly stimulated young people to think for themselves about the doctrine of nonconformity.

As they felt the stress of these influences, the Brethren vigorously resisted modification of their practice of plainness in dress and appearance. Not only was commitment to this aspect of nonconformity deeply rooted in their previous history, but it received powerful if somewhat paradoxical support from the advance of second-work holiness among them.

This outcome might not have been anticipated by an observer of the coming of second-work holiness into the life of the Brethren. One reason why holiness teaching in Kansas caused consternation among parts of the brotherhood there and elsewhere was the tendency of such teaching to encourage individualism in Christian experience. Theoretically, at least, those entirely sanctified or prefected in heart had less need to rely upon the guidance or counsel of the Brethren community in defining the life of obedience. They would be inclined, or at least tempted, to express their perfectionism in individualized decisions about the validity of plain dress.

Some early Brethren perfectionists did express their individualism by severing connections with their "plain" background, but that radical phase of the holiness movement gradually subsided within the brotherhood. This was due in no small measure to the influence of some of the foremost holiness leaders, who vigorously defended the historic nonconformist life-style of the Brethren.[28]

Noah Zook was one of the most influential of these leaders. Though he proclaimed holiness experience far and wide and, in the process, displayed a breadth of spirit and association which troubled some of his church colleagues, he spoke out strongly in support of nonconformity in appearance.

> We are not only separated from the world because we do not join oath-bound secret orders, and because we are not seeking after the wealth of this world, but we are also separated by our general appearance in way of apparel. While the Scripture gives no special form or cut of clothes, yet inspired teaching is clear on this line that we as believers should not be conformed to this world . . . . Many people who profess to be Christians are still slaves to fashion and are following the world in wearing gold and pearls and costly array so strictly forbidden by the inspired apostles.[29]

Another early perfectionist, John Zook, after summarizing his understanding of the holiness experience and conditions necessary to retain it, noted: "Our adornment must be modest, and the face should not be disfigured."[30] On another occasion he was more specific:

> There is no merit of salvation in a uniform dress. But a modest uniform in dress is most surely a great safeguard against drifting into hurtful fashions. May our people never discard the time-honored uniform in dress,—for it is modest, sanitary and safe. While some of our dear people have given way on this point, my conviction as to its necessity as a safeguard and protection against becoming votaries of fashion has grown stronger.[31]

Many second-generation holiness leaders such as Orville Ulery, Lafayette Shoalts, and Henry Landis concurred with the nonconformist views of Noah and John Zook.[32] Orville Ulery, for example, one of the most forceful advocates of perfectionism, strongly supported nonconformity in dress. In his words:

> Our evidence of separation, to be scripturally complete, must not only show a difference from the world, but should also be that which will reprove and condemn the vanity of the world; that which will visibly witness to our attachment to Christ, and be that which becometh or is in harmony with our profession of godliness. In simple words, to meet fully . . . all the teaching of Scripture in the matter of separation in appearance and dress, requires some form or standard of dress, which by some general church sanction, custom or universal use, is openly and generally recognized as the mark of a professing Christian.
>
> In our accepted and time practiced mode of dress, the Brethren in Christ have such a generally recognized mark.[33]

This strong commitment of holiness leaders to the historic Brethren position on nonconformity created the expectation that holiness experience would reinforce that position. As a result the holiness message which potentially could have nurtured a divisive individualism now became a means to enforce conformity to traditional Brethren practices; holiness and nonconformity went hand in hand. A correspondent reporting a Lancaster County meeting noted: "The Word presented was plain and distinct, pointing the saints to Holiness and separation from the world, . . ."[34] Another member wrote: "The baptism of fire will burn out of our hearts selfishness and hatred. It burns out the desire to look like the world, gives a real hatred for it, . . ."[35] As previously noted, holiness also supported nonconformity in the Roxbury camp-meeting movement.[36]

The most conclusive evidence that the Brethren joined perfectionism to their historic concern for nonconformity in personal appearance appears in the 1937 revision of their doctrinal articles. These revised statements both endorsed sanctification as an instantaneous experience subsequent to justification and prescribed specific church uniforms for men and women.[37] The underlying assumption was that perfectionism would reinforce nonconformity and other doctrinal distinctives of the Brethren. Succinctly stated, the view of the brotherhood at the time was that "Entire sanctification . . . acts as a guiding force leading one in the ways of the church, for after all, these are the ways of the Scripture and of the Spirit."[38]

Adoption of Church Uniforms

The adoption of church uniforms for both men and women was the culmination of a long struggle by the Brethren to preserve their historic practice of nonconformist dress. Between 1904 and 1937 the dress question repeatedly came before General Conference, indicating that influences opposing traditional dress practices were at work.

Pennsylvania was the focus of special concern to strengthen the commitment of the brotherhood to nonconformist dress. In 1913 Pennsylvania districts raised questions about "the . . . pride and deviation from the adopted teaching of the Brotherhood in respect to apparel, social relations, occupations, etc."[39] At Messiah Bible School and Missionary Training Home, administrators were perplexed about what to promote and teach concerning nonconformity in personal apparel.[40] In response to these expressions of concern, Pennsylvania State Council urged districts to close their churches to visiting missionaries, ministers, and evangelists who were "not in order with reference to the Plain Modest apparel" previously endorsed by the brotherhood. The council also requested General Conference to make a comprehensive statement of the principle of nonconformity.[41]

Another very different facet of the nonconformity issue came to the attention of the Pennsylvania Brethren. Some members regarded the visible forms of nonconformity as evidence of a changed heart when, in fact, persons practicing nonconformity might be neither saved nor sanctified. Pennsylvania State Council believed that lack of adequate Bible teaching on nonconformity was the explanation for this inconsistency.[42]

When General Conference considered these Pennsylvania concerns, the current official statement on the dress question read:

> Our apparel is therefore to be plain, not costly, but such as becometh those professing godliness. We have no express command in God's word as to what the cut of our clothing shall be, yet it does teach that we should not be conformed to this world, and uniformity, as much as possible, is essential to maintain the simplicity and plainness, which is [sic] so necessary among God's people as a mark of separation from the world.[43]

That statement obviously was unsatisfactory to the Pennsylvania membership so Conference appointed a committee to formulate a response to their concerns.[44]

This 1913 debate on plain dress marked the beginning of an eventually successful effort to adopt church uniforms for men and women. In the absence of such uniforms, teaching, example, and social pressure had combined to maintain a large measure of uniformity in dress. At the same time, individuals or regions deviating somewhat from generally accepted norms did not technically violate General Conference rulings. The wearing of the necktie, for example, was controversial in the late nineteenth century, but even some ministers wore it.[45] In the Black Creek District, a highly respected elderly member wore a four-in-hand tie under his full beard. No one knew this until it was made known in defense of a younger man who was in danger of being put out of the church because he wore a similar tie.[46]

The absence of specific statements of position on this and other aspects of dress had given the Brethren some degree of flexibility amid the social changes of the early twentieth century. Now they had the options of either continuing to stress nonconformity while tolerating some variations from uniformity, or they could draw a sharply defined line making nonconformity synonomous with uniformity.

General Conference, in spite of the appeals from Pennsylvania, declined to change the official position on plain dress. The new Constitution and By-Laws of 1915 merely reproduced the dress statement of 1904.[47] But pressure for a dress standared continued to mount. In 1919 Canada Joint Council authorized a committee of bishops to propose "certain nonconformity standards" to General Conference.[48] When this petition reached the floor of Conference, similar petitions from Iowa and Pennsylvania were on the agenda.[49] California was also concerned about the loss of church identity, and the Upland Church Council admonished its members to "more strictly adhere to the former conviction of the church."[50]

In its report the committee appointed by Conference of 1920 to respond to the dress petitions stood by the historic position of the brotherhood. The report asserted that the Scriptures prescribed no specific form of dress and that to adopt one and require everyone to conform "would be legalistic and lead to formalism." The committee statment concluded with a typical admonition for members "to adhere to the form of simplicity and plainness in dress which has existed under the sanction and usage of the Church in the past, . . ."[51]

Here the matter officially rested through two more revisions of the church manual of polity and doctrine, but another wave of concern for nonconformist dress soon swept parts of the brotherhood.[52] In 1929 Pennsylvania State Council, backed by petitions from Bucks and Montgomery District and Messiah Bible College, once again sought to persuade Conference to adopt a dress standard by offering the following proposals:

> Sisters shall refrain from unscriptural dressing and bobbing of hair; they shall not wear low necked, sleevless [sic] or short dresses, adult sisters shall have their dresses not more than eight inches from the floor and the younger sisters not more than ten inches; they shall not wear flesh colored or fancy stockings; their bonnets shall be made of plain materials, without trimmings, and conform to the size of the head; and they shall adhere more carefully to the form of prayer veiling used by our sisters in former years:
>
> The brethren shall wear the coats with the military collar and refrain from wearing neckties, creased hats, colored hats, cuffs and studs;
>
> Brethren and sisters alike shall refrain from the unscriptural wearing of gold and the display of jewelry.[53]

The committee of Conference considering these proposals quickly realized that their adoption would conflict with the Constitution and By-Laws, which disavowed a specific dress standard. Its report, however, did endorse part of the Pennsylvania proposals including rejection of the necktie.[54]

By the following year this committee had second thoughts. Its 1930 report noted that for nearly sixty years General Conference refused to endorse a uniform standard of dress. The report accordingly reverted to that position and confined itself to general principles based upon familiar New Testament texts. These principles prohibited costly, conspicuous, or fashionable apparel including flesh-colored outer garments, artificial hair styling—"bobs, waves, curls, and men's fashionable and unbecoming haircuts"—and the wearing of gold. Missing was any reference to the necktie and various other Pennsylvania proposals such as the erect or "military" collar for men.

Conference not only adopted this revised report reflecting the historic reluctance to legislate a church uniform but had it printed in leaflet form for distribution to all members. This document covered a broad spectrum of nonconformist concerns—growing and trafficking in tobacco, courtship, language, political affiliation, building and furnishing homes—in addition to personal appearance.[55]

In 1933 Messiah Bible College helped to keep the dress standard issue alive by securing Pennsylvania State Council approval for a campus dress policy. Its trustees presented the following rationale for such a policy:

> The problem of Messiah Bible College in respect to the attire of its students is unique, in that students come from various sections of the Brotherhood, and students are admitted who have no connection with the Church which sponsors the school, and in some cases the student makes no profession of being a Christian.
>
> The drift toward conformity to worldly styles in dress in the Brethren in Christ Church has been so rapid and apparent that it has affected the student body of the school. Therefore it becomes necessary that a pace be fixed and a standard prescribed for those who are members of the Church, as well as those who are not.[56]

Hoping to halt the campus drift toward worldly conformity, the college proposed dress standards for men and women, with stricter requirements for students holding Brethren membership. The standard for male members included the erect collar and discouraged the necktie; for women members it included the cape, high neck lines, and low hemlines measured in specific inches. Pennsylvania State Council expressed its support by endorsing these standards for the college community.[57]

Other areas of the brotherhood shared the perplexities of Messiah Bible College in applying the principle of nonconformity in dress. Rapho District, for example, was alarmed by "a very marked worldward tendency in conformity to the world in recent years." The district noted with dismay that this tendency was even invading the floor of General Conference and called for action to safeguard the future church from "the invasion of worldly, immoral, and inconsistent dress, and worldly conformity, at all . . . General Conference assemblies, . . ."[58] Conference declined to become involved in this matter, which would have required specific definitions of worldly dress.

In 1934 an Ohio-Kentucky Joint Council request to revise the Constitution and By-Laws began a process of which one outcome would be the specification of church uniforms.[59] General Conference spread the request on the minutes, and its 1935 successor named a committee of twelve to undertake the revision.[60] This "Revision Committee," composed of relatively young men, led the brotherhood in a major departure from past policy regarding nonconformist dress.[61]

Before adopting a new Constitution and By-Laws, Conference examined and debated two tentative editions of the revision. In the doctrinal section of each, an article on "Separation" preceded one on "Christian Apparel."[62] The former dealt broadly with nonconformist principles; the latter confined itself to dress. The texts of these articles, as adopted by Conference in 1937, were practically identical with those proposed in the first tentative edition. This indicates that those in opposition to specific church uniforms were unable to muster the strength needed to influence the voting on the issue.

In approving the article on Christian apparel, General Conference prescribed the first specific church uniforms. The introductory part of the statement on apparel asserted that "modesty, simplicity and nonconformity" in dress were clearly taught in 1 Peter 3:3-5 and I Timothy 2:9-10. Modesty required adequate covering of the body, simplicity prohibited excessive articles of dress for ornamentation, and nonconformity reflected Christian principles rather than standards of godless fashion.

Principles, according to the article, require interpretation, and a distinctive church garb "prescribed with a proper consideration for varied conditions and needed adaptations" would preserve clear scriptural principles, prevent drifting toward worldly and degrading fashions, testify for Christ, and provide a protection for both the individual and church.[63] On these assumptions, the Brethren broke with their historic precedent and adopted the following church uniforms:

For the Brethren
1. Suits of plain material with the erect collar are considered our uniform.
2. The wearing of silver, gold, precious stones or other forms of ornament and apparel for adornment, (such as the tie) is not consistent with the principles of separation and non-conformity as taught in the Word of God.

For the Sisters
1. Dresses of plain material which modestly cover the body and include the cape are considered our uniform.
2. The wearing of silver, gold, precious stones or other forms of ornament and apparel for adornment, or artificial efforts to beautify or bedeck the face or hair are likewise not consistent with the principles of separation and non-conformity as taught in the Word of God.[64]

This article on Christian apparel made one significant concession to members engaged in employment where the church uniforms was not permitted. They could "conform [while on duty] to the uniform required by their employers . . . provided the principle of modesty . . . [was] not violated." This meant that the cape could be discarded and the necktie worn while on duty in employment, although the latter concession appeared to clash with the definition of the tie as an article of adornment inconsistent with "the principles of separation and non-conformity as taught in the Word of God."[65] In other words, biblical principles of dress as interpreted by the Brethren could be bypassed by an employee while on duty, but they applied to that employee at all other times.

Some critics of the work of the 1935 Revision Committee have tended to overlook the fact that the article on apparel appeared in the doctrinal section of the Constitution and By-Laws and not in the section on membership requirements. This is an important distinction. Prescribed dress uniforms originally were meant to be goals for members. The committee did not intend to make them standards of discipline. This distinction proved to be difficult to maintain, however, and some areas of the brotherhood tended to view church uniforms as membership requirements.[66]

In 1937 General Conference easily mustered the two-thirds vote necessary for approval of the dress standards.[67] The brotherhood now believed that the time-honored reliance upon admonition and example to preserve nonconformist traditions could no longer stem the drift toward worldly conformity; doctrinal legislation setting forth specific standards of dress would, hopefully, meet the need.

Time would wither these high hopes for the perpetuation of dress standards, but few church leaders appear to have foreseen that outcome. The Revision Committee noted with gratification that more young men appeared in plain vests at the next General Conference.[68] Also, coincidentally or otherwise, church growth spurted upward. In the three years beginning in 1937, membership increased by a total of 795 as compared to 541 for the entire preceding decade.[69]

Life Insurance and Social Security

The Brethren entered the twentieth century firmly resisting sentiment to modify their long-standing opposition to life insurance.[70] Kansas was one center of dissatisfaction with the restrictive policy on life insurance. For a time the Kansas Brethren permitted life insurance without discipline, although they later expressed agreement with Conference rulings.[71] California was also perplexed about the position of the church on life insurance.[72] On the other hand, areas of the brotherhood such as Ohio and Canada strongly supported that position.[73]

By the 1920s a considerable number of members had their lives insured, and a few were reported to be selling insurance. This situation disturbed the Canadian Brethren, who pressed General Conference to place such persons on a suspended membership list, to be followed by eventual disfellowship if the insurance was not dropped.[74]

Conference responded partially by accepting the principle of the suspended membership list but limited it to "all ordained Church officials and members of Conference."[75] This distinction was difficult to maintain, and Conference struggled for several years to clarify the ruling. The final effort to do so reaffirmed the historic objection to life insurance by asserting:

> That the very purpose of self protection as sought in life insurance, or
> kindred agencies, hinders a life of faith and trust in God . . . clearly taught in

His word, and also evidenced by definite dealings of the Spirit of God in convicting individuals of this lack of faith by trusting in the arm of flesh, and in witnessing, with exceeding joy, to those who had surrendered their dependence on human agencies, to confidence and faith in God who said "Take no thought for your life" and "Cast all your care upon Him for He careth for you."[76]

Ministers, other officials and legislative representatives, the statement maintained, should be in a position "to clearly reflect by precept and example the declared belief of the Church on this question. . . ."

In taking this position General Conference launched the brotherhood upon two decades of a double standard of life insurance, one for officials and one for lay members. Loyalty backed by the threat of discipline held the former in line; loyalty alone restrained the latter. When a district elected an insured member to official position, he had to cancel any life insurance to establish his eligibility for service.

Although Conference tried to stem the tide of life insurance, it made some concessions to the emerging social and economic realities of the new industrial society. In 1926 Brethren employees gained approval to conform to legal requirements for workmen's compensation in the state or province of their employment.[77]

In the midst of this insurance ferment, some members began to advocate a plan for church-related financial security in lieu of life insurance. The problem involved had been illustrated as early as 1907 by an appeal for funds to bury a member in Philadelphia. This particular member, a woman, died destitute because she gave up her life insurance when she joined the brotherhood. The author of the appeal expressed his agreement with the stand of the church on life insurance but added: "Now, under these conditions, it is our duty as brethren and sisters in Christ to see that she is buried properly. Now in Jesus' Name I plead for help." He backed this appeal by pointing out that many of the Philadelpha members were poor.[78]

How fully readers grasped the implications of this incident is unknown, but it emphasized an important principle. When the brotherhood directed members to detach themselves from "worldly" economic structures around them, their theoretical understandings of church and brotherhood implied that the group assumed responsibility to assist the member in need. Now, as the cost of caring for the aged, widows, and orphans began a relentless upward spiral, members with material abundance could not gracefully exhort their less fortunate brethren and sisters to "Consider the lilies of the field." There were other clear New Testament principles to be accounted for such as: ". . . for as many as were possessors of land or houses sold them, . . . and distribution was made unto every man according as he had need."

Some members saw the inconsistency of condemning life insurance without providing a systematic church-related alternative. In 1926 General Conference reaffirmed its opposition to life insurance but simultaneously passed the following resolution: "That since it is the work of the Beneficiary Board to provide for members in need, General Conference instruct said Board with a plan whereby the needs of such may be met, . . ." The resulting plan provided for monthly assessments of twenty-five cents from each member of the brotherhood, with the accumulating principal to remain intact for the five years of the plan. During those years the Beneficiary Board was free to disburse the interest of the fund.[79]

This proposal, which envisioned a fund of $75,000, met with skepticism. Kansas State Council had little faith in the plan and observed that it was receiving poor support. The Kansas Brethren also noted that members were insuring their lives in spite of the "not allowed" in Conference rulings and urged that this wording be changed to "not encouraged."[80]

The California Brethren likewise were unconvinced of the practicality of the 1926 plan to care for needy members.[81] A few years later the Pacific Coast District Council discussed an elaborate alternative for an organization to be known as "'The Saving Fund of the Brethren in Christ Church.'" Its purpose was to cover funeral expenses and to provide other substantial help when the husband or wife of a family passed away, thus providing a substitute for life insurance.[82] This proposal produced no tangible results.

National social legislation during the depression of the 1930s posed new problems for Brethren relationships to the economic and political structures of society. Such legislation took the form of social security programs involving government relief, pensions, unemployment insurance, death benefits, and family allowances. In both Canada and the United States, the Brethren reaction to such social welfare programs was initially negative and then shaded gradually into full acceptance.

By 1936 the Canadian Brethren were wrestling with the issue of state relief and old age pensions. Early sentiment was strongly against accepting these benefits. As with life insurance, however, some members urged that opposition to them be coupled with a church-sponsored alternate plan to care for the needy poor. Since General Conference had created the Beneficiary Board to work in this area, the Canadian brotherhood called upon the church to rally to support of that agency.[83]

After studying the social security issue for several years, Canada Joint Council still believed that state relief and old age pensions were incompatible with the principles of separation and nonresistance to be followed by Christians as "pilgrims and strangers on earth and called to a heavenly citizenship." These public benefits, the council believed, tended to destroy the independence, thrift and self-respect of individuals, to undermine the responsibility of children for their parents, and to make the church careless in her duty towards the needs of the poor.[84] For these reasons Canada Joint Council not only opposed state relief and old age pensions but also petitioned General Conference to join in opposing social security benefits.[85]

Conference responded to this Canadian proposal by naming a study committee. The study assignment was complex, for by now the United States Brethren were also involved with state relief and other social security reforms of the "New Deal" launched by the Franklin D. Roosevelt Administration.[86]

When the final report of this committee came to Conference, it was a landmark in the relationships of the Brethren to the national societies of which they were a part.[87] The report revealed that, in the midst of unprecedented economic depression, "a very great number" of members had accepted state relief. Some, relying upon the historic Brethren tradition of mutual aid, looked to the church for the needed help, but such help, when given at all, "proved wholly inadequate to meet the needs."

The report rejected the concept of a relationship between spirituality on the one hand and wealth or poverty on the other. It asserted: "The Bible and history clearly prove that poverty and wealth have existed side by side from the earliest antiquity, and while some have been blessed with the stewardship of wealth, other persons, equally as industrious and sometimes possessing better and more pleasing Christian character, have remained poor; . . ." The report also acknowledged that there was no escape from the admission that economic problems now demanded increased thought and planning and added: "It is not enough, therefore, that we pray, 'Give us this day our daily bread.'"

Of eight resolutions offered by the committee, three summarized the emerging Brethren sense of direction in a rapidly changing world.

That it shall not be deemed sinful, nor incompatible with our beliefs, to accept aid (when needed) from the state which we, by paying our taxes, have helped to provide for such civil activities. Nevertheless, we believe that the Scriptures show a more excellent way.

That we, who are blessed with this world's goods, will do our Christian duty to our brethren who are not so blessed. . . .

That we, who have not been so fortunate as our brethren referred to above, will not be satisfied until we have made the most of our opportunities, and we shall endeavor, by the grace of God, to trust more and more by a living faith in Him who has said, "The cattle upon the thousand hills are mine," [*sic*] rather than to lean upon the arm of flesh.

In accepting these resolutions, the Brethren recognized the principle that Christians are citizens of two worlds. Their understanding of the church as a visible community whose members should love and support each other spiritually and materially was not repudiated, but Conference acknowledged that such members also had a legitimate relationship to the structures of society. Whatever their reservations about the coercive functions of government, the Brethren now perceived themselves to be responsible tax-paying supporters of its welfare functions, and therefore proper recipients of its welfare benefits.

One other form of social welfare troubled the Canadian Brethren. This was the family allowance, a system of payments of public funds scaled to family size, initiated after the Second World War. At first the Canadians opposed this policy as involving possible political entanglements and a tendency to undermine parental responsibility.[88] Five years later they made the issue a matter for decision by individual conscience.[89]

The growing complexities of modern life also led the Brethren to conclude that their traditional position on life insurance was untenable; the old, simpler definitions of the relationship of the Christian to society no longer applied. In 1929 they struggled to distinguish between acceptable and unacceptable forms of insurance. Acceptable insurances, they concluded, were fire, hail, storm, theft, automobile, accident, workman's compensation, medical, building and loan, and nonspeculative investment policies; unacceptable was "all speculative life insurance bearing a premium after death."[90]

This distinction continued as official policy until 1951. Then, acknowledging that "the past-declared policy of our church on the matter of life insurance . . . [did] not adequately reflect present-day needs and conditions," and that it discriminated unequally between officials and laity, the Brethren rescinded their historic policy and referred the question to the conscience of the individual.[91] This concluded the life-insurance controversy which had extended over three-quarters of a century.

Use of Musical Instruments

For many years the Brethren opposed the use of musical instruments in worship. Even small Sunday school and mission assemblies, which found a cappella singing very difficult, technically violated General Conference rulings when they ventured to use pianos or organs. Early in the century the Conference made a serious effort to enforce the anti-instrument rulings in city missions.[92]

With the passage of time, factors such as singing schools, the teaching of vocal and instrumental music in the church schools, and the introduction of the radio into Brethren homes combined to raise the level of musical interest and to create awareness of the potential of musical instruments. These circumstances produced recurring challenges to the exclusion of instruments from Brethren worship and nurtured the tendency to circumvent the official policy when it proved to be especially burdensome in local situations.

Many mission congregations, for example, eventually used pianos or organs. These congregations answered administratively to the Home Mission Board rather than to district officials. Members of that board learned by practical experience the difficulties of mission singing without instruments, and they backed the missions in their use.

The presence of instruments in mission congregations occasionally created awkward situations. When, for example, Beulah Chapel in Kentucky was dedicated in the early 1940s with furnishings including a piano, the bishop who performed the dedication agreed to do so only on the condition that the instrument would not be used during the service. Because of their great respect for this bishop, the congregation acquiesced with his wishes, but they were unhappy to be deprived of their piano on such a significant occasion.[93]

In spite of this double standard in the use of musical instruments, Conference continued to reaffirm its traditional opposition to their use in worship. This was not only due to the fear of worldliness, but also to the belief that instruments detracted from the quality of congregational singing. In 1921 Conference asserted that "the safe course for the Brethren in Christ Church to pursue is to confine ourselves to the use of vocal music only, in connection with worship in our public assemblies."[94] A similar ruling sixteen years later added the exhortation that "Every congregation should give due attention to the cultivation of sacred vocal music. Hymns or spiritual songs, proper to the occasion, should be chosen."[95]

Like life insurance, musical instruments would not go away. By the middle of the century, sentiment favoring their use was growing rapidly. In 1951 the instrument question again came to General Conference. This time a large majority voted for district option in the use of instruments. Conference simultaneously nullified all past dedicatory rituals which had banned instruments from specific churches or institutions.[96]

The history of the Brethren in Christ doctrine of nonconformity through four decades after 1910 reveals that official statements of policy about it were often rear-guard actions against the advance of change. Although a policy statement often slowed the pace of change, the direction of that change was not reversed. Nonconformity in dress seemed to have the greatest staying power, but even in this instance the official endorsement of church uniforms was deceiving. Powerful forces culminating after the mid-century soon paved the way for a radical departure from uniformity in dress.[97]

NOTES:

[1] See Appendix C.

[2] I. J. Ransom, "Our City Missions and Their Relation to Plain Dress," *Visitor*, XIX (April 15, 1905), 4-5; Noah and Mary Zook, "A Review," *Visitor*, XXII (January 15, 1908), 8.

[3] [George Detwiler], *Visitor*, XX (December 1, 1905), 3.

[4] Mary Wismer, "Another Partial Answer," *Visitor*, XX (January 15, 1906), 7.

[5] J. D. Keefer, "A Definite Answer—Unwillingness," *Visitor*, XX (February 15, 1906), 7.

[6] An Ohio member, quoted by Detwiler, *Visitor*, XX (April 2, 1906), 3.

[7] Rapho District Council Minutes, August 11, 1910, Article 6; *Ibid.*, February 9, 1911, Article 14.

[8] *Ibid.*, February 8, 1912, Article 18.

[9] [George Detwiler], *Visitor*, XXVIII (November 16, 1914), 5; "The Automobile," *Visitor*, XXXII (July 1 & 15, 1918), 27 selected article.

[10]D. V. Heise, "Then and Now," *Visitor*, XXIV (February 21, 1910), 6; Jacob Zercher, "Twenty-One Reasons," *Visitor*, XXVII (January 13, 1913), 6-8.

[11]*Manual of the Brethren in Christ Church of the United States of America, Dominion of Canada, and Foreign Countries* (Lancaster, Pa.: Examiner Print, 1916), p. 20.

[12][George Detwiler], "As To Moving Picture Shows," *Visitor*, XXVI (February 5, 1912), 2.

[13]H. W. Landis, "Des Moines, Iowa," *Visitor*, XXVIII (February 9, 1914), 14.

[14]See Chapter III.

[15]*General Conference Minutes*, 1912, Article 43, pp. 114-15.

[16][George Detwiler], "As To Moving Picture Shows," *Visitor*, (February 5, 1912), 2; "The Greatest Religious Menace," *Visitor*, XLVIII (August 19, 1935), 262-63 selected article. Surviving photographs of nineteenth-century church leaders give the impression that not all of them felt personally bound by the official ban against photography.

[17]*General Conference Minutes*, 1921, Article 7, p. 9.

[18]*Ibid.*, 1940, Article 29, p. 46.

[19]*Ibid.*, 1941, Article 25, p. 36.

[20]*Ibid.*, pp. 36-37.

[21]*Pennsylvania State Council Minutes*, April 7, 8, 1948, Article 13, p. 29.

[22]*General Conference Minutes*, 1948, Article 45, pp. 114-15.

[23]*Ibid.*, 1949, Article 13, p. 39.

[24]*Ibid.*, p. 40.

[25]*Ibid.*, 1954, Article 19, pp. 35-36.

[26]*Michigan District Council Minutes*, November 5, 1949, Article 13, p. 13. Not all congregations permit pictures to be shown in their church buildings as of the time of this writing (1976).

[27]*General Conference Minutes*, 1951, Article 21, pp. 42-43.

[28]See Chapter XI and Alderfer, "Mind of the Brethren," pp. 255-58.

[29]Noah Zook, "Separation," *Visitor*, XV (October 1, 1901), 362. See also Noah and Mary Zook, "A Review," *Visitor*, XXII (January 15, 1908), 8.

[30]J. R. Zook, *Holiness and Empowerment*, p. 28.

[31]J. R. Zook, "'A Good Soldier for Jesus,'" *Visitor*, XXXI (August 13, 1917), 10.

[32]The present writer knew most of the prominent church leaders of the 1930s and 1940s personally and sat under many of their ministries.

[33]O. B. Ulery, "Separation from the World (In Dress)," *Visitor*, XLIX (January 20, 1936), 21.

[34]"Florin, Pa.," *Visitor*, XXXIII (March 8 and 22, 1920), 14.

[35]Adda G. Wolgemuth, "The Baptism of the Holy Ghost and Fire," *Visitor*, XLIII (December 1, 1930), 22.

[36]M. E. W., "Gleanings from the Roxbury Revival," *Visitor*, XLVIII, (November 11, 1935), 361; *Roxbury-25th Anniversary*, p. 14.

[37]*Constitution and By-Laws*, 1937, pp. 15-16, 22-24.

[38]Alderfer, "Mind of the Brethren," p. 258.

[39]*Pennsylvania State Council Minutes*, April 9, 1913, Article 2, pp. 5-6.

[40]*General Conference Minutes*, 1913, Article 40, p. 59.

[41]*Pennsylvania State Council Minutes*, April 9, 1913, Article 3, p. 6.

[42]*Ibid.*, Article 2, p. 5.

[43]*General Conference Index,* p. 282. This statement was published in 1904.

[44]*General Conference Minutes,* 1913, Article 40, pp. 59-60.

[45]William H. Boyer to a Dear Bro. in Christ, August 21, 1897, Church Archives; Picture of Henry Davidson, Church Archives.

[46]Told to the present writer by Asa W. Climenhaga who grew up in the Black Creek District.

[47]*Constitution and By-Laws of the Brethren in Christ* . . . Revised According to a Decision of General Conference of 1914 . . . and also a Decision of General Conference of 1915 . . . . Article 12, pp. 57-58.

[48]*Canadian Joint Council Minutes,* September 11, 1919, Article 7, p. 46.

[49]*General Conference Minutes,* 1920, Article 29, p. 41.

[50]Upland Church Council Minutes, March 2, 1920, Article 7, p. 87.

[51]*General Conference Minutes,* 1921, Article 7, p. 9.

[52]1922 and 1924 revisions of the *Constitution and By-Laws; Pennsylvania State Council Minutes,* April 7, 1927, Article 14, p. 14; *Canadian Joint Council Minutes,* September 13, 1928, Article 13, p. 71; *ibid.*, September 12, 1929, Article 5, p. 75.

[53]*Pennsylvania State Council Minutes,* April 4, 1929, Article 2, pp. 7-8.

[54]*General Conference Minutes,* 1929, Article 31, p. 46.

[55]*Ibid.*, 1930, Article 5, pp. 15-19.

[56]*Pennsylvania State Council Minutes,* April 5 and 6, 1933, Article 20, p. 26.

[57]*Ibid.*, p. 28-30.

[58]*Ibid.*, April 3 and 4, 1935, Article 11, p. 23.

[59]*General Conference Minutes,* 1934, Article 38, pp. 62-65.

[60]*Ibid.*, 1935, Article 7, p. 13.

[61]Data compiled from surviving committee members, obituaries, and families of deceased members reveal that five were in their thirties, two in their forties, four in their fifties, and only one in his sixties.

[62]*Constitution and By-Laws,* 1937, pp. 20-24.

[63]*Ibid.*, 1937, pp. 22-23.

[64]*Ibid.*, pp. 23-24.

[65]E. J. Swalm to C. O. Wittlinger, February 2, 1974; C. W. Boyer to C. O. Wittlinger, February 1, 1974. Both Swalm and Boyer were members of the Revision Committee.

[66]C. W. Boyer to C. O. Wittlinger, February 1, 1974; *Canadian Joint Council Minutes,* September 11, 12, 1940, p. 223.

[67]E. J. Swalm to C. O. Wittlinger, February 2, 1974.

[68]C. W. Boyer to C. O. Wittlinger, August 4, 1973.

[69]See Appendix C. There is, of course, no way to prove that nonconformist legislation stimulated this accelerated growth.

[70]*General Conference Minutes,* 1905, Article 17, p. 14; *ibid.*, 1908, Article 29, p. 18.

[71]*Kansas Joint Council Minutes,* April 3, 4, 1907, Article 4, pp. 2-3; *ibid.*, April 2, 3, 1924, Article 18.

[72]*Pacific Coast District Council Minutes,* March 11, 1927, Article 6, pp. 11-12.

[73]*Ohio State Council Minutes,* March 19-21, 1914, Article 12, p. 10; *Canadian Joint Council Minutes,* September 8, 1927, p. 68.

[74]*Canadian Joint Council Minutes,* September 8, 1927, p. 68.

[75]*General Conference Minutes,* 1928, Article 34, pp. 61-62; *ibid.,* 1929, Article 27, p. 44.

[76]*Ibid.,* 1930, Article 32, p. 58.

[77]*Ibid.,* 1926, Article 7, pp. 10-11.

[78]Peter Stover, "Special Notice," *Visitor,* XXI (November 15, 1907), 4.

[79]*General Conference Minutes,* 1926, Article 7, p. 11.

[80]*Kansas State Council Minutes,* April 6, 7, 1927, Article 21, pp. 21-23.

[81]*Pacific Coast District Council Minutes,* March 11, 1927, Article 6, pp. 11-12.

[82]*Ibid.,* March 8, 1929, Article 9, pp. 22-24.

[83]*Canadian Joint Council Minutes,* September 10, 1936, p. 147.

[84]*Ibid.,* September 14, 15, 1938, p. 182.

[85]*General Conference Minutes,* 1939, Article 53, pp. 89-90.

[86]*Ibid.,* 1941, Article 11, p. 15.

[87]*Ibid.,* 1943, Article 18, pp. 25-28.

[88]*Ontario Joint Council Minutes,* "Unfinished Business," September 1-3, 1945, Article 4, p. 42.

[89]*Ibid.,* 1950, p. 97.

[90]*General Conference Minutes,* 1929, Article 29, p. 45.

[91]*Ibid.,* 1951, Article 19, p. 37.

[92]*Ibid.,* 1901, Article 25, p. 14.

[93]Albert H. Engle interview, June 3, 1974. Engle was the superintendent of the Kentucky mission work.

[94]*General Conference Minutes,* 1921, Article 7, p. 10.

[95]*Ibid.,* 1937, Article 5, p. 13.

[96]*Ibid.,* 1951, Article 19, p. 39.

[97]See Chapter XIX.

The Peace Testimony
And Total War

Like many of their contemporaries, the Brethren in Christ did not clearly foresee the catastrophic wars toward which the Western World was moving in the early twentieth century. As a result they faced the military draft and mobilization of national resources for total war with little warning and experience to help them cope with such tremendous challenges to their nonresistant faith.

World War I: Nonresistance and Relief

When World War I began in 1914, *Visitor* Editor Detwiler was appalled as he observed Christians rallying under the flags of opposing armies.

> What a spectacle! Christs on the British side shooting or bayonetting Christs on the German side for Paul said "Christ liveth in me." . . . What an insult to our blessed Savior and Lord to associate Him with such horrible work, yet that is what we attribute to Him when we say His true children are engaged in this licensed wholesale murder.[1]

At the time when Detwiler wrote, Canada was already at war, but the United States had proclaimed neutrality and hoped to avoid involvement. Draft laws for both countries were still in the future. This may explain why General Conference did not appear to be greatly concerned about the doctrine of nonresistance from 1914 through 1916.

By May of 1917, however, the United States was also at war. Congress passed the Selective Service Act while General Conference was in session, and the Canadian Parliament was about to pass the Military Service Act.

These circumstances made the Brethren uneasy, and they gave the question of nonresistance "considerable attention."[2] Elkhart District, Indiana, requested that an article on nonresistance be placed on record with the United States Government in Washington.[3] Conference responded by approving a lengthy statement entitled, "The Principles of a Non-Resistant."[4] That document defined a nonresistant as:

> One who maintains that no resistance should be made to constituted authority, even when unjustly or oppressively exercised.
> [and]
> One who advocates or practices absolute submission, and holds that violence should never be resisted by force.

The remainder of the document was a compilation of scriptural passages supporting these principles and relating them to individual relationships, the home, the church, business, the state, and military service.

Conference also provided a church membership certificate for the use of young men applying for military exemption. By identifying the brotherhood as "the Brethren in Christ Church formerly known in the United States as 'River Brethren' and known in Canada as 'Tunkers'," this certificate sought to anticipate the needs of men in both Canada and the United States.[5]

When the war began both the Canadian and United States brotherhoods believed that their nonresistant faith was a matter of historic record with their respective governments. As early as 1912, however, Canada Joint Council had begun contacts with officials of the Dominion Government to clarify the status of conscientious objectors in the event of war.[6] As late as 1917 the United States Brethren allowed the Conference of that year to pass without authorizing similar contacts. They assumed that the church was registered in Washington as a nonresistant body, and they also understood that the Selective Service Act made adequate provision for religious conscientious objectors.[7]

Although Conference failed to initiate government contacts, the non-resistant churches of Lancaster County—Church of the Brethren, Mennonites, and Brethren in Christ—soon sent a joint delegation to Washington to secure information about the draft law. Bishop Christian N. Hostetter represented the Brethren in Christ in this delegation.[8] In addition to seeking draft information, the delegation was to notify the government that the churches represented were "conscientiously opposed to . . . military service in any form, believing that all such service under the military arm of the government, whether in combatant or non-combatant capacity, is conflicting with the Bible doctrine of non-resistance."[9]

This resolution appeared in the *Visitor,* but it did not, of course, have the force of a General Conference ruling. The result was that in both Canada and the United States men faced the first impact of the draft laws without clear Conference guidance for their response to the issue of noncombatant service.

As part of the British Empire, Canada became involved in the war soon after it began, and the Canadian brotherhood felt its full psychological impact some years before the United States Brethren. The Canadians, however, were somewhat better prepared, for as directed by Canada Joint Council, David W. Heise had secured a copy of the law providing for military exemption.[10] His investigations indicated that there was adequate legal provision for religious objectors, but he thought that a fine or tax might be levied upon those exempted. To strengthen the case for exemption, Canada Joint Council strongly recommended that all members of the Canadian brotherhood refrain from taking any active part in political elections.[11] This action reflected the understanding that the Canadian Government regarded the exercise of the franchise as inconsistent with the nonresistant position.

In the second year of the war, as conscription appeared imminent, Black Creek District sought to clarify its positon on compulsory military service.[12] Later, that district named a delegation to approach the Canadian Government and claim military exemption should a conscription emergency arise before the next meeting of Canada Joint Council.[13] When the latter body convened, it endorsed the preliminary work of Black Creek District and appointed Fred Elliott and Asa Bearss to communicate with the government on behalf of military exemption for the Canadian Brethren.[14]

These men drew up a petition which sought to clear the nonresistant position from charges of disloyalty and to give assurance of willingness to pay fines imposed in lieu of military service. The statement read:

> Whereas the principles of the said church (Tunker) remain unchanged, we as loyal, law abiding citizens in every respect, remembering past privileges and hoping for their continuance are willing and will gladly submit to any commutation measures that may be imposed in lieu of, and outside of direct military service. We respect our National Emblem, and in accordance with

our Faith and Practice we are subject to the higher powers, and obey magistrates and uncomplainingly submit ourselves to every good work for the Lord's sake, as long as it is not in violation of the fundamental teachings of Christ as interpreted by the aforesaid Tunker Church . . . . Our opposition to war is not founded upon disloyalty to our Government, but upon the conviction that the Gospel of Christ is the Gospel of Peace.[15]

In an emotionally charged wartime atmosphere, the Canadian brotherhood encountered difficulties. The Military Service Act of October 13, 1917, provided exemption from combatant service for any member of an organized religious denomination "existing and well recognized in Canada at such date," whose tenets of faith prohibited such service.[16] Missing, however, was provision for conscientious objection to wearing the military uniform and to performing noncombatant service under military command, both of which were basic considerations for the peace position of the Canadian Brethren.[17]

An important part of the act provided that anyone who voted at a Dominion election held subsequent to October 7, 1917, forfeited his right to exemption from military service on conscientious grounds. This provision confirmed the impression of the Canadian Brethren that the exercise of the franchise was inconsistent with their nonresistant faith.

In the fall of 1917, conscription of all unmarried men from eighteen to thirty-four began under the Military Service Act. Drafted men could apply for exemption under several categories including agricultural employment and conscientious objection to bearing arms. Most Brethren young men were farmers so the exemption boards did not deal with their applications on the basis of conscientious objection alone.[18] This prevented an immediate crisis between government requirements and the nonresistant commitment of the Canadian Church.

By the spring of 1918, however, the intensification of the war caused the Canadian Government to adopt the more stringent policy of conscripting every man from twenty to twenty-three. The first member of the Canadian brotherhood called was Ernest Swalm of Duntroon, Ontario, whose official summons directed him to report within a week for the military draft at Hamilton, Ontario. Information about the new conscription policy was limited and confusing; he could discover no basis for appeal nor even assurance that the previous legal provision for the exemption of conscientious objectors was still in force.[19]

Swalm's family was a closely knit unit. The father, furthermore, who had only one hand, faced a major crisis as the son whose help was needed for farm operations prepared to depart. As they did the chores together for one of the last times, Isaac Swalm put his arm around his son's neck, wept, and said:

> "I would far rather get word that you were shot, that I should never see you again after you leave home, than to have you come home again, knowing that you compromised and failed to live up to the convictions that you had. Though it would be very hard for me to lose my only son, and it would mean a lot, I'd rather know that you honored your convictions if it cost you your life, and I must spend the rest of my days without you."

Later in life the son commented that his father's courage "put a buoyancy in my soul that I cannot describe."[20]

After a sorrowful departure from home and loved ones, the young Swalm proceeded to the military base at Hamilton. Here he announced and steadfastly maintained his determination to stand by his nonresistant convictions. The officers tried by every means—flattery, ridicule, and intimidation—to break his resolve, all to no avail. When ordered to put on the uniform, he courteously refused. Instead, he offered to serve in any kind of medical or relief work if he could do so as a non-uniformed civilian. Eventually, and without resistance on his part, he was stripped of his civilian suit and clothed in army fatigues. Later, he was court-martialed and sentenced to two years in prison at hard labor.[21]

In the meantime Canadian Brethren leaders such as David Heise and Mennonite leaders such as Samuel F. Coffman were laboring to clarify the legitimate exemption status of conscientious objectors who belonged to the Historic Peace Churches. Coffman declared that he would follow Swalm's case to the Privy Council in England before he would be defeated.[22]

Finally, after four weeks in jail, the prisoner received word that the Canadian Government had recognized the exemption privileges conferred in the past upon members of nonresistant denominations. Accordingly, the Minister of Justice expunged the sentences of these men, the army granted them indefinite leave without pay, and they returned to their homes.[23]

Other Tunker draftees followed Swalm in refusing both combatant and noncombatant service. William Charlton and Earl M. Sider received their draft calls on the same day in May, 1918, and found themselves together at base camp in Toronto. Upon refusing the uniform, pressures were applied to try to change their minds. For a time they were locked in a small room, known as the "clink," and fed poorly and sparingly. Breakfast was oatmeal without milk or sugar, lunch was fish, usually poorly cleaned, and supper was soup.[24]

Army officers, who visited them from time to time, tried different tactics, including threats of shooting, to persuade them to join the military. When they appeared before a military court, David Heise was present and pled their case. The court refrained from questioning either man, and the next day they received official leaves of absence on the grounds of religious conviction.[25]

Two other men drafted in 1918, J. Henry Heise and Charles H. Wright, refused the uniform. Like the other draftees mentioned, they were pressured to renounce their nonresistant position. Upon refusal to do so, they were sentenced to two years less one day at hard labor. While serving this sentence, working ten hours a day removing snags (stumps) on a prison farm in northern Canada, church leaders discovered errors in their registrations on file in Ottawa. When these were brought to the attention of the military authorities, they granted releases to both conscripts.[26]

Another Canadian draftee, Frank Carver, was requested to sign a declaration that he "would die for King and Country." He declined on conscientious grounds, refused the military uniform, and spent two weeks in military detention.[27]

The experiences of these men illustrate the strong commitment of the Canadian Brethren to nonresistance during World War I. Their men could not conscientiously accept either combatant or noncombatant service under military command; they perceived rejection of the military uniform to be the point at which to take their stand.

In the United States the brotherhood faced military conscription soon after the country entered the war in April of 1917. The Selective Service Act provided exemptions for persons conscientiously opposed to war because of the existing creed or principles of a well recognized religious sect to which they belonged. Such objectors, however, were liable for service in any capacity that the President declared to be noncombatant.[28]

President Woodrow Wilson designated the Medical Corps., the Quartermaster Corps, and the engineering services as appropriate alternatives for conscientious objectors to combatant service. This directive also prescribed the treatment of men who could not conscientiously accept even noncombatant assignments. They were to be segregated from other draftees in camp but were not to be mistreated.[29]

Later, men who refused noncombatant service gained some nonmilitary service options. These included enlistment in the Friends'

Reconstruction Unit which rebuilt devastated French villages and cared for homeless women and children, work in hospitals which rehabilitated badly wounded or maimed soldiers for civilian life, and furloughs to farm or work in industry.[30]

Because the draft law provided deferments on the grounds of dependents or farm employment, some conscientious objectors among the Brethren could receive exemptions on one or both of these grounds without confrontations about their nonresistant convictions.[31] Graybill Wolgemuth of Rapho District in Pennsylvania, for example, received his draft summons, passed the required physical examination, but then received exemption for farm work. Since a high proportion of the Brethren were farming at that time, other young men had similar experiences.[32]

Three other Pennsylvanians who were not farmers each responded differently when drafted. Harry L. Brubaker was a factory worker when he was called up and sent to Camp Meade, Maryland. When he refused both the uniform and noncombatant service, he was segregated with other conscientious objectors and kept under guard for many months. After the farm-furlough option became available late in July 1918, he went to work on a Maryland farm. Harry L. Fishburn was driving a truck when drafted and sent to Camp Lee, Virginia. Here, among a population of some 80,000 men, he found only one other conscientious objector. Fishburn accepted noncombatant service as an orderly in the base hospital. After the Armistice in November 1918, he continued in this role until August 1919, caring for the wounded and disabled soldiers returned from overseas.[33] Henry S. Miller, drafted from his job as a creamery worker entered the medical corps but received his discharge before completing a year of service.[34]

C. Benton Eavey, a member of the faculty of Messiah Bible School, received his draft call in August 1918. He refused military service and requested assignment in relief work under the Friends' Service Committee. Upon being accepted, Eavey spent nearly a year in France, distributing food, clothing, furniture, and tools in the devastated area around Rheims.[35]

Two other men received draft summons in Southern Ohio where, like Canada and Pennsylvania, the doctrine of nonresistance appears to have had strong support. In this instance both draftees were farmers. Rolla L. Wenger, drafted in the summer of 1917, was confused about the procedures to be followed by conscientious objectors. At first he simply remained at home, but when he receive a second summons, he reported to camp. Although he refused the uniform, officers forcibly put it on him. He then yielded to pressure for noncombatant service as hospital orderly in the camp, although he had some misgivings about the situation. In his words:

"First I had decided to accept no service of any kind but after they had put the uniform on me and given the good job as an orderly, I decided to work as an orderly as long as I could do it conscientiously. I had violated my convictions by accepting any military service, so when I was chosen to do overseas service, I refused regardless of the results."

Because of this stand he faced a court-martial and was sentenced to fifteen years in Fort Leavenworth Prison, Kansas, where he served nine months before release with a dishonorable discharge.[36]

Rolla's young brother, Samuel S. Wenger, was drafted and reported to camp in September, 1918. Here, in spite of threats and indignities, such as having his Bible snatched from his hand and thrown to the ground, he refused the military uniform. When asked in military court whether he could conscientiously farm in France behind the battle line, he stated that he could do so. Convinced that his stand was based upon conviction rather than fear of danger, the military authorities released him to do alternate service at a county home in Ohio.[37]

These case histories of young men who were painfully involved in the attempt to reconcile their consciences with military conscription present a sample of responses made by Brethren draftees in Canada, Pennsylvania, and Ohio. All of these men refused combatant service. One of the two men who accepted a noncombatant role later reversed his decision and accepted a prison sentence.

Response to the draft varied in Brethren constituencies west of Ohio. The Kansas Brethren decided in council that the interpretation and application of the principles of nonresistance as set forth by the church should be "a matter for the individual member to determine upon conscience."[38] Most young men of draft age in the Kansas Church were eligible for exemption because of dependents or farm employment.[39] Two of the three known to have been drafted there, Charles Engle and Clarence Byer, accepted noncombatant service in the Medical Corps. The latter subsequently reversed his decision when he learned that he might be called upon to bear arms in an emergency.[40] A third man, Edgar Heise, could not conscientiously accept any form of service and rejected the military uniform.[41]

Like the Kansas Church, the California Brethren took no official stand on the course to be followed by men drafted from their midst. One young man could not recall having heard a single message outlining the Brethren position on war prior to his summons to register for the draft. When the registration officer, who knew about the Brethren doctrine of non-resistance, asked him whether he took the "C. O." position, he replied, "What's that?"[42] Men known to have been conscripted from Brethren homes in California registered two to one in favor of combatant service as compared to noncombatant. There is no available evidence that any refused the military uniform.[43]

The preceding analysis of the response of the United States Brethren to military conscription indicates that they were aware of the historic peace position of the brotherhood and that a high percentage of them endeavored to be loyal to it.[44] Some of them felt, however, that their churches had not taught the doctrine of nonresistance very clearly, and quite a number reported that the Brethren provided no spiritual ministry to them while they were in camp or prison.[45]

The issue of contributing money for military purposes was a phase of nonresistance to which the Brethren had given little forethought. In Canada, Wainfleet District saw no compromise in wartime donations to the government if the funds were used for charitable purposes, but the purchase of Victory Bonds was another matter.

A government proposal resolved the Victory Bond dilemma. Purchasers with nonresistant convictions were assured that none of the purchase money would be used for war purposes or sent outside of Canada. Wainfleet District then decided that members could buy Victory Bonds without violating the tenets of the church, provided such bonds were properly stamped and distinguished as "Tunker Bonds to be used for relief purposes."[46] Canada Joint Council approved this action in principle by declaring itself "in favor of showing appreciation in a monetary way of the benefits received by the church in connection with the Military Service Regulations."[47]

Possibly because the period of their country's involvement in the war was short, the United States Brethren do not appear to have had difficulty with the Liberty and Victory Loans.

One further gesture of cooperation with government in wartime was compatible with the Brethren conscience. When President Woodrow Wilson proclaimed May 30, 1918, as a day of public humiliation, prayer, and fasting, General Conference resolved to observe the proclamation and to spread it on the minutes.[48]

There are intimations that at least a few Brethren were perplexed about reconciling high wartime profits with their nonresistant position. Enos Hess, in an article entitled "The War and Our Attitude," forcefully stated the issue:

Shall we who claim heavenly citizenship and act indifferent [sic] to national citizenship be permitted to enhance our material accumulations by virtue of the high price of farm products when in many instances the prices that prevail have resulted from the spirit of covetousness taking advantage of the situation and forcing the prices up on account of conditions brought about by the war?[49]

Hess questioned whether a nonresistant could consistently convert wartime profits into "increased luxuries or accumulations" because, in his view, they were in a sense "blood money." He challenged members to pledge themselves to operate their businesses for a year with as little capital investment as possible, to live frugally during that period, and to contribute the year's profits for the "advancement of Christ's kingdom."[50] Some twenty members took this pledge at the General Conference of 1917 in Detroit, Kansas.[51] The topic "Correct Business Methods for the Christian Farmer with the Prevailing War Prices," which appeared the following year on the Bible Conference program of Messiah Bible School, suggests similar concern about wartime profits.[52]

Another outcome of the Brethren stand on nonresistance was their increased sense of responsibility to help meet the needs of suffering people in other lands, needs greatly accentuated by the scourge of war. At least some of them had developed prior concern about mass suffering. John Forney served in 1900 as president of the India Famine Relief Association of Dickinson County, Kansas.[53] Editor Detwiler promoted Sunday school and individual giving for India famine relief, channeling contributions through his office to various relief agencies.[54] When war came he described feelingly the massive suffering among the war refugees from the European battle fronts.[55] The next year the members of Markham District listened to a paper dealing with military affairs, exemption law privileges, and "the duty we owe to our destitute neighbors in Belgium."[56]

These incidents reveal the growing Brethren awareness of a connection between refusal to destroy lives in war and responsiblity to save lives ravaged by war. This perception is apparent in the formation of the Non-Resistant Relief Organization by Canadian Mennonites and Brethren in

Christ. Its purpose was to raise a Memorial Fund to present to the Dominion Government in recognition of religious liberty and for the purpose of relief work necessitated by the war.[57]

A few months later the General Executive Board responded to numerous inquires about how the church could do effectual relief. It sought to rally the brotherhood to support the principle that consistent nonresistance required commitment to the saving of men's lives.[58] In an appeal entitled *An Organized Effort For the Relief of Sufferers in the War Stricken Countries,* the board wrote:

> But as we view war with all its horrors of bloodshed, suffering, and death, our first thought of taking part is repulsive. As we ponder, however, may we remember the words of the Master, who said that "He came not to destroy men's lives, but to save them." How tender this expression, how appealing, and in keeping with all that Jesus said or did. With these words in mind, let us think of the millions of hungry, almost naked, destitute, and formerly rich men, women, and children, made homeless by war's destruction. In Belgium, France, Russia, Syria, Armenia, in all the battle-torn countries, including Palestine—the birthplace of Jesus—are millions of these poor sufferers, who upon bended knees, with uplifted hands and upturned faces, are crying for help and rescue.[59]

Noting that the Brethren were too few to undertake their own relief program and that General Conference had approved the American Relief Board to receive contributions for Armenian and Syrian relief, the Executive Board endorsed the American Friends' Service Committee as the channel for giving to relief needs in Europe. Bishops and overseers throughout the brotherhood were to appoint solicitors to receive contributions for these two agencies. Within less than a year, this appeal produced $13,577, and Conference heartily encouraged continued giving for relief and reconstruction.[60]

World War II: Nonresistance

During the lull between the wars, the Brethren kept their nonresistant concerns alive. Canada Joint Council appointed the Canadian bishops as an executive board to deal with the government in military and civil affairs requiring attention between the annual councils.[61] General Conference directed that questions on nonresistance be included in future ministerial examinations and also authorized publication of a tract on this doctrine.[62]

When international tensions began to rise in the 1930s, the tempo of Brethren concern for their nonresistant faith increased. In 1938 General Conference named two committees to contact the authorities of the Canadian and United States Governments to "bring to their minds the faith and doctrine of nonresistance as believed in and taught by this religious denomination since its origin . . . ."[63] Leaders were taking no chances that the lack of adequate liaison with government during World War I would be repeated.

These committees prepared and used the same "Memorial and Redeclaration of Non-resistance," adapted for submission to their respective governments. This document stated that:

> From our earliest history our people have accepted and taught the principles of non-resistance, . . . believing it to be a clear and definite teaching of God's Holy Word and exemplified on the earth by the self-sacrificing service, life, voluntary suffering, and vicarious death of the Son of God, Jesus Christ, our Lord and Savior.

After listing various supporting Scriptures, the statement continued:

> In view of the definite teaching of these and many other like scriptures, we, the Brethren in Christ Church, wish to reaffirm our sincere acceptance of an obedience to the principles and doctrine of non-resistance as taught in God's Word, and again declare that we cannot violate our God-given convictions against participation in carnal warfare or warlike activites.

The memorial concluded with an expression of Brethren loyalty to government and prayerful concern for national well-being.[64]

The next year General Conference created a Nonresistance Committee. Its function was to keep the issue of nonresistance alive through programs, literature, and otherwise.[65]

In 1940 Conference met in an intensifying wartime atmosphere. Canada had entered the conflict against Germany and Italy, and the United States was feverishly rearming and on the verge of the first peacetime conscription in its history. In view of these circumstances, Conference authorized the Peace Committee, successor to the Nonresistance Committee, to act on any problem or emergency that might arise in connection with the war, draft, or war relief problems. Conference also requested that a sermon on nonresistance be preached in every congregation of the brotherhood in the United States during the coming year.[66]

This action implied that the United States brotherhood needed to place special emphasis upon the doctrine of nonresistance, which suggested that the Canadian Brethren were again leading in the promotion of that doctrine. In fact, as early as 1935, with "war clouds hovering and the spirit of enmity . . . increasing almost daily," Canada Joint Council formulated procedures for granting membership certificates to be used in requests for exemption from military service.[67] In 1939 the council ordered a census of men in the draft age and created a Committee on Nonresistance to assist men called for military service and to do whatever else seemed necessary to meet emergencies arising out of the war. It also took steps to bring church membership lists up-to-date, so that persons living inconsistent lives would not bring disrepute upon the brotherhood by seeking military exemption.[68]

This concern to clarify the basis for granting membership certificates led the Canadian Church to formulate a membership standard applicable to both men and women. The standard made attendance and support of the program of the church a prerequisite for unqualified membership and also identified types of conduct unacceptable for members. Significant among the latter in view of church-state tensions accentuated by war were "participating in political election campaigns, exercising . . .[the] franchise, serving on juries, taking civil oaths, suing at the law, enlisting for military services."[69]

While the Canadian Brethren sought to protect the integrity of their nonresistant witness, they were also making common cause with other peace churches. In July of 1940 their Peace Committee met at Waterloo, Ontario, with representatives from various branches of the Mennonite Church and reported: "The fellowship and oneness of spirit enjoyed at that conference was [sic] indeed precious and our ideas were confirmed that we have a mutual problem." An important consequence of that meeting was the sending of a delegation to interview leaders of the Canadian Friends about their attitude toward military service. This exchange of views led to the union of the Friends with the various Mennonite groups and the Brethren in Christ in the Canadian Conference of Historic Peace Churches under the chairmanship of Ernest Swalm.[70]

That agency then sent a delegation to Ottawa to discuss with the Canadian Government the status of conscientious objectors and the possibility of arranging for constructive civilian service for them. As Swalm, a member of the delegation, reported: "We stated that we were not satisfied to take a negative position, but wished to make some positive contribution to the country's welfare, provided this could take the form of constructive civilian work under civilian control." The first government official who met the delegation seemed interested and sympathetic.[71]

In the United States, meanwhile, the Brethren were also moving toward cooperation with other Historic Peace Churches. After passage of the Burke-Wadsworth Selective Service Act in September 1940, the Brethren in Christ joined the Mennonites, Friends, and Church of the Brethren in a peace convention. Finding themselves in agreement about nonresistance, these churches created a central Washington office, The National Council for Religious Conscientious Objectors, which later became The National Service Board for Religious Objectors. Paul C. French of the Friends' Service Committee took charge of the agency, which was recognized by Selective Service as the clearing house for problems of the nonresistant churches.[72]

In this period the Brethren were also entering a cooperative relationship with the Mennonite Central Committee, an agency formed in 1920 when North American Mennonites united to send relief to their famine-stricken brethren in Russia.[73] During World War II it administered a vast program of war relief and played a major role in Civilian Public Service.[74] In 1940 General Conference designated MCC as the channel for contributions to war relief.[75] Subsequently, Jesse W. Hoover served as Brethren in Christ liaison man with that agency.[76] In 1942 the Brethren in Christ Church became a full member of MCC, with Hoover serving as secretary of its Peace Section.[77]

By the early 1940s, the United Zion Church was cooperating with the Brethren in Christ in matters relating to the draft and war relief. In 1941 the former group had a representative on the Peace Committee, which now became the Relief and Service Committee.[78]

The draft regulations in both Canada and the United States provided for conscientious objectors to render service of national importance without bearing arms, but the precise nature of such service was unclear. In Canada Major General Leo R. Laflecke, Deputy Secretary of War, at first insisted that noncombatant service alone would satisfy the regulations. In a tense, lengthy conference with a delegation from the Historic Peace Churches, he was adamant. The chairman of the delegation stated that the groups which they represented could not accept any form of military service. To this Laflecke responded sternly, "'What will you do if we shoot you?'" The reply was: "We will die before we will become a part of the army."[79]

Faced with this impasse, the delegation sought out an acquaintance of Friends' background, who was influential in the Dominion Government. He secured for them a direct audience with the Honorable James G. Gardiner, Minister of War. Gardiner proved to be more open to consider the position of the Peace Churches and assured the delegation that civilian service of national importance was possible. This meeting proved to be decisive for the treatment of conscientious objectors in Canada.[80]

As the Canadian plan unfolded, it provided for objectors to serve in camps financed by the government which provided food, lodging, medical care, and transportation at times of draftee assignment and release. In addition each man received fifty cents a day, with slightly higher rates for cooks, straw bosses, timekeepers, and truck drivers. This program, known as Alternate Service Work, included projects such as road building, land clearance, reforestation, and fire fighting.[81]

The first draftees to enter the ASW camps in August, 1941, served a four-month term, but changes in the regulations later froze objectors in the service for the duration of the war.[82] These men represented a wide range of religious groups in addition to those from the Historic Peace Churches. Most of the draftees objected to military service for religious reasons, but a few were political pacifists protesting the uselessness of war and advocating social reform.[83]

The Canadian Government financed and operated the camps, but the Conference of Historic Peace Churches provided pastoral care for the men. This was done through ministers who served as religious directors of the camps. Each director had responsibility for a camp or, in some cases, a group of camps among which he moved somewhat as a "circuit rider." In British Columbia, with approximately twenty camps of fifty men each, one complete pastoral circuit required about a month and covered six or seven hundred miles by boat, rail, automobile, and on foot. When the religious director was not in camp, the men conducted their own services.[84] Two Brethren leaders, Ernest Swalm and Edward Gilmore, gave much time to the religious program of the camps in British Columbia, the latter serving for an extended period as religious director in that region.[85]

Under the ASW program the Canadian Brethren bore a relatively light financial burden on behalf of their draftees. Prior to the summer of 1942, the cost was thirty-five cents for each church member. This assessment supplied funds for the Conference of Historic Peace Churches to send delegations to Ottawa and to provide religious directors for the camps.[86]

By 1943 the Canadian Government was approving contracts for conscientious objectors to serve on farms and in certain non-war industries approved by the Historic Peace Churches. These draftees received increased financial income in their new assignments even after a substantial deduction from their earning was made for the Red Cross.[87] Eventually, conscription regulations also made provision for the dependents of these men.[88] When General Conference met in the summer of 1945, the ASW camps were closed, and the men were completing farm and industrial contracts in their home communities.[89]

These provisions for ASW proved to be generally satisfactory to the Canadian Brethren, and the Conference of Historic Peace Churches sent a delegation to Ottawa to express their thanks for them. This delegation met with William Lyon Mackenzie King, Prime Minister of Canada, and expressed gratitude for provisions made for all conscientious objectors. A member of the delegation later wrote: "The Prime Minister's kind remarks and his courteous reception will always be remembered."[90]

The relatively simple and effective Canadian solution to the problem of the conscientious objector was not duplicated in the United States. Prior to passage of the United States conscription act, Historic Peace Church representatives went to Washington repeatedly to clarify their nonresistant position with government officials and to find a way for conscientious objectors to render constructive service in the event of a national emergency. As a result of these overtures, the conscription act provided that men conscientiously opposed to war in any form could render alternate service of national importance under civilian direction.[91]

Soon after passage of that act, Lieutenant Colonel Lewis B. Hershey, a Selective Service official, asked Paul French of the Friends' War Problems Committee whether the Historic Peace Churches would assume responsibility for all conscientious objectors who elected alternate service. Hershey pressed for an early answer and requested the Historic Peace Churches to prepare specific proposals for consideration by Selective Service.[92]

In response to this request, the National Council for Religious Conscientious Objectors submitted detailed proposals to the President's Advisory Committee on Selective Service and to Clarence Dykstra, the newly appointed Director of Selective Service.[93] These proposals included three types of projects: (1) those directly under and financed by governmental agencies; (2) those administered by church service agencies in cooperation with governmental agencies, and with shared finances; (3)

those administered and financed by church service agencies.[94]

President Franklin Roosevelt swept away tentative agreement on these proposals by his immediate and aggressive opposition to them. Although he later changed his mind, he at first even opposed the use of the men to reactivate the soil conservation work begun by the Civilian Conservation Corps under the New Deal because he thought that would be too easy for conscientious objectors. Instead, he proposed somewhat vaguely that army officers should drill them.[95]

The President's positon posed a dilemma for the Historic Peace Churches. Director Dykstra of Selective Service asked whether they would be prepared to administer all conscientious objector camps and assume the major costs involved, with the men serving without pay. The only alternative foreseen by Dykstra was a Congressional appropriation, in which case the government would probably retain full control of the program.[96]

Faced with this unforeseen "all or none" decision, the Peace Churches chose the former on an experimental basis for six months. As the plan finally evolved, the government agreed to furnish the camps, technical supervision, cots, bedding, mess kits, medical care, and transportation at times of assignment and release. The churches would provide camp direction, subsistence, religious ministry, education, recreation, and discipline. Estimated costs to the associated churches for the six-month period were fifty cents a member.[97]

This plan presented heavy administrative burdens for the associated churches, in addition to the expanding financial costs involved. Their representatives believed, however, that its acceptance was essential to the integrity of their nonresistant witness, for they feared the consequences of government-administered camps, although that plan worked well in Canada.[98] As a member of the Relief and Service Committee observed: "To refuse this plan because it costs money, would give the government the right to question the sincerity of our conscientious scruples."[99] The Peace Churches accepted the plan, and on May 22, 1941, nine Brethren in Christ and Mennonite men arrived at the former Civilian Conservation Corps camp at Grottoes, Virginia, one of the first three camps established under Civilian Public Service, and shared in reactivating a soil conservation program.[100]

Representatives of Selective Service and the Historic Peace Churches met again in September 1941, at Winona Lake, Indiana, to review the outcomes of the experimental program. Selective Service spokesmen expressed satisfaction with the camps. They also emphasized that church financing strengthened the case for this alternate program for conscientious objectors, and that the necessity for the men to donate their time helped to eliminate insincere individuals. On the critical financial issue, they were sure that federal financing for the camps could be secured but warned that the government would direct and control the spending of the funds. Once again, the church representatives committed their constituencies to bear the increasing financial burdens.[101]

Typical Civilian Public Service Camp, Sideling Hill, Pennsylvania.

This experimental arrangement for financing CPS largely from funds provided by the cooperating churches later became permanent. In testimony to the strength of their nonresistant convictions, the respective constituencies accepted the heavy administrative and financial obligations imposed upon them; many of their young men gave similar testimony by serving without pay other than small allowances provided from church and family sources.[102]

When the drafting of fathers began, many wives and children shared the financial hardships. One Brethren draftee summarized the financial stresses of CPS:

> Most men averaged from two to four years working without any compensation. This represented to all of them, especially in the days when wages were at an all-time high, a loss of thousands of dollars. Many had been in college preparing for a future vocation. Some of these had school debts. Other men were married and had one or more children whose support they could no longer provide for. These dependents who had no source of income could apply for support from the church constituency who made provison for it, but many chose not to add this additional burden to the church's already heavy financial program.[103]

In contrast the men in military service had their G. I. (Government Issue) Bill of Rights guaranteeing them reemployment and educational benefits upon return to civilian life, while the conscientious objectors had no comparable assurances of future security.[104]

When General Conference assembled in 1942, the CPS camps were not yet a year old, but the costs for the program had already increased from fifty cents to three dollars for each church member. The Relief and Service Committee, however, had met collectively in the Conference interim with the bishops and leaders of the Pennsylvania churches and had found enthusiastic support for the camp program in spite of its increasing costs. That group had discussed the personal financial needs of CPS men serving indefinitely without pay and had encouraged home districts and congregations to care for those needs.[105] In reporting this information to Conference, the Relief and Service Committee also noted the MCC appointment of Henry H. and Elizabeth Brubaker as the first Brethren in Christ camp director and matron, serving at Placerville, California.[106]

One of the depressing aspects of CPS camp experience was the feeling of many men that digging post-holes, planting trees, grading roadbanks, and similar projects was not really "work of national importance" in an age of crisis.[107] Representatives of the Peace Churches sought to secure the approval of Selective Service for detached service projects offering more creative challenge.

By the summer of 1943, they had made some progress in this direction. Selective Service approved projects such as dairy farming, milk testing in which a man moved daily from farm to farm, and employment as attendants in mental hospitals.[108] The government eventually approved other imaginative options, including public health projects such as hookworm control, conventional forest-fire fighting, specialized "smoke jumping" in which men parachuted into the fire areas, "guinea pig" experiments on volunteers for medical research, and hospital work in Puerto Rico.[109]

These alternative projects, which provided living costs and often other financial benefits for the men, helped to reduce the mounting Brethren budget for CPS.[110] In spite of this measure of relief, the financing of the program caused concern because the funds had to be raised in addition to those normally required for the institutions and missions of the brotherhood. For the year ending May 1, 1945, Brethren contributions to MCC totaled approximately $31,000. Some of this amount was dependency payments at the rate of thirty-five dollars per month for mother and child and ten dollars for each additional child.[111]

The Brethren leadership, while not unmindful of the limitations of CPS, shouldered its burdens with fortitude and regarded it as a success. Christian N. Hostetter, Jr., one of the principal supporters of the program, summarized its outcomes:

> In the minds of many observers Civilian Public Service constituted the most effective witness against war ever presented in American life.
>
> While the new program had many faults, it represented for the emergency of World War II the church's best efforts to stand by the young men who believed in and desired to practice the doctrine of Biblical Non-resistance.[112]

In 1943 the Relief and Service Committee noted that its members had made numerous visits to the CPS camps and reported: "The spirit of these boys was excellent almost without exception. Their willingness to sacrifice with joy is an example to all of us."[113]

When described by the draftees themselves, the base camp experience in CPS left much to be desired. As Wendell Harmon, a California draftee, perceived it:

> Men who had arrived in camp charged with high idealism soon . . . lost interest in everything they had ever hoped to accomplish by being a conscientious objector. The worthless work programs and poor supervision caused men to lose interest in their work and to fall into bad work habits. The rigid and often unnecessary restrictions produced restiveness, and the barring of the possibility of relief work brought on an attitude of defeatism. Men who had come to camp as outstanding Christian characters decided it wasn't worthwhile, and, due largely to lack of contact with their home churches and with older Christians, became immoral and disinterested.

Although outside observers looked on the CPS program as a glorious opportunity for Christian fellowship and united action, the men in the camps knew better. They knew the possibility was present, but they also knew that the pull was in the opposite direction. It required a constant effort to combat that pull.

But by far the majority of the men made the effort. They constantly sought new ways of making the long interminable days of their camp detainment as profitable as possible.[114]

When, to the problems enumerated, was added the debilitating effect of being unable to provide financially for themselves and their loved ones, the fact that base camp experience could make or break men spiritually and psychologically is not surprising. One perceptive campee concluded that the strongest stabilizing influence was a strong spiritual faith supported by a settled belief that he was standing for the right. A man needed the strength of the assurance that simply by his presence in camp instead of in the military establishment he was giving "silent witness and affirmation to the fact that the Way of Peace was worth standing for."[115] Another campee who basically agreed with Harmon's analysis of the base camp situation concluded that:

> On the whole, the base camp accomplished its purpose. It was intended to be a channel of activity sanctioned by the government which would substitute for participation in war. It was not all the government wanted. It was not all the peace churches hoped for. It was a compromise between a majority in power and a minority seeking privileges.[116]

In contrast to many base camps, detached service projects opened more meaningful areas of service to conscientious objectors. Their work in mental hospitals, for example, attracted national attention. Eleanor Roosevelt, wife of the President of the United States, visited the New Jersey State Hospital of Marlboro and interviewed six of the men in the unit assigned there. Later, she reported the interview in her newspaper column "My Day."

> "We met here with some of the . . . conscientious objectors . . . who have volunteered to serve in hospitals for mental cases. They are a very fine group of young men and bring a spiritual quality to their work because of their religion. In many ways, this is probably raising the standard of care given the patients."[117]

When the war ended, additional meaningful service projects in overseas relief and reconstruction became available to draftees who could not conscientiously enter the military establishment.

From the Brethren in Christ standpoint, CPS is the story of approximately 136 men known to have rejected any form of military service. On the other hand, a considerable number of United States draftees, and a smaller percentage of those in Canada, entered combatant service, thus repudiating completely the historic peace position of the Brethren. There were also men in both countries who wore the military uniform as noncombatants.

Among the latter were those who acted thoughtfully and conscientiously. Some believed, for example, that unarmed service in the medical corps, sharing the dangers of war, was a greater opportunity for Christian witness and contribution to the welfare of mankind than entering ASW or CPS. One noncombatant explained his stand to a Brethren leader.

> You mentioned that to do this work I would have to be part of the army, the purpose of which is aggression. But on the other hand, it seemed to me we could not ask the Government to create a civilian force for this work . . . the Medical Corp [sic] although part of the army is recognized by all nations to be of a different nature to the extent that international law forbids the attacking of Medical Units.
>
> You mentioned also that working in this corp [sic] would release other men to fight. But is that not true no matter what I do under our present centralized state?
>
> Now I know that from the official church standpoint I have compromised on the doctrine of nonresistance . . . . It makes me feel very badly when I think of this. But on the other hand I can say from my heart that even in this I have done what I believed to be my responsibility and duty as a child of the King.[118]

The number of Brethren men who accepted combatant and noncombatant service in the United States armed forces is unknown, but it may have been comparatively large. Canada, with approximately one-fifth as many male members as the United States, had a total of eighty-five ASW men, which constituted about eighty-five percent of all Canadian Brethren draftees.[119] Hypothetically, therefore, had draft regulations, draftee responses, and all other factors been the same in both countries, the United States male membership would have yielded more than 400 men for CPS. While this hypothesis cannot be tested in the absence of statistics of total Brethren draftees in the United States, it encourages the inference that their number was considerably larger than the 136 men who entered CPS.

Different areas of the brotherhood varied in their degree of commitment to the historic Brethren position on nonresistance. This suggests the probability that local leadership played a crucial role in determining the attitudes of young men in the draft ages. The more supportive areas were Canada, most of Pennsylvania, Ohio, Michigan, Iowa, and Kansas.[120] Least supportive were Oklahoma, Indiana, and Illinois.[121] California was divided, but a significant number of men drafted from that area elected CPS.[122]

By 1942 the Relief and Service Committee was deeply concerned about

Six Brethren in Christ leaders cited by the men who served in Alternate Service (Canada) and Civilian Public Service (United States) as "outstanding champions of the cause of non-resistance." Top row, left to right: Ernest J. Swalm, Christian N. Hostetter, Jr., Jesse W. Hoover. Bottom row, left to right: Henry G. Brubaker, Henry N. Hostetter, Orville B. Ulery.

the flow of young men from Brethren backgrounds into the armed services. In the view of the committee, it was "distinctly contrary to the position of the Church to accept service of any nature with the armed force, as Chaplain, in the Medical Reserves, or in any other capacity." Hinting that this was due partly to the weak support of nonresistance by church leaders, the committee proposed to come "to the assistance of such leaders, calling upon the Examining Board for help in coping with the problem if necessary."[123]

This proposal to call leaders to account was not, in the judgment of the committee, a sufficient response to the breakdown of support for nonresistance among the United States Brethren. It accordingly requested approval for one of the most sweeping disciplinary actions in the history of the brotherhood. Preambles of the committee's report noted that the Brethren had always opposed military service and support for war, that the governments of both Canada and the United States had made alternate service provision for conscientious objectors, and that acceptance of military service betrayed the doctrine and practice of the church. Conference then adopted the following policy:

> RESOLVED, that any member who violates these principles by accepting military service, combatant or non-combatant, automatically declares himself to be out of fellowship with the Brethren in Christ Church, and suspends his membership; and,
> RESOLVED, that this become effective July 1st, 1942, and is not to be retroactive; and, be it further
> RESOLVED, that any member who accepts military service shall only be re-instated in fellowship upon satisfactory acknowledgement of his error and declaration of his acceptance of the Bible teaching on this doctrine of non-resistance, and being in harmony with the tenets of the Church.[124]

The resolutions jolted the brotherhood. The Kansas Church took action to provide more competent counsel and assistance for members in the draft age.[125] In California, where conscientious objectors were dividing between noncombatant service and CPS, the disciplinary action created a painful dilemma. The California Brethren solved their problem by accepting the principle of membership suspension for men who accepted military service and then, by interpretation, stripping the suspension of punitive implications. A suspended member was not relieved of "Church membership and its attendant responsibilities," nor deprived of "Church privileges and Christian fellowship." He could continue to vote and receive communion in the congregation and would be reinstated to full fellowship upon the basis of his personal testimony alone.[126]

The context in which this position gained approval reflects the division in the California Church. A defense of combatant military service was not the issue; the California Brethren considered themselves nonresistant, but many did not object to the military uniform as such. This latter group perceived noncombatant service, such as the medical corps or chaplaincy, to be demonstrations of Christian compassion. A trained nurse in the Upland congregation, for example, entered the medical corps as a matter of conviction and eventually advanced to the rank of second lieutenant.[127]

As noted, the California Brethren neutralized among themselves the attempt of General Conference to enforce nonresistance as a condition for church membership, but they decided, nevertheless, to press for reconsideration of the disciplinary action.[128] In this they were supported by the Oklahoma Church which was "unable to understand why a brother who has convictions and feels that he can do a greater degree of service for his Saviour by going in as a noncombatant should be suspended as a member."[129] A Pennsylvania petition stressed another aspect of the problem by pointing out that the disciplinary policy failed to consider the inconsistency of members engaged in "war work."[130]

Faced with this barrage of petitions, General Conference of 1943 perceived that the noncombatant issue was not settled. It accordingly named a committee of ten to consider the several petitions. After an exhaustive all-night session, this committee brought in a report which reflected agonizing compromise.[131] The proposals provided that any member accepting combatant military service thereby declared himself out of fellowship with the Brethren in Christ Church and "voluntarily" resigned his membership. Succeeding preambles condemned both noncombatant service and war or defense work defined as "any work or industry which directly supports the war through the manufacture, construction, or production of war goods . . . plant or equipment which are used for destruction."[132]

The final, crucial resolution, however, was a marked retreat from the discipline endorsed by the preceding Conference. It read:

"Resolved, That members who compromise loyalty to the doctrine of the church by accepting employment in defense or war work or by entering noncombatant military service have the disapproval of the church, and that officials and leaders of congregations or districts where such conditions obtain be made responsible to deal with those at fault in much love, forbearance and kindness, endeavoring to remedy the situation by prayerful instruction, guidance, counsel, or discipline as deemed necessary."[133]

This revised policy continued in effect until 1948, at which time the Examining Board initiated a move to strengthen the nonresistant position of the church. Noting that the war hysteria of recent years had subsided, the board emphasized the need to declare anew the position of the brotherhood on military service. It then offered a declaratory statement against such service, both combatant and noncombatant, as well as participation in defense work. Members who violated these positions of the church became transgressors subject to loss of membership. They could regain membership only by satisfactorily acknowledging their error, accepting the Bible teaching on nonresistance, and subscribing to the tenets of the church.[134]

The report of the Examining Board also stressed the lack of unified leadership support for nonresistance and the responsibility of the church schools for stronger teaching of the doctrine. With the hope of rallying leaders and the schools to more effective support for nonresistance, General Conference ruled that harmony with the declared position of the church on military service and defense work was a requirement for anyone who served as a bishop, minister, licensed minister, deacon, home or foreign missionary, or faculty member in a church school. Conference further ruled that acceptance of the doctrine and principles of nonresistance would thereafter be an unavoidable requirement for church membership.[135]

If legislation could have safeguarded the doctrine of nonresistance, these decisions of General Conference appeared adequate to achieve that goal. In the decade of the 1940s, furthermore, the brotherhood committed itself to a strong teaching ministry—an "indoctrination movement"—to acquaint youth more fully with nonresistance and other doctrines of the Brethren faith.[136] The outcome of all of these measures, however, disappointed the advocates of nonresistance, for a high percentage of postwar Brethren in Christ draftees in the United States continued to elect military service.[137]

This situation is perplexing, for the postwar period opened to conscientious objectors many alternate overseas service options, in addition to expanding creative project opportunities in the homeland. No longer did the draftee face the frustrations of the CPS base camp experience. Now he could share directly in feeding the hungry, housing the homeless, clothing the destitute, and healing the sick. But he still had to do these things at considerable personal sacrifice of time and money. Amid the increasing affluence of postwar society, the pull of economic self-interest must have been very strong, but only the individual draftee who chose the military in preference to alternate service knew his motives for doing so.

What happened to loyalty to the doctrine of nonresistance after the end of CPS in 1947 is clearer than why it happened. A survey of United States draftees for the period from 1951 through 1957 reveals that of the 313 men conscripted from Brethren congregations under the 1950 and subsequent Selective Service Acts, 149 or forty-eight percent chose some type of military service while 164 or fifty-two percent chose some form of alternate service. Perhaps even more revealing is the fact that only thirteen of the 149 men entering the armed services elected a noncombatant branch; thus 136 made no profession whatever of nonresistant conviction.[138]

The following percentage breakdown of the preceding statistics by regional conferences is also significant:

	Alternate Service	Military Service
Central Conference	65.8	34.2
Midwest and Pacific Conferences	57.1	42.9
Allegheny Conference	55.4	44.6
Atlantic Conference	42.2	57.8

These data show that the western region of the brotherhood had moved toward stronger support for the nonresistant position, while that part of Pennsylvania in which the Brethren originated was the least supportive of it.

Noting that only twenty-six of the 149 Brethren men entering military service during the seven-year period covered by the survey had been disciplined under the ruling of 1948, the Peace, Relief, and Service Committee saw no alternative but to recommend that all previous Conference actions terminating the membership of such persons be repealed.[139] Conference agreed and endorsed the following substitute policy: ". . . we reaffirm our position as believers in Biblical Non-resistance and that the teaching ministry of the church, through preaching, teaching and personal counseling in the local congregations give continued and strengthened emphasis to the peace position of the church, and that efforts to redeem and restore those who violate these principles be made with patient, persistent and charitable concern."[140]

The attempt to legislate conformity to the historic position of the brotherhood on nonresistance had failed.

World War II: Relief and Service

Experiences of the Brethren during World War I quickened their sensitivities to war-related human needs and also caused them to consider the positive implications of their nonresistant faith. As a result, World War II found them ready to think and act more forcefully in war relief. This is illustrated by the following statement of Harold Martin who entered CPS and later became the first director of the hookworm-control project in Florida:

> A positive peace program is our only objective if we oppose war. Present mission and church budgets and programs may not be curtailed, else we shall remove the roots in our efforts to grow more branches. A tremendous reconstruction program will be needed when the war is over. Increased earnings by higher prices and additional wages cannot be avoided but make it mandatory that offerings and sacrifices be increased so that our belief in non-violence is perpetuated now and for the years to come . . . .[141]

Following General Conference of 1940, a member of the Peace Committee vigorously urged the Brethren to support the cause of war relief. Noting that massive war suffering made the combined efforts of all relief agencies seem like a feeble gesture, he hoped for "more than a generous response" to extend a helping hand in the name of Christ.[142]

As was true of nonresistance, the Canadian Church led the way by contributing more than one dollar a member to relief work during the 1940-1941 Conference year. Spurred by this example, Conference adopted a relief budget of not less than one dollar a member for the United States Brethren, the cumulative funds to be disbursed through MCC channels.[143]

These actions of General Conference of 1941 set the pattern for Brethren giving to war relief. Because of the continuing heavy financial demands of the CPS program, total United States relief giving suffered. In 1944-1945, for example, with a membership of approximately 5,000, the United States Brethren gave $30,811 for CPS and only $4,800 for relief.

During the same period approximately 1,000 Canadian members gave $1,851 for the dependents of conscientious objectors and $2,917 for relief.[144] In addition to cash, relief contributions included gifts in kind of unknown dollar value.[145] While the combined financial totals may not seem large, they must be interpreted in light of a total membership of approximately 6,000 faced with the sudden necessity to raise this money in addition to prior church-related financial commitments.

No one, furthermore, can measure the dollar value of the extensive unremunerated time invested by peace leaders and pastors in promoting and administering the war-related responsibilities of the brotherhood, to say nothing of the vast amounts of time given by conscientious objectors at great personal financial sacrifice. A report of the National Service Board for Religious Objectors revealed that the total group of CPS men under all agencies performed the following amount of work from May 15, 1941 to December 31, 1945:

3,132,970 man days worked on projects
4,819,953 man days overall, including furlough, sick leave, etc.
$8,033,265.00 value of work by C.P.S. men on basis of $50 per month base pay.[146]

In response to a growing awareness of human need, some Brethren young people who were not subject to conscription eventually began to volunteer blocks of their time in overseas relief; later MCC developed a homeland service program known and administered as "Voluntary Service."[147]

As early as 1940, MCC appealed for a voluntary Brethren in Christ relief worker to serve in France; several responded but none actually went.[148] Later, MCC selected one of its members, Jesse Hoover, who represented the Brethren in Christ, to familiarize himself with relief work by going abroad and, upon his return to the homeland, to promote voluntary relief service. Hoover reached his assigned post in France in March 1941. His activities centered in the southeastern part of the country where he shared in founding an MCC convalescent home for war-refugee children.[149] In a letter home he described the project:

There are 18,000 refugees in this one camp and conditions are plenty bad as you can well imagine. For one thing there is much sickness and although there is a hospital to which they send the worst cases, it is not adequate for the needs of the camp. So we are founding a home for children who have been in the hospital and are recovering, but are not able to stand the exposure of the camp. They are sent from the hospital before they should be in order to make room for others, so that is the function of this Home.[150]

Having one of their own members in the midst of war suffering and devastation personalized both financial war relief and personal relief service for the Brethren. Hoover returned from France shortly before the United States entered the war with Germany, and his coast-to-coast itinerary among the MCC constituencies gave the brotherhood an eye-witness account of the significance of war relief efforts.[151]

Although MCC thereafter repeatedly asked the Brethren to furnish voluntary relief workers for service abroad, none volunteered until 1945. In September of that year, however, Elsie Bechtel from Ohio entered relief work in France.[152] Some weeks before sailing she explained her motives:

Regardless of how we feel about war, there are thousands of people who have made what we call the supreme sacrifice. We must admit that we, with the rest of the country, receive certain temporal advantages because they gave their lives to make our country politically free. We are selfish, indeed, if we do nothing to compensate.

Relief Service gives us a chance to test and put into practice one of the important Christian beliefs. We have been saying very loudly that love is the greatest thing in the world. I doubt if many of us have realized this other than as a theory.[153]

Both Hoover and Bechtel served the relief cause in different capacities as isolated individuals. By the summer of 1946, General Conference had before it an MCC proposal for a Brethren relief program in the Philippines. The Relief and Service Committee strongly supported this proposal, noting that the brotherhood had "not yet met the challenge of personal service in war sufferers' relief to any significant measure." Advantages perceived by the committee included the possibility that the project would develop into a continuing spiritual mission. Conference accepted the proposal.[154] Within a year six Brethren relief workers were in the Philippines under MCC. In conjuction with the Relief and Service Committee, that agency also sponsored Jesse Hoover as "commissioner" to serve in the Philippines in the interest of the Brethren in Christ and elsewhere in the Far East in the interest of MCC. Hoover was to investigate the possibility of a special Philippine relief project "more distinctly our own," that is, Brethren in Christ.[155]

Later Ray I. Witter, chairman of the Foreign Mission Board joined Hoover in the Philippines to assess the possibilities for mission work there.[156] Although no permanent mission program resulted, the investigation dramatized the Brethren concern to combine a spiritual, evangelistic ministry with the material aspects of relief work. Jesse Hoover strongly promoted this concern within MCC circles.[157]

For a time the Philippines drew the greatest concentration of Brethren relief workers, but representatives of the brotherhood also went to various other parts of the world. In the summer of 1949, for example, four were in the Philippines, one in Okinawa, one in India, one in Holland, and three in Germany; six of the ten were women.[158] Among those in Germany were Norman and Eunice Wingert, who were beginning a unique relief career spanning many years and extending to three continents.

Not all Brethren voluntary service workers went overseas. Some chose to serve on projects in the homeland for summers or more extended periods of time.

Voluntary service in the homeland, which also attracted women as well as men, began on a small scale before the close of the war. One of the first women's units was at the State Hospital of Mental Diseases at Howard, Rhode Island. Nineteen members of this unit were students of Mennonite and Brethren in Christ colleges and academies; five were from Messiah Bible College and Academy at Grantham, Pennsylvania. The women worked eight-hour shifts as ward attendants and spent approximately eight hours per week in studies such as Mental Hygiene and Psychiatry, International Relief, and other activities including religious services. In this instance the objective of the volunteers was to engage in some form of Christian service during the summer, while earning income for school expenses.[159]

At first MCC planned and provided general oversight of the VS projects which were designed to benefit the suffering and underprivileged. Some projects paid wages while other did not. After June 1949, when volunteers received only maintenance and nominal support from the MCC treasury, the Peace, Relief and Service Committee budget reimbursed MCC at the rate of $50.00 a month for each Brethren volunteer.[160]

The Relief and Service Committee began to promote VS strongly in the late 1940s, and appealed to young people free from military conscription to help meet pressing human needs. In 1947 Conference approved the following recommendation: ". . . that we continue to sponsor voluntary service projects, as a more direct expression of the second-mile principle, as a reflection of our continuing concern for the needs of the world, and as an initiatory step into full-time Christian service."[161]

Voluntary Service projects offered a wide variety of experiences and utilized many different talents and skills. During the summer of 1946, for example, a voluntary service group of eight women worked in cooperation with the MCC public health unit of selected draftees at Gulfport, Mississippi. These women held Bible schools for both black and white children and supervised play periods in two crowded urban districts. Other volunteers arrived to serve longer terms at other tasks.[162]

When the Gulfport draftees were discharged with the termination of CPS in 1947, MCC officially designated the project as a VS unit and adapted the program and financing accordingly.[163] At least four Brethren young men and women gave voluntary service at Gulfport.[164] Among them were Harold and Ruth Davis who elected to spend their first year of married life in VS and later reflected upon the implications of that experience:

> Camp London . . . became home for a year. . . . Community service projects were many, both large and small: home building and wiring (where electricity was available), directing recreation in segregated black schools, donating blood for a critically ill mother and caring for her newborn baby at Camp while she was hospitalized, working with the County Health Department in rodent control, helping to sew dresses of feed bag material for a black teacher who was going to summer school, assisting members of a black congregation to build a new church, trying to impress the virtues of sanitation and cleanliness upon some families, singing to patients at the local hospital, giving baths to an invalid woman, tutoring a twelve-year-old boy who was struggling unsuccessfully with third grade reading and arithmetic, and on and on!
>
> . . . the intervening twenty-seven years could not erase the memories, mental pictures, friendships, and lessons of those experiences. It may sound trite, but its very true—our lives could never be the same, because we gained much more than we gave.[165]

The concept of voluntary service was imaginative. Soon the Home Mission Board perceived its possibilities and appealed for persons who did not feel called to full-time mission service to give blocks of time to missions or to support others who could do so.[166] The board offered many opportunities including mechanical work of all kinds, various technical and professional services, and "the highest grade of mission work."[167]

Brethren young men and women here and there still continue to respond to the call to volunteer periods of their time for services to church and humanitarian projects. While MCC and other service agencies attract some of the volunteers, others accept assignments in Brethren in Christ home and overseas missions and churches, as well as in the educational and benevolent institutions of the brotherhood in North America. Among them are mechanics, farmers, secretaries, nurses, doctors, teachers, and individuals with various other skills.

A phenomenon of recent years is the increase in the average age of the volunteers. These now include some older men and women who, after retiring from their normal vocations, welcome the call to give additional years of service under church agencies.

War Finance and War Work

To a greater degree than the first great war, World War II forced the Brethren to wrestle with the implications of national drives to raise money for war purposes, and with the implications of employment in industries related to the war effort. Neither the purchase of war bonds nor profit from war-related employment seemed compatible with their peace testimony. Some aspects of Civilian Defense also posed potential problems, but these did not become acute because the war remained outside of the Westen Hemisphere. Unlike the foregoing activities, blood donations for the benefit of the wounded, both civilians and soldiers, raised no basic issues of military involvement.

In 1942 the Relief and Service Committee, anticipating pressures to enlist members of the brotherhood in war-related activities, endorsed detailed MCC guidelines to govern the response of the Peace Church constituencies to such pressures. An introductory statement expressed the hope that these constituencies could avoid participation in war finance and civil defense by providing constructive alternatives, even as the men in civilian public service contributed work of national importance in lieu of participation in war. Some of the guidelines called the constituency memberships to consistent Christian living, sacrificial giving to church programs, CPS, and wartime relief, and prayer for rulers. Others stressed loyalty to the principle of nonparticipation in all forms of military service, defense work, and the purchase of war bonds and stamps. The purchase of bonds and saving stamps for civilian government purposes was encouraged.[168]

Both the Canadian and United States Governments eventually accepted the suggestion of the Historic Peace Churches for the issuance of special war certificates or bonds guaranteeing that the purchase money would be used for purposes compatible with the nonresistant position. In Canada the purchaser had the option of either a special non-interest-bearing certificate or a regular interest-bearing bond with a sticker indicating that use of the revenue was restricted to relief and reconstruction.[169] The total amount of Canadian Brethren investment in certificates and bonds is unknown because it is merged into the $4,672,410 subscribed by the total constituencies of the Canadian Historic Peace Churches.[170]

In the United States the problem of relating to government war-fund drives was conditioned by the heavy Historic Peace Church investment in CPS. The assumption that the financial support of conscientious objectors engaged in "work of national importance" should be considered a major contribution to the needs and well-being of the nation appeared to be logical.

The first move of the Peace Committee, therefore, was an attempt to obtain United States Government recognition of the extensive contributions to national and international welfare through CPS and overseas relief, in lieu of purchases of war bonds. To implement this effort General Conference authorized "certificates of contribution" in the amounts of five, ten, twenty-five, fifty, and one-hundred dollars. The individual making a contribution received the certificate as a receipt to be presented to solicitors for war-bond purchases and donations to organizations such as the Red Cross.[171] Following Conference of 1941 the Relief and Service Committee, successor to the Peace Committee, also made available ten-cent stamps as receipts for small-scale contributions; fifty accumulated stamps could be exchanged for a five dollar certificate.[172]

Increasing pressure for nonresistant people to subscribe to the war-fund drives caused MCC to strive for an issue of Civilian Government Bonds to be purchased instead of Defense Bonds. This proposal gave the Relief and Service Committee some concern. Recognizing the frailties of human nature, the committee speculated that Brethren members might be tempted to reduce their contributions to CPS and relief in favor of investment in Civilian Government Bonds.[173] The Federal Government eventually agreed with MCC on a plan permitting people of nonresistant faith to purchase bonds issued for civilian government purposes only.[174]

Like the purchase of war bonds, employment in war-related industries was a concern of the Historic Peace Churches. Difficulties of definition complicated this problem. An industry producing arms or munitions lent itself to easy identification. In time of mobilization for total war, however, many industries were war-related in varying degrees. Was a shoe factory, for example, a war industry if some or even all of its production was military footwear? An added complication was the high wage scale which resulted from the need for increased production of all kinds of goods. There was apparent inequity when a conscientious objector serving in CPS received only subsistence while another deferred objector, possibly a tool and die expert, received a higher income than ever before.

In facing these problems the Brethren recognized that "a certain amount of latitude was . . . necessary." When a factory went on full-time war production, it seemed obvious that the nonresistant Christian should resign his position. The Relief and Service Committee offered the following guidelines to assist employees to make decisions when the issues were less clear:

(1) Avoid anything in any sense questionable.
(2) Definitely and earnestly consult God, with open heart to receive the truth.
(3) As much as possible give extra wartime profits to relief and other charitable causes.
(4) Seek to maintain a tender conscience on all things related to the Total War Effort.
(5) When uncertain, seek counsel from those who are in a position to know more fully the implications of a given course.[175]

The measure of ambiguity involved in war or defense work had made difficult the inclusion of such work in the strong disciplinary action of the Conference of 1942.[176] Its omission from that action, however, was not easily justified. Two of three petitions which later called for reconsideration of the 1942 action pointed out the inequity of suspending the membership of men who accepted noncombatant military service while ignoring men engaged in war industry.[177] The disciplinary compromise of 1943, therefore, coupled war work with noncombatant military service under the disapproval of the church. Persons engaged in either activity were to be dealt with in the same way, that is, with loving, prayerful counsel and discipline "as deemed necessary."[178]

Labor Union Affiliation

Another industrial problem involving the peace testimony of the Brethren was labor union affiliation. Historically, the brotherhood had opposed union membership, but the rapid industrialization of society forced members and leaders to come to grips with the issue in a new and realistic way.

In 1933 the labor union question arose in Pennsylvania State Council when a district asked what a member should do when required to pay union dues or forfeit his job. To this query the council replied somewhat ambiguously that he sould "assume no obligations or submit to no practices contrary to God's Word or to the practice of the church." The context for this council directive did not imply, however, that a member using his discretion about paying union dues would be subject to discipline.[179]

Soon the labor union question reached the floor of General Conference where a special Committee on Labor Union Affiliation recommended the preparation of a tract clearly defining the Brethren understanding of the Scriptures in this matter.[180] This completed document opposed union membership on three grounds—nonresistance, separation, and freedom of conscience.[181] It focused the nonresistant issue as follows:

> We grant that Organized Labor prefers to seek its objectives through negotiation and peaceful methods whenever possible. But back of the technique of Peace, lies also the technique of Force. . . . The Christian might easily support the program of Labor in seeking fair and right objectives through peaceful methods. But when such means fail, . . . can the Nonresistant Christian who wishes to follow the Scriptural teachings . . . , then cooperate in the use of forceful measures, which are coercive, and retalitory [sic] and perhaps violent in nature?

To the authors of the tract, the answer was self-evident; Scripture and unionism were irreconcilable.

This document also argued that union membership violated the principle of separation from the world:

> We believe this principle of Separation applies particularly in regard to association or affiliations into which a Christian may enter, and to which he may be required to give definite pledges of loyalty and support. In II Corinthians 6:14, we have the admonition, "Be not unequally yoked

together with unbelievers," which we believe applies very clearly on this point. By this . . . we understand that the true Christian ought not to affiliate himself with those who make no profession of Christianity, in such a way as to obligate himself to a course of action that would violate Scriptural teaching and the dictates of his conscience.

Finally, the tract maintained that the closed shop, if sought by intimidating and coercing workmen, violated freedom of conscience, "an inalienable and sacred human right." Such violation of the rights of the individual was not "in harmony with the spirit of Christ, which all true Christians should manifest in their dealings with their fellow men."

This tract took pains to point out that its purpose was not to condemn members of labor unions who believed that such membership was consistent with a profession of Christianity. Rather, the intent was to appeal for understanding and recognition of workers who, because of religious conviction, felt that they could not join labor unions. The tract, furthermore, made what proved to be a fruitful suggestion that workers conscientiously opposed to union membership could pay a sum equivalent to, or greater than, the union dues to some charitable cause upon which they and the union would mutually agree.

Soon after release of this tract, members of the committee began to receive calls to assist Brethren members with labor union problems. Attempts to render assistance at the level of local unions revealed the necessity for contacts with national labor leaders.

The General Executive Board accordingly commissioned Orville Ulery and Clarence Boyer to go to Washington and contact the heads of national labor organizations. These men interviewed L. G. Hines, General Secretary of the American Federation of Labor, since it was a local of this organization with which they had reached an impasse in attempting to present the problem of conscientious objection to union membership. Two Mennonite bishops joined them on this occasion.[182]

Hines received the joint Brethren in Christ—Mennonite delegation sympathetically and promised to use the influence of his office on their behalf. Subsequent Brethren and Mennonite agreements with local American Federation of Labor unions confirmed that he had acted in good faith.[183]

During the 1939-1940 General Conference year, both the United States Senate and House of Representatives conducted hearings on possible amendment of the National Labor Relations Act. Bishop Orville Ulery and Mennonite Bishop John L. Stauffer appeared before the appropriate Senate committee, testified to the common position of their respective constituencies on labor union affiliation, and appealed for statutory provision recognizing religious conviction against union membership. The comparable committee of the House of Representatives later requested permission to include the Ulery-Stauffer testimony in their records.[184]

Thereafter the Brethren continued to cooperate with the Mennonites in labor union matters.[185] One result of this cooperation was the preparation of a joint expression of position on industrial relations. Unlike the previous statement of the Brethren in Christ, which set forth objections to labor unions only, the joint document identified unacceptable practices of both management and labor. Its keynote was the conviction that "industrial strife, unfair and unjust practices by employers or employees and every economic and social condition and practice which makes for suffering, or ill-will among men is [sic] altogether contrary to the teaching and spirit of Christ and the Gospel."[186] The statement continued:

> We believe the industrial conflict to be a struggle for power with which to achieve social justice, whereas Biblical nonresistance enjoins submission even to injustice rather than to engage in conflict. . . .
>
> As employers we can have no part in manufacturers or employers associations in so far as they are organized for the purpose of fighting the labor movement, using such well-known methods as the lockout, the blacklist, detective agencies, espionage [and] strike-breakers. . . .
>
> As employees we can have no part in labor organizations in so far as their sanctions ultimately rest on force, making use of such well-known methods as the monopolistic closed shop, the boycott, the picket line, and the strike.
>
> As agriculturists we can have no part in farmers' organizations in so far as they are organized for monopolistic or coercive purposes, ultimately employing such methods as the boycott and strike.[187]

Conference adopted this statement as a basis for negotiations with labor officials when Brethren members sought release from union membership. Such release would be conditional on the payment of the equivalent of membership dues to a mutually agreeable benevolent agency.[188]

After 1941 a new Brethren in Christ Industrial Relations Committee continued to work along the lines marked out by its predecessor.[189] As cases of individual employees came to the attention of this agency, it became increasingly skillful in coping with their problems. Its members also held meetings with local, regional, and national leaders of the

American Federation of Labor and the Congress of Industrial Relations. For the most part these leaders proved to be quite understanding of a position apparently new to most of them.[190] In 1946 William Green, President of the American Federation, wrote to the secretary of the committee as follows:

> I received and read your letter dated March 7 with deep interest. We have endeavored to deal with the problems which have been presented from time to time by the members of the Mennonite and Brethren in Christ Churches who secure employment in plants where the workers have negotiated closed shop agreements. In each instance I have advised our workers to respect conscientious objection on the part of the members of these religious organizations to taking union obligations and to subscribing to the closed shop principle. We do that in the interest of harmony and cooperation.[191]

Some years later representatives of the Mennonite and Brethren in Christ Industrial Relations Committees negotiated an agreement with the United Automobile Workers, a powerful affiliate of the Congress of Industrial Organizations. This demonstrated the penetration of Mennonite—Brethren in Christ influence into the second of the two great labor organizations of the United States.[192]

The responsibility for carrying a nonresistant witness into the industrial world passed in 1953 to a new Committee on Social and Economic Relations.[193] Over a period of six years, this committee assisted a few individuals who faced union membership problems.[194] Thereafter the labor union issue gradually faded into oblivion; from 1960 to 1962 the committee received no appeals for assistance so it did not report to General Conference.[195]

In succeeding years, although it occasionally reminded Conference of its original function, the attention of the committee shifted to other social and economic concerns such as affluence, race relations, poverty, and population pressures. Labor union membership apparently ceased to be significant ethical concern among the rank and file of the Brethren in Christ membership.[196]

Effects of the Great Wars

From their agonizing confrontation with government in wartime, the Brethren, together with the other Historic Peace Churches, produced the most massive organized nonresistant testimony in modern times. ASW and CPS undoubtedly had serious faults and limitations, but they witnessed to the fact that both Canada and the United States had minorities of otherwise loyal citizens who could not in good conscience reconcile their destruction of fellow human beings in war with their understanding of obedience to the teachings and example of Christ.

Another effect of the great wars was the developing of working Brethren relationships with other Historic Peace Churches. It was the pooling of conviction, experience, talent, and resources from these various constituencies which gave weight to their common peace concerns. Especially significant for the Brethren in Christ was their affiliation with the Mennonite Central Committee. Since the beginning of this affiliation early in World War II, it has been a dynamic influence in the life and ministry of the brotherhood.

The struggle to give their peace testimony in the midst of total war also made the Brethren more aware of the political realities of the societies of which they were a part. Prior to 1914 they thought of their relations to government largely in non-political terms, as did Samuel Zook when he visited a government school for Indian children in Arizona and found his heart moved "with gratefulness to God for the principles of a Christian Government to reach out after those heathen children."[197] Also, when the pre-war Brethren made their rare comments about political leaders, they either criticized or applauded the ethical views or conduct of public officials. On the one hand, for example, they criticized President Theodore Roosevelt when he reviewed troops on the Lord's Day and, on the other hand, commended him for speaking out against lax divorce laws.[198] Again, when *Visitor* Editor Detwiler commented on the candidates in the Presidential campaign of 1904, he perceived them primarily in the light of their positions on the prohibition question.[199]

This tendency to think of government in non-political terms is understandable in the light of the historic Brethren detachment from politics and government. Over the years they had spent much time trying to establish boundaries between political and non-political issues and conduct, on the assumption that the former category was a part of the "world." They might support prohibition at the polls because this was a "moral" rather than a "political" question, and they might elect or serve as a school director because that office was "non-political." When, however, a Saskatchewan member stood for election to Parliament and won a seat, Canada Joint Council took disciplinary action and also referred the matter to General Conference. The result was a Conference ruling that any member who accepted or continued in a seat in Parliament or any other legislative assembly suspended himself from full fellowship and communion privileges until he retired from such position and publicly confessed the impropriety of his action.[200]

The latter incident occurred between the two world wars, indicating that World War I had not shaken the Brethren determination to stand aloof from political participation. But conscription in the course of two wars did force them to deal with government concretely rather than abstractly. They had to meet and defend their nonresistant position with high government officials, and they explored possibilities to influence legislation through contacts with politicians and legislative committees.

Their wartime experiences, furthermore, forced the Brethren to decide what they could conscientiously do for government when many fellow-citizens were giving largely of their energies, time, and even life and limb for national security. The days when the brotherhood could view government abstractly from afar ended in the holocaust of total war.

Finally, the stresses of total war revealed that loyalty to the Brethren doctrine of nonresistance could not be taken for granted. The large number of draftees, especially in the United States, who entered military service during and after the second war, and the division of leadership on the issue of noncombatant service, demonstrated widespread uncertainty about the meaning and validity of the peace testimony as the brotherhood passed the mid-century.

NOTES:

[1][George Detwiler], *Visitor*, XXVIII (October 5, 1914), 4.

[2][George Detwiler], "Conference Notes," *Visitor*, XXXI (June 4, 1917), 4.

[3]*General Conference Minutes*, 1917, Article 25, pp. 66-67.

[4]*Ibid.*, Article 60, p. 114.

[5]*Ibid.*, Article 25, p. 67.

[6]See later in this chapter the discussion of this and succeeding contacts.

[7][George Detwiler], "Conference Notes," *Visitor*, XXXI (June 4, 1917), 4.

[8]*Ibid.*; C. N. Hostetter, "Conscription Information," *Visitor*, XXXI (September 10, 1917), 6-7.

⁹C. N. Hostetter, "Conscription Information," *Visitor*, XXXI (September 10, 1917), 6-7.

¹⁰*Canadian Joint Council Minutes*, September 12, 1912, p. 30.

¹¹*Ibid.*, September 11, 1913, pp. 31-32.

¹²*Black Creek District Council Minutes*, February 4, 1916, Article 9.

¹³*Ibid.*, January 20, 1917, Article 7.

¹⁴*Canadian Joint Council Minutes*, September 13, 1917, p. 41.

¹⁵*Petition of the "Tunker" Church to the Exemption Boards*, (September 1917), quoted by Sider, "Brethren in Canada," p. 173.

¹⁶The relevant parts of this act are in Walter G. Kellogg, *The Conscientious Objector* (New York: Boni and Liveright, 1919), p. 11.

¹⁷See this portion of the act quoted by L. J. Burkholder, *A Brief History of the Mennonites in Ontario* (Toronto: Livingstone Press, 1935), p. 260.

¹⁸E. J. Swalm, comp., *Nonresistance*, p. 27.

¹⁹*Ibid.*, pp. 28-29.

²⁰*Ibid.*, pp. 28-31.

²¹*Ibid.*, pp. 33-48.

²²*Ibid.*, pp. 28-29, 38.

²³Burkholder, *Mennonites in Ontario*, p. 269.

²⁴Earl M. Sider to C. O. Wittlinger, February 6, 1976; Ray D. Bert "Brethren in Christ 'Peacemakers' and World War I" (unpublished paper in Church Archives), pp. 10-12.

²⁵Earl M. Sider to C. O. Wittlinger, February 6, 1976; Bert "Brethren 'Peacemakers,'" pp. 11-12.

²⁶Charles H. Wright to C. O. Wittlinger, January 22, 1976; Bert, "Brethren 'Peacemakers,'" pp. 12-14.

²⁷Frank Carver to C. O. Wittlinger, July 29, 1974.

²⁸The relevant parts of this act are printed in Kellogg, *Conscientious Objector*, p. 17.

²⁹*Ibid.*, pp. 17-21.

³⁰*Ibid.*, pp. 31-32, 75.

³¹C. N. Hostetter, "Conscription Information," *Visitor*, XXXI (September 10, 1917), 7.

³²Graybill Wolgemuth to C. O. Wittlinger, January 3, 1974.

³³Harry L. Brubaker to C. O. Wittlinger, February 23, 1974; Bert, "Brethren 'Peacemakers,'" pp. 2, 9-10, 15-16.

³⁴Anna Verle Miller interview, March 10, 1978.

³⁵*Ibid.*, pp. 2, 14-15; C. B. Eavey, "A Letter from France," *Visitor*, XXXIII (January 12, 1920), 14-15.

³⁶Bert, "Brethren 'Peacemakers,'" pp. 17-18.

³⁷*Ibid.*, pp. 16-17.

³⁸Kansas Joint Council Minutes, April 4 and 5, 1917, Article 17.

³⁹M. M. Book to C. O. Wittlinger, July 13, 1973; Christ Frey to C. O. Wittlinger, August 27, 1973.

⁴⁰Charles E. Engle to C. O. Wittlinger, August 2, 1974; Clarence Byer to Isaiah B. Harley, January 24, 1926, copy in C. O. Wittlinger files.

⁴¹Edgar Heise to C. O. Wittlinger, August, 1974.

⁴²Paul E. Engle to C. O. Wittlinger, January 5, 1974; Paul E. Engle, draft statistics and notes on World War I, C. O. Wittlinger files.

⁴³Paul E. Engle to C. O. Wittlinger, August 1, 1974.

[44]Data are unavailable for draftees from Indiana, Illinois, Iowa, and Oklahoma.

[45]See Bert, "Brethren 'Peacemakers,'" and previous citations documenting the experiences of Brethren draftees.

[46]*Wainfleet Council Minutes,* July 30, 1918, Article 5; *ibid.*, October 29, 1918 (meeting of officials only); *ibid.*, November 5, 1918, Article 1.

[47]*Canadian Joint Council Minutes,* September 12, 1918, p. 43.

[48]*General Conference Minutes,* 1918, pp. 62-63.

[49]E. H. Hess, "War and Our Attitude," *Visitor,* XXXI (June 18, 1917), 6.

[50]*Ibid.*

[51]*Ibid.*

[52]"Ninth Annual Bible Conference at Grantham, Pa.," *Visitor,* XXXII (January 14, 1918), 6.

[53]M. B. Fuller, "Corn Report," *Visitor,* XIII (July 1, 1900), 255.

[54][George Detwiler], *Visitor,* XIII (July 15, 1900), 274-75.

[55][George Detwiler], "War's Doing," *Visitor,* XXIX (May 3, 1915), 2-3.

[56]Markham District Council Minutes, January 28, 1916, Article 9.

[57]Broadside, Asa W. Climenhaga Papers.

[58]*General Conference Minutes,* 1919, Article 9, pp. 13, 14.

[59]Pamphlet, Church Archives, p. 2.

[60]*General Conference Minutes,* 1919, Article 9, pp. 13, 14.

[61]*Canadian Joint Council Minutes,* September 11, 1919, p. 47.

[62]*General Conference Minutes,* 1919, Article 12, p. 20; *ibid.*, 1931, Article 32, pp. 49, 50.

[63]*Ibid.*, 1938, Article 50, p. 87.

[64]*Ibid.*, 1939, Article 10, pp. 16-21, For the Canadian Memorial and accompanying documents, see *ibid.*, 1940, pp. 139-44.

[65]*Ibid.*, 1939, Article 10, p. 21.

[66]*Ibid.*, 1940, Article 17, pp. 29-30.

[67]*Canadian Joint Council Minutes,* September 12, 1935, p. 128.

[68]*Ibid.*, September 13-14, 1939, pp. 193, 194.

[69]*Ibid.*, September 11-12, 1940, pp. 221-23.

[70]*Ibid.*, pp. 220, 223-24; E. J. Swalm, in Wendell E. Harmon, ed. *They Also Serve (n.p., n.d.), p. 44.*

[71]*Canadian Joint Council Minutes,* September 11-12, 1940, pp. 223-24.

[72]*General Conference Minutes,* 1941, Article 14, pp. 17, 18; Henry G. Brubaker, "Peace Convention," *Visitor,* LIII (October 21, 1940), 338; C. N. Hostetter, Jr., in Swalm, *Nonresistance,* pp. 61-62.

[73]Hereafter referred to as "MCC." It included membership from the various Mennonite branches and eventually the Brethren in Christ.

[74]*Mennonite Encyclopedia,* III, 606. Civilian Public Service is discussed later in this chapter.

[75]*General Conference Minutes,* 1940, Article 17, p. 30.

[76]C. N. Hostetter, Jr., in Swalm, *Nonresistance,* pp. 61-62.

[77]*General Conference Minutes,* 1942, Article 12, pp. 20-21.

[78]*Ibid.*, 1941, Articles 14, 16, pp. 18, 21.

[79]E. J. Swalm to C. O. Wittlinger, July 20, 1974.

[80]*Ibid.*

[81]*General Conference Minutes,* 1942, Article 12, 23-24; Edward Gilmore, in Swalm, *Nonresistance,* pp. 76-78. Alternate Service Work is frequently referred to hereafter as "ASW."

[82]*General Conference Minutes,* 1942, Article 12, p. 23.

[83]Edward Gilmore, in Swalm, *Nonresistance,* pp. 78-79.

[84]*Ibid.,* p. 79.

[85]*General Conference Minutes,* 1943, Article 12, p. 18.

[86]*Ibid.,* 1942, Article 12, p. 24.

[87]*Ibid.,* 1943, Article 12, pp. 18-19.

[88]*Ibid.,* 1944, Article 12, pp. 19-20.

[89]*Ibid.,* 1945, Article 12, p. 33.

[90]J. B. Martin, in Swalm, *Nonresistance,* p. 70.

[91]Jesse W. Hoover, in Harmon, *They Also Serve,* p. 5.

[92]*Ibid.,* p. 6.

[93]*Ibid.*

[94]*Ibid.,* pp. 49, 51.

[95]*Ibid.,* p. 51.

[96]*Ibid.;* Henry G. Brubaker, "Non-Resistance is Not Too Expensive," *Visitor,* LIV (January 27, 1941), 18.

[97]Jesse W. Hoover, in Harmon, *They Also Serve,* p. 51; Henry G. Brubaker, "Non-Resistance is Not Too Expensive," *Visitor,* LIV (January 27, 1941), 18.

[98]E. J. Swalm To C. O. Wittlinger, July 20, 1974.

[99]Henry G. Brubaker, "Non-Resistance is Not Too Expensive," *Visitor,* LIV (January 27, 1941), 18.

[100]"Fifth Year of C. P. S. Begins," *Visitor,* LVIII (May 21, 1945), 162; Melvin Gingerich, *Service for Peace: A History of Mennonite Civilian Public Service* (Akron, Pa.: Mennonite Central Committee, 1949), p. 66. Civilian Public Service is generally referred to hereafter as "CPS."

[101]Henry G. Brubaker, "Civilian Public Service Convention," *Visitor,* LIV (September 22, 1941), 290.

[102]Eber B. Dourte, in Swalm, *Nonresistance,* pp. 109-10.

[103]*Ibid.*

[104]The Brethren in Christ eventually planned for and strove to facilitate the social and financial rehabilitation of CPS men into civilian life and provided modest educational assistance to those who wished to continue or begin educational programs. See the reports and recommendations of the Relief and Service Committee and its successor, the Peace, Relief, and Service Committee, in *General Conference Minutes,* 1944-1949.

[105]*Ibid.,* 1942, Article 12, p. 18.

[106]*Ibid.,* p. 19.

[107]Dourte, in Swalm, *Nonresistance,* p. 112.

[108]*General Conference Minutes,* 1943, Article 12, p. 17.

[109]Swalm, *Nonresistance,* pp. 85-155; Harmon, *They Also Serve,* pp. 2-42.

[110]*General Conference Minutes,* 1943, Article 12, p. 17.

[111]*Ibid.,* 1945, Article 12, p. 33; *ibid.,* 1944, Article 14, p. 22.

[112]C. N. Hostetter, Jr., in Harmon, *They Also Serve,* p. 12.

[113]*General Conference Minutes,* 1943, Article 12, p. 17.

[114]Wendell Harmon, in Harmon, *They Also Serve,* p. 8.

[115]*Ibid.,* p. 11.

[116]Dourte, in Swalm, *Nonresistance,* pp. 112-13.

[117]Quoted in "First Lady Visits Marlboro, N. J. Hospital," *Visitor,* LVI (February 15, 1943), 50.

[118]Private correspondence of E. J. Swalm, December 9, 1943, quoted by Sider, "Brethren in Canada," pp. 190-91.

[119]*General Conference Minutes,* 1947, "Church and Sunday School Statistical . . . Report, 1947"; lists of ASW and CPS men in Harmon, *They Also Serve,* pp. 47, 56-60. Ernest Swalm estimates that at least eighty-five percent of Brethren draftees in Canada entered ASW. E. J. Swalm to C. O. Wittlinger, July 20, 1974.

[120]E. J. Swalm to C. O. Wittlinger, May 28, 1974. Swalm, a leading member of the Relief and Service Committee, traveled widely throughout the brotherhood, which he probably knew and understood at that time as well or better than any man of his generation.

[121]*Ibid.;* Ira Eyster interview, June 30, 1974. Eyster went into noncombatant service from Oklahoma.

[122]Paul E. Engle to C. O. Wittlinger, January 5, 1974.

[123]*General Conference Minutes,* 1942, Article 12, p. 22.

[124]*Ibid.,* Article 13, p. 26.

[125]*Kansas State Council Minutes,* April 8, 1943, Article 6, pp. 10-11.

[126]*Pacific Coast Branch Council Minutes,* 1943, Article 11, pp. 29-31.

[127]Alvin Burkholder interview, February 2, 1974.

[128]*General Conference Minutes,* 1943, Article 51, p. 85.

[129]*Ibid.,* pp. 84-85.

[130]*Ibid.,* p. 86.

[131]The present writer recalls this occasion as one of the tensest moments in his memories of several decades of attendance at General Conference.

[132]*General Conference Minutes,* 1943, Article 52, p. 87.

[133]*Ibid.*

[134]*Ibid.,* 1948, Article 23, pp. 56-57.

[135]*Ibid.,* p. 57.

[136]See Chapter XVII for an account of the Indoctrination Movement.

[137]In Canada conscription ended in 1946, but it continued in the United States, except for a brief period after expiration of the Burke-Wadsworth Selective Service Act on March 31, 1947, until establishment of the all-volunteer army in 1973.

[138]*General Conference Minutes,* 1958, Article 16, pp. 41-42.

[139]In 1947 the Peace, Relief, and Service Committee became the successor to the Relief and Service Committee.

[140]*General Conference Minutes,* 1958, Article 16, pp. 42-43.

[141]Harold S. Martin, "Positive Peace," *Visitor,* LV (February 16, 1942), 72.

[142]O. B. Ulery, "War Refugee Relief," *Visitor,* LIII (July 29, 1940), 250.

[143]*General Conference Minutes,* 1940, Article 17, p. 30.

[144]*Ibid.,* 1945, Article 12, pp. 33-34.

[145]*Ibid.,* p. 36.

[146]"Work Performed by CPS Men," *Visitor,* LVIII (May 21, 1945), 162.

[147]Kenneth B. Hoover interview, August 23, 1976. Voluntary Service will frequently be referred to as "VS."

[148]*General Conference Minutes,* 1941, Article 14, p. 18.

[149]*Ibid.;* Jesse W. Hoover interview, December 1, 1974.

[150]J. W. Hoover, "Excerpts from Letters," *Visitor,* LIV (June 2, 1941), 175.

[151]"Brother Jesse Hoover on Speaking Tour," *Visitor,* LV (January 19, 1942), 38.

[152]"Workers Arrive in France," *Visitor,* LVIII (October 8, 1945), 322.

[153]Elsie C. Bechtel, "Why We Should Support Relief Service," *Visitor,* LVIII (July 19, 1945), 229.

[154]*General Conference Minutes,* 1946, Article 18, p. 42.

[155]*Ibid.,* 1947, Article 16, pp. 43-44.

[156]*Ibid.,* 1948, Article 25, p. 67.

[157]Jesse W. Hoover interview, December 1, 1974.

[158]*General Conference Minutes,* 1949, Article 18, p. 44.

[159]"Women's Unit at Howard, Rhode Island," *Visitor,* LVII (July 3, 1944), 210.

[160]*General Conference Minutes,* 1949, Article 18, p. 48.

[161]*Ibid.,* 1947, Article 16, p. 41.

[162]Gingerich, *Service for Peace,* p. 263.

[163]*Ibid.*

[164]*General Conference Minutes,* 1949, Article 18, pp. 44-45.

[165]Personal statement by Harold and Ruth Davis, March 1976. C. O. Wittlinger files.

[166]*General Conference Minutes,* 1949, Article 28, p. 87.

[167]*Ibid.,* 1954, Article 37, p. 99.

[168]"Our Attitude as Nonresistant Christians in the Present Situation," *Visitor,* LV (February 2, 1942), 49.

[169]"The Civilian Bond Purchase Plan," *Visitor,* LV (July 20, 1942), 234.

[170]Sider, "Brethren in Canada," pp. 198-99.

[171]*General Conference Minutes,* 1941, Article 16, p. 21.

[172]Henry G. Brubaker, "Peace Committee Changes Name," *Visitor,* LIV (July 23, 1941), 226. MCC either adopted or originated this plan. See "M. C. C. Certificates and Stamps and Civilian Government Bonds," *Visitor,* LV (March 30, 1942), 112-13.

[173]*General Conference Minutes,* 1942, Article 12, pp. 21-22.

[174]"The Civilian Bond Purchase Plan," *Visitor,* LV (July 20, 1942), 234. There are no known statistics on Brethren purchases of United States bonds.

[175]*General Conference Minutes,* 1942, Article 12, p. 22.

[176]*Ibid.,* Article 13, p. 26.

[177]*Ibid.,* 1943, Article 51, pp. 84-86.

[178]*Ibid.,* p. 87.

[179]*Pennsylvania State Council Minutes,* April 5 and 6, 1933, Article 12, pp. 21-22.

[180]*General Conference Minutes,* 1938, Article 25, pp. 37-38.

[181]"The Christian's Attitude Toward Organized Labor (Considered from the Nonresistant Viewpoint)," *Visitor,* LI (October 24, 1938), 339-40.

[182]*General Conference Minutes,* 1939, Article 12, pp. 22-23.

[183]*Ibid.*

[184]*Ibid.,* 1940, Article 13, pp. 24-25.

[185]*Ibid.*

[186]*Ibid.*, 1941, Article 18, pp. 25-26.

[187]*Ibid.*

[188]*Ibid.*, pp. 27-28.

[189]*Ibid.*, 1942, Articles 5 and 15, pp. 12, 33. Several years later Conference invited the United Zion and United Christian Churches to name associate members of this committee.

[190]See the annual reports of the committee after 1942.

[191]Letter from William Green to C. W. Boyer, quoted in *General Conference Minutes,* 1946, Article 16, p. 37.

[192]*General Conference Minutes,* 1952, Article 14, p. 45.

[193]*Ibid.*, 1953, Article 24, p. 42.

[194]Annual reports of the Committee, 1954-1959.

[195]*General Conference Minutes,* 1963, Article 17, p. 48.

[196]Annual reports of the Committee, 1964-1969; C. W. Boyer to C. O. Wittlinger, August, 15, 1976.

[197]"A Western Mission Tour," *Visitor,* VI (March 1, 1893), 75.

[198][George Detwiler], *Visitor,* XVI (October 15, 1902), 394-95; *General Conference Minutes,* 1905, Article 16, pp. 12-13.

[199][George Detwiler], *Visitor,* XVIII (August 1, 1904), 2.

[200]*Canadian Joint Council Minutes,* September 13, 1923, p. 55; *ibid.*, September 11, 1924, p. 58; *General Conference Minutes,* 1924, Article 24, p. 37.

XVII

The Christian
Education Movement

During the first half of the twentieth century, the Brethren in Christ continued to develop Sunday school work and launched various other Christian education enterprises. As opposition to the Sunday school waned, questions arose about new activities such as young people's societies and young people's conferences. Gradually the brotherhood adjusted to previously unfamiliar forms of Christian education, somewhat as *Visitor* Editor Davidson did to a children's meeting in 1890 when he observed that it was "something new among the brethren . . . yet it seemed to be a fitting recognition of the duty of the church in that direction."[1]

Advance of the Sunday School

In 1910 the Sunday School Board reported thirty-one Sunday schools with an average attendance of eighty-five.[2] These data suggest that Sunday school had not yet found a place in a majority of Brethren congregations. Its supporters looked forward hopefully to the day when it would do so, and the Sunday school meeting at General Conference of 1921 adopted the motto:

For CHRIST and the CHURCH
"OUR MOTTO"
A Sunday School in EVERY Church
On EVERY Sunday
For Everybody, and Everybody in the
Sunday School.

The meeting closed with the observation that ". . . interest is growing in this phase of gospel dissemination."[3]

Sunday school work gradually advanced until all congregations, large and small, took its importance for granted.[4] One factor facilitating this advance was the regionalization of Sunday school activity. Following the precedent of state, provincial, and joint council mission boards, regional Sunday school boards were formed. Kansas had such a board in the early 1890s.[5] Other regions of the brotherhood eventually followed the Kansas example.[6] In 1941 General Conference assumed oversight of regional Sunday school work by integrating the duties of state and joint council boards with those of the General Sunday School Board.[7]

While the regionalization of Sunday school work proceeded, the General Sunday School Board continued to play a significant role in the Sunday school movement.[8] During its first decade the board emphasized the importance of the Sunday school in building church membership and stimulating missionary spirit and giving; it also encouraged teachers' meetings, promoted conferences, and published statistics.[9]

Soon the board saw the need for some instrument by which schools could evaluate and improve their work. In 1921 Conference approved the first Sunday School Standard with twelve goals for Sunday school improvement.[10] Among them were missionary and temperance instruction, teacher training, evangelism, and good attendance records.[11]

By the late 1930s this Sunday school standard had become inadequate because of uncertainty and lack of uniformity in the interpretation of its requirements. To clarify this confusion the General Sunday School Board prepared a major revision of the document.[12]

The revised standard strongly emphasized the denomination. Superintendents and teachers were to be loyal in word and practice to the doctrines of the church. Other guidelines stressed requirements and benefits of church membership and emphasized teaching and giving in relation to the educational, publishing, benevolent, and missions activities of the brotherhood. In its strong denominationalism, the standard of 1938 went far beyond its predecessor of 1921.[13]

Teacher training was another major goal in the 1938 standard. Local Sunday school leaders were asked:

> Has a Teacher Training Class been conducted in your school during the year?
> Or have at least 25% of your regular teachers been enrolled in a T. T.

correspondence course from one of our Church Schools?

Or do 50% of your regular teachers already hold a T. T. certificate or diploma?

Serious emphasis upon teacher training had begun previously with preparation of the 1915 Teacher's Training Course, which devoted about two-thirds of its contents to Bible study and the remaining one-third to the Sunday school, the pupil, and the teacher.[14] Messiah Bible School subsequently experimented with the course in its winter term and later published it for campus use and for the benefit of the church generally.[15]

For more than a decade this course met an important need in the Sunday school movement. Approximately 300 students eventually graduated from it with appropriate certificates.[16] In addition, the Extension Department of Messiah Bible School gradually introduced other teacher training courses such as Life of Christ, Religions of the World, and Christian Doctrine.[17]

The teacher-training movement advanced on a new path in the 1930s when the educational institutions of the brotherhood affiliated with the Evangelical Teacher Training Association of Chicago. Clarence H. Benson founded this agency with the express purpose of upgrading the quality of Sunday school training. By the late 1930s courses of the ETTA were available through the church schools, and General Conference endorsed this training program.[18]

In the 1940s the enlarged Sunday school movement required guidelines to define the relation of the schools to the local church organization. Pennsylvania State Council prepared "Rules to Regulate the Church Sunday Schools," but while the General Sunday School Board worked on the same project, the council deferred action for two years.[19] The combined efforts of these two agencies produced a comprehensive manual entitled *Our Sunday School at Work: Handbook of Organization and Administration.*[20]

Concerns about Sunday school literature paralleled these interests in teacher training and better organization and administration. Early hopes for a denominational literature proved to be unrealistic for a small denomination, so Conference approved a Brethren imprint on Mennonite materials.[21]

At first some of the Sunday schools had difficulty in understanding the imprint arrangement.[22] The Publication Board accordingly sought to extend the use of the approved literature by an appeal asserting that where used it was meeting with general satisfaction.[23]

The hesitation to accept the approved literature was due partly to misunderstanding, but it may also have reflected the preferences of some schools for other materials. Of fifty-four schools reporting statistics in 1913, thirty-eight used only the imprinted materials. David C. Cook of Chicago headed the list of other sources of supplies.[24]

In spite of General Conference approval of Mennonite literature, the Brethren were never entirely satisfied with imprinted Sunday school materials. In 1916 Indiana and Michigan Joint Councils both expressed dissatisfaction with the imprinted take-home papers.[25] Five years later the Publication Board recommended that the Brethren undertake production of their own literature.[26]

Soon after Conference authorized this project *Visitor* Editor Vernon Stump began to prepare expository lesson notes as a beginning of an original Brethren Sunday school literature. It quickly became apparent, however, that the hope of preparing lesson quarterlies was unrealistic.[27] Noting the limited number needed and the efforts which would be required to produce them, the Publication Board accordingly deferred action for the time being, and this deferment proved to be permanent.[28]

Although rejecting the publication of quarterlies, the Publication Board did create take-home papers.[29] *Sunbeams* served the needs of small children and *The Youth's Visitor* those of older children.[30] Acquisition of a Brethren press in 1920 and the hope that sales of these largely non-sectarian papers would make them self-sustaining explain the take-home paper venture.[31] The board eventually launched a third paper, *The Sunday School Herald,* designed for young people and adults.[32]

In 1958, due to increased production costs and a limited market, all three papers terminated as Brethren in Christ publications.[33] Take-home papers distributed thereafter under the auspices of the Publication Board originated outside of the brotherhood.

As early as 1912 the Brethren were aware of the graded lesson movement, but they had reservations about it. These were primarily theological rather than pedagogical. They also recognized the limitations of using graded lesson materials in which they had no pre-publication editorial voice.[34]

Graded lessons, however, were too pedagogically sound to be ignored entirely. In 1940 Pennsylvania State Council noted the need for lesson material better adapted to the younger children. The council also petitioned the General Sunday School Board to investigate the advisability of adopting a graded system of instruction for the brotherhood.[35] Later, Henry G. Brubaker, a member of the board, ably reviewed in the *Visitor* the history and pedagogical implications of the graded lesson movement.[36]

In response to interest in graded lessons, the Sunday School Board recommended the All Bible Graded Series edited by Clarence Benson and published by Scripture Press. The board noted that these materials were Bible centered and "reasonably safe in so-called fundamental doctrines." It also cautioned the Sunday schools against hastily dropping the Uniform Sunday School Lessons, in view of a pending attempt to grade them for a younger age group.[37]

In spite of their pedagogical soundness, graded lessons had practical limitations for small Sunday schools with a limited number of classes. With some exceptions, Brethren schools of that period had average attendances of fewer than one hundred pupils, and the uniform lessons appeared to offer the greatest advantages for most of them.[38] Graded lessons continued, however, to be a live issue with some Sunday schools. This situation eventually caused the General Sunday School Board to endorse another graded series, Gospel Light, in addition to the All Bible Graded Series.[39]

By the mid-century the long-standing arrangement for the use of imprinted Mennonite Uniform Lesson quarterlies was causing considerable dissatisfaction. The reasons for this were "the lack of definite spiritual emphasis and applications which our people appreciate," that is, the new birth and second-work holiness, as well as the strong Mennonite emphasis in the materials.[40] An exhaustive study of other literature led to a unanimous joint decision by the Publication and Sunday School Boards to discontinue the Mennonite quarterlies and substitute those of the Christian and Missionary Alliance.[41]

The latter were attractive because of their generally acceptable doctrinal emphases on holiness, pre-millennialism, simplicity in dress, immersion baptism, and neutrality on the war question. Findings of the study also stressed the pedagogical quality of the materials and noted that they were largely free from the distinctive denominational emphasis which made the Mennonite literature objectionable.[42] General Conference agreed with the proposed change of literature, which resulted in a new imprint series known as "Word of Light."[43]

These materials continued in use until 1970. At that time, a new preference having developed for David C. Cook materials, the brotherhood discontinued use of the Christian and Missionary Alliance literature in favor of a Word of Light imprint on the Cook literature.[44]

The complicated problem of a satisfactory curriculum literature was only one of many facets of the Sunday school movement as it became a principal means for community outreach and evangelism. In 1937 General Conference recognized the responsibility of the Sunday school "to reach the unreached in its community" and charged it to "make definite and regular efforts to this end."[45] Concern for community outreach became especially pronounced during the 1940s.[46] The first article in *Forward,* a promotional periodical launched by the General Sunday School Board in 1948, was entitled "Evangelism in the Sunday School."[47]

One of the major techniques for outreach was an annual "Forward Enlargement Campaign." This began in 1949 as the "Forward Sunday School Contest" stressing more regular attendance by enrolled scholars, the bringing of visitors, and special efforts to enroll new members. Schools were divided into three categories, based upon average attendance in 1948, to compete for prizes and awards.[48] The first contest produced a total attendance gain of 763 for the year.[49] There was also evidence that it had been a direct influence in adding a number of members to the church.[50]

The resulting Sunday school enthusiasm encouraged another contest in 1950. When these results were tabulated, some Sunday schools had accomplished the seemingly impossible. At Dayton, Ohio, average attendance for the six Sundays of the competition jumped from 186 to 267. A Dayton contest reporter observed: "We feel that the contest as a whole was a tremendous success . . . and that the dear Lord rewarded our efforts much greater than we expected."[51]

A rural Canadian school almost doubled its attendance during the first Sunday of the contest, to the amazement of those previously skeptical about increasing attendance in their rural community.[52] The bishop of the district noted that the contest had "done something to almost every member in the church that needed to be done. It fired them with new enthusiasm, encouraged them to deeper consecration and widened their horizons."[53] Many other Sunday schools reported benefits from the contest.[54]

Following these experiments which produced the annual Forward Enlargement Campaign, the General Sunday School Board also explored possibilities for a national Sunday school convention. The first such convention was held at Roxbury Holiness Camp Grounds in July 1951.[55]

In a sense this convention was a national counterpart of previous regional Sunday school conventions conducted by the Brethren, but there was a significant difference. For some years the General Sunday School Board had been following the meetings and activities of the National Sunday School Association, on whose advisory council Paul W. McBeth, a member of the board, served for a number of years.[56] His presence on the council had facilitated cooperation by the Brethren in Christ with the NSSA in projects such as National Sunday School Week.[57] It also gave him opportunity to meet nationally known Sunday school leaders, who began to appear on platforms of the brotherhood, such as that of the first National Sunday School Convention.[58] These leaders enlarged the Sunday school vision of the Brethren and exposed them to contemporary pedagogical developments in Sunday school work. The second National Sunday School Convention, which also featured non-Brethren speakers, had 702 registered delegates and hundreds of other attendants.[59]

Although the General Sunday School Board sponsored several other national conventions, this activity did not become an annual feature of the Sunday school movement. The conventions, however, achieved their goals which were the enlargement of vision, the stimulation of enthusiasm, and the attainment of greater efficiency in Sunday school work.[60]

Another development closely related to the Sunday school movement was the daily vacation Bible school. The first known schools of this type began in 1928. Albert Engle and his staff employed them in pioneer mission work in Kentucky.[61] In the same year Christian N. Hostetter, Jr. began a similar school at Refton, Pennsylvania.[62] Twenty-five years later it had a record enrollment of 225 and an average attendance of 201.[63]

In 1929 the Grantham District in Pennsylvania conducted a vacation Bible school which is illustrative of the early schools.

At the sound of the bell the children marched into the chapel singing "Onward Christian Soldiers." These first fifteen or twenty minutes were our worship period during which we sang, quoted our scripture passage . . . and had prayer.

After this there were classes at which time the teachers conducted the story hour, where the Bible lesson for the day was studied. Memory work and hymn study came in this period. Then there was recess and again classes convened for the hand work period. This consisted in preparing notebooks, making scrap books for the mission fields, preparing postals for use by missionaries, making rose bowls for the shutins [sic], . . . The period which followed this was another chapel session where announcements were made and closing exercises conducted. Dismissal was at 11:30.[64]

This two-week school closed with a public evening program featuring the work of the children.

Other Brethren churches were quick to organize vacation Bible schools, and the movement spread rapidly throughout the brotherhood. A 1948 survey revealed at least sixty-six schools with an enrollment of 7,911 and an average attendance of 6,275. This survey also reported that "scores of children accepted Christ in special decision services, also many consecrated themselves for Christian service."[65]

Together with the vacation Bible school movement, the Sunday school program advanced. At the mid-century all established Brethren congregations conducted Sunday schools, and some areas had extension schools.[66] In 1954, after ten consecutive years of increasing attendance, the total Sunday school enrollment throughout the brotherhood was 17,844 with an average attendance of 13,987.[67] This enrollment was more than twice the total number of church members.[68] The Sunday school zeal of the mid-century is expressed in an excerpt from a General Sunday School Board report:

> In our S. S. enrollment, which is more than twice our Church membership, and in our V.B.S. enrollment, is perhaps, our most fertile field for evangelism and church extension. Let us thank God as we view the accomplishments of the past; and with "Forward" as our rallying cry, let us "take courage" as we dedicate ourselves anew to the great unfinished work which still lies before us.[69]

In 1963 General Conference celebrated with appropriate activities and ceremonies one hundred years of Sunday school work, and the Board of Christian Education marked this centennial with a special issue of *Forward*.[70]

The Youth Movement

Although the Sunday school served all age groups, a supplemental program for young people began to emerge in the early twentieth century. In 1907 John Myers advocated young people's meetings, but he stressed

---

Opposite page: Chicago Mission Summer Bible School staff and students, 1961. Superintendent Carl Carlson, third from left in first standing row, with his wife, Avas, to his immediate right.

that "the old members" should be present to look on, give their testimonies, and show their appreciation of the work "just as much as we do on the farm."[71] Whether such meetings actually began that early is unknown, but the Upland congregation had a "young people's league" by 1910.[72]

Young people's meetings gradually appeared in other areas of the brotherhood. Manor-Pequea District in Pennsylvania had a youth program by 1918.[73] About a decade later Fairview, Ohio, conducted Sunday evening programs of Bible study for young people and others, and Markham District in Ontario experimented with young people's meetings on Sunday evenings as a preliminary to the worship service.[74] This Markham plan for scheduling such meetings as a preliminary part of the Sunday evening service later became the typical arrangement for young people's meetings.

This advance of youth activity aroused considerable adult opposition. Some of it may have reflected typical Brethren suspicion of innovation. Much of it, however, was probably due to the fear that young people were more susceptible than mature adults to "worldly" influences; these influences might enter the church through an activity under youth direction. In one Canadian congregation, for example, adults prevented the formation of a young people's society until the late 1940s and then permitted it only on condition that they would dominate it. In spite of opposition in some localities, there were at least seventy young people's groups by 1946.[75]

The local youth program developed an organizational pattern with a chairman and secretary, a program committee, and an adviser. These organizations were referred to as "societies," and their programs were essentially Bible studies with various individuals discussing aspects of a program subject.

Since persons of all ages participated, and young and old were not separated in seating, young people's societies were actually total congregations functioning somewhat more informally than in the latter part of the Sunday evening services. The societies, however, did provide new opportunities for young people to develop capacities to think and speak about biblical subjects and to act in leadership roles as officers and members of program committees.

As young people's societies multiplied, the problem of supplying appropriate program materials for them arose. Early planning committees had to depend upon materials in non-Brethren publications and upon the resourcefulness of local ministers and lay leaders.[76] In 1921, when *The Youth's Visitor* began publication, the Fairview Bible Study Committee of Dayton District, Ohio, provided a column of youth program materials previously developed for use in that district. This column continued for several years.[77]

By 1931 the number of young people's societies had increased significantly, and General Conference assumed responsibility for supplying them with authorized program materials; it appointed a Young People's Topic Committee to prepare a list of topics with "sufficient" program helps and instructed the committee to make these materials available to the brotherhood.[78]

The first program outlines, which began appearing in the *Evangelical Visitor* in 1932, stressed both doctrinal and practical instruction.[79] A sample of the topics for the first quarter of 1932 included: "The Word of God"; "Remarkable Conversions and Their Results"; "Sin"; and "Self Denial."

Following a poor response to a questionnaire sent to the congregations, the committee brought a pessimistic report to General Conference.[80] That body, however, approved continuance of the program outlines and admonished the church to adopt them in whole or in part. Those who found them unsatisfactory were urged to offer constructive criticisms.[81] From these humble beginnings the topics, later known as "Christian Life Bible Studies," gradually gained recognition and became a basic resource of the young people's movement.[82]

During the early years of the youth movement, another innovation, the young people's conference, appeared under the sponsorship of local areas of the brotherhood. The Kansas Brethren held the first such conference in 1926 at a camp near Manhattan, with an enrollment of eight-five.[83] Its theme was "Living with a Purpose," and the program stressed Bible study, missions, vocational guidance, and aspects of practical living, in addition to song services and recreation. The principal speakers included Asa W. Climenhaga, Alma B. Cassel, David F. Shirk, and Amos D. M. Dick.[84]

Although Kansas pioneered the young people's conference, the most ambitious venture of this kind began in 1933 under the sponsorship of the Grantham District in Pennsylvania. This Grantham Youth Conference received enthusiastic support from churches in Pennsylvania and neighboring states.[85] By 1934 it evolved into two separate conferences for younger and older age groups, with a total enrollment of more then 300.[86] Youth conferences continued at Grantham for several decades. Inspired by Kansas and Pennsylvania, other areas of the church, including Ontario, Michigan, Ohio, California, and Oklahoma, soon organized similar conferences.[87]

Beginning in Ohio in 1948, another conference movement, designed to serve the needs of young married people, began to spread across the brotherhood. The young married people's conference stressed the development of spiritual home life, wholesome marital adjustment, and child rearing. Soon after the mid-century, such conferences assembled annually in widely separated localities including Pennsylvania, the Midwest, and California. That they met a basic need is revealed by enrollments which, in some instances, included as many as 100 couples.[88]

In 1950 another Christian education ministry, Kenbrook Bible Camp, emerged from an idea nurtured by the Fairland Sunday School of Cleona, Pennsylvania. Here a group of interested persons formed a non-profit corporation and launched the camp in a beautiful natural setting of woodland and stream. Its program emphasizing Bible, music, and camp-lore extended over several weeks. The total age group served was from nine to sixteen, with each group of boy or girl campees remaining for one week. Those responsible for the camp sought to select instructors and counselors committed to the basic project goal which was "the salvation and Christian growth of our boys and girls."[89] The Kenbrook facilities have expanded over the years, and the camp continues to offer a dynamic program.

Although many youth activities received their primary impetus from local or regional agencies, General Conference continued to play an active role in the youth movement from time to time. Soon after creating the committee to provide program materials for young people's meetings, Conference took up the task of formulating a constitution for youth societies.

In 1934 the General Executive Board had stressed the need for a written constitution to define the relation of the local society to the church. As adopted by General Conference the following year, this constitution named the organization the "Brethren in Christ Young People's Society." Its president was to be of good Christian standing and in harmony with church doctrines. The district council exercised supervision through an adviser serving as an ex-efficio member of all committes. One article of the constitution specified that "This Society owes allegiance to the Church of which it is a part . . . ."[90] Another stated the objectives as follows: "to promote vital Christian living and consecrated service to God among its members; to become better acquainted with the inspired Word of God; and to train for more effective work in the Church."

The year after the constitution went into effect, General Conference ruled that one day of the tent program at its annual meeting should be devoted to the interests of young people.[91] This set a precedent followed for many years and helped young people to feel that they were a part of the life of Conference.[92]

In 1937 General Conference took another major step in the development of the youth program by creating a Board for Young People's Work. This board took over the functions of the former Young People's Topics Committee; it was also responsible to promote and encourage organized young people's work throughout the church and to function in an advisory capacity in relation to such work. Other duties were cooperation in arranging and holding young people's conferences, promoting youth work and youth programs at annual Conferences, and serving as a center "to which young people . . . [could] appeal concerning the various problems relative to life."[93]

The new board promptly initiated a project in which the young people of the brotherhood joined annually to raise funds for a special Christian enterprise. The first project set a goal of $400 to assist Charles and Mary Eshelman to attend Cornell University to acquire additional education needed for service on the Africa mission field.[94]

The second project was a budget to send the third foreign mission deputation to Africa and India.[95] This fund-raising campaign produced approximately $2,000 in depression times.[96] In recognition of such strong youth support, Conference named the secretary of the Board for Young People's Work, Henry N. Hostetter, to serve as one of the two members of the deputation.[97]

Of the many other youth projects, one is of special interest. This provided small monthly allowances to Brethren draftees serving in United States Public Service Camps during a few years of World War II.[98] In those particular years, the board sponsored separate projects for the Canadian young people's societies.[90]

Several important developments occurred in the 1950s. One was adoption of the name "Christ's Crusaders" for the young people's organization of the brotherhood.[100] Ernest Boyer, a youth leader, explained its significance.

. . . this name recognizes Christ as the essential leader of every phase of the program. In addition, the word "Crusaders" is included, making clear the aggressiveness that is essential if our youth groups are to make an impact for Christ. Webster defines "crusade" as an "enterprise undertaken with zeal and enthusiasm." Thus, prayerfully, the Commission on Youth recommended that our Brethren in Christ youth groups be known as "Christ's Crusaders;" with the Christian message as our "enterprise" we will aggressively proclaim His message with zeal and enthusiasm."[101]

Adoption of the new name implemented the concept of an overall Brethren in Christ youth organization which expressed itself principally although not entirely through local young people's societies. The name also personalized the youth program; it connoted people rather than organization and function, and its prompt adoption all across the brotherhood witnessed to its appeal.

Another change in the 1950s was the beginning of an annual Christ's Crusaders Day, a Sunday during which youth received special recognition in the life of the church, as well as opportunities to participate in activities planned especially for the occasion.[102] Reports from the first such day indicate that many churches participated with enthusiasm. One Crusader noted: "This was a day of actually being a Christ's Crusader. It was not a day of listening, but a day of application and participation."[103] Another reported: "Christ's Crusaders Day was when I finally got my mother, father, and two sisters to church. I also received many blessings."[104]

A Bible quiz program begun during 1956-57 was a significant addition to the youth program. Organized on a regional conference basis with playoffs at General Conference, it aroused much enthusiasm. During the first year of this quiz program, several church leaders expressed the opinion that sponsoring it was the best thing that the Commission on Youth ever did.[105]

Expanding youth activities created the need for the improved training of young people's leaders. This led to a Youth Leadership Institute preceding the second annual Sunday School Convention in 1952.[106] In 1954 the Commission on Youth also sponsored a national Christ's Crusaders Congress in Pennsylvania preceding General Conference, with Robert A. Cook, President of Youth for Christ International. as the keynote speaker.[107] Two other congresses followed in California and Pennsylvania.[108]

The decade of the 1950s also witnessed a reappraisal of the youth programs in the local churches. Two problems were emerging. In the first place, the traditional young people's society did not meet the needs of all of the youth of the congregation, especially the younger age group for whom the programming was too mature. Second, Sunday evening services planned partly by the young people and partly by the congregational leadership sometimes lacked the vitality and inspiration essential to an effective evangelistic contact with the communities in which Brethren in Christ churches were located.

Separation of the Christ's Crusaders meeting from the Sunday evening service was one obvious possibility for change. By the summer of 1953, an increasing number of congregations were scheduling young people's meetings separate from and prior to the Sunday evening service.[109] This trend continued until the traditional young people's society combining youth and adults, which had served the Brethren for two decades, practically disappeared.

A concern to provide more adequately for junior and intermediate youth led to a study of possibilities for instituting a Christian club program graded for different age levels. Such a program required youth manuals which could be adapted for both urban and rural churches.[110] When the preparation of such materials by a small denomination appeared to be impracticable, the search for an acceptable existing youth club program began.

One promising possibility was affiliation with the interdenominational, evangelical Christian clubs known as "Pioneer Girls" and "Christian Service Brigade." Negotiations with the Chicago headquarters of these groups revealed that their administrators would welcome the affiliation of the Brethren in Christ.[111]

Pioneer Girls posed no significant doctrinal or practical problems. In 1954 the Commission on Youth reported to General Conference that a careful study of the Pioneer Girls literature indicated that it was "oriented in the direction of a spiritual, evangelical ministry . . . and . . . with minor modifications . . . could be used with profit in the Christian education program of our local churches." On the basis of this report, Conference authorized the Commission on Youth to make the program available to the brotherhood.[112]

Unlike Pioneer Girls, the Christian Service Brigade posed perplexing problems. These were due to what appeared to be militaristic overtones in the program. Its history and some of its terminology, such as "brigade" and "battalion," had military connotations, and its uniform resembled that of a soldier. Although optional for affiliated groups, the uniform received considerable pictorial prominence in the literature.[113] In view of these circumstances, the commission hesitated, but General Conference authorized it to make this boys' program available if further negotiations could resolve the most outstanding difficulties.[114]

Administrators at Brigade headquarters subsequently gave assurances that a pending revision of their literature would make it more compatible with Brethren concerns, especially by reducing the pictorial prominence of the uniform. These administrators pointed out, however, that there was no feasible way to eliminate all verbal parallels with military terminology without drastic changes which would destroy the integrity of their organizational structure. The commission understood this; furthermore, there was New Testament precedent for the use of militaristic language such as "good soldier" and "armor of God" to describe aspects of the Christian life.

After careful consideration of the total situtation, the Commission on Youth decided in favor of affiliation with the Brigade program. Prior to recommending it to the brotherhood, however, the commission prepared guidelines to assist local churches to adapt the activities and literature wherever these might involve questions related to a nonresistant faith.[115]

By the summer of 1955 the program for boys from ages eight through eleven years of age was ready for implementation in those churches desiring boys' clubs.[116] Brigade units for older boys became available later.

The Indoctrination Movement

Another phase of the Christian education movement developed in the 1940s when the Brethren became engaged in an indoctrination program to reinforce the tenets of their historic faith. Indoctrination in itself was not new to them; they had always emphasized it. In 1929, for example, the California Church requested a children's book stressing "the teachings of our church doctrines," and Conference responded with *Questions and Answers in Bible Instruction.*[117] A few years later the Pennsylvania Brethren expressed the need for Sunday school literature in harmony with the church.[118] These examples of indoctrination concern could be multiplied; what made the indoctrination movement of the 1940s unique was its scope and intensity.

In the previous decade the Brethren had expended much energy revising doctrinal statements to counter social change, only to discover that new statements did not assure church loyalty.[119] Church membership statistics indicated problems. These statistics spurted upward in the late 1930s, leveled off between 1940 and 1942, and then declined steadily until 1946. Sunday school enrollment also dipped sharply from 1940 to 1945.[120]

In the 1940s World War II and social change brought heavy pressures to bear upon the youth of the brotherhood, some of whom were being lost to the group.[121] Brethren leaders, therefore, became deeply concerned about the indoctrination of their young people. A strong supporter of non-resistance wrote in 1944:

> . . . we are challenged with respect to indoctrination. We are always in danger with our sincere efforts to evangelize the heathen abroad, of neglecting to indoctrinate our boys and girls and thus they grow up not knowing what their fathers stood for. Since we have this fundamental doctrine [nonresistance] let us not be ashamed to indoctrinate our youths. The church of yesterday did it. That is why we stand on it today, let us do as much for the church of tomorrow.[122]

In 1943 the Relief and Service Committee noted the lack of an adequate literature to promote nonresistance and recommended that "every available means" be used for the production, promotion and diffusion of such literature.[123]

In that same year the General Sunday School Board, facing declining enrollments in the Sunday schools, lent its support to the growing indoctrination sentiment. It reported: "We are conscious of the need of implanting into the minds of our children a knowledge of the Word of God in general and in particular of Bible doctrine as interpreted and believed by the Church; . . ." To help meet this need, the board recommended wider use of the booklet *Questions and Answers in Bible Instruction.*[124]

Other boards added their voices to the indoctrination chorus until it seemed to resound from every side. The General Education Board noted "a greater need than ever before that our youth be indoctrinated in the teachings of the Bible" and urged the church schools to make more adequate provision for it.[125] The Publication Board sensed "the need for producing constantly more of our own materials for reading as well as for more formal study if we are to preserve our cherished doctrinal standards, and perpetuate them intact to future generations."[126] And the Board for Young People's Work felt that the interests of young people required "a more careful and systematic program of instruction in the doctrines and practices of the church, . . ."[127]

The columns of the *Evangelical Visitor* also reflected the rising tide of interest in indoctrination. In "Faithful Indoctrination," Editor Jesse Hoover noted that the Brethren had largely failed to give the outside world and even their own youth a coherent understanding of their faith. He observed: "We have only touched the fringes in our indoctrination."[128] Another writer who defended the principle of indoctrination and a program to implement it observed:

> If they [the young people] are to pledge constant loyalty to our church code of basic and abiding principles and doctrines, we owe them a philosophical interpretation which portrays and clarifies the worthwhileness of the basic nature of the doctrines and practices which are to be perpetuated. They want to be instructed in and imbued with the principles and doctrines of the Brethren in Christ, so that they might understand as well as believe.[129]

In 1943, in the midst of this widespread concern for indoctrination, California State Council called attention to "the duty of the Church to teach and indoctrinate especially its young people and its new converts in the doctrines and teachings of the Scriptures and in the practices which the Church has adopted for the carrying out of these principles." The council requested suitable indoctrination materials. Conference responded by appointing a Committee on Preparation of Doctrinal Literature.[130]

By the summer of 1944, this committee was ready with a detailed outline for a concise source book on doctrines and practices, suitable for mature young people and adults.[131] When Conference assembled in 1945, the book entitled *Manual for Christian Youth* was off the press.[132]

Excerpts from the introduction to the *Manual* make its purpose clear:

> Who are the Brethren in Christ? Where did they come from? What do they believe? Where are they located? Why does this Church exist apart from others?
>
> Have you ever been asked these or similar questions? . . . Could you, as a member of the Church, give a reason for our beliefs and practices? . . .
>
> . . . We propose to give you an intimate acquaintance with this body of believers.[133]

The book included four main sections describing doctrine, Christian experience, practices of the Christian life, and the ordinances respectively. It was, in fact, a concise compendium of what the Brethren understood themselves to be in the mid-1940s. A workbook to facilitate its use soon followed.[134]

While this committee was at work, General Conference created another agency, the Indoctrination Committee, to correlate the indoctrination efforts of the Education Board and the Board for Young People's Work.[135] The new committee concluded that materials created by the Committee on Preparation of Doctrinal Literature, together with pre-existing pieces of Brethren literature, were adequate for indoctrination purposes; it perceived its task to be the development of methods for the use of that literature.[136]

The Indoctrination Committee soon circulated a questionnaire to all ministers and bishops, seeking reasons for laxness in indoctrination and soliciting suggestings for solution of the problem. From the large number of replies, it drew several conclusions. Parents, General Conference, local churches, and the church schools shared responsibility for the inadequacy of doctrinal instruction. Lack of uniformity in ministerial teaching and a ministerial system with no prescribed unifying preparatory study also hindered an efficient teaching program. The committee, furthermore, found the brotherhood emphasizing experience and emotion without a strong supporting emphasis upon doctrinal instruction, discerned a lack of loyalty in teaching and practice by church leaders and parents, and noted that the "must" without the "why" sometimes characterized teaching and practice.[137]

In view of the problems revealed by this questionnaire, the committee presented corrective proposals. One was that ministerial candidates should complete a required study course prior to ordination or licensure. Other proposals called upon bishops and local leaders to consider how they might give greater emphasis to indoctrination, offered the assistance of the committee in developing indoctrination programs, and appealed to the church colleges to strengthen their doctrinal courses and to enroll as many Brethren students as possible in those courses. By approving these numerous proposals, General Conference declared its support for the most far-reaching indoctrination efforts in the history of the brotherhood.[138]

There is little evidence that the indoctrination movement of the 1940s significantly affected the Brethren movement. Although the church membership decline ended in 1946, no connection between this and indoctrination can be established. As late as 1948 the Indoctrination Committee expressed disappointment with the limited use of doctrinal literature; its statement implied that few local churches participated seriously in the indoctrination effort.[139] The rapid changes in Brethren life in the 1950s suggest that the previous indoctrination effort had only superficial results.[140]

The Board of Christian Education

One factor which caused the indoctrination movement to decline was its submergence in a mid-century reorganization of church boards and committees. From 1910 to 1940 such agencies had multiplied and, in some cases, developed overlapping functions. The indoctrination program focused attention on this problem; by 1946 four boards and two special committees were involved in the selection, creation, and use of doctrinal literature.[141] Conference accordingly created a Correlation Committee which recommended the merger of the Committee on Preparation of Doctrinal Literature and the Indoctrination Committee. At the same time, the committee questioned the need for the resulting agency because several church boards had assignments relating to Christian education.

The next year Pennsylvania State Council questioned overlapping functions of church boards and noted that some boards were so overworked that board members could no longer serve effectively. The work-load problem was critical for boards administering programs wherein "many consecrated workers . . . [were] giving full time and pouring out their lives in self-sacrificial service."[142] This was an obvious reference to the mission boards. Since a real problem was apparent, Conference named a Committee for the Re-Study of Church Board and Committee Effectiveness.[143]

In its first report this committee recommended the merger of three boards working directly in the field of Christian education—General Sunday School Board, General Education Board, and Board for Young People's Work.[144] Later, the committee concluded that the Education Board should continue its independent role as the Board for Schools and Colleges, but the General Sunday School Board and Board for Young People's Work should merge into a Board of Christian Education. In addition to assuming the duties of the merged boards, the new agency would absorb those of the Indoctrination Committee.[145]

As this merger plan was finally approved by General Conference, the new Board of Christian Education had the following duties:

> . . . to provide and promote an effective program of Christian education through the various teaching agencies of the local church, and through other agencies such as regional or general Sunday School Conventions and Youth

Conferences. The Board shall also lend its encouragement and assistance in the establishing of agencies for carrying on the teaching ministry in new communities.[146]

To carry out these duties, the board was authorized to organize into commissions and appoint a salaried executive secretary. In the "selection, approval, or preparation of literature or teaching materials," it would collaborate with the Publication Board in a joint Curriculum Committee.[147]

The nine-man Board of Christian Education organized immediately into three commissions—Sunday school, Youth, and Home.[148] Paul McBeth became the first full-time executive secretary, serving both the board and its commissions. *Forward* magazine, originally launched to promote Sunday school work, now became the voice of the Board of Christian Education.[149]

While the Commissions on Sunday School and Youth respectively carried on the work of previous boards, the Commission on Home developed a new program. Its assignment was to foster Christian training in the home and to provide help for parents; it might also function in the field of young married people's conferences.[150]

One of the first acts of this commission was a survey of Brethren family life. It also began a bibliography of materials on courtship, marriage, and home life, and, in 1952, sponsored the first Brethren in Christ observance of National Family Week.[151] Other home-related projects such as family-life conferences followed from time to time.[152] To provide operational structure, Conference recognized local deacons as the channel of communication between the commission and the families of the brotherhood.[153]

During its early years the Board of Christian Education encountered difficulties, especially financial, as it sought to improve its plan of operation and to justify mounting costs for increased services. These services were not always well understood nor welcomed at the grassroots level of church life. As the role of the Board became more clearly defined, however, and its operations more efficient and relevant to local church needs, the brotherhood responded with growing appreciation and better financial support for its work.[154]

Ministerial Education

While the Brethren in Christ promoted education through church schools and local congregations, they also faced the issue of the educational growth of ministers and ministerial candidates. Gradually their awareness of the need for such preparation increased until they decided to make specific educational requirements for ministerial service.

Long before they became concerned about ministerial education, the Brethren stressed the doctrinal loyalty of ministers. In 1878 General Conference provided that persons elected to the ministry should be examined "as to their sentiments on the doctrine as held forth by the brethren" before they could be ordained.[155] Two decades later Conference appointed an examining committee of three to assure the doctrinal soundness of persons sent out on general church ministries.[156] This agency, later known as the Examining Board, eventually became responsible for the doctrinal examination of all bishops, pastors, and ministers.[157] Beginning in the 1930s it also began to promote ministerial education.

The Examining Board at first had neither official prerogative nor precedent for its latter role. In 1939 it took a cautious step by advising all ministers to read *Homiletics and Pastoral Theology* by Aaron M. Hills.[158] Concerning that book the board observed: "His theology is sound, his instruction is timely, his illustrations convincing, and every page will present some truth of profit, and its reading will cause you to respect your calling, to sense your great responsibility, and to instruct you to better minister to those you serve."[159]

The following year the board tested support for what it had done by asking General Conference to judge the advisability of future recommendations of this kind. After receiving a favorable Conference expression, the board continued to make suggestions for ministerial reading.[160] In doing so it endeavored to make clear that these readings were not to take the place of "the revelations of the word of God through the Spirit, and a Spirit-filled life."[161] In one instance the board exhorted: "Above all continue to study and preach the Word which is forever settled in Heaven."[162]

The dearth of Brethren theological literature hindered denominationally oriented ministerial education. To make the most of the limited materials available, the Examining Board promoted the writings of Frances Davidson, Henry Smith, Peter Wiebe, Jesse Engle, William Baker, and Avery Long. These were all old books still in print in the early 1940s.[163]

Amid the ferment of the Indoctrination Movement, the Examining Board took a more positive step in ministerial education. It proposed for study the *Constitution-Doctrine, By-Laws and Rituals* of the 1930s and the later *Manual for Christian Youth;* furthermore, it requested ordained ministers under forty-five and all licensed ministers to report the outcomes of this study on a prepared questionnaire.[164] Approximately fifty of 124 questionnaires were returned prior to General Conference of 1946. Although acknowledging that the project produced some criticism, the board concluded that it had been quite worthwhile.[165]

By 1950 General Conference was ready to support a stronger commitment to ministerial education, and it created the Ministerial and Examining Board to replace the Examining Board. The new name indicated that the agency would perform functions beyond that of examining officials for doctrinal soundness. These included establishing standards for ministerial ordination and certifying when these standards had been met. The educational phase of board activity was made clear by the following statement: "A satisfactory completion of a prescribed study course or its equivalent shall be a necessary requisite for ordination." In addition the board could hold ministerial conferences and study sessions throughout the brotherhood.[166]

In its first attempt at obligatory ministerial education, the board renewed its 1945 proposal for a study of the *Constitution-Doctrine, By-Laws and Rituals* and the *Manual for Christian Youth*. Satisfactory completion of this study became a requirement for both ordination and renewal of ministerial license.[167]

Exercising another prerogative granted in 1950, the Ministerial and Examining Board cooperated with the Board for Schools and Colleges in planning and promoting education for the benefit of ministers, evangelists, and mission workers.[168] The two boards acted jointly under this mandate for the first time in 1952 when they sponsored a three-day January seminar at Messiah College. All active ministers in Ontario and Central and Eastern United States were to attend at the expense of their respective congregations. Licensed ministers, theological students, and missionaries were also invited. Program emphases included sermon building, church administration, pulpit etiquette, pastoral work, the Sunday school, and physical plant. More than 150 persons registered.[169]

As concern for ministerial education grew, the Ministerial and Examining Board shifted its attention to a two-year collegiate program.[170] The proposed studies included core courses in English and Bible plus a distribution of courses in eight other fields including pastoral theology, church history, and evangelism. Young men professing calls to the ministry were to consider this curriculum minimal. Ordained and licensed ministers in service and unable to attend the day classes of the church colleges could take night or extension classes and correspondence courses.[171]

The Ministerial and Examining Board soon perceived that flexibility was needed to administer requirements which many active ministers had not met, and which, because of age or other factors, a considerable number could not meet. To cope with these realities the board individualized the application of the requirements while the transition to a minimally educated ministry proceeded. The board also strongly stressed that candidates for ordination or re-licensing should take their collegiate work in the church colleges.[172]

In view of the increased number of men considering the ministry who were enrolling in college programs, General Conference encouraged Messiah College to develop a five-year curriculum leading to the bachelor of theology degree.[173] A considerable number of ministers and ministerial candidates earned this degree after completing four-year baccalaureate programs, but it never became a requirement for ordination.[174]

As emphasis upon ministerial education increased, some ministerial candidates began to look beyond college to seminary. As late as the 1950s, the Brethren in Christ did not urge their ministers to proceed beyond college, so the surge of interest in seminary work posed the problem of where ministerial students should enroll. Noting that the selection of a seminary involved "many matters of serious import," the Ministerial and Examining Board advised interested students to seek an evangelical institution with a holiness emphasis, and one which was sympathetic to or tolerant of other distinctive Brethren in Christ doctrines.[175]

Experience proved that no seminary adequately met these specifications. This was due to the inability of any one institution to meet the need of the Brethren to promote their unique theology combining elements of Pietism, second-work sanctification, and Anabaptism. Because many Brethren did not perceive these distinctive perspectives to be equally important, they tended to polarize into two groups. Some leaders preferred a Wesleyan seminary even if it neglected Anabaptism; others preferred an Anabaptist seminary even if it neglected Wesleyanism.

Before they fully perceived the magnitude of this problem, the Brethren hopefully began to explore possibilities for a seminary affiliation which would give them some voice or influence in the education of their ministeral candidates. Such an affiliation would also provide a common theological and community experience for students who would eventually be called upon to understand and interpret the identity of the Brethren in

Christie.[176]

The most immediate prospect for a Brethren seminary affiliation was with the Associated Mennonite Biblical Seminaries in Indiana. Christian Hostetter, Jr., who had close relationships with Mennonite leaders, shared in the planning stages of this venture to unite Mennonite and similar bodies in a cooperative seminary effort. When General Conference met in June 1958, the new seminary program was about to begin, and the Ministerial and Examining Board pressed for immediate steps toward Brethren affiliation with it.[177]

The board presented various arguments to support its position. One was the openness of the Mennonites to a full or partial seminary affiliation by the Brethren in Christ. Another was the "distinct similarity in position and view between the Mennonite groups and the Brethren in Christ in areas of doctrine and practice."

These arguments impressed Conference sufficiently to secure its approval for further study of "doctrinal involvements, curriculum, financial obligations, steps necessary for affiliation, and the searching out and preparing of the proper person to represent the Brethren in Christ on the staff of the Seminary . . . ." In addition, Conference appointed Christian Hostetter, Jr., to serve as liaison officer between the Brethren and the Associated Seminaries and advised ministerial candidates to consider study there.[178]

This authorization for further investigation of a possible seminary affiliation did not include plans for implementing the study. As a result, the Board for Schools and Colleges, which shared with the Ministerial and Examining Board responsibility for ministerial education, brought a new and more cautious recommendation to the succeeding Conference. This called for a seminary study committee representing those two Boards and the newly created Board of Bishops. The committee would conduct an investigation of various seminaries and bring recommendations to Conference "relative to affiliation with the Associated Mennonite Seminaries and/or any other seminaries which they . . . feel would be an asset in the furtherance of the Church."[179]

When General Conference assembled in 1959, the Committee on Seminary Study laid before it the results of a questionnaire completed by twenty-two individuals who had studied or were studying at fourteen different seminaries. In general, these men felt that the Brethren should do more to prepare their own ministers, especially for service in small and rural churches. The questionnaire returns indicated the need for a better understanding of Brethren in Christ history, doctrines, program, polity, and administration. Only two of the twenty-two men surveyed favored denominational affiliation with the seminaries in which they had enrolled, and these two represented different institutions.[180]

In the light of this survey, Conference instructed Messiah College both to continue and to improve its fifth-year program leading to the bachelor of theology degree, with special emphasis upon Brethren in Christ doctrine, polity, and practice, and with opportunity for pastoral apprenticeships. In addition, the college was to make serious efforts to gain credit for this year of study from some approved seminary. Goshen College Biblical Seminary was the first to grant such credit.[181]

Since Conference was not ready for a decision on seminary affiliation, it decided "as an interim guidance provision" to endorse Asbury Theological Seminary at Wilmore, Kentucky, and Mennonite Biblical Seminary at Elkhart, Indiana, as preferable for the attendance of persons planning for pastoral work in the Brethren in Christ Church. The former was an established seminary with a Wesleyan theology; the latter was a young institution in the Anabaptist tradition.[182]

General Conference of 1959 also approved continuation of the seminary study, but the matter lay dormant until 1964 when it was revived by the Board of Administration. That board was planning to provide tuition scholarships for ministerial candidates attending approved seminaries, and it assumed that the previous 1959 interim approval of Asbury Theological Seminary and the Mennonite Biblical Seminary was still valid. In addition to these two seminaries, Conference added Western Evangelical Seminary, a Wesleyan-oriented institution in Oregon, to the approved list. This action recognized that the other approved seminaries were far removed from the churches of the Pacific Conference. Also, since Mennonite Biblical Seminary was becoming increasingly interrelated with Goshen College Biblical Seminary in the Associated Mennonite Biblical Seminaries, Conference approved the latter.[183]

The Brethren did not live comfortably with a multi-seminary policy. In many ways the situation resembled their struggle to adapt for their own use Sunday school literature prepared by others.[184] Just as they lacked the numerical strength and financial resources to justify production of their own literature, so they lacked membership and finance to establish their own seminary. The next best alternative still seemed to be a denominational affiliation with a single seminary.

With this end in view, the Board of Administration vigorously pursued an investigation of possibilities for such an affiliation. Its seminary committee sent visitation teams to various seminaries.[185] Considerations such as location and administrative structure discouraged the formation of official relationships with some of these. Where such considerations were not crucial, however, the Wesleyan-Anabaptist tension within the ranks of the Brethren precluded affiliation with a single seminary.

When General Conference assembled in 1967, the Board of Administration reported that its study had not led to agreement upon a single seminary where the Brethren in Christ could develop "a center and sense of community." This acknowledgement of failure prefaced a recommendation to endorse still another seminary. By adopting this recommendation Conference added Ashland Theological Seminary, at Ashland, Ohio, an institution with theological roots in the German Baptist Brethren (Dunker) movement, to the previously approved list.[186]

In failing to achieve a seminary affiliation, the denomination automatically avoided the financial burdens which this would have entailed. Although seminarians receive some personal financial grants from brotherhood sources, the institutions in which they enroll must assume responsibility for financing that portion of their education not covered by tuition.[187]

Lack of a seminary affiliation poses some problems for the life of the Brethren. With no institution enrolling a sufficient number of seminarians to provide a clear sense of Brethren in Christ community and identity, the church is deprived of an important unifying influence.[188] The brotherhood, furthermore, has no voice or representation in the training of its ministerial students.

Under present circumstances it is difficult to explain to a prospective seminarian why he should confine himself to one of four institutions, each enrolling a few Brethren students. The Canadian Conference, for example, has its own ministerial committee and ministerial fund, with the result that most Canadian ministerial students now pursue their studies in Canada rather than at any of the approved seminaries in the United States.[189] Under these circumstances, the church tends to move progressively further away from the "center and sense of community" previously deemed advisable for its seminarians.

The lack of a single seminary affiliation offers one minor advantage—the opportunity for seminarians to contact and, in some instances, to render pastoral service in churches in various regions of the brotherhood. If there were but one approved seminary, only Brethren churches within its general vicinity could benefit from the contributions of the ministerial students enrolled.

Few leaders of the denomination are fully satisfied with the present state of ministerial education. There is, however, consensus about the need to build bridges of understanding and mutual respect between seminarians of different backgrounds. As a means to this end, Brethren in Christ leaders periodically join with them as a total group in seminars or institutes. These are held biennially and each seminarian is urged to attend two, with costs of attendance borne by the church. This program appears to be fostering unity in the midst of diversity.[190]

NOTES:

[1][Henry Davidson], "General Conference," *Visitor*, III (June 1, 1890), 161.

[2]*General Conference Minutes*, 1910, Article 6, p. 9. See Chapter X for the beginning of Sunday school work.

[3]*Ibid.*, 1921, p. 59.

[4]C. W. Boyer, "Significant Developments in Brethren in Christ Sunday School Work, 1932-1952," *Forward*, V (Spring, 1953), 10.

[5]Kansas Joint Council Minutes, March 18, 19, 1892, Article 16.

[6]*Pennsylvania State Council Minutes*, 1924, Article 6, pp. 12-14; *Canadian Joint Council Minutes*, September 8, 1927, p. 67.

[7]*General Conference Minutes*, 1937, Article 36, p. 57.

[8]*Ibid.*, 1941, Article 38, pp. 61-64.

[9]*Ibid.*, 1913, Article 14, p. 23; *ibid.*, 1917, Article 6, pp. 8-10; *ibid.*, 1918, Article 26, pp. 36-37.

[10]*Ibid.*, 1921, Article 35, p. 40.

[11]*Ibid.*, 1921, Article 40, p. 55.

[12]*Ibid.*, 1938, Article 39, pp. 62-64.

[13]The board again revised the standard in 1954.

[14]See Chapter X for the introduction of this course.

[15]*General Conference Minutes*, 1919, Article 14, p. 25.

[16]Alma B. Cassel, "Brethren in Christ Sunday Schools in the Twentieth Century, 1911-1963," *Forward*, XV (July, August, September, 1963), 15.

[17]*General Conference Minutes*, 1922, Article 41, p. 47.

[18]*Ibid.*, 1938, Article 39, pp. 58-59.

[19]*Pennsylvania State Council Minutes*, 1943, Article 9, pp. 16-22; *General Conference Minutes*, 1944, Article 73, p. 108.

[20](Nappanee, Indiana; E. V. Publishing House, 1946).

[21]See Chapter X for the initial adoption of this Mennonite literature.

[22]John A. Stump, "Special Notice," *Visitor,* XXIII (February 15, 1909), 3.

[23]*General Conference Minutes,* 1910, Article 46, pp. 48-49; *ibid.,* 1911, Article 71, p. 75.

[24]*Ibid.,* 1913, Article 14, p. 23.

[25]*Ibid.,* 1916, Article 37, pp. 74-75.

[26]*Ibid.,* 1921, Article 35, p. 40.

[27]C. W. Boyer to C. O. Wittlinger, June 9, 1976.

[28]*General Conference Minutes,* 1922, Article 11, p. 13.

[29]*Ibid.*

[30]See the files of these publications in the Church Archives.

[31]*General Conference Minutes,* 1923, Article 14, p. 19; *ibid.,* 1925, Article 17, p. 32; *ibid.,* 1931, Article 27, p. 46; *ibid.,* 1932, Article 29, p. 56.

[32]V. L. Stump, "Editorial," *The Sunday School Herald,* I (January, 1937), 4.

[33]*General Conference Minutes,* 1963, Article 27, pp. 105-6.

[34][George Detwiler], "Criticism on Graded Lesson System," *Visitor,* XXVI (June 3, 1912), 15.

[35]*Pennsylvania State Council Minutes,* April 3-4, 1940, Article 10, p. 24.

[36]Henry G. Brubaker, "Graded Sunday School Lessons," *Visitor,* LIV (April 7, 1941), 106.

[37]*General Conference Minutes,* 1941, Article 38, pp. 63-64.

[38]Henry G. Brubaker, "The Improved Uniform Sunday School Lessons," *Visitor,* LIV (May 19, 1941), 159.

[39]*General Conference Minutes,* 1944, Article 73, p. 109.

[40]Curriculum Committee Report to the Publication and General Sunday School Boards, January 25, 1950, Paul W. McBeth files; C. W. Boyer to C. O. Wittlinger, September 28, 1974; Paul W. McBeth interview, October 8, 1974.

[41]Curriculum Committee Report.

[42]Minutes of a joint meeting of the Sunday School Board, the Publication Board, and the Curriculum Committee, January 25, 1950; Curriculum Committee Report.

[43]John N. Hostetter, "History of Sunday School Literature," *Forward,* XV (July, August, September, 1963), 23.

[44]*General Conference Minutes,* 1969, Article 23, p. 106; *ibid.,* 1970, Article 22, p. 99.

[45]*Constitution and By-Laws,* 1937, p. 78.

[46]C. W. Boyer, "Significant Developments in Brethren in Christ Sunday School Work, 1932-1952," *Forward,* V (Spring Issue, 1953), 10.

[47]Glenna McClure, *Forward,* I (Autumn Issue, 1948), p. 1.

[48]"Join the Forward Sunday School Contest," *Forward,* I (Summer Issue, 1949), 1.

[49]C. W. Boyer, "Good News! Another 'Forward' Sunday School Contest," *Forward,* II (Summer Issue, 1950), 1; *General Conference Minutes,* 1950, Article 30, p. 80.

[50]*General Conference Minutes,* 1950, Article 30, p. 80.

[51]"Dayton, Ohio Sunday School has the Largest Increase of Any Sunday School. How Did They Do It?" *Forward,* III (Winter Issue, 1951), 2.

[52]E. J. Swalm, "Thanks to the General Sunday School Board," *Forward,* III (Winter Issue, 1951), 1.

[53]*Ibid.,* p. 5.

[54]*Forward,* III (Winter Issue, 1951), pp. 4-8.

[55]Grace Herr, "Sunday School Convention Echoes," *Forward,* III (Summer Issue, 1951), 1.

[56]Paul W. McBeth interview, August 3, 1976. In 1952 General Conference approved the affiliation of the Board of Christian Education with the National Sunday School Association and confirmed Paul McBeth as the denominational representative on the advisory council of the NSSA. *General Conference Minutes, 1952,* Article 34, pp. 72-73.

[57]P. M. "Looking Ahead for '51," *Forward* III (Winter Issue, 1951), 2.

[58]Grace Herr, "Sunday School Convention Echoes," *Forward* III (Summer Issue, 1951), 7.

[59]Gloria Hope, "Youth Leadership and Sunday School Convention Is Bigger and Better," *Forward,* IV (Summer Issue, 1952), 1, 3.

[60]C. W. Boyer, "Significant Developments in Brethren in Christ Sunday School Work, 1932-1952," *Forward,* V (Spring Issue, 1953), 10.

[61]Albert H. Engle interview, October 30, 1974.

[62]C. N. Hostetter Jr., "Vacation Bible School Deductions," *Visitor,* XLVI (October 23, 1933), 340. See his analysis of VBS goals in this article.

[63]Cyrus G. Lutz, "Our First Daily Vacation Bible School at Refton Completes 25 Years," *Forward,* VI (Fall Issue, 1953), 2.

[64]Mrs. Ernest M. Frey's report in Enos H. Hess, "The Vacation Bible School," *Visitor,* XLII (August 19, 1929), 9.

[65]"Over 7,900 Enrolled in Brethren in Christ Summer Bible Schools During the Year," *Forward,* I (Autumn, 1948), 7.

[66]"Church and Sunday School Statistical and Financial Report," *General Conference Minutes, 1958,* insert in back.

[67]*General Conference Minutes, 1955,* Article 33, p. 64.

[68]*Ibid.,* and insert in back.

[69]*Ibid.,* 1949, Article 27, p. 78.

[70]*General Conference Minutes, 1963,* Article 24, pp. 83-85; *Forward, Centennial Issue,* (July, August, September, 1963).

[71]John H. Myers, "The Lord's Commission," *Visitor,* XXI (August 15, 1907), 9-10.

[72]*Upland Council Minutes,* September 20, 1910, Article 4, p. 33; and March 21, 1911, Article 11, p. 37.

[73]Henry N. Hostetter to C. O. Wittlinger, June 2, 1976.

[74][Ohmer U. Herr], "Historical Sketches of the Advancement of Programs for Bible Study Services, Constitutional Provision for Young People's Meetings & Institution of the Board for Young People's Work in the Brethren in Christ Church," pp. 2, 3, MS in Church Archives; Markham District Council Minutes, February 6, 1925, Article 18.

[75]E. Morris Sider interview, August 21, 1976. Young People's Society Roster, Board for Young People's Work Records, Church Archives.

[76]Herr, "Historical Sketches," p. 2.

[77]*Ibid.,* pp. 3-4.

[78]*General Conference Minutes,* 1931, Article 28, p. 48.

[79]Herr, "Historical Sketches," pp. 5-7; *Visitor,* XLV (January 4, 1932), 16.

[80]*General Conference Minutes,* 1932, Article 5, p. 10.

[81]*Ibid.,* p. 11.

[82]*Ibid.,* 1940, Article 53, p. 89.

[83]*Kansas State Council Minutes,* 1927, Article 17, p. 16.

[84]*Young Peoples Conference of Kansas Brethren in Christ . . . Manhattan, Kansas,* August 16-19, 1926; *Kansas State Council Minutes,* April 6-7, 1927, Article 17, p. 16.

[85]Naomi T. Brechbill interview, November 20, 1974; Mary A. Stoner interview, November 21, 1974. Both interviewees helped to organize the first Grantham young people's conference. See also Grace M. Stoner, "Grantham Youth Conference," *Forward,* IV (Spring, 1952), 10.

[86]"Young People's Conference Report," Grantham District Records, Church Archives.

[87]*Canadian Joint Council Minutes,* September 19, 1936, pp. 144-45; *Michigan District Council Minutes,* November 15, 1937, Article 17, p. 21; *Ohio-Kentucky Joint Council Minutes,* March 12-14, 1942, Article 21, pp. 21-25; *Pacific Coast Branch Minutes,* March 13, 1941, Article 10, pp. 24-26; Ira M. Eyster, "Oklahoma Youth Conference," *Forward,* IV (Spring 1952), 11.

[88]*Ohio-Kentucky Joint Council Minutes,* March 17-19, 1948, Article 12, p. 21; Kenneth B. Hoover, "Grantham Young Married People's Conference," *Forward,* IV (Spring, 1952), 11; Ernest U. Dohner, "Young Married People's Conference," *Forward,* IV (Spring, 1952), 11; Wendell Harmon, "California Chose Snow-Peaked Mountains for Their Young Married People's Conference," *Forward,* IV (Spring, 1952), 9.

[89]Alfred Crider, "Kenbrook Bible Camp," *Forward,* IV (Spring, 1952), 10.

[90]*General Conference Minutes,* 1934, Article 60, p. 89.

[91]*Ibid.,* 1935, Article 39, p. 69.

[92]*Ibid.,* 1936, Article 14, p. 24.

[93]*Constitution-Doctrine, By-Laws and Rituals of the Brethren in Christ Church.* Adopted at the General Conference held at Cross Roads Church, Florin, Pa., June 4, 1937, pp. 68-69.

[94]*General Conference Minutes,* 1938, Article 20, pp. 27-28.

[95]General Conference authorized previous foreign mission deputations in 1909 and 1919.

[96]*General Conference Minutes,* 1939, Articles 20, 21, pp. 37-40; *ibid.,* 1941, Article 48, p. 83.

[97]*Ibid.,* 1939, Article 33, pp. 56-57; *ibid.,* 1946, Article 26, p. 69. Hostetter was later transferred to the Foreign Mission Board.

[98]*Ibid.,* 1942, Article 46, p. 89; *Ibid.,* 1943, Article 47, p. 82.

[99]*Ibid.,* reports and recommendations of the Board for Young People's Work for the years 1942-1947.

[100]*Ibid.,* 1952, Article 34, p. 77.

[101]Ernest Boyer, "What Is a Name?" *Forward,* V (Fall, 1952), 10.

[102]*General Conference Minutes,* 1953, Article 32, p. 64.

[103]Helen L. Dodson, "It Really Happened on Christ's Crusaders Day," *Forward,* VI (Spring, 1954), 7.

[104]*Ibid.*

[105]Commission on Youth Minutes, 1957, Article 3. The origin of this commission is explained later in the chapter. This annual Bible Quiz continues as of the date of this writing.

[106]*General Conference Minutes,* 1952, Article 34, p. 66.

[107]*Ibid.,* 1953, Article 32, p. 63; "Christ's Crusaders Congress," *Forward,* VI (Winter, 1954), 2.

[108]*General Conference Minutes,* 1954, Article 34, p. 71; *ibid.,* 1957, Article 26, p. 42.

[109]*Ibid.*, 1953, Article 32, p. 60.

[110]*Ibid.*, 1952, Article 34, pp. 76-77.

[111]Commission on Youth Minutes, June 1953, Article 19; *ibid.*, June 1954, Article 15; ibid., December 1954, Article 12, Church Archieves.

[112]*General Conference Minutes,* 1954, Article 34, p. 71.

[113]Personal knowledge of the present writer.

[114]*General Conference Minutes,* 1954, Article 34, p. 72.

[115]Commission on Youth Minutes, June 1954, Article 15, Church Archives. As secretary of the Commission on Youth, the present writer was in close touch with the negotiations for boys' and girls' club programs.

[116]*General Conference Minutes,* 1955, Article 33, p. 66.

[117]*Pacific Coast District Council Minutes,* March 8, 1929, Article 7, p. 22.

[118]*Pennsylvania State Council Minutes,* April 9, 1931, Article 6, p. 13.

[119]See Chapters XV and XVI.

[120]See Appendix C and the statistical inserts in General Conference Minutes, 1941-1946.

[121]Henry G. Brubaker, "The Urgency of God Power," *General Conference Minutes,* 1941, p. 4. See also the section on "An Unexpected Catalyst for Change" in Chapter XIX.

[122]E. J. Swalm, "Evaluation and Challenge of Our Peace Activities," *Visitor,* LIV (December 1, 1941), 370, 380.

[123]*General Conference Minutes,* 1943, Article 13, p. 21.

[124]*Ibid.*, Article 35, p. 56.

[125]*Ibid.*, 1942, Article 37, p. 70.

[126]*Ibid.*, 1944, Article 35, p. 59.

[127]*Ibid.*, 1944, Article 74, p. 110.

[128]*Visitor,* LVIII (January 29, 1945), 35.

[129]H. G. B., "Concerning a Program of Indoctrination," *Visitor,* LVIII, (March 12, 1945), 83.

[130]*General Conference Minutes,* 1943, Article 53, pp. 87-88; *ibid.,* Article 5, p. 12.

[131]*Ibid.*, 1944, Article 8, p. 13.

[132]*Ibid.*, 1945, Article 7, p. 22.

[133]*Manual for Christian Youth: Doctrines and Practices Based Upon the Holy Scriptures as Taught By the Brethren in Christ Church* (Nappanee, Ind.: E. V. Publishing House, 1945), p. 10.

[134]*General Conference Minutes,* 1946, Article 7, p. 22; [Jesse F. Lady], *Workbook to Be Used with the Manual for Christian Youth* (Nappanee, Ind.: E. V. Publishing House, n.d.).

[135]*General Conference Minutes,* 1944, Article 74, pp. 110-11.

[136]*Ibid.*, Article 75, pp. 111-12.

[137]*Ibid.*, 1945, Article 10, pp. 24-25.

[138]*Ibid.*, p. 27.

[139]*Ibid.*, 1948, Article 14, pp. 32-33.

[140]See Chapter XIX for changes made by the Brethren in Christ in the 1950s.

[141]*General Conference Minutes,* 1946, Article 7, p. 23.

[142]*Pennsylvania State Council Minutes,* April 2-3, 1947, Article 10, p. 27.

[143]*General Conference Minutes,* 1947, Article 9, p. 29.

[144]*Ibid.*, 1948, Article 9, p. 26.

[145]*Ibid.*, 1949, Article 8, p. 28.

[146]*Ibid.*, 1951, Article 15, p. 29.

[147]*Ibid.*

[148]*Ibid.*, p. 23.

[149]P. W. M., "Editorially Speaking," *Forward*, IV (Spring Issue, 1952), p. 2.

[150]*General Conference Minutes*, 1951, Article 15, p. 30.

[151]*Ibid.*, 1952, Article 34, p. 62.

[152][Ohmer U. Herr], "Would You Like the Benefits of a Christian Home Conference in Your Congregation?", *Forward*, VII (Summer Issue, 1955), 13.

[153]*General Conference Minutes*, 1965, Article 22, p. 86; *Manual of Doctrine and Government of the Brethren in Christ Church* (Nappanee, Ind.: Evangel Press, 1961), p. 129.

[154]The gradual development of boards of Christian education at regional and congregational levels also improved constituency relationships with the General Conference Board of Christian Education.

[155]*Church Government*, 1887, p. 17.

[156]*General Conference Minutes*, 1899, Article 9, pp. 6-7.

[157]*Ibid.*, 1910, Article 36, p. 39.

[158]Misspelled "Mills" in *General Conference Minutes*.

[159]*General Conference Minutes*, 1939, Article 27, p. 48.

[160]*Ibid.*, 1940, Article 31, p. 48; *ibid.*, 1942, Article 23, p. 48; *ibid.*, 1944, Article 22, p. 31.

[161]*Ibid.*, 1942, Article 23, p. 48.

[162]*Ibid.*, 1944, Article 22, p. 31.

[163]*Ibid.*, 1943, Article 23, p. 37. Although his name was not specifically mentioned, the writings of William Baker were obviously intended for inclusion.

[164]*Ibid.*, 1945, Article 20, pp. 53-54.

[165]*Ibid.*, 1946, Article 23, p. 53.

[166]*Ibid.*, 1950, Article 10, p. 29. Beginning in 1908 a ministerial meeting was held for many years in conjunction with General Conference, and eventually the Examining Board became responsible for it. *Ibid.*, 1937, Article 5, p. 14.

[167]*Ibid.*, 1950, Article 25, p. 57.

[168]*Ibid.*, 1950, Article 25, p. 57.

[169]*Ibid.*, 1951, Article 24, p. 64; *ibid.*, 1952, Article 38, p. 110. Later ministerial seminars were held in other areas of the brotherhood such as Canada and Ohio.

[170]*Ibid.*, 1953, Article 36, pp. 102-3. Two years earlier Conference approved in principle a suggested collegiate program for ministers and missionaries. *Ibid.*, 1951, Article 36, p. 69.

[171]*Ibid.*, 1953, Article 36, pp. 102-3.

[172]*Ibid.*, 1954, Article 38, pp. 105-6; *ibid.*, 1955, Article 37, pp. 113-15.

[173]*Ibid.*, 1949, Article 11, p. 37.

[174]Lists of Th. B. graduates in the Messiah College commencement programs beginning with 1952.

[175]*General Conference Minutes*, 1955, Article 37, p. 114.

[176]*Ibid.*, 1957, Article 28, p. 98.

[177]*Ibid.* Sponsors of this associated seminary program envisioned eventual par-

ticipation by the (Old) Mennonites, the General Conference Mennonites, the Mennonite Brethren, and the Brethren in Christ.

[178]*General Conference Minutes,* 1957, Article 28, p. 98.

[179]*Ibid.,* 1958, Article 30, pp. 126-27.

[180]*Ibid.,* 1959, Article 29, pp. 108-9.

[181]Harold S. Bender to C. O. Wittlinger, May 16, 1962, files of the Dean of Messiah College. Some other seminaries followed this example, but young men who completed seminary degrees in two years after the Th. B. reported dissatisfaction with the interrelationship between the two programs; furthermore, those interested in the Th. B. as a finishing program were too few to justify its continuance for this purpose.

[182]*General Conference Minutes,* 1959, p. 109.

[183]*Ibid.,* 1964, Article 21, pp. 72-73.

[184]See Chapter X.

[185]The present writer served as a member of four of these teams.

[186]*General Conference Minutes,* 1967, Article 19, p. 63. This action is explained by the presence of a Brethren in Christ scholar, Owen H. Alderfer, on the faculty of the Ashland Theological Seminary.

[187]*General Conference Minutes,* 1971, Article 19, pp. 94-95; *ibid.,* 1972, Article 19, p. 98.

[188]This problem of unity and identity has taken on new dimensions in recent years as an increasing number of pulpits are filled by persons who have had neither a unifying seminary experience nor the experience of growing up within the Brethren in Christ tradition.

[189]*General Conference Minutes,* 1970, Article 18, p. 57; Alden Long interview, May 16, 1976. Long is chairman of the Ministerial Credentials Board.

[190]Alden Long interview, May 16, 1976.

XVIII

Expanding Mission Outreach

Rural Missions

As a rural people the Brethren in Christ first expressed their interest in missions and evangelism through preaching ministries in rural settings. Migrations of Brethren families seeking improved economic opportunities in new localities provided bases from which itinerant evangelists carried the gospel into surrounding areas.[1] From time to time General Conference or state councils recognized clusters of pioneering families and new converts as "missions" until they grew into fully organized church districts or migrated elsewhere. In 1903 there were three rural missions, one in each of the states of Michigan, Arizona, and California.[2] By the 1920s the Brethren had begun other rural missions in Virginia, Kentucky, Ontario, and Pennsylvania.

The first rural mission sponsored by General Conference began at Carland, Michigan, in the 1890s.[3] This work progressed slowly, but by 1920 it was an organized church district with a resident bishop.[4] Mission activity later expanded into the vicinity of Gladwin, Michigan, where two mission churches were active by the 1930s.[5]

The Brethren also made a few feeble attempts to begin a mission in Virginia prior to 1917.[6] In that year, however, the Home Mission Board laid the foundations for a permanent mission program in that state. Denny and Marie Jennings, native Virginians who embraced the Brethren faith in Buffalo, New York, pioneered the work under the board's direction. Carrying a burden for their own people, they took up residence at Sylvatus, Virginia, in 1917 and launched a mission.[7]

These Virginia mission pioneers were prepared for material sacrifice, for when opposition forced them to vacate "the cozy little home" first secured for a mission station, they spent the following winter in a renovated stable.[8] Later, after some Pennsylvania members purchased a site and erected suitable mission buildings, including a chapel, the Jennings responded:

> We feel very unworthy of the home and comforts the Brethren have placed here for us workers but we are thankful for them and know God will bless each one of you for we know it is done as unto Jesus. We are not, however, tied to the comforts of life for when Father says again go on farther into the hills and mountains, take a log cabin or anything for the sake of Jesus gladly will we go.[9]

Mission interest in Kentucky first developed among the Ohio Brethren, some of whom crossed the border on preaching ministries from time to time. For a few years Walter Reighard resided at Garlin and gave temporary pastoral leadership to the work. Later, in 1927, Albert and Margie Engle began seventeen years of mission service in that state.[10] When they arrived and took up residence at Garlin, they found only a few Brethren members.[11] Within ten years an increased membership was scattered in seven or eight communities, and the mission staff had expanded to eleven persons.[12] By 1937 three churches formed centers from which the work fanned out through the surrounding country.

The early Kentucky missionaries carried heavy spiritual and physical burdens. In 1937 the Engles and one co-worker at Garlin ministered at twelve regular preaching appointments and twenty-one prayer meetings each month. In the same period they shared in four Sunday schools, directed vacation Bible schools, participated in revival and tent meetings, and conducted funerals (five in one weekend). Albert Engle simultaneously served as field superintendent for the entire Kentucky work and Margie Engle, a registered nurse, frequently ministered to the sick.[13]

In 1894 mission work began near Brantford, Ontario, when the Canadian Mission Board sent Asa Bearss and Christian Winger to conduct a revival meeting in Houghton Township of Norfolk County.[14] As a result of that campaign, six members of the community united with the Brethren. For several decades ministers from Black Creek District supplied the mission pulpit on a monthly basis. When efforts to secure a resident pastor failed, the work eventually declined.[15]

In the late 1920s, John Nigh of Springvale, Ontario, revived interest in the mission by traveling some fifty miles weekly to conduct prayer meetings in community homes. After two years of these services, summer tent meetings gave new impetus to the enterprise.[16] The following report reflects the outcomes of a 1931 tent campaign sponsored by the Home Mission Board: "Backslidden members were re-instated and hardened sinners, under deep conviction confessed their sins, sought for pardon and were graciously delivered."[17]

The second pitching of the tent was in nearby Walsingham Township, a community noted for bootleggers who created serious problems for the police. When many of these hardened lawbreakers became converted and changed their life-styles, police spokesmen observed that this spiritual awakening accomplished what they had been trying to do for years.[18] Under these auspicious circumstances, the mission board assigned Walter Taylor and his wife as the first resident workers at the Houghton Mission.[19] After less than three years of service, Taylor died; his six pallbearers had been converted and joined the brotherhood under his ministry.[20]

Another significant rural mission development resulted from the "Saxton Revival" in Blair and Bedford Counties, Pennsylvania, a dynamic movement which reached its peak in the 1930s. Herman and Laura Miller, who launched the Altoona Mission early in the previous decade, helped to prepare the way for the revival.[21] In the late 1920s this mission became the church home of Harry and Minney Fink and Roscoe and Lillian Ebersole, who energetically propagated their faith among their neighbors.[22]

In the fall of 1931 the Finks and Ebersoles accepted an invitation to hold home prayer meetings in Saxton, southeast of Altoona. When homes proved inadequate to accommodate the crowds, the meetings moved to Weaver's Grove, a picnic grounds four miles from town. Here the simple pavilion had open sides, and inclement weather soon created the need for an indoor meeting place. The trustees of the Saxton Grange granted permission for the group to use the grange hall.[23]

People now flocked to the services until the hall could not begin to contain them. Iola Dixon, who played an active role in the revival, described one of the services.

"We went early and found the room well filled with people. They came in the front door and then the side door until every vacant place was taken.

Many of us were holding people on our laps. Some were sitting on the floor. People listened through the windows. One man who had a marvelous conversion stuck his head in the window to testify of God's saving grace.

"The new converts could not wait to testify. The love and grace of God flowed in waves. There was something here you could see and feel that was not of this world. It was the power of the Holy Spirit working from the inside of redeemed people. Nobody was bored or cared about the time. You wanted the service to go on forever. It was the nearest thing to heaven I expect to experience in this life."[24]

These grange hall meetings continued for five weeks with a strong emphasis on conversion, sanctification, and healing.[25] Ebersole and Fink reported some outcomes:

In all over 200 found Jesus, among . . . [whom] were . . . [backsliders], who were reclaimed, and many others who were born again—bootleggers, gamblers, adulterers; and young men who conducted a broadcasting orchestra at Altoona were gloriously saved and delivered from the drink habit. It is claimed that one man was sober this Christmas for the first time in 22 years. Also quite a number of well-to-do folks found the Lord.[26]

The Saxton Revival aroused strong opposition. Meetings in the grange hall terminated after five weeks because the building burned down. In the opinion of the workers, this fire was an act of arson intended "to get rid of us."[27] Many times they were jeered and mocked and once, by implication, threatened with tarring and feathering.[28] At a later meeting in the Clear Creek area, someone set off a dynamite blast which showered a sleeping revivalist with sawdust and gravel.[29] On another occasion thieves stole and burned the workers' bedding.[30]

Opposition, however, did not deter the intrepid revivalists. When the grange hall burned, the Saxton meetings were briefly interrupted and then moved to a garage.[31] This structure had a ground floor, and during periods of rainfall water had to be dipped up and new sawdust shavings put down on the mud. A pot-bellied stove supplied the heat, but little was needed because of the tightly packed crowds.[32]

The main thrust of the revival at Saxton occurred in the early 1930s.[33] By June of 1932 it had produced a forty-member congregation. This caused the Home Mission Board to assign Roscoe and Lilian Ebersole and Iola Dixon as mission workers and to proceed with the erection of a church building. Although Saxton was the focus of the awakening, revival influences radiated into nearby communities. By the end of the decade, continuous evangelistic efforts had produced a number of small mission congregations in Blair and Bedford Counties.[34]

Mission work at sub-zero temperatures. Heated "caboose," North Star Mission, Saskatchewan, about 1950. Florence Faus standing outside; Pearl Jones seated inside.

The preceding sketch of rural mission activities shows that the Brethren had become deeply involved in this type of endeavor by the 1930s.[35] During the next two decades, they expanded their mission efforts into several other states where they now have organized churches—Oregon, Tennessee, and New Mexico.

A few Brethren had found their way to Oregon by the 1890s, but they lived in isolation from the rest of the brotherhood and conducted no services of their own.[36] In 1918 the Home Mission Board sponsored an Oregon tent meeting conducted by Jesse Eyster and others and reported: "There were quite a number of conversions and some have united with the

Church."[37] What happened to these new members is not clear, for no record of an Oregon mission before 1945 exists. By that year a group of members from the California Church, who had recently moved to Grants Pass, Oregon, were functioning as a mission congregation. The Home Mission Board assumed active supervision of this work and assigned Benjamin M. Books as mission pastor.[38]

A decade later the Brethren launched a mission program in Tennessee. Evangelistic outreach by the Kentucky Church combined with interest on the part of Ohio-Kentucky Joint Council to prepare the way for this venture. Following three tent meetings in 1954, the Home Mission Board studied the field and assigned Dortha Dohner as a temporary worker in DeRossett. By June of 1955 the board concluded that this area was "in need of a balanced evangelical testimony" and that it promised to be a fruitful field for mission enterprises. Conference agreed and DeRossett became a mission pastorate.[39]

As early as the 1880s, the Brethren had seriously considered a mission to the American Indians.[40] In 1945 such a mission finally began when Lynn and Eleanor Nicholson launched a work among the Navajos in New Mexico. The young couple viewed this Indian tribe with both Christian concern and sociological insight, as illustrated by the following comments:

> The Navajos offer a tremendous challenge to present-day American Christians. Here, within our borders, is a tribe of perhaps sixty-thousand people, speaking a strange language, having contact with America, yet not a part of America, having known modern Christianity for many years, yet not convinced of the truth, value or sincerity of that Christianity. A tribe of self-supporting, hard-working, independent, proud, yet poverty-stricken people, who living in a hard and barren country, where life is a constant struggle, can still laugh, and sing as they go their way.[41]

After studying the Navajo language and the people, the Nicholsons secured a mission site near Bloomfield, New Mexico, and began to construct a home, school, and church.[42] While the work proceeded they engaged in home visitation, reading the Scriptures, singing hymns in the Navajo language, and presenting a gospel witness with the help of phonograph records in the Navajo tongue. During 1948 three Indians professed conversion, a development which greatly encouraged the missionaries.[43]

One of the most pressing problems of the mission was an assured water supply which could come only from a well. After drilling to a depth of 166 feet without results, the mission purchased a new drilling rig, and with Nicholson doing all of the work himself, finally struck water with a flow of fifteen gallons per hour. This was adequate for immediate needs but provided no reserve for the expansion of facilities.[44]

Another urgent need was provision for medical care. The nearest doctor was forty-five miles away and the only satisfactory hospital sixty-five miles. Transporting sick and injured Navajos such distances was difficult at best, and very hazardous when winter roads magnified the problems. On one occasion the mission car became involved in an accident while racing to the hospital with a woman in labor; fortunately, the car could proceed and reached its destination before the woman delivered.[45]

These circumstances demonstrated the need for medical facilities at the mission. By 1953 a medical clinic staffed by nurses served 900 different persons in one year. That year the mission also dedicated the first units of a four-wing hospital complex.[46] In 1956 it passed another milestone when General Conference assigned Alvin Heise, the first of a succession of medical doctors, to the mission staff.[47] Due to the development of other medical facilities in the area, the mission discontinued its medical program in July 1976.[48]

City Missions

While the Brethren were founding and expanding rural mission programs, they also widened their city mission outreach. Five years after the opening of the Chicago work in 1894 additional missions were active in Des Moines, Iowa; Buffalo, New York; and Philadelphia, Pennsylvania.[49] By 1925 the number of city missions had increased to ten and by the mid-century to fourteen.[50]

The crowds and complexities of city life contrasted sharply with the rural agricultural experiences of a people who did not become involved with city mission work until the late nineteenth century. Yet the cities drew them; they had a burden to share their faith with the multitudes. When they entered urban communities, however, they often had to adapt themselves to circumstances which they had not anticipated. Depending upon the particular situation, the urban missionary might give largely of his or her time to one or more ministries, such as children's work, prison visitation, hospital and home visitation of the sick, feeding and housing destitute transients on "skid row," or to other activities which would now be considered social service.[51]

City missionaries, of course, generally became simultaneously involved with a variety of ministries in addition to conducting regular services in mission halls. Some found themselves in unexpected and unique situations, as illustrated by a 1914 report from the San Francisco Mission: "In October we were privileged to hold a few services aboard the battleship Pittsburg [sic], where we found a Bible Class of about twenty young men, some of them in possession of a bright experience."[52]

The complexities of city mission work puzzled the Brethren and gave rise to different opinions about how to define it. In 1910 General Conference struggled with the problem of definition. It concluded that no one type of activity could be designated as city mission work to the exclusion of all others but that work carried on in sections of the city "where the multitudes can be reached" should be regarded as city mission work in the fullest sense and therefore more freely encouraged.[53]

This definition placed a premium upon what today would be called "inner city" work. Since most of their city missions began before the massive northward migration of southern blacks, the Brethren perceived native-born and immigrant whites as their mission field. With one exception, a short-lived Boston mission to Armenians, they made no self-conscious effort to reach specific urban minorities.

The Boston work was the outcome of an abortive attempt to launch an overseas mission in Armenia.[54] When that venture succeeded only in raising a fund for Armenian orphan relief, the Home and Foreign Mission Boards collaborated in 1921 to launch a mission to the Armenian community in Boston.[55] In this they had the assistance of two Armenian couples.[56] The resulting cooperative relationship continued until 1926 when the Armenian mission staff voluntarily relinquished further financial assistance from the Brethren. Although that staff desired to continue to work under the auspices of the brotherhood, the relationship became increasingly tenuous until it ceased altogether.[57]

The preceding survey of rural and city missions reveals the vigor of home mission interest among the Brethren in the first half of the twentieth century. Dedicated men and women often sacrificed material comforts, and some practically burned out their lives in response to the Great Commission. Their combined efforts had important results.

One was the growth of the Brethren in Christ Church, accompanied by an infusion of new blood. Mission converts helped to account for the gradual increase of membership statistics from 1910 to 1950. As early as

1937, furthermore, a number of self-supporting churches traced their origins back to mission stations. These included congregations such as Mooretown, near Sandusky, Michigan; Lancaster and Chambersburg, Pennsylvania; and Des Moines, Iowa.[58] Since the home mission effort absorbed large amounts of time, talent, and money, the resulting membership gains to 1950 may have been more modest than some observers might have expected.

Any assessment of the home mission impact upon church extension to the mid-century must take into account the deep commitment of the brotherhood to its historic distinctives. Most Brethren of that period were not prepared to modify practices such as plain clothing, the prayer veiling, and abstention from tobacco in order to gain church members. When, for example, some of the first city mission workers reported that plain dress requirements repelled converts from membership, and requested a solution to the problem, Conference made clear that those requirements must stand.[59] On the other hand, both rural and city missionaries often believed in and vigorously reinforced Brethren distinctives; they accepted as necessary the resulting loss of non-conforming converts to other churches.[60] In that respect they faithfully represented the position of the brotherhood as reflected in a 1932 report of the Home Mission Board:

> Church extension by the Brethren in Christ is a difficult task not only because of the direct opposition of Satanic forces, but the fact that we stress unpopular and neglected truth and endeavor to have our people observe the "all things" of divine revelation makes our task doubly difficult. In spite of the difficulties, however, we are encouraged by the evidence of definite progress.[61]

Brethren distinctives were not, of course, the only factors limiting contributions of city and rural missions to the growth of the church. Some pioneer mission evangelists appear to have been more effective in winning converts than in nurturing and building them into stable congregations. City and rural missions, furthermore, made a significant impact upon large numbers of people who, for a variety of reasons, may never have considered affiliation with the Brethren. Many of those who professed conversion under mission ministries were members of other denominations, who simply carried the influence and inspiration of those ministries back to their home churches. Some city missions, contacting large numbers of transients, could not measure the long-range effects of their efforts, as illustrated by the following 1914 San Francisco Mission report:

> Concerning the conversions during the year, it would be impossible to give any number, on account of the transcientness [sic] of so many with whom we deal. For illustration—on New Year's eve, there came into the meeting a man whom none of us recognized and whose testimony ran something like this—"I was converted last New Year's eve in this mission. I have not been here since. My wife and I have been conducting a mission up in the mountains, and at this present moment my wife is no doubt preaching the Gospel to the mountaineers. As long as I am within reach, I expect to visit this mission every New Year's eve."[62]

Whatever else may be said about the home missions of the Brethren, they clearly represented a major enterprise of the group. At the mid-century 108 missionaries served under the Home Mission Board in fourteen cities and forty-three rural communities. During the year reported, they conducted forty Sunday schools and approximately 150 regular services weekly with a total average attendance of 3700. In addition they held children's and young people's meetings, week-day Bible schools, and forty-four revivals with 1761 seekers at public altars. Church accessions from these endeavors, however, totaled only fifty-five for the year.[63]

Missions in Africa

Like home missions, the overseas missions of the Brethren in Christ expanded during the first half of the twentieth century. In Africa Henry P. Steigerwald and his successor, Henry H. Brubaker, followed in the footsteps of Jesse Engle to provide able administrative leadership for the growing program. The high esteem in which the brotherhood held these men is attested by the fact that each was retained as field superintendent for more than twenty years.[64]

By the mid-century the work begun in 1898 in the Matopo Hills had produced four more mission stations—Mtshabezi and Wanezi in Southern Rhodesia (now Rhodesia), and Macha and Sikalongo in Northern Rhodesia (now Zambia).[65] Two decades later fifty-five white missionaries and 177 national workers staffed missions in Rhodesia with 152 churches and a membership of 4,646. At the same time, twenty-nine white missionaries and seventy-three national workers staffed missions in Zambia with forty-nine churches and a membership of 1,290.[66]

Direct evangelism was always a major concern of the overseas missions, but the need of Africans for education and medical services made heavy demands upon the mission program. At first from their own resources, and later with government financial grants, the missions gradually provided elementary schools for their respective areas. Almost immediately after the Jesse Engle missionary party arrived on the site of Matopo Mission, they began a school for the local children.[67] A decade later one missionary and one native teacher instructed eighty children in the Matopo Church. Sixteen of the group boarded on the mission compound; the remainder came from the native villages for two of the three daily sessions.

Sindebele was the principal medium of instruction, except in arithmetic, in which English was used as much as possible. Reading instruction concentrated on mastery of the Bible in native dialect, a methodology which the Inspector of Schools from the Department of Education in Salisbury, Southern Rhodesia, regarded as "admittedly primitive" but relatively effective. When not in school the students received industrial training—farming, brickmaking, thatching, gardening, and household service for the boys; household service, kitchen work, gardening, and dairying for the girls. The Inspector noted: "I was favorably impressed with the obedience, alacrity and cheerfulness with which the students carry on their duties." He regretted, however, that only three students were enrolled for the formal study of English.[68]

By 1909 Mtshabezi also had a boarding school for boys and was beginning a girls' school which General Conference had encouraged for several years.[69] The latter had its own resident trustees who were responsible to the mission board in America. Its curriculum included all branches of a common education as well as practical work in "seamstressy, culinary and general house-work, gardening and plant culture, hygiene and sanitary habits . . . ." The life-style of the Brethren in the homeland thousands of miles away expressed itself in one policy—"Games of no kind shall be allowed."[70]

Here, as at Matopo, instruction was in Sindebele, with books in the kindred Zulu tongue. The Inspector of Schools found fully half of the students able to read from the Zulu Bible, some with fluency. In addition to reading, their studies included spelling, arithmetic, and singing as well as practical arts. The Inspector observed: "The general conduct of the work of this mission struck me very favorably; and the school is in the hands of a skilled and experienced teacher [Mrs. Harvey J. Frey], and may be expected to produce good results especially when further progress allows more attention to be given to the teaching of English."[71] On the basis of this report, the Department of Education gave both the boys' and girls' boarding school programs first-class standing.[72]

The growth of the school systems at the mission stations is illustrated by 1953 statistics from Mtshabezi. There were 270 girls in the boarding school and 278 boys and girls in the day school. Four outschools supervised from the station enrolled an additional 300 students. The teaching staff included two missionaries and twenty-four Africans.[73]

In addition to boarding and day schools at the mission compounds, circuits of outstation schools developed within areas assigned by the Rhodesian Government to the Brethren in Christ. The African men who staffed these schools received their training in a teacher-education program at Matopo Mission.[74] These outstation teachers, functioning under missionary supervision, often provided preaching ministries in addition to their educational duties. With the passage of time, however, other and usually older Africans tended to assume the preaching responsibilities.[75]

By 1950 the Brethren in Christ were responsible for scores of elementary schools. As the general educational level of the Africans rose, however, the missions gradually transferred these elementary schools to government control and concentrated on secondary education.[76]

The missions were well along with the development of an elementary school system before they developed professional medical facilities. Because of sheer necessity, some of the early missionaries, men and women, provided amateur medical services such as bandaging wounds, extracting teeth, and dispensing home remedies for illnesses.[77] Professional medical work began at Mtshabezi Mission in 1924 when two trained nurses, Martha Kauffman and Grace Book, arrived on the field.[78] Medical clinics staffed by professional nurses then became an important phase of the mission program, and farsighted mission supporters looked forward to the day when doctors would also be available.

Few Brethren in Christ entered medical schools prior to the mid-century so the mission board endeavored to start a fund to educate a missionary doctor. The immediate incentive for this project was an appeal from the India field for a woman physician; a candidate was available but could not finance her medical education.[79] The project made little headway until it was stimulated in 1937 by the donation of $100 to begin a "Medical

Student Preparation Fund."[80] By that time the mission board was striving to place a doctor on each the overseas mission fields.

This hope for mission doctors moved slowly toward fulfillment. In 1950 three prospective candidates were in medical school, but the most advanced was still a minimum of a year away from readiness for appointment. At that time Alvan Thuma, M.D., who had recently completed medical school, volunteered to staff the small hospital under construction at Mtshabezi Mission.[81] In the words of a veteran missionary, the arrival of the Thumas on the field a short time later was "A great day for the African work."[82]

Within a few years Northern Rhodesia also had a hospital at Macha Mission. Alvan Thuma, who had pioneered the development of the Mtshabezi hospital, went north in 1954 to open and staff the Macha hospital unit, while Virgina Kauffman, M.D., took over his medical responsibilities at Mtshabezi.[83] During the following decade, the Macha Hospital added a School of Nursing with Eva Byers, M.S., serving as the first directress; the first class of nurses graduated in 1969.[84]

The missionaries used both education and medical work as means to evangelize and extend their Christian witness. They always, however, stressed direct evangelism and church extension through preaching and village visitation. In recent years the sale of Christian literature through bookstores in both Rhodesia and Zambia has become another important medium for Christian witness. In 1969, the Matopo Book Centre in Bulawayo had fifteen full-time employees and did a gross business of $365,000, a figure which increased to $850,000 in June of 1976. Profits provide support for evangelists and Christian colporteurs to sell and distribute Christian literature.[85]

One of the great concerns of the missionaries was to see converts advance in Christian maturity and minister to their own people. As early as 1921 three unordained national overseers were appointed to supervise circuits of outstation churches. These men functioned administratively under the American missionary bishop.[86] Their ordination in 1944 as the first national ministers marked a milestone in the history of the work.[87]

Four years later the dream of a Bible school to train nationals as pastors and evangelists came true when the Wanezi Bible School opened its doors with Arthur Climenhaga as superintendent and Anna Engle as teacher. The sense of need for this program of pastoral training was so strongly felt on the field that preparations were made to begin it if only one student enrolled, but four did so.[88] The school, later known as Ekuphileni Bible

Institute relocated in 1969 at Mtshabezi.[89]

When Zambia and Rhodesia became independent in 1964 and 1965 respectively, the white-dominated government of the latter restricted the free movement of Zambians across the border. As a result the missions in Zambia launched the Choma Bible Institute which graduated its first three students in 1969.[90] Beginning in 1956, the work of the Bible institutes on the field was supplemented by sponsorship of a few African students for academic programs abroad, especially at Messiah College.[91]

As Africans developed their professional and administrative capacities, they gradually assumed more responsible roles in the schools and in the general work of the church. The elections of Philemon Kumalo in 1970 as the first African bishop in Rhodesia and of William Silungwe in 1976 as the first African bishop in Zambia dramatically illustrate how far this assumption of responsibility by Africans has progressed in recent years.[92]

The significance of these elections of Africans to the highest church offices can only be appreciated against the background of the long process of transition from paternalistic mission to independent church. For many years after the Brethren began work in Africa, the missionaries exercised administrative supervision of the church community.

For the first few years this supervision was exercised with each mission station functioning as an administrative unit under the mission board in America. Then, in 1906, "the brethren and sisters of the Brethren in Christ Church of Southern Rhodesia, South Africa, met in Joint Church Conference to consider the advancement of the work in South Africa."[93] This first African General Conference was similar to the councils with which the Brethren were familiar in the homeland.

For many years this conference, in which the missionaries played the predominant role, was administratively responsible through the mission board to the General Conference in America. The concept of an independent church meant that African and European would eventually have equal status in this African General Conference and that it would be fully autonomous, not only in the choice of a bishop but in all other matters relating to the African church.

After the mid-century, progress toward development of an independent church accelerated. Not only were Africans growing in competency for leadership, but the independence movements of the time created a climate which raised questions about the indefinite continuance of mission programs.

Under these circumstances, Arthur and David Climenhaga, who in turn filled the joint offices of Superintendent and Bishop of the Africa Mission field, gave strong administrative leadership to the movement for church autonomy.[94] In 1964 another milestone was passed when the Brethren in Christ Church in America transferred to the Brethren in Christ Church in Africa full responsibility for church organization, Christian nurture, and evangelism. Nationals and missionaries thereafter worked with and under each other as partners in the midst of the racial and political agitation which accompanied the independence movement on the African continent.[95]

In 1973 political tensions necessitated another major administrative change. By this date difficulties encountered in crossing the border between Rhodesia and Zambia made impracticable the continuation of a unified African General Conference. At the last such Conference in 1973, which celebrated the seventy-fifth anniversary of Brethren in Christ missions in Africa, the church in Zambia and the church in Rhodesia mutually agreed to separate administratively, with each functioning thereafter as a General Conference.[96]

Missions in India

When Henry Smith died of smallpox in 1924 after a decade of mission work in India, his leadership responsibilities passed to Amos Dick. Together with his wife, Dick gave a lifetime of service in that country and bore heavy burdens imposed upon the mission program by earthquakes, changing river courses, and anti-European political agitation. In 1935 General Conference authorized his ordination as bishop of the India mission field.[97]

By 1918 the Brethren in Christ had three mission stations in India—Saharsa, Madhipura, and Supaul.[98] In that country, caste, sophisticated religious systems, and indigenous customs made the task of Christian evangelism much more difficult than it was in Africa.

The missionaries baptized their first two converts in 1917.[99] After five years of ministry, the Saharsa and Madhipura stations reported two nationals in full church membership with four in inquirers' classes, while Supaul reported sixteen "adherents."[100] The following year ten new members joined the infant church.[101]

During those early years the missions developed basic patterns of Christian witness which characterized the work for decades. In addition to the program of religious services at the mission stations, the missionaries went into nearby villages holding Sunday schools for children and open-air meetings for adults. When Indian male helpers became available, they conducted many of the latter meetings. Female missionaries assisted by native "Bible women" found a special field for service among the village women from whose homes non-family males were rigidly excluded. From time to time missionary parties went into the interior, pitched a tent for living quarters, and ministered for a period of weeks in the surrounding villages. They also witnessed to the people at the markets and religious festivals.[102] In addition to this spoken witness, the missionaries distributed gospel literature.[103]

Like the missionaries in Africa, the workers in India promptly began to minister to the medical and material needs of the people. Early in the history of the work they supplied medicines to the sick, and medical dispensaries soon became a part of the program.[104] At special times such as Christmas, the missionaries gave cloth and grain to poor people. Famine conditions increased their concern for the well-being of the poor.[105] Eventually the missions became involved in large relief programs. In 1958, for example, the Saharsa station alone distributed weekly wheat rations to more than 300 people including fifteen to twenty lepers.[106]

By 1918 the missionaries were experimenting with institutional ministries. A boys' school launched at Saharsa proved short-lived because it had to employ Hindu teachers who were unreliable during the anti-white movement of the 1920s.[107] Orphanage work proved to be a more effective ministry. In 1919 the missionaries were caring for a motherless boy and looking forward hopefully to the founding of an orphanage.[108] This hope soon materialized with the launching of orphanages for both boys and girls, together with schools to educate them.[109] Young people who grew up in these institutions became the principal source of members for the church as it developed to the mid-century.[110] One year, for example, eighteen orphanage boys and girls accepted baptism.[111]

In addition to orphanage children, the missions sought to provide shelter and care for destitute widows, one of India's saddest problems.[112] This effort developed into a widows' home at Saharsa, which was filled to its limited capacity by 1939.[113]

For many years the medical work of the India Mission had only minimally trained personnel. Effie Rohrer, who accompanied the Henry Smiths, had the advantage of a prior course in practical nursing.[114] Several years later Ruth Byer arrived and took charge of the dispensary work at

Saharsa. After her second furlough in America and marriage to Allen Foote, she took a year of training in midwifery in London before returning with her husband for further service in India.[115] Other early missionaries with no medical training found themselves in situations which required them to make diagnoses, prescribe medicines, set broken bones, and perform minor operations.[116]

In 1938 the medical work advanced significantly when Leora Yoder, the first registerd nurse, arrived on the field. She had stopped en route in London for a year of specialized training in midwifery.[117] Statistical evidence of her impact upon the medical work is the total of 36,000 day-treatments given at the Saharsa dispensary in 1940.[118] Three years later the dispensary provided about 40,000 treatments, in addition to several hundred house calls.[119]

In 1953 General Conference approved George Paulus, M.D., as the first missionary doctor for India.[120] His arrival on the field the next year fulfilled a hope which had been kept alive for decades.[121] Within a few years the Madhipura Hospital served nearly 18,000 patients during a twelve-month period. Of these treatments 3,550 were for tuberculosis and 4,700 for leprosy, two of India's deadly scourges in which the hospital attempted a measure of specialization.[122]

Although the missionaries in India labored with great dedication, the work encountered many serious obstacles. Two days before the death of Henry Smith the meandering course of the Kosi River invaded the Madhipura Mission Compound and forced the missionaries to evacuate.[123] In 1934 a great earthquake shook Bihar Province and, during its eight minutes of duration, wrecked part of the Supaul station, damaged Saharsa, and practically demolished the mission rest home in Darjeeling.[124] Two years later the Kosi River, again rampaging and sometimes changing course as much as seventy-five feet per day, forced evacuation of the Supaul Mission Compound.[125]

In addition to natural disasters, the missionaries had to cope with the surge of anti-foreign sentiment generated by the home-rule movement in India. This reached a peak during World War II and at times placed the lives of the missionaries in jeopardy. Several times in 1942 mobs of nationalists, infiltrated by Communists, threatened to kill and loot at the mission compounds. Once a military police escort temporarily removed the missionaries from the stations until tensions subsided sufficiently for them to return.[126] In Madhipura a hostile mob forced Charles Engle to march to the marketplace. In the midst of the shouting, jeering crowd, he walked alone, wearing the white home-spun cap, symbol of the Congress party. One observer later said, "His face looked like the face of Jesus as he walked."[127] Surprisingly, when the procession reached the local headquarters of the Congress Party, its leaders rebuked the mob, apologized to Engle, and assured him safe passage back to the mission station.[128]

Concerning those experiences, one missionary later reminisced:

> "When I recall those terrible days, I think of the song, 'And are we yet alive.' During those days I often found myself singing, not 'Safely through another week,' but 'safely through another hour, God has brought us on our way.' They were indeed days of miracles. I purposely did not keep a diary, because I wanted to forget things. Others said they neither kept a diary nor could they forget. One thing stands out in my memory, though, God seemed to be very near—His presence real, and answered prayers every minute."[129]

In spite of all obstacles, the mission program forged ahead, and the church grew slowly. In 1939, when the Silver Jubilee of the India work was celebrated, 151 baptisms had been administered and the Christian community numbered 200.[130] Appropriately, the jubilee celebration took place at Saharsa where, in 1914, the second missionary party led by Henry Smith laid the foundations for a continuing mission under the auspices of the Brethren in Christ.[131]

Although the missionaries who celebrated in 1939 could not know it, the decade following the Silver Jubilee would provide opportunity for significant expansion of the church among the Santals, a people who were not locked into the caste system. This was an important consideration, because caste had always been a great hurdle for Indians who considered accepting Christianity. Conversion made them outcastes among their people; its traumatic implications cannot easily be grasped by the Western mind. These circumstances help to explain why most converts prior to the mid-century were from lower or depressed classes whose members had the least to lose by conversion.[132]

The mission to the Santals began in 1945. Charles Engle, stationed at Madhipura, contacted some Santals who had moved into Bihar Province.[133] They were an animistic people of uncertain origin who, although somewhat influenced by caste, were not bound by it as were the Hindu masses.[134] Some were already Christians when Engle encountered the group.[135] Soon after that initial encounter, he administered baptism to a young Santal man whose sister was also comtemplating baptism.[136]

With the passage of time, the number of Santal converts increased. Benjamin Mirandi, a Santal Christian, became an effective evangelist to his people. One one occasion, an observer wrote of him and his influence:

> Benjamin Mirandy [sic] looked like a prophet as he stood with a blanket draped over his spotlessly white garments. His eyes flashed for he was proclaiming in power the Word of God to his people. And it pleased the Lord to save those who believed. First came Jatha, a young man who was baptized in the stream near Khanua village. Soon he brought four others to the Lord and they too were baptized. Then two young women came. . . . Thus a new church has taken birth among the Santals.[137]

By the time these comments about Mirandi were written, a new mission, Banmankhi, had been located within easy access of the Santal villages, and it soon added a medical dispensary.[138] The resulting concentration of witness and service upon the Santal work largely accounts for the fourfold increase of the Indian church during the three decades following the Silver Jubilee. By 1968 the membership in Bihar Province numbered 820 divided among twenty-seven congregations. The evangelistic staff at that time included fourteen nationals and thirteen missionaries.[139]

In addition to expansion among the Santals, the mid-century witnessed the beginnings of new forms of mission endeavor. One was the opening of a bookshop and reading room at Saharsa. Within three months more than five thousand persons visited this room, and twelve enrolled in correspondence courses through its ministry.[140] In this period also Allen and Leoda Buckwalter engaged in a gospel radio ministry sponsored by the Evangelical Radio Fellowship of India, and Joseph and Marietta Smith were active in work among university students in Delhi.[141]

After the mid-century, the administrative leadership in India passed successively to William Hoke, Arthur Pye, and Harvey Sider. As in Africa, this was a time when the mission executives and their associate missionaries labored to nurture the emerging church.

In 1967, after study and preparation involving missionaries and Indian church leaders, a constitution for a Brethren in Christ Church in India went into effect. This constitution provided for a church chairmanship rotating among four regional superintendents. The first Indians to hold these offices were Hem K. Paul, Surendra N. Roy, Patros Hembrom, and Sohan Lal Bara. Indians were also replacing missionaries in other administrative posts.[142]

Early in the 1970s, Madhipura Christian Hospital affiliated with the Emmanuel Hospital Association, an evangelical board created to assure a continuing ministry of the fifteen Christian hospitals in India.[143]

As an autonomous church emerged in India, the church in America shifted to a supportive role. A few missionaries with specialized gifts and training participate in the life and work of the Indian church, and a limited amount of American funds goes to certain of its ministries.[144]

In 1974 the India Mission officially terminated and the Brethren in Christ Church in India became fully autonomous. At that time church membership had passed the 1,000 mark.[145]

The story of overseas missions of the Brethren in Christ includes cooperation with other church groups which have been loyal partners in these enterprises. For many years the United Zion and United Christian Churches liberally supported the mission program financially and, on occasion, with personnel. In 1930 a General Conference action acknowledged this support:

> Resolved, That this Conference hereby wishes to extend its thankfulness to God for these special leadings of [the] Holy Spirit in the hearts and minds of the members of the aforesaid religious bodies; and further more [sic] extends heartfelt appreciation for these efforts and hopes that this same spirit of cooperation may continue until . . . the dead in Christ shall rise, and those who are alive shall be caught up with the Lord . . . .[146]

Since the 1930s these churches have had representatives on the Brethren in Christ boards responsible for overseas mission work.[147]

Effects of Mission Advance

Like home missions, overseas missions were a dyamic spiritual influence in the life of the brotherhood during the first half of the twentieth century. Mission interest was not restricted to the mission boards; other church agencies became actively involved both at home and abroad. The Board for Young Peoples Work and its successor, the Board of Christian Education, sponsored youth projects which raised many thousands of dollars for mission enterprises. Organizations of the brotherhood—the Men's Fellowship and the Nurses' Association—promoted similar projects among their special constituencies.[148]

Beginning in the mid-1940s, women across the church joined in organizing prayer circles to pray for and promote missions. This grassroots movement produced the Women's Missionary Prayer Circle Committee functioning as an auxiliary of the two mission boards and their present unified successor, the Board for Missions.[149] The impact of this women's movement upon the advance of missionary work can hardly be overemphasized. Not only did the women who shared in it arouse mission interest on the part of large numbers of church members, but by their special projects and in other ways, they drew the attention of the church to the cutting edge of the mission enterprise. In the words of a mission executive: "They helped to make things happen."[150]

Women's sewing circles throughout the brotherhood have also contributed significantly to missions. Their work is now correlated on a general church level through the Women's Missionary Sewing Auxiliary functioning in conjunction with the Board for Missions. The two years preceding General Conference of 1974 illustrates the present scope of sewing circle activity. During this period the women completed major sewing projects for the Navajo Mission, Fellowship Chapel in New York, and Macha Hospital in Zambia. In addition they collected children's clothing and layettes for those who suffered loss in the 1972 Nicaraguan earthquake and supported various other missions and institutional enterprises.[151]

During the first half of the twentieth century, Brethren in Christ missions reflected a strong urge to spread the gospel, but they also served as a stabilizing influence during a difficult period in the life of the brotherhood.[152] Preceding chapters have shown that powerful forces were transforming traditionalism, embodying past Brethren commitments, into what many members later regarded as legalism. Evidences of this transformation included the attempt to legislate conformity to non-resistance, the prescription of specific church uniforms, and the precise definition of the doctrine of sanctification to eliminate the remaining flexibility in its interpretation.

The developments in this transition were divisive. Paralleling them, however, was the growing mission movement which was both noncontroversial and spiritually dynamic. Thus, at a time when the Brethren in Christ were preoccupied with internal difficulties and differences, and veering toward legalistic solutions to their problems, they had a unifying bond in their growing sense of responsibility to share the gospel. At the same time missions, joined with concern for local church outreach through the Sunday school and other forms of community evangelism, helped to prepare the brotherhood for the reappraisal of their identity which occurred during the second period of transition.

NOTES:

[1]T. A. Long, "The Mission Spirit," *Visitor,* XXIV (June 13, 1910), 7.

[2]*General Conference Minutes,* 1903, Article 44, p. 25.

[3]See Chapter IX.

[4]*General Conference Minutes,* 1920, Article 39, p. 47.

[5]*Ibid.,* 1937, Article 33, p. 51.

[6]See Chapter IX.

[7]*Handbook of Missions Home and Foreign of the Brethren in Christ Church,* 1918, pp. 69-70; *ibid.,* 1950, p. 33.

[8]*Ibid.,* 1919, p. 64; *General Conference Minutes,* 1919, Article 40, p. 52.

[9]*Handbook of Missions,* 1919, p. 54.

[10]Albert Engle interview, December 27, 1974.

[11]C. N. Hostetter, Jr., "Rural and City Missions," *Visitor, Fiftieth Anniversary,* p. 63.

[12]*Ibid.; General Conference Minutes,* 1937, Article 33, p. 51.

[13]*Handbook of Missions,* 1937, pp. 78-82.

[14]A. Bearss, "A New Field—Ontario," *Visitor,* VIII (March 15, 1895), 91.

[15]*Canadian Joint Council Minutes,* 1919, p. 45; Sider, "Brethren in Canada," p. 133.

[16]Sider, "Brethren in Canada," p. 134.

[17]*Canadian Joint Council Minutes,* 1931, p. 83.

[18]Sider, "Brethren in Canada," pp. 134-35.

[19]*General Conference Minutes,* 1931, Article 19, p. 32.

[20]C. N. Hostetter, Jr., Rural and City Missions," *Visitor, Fiftieth Anniversary,* p. 63.

[21]*General Conference Minutes,* 1921, Article 37, p. 48.

[22]E. Morris Sider, *Fire in the Mountains,* pp. 23-33; *Memoirs of Elder and Mrs. Harry Fink,* by S. Gerald Weaver (n.p., n.d.), p. 8.

[23]Sider, *Fire in the Mountains,* pp. 31-39; *Fink Memoirs,* pp. 9-10.

[24]S. Iola Dixon quoted by Sider, *Fire in the Mountains,* p. 41.

[25]Roscoe Ebersole and Harry Fink families, "Saxton, Pa.," *Visitor,* XLV (February 1, 1932), 43.

[26]*Ibid.* The *Fink Memoirs* place this total between 122 and 127.

[27]Roscoe Ebersole and Harry Fink families, "Saxton, Pa.," *Visitor,* XLV (February 1, 1932), 43.

[28]Sider, *Fire in the Mountains,* p. 47.

[29]*Ibid.,* p. 87.

[30]*Ibid.,* p. 88.

[31]*Fink Memoirs*, p. 10.

[32]Sider, *Fire in the Mountains*, pp. 43-44.

[33]*General Conference Minutes*, 1932, Article 22, pp. 38-39; *ibid.*, Article 23, p. 40.

[34]*Handbook of Missions*, 1940, p. 2.

[35]This sketch does not include all rural missions begun before 1940. Among them, for example, were Iron Springs, Pennsylvania, and North Star, Saskatchewan.

[36]See Chapter VIII.

[37]*Handbook of Missions*, 1919, p. 57.

[38]*General Conference Minutes*, 1945, Article 24, pp. 75, 84.

[39]*Ibid.*, 1955, Article 36, pp. 104, 111.

[40]*Ibid.*, 1887, Article 9, and 1889, Article 20.

[41]*Handbook of Missions*, 1946, p. 31.

[42]*Ibid.*, 1948, pp. 30-31; *ibid.*, 1949, p. 100.

[43]*Ibid.*, 1948, p. 31; *ibid.*, 1949, p. 100.

[44]*Ibid.*, 1948, p. 31; *ibid.*, 1949, p. 101. An adequate water supply was finally found in 1957. J. Wilmer Heisey interview, August 25, 1976.

[45]*Ibid.*, 1949, pp. 100-1.

[46]*Ibid.*, 1953, p. 90; *ibid.*, 1954, p. 24; *General Conference Minutes,*1952, Article 37, p. 98.

[47]*General Conference Minutes*, 1956, Article 29, p. 90.

[48]J. Wilmer Heisey interview, August 25, 1976.

[49]*General Conference Minutes*, 1897, Article 19, p. 7; *ibid.*, 1898, Article 19, p. 7; *ibid.*, 1899, Article 26, p. 11.

[50]*Ibid.*, 1925, Article 39, p. 72; *ibid.*, 1950, Article 31, p. 85. General Conference of 1928 distinguished between missions and mission pastorates. The latter depended upon their local fields or congregations for a significant measure of financial support; they could not solicit offerings from the church-at-large. Behind the mission pastorate concept was the hope of accelerating the development of financially self-sustaining churches. *Ibid.*, 1928, Article 6, pp. 10-11.

[51]*Ibid.*, 1912, Article 70, p. 181.

[52]*Ibid.*, 1914, Article 47, p. 86.

[53]*Ibid.*, 1912, Article 70, pp. 181.

[54]*Ibid.*, 1913, Article 16, p. 47; *ibid.*, 1918, Article 25, p. 35; *ibid.*, 1919, Article 41, p. 61; *ibid.*, 1920, Article 40, p. 51.

[55]*Ibid.*, 1921, Article 36, pp. 43-44.

[56]*Ibid.*, 1922, Article 37, p. 36.

[57]*Ibid.*, 1926, Article 41, p. 72; *ibid.*, 1937, Article 18, p. 34.

[58]C. N. Hostetter, Jr., "Rural and City Missions" *Visitor, Fiftieth Anniversary*, p. 47.

[59]*General Conference Minutes*, 1905, Article 32, p. 25.

[60]*Handbook of Missions*, 1919, p. 55; *ibid.*, 1934, p. 34; *ibid.*, 1937, p. 87; Albert Engle interview, January 25, 1975; Esther Ebersole interview, January 21, 1975. The present writer grew up near Buffalo, N. Y., and recalls vividly the strong emphasis which the Buffalo Mission placed upon Brethren distinctives in the 1930s.

[61]*General Conference Minutes*, 1932, Article 12, p. 38.

[62]*Ibid.*, 1914, Article 67, p. 86.

[63]*Ibid.*, 1950, Article 31, p. 85.

[64]*Ibid.*, 1908, Article 50, p. 53; *ibid.*, 1929, Article 52, p. 69; *ibid.*, 1951, Article 36, p. 75.

[65]*Handbook of Missions,* 1951, p. 6.

[66]*Ibid.,* 1969, pp. 9, 22.

[67]*General Conference Minutes,* 1899, Article 31, p. 13. Conference named Frances Davidson to superintend the school.

[68]"Report, J. B. Brady, Inspector of Schools, to the Director of Education, Salisbury, August 27, 1909," *Visitor, Fiftieth Anniversary,* pp. 50-51. Mary Brenaman Brechbill supplemented the industrial training data.

[69]*General Conference Minutes,* 1906, Article 55, p. 36.

[70]*Ibid.,* 1909, Article 82, pp. 100-103.

[71]"Report, L. H. Foggin, Inspector of Schools, to the Director of Education, Salisbury, August 24, 1909," *Visitor, Fiftieth Anniversary,* p. 51.

[72]"George Duthie, Director of Education, Salisbury, to The Rev. H. J. Frey, Mtshabezi Mission, Sept. 8, 1909," *Visitor, Fiftieth Anniversary,* p. 51.

[73]*Handbook of Missions,* 1954, p. 68.

[74]*General Conference Minutes,* 1909, Article 81, p. 100.

[75]Mary Brenaman Brechbill interview, January 23, 1975.

[76]Ruth Hunt Wolgemuth interview, January 23, 1975. For a detailed study of Brethren mission education in Rhodesia, see John Norman Hostetter, "Mission Education in a Changing Society: Brethren in Christ Mission Education in Southern Rhodesia, Africa, 1899-1959" (Ed. D. dissertation, State University of New York at Buffalo, 1967).

[77]Mary Brenaman Brechbill interview, May 26, 1976.

[78]*General Conference Minutes,* 1924, Article 19, p. 31; *Handbook of Missions,* 1969, p. 9.

[79]*General Conference Minutes,* 1933, Article 31, p. 39.

[80]*Ibid.,* 1937, Article 30, p. 47; *ibid.,* 1942, Article 17, pp. 36-37.

[81]*Ibid.,* 1950, Article 29, pp. 71-72.

[82]Mary Brenaman Brechbill interview, January 23, 1975.

[83]*Handbook of Missions,* 1955, pp. 13, 30.

[84]*Ibid.,* 1970, p. 15.

[85]*Ibid.,* pp. 8, 16; J. Wilmer Heisey interview, August 19, 1976.

[86]Engle, *et. al., There Is No Difference,* p. 183.

[87]H. H. & Grace Brubaker to C. N. Hostetter, August 15, 1944. C. N. Hostetter Papers.

[88]*Handbook of Missions,* 1949, pp. 52-53.

[89]*Ibid.,* 1970, p. 10.

[90]*Ibid.,* p. 17.

[91]Jonathan Muleya, the first African selected for this study abroad, enrolled in Messiah College in 1956. Data from College Registrar's Office.

[92]*Handbook of Missions,* 1970, p. 13; *Newsletter of Brethren in Christ Missions,* XVII (October 1976).

[93]*General Conference Minutes,* 1907, Article 40, p. 40.

[94]*Ibid.,* 1951, Article 36, p. 75; *ibid.,* 1959, Article 27, p. 91.

[95]*Ibid.,* 1964, Article 28, p. 112; *ibid.,* 1965, Article 27, p. 111.

[96]Information supplied by the Brethren in Christ Mission Office, Elizabethtown, Pennsylvania.

[97]*General Conference Minutes,* 1935, Article 31, p. 59.

[98]*Handbook of Missions,* 1918, p. 26.

[99]Amos D. M. Dick interview, February 15, 1975.

[100]*Handbook of Missions,* 1918, pp. 26, 33, 37.

[101]*Ibid.,* 1919, p. 23.

[102]*Ibid.,* 1918, p. 26; *ibid.,* 1919, pp. 21-22, 28-30; Amos D. M. Dick interview, February 15, 1975.

[103]*Handbook of Missions,* 1921, p. 31.

[104]Engle, *et. al., There Is No Difference,* p. 241; *Handbook of Missions,* 1919, p. 22.

[105]*Handbook of Missions,* 1919, p. 22; Engle, *et. al., There Is No Difference,* p. 244.

[106]*Handbook of Missions,* 1959, p. 34.

[107]*Ibid.,* 1919, p. 23; *ibid.,* 1928, pp. 33-34.

[108]*Ibid.,* 1919, p. 26.

[109]*Ibid.,* 1929, pp. 30-31. The orphanage schools gained official accredited standing.

[110]Amos D. M. Dick interview, February 15, 1975.

[111]*Handbook of Missions,* 1929, p. 31.

[112]*Ibid.,* 1928, p. 34.

[113]*Ibid.,* 1940, p. 110.

[114]Engle, *et. al., There Is No Difference,* p. 383.

[115]*Ibid.;* Hannah Foote to Miriam Bowers, March, 1975. Information transmitted by Miriam Bowers.

[116]Amos D. M. Dick interview, February 15, 1975.

[117]*General Conference Minutes,* 1938, Article 32, p. 45.

[118]*Handbook of Missions,* 1941, p. 55.

[119]*Ibid.,* 1944, p. 109.

[120]*General Conference Minutes,* 1953, Article 34, p. 79. George Paulus was a son of Brethren in Christ missionaries to India —George and Blanche Paulus.

[121]*Handbook of Missions,* 1955, p. 46.

[122]*Ibid.,* 1960, p. 61; *General Conference Minutes,* 1960, Article 25, p. 73.

[123]*Handbook of Missions,* 1925, p. 32; Engle, *et. al., There Is No Difference,* p. 246.

[124]*Handbook of Missions,* 1934, pp. 81-82, 84, 87-88.

[125]*Ibid.,* 1939, pp. 50-52.

[126]Amos D. M. Dick interview, February 15, 1975.

[127]Engle, *et. al., There Is No Difference,* p. 258.

[128]*Ibid.*

[129]Quoted in *ibid.,* p. 259.

[130]Amos D. M. Dick interview, February 15, 1975.

[131]*Handbook of Missions,* 1940, p. 109.

[132]*Ibid.,* 1944, p. 101.

[133]*Ibid.,* p. 107.

[134]Amos D. M. Dick interview, February 15, 1975.

[135]*Handbook of Missions,* 1945, p. 56.

[136]*Ibid.,* 1946, p. 128.

[137]*Ibid.,* 1951, p. 65.

[138]*Ibid.*

[139]*Ibid.,* 1969, p. 29.

[140]*Ibid.,* 1962, p. 63.

[141]*Ibid.*, 1960, p. 62; *ibid.*, 1969, pp. 29-34.

[142]*Brethren in Christ Missions Yearbook* (Elizabethtown, Pa.: Brethren in Christ Missions, 1971), p. 7; *Missions Photo Album,* 1975-1976 (Elizabethtown, Pa.: Brethren in Christ Missions, 1976), pp. A-13, 14.

[143]*Missions Yearbook,* 1971, p. 7; J. Earl Musser interview, August 20, 1976.

[144]J. Wilmer Heisey, "Brethren in Christ Missions/An Overview," *Missions Yearbook,* 1974, p. 74.

[145]*Ibid.*

[146]*General Conference Minutes,* 1930, Article 17, pp. 36-37.

[147]*Ibid.*, 1937, Article 30, p. 46. The original Foreign Mission Board became the Board for World Missions in 1960 and later, after merger with the Board for Home Missions and Extension and the Peace, Relief and Service Committee, it became the Board for Missions.

[148]The Brethren in Christ Men's Fellowship is an organization of laymen which seeks in various ways to facilitate the witness and program of the brotherhood. It is coordinated by an official General Conference commission amenable to the Board of Bishops. The Brethren in Christ Nurses' Association is an unofficial organization functioning with the goodwill of Conference to promote the medical programs of the church.

[149]*General Conference Minutes,* 1947, Article 11, p. 32.

[150]J. Wilmer Heisey interview, August 13, 1976.

[151]*General Conference Minutes,* 1974, Article 22, p. 98.

[152]During the period 1878-1966, 711 persons served under General Conference appointment in Home Mission ministries. During the period 1897-1966, 243 persons served overseas under General Conference appointment. *Handbook of Missions,* 1967, pp. 101-20.

Part Four

The
Second Period of Transition

1950 — 1975

XIX

The Quest for a
New Brethren in Christ Identity

As the Brethren in Christ passed the mid-century, they were in the preliminary stage of a second period of transition which significantly changed their life-style. By the end of the 1950s, they had completed the major transitional changes, although many implications of these changes continued to unfold thereafter.

This second period of transition differed in two respects from the first which began about 1880. The changes of the earlier period came gradually during approximately thirty years (1880-1910); only the perspective of history reveals their cumulative impact as a force altering the life of the brotherhood. In the second place, the men and women who advocated those changes did not perceive them as directed toward the creation of a new group identity; rather, they saw them as means to vitalize and strengthen the historic understanding which the Brethren had of themselves and their mission in the world. In contrast, the changes of the second period of transition came quickly and abruptly, and they were, at least for some members, a self-conscious attempt to alter the nature of the Brethren movement as it had developed in the 1930s and 1940s.

These circumstances further explain why the preceding years from 1910 to 1950 are best understood as a period of adjustment. During that time the Brethren labored to integrate old and new values without intending to disrupt the essence of their historic faith and life-style. By the 1950s, however, some of them were beginning to believe that only a radical break with the past could give their movement a new and viable identity. The two remaining chapters are the story of the quest for that identity.

New Ecumenical Relationships

A sense of uneasiness and uncertainty had begun to permeate the ranks of the Brethren as they approached the mid-century. Some of them wondered why their message made so little impact upon communities contacted through their congregations. Church membership statistics, except for a brief upward spurt in the late 1930s, plateaued and gave no evidence of vitality; whatever the members in established churches had, few non-members seemed to want it. Furthermore, although the realization dawned slowly because of offsetting membership gains in home missions, leaders eventually perceived that their message and life-style were not convincing to their own children, many of whom were repudiating their parents' faith.

These circumstances caused growing concern. Many members recalled the decade of the 1930s when the brotherhood attempted legislative reinforcement of its historic distinctives, as well as the following decade when indoctrination received major attention. They were also aware of the vigorous revivalism, Sunday school and youth work, holiness preaching, and mission emphasis of the several decades preceding the mid-century. Yet, in spite of all this, the brotherhood appeared to be relatively unsuccessful both in reaching the "lost" and retaining the "saved."

As feelings of uncertainty about the viability of the Brethren message grew, there was no unanimity as to what should be done to remedy the situation. Many members, indeed, were unaware of an approaching identity crisis. They appeared secure in their understanding of the church and its mission. If there was need to spur the advance of their movement, the methodologies of the past would be adequate if properly utilized.

On the other hand, an increasing number of members began to speculate that a change in the group's self-image or identity might be needed. Perhaps, some thought, a solution to the problem could be found if the brotherhood moved closer to the main stream of contemporary evangelicalism represented by the National Association of Evangelicals and the National Holiness Association. General Conference of 1947 decided to explore this possibility and named a committee to study the "desirability and feasibility" of affiliating with these organizations.[1]

In a 1948 preliminary report, the committee summarized the advantages of such affiliations. These included strengthening the witness of both the Brethren in Christ and the national associations in matters of common belief and concern, making the Brethren more widely known, and making available to them new sources of spiritual inspiration and fellowship.[2]

The report omitted any direct reference to possible disadvantages of the proposed relationships and specifically stated that neither of the national associations "would necessarily detract from our identity as Brethren in Christ, nor from our highly cherished and distinctive full-Bible testimony and practices, . . ."[3] What the committee intended by inserting "necessarily" in this report is a matter of conjecture. That word is the only hint that the affiliations under study might have had potential to alter the distinctives and identity of the Brethren.

These recommendations to affiliate with the NAE and NHA were spread on the minutes of General Conference for a year of study. Members were urged to read the literature of the two organizations, especially *United Evangelical Action* published by the NAE, and to attend their conventions.[4]

In 1949 General Conference approved the affiliation of the Brethren in Christ with NAE. By that time, however, misgivings were surfacing—"a conscientious and worthy difference of opinion on the matter." Surprisingly, the opposition concentrated especially on the NHA, and Conference postponed a final vote on that affiliation until 1950, at which time it, too, was approved.[5]

One of the objections to affiliation with these national organizations is self-evident. The Brethren in Christ had never become officially involved with the mainstream evangelical and holiness movements. These movements were uncommitted to the historic Brethren understanding of the church as a visible community with a common faith and life-style expressed in distinctives such as nonresistance, nonconformity in dress, the prayer veiling, and feet washing. Except for limited collaboration with the Quakers during World War I, and with Mennonites through the Mennonite Central Committee since World War II, the group had little precedent for ecumenical relationships. Some members, therefore, perceived the prospect of formal affiliation with "worldly" evangelical and holiness churches to be a compromise of the group's historic identity. What, they wondered, could such relationships add to a church with an evangelical and holiness message plus commitment to the "all things" which Christ called his followers to observe?

There was, however, a new leaven at work causing other members to see the NAE and NHA affiliations in quite a different light. Charlie B. Byers, the first official representative to the NAE, came home impressed by the "rich fellowship of these many brethren drawn from many Evangelical

Denominations." He reported that much stress was put on prayer and "was compelled to believe that God is using this organization to accomplish that which is impossible for any one particular denomination to do, especially in the field of missions, radio, and Christian education."[6]

Similarly, Ohmer U. Herr, the first official representative to the NHA, reported that convention to have been "an occasion very definitely blessed of the Lord." He noted with approval that the association was launching "an active program of evangelism for holiness with increased enthusiasm and sacrificing Spirit-filled personnel."[7]

Some years later another leader noted that in the NAE Bible-believing and Bible-loving churches joined hands for fellowship and service. Their united effort had helped to keep the channels of the air open for gospel broadcasting, aided mission boards to overcome obstacles to their work, and caused the Christian testimony against the evils of the day to be "spoken more clearly and heard more widely because of a united voice." He then described the NAE impact upon the grassroots life of the Brethren. "For the Brethren in Christ Church this fellowship has helped to fire the hearts of bishops, ministers and laymen, to make our Sunday schools more effective, to improve the functioning of our church schools and college and to fan and fuel the flame for evangelism and personal witnessing."[8]

This was a perceptive judgment. More and more Brethren were coming under direct and indirect influences flowing from the NAE and NHA. Some served as members of commissions of the national associations; others worked in or through associated agencies such as the National Sunday School Association and the Evangelical Foreign Mission Association. A number rose to high office; for example, Henry Ginder became president of the NHA and Charlie Byers secretary. Several Brethren leaders served as chairman of NAE commissions: Arthur Climenhaga, Theology; Alvin Burkholder, Stewardship; and Christian Hostetter, Jr., World Relief.

Office holding was but one way through which the Brethren absorbed the influences of the NAE and NHA. Members who attended meetings and conventions of these organizations were impressed by the messages given and also found themselves in informal contact with leaders from a wide variety of evangelical and holiness denominations. In these settings they discovered common interests and areas of agreement and learned about the spiritual progress and problems of heretofore unfamiliar churches. Leaders from various evangelical and holiness groups also appeared on Brethren in Christ platforms at General Conference, conventions, and holiness camps, where their charisma, spiritual zeal, and viewpoints impressed many members who had never attended NAE and NHA meetings. As a result of this combination of circumstances, the misgivings about affiliations with these organizations receded into the background.

In recent years misgivings about the NAE relationship have revived because of the way that organization integrates evangelicalism with United States nationalism and politics. The Canadian Brethren, for example, cannot feel spiritually at home in the atmosphere created by such integration. Canadian evangelicalism finds its ecumenical expression in the Evangelical Fellowship of Canada, with which the Canadian Conference of the Brethren in Christ identifies.[9]

An Unexpected Catalyst for Change

In a way that could not have been foreseen, the 1950 NAE convention in Indianapolis became a catalyst for change in the life of the brotherhood. A group of Brethren leaders attending the convention and lodging in the same hotel assembled one evening in a hotel bedroom suite. The spiritual enthusiam and success orientation of the convention had moved them deeply. Although their thoughts were unknown to each other prior to this unplanned meeting, they were individually comparing what they had seen and heard with their perceptions of the spirit and program of their own movement, and the comparison depressed them. Seated informally on chairs, beds, and floor, men who had labored together for many years on behalf of the Brethren in Christ opened their hearts to each other and shared pent-up frustrations and doubts about the outcomes of their efforts.[10]

No one had anticipated this unusual situation. One participant described the meeting as "simply a get-together . . . after the evening service. Nothing was planned. We just . . . got to talking." On into the night and the early hours of the next day, the men talked, wept, and prayed. They were not critical of nor bitter about the brotherhood but rather deeply disturbed about its apparent lack of meaningful impact and progress.

The following statements illuminate the concerns and atmosphere of the meeting. One participant noted:

> In this informal setting the whole program of the Church was discussed, particularly with emphasis on future progress, growth and spiritual life. There were deep emotional feelings expressed with tears on the part of some of the men. One statement I recall was that our brotherhood was known by some other groups as a legalistic group, which shocked some of us. Many aspects were discussed, including youth work, a stronger pastoral leadership, the possibility of a . . . [better] supported ministry and a greater evangelistic and outreach emphasis.

Another recalled his impressions:

> There was unanimity within the group that we had come into legal bondage. Now of course you've got to take the setting to get the impact of that. We were with a group of evangelicals. For the first time in most of our lives, we began to fellowship with that type of people . . . in a setting where we felt the velocity of it [the evangelical movement] . . . . For once the feeling really took hold . . . that we had been feeling almost wrongly about the outside, and we found that they had a peculiar liberty and an opportunity for ministry that we did not have. We had closed the door on ourselves. . . . We had followed a course of procedure that had almost ended in an isolated ministry. Now how could we get out of it?
>
> I remember clearly the sobbing and praying that went on there between twelve and one o'clock at night. . . . It wasn't a case of finding fault with the Brethren in Christ Church. . . . I think I am safe in saying that there wasn't a degree of antagonism there; it was a case of finding a . . . ministry.

Although the discussion ranged widely, it focused sharply upon two issues. One was the tradition of a self-supporting ministry with its attendant limitations. Pastors who had to give much of their time to earning a living could not devote their best energies to their pastorates. The consensus of the group was that men should be encouraged to enter the ministry on the assumption that they would be provided with financial support adequate to permit full-time pastoral service.

A second major problem was that of assimilating converts into the life of the brotherhood. The men who opened their hearts to each other at Indianapolis were deeply concerned about the lack of church growth, and especially about the many youth from Brethren homes who were forsaking their parents' faith. As one leader noted: "The Church was losing them left and right."

The group perceived these two problems as interrelated. A strengthened pastoral system would only produce frustration if church rules and regulations created a setting in which converts from non-Brethren backgrounds could not be assimilated into congregational life.

This Indianapolis meeting was one of the first times that such a group of leaders sat down together simply to share their inmost feelings with one another. Precisely because the meeting was unplanned and unofficial, those who participated achieved an unusual degree of openness. As one member remarked: "We almost scared ourselves."

While the discussion produced no grand strategy for dealing with the problems of church life, the realization that a group of leaders had common frustrations and concerns was one factor helping to pave the way for a major transition in the life of the Brethren. That transition would have eventually come in any event, but the Indianapolis meeting helped to give it both impetus and form. Inevitably, the men who shared in that meeting in the context of vibrant, articulate, contemporary evangelicalism entered the period of transition with mainline evangelical church models and life-styles impressed upon their minds.

General Conference and a Decade of Change

When the Brethren assembled in General Conference at the mid-century, they stood on the threshold of an unprecedented period of change.[11] By the close of that decade, they had officially abandoned or modified many aspects of their historic attitudes and practices. This process, which involved continual and often tense confrontation between traditional and progressive points of view, was exceedingly painful.[12] How they managed to complete it without serious schism would be a fascinating problem for a study of group dynamics.

There is no way to determine how many members of the General Conference which convened in 1950 shared the concerns which had surfaced spontaneously among a few leaders at Indianapolis. What is clear, however, is that those leaders played an active role in directing the attention of Conference to those concerns.

In the first place, John N. Hostetter, who had been in the Indianapolis meeting, focused the broad issues in his Conference sermon, "The Holy Ghost and Us." On the basis of consultation with a population expert, he concluded that during the twenty years from 1929 to 1949 the growth rate of the Brethren in the United States and Canada reflected the actual loss of 1,000 youth born into their homes. During the same two decades, giving for home and foreign missions and the operational budgets of educational institutions increased nearly three hundred per cent. In comparing these data, Hostetter observed that the group seemed to know "better how to handle dollars than to deal with the souls of men or women." He also suggested that the Brethren may have tended to assume that unlikeness to others constituted their testimony and witness, and that they accordingly failed to speak as fervently and warmly of the person of the Lord Jesus as they should have.[13]

This was a startling suggestion to make to a people who had held both their historic heritage and evangelism in high regard, but Hostetter was not finished. He had recently reviewed a book on the smaller denominations in America. Expecting to find the Brethren in Christ listed with the holiness bodies, he was amazed to discover them obscurely placed among the legalistic groups.[14] Then he pressed home the point of legalism versus spirituality:

> It might be something for us to think about that those observing us from without look upon us as being of the legal type. This fact must be remembered . . . it requires less sacrifice to be legal than to be spiritual.
>
> Brethren and sisters in the Lord, the time is short. Men and women, eternity bound souls are rushing toward the great abyss that lands them in eternity.

Hostetter's inferences were clear. It was high time, he believed, for the Brethren to substitute aggressive spiritual concern and evangelism for preoccupation with what at least some members perceived to be unproductive legalism. His message expressed the spirit of what one writer has called "the spiritual revolution" in the Brethren movement.[15] The Conference sermon of 1950 did not create the revolution; that was already underway in the hearts and minds of at least some members. The sermon did, however, place the theme of that revolution clearly before the brotherhood.

A second illustration reflecting concerns expressed at the Indianapolis meeting was a recommendation from the General Executive Board to create a pastoral stationing committee. Although as early as 1940 General Conference authorized congregations to shift from the multiple ministry to individual pastors, there was no church agency to promote and assist the transition.[16]

To meet this need the Conference of 1950 created a Committee on Pastoral Stationing whose duty it was "to seek out, encourage and, on request from congregations or district boards, station men, called of God and approved by the church; . . ." Furthermore, while the 1940 Conference action had stressed that no pastoral service should be "on a commercialized or professionalized basis," the 1950 plan called for financial support needed to enable pastors to give "the time, care, and attention, deemed advisable to extend the borders, and pastor the flocks, even to full time when necessary."[17]

The context of the latter action makes clear that the day of the full-time, salaried pastor was at hand. In a highly competitive society, and with expanding church programs, the Brethren concluded that they could not carry on with pastoral arrangements designed for an age that was rapidly passing.

General Conference might have instituted the new pastoral plan at that time had there been no prior meeting of church leaders at Indianapolis; there was, however, a direct personal link between that meeting and the pastoral plan. Charlie Byers, one of the men who had met at Indianapolis, was assistant chairman of the General Executive Board which brought the new pastoral recommendations, and he sponsored them on the floor.[18] Byers also became chairman of the new Pastoral Stationing Committee of which John Hostetter served as secretary.[19]

A third illustration of how the kinds of concerns expressed at Indianapolis focused in the life of the Brethren was the formation of an agency which came to be known as the "Church Review and Study Committee." Its assignment was to study the "state, function, and work of the general church" and to report findings and recommendations to General Conference.[20] Half of its twelve members had been in the Indianapolis hotel-room meeting.[21] Throughout the decade of the 1950s, this committee led the brotherhood through sweeping changes in attitudes and life-style.

Christian Hostetter, Jr., had the task of bringing the 1951 General Conference sermon. As a member of the Church Review and Study Committee, he was well aware of the pending debate about the merits of Brethren traditionalism. In four days of meetings, the committee had discussed the positions of the brotherhood on Christian apparel, the prayer veiling, baptism, life insurance, the use of musical instruments, wedding ceremonies, and various other matters.[22]

This Conference, to which the Church Review and Study Committee would also bring its first report and recommendations, assembled at the Free Methodist Camp Ground in Manhattan, Kansas. Even the natural elements created an atmosphere of uneasiness and stress. Heavy rains accompanied by lightning muddied the ground underfoot and raised an adjacent river to flood stage, threatening to inundate the campsite.[23]

In attempting to set the tone for the Conference, Hostetter strongly supported improved pastoral service with adequate financial support and also warned the assembly against the dangers of ritualism, lukewarmness, and traditionalism. Significantly, he perceived traditionalism to be the principal peril, noting that the New Testament church had great difficulty freeing itself from tradition in the form of circumcision. He closed his message with a ringing call to spirituality and evangelism:

> Our basic problem is spiritual. The Church must win more men to Christ. We must lead our people in spirituality, service and stewardship. We must challenge them to a plane of living where "they count not their lives dear unto themselves." If we lead them deep enough with God, they, like Paul, will not covet silver or gold, but will labor, share and give for the Master.[24]

The initial report of the Church Review and study Committee postponed some delicate and debatable issues, but its ten recommendations did include a number which were highly controversial.[25] Probably by design, the committee first presented a noncontroversial proposal entitled "Challenge to a New Passion for Evangelism." This recommendation struck a note agreeable to all and psychologically united the Conference body. The following excerpt from its preface is one of many evidences of the growing concern of the Brethren for spiritual renewal and more forceful evangelism:

> From many parts of the world come evidences of the rustlings of revival. Men and women are on their faces in heart searching intercessory prayer claiming the promises of the Word. . . .
>
> God is answering. The church is being revived. Believers are being impassioned for service. . . .
>
> Will we not as a church rise to meet the challenge? We believe the return of our Lord is near. We want to see our sons and daughters saved and dedicated to His service. We want to see our Sunday School boys and girls in the fold. Our neighbors and friends are too precious to be lost. . . . To each of us personally comes the question, what am I doing?

After this moving introduction, Conference approved a comprehensive plan for personal and congregational evangelism.

The euphoric feelings created by emphasis upon spirituality and evangelism quickly evaporated when the committee next proposed to delete the description of distinctive church uniforms from the doctrinal literature of the brotherhood and to introduce more flexibility in the wearing of the prayer veiling.[26] Anticipating serious conservative reaction to these proposals, the committee had named Henry Ginder, bishop of Rapho District, one of the most conservative districts in Pennsylvania, to sponsor them.

As the Conference body grasped the implications of the sponsorship, the atmosphere on the floor became tense. When Bishop Ginder was asked point-blank whether passage of the recommendation would eliminate prescribed church uniforms, he replied simply and clearly: "Yes, if the recommendation passes, there will be no prescribed uniforms."[27]

The debate on this question was undoubtedly one of the most dramatic and significant in Brethren history. Strong and sometimes emotional speeches were made for and against the recommendation. As can easily happen in debates which stir deep emotions, some speeches exposed elements of inconsistency, which prompted one veteran churchman to remark dryly: "I see that the conservatives are conservative in spots and that the liberals are liberal in spots."[28]

When the debate concluded, Conference was unwilling to go as far as the recommendation on a church uniform proposed. It accordingly recommitted the question for further study and thus made clear that the committee should bring a more conservative report the following year.

Although the report the following year strongly emphasized non-conformist principles, it was, in fact, a compromise which indicated that the committee was unshaken in its resolve to press for a more flexible doctrine of Christian apparel. While recognizing that the cape dress for women and the erect collar for men continued "to have value," the report went only so far as to "encourage" the wearing of church uniforms. It proposed deletion, furthermore, of the 1937 doctrinal statement which described the necktie as a form of apparel inconsistent with "the principles of separation and non-conformity as taught in the Word of God."[29]

The ensuing debate indicated that many members of Conference still thought the report too liberal. As one debater remarked, however, it probably divided the brotherhood as little as possible under the circumstances, and his viewpoint prevailed.[30] The resulting Conference action was so crucial in providing the basis upon which the Brethren would learn to live together in spite of their differences about nonconformity that its substance is reproduced in full. The committee offered the following rationale for its proposals:

> The Brethren in Christ Church has periodically given instructions and guidance to her constituents in regard to Christian apparel in order to present a consistent and effective testimony of Christ to the world.
>
> We feel there is a common desire on the part of our Church to continue to uphold the Biblical teachings of modest apparel, since the Word of God sets forth abiding principles of modesty, simplicity, and non-conformity.
>
> Some of the practice [sic] of the Church in the past have given an effective testimony, and have helped to preserve these principles in a practical interpretation, such as the wearing of the cape for the sisters, and suits with the erect collar for the brethren, which continue to have value and are worthy of encouragement.
>
> We are, however, experiencing the inevitable transition from a rural to an urban type of life with its industrial and professional responsibilities; necessitating flexibility in the interpretation and practices of our standards.

Against the background of this rationale, General Conference deleted the description of church uniforms from its doctrinal literature and substituted the following:

> Positive teaching is given in God's Word against the wearing of jewelry. (1 Tim. 2:9, 1 Peter 3:3) Christians are enjoined not to wear gold or pearls or that which is termed costly array. Gaudy and fashionable articles of clothing that are worn for adornment violate the teaching of simplicity and separation.
>
> The Word of God clearly teaches that women should have long hair. (1 Cor. 11:15) As defined in Holy Writ, it is a shame for a woman to be shorn (1 Cor. 11:6). The wearing of a devotional veil by Christian women is taught in 1 Cor. 11:5-6. The significance and meaning of the head covering should not be overlooked when arranging the hair. The use of artificial means to beautify the face is not the true method to attain real beauty, and such practices are not consistent with simplicity and separation. Christian women should wear garments of plain materials and quiet patterns which modestly cover the body.
>
> Therefore, to promote adherence to the teachings of the Holy Scriptures on simplicity and modesty we encourage the wearing of the cape for the sisters and the suits with the erect collar for the brethren.[31]

Other 1951 proposals of the Church Review and Study Committee related to wedding ceremonies. Simple Brethren church buildings without musical instruments were having difficulty competing with more aesthetic churches of other groups as settings for the weddings of the youth of the brotherhood. The committee accordingly cautioned against "the increasing tendency toward elaborate weddings" and urged that the ceremonies be performed in the churches of the brotherhood. It also recommended that members neither give nor wear wedding rings and that ministers avoid performing marriages in which ring ceremonies had to be used.[32]

These particular proposals indicate that the Church Review and Study Committee was not always on the side of change. In this instance it endeavored to reinforce the traditional disapproval of elaborate weddings and the wedding ring which the Brethren had always classified as jewelry condemned by the New Testament.

Possibly to the surprise of General Conference, the injunction against ministers using ring ceremonies in performing marriages encountered difficulty. Various ministers frankly acknowledged that they used such ceremonies, or at least were party to them, when marrying non-members of the Brethren in Christ Church. In view of this revelation Conference referred the wedding proposals back to the committee for further study.

When the wedding question returned to the floor of Conference in 1952, the only significant change in the substance of the committee recommendations was a milder reference to ring ceremonies. Instead of the blunt statement of 1951 that ministers should "not perform" ring ceremonies, they were now merely "urged to use" rituals without such ceremonies. Like the compromise on Christian apparel, this change introduced ambiguity which permitted a considerable measure of individual discretion.

When General Conference approved two other proposals in the 1951 report of the Church Review and Study Committee, it terminated debates which had been in progress for three-quarters of a century. One of these recommendations made life insurance a matter of individual conscience for officials as well as laymen; the other permitted districts, congregations, and church institutions to exercise local option in the use of musical instruments in worship.[33]

An innovative proposal in 1951 was a plan of associate membership for certain persons, such as those divorced and remarried, who could not immediately meet full membership requirements. The committee urged adoption of the plan as an intermediate step in bringing converts into the brotherhood. Its report spelled out in detail both the requirements and privileges of associate membership. Critics of the plan stressed the dangers of a double standard of membership, but Conference supported the committee.[34]

When General Conference convened in 1953, the Church Review and Study Committee was ready with new and difficult issues. One was a proposal to modify the requirement of rebaptism for membership applicants who had been baptized by forms of believer's baptism other than trine immersion.[35] Like plain dress, such rebaptism was often a stumbling block for individuals who might otherwise have united with the Brethren. This requirement for rebaptism implied that any form of believer's baptism other than trine immersion was not a valid public testimony to a personal experience of salvation, that is, to a profession of mature, personal faith in Christ. For some Christian men and women satisfied with their previous baptisms, the requirement of rebaptism would violate their sense of personal integrity.

The committee sought to make clear that its proposals did not compromise on the importance of water baptism for converted individuals nor question trine immersion as the most appropriate mode of baptism. Thus far the report rested solidly upon the historic faith, but then it moved to highly controversial ground with the following recommendation: ". . . that the Brethren in Christ Church accept into membership, upon the basis of their testimony, Christians who have been previously baptized by a mode of believer's baptism other than trine immersion."[36]

After much debate Conference adopted the recommendation, but the issue was not yet settled; Ohio-Kentucky Joint Council brought up the question again in 1954. The council petition did not challenge the substance of the previous decision but proposed to amend its wording by adding qualifying clauses waiving the requirement for rebaptism only if such rebaptism violated the personal conscience of the membership applicant.[37]

This proposal opened the way for another vigorous debate. Some members of Conference still objected to any mode of baptism which did not involve immersion; they could not, in other words, accept sprinkling or pouring. One debater even saw the possibility of the Brethren accepting infant baptism. As the debate proceeded, Conference became so confused about the meaning of believer's baptism that it named a committee to study this question and report back the following year; it also passed the amendment proposed by Ohio-Kentucky Joint Council.[38]

In 1955, when the referral committee defined believer's baptism as that administered to the individual "after . . . he himself has exercised and professed faith in Christ as his personal Saviour," Conference was satisfied.[39] Thereafter persons baptized by any mode of believer's baptism could unite with the brotherhood without rebaptism if such rebaptism violated their consciences. Conference officially eliminated this conscientious qualification in 1974.[40]

By the mid-1950s the Church Review and Study Committee had led the brotherhood through a major reappraisal of basic historic positions on matters such as nonconformity, the use of musical instruments, life insurance, and baptism. It had also begun to work on one of the thorniest issues of all—a new pastoral and administrative system. In this task it was assisted by a Committee on Executive Administration created in 1953.[41]

These committees reported jointly to Conference in 1954 and outlined proposed duties for future pastors and bishops. Long range goals were: substitution of full-time pastors for the traditional multiple-ministry, a decrease in the number of bishops, and vitalization of the offices of both pastors and bishops. The direction in which Conference would ultimately go was revealed by its adoption of the following principles:

> . . . that every bishop plan to develop pastoral leadership in the pastor of each congregation under his supervision, according to the full provision of the aforementioned duties of pastors, . . .
>
> . . . that bishops seek to arrange for the support of full time pastors, . . .
>
> . . . that the brethren now serving as bishops be alerted to the possibilities of serving as pastors or evangelists, or in other fields of Christian service, as and when their pastors assume leadership to the point of proper care of their congregations. . . .
>
> . . . that for the purpose of achieving our goals, this General Conference declare a moratorium on the election of bishops. . . .
>
> . . . that the General Conference authorize the Committee on Executive Administriation to make a study relative to decreasing the number of church districts, including also the methods by which the bishops shall be chosen and their duties apportioned, and that they report to the Church Review and Study Committee for joint-report to the Conference of 1955.

A related recommendation directed the General Executive Board to call a convention of bishops "for the purpose of better understanding and cooperation in achieving these objectives."[42]

At the time of the adoption of these resolutions, approximately twenty-five active bishops served more than thirty organized districts in the United States and Canada.[43] Obviously, decreasing the number of bishops and combining districts would involve a great deal of personal and regional stress. Recognizing this and many other complications involved in such drastic changes, Conference decided that bishoprics should not be changed before 1957.[44]

By 1956 the joint committees were ready with a detailed plan of administration based upon a study of the administrative structures of numerous evangelical and holiness churches. In addition to proposals for the duties of pastors, bishops, and local church boards, the recommendations called for full-time bishops with five-year terms. A special Bishops' Nominating Committee would select these bishops, subject to confirmation by General Conference. There would be six regional conferences—Atlantic, Allegheny, Canadian, Central, Midwest, Pacific—each served by a bishop. Under the oversight of their bishops, congregations would be recognized as self-governing units subject only to the rulings of General Conference. A new Board of Administration would have general oversight of the governmental phases of church life.[45]

Such sweeping modifications of a church governance pattern which had evolved over a period of approximately 175 years had breath-taking implications. Not surprisingly, some members feared that the new plan might concentrate power in too few hands and thus undermine the democratic procedures to which they were accustomed.[46] But Conference as a whole was ready for the change and voted for its immediate implementation.[47]

General Conference of 1957, therefore, created the proposed Board of Administration and elected the first regional conference bishops.[48] As of that Conference, the General Executive Board as well as state, provincial, joint, and district councils ceased to exist.

These rapid changes in the faith, life-style, and governance of the Brethren tended to build momentum for further changes. Leaders had to consider constantly how to respond to new situations indicating continuing departure from historic positions. Some women, for example, began to modify their practice of the prayer veiling by adopting conventional headdress. This adjustment started a trend which led eventually to many women worshipping with uncovered heads, cutting their hair, and adopting conventional hair styling. Jewelry, especially the wedding band, also began to appear in brotherhood circles.

In an effort to preserve the concept of the prayer veiling, the Church Review and Study Committee had offered General Conference of 1956 a new statement of position on that issue. The recommendation strongly supported the principle of the covered head for women in religious activities, but recognized by inference that uniformity of practice in wearing the veiling was nearing an end. After stressing the primacy of applying the principle in public worship settings, the committee inserted the following significant passage:

> The form of head covering for the woman is not specifically prescribed in Scripture. This suggests that the guidance given by the Church in this matter should seek primarily to promote commitment to principle. It is recognized that the form of head covering or veiling generally approved by the church embodies the scriptural principle, but is not necessarily the only Biblical form of covering. A concern for the welfare of and unity of the group should be expressed in careful restraint with regard to adaptations in the application of this principle.

In conclusion, the report recognized the possibility of difference of conviction and practice regarding the veiling and called upon members who disagreed on the matter "to manifest genuine Christian courtesy and love toward each other."[49] Once again Conference was unwilling to go as far as the Church Review and Study Committee proposed. One debater who supported a more conservative statement commented: "There is no end to compromise except the bottom."[50]

The committee accordingly reviewed and modified its work to make it more acceptable. Its 1957 report deleted the stronger emphasis upon the wearing of the veiling in public as compared to private worship, removed the passage recognizing the validity of various forms of the veiling, and eliminated the reference to differences in conviction and practice concerning it. In addition the statement sought by a rhetorical question to encourage women to continue wearing long hair. It asked: "'When God says long hair is a glory to a woman and shorn hair is a shame for her, why should any heart that loves Him seek to get as far away as possible from that which He calls a glory and try to get as close as possible to that which He calls a shame?'" In this modified form, General Conference of 1957 approved the new statement on the prayer veiling.[51]

Soon the new Board of Administration became involved with problems arising from the period of transition.[52] One was increased use of the wedding ring in spite of the 1951 General Conference reaffirmation of historic opposition to the wearing of jewelry. Conference requested the board to respond to a Pennsylvania State Council petition for "some constructive declaration as to how this increased tendency toward the wearing of the wedding ring may be halted and what course a church leader should follow if his people should fall prey to such practices."[53]

When the board reported in 1958, differences of opinion about the wedding ring could not be overlooked. As happened so often throughout the history of the Brethren movement, the proposed solution to a problem made provision for differences of conviction, while seeking to preserve fellowship and brotherhood. The report read:

> Because of this historical experience out of which our convictions regarding the wedding ring have come, it appears that although for some, because of geographical or cultural reasons, the wedding band holds real meaning, for others such a practice may be motivated by a desire for adornment as taught against in 1 Peter 3.
>
> [Recommendation 1] . . . the Church continue her Biblical and historical stand against the wearing of jewelry, . . .
>
> [Recommendation 2] . . . that we exercise due Christian charity with respect to the conscience of those who do not regard the wedding band as such. Colossians 3:12-13.

General Conference had reservations about the report and referred it back to the Board of Administration. At a later session, however, Conference adopted these recommendations, thus placing the wedding ring in that broadening area of decision governed by individual conscience.[54]

As early as the mid-1950s, changes already made in Brethren beliefs and practices had indicated that a revision of the *Consitution-Doctrine, By-Laws and Rituals* adopted in 1937 would be necessary. In response to this need, Conference made the Church Review and Study Committee responsible for the revision, a task which it completed in 1961. The changes in Brethren life discussed above, as well as other changes, were included in the new 1961 *Manual of Doctrine and Government.*

The Revolution in Church Architecture

A visible but almost unnoticed and little understood aspect of the transition of the 1950s and 1960s was a revolution in the architecture of

Brethren houses of worship.[55] As this revolution proceeded, congregations moved from simple, unadorned meetinghouses into typical Protestant church edifices.[56]

The shift toward a conventional church architecture was slow and unplanned. In the early 1950s, as if by prophetic insight, *Visitor* illustrations began to include church structures contrasting strikingly with those of the brotherhood. In 1951 the paper unveiled a new masthead which featured a profile drawing of a large church with a tall spire topped by a cross.[57] Thereafter imposing church buildings appeared from time to time in other contexts. One illustration featured a group of young people with neckties and modern hairstyling seated in front of a large gothic window through which light streamed onto a Bible superimposed upon the group.[58] In 1954 the periodical introduced another new masthead with a spired church.[59]

The acceptance of these illustrations without challenge suggests that new thought patterns were emerging. The time was at hand when the implications of substituting "church" for "meetinghouse" in the vocabulary of the brotherhood, a process already completed, would emerge more clearly. In the early tradition, "to go to meeting" symbolized assembling with people—God's people—in personal fellowship encounter. In the vocabulary of the mid-1950s, "to go to church" tended to emphasize a place with special religious significance.

When the Brethren concluded that their simple, traditional meetinghouses had no particular merit, mainline Protestantism offered a broad range of possibilities for imitative church architecture.[60] As a veritable wave of building and remodeling of houses of worship spread across the brotherhood, the architectural guidelines were not formulated out of a consciously understood theology of worship rooted in the history of the group, but rather out of observations of architectural practices of other denominations.

One obvious trend in the early stage of this architectural revolution was the arrangement of pews facing toward a pulpit on a raised platform at the end of the assembly room. No new church retained the side-of-the-room location for the ministerial center. Gone was the circle symbolism of gathered, sharing brethren and sisters seated appropriately for worship and fellowship. In its place was the leader on an elevated platform, with all members of the congregation facing him. Although a departure from previous worship practices, the new arrangement did lend itself to a symbolism in which the preaching pulpit or open Bible was the central, integrating theme.

A side-effect of the new architecture was the development of a special vocabulary to describe it. The term "sanctuary," came into common use, partly, no doubt, because of the need to distinguish the worship area of the structure from Christian education and social rooms. Even more than "church," the word "sanctuary" tended to identify God's presence with place and structure rather than with assembled brethren and sisters.

Another term acquiring new significance in the continuing architectural revolution is "altar."[61] Long before the 1950s the "altar call" and "going to the altar," as well as "altar service," had become familiar expressions in Brethren revivalism. These terms merely indicated, however, that the space at the front of the assembly room had practical usefulness for

General Conference in session at the Upland Church, California, 1965. Note the architectural features and especially the divided chancel which is appearing here and there in churches across the brotherhood. The moderator, Bishop Charlie Byers, is behind the preaching pulpit on the left.

counsel and prayer with persons manifesting spiritual needs. There was no architectural symbolism suggesting that God was present at the altar in a sense that He was not present elsewhere.

In recent years the worship center or liturgical altar has appeared in a number of new churches. To make space for a central platform altar, the pulpit is placed to the left of the worshippers while a lectern balances it architecturally on their right. Neither the early circle of gathered brethren and sisters nor the later preaching pulpit, symbolic of the open Bible, is then the central, integrating focus of worship. That function is now assumed architecturally by the altar, the central or holiest place in the sanctuary.

The introduction of a liturgical altar is a striking example of how a group with a "house church" origin, which historically stressed the gathering of God's people rather than place or structure in worship, seems to be gradually feeling its way toward increasing accommodation to liturgical Protestant church architecture. Symbolically, this architectural form suggests that a pietistic emphasis upon the individual's relationship to God takes precedence over brotherhood and the concept of the church as a gathered, visible community of believers.

Who Were the Brethen in Christ in the 1960s?

Had such a question been widely asked across the brotherhood in the 1960s, many members would have undoubtedly replied that they did not know. Much of what they had believed, taught, and practiced was in a state of flux. Individuals, congregations, and regions shared the trauma of an uncertain identity. It is remarkable that the group stayed together. When a leader of another church observed that his people could not have made such changes without splitting, a Brethren churchman replied: "Perhaps you were large enough to split. We were too small, so we had to stretch."[62]

This answer may have included an element of truth, but deeper and more fundamental factors, which can only be conjectured, account for the survival of unity in the midst of diversity in the 1960s.[63] At one point the shadow of schism appeared and spread but ultimately subsided. Membership losses were relatively small.[64] By 1960, furthermore, the membership graph had begun a sharp upward turn to mark the beginning of the most significant fifteen-year period of growth in the history of the brotherhood.[65]

Many individuals may have been confused about the identity of the Brethren in Christ in the 1960s, but the 1961 *Manual of Doctrine and Government* reveals that their official postion had shifted significantly toward the image of the typical evangelical-holiness denomination. In 1950 the leaders assembled at Indianapolis had poured out their concerns to each other in the context of a convention of articulate, success-oriented, evangelical churchmen. Those frustrated Brethren in Christ were impressed by the evangelical church models set before them at that time. Later, fraternization with NHA churches gave the brotherhood greater awareness of holiness models of church life. It is not surprising, therefore, that the guidelines for the second period of transition came to the Brethren from outside of their movement rather than from searching reappraisal of their own historical roots and theology.

The 1961 *Manual of Doctrine and Government* illustrates the nature of the transition. In the new constitution, The Apostles Creed, with addition of the phrase "the sanctification of believers," became the creed of the Brethren. The constitution, furthermore, conformed to typical, evangelical Protestantism, in recognizing only two "general ordinances, believer's baptism and the Lord's Supper."[66] Feet washing had yielded its place as an ordinance and, together with the prayer veiling and holy kiss, was classified with "scriptural practices . . . which should be observed in church life and practice."[67]

Perhaps the most striking example of a shift in the official position of the group was the formulating of a doctrine of the invisible church. The 1961 *Manual* states: "The Church is composed of all those in every nation who through saving faith in Christ have entered into spiritual union with Him."[68]

While the early Brethren would not have denied this statement, they placed the emphasis elsewhere. In their understanding of the New Testament, the church must become visible in the gathered fellowship of born-again believers in which, through loving concern and redemptive discipline, each member assists the others to perfect their obedience in the Christian walk. For them "saving faith in Christ" could not be detached from carefully nurtured, personal relationships and a common Christian ethic and life-style embodying the meaning of obedience. Acceptance of responsibility to observe the "all things" which Christ commanded was inseparable from this understanding of the church. In contrast, the 1961 definition of the church made profession of faith rather than obedience the basic criterion for identifying the Christian.

Amid the uncertainties of the 1960s, members differed among themselves about the significance of their historic distinctives such as the prayer veiling, nonconformity in personal appearance, feetwashing, and nonresistance. The 1961 *Manual* summarized the theoretical bases for these beliefs but gave relatively little guidance for their practical application in an increasingly complex society. Preceding the *Manual* was the transitional legislation of the 1950s which stressed the preservation of "principles" while sweeping away many of the specifics reflecting the previous group understanding of how the principles should be applied. By the 1960s, furthermore, practice was already modifying a number of the specifics which the legislation of the 1950s did seek to retain, and individual conscience was increasingly becoming the final authority in the application of principles.

Another factor which is important for an understanding of this period was a widely-held interpretation of the 1930s and 1940s as a time when the church fell into bondage to legalism. The fear of perpetuating a legalistic trend made difficult the development of a positive church discipline for the post-1950 era. From one point of view, therefore, the transition of the 1950s was a rapid repudiation of the past without a clear conception of the desired future.

The unique situation eventually produced by this combination of factors may be illustrated by what happened to the practice of nonconformity in personal appearance. By the 1970s a perceptive observer of many congregations and special gatherings, such as camp meetings, would have noted a wide spectrum of dress and style. At one end of it were men and women wearing the traditional church uniforms, and women the prayer veiling; at the other end were men and women wearing conventional clothing, hair styles, and jewelry, and women with uncovered heads. Had the observer last contacted the Brethren in 1950, he or she might have been tempted to paraphrase some famous words from another context: "Seldom in the history of small churches have so many changed so much so soon."[69]

In summary, as the Brethren in Christ passed through their second period of transition, they differed a great deal about the implications of what was happening to them. Now, with the perspective of history, it is clear that the forming of new ecumenical relationships, the unplanned Indianapolis meeting of church leaders, the reform legislation of General

Conference, the new *Manual of Doctrine and Government,* and the revolution in church architecture combined to move the group toward a typical, evangelical-holiness position.

The sweeping changes of the 1950s, furthermore, nurtured an indivdualistic Pietism which accentuated the historic emphasis of the Brethren upon subjective Christian experience but which was less compatible with their ties to Anabaptism. In other words, their emphasis on piety increased while their emphasis on obedience decreased.

NOTES:

[1]*General Conference Minutes,* 1947, Article 24, p. 77. These organizations are referred to hereafter as "NAE" and "NHA." The National Holiness Association adopted the name Christian Holiness Association in 1971.

[2]*Ibid.,* 1948, Article 11, pp. 30-31.

[3]*Ibid.,* p. 31. The Brethren had previously made some use of NAE services in the fields of foreign missions and Christian education.

[4]*Ibid.*

[5]*Ibid.,* 1949, Article 10, p. 32; *ibid.,* 1950, Article 13, p. 36.

[6]*Ibid.,* Article 24, p. 55.

[7]*Ibid.,* 1951, Article 30, p. 56.

[8]C. N. Hostetter, Jr., "N. A. E. and the Church," *Visitor,* LXXI (June 16, 1958), p. 2.

[9]Roy V. Sider to Carlton O. Wittlinger, May 28, 1975.

[10]This account of the Indianapolis hotel-room meeting is based upon interviews with or letters from Charlie B. Byers, Paul W. McBeth, John N. Hostetter, Erwin W. Thomas, Samuel Wolgemuth, Ray M. Zercher, and Carl J. Ulery, all of whom were present. Christian N. Hostetter, Jr., served as the discussion leader, but his health at the time of this writing did not permit an interview.

[11]For an analysis of pre-1950 factors paving the way for this decade of change, see Frank Demmy, "The Spiritual Revolution in the Brethren in Christ Church as a Prelude to a Decade of Reorganization" (history honors paper, Messiah College, 1974).

[12]"Traditional" and "progressive" are used here to differentiate reluctance to change from support for change.

[13]*General Conference Minutes,* 1950, Article 3, pp. 10-13.

[14]See Elmer T. Clark, *The Small Sects in America* (Rev. ed.; New York: Abingdon-Cokesbury Press, 1949), pp. 211-12.

[15]Demmy, "Spiritual Revolution."

[16]*General Conference Minutes,* 1940, Article 18, pp. 30-33.

[17]*Ibid.,* 1950, Article 29, pp. 79-80.

[18]Charlie B. Byers to Carlton O. Wittlinger, March 26, 1974.

[19]*General Conference Minutes,* 1950, p. 25.

[20]*Ibid.*, Article 11, p. 31.

[21]See *Ibid.*, for the personnel of the committee, which included six of the eight men listed in note 10 as attendants at the Indianapolis hotel meeting.

[22]Church Review and Study Committee Minutes, April 9-12, 1951, Church Archives.

[23]*General Conference Minutes,* 1951, p. 181.

[24]*Ibid.*, 1951, pp. 9-12.

[25]*Ibid.*, Article 19, pp. 33-41.

[26]See Chapter XV for a discussion of the church uniform question.

[27]The present writer was a member of the 1951 General Conference and heard the debate.

[28]Statement by Ernest Swalm.

[29]*General Conference Minutes,* 1952, Article 18, pp. 36-37.

[30]Personal recollection of the present writer.

[31]*General Conference Minutes,* 1952, Article 18, p. 37.

[32]*Ibid.*, 1951, p. 40.

[33]*Ibid.*, pp. 37-39. For further reference to these historic debates, see Chapter XV.

[34]*Ibid.*, pp. 38-39.

[35]"Believer's baptism" is used here to signify baptism accompanied by a personal confession of faith in Christ, in contrast with infant baptism in which the subject is unable to make such a personal confession.

[36]*General Conference Minutes,* 1953, pp. 31-32. The present writer heard this debate.

[37]*Ibid.*, 1954, pp. 120-21.

[38]General Conference Debates, 1954. Since 1954 the principal debates are preserved on tape. David M. Scott, one of the present writer's students, analyzed and summarized the 1954-1958 debates on the work of the Church Review and Study Committee.

[39]*General Conference Minutes,* 1955, Article 15, p. 34.

[40]*Ibid.*, 1974, Article 10, p. 21.

[41]*Ibid.*, 1953, Article 13, p. 25.

[42]*Ibid.*, 1954, Article 15, pp. 26-29.

[43]*Ibid.*, pp. 132-33.

[44]*Ibid.*, 1955, Article 16, p. 35.

[45]*Ibid.*, 1956, Article 14, pp. 30-36.

[46]General Conference Debates, 1956.

[47]*General Conference Minutes,* 1956, Article 14, p. 36.

[48]These were Henry Ginder, Atlantic Conference; Charlie Byers, Allegheny Conference; Carl Ulery, Central Conference; Alvin Burkholder, Midwest and Pacific Conferences; and Ernest Swalm, Canadian Conference.

[49]*General Conference Minutes,* 1956, Article 15, pp. 39-40.

[50]General Conference Debates, 1957.

[51]*General Conference Minutes,* 1957, Article 13, pp. 37-38.

[52]*Ibid.*, 1957, Article 35, pp. 116-17.

[53]*Ibid.*

[54]*Ibid.*, 1958, Article 11, p. 32.

[55]This section utilizes Demmy, "Spiritual Revolution," and C. O. Wittlinger, "Thoughts on the Worship Setting," *Visitor*, LXXXII (April 21, 1969), 5, 11, 14.

[56]See Chapter V for a description of the early meetinghouses and worship practices.

[57]*Visitor*, LXIV (Jan. 8, 1951), 1.

[58]*Ibid.*, LXIV (April 16, 1951), 13.

[59]*Ibid.*, LXXVIII (January 4, 1965), I.

[60]The vocabulary change from "meetinghouse" to "church" occurred long before the revolution in church architecture.

[61]See Chapter V for the history of these terms.

[62]Charlie B. Byers to Carlton O. Wittlinger, June 3, 1975.

[63]See Chapter XX for further comment about this phenomenon.

[64]One congregation in Philadelphia eventually withdrew from the Brethren in Christ to form the Calvary Holiness Church. Groups of members also withdrew from congregations near Massillon, Ohio, (Sippo Valley); Hanover, Pa.; and near Millersburg, Pa. (Free Grace), but no transfer of church property occurred.

[65]See Appendix C.

[66]*Manual of Doctrine and Government*, 1961, p. 11. The Church Review and Study Committee began its revision of the constitution with a preference for "Eucharist" rather than "Lord's Supper." See Church Review and Study Committee Minutes, December 31, 1957.

[67]*Manual of Doctrine and Government*, 1961, pp. 11-12.

[68]*Ibid.*, p. 22.

[69]Part of quotation suggested by a statement by Winston Churchill.

New Trends and Ventures

Missions in the Homeland

The historical development of Brethren in Christ missions at home and abroad involved considerable trial and error. This caused insecurity and stress for missionaries carrying out assignments "away from home" under the supervision of boards with members scattered across the brotherhood.

By the 1950s two new trends indicated that the Home Mission Board was aware of the need to improve mission administration and to care more adequately for the well-being of workers. One was a shift of emphasis in the staffing of mission stations. For many years the typical staff included a married couple and one or more "single sisters," occupying common housing and susceptible to potential stress in interpersonal relations.[1] Eventually, the board concluded that its assignments could best be carried out by pastoral couples who lived in their own homes while developing church programs. The objective was to build mission congregations with the assistance of both new converts and more mature Christians who chose to become identified with the program. As this trend increased, the assignment of single women to mission stations declined.[2]

Simultaneously with this development of mission pastorates, the "institutional mission" emerged. This was a program which developed ministries too large and complex to fit into a plan of congregational administration. Some of these institutional missions had little or no congregational base; they were conducted by "imported workers," each with an assigned task. The administrative implications for such enterprises were basically different from those for typical mission churches functioning as congregations under the supervision of a mission board appointed by General Conference.[3]

As the Home Mission Board realized that it was operating two very different types of programs, it sought to provide institutional missions with leadership and management more specialized than that required for the traditional mission church. Circumstances at the Navajo Mission in New Mexico paved the way for the first institutionalization of a home mission station. By 1958 the combined evangelistic, educational, and medical programs of that mission made it unique, and administrative

Airview of Navajo Mission, Bloomfield, New Mexico, 1962.

arrangements applicable to other missions no longer met its needs. General Conference accordingly granted it institutional status and authorized its incorporation under the laws of New Mexico as the "Navajo Brethren in Christ Mission." Thereafter, it functioned with its own board of directors which included representatives from the Midwestern and Pacific Conferences, as well as from the Board for Home Missions and Extension.[4]

In the following decade General Conference institutionalized two other mission projects—the Life Line Mission in San Francisco, California, and the Montreal Lake Children's Home in Saskatchewan. The former was an inner-city mission serving large numbers of poor, sick, and often transient people. It conducted large-scale feeding and lodging projects, a medical clinic, and a vigorous evangelistic program. The following passage from an annual report reflects its spirit and scope:

> This scripture [Galatians 6:9] is often encouraging as we serve endless lines of people who are hungry, sick, destitute, homeless and, seemingly, hopeless.
>
> Tons of food have been prepared and served, thousands of pills have been prescribed and dispensed, hundreds of people have been prayed with and counseled, thousands have . . . [sat] under the ministry of the Word . . . .[5]

Since, like the Navajo Mission, the Life Line Mission could not operate effectively under the administrative pattern of typical home missions, General Conference officially institutionalized it in 1965 under the general oversight of the Board for Home Missions and Extension.[6]

Montreal Lake Children's Home, the northern outpost of Brethren missions, is a unique ministry to North American Indian children. The Northern Canada Evangelical Mission founded the home in the early 1950s to provide boarding facilities for these children from Northern Saskatchewan while they attended a government school at Timber Bay on the east shore of Montreal Lake. In June of 1969 the Brethren in Christ assumed full responsibility for this project, which, during the ensuing school year, operated at capacity with sixty-four students and a staff of thirteen. The purpose of the home was to provide a wholesome Christian environment for these Indian young people seeking to gain an education. In accepting responsibility for the project, General Conference gave it institutional status with its own administrative board, including, in addition to Brethren in Christ, representatives from three Mennonite groups in Saskatchewan.[7]

At the present time, the Board for Missions is developing an alternative and more flexible administrative pattern for institutional mission programs. Although corporate mission management proved to be particularly helpful in the development of physical plant, it had limited capacity to create viable people-centered programs and ministries. In view of this weakness, more recent institutional ministries in the Bronx, New York, and in Labish Village, Oregon, do not depend upon boards of directors. Instead, the Board for Missions assists local administrators to develop programs and support for mission personnel to fit their individual talents and needs.[8]

Dedication of the Ridgemount Church, Hamilton, Ontario, 1959. This was the pilot project for the contemporary Brethren in Christ extension-church movement.

Church Extension

During the 1920s General Conference became concerned about the lack of serious district commitment to church growth and extension. Some proposals to overcome lethargy at this level of church life proved to be too radical or innovative to gain general acceptance. Conference did, however, create a Church Extension Board authorized to enter organized districts to investigate the lack of church growth and extension and to promote more effective efforts in these areas of concern.[9] Although the direct outcomes of this flurry of attention to district outreach were not impressive, the resulting publication of annual district membership statistics was significant. Thereafter the Brethren had one kind of index to test the vitality and impact of their movement.

During approximately four decades after 1928, efforts for church extension employed familiar techniques such as home missions, tent meetings, revival meetings, youth programs, and Sunday schools. In the late 1950s, however, the brotherhood began to experiment with extension churches planted in new communities previously without a Brethren in Christ witness.

The first such extension church was Ridgemount in Hamilton, Ontario. In 1957 Ontario Joint Council, the Home Mission Board, and General Conference all endorsed this project.[10] The $50,000 building program consummated with dedication of a new church edifice in October 1959.[11]

Ridgemount was a pilot project for the founding of other extension churches. After the six new regional conferences began to function in 1957, they developed administrative arrangements to plan and promote church extension. Each conference formed a Church Extension Board which, together with the conference bishop, was responsible to investigate promising locations and pastoral possibilities for new extension churches. To provide financial underwriting for such churches, each regional conference also created a Church Extension Fund to receive and solicit cash investments at appropriate interest rates. The presence of the regional conference bishops on the General Conference Board for Missions provided liaison with that agency, one of whose full-time staff became Director of Extension Churches.[12]

This extension church movement embodied an imaginative concept. Locate a pastor or pastoral family in a promising community where a potential building or site for a church is available; start a church work from "scratch" as one might launch a new business enterprise; when a congregational nucleus develops, borrow from the appropriate church extension fund and erect a self-amortizing church building. This concept came to the Brethren in Christ from other denominations which were applying it with marked success.

Experience with this concept soon taught the Brethren that some of its financial presuppositions would require modification in their circles. New churches which borrowed most of the capital to erect church buildings often found themselves in financial difficulty. This caused Brethren leaders to perceive that the general church should assume more direct financial responsibility for the extension program. As one means of discharging this responsibility, the sponsoring regional conference now conducts a conference-wide solicitation to provide an initial building grant for each new extension church.[13]

In spite of the need for trial and error learning, the extension church movement advanced. Before the close of the 1960s, more than a dozen new churches were ministering in Canada and the United States, and the number was increasing.[14]

While regional conferences usually sponsored church extension, some congregations have experimented with the "parent-church" concept. A few strong congregations, such as the one at Grantham, Pennsylvania, have been instrumental in starting new churches in adjacent communities. In the early 1970s a group of Grantham members began services in a vacated church building three miles to the south in the small town of Dillsburg. This venture produced a new congregation known as the Dillsburg Brethren in Christ Church.[15]

One important result of recent church extension has been the infusion of new blood and new families into the Brethren movement. This comes at a time when some of the older, rural churches of the brotherhood are struggling to hold their own numerically and when the surge of rural mission expansion so conspicuous in the first half of the century has subsided.

These developments have important consequences for Brethren in Christ identity. As traditional and family bonds weaken, the brotherhood seeks to offer a viable, biblical challenge to the many newcomers entering the group. Under these circumstances, the quest for a clear conception of group identity takes on special significance.

Evangelism in the Local Church

Since the mid-century, traditional evangelistic meetings of two or more weeks have gradually yielded to other approaches in local church evangelism. Some churches still hold one-week or ten-day meetings, but the trend is toward shorter periods, such as long weekends, with more emphasis upon spiritual renewal than upon evangelism. Several factors contributed to this change.[16]

One was the multiplication of congregational services and activities in recent years. In the first half of the century, the typical congregational schedule included morning and evening Sunday services, plus a mid-week prayer meeting. The protracted evangelistic meeting; therefore, was non-competitive; it merely replaced existing services and filled in the remaining evenings of the week.

Another factor was the increasing involvement of Brethren members in community life and activities. This was partly due to social changes which multiplied opportunities for such involvement. It also reflected, however, a modification of the social isolation developed out of a movement built primarily upon work and worship. Until relatively recent times, many members avoided participation in social and recreational community activities which were thought to foster worldliness and the "unequal yoke" with unbelievers.[17] This attitude no longer prevails widely within the brotherhood, and many members carry heavy schedules of community activities. Such schedules are not compatible with regular attendance at protracted evangelistic meetings.

A third factor militating against extended evangelistic meetings was their increasing inability to attract significant numbers of non-Christians. In an age when life was simpler and more leisurely, when the competition from community activities and television was not what it is today, the protracted meeting attracted wide community interest and attendance; it was a great social event. Respected evangelists attracted large crowds night after night, and the people who came were not clock conscious as are most church attendants today. One evangelist leader reminisced:

> Really, from the standpoint of a preacher, those were the good old days. Those were the days, you know, when you could preach everything you thought about and maybe some things you didn't think about. The sermons were long; you could preach as long as you liked. . . . We counted . . . on the preaching and the praying of those days to bring . . . conviction and the turning of people to the Lord . . . . That of course, has changed.[18]

While the protracted meeting of at least two weeks lingered in some circles, the brotherhood as a whole began to explore other and more personalized methods of evangelism. This development went forward more rapidly after 1957 when the new Board of Bishops was made responsible to provide leadership in evangelistic outreach.

Until 1967 the bishops acted jointly as a commission on evangelism. In that year General Conference created a new office, Director of Evangelism, "for the purposes of coordinating and promoting the revivalistic and evangelistic concerns of our brotherhood" and directed the Board of Bishops to select one of their number to fill it. That board responded by naming Bishop Henry Ginder of the Allegheny Conference as the first Director of Evangelism.[19]

Soon after his appointment, Bishop Ginder directed the first major experiment of the Brethren with the newer methods of evangelism, which he called "The Witness and Win Program." This utilized Nate Krupp's book *You Can Be A Soul Winner—Here's How,* which a businessman provided for all pastors. At the time there was concern because the Brethren had been doing fairly well in witnessing but not too well in winning. "Witness and Win" was the first general, organized effort to awaken the brotherhood to concern for personal, one-to-one visitation evangelism, as it is sometimes called. A few congregations such as that at Sherkston, Ontario, responded well to this innovation. On the whole, however, it did not produce wide lay involvement in community evangelism.

From this first loosely organized attempt to stimulate lay evangelism, the brotherhood moved on to more highly organized programs in use by other groups. Campus Crusade with its "Four Spiritual Laws" provided one model, and the Coral Ridge program developed by James Kennedy of the Fort Lauderdale Presbyterian Church in Florida, provided another. The latter stressed on-the-job training with two trainees accompanying a leader experienced in home visitation evangelism. The expectation was that the trainees would eventually become leaders of other similar groups of trainees.

In 1970 the Coral Ridge program received a strong impetus when the Brethren in Christ Men's Fellowship financed the attendance of twelve men, two from each Regional Conference, at the James Kennedy evangelism clinic at Fort Lauderdale.[20] As a result, some Brethren congregations have employed the Kennedy approach with marked success. The congregation at Carlisle, Pennsylvania, for example, won the Class A award of the denomination for Sunday school growth during a year when they were not consciously engaged in the annual contest to achieve growth.

Their Sunday school simply grew as a result of home-visitation evangelism, which added new members and families to the congregation.

Two other evangelistic techniques used more recently are the Home Bible Study and the Lay Witness Mission. The former encourages new Christians to invite friends into their homes for Bible study in the book of First John, with emphasis on evangelism rather than Christian nurture. Lay Witness Mission stresses an intensive weekend of evangelistic meetings under the direction of a team of laymen coming from outside of the congregation.

Some growing congregations have not concentrated on one method of evangelism. An example is the Highland congregation, near West Milton, Ohio, which, with an eclectic approach to community outreach, tripled its membership during a recent five-year period.

These experimental approaches to new methods of evangelism conformed to the counsel of the Director of Evangelism, who had urged congregations to continue the traditional evangelistic meetings until they had something better with which to replace them. In his view, the gradual development of evangelistic "outreach"—witnessing to the unconverted "on their own turf"—provided opportunity to shift the emphasis of the earlier type of meetings toward Christian renewal and growth, that is, "inreach" which he came to perceive as the wellspring of evangelism. Due to his leadership, as well as to other factors, the contemporary Brethren in Christ Church presents a panorama of evangelistic activity reflecting congregational individuality in the choice of new or old methodologies and, in many instances, a blending of elements from both.

Radio Broadcasting

By the early 1950s various groups of Brethren were entering the field of radio evangelism. In one year they spent approximately $24,000 for program production alone.[21] By the summer of 1954, they had twenty-four different broadcasts, and some members in Franklin County, Pennsylvania, were experimenting with a telecast.[22] This flurry of activity and investment aroused the interest and concern of General Conference which, perceiving the need for "corresponding organization and supervision," named a Commission on Radio to function under the General Executive Board.[23]

This commission promptly turned its attention to the possibility of a denominational broadcast. Having secured General Conference approval for exploratory work, the commission moved rapidly and selected Southern Ohio as the site for development of a sample program. This was taped at Springfield where the ministerial services of Owen Alderfer, pastor of the Springfield Congregation, were available. General Conference of 1954 agreed to hear the program which was released on the floor under the caption, "The Hour of Power." Although the broadcast title was not fully satisfactory, Conference authorized the commission "to make arrangements toward the organization of a denominational broadcast of the Brethren in Christ Church."[24]

Production of a denominational broadcast proved to be a formidable undertaking. By 1955, furthermore, it was clear that local broadcasters would not readily surrender their autonomy in program production. The commission felt compelled to live with this reality and reported to Conference as follows: "It should be kept clearly in mind that the proposed denominational broadcast is not intended to replace current programs which are locally sponsored, but that it will rather operate in conjunction with such broadcasts in extending the outreach and effectiveness of the radio ministry of the Brethren in Christ Church."[25]

By the summer of 1956 the denominational broadcast, now captioned "Gems of Grace," was ready for release on weekly tapes.[26] Owen Alderfer, then a faculty member at Upland College, was the radio minister. Some of his faculty colleagues were highly qualified in various phases of radio program production; furthermore, Upland College in conjuction with the Upland Church could provide quality music to support radio programming. These factors combined to make Upland, California, the point of origin for the broadcast. The initial funding came from Christ's Crusaders, the General Executive Board, and Upland College.[27]

After launching the new venture, the Commission on Radio informed General Conference that its one concern had been "to make the broadcast reach the most sinners for Christ, and strengthen the most believers in Christ." It also asserted that the programs would radiate a true spirit of evangelism and expressed confidence that they would be aired in the respective areas of the brotherhood.[28]

These hopes did not come to fruition. Radio stations were not generally interested in presenting the broadcasts on free time, and few areas of the brotherhood were willing to provide the needed financial sponsorship.[29] During the Conference year from 1957 to 1958, the number of stations airing the programs declined form eighteen to nine.[30]

These circumstances did not appear to justify the effort and expense required to keep Gems of Grace on the air. Subsidies from several church boards and the limited remuneration of the program staff could not continue indefinitely. In 1958 when the Commission on Radio saw no future prospect for adequate constituency support and also received notice that key numbers of the production staff would be unavailable after September 1, 1958, it bowed to the inevitable. Conference accordingly approved the commission's recommendation to suspend Gems of Grace as of the September date and suggested that the regional conferences assume responsibility for radio broadcasting within their respective jurisdictions.[31]

The termination of Gems of Grace did not end interest in a denominational broadcast which could be made available to local areas of the brotherhood.[32] An existing broadcast, The Gospel Tide Hour, originating in Chambersburg, Pennsylvania, under the direction of Bishop Charlie Byers, seemed to offer possibilities for adaptation to the needs of local regions desiring a Brethren in Christ broadcast. The production staff would finance release of the program in such regions provided they could promote it by mailings, rallies, and other methods of contact. Any congregation wishing to contract for its release could make the necessary arrangements under the supervision of the Commission on Radio. The commission reported this information without recommendation to General Conference, which accepted the report but took no further action on the broadcast issue.[33]

This somewhat indirect promotion of The Gospel Tide Hour by the Commission on Radio did not give that broadcast a monopoly of attention. By 1961 seven other Brethren programs were on the air.[34] While the commission continued to encourage such radio services generally, it sounded a warning about the flow of funds to support non-Brethren broadcasts. This warning resulted in part from an exposure of fraud in one nationally known program. The commission also urged pastors to seek to identify questionable religious broadcasts and to warn their congregations to be on guard against them.[35]

Soon the Commission on Radio began to look more searchingly at the cost and quality of Brethren radio programs. It expressed concern about overlapping programs and duplication of effort through the use of time, talent, and finances. The commission, furthermore, stressed the importance of airing programs whose quality would "enhance the Kingdom of God and do the most good for the Brethren in Christ Church and her institutions." General Conference responded to these concerns by requiring that all regular broadcasts in the name of the Brethren in Christ Church should be registered with the Commission on Radio and that only registered programs should be entitled to commission recognition and promotion.[36]

In 1964, to meet the need for a more clearly defined radio voice of the brotherhood, General Conference endorsed The Gospel Tide Hour as the official radio broadcast of the Brethren in Christ Church. The program had been on the air for seventeen years and continued to expand in outreach and to improve in quality; it had also incorporated as the Gospel Tide Broadcasting Association. Conference therefore authorized the Commission on Radio to establish a working relationship with the corporation so that the broadcast might be made available to the entire brotherhood.[37] This was done without recourse to financial underwriting by the church; the broadcast relies upon offerings received by mail.[38]

Gospel Tide programs are aired within all regional conferences. Since the fall of 1974, the programs have also been released from a Swaziland transmitter which reaches all of Africa from the equator to the Cape of Good Hope, in which area the Rhodesia and the Zambia Brethren in Christ churches are located. In addition to communications from listeners in Africa countries, the broadcast office receives letters from as far away as India and Pakistan.[39]

New Missions Abroad: Japan

During the early 1950s a surge of interest in new missions abroad moved the brotherhood. Official mission ventures in Israel and Mexico proved to be shortlived, but those in Japan, Cuba, and Nicaragua produced indigenous churches affiliated with the Brethren in Christ in North America.

Interest in a mission to Japan began in the early 1950s when Samuel Wolgemuth made a trip around the world and developed a burden for the spiritual welfare of the Japanese people. Upon his return, he accepted an invitation to speak to the Upland Brethren in Christ Church in California about the religious situation in Japan.[40]

In 1951, after hearing Wolgemuth, the Upland Brethren in Christ's Men's Fellowship sponsored a gospel team to tour Japan. Three young men, Royce Saltzman, Gordon Johnson, and Peter Willms made the tour. In addition to speaking and singing, they were interested in possibilities for

Brethren in Christ mission work.[41]

When the team arrived home, its members shared their concern for the spiritual welfare of the Japanese. Peter Willms and his wife, Mary, spoke to churches in various parts of the country, stressing the great potential for mission work in Japan.[42] These reports prompted General Conference to authorize a study of mission possibilities in that country, with the understanding that the Foreign Mission Board could open a work if circumstances appeared to justify this step.[43]

Following the Conference of 1952 Carl Ulery, a member of the mission board, visited the mission fields in Africa and India and stopped en route in Japan. There he consulted with Samuel Wolgemuth, Youth for Christ Director in that country, and they decided that the city of Hagi, population 50,000, on the western coast of Yamaguchi-ken Prefecture (Province) in southern Japan would be a promising site for a Brethren in Christ mission.[44]

When Ulery returned, he contacted Peter and Mary Willms about the possibility of pioneering a Brethren in Christ mission in Japan to which the husband had felt called for several years.[45] The young couple agreed to go, and General Conference of 1953 confirmed them as missionaries.[46] After their arrival in Japan, they shared in the World Congress on Evangelism sponsored by Youth for Christ in Tokyo. Gospel team witness was a phase of the Congress program, and the Willms, together with a few other persons including an interpreter, comprised a team which ministered in street meetings and in the town hall at Hagi.[47]

After these meetings the Willms located in Hagi, began Bible classes in their home, and engaged in street meetings and literature distribution. Soon several seekers met regularly with the missionaries. These seekers eventually made a profession of Christian faith, received water baptism, and became the nucleus for the first Brethren in Christ mission congregation in Japan.[48]

From Hagi the work spread to other cities in Yamaguchi-ken Prefecture. In 1963, in order to maintain contact with church members moving to Tokyo, John and Lucille Graybill, who had been working in the city of Nagato, relocated in the Japanese capital to give leadership in the development of a new church there.[49]

As the Tokyo work grew in temporary quarters, the need for a permanent meeting place increased, but the financial burden of providing it seemed almost insurmountable. At $100,000 in United States currency for a plot of land fifty by one hundred feet, building prices were the highest in the world.[50]

Believing that God would help them, the small group of believers moved forward with the church project. Financial assistance for the purchase of a small lot came from United Zion, United Christian, Mennonite, and other sources, in addition to Brethren in Christ; consequently, only $25,000 of the $93,000 purchase price had to be borrowed. By sacrificial giving, tearing down an old house to build with used lumber, and doing the work themselves, the congregation completed the Koganei Church, a tangible symbol of the brotherly cooperation of several American Churches with a young but growing community of Christian believers in Japan.[51]

During the early years of Brethren mission work in that country, the missionaries provided the basic leadership. As time passed Japanese Christians increasingly assumed leadership responsibilities, and the missionary role rapidly became one of assisting the Japanese Church to carry out its plans. Missionaries now serve as consultants to church leaders, provide instruction in the Bible and in conversational English, share in home visitation, and help to open new points for Christian witness.[52]

One major sign of the growing maturity of the Japanese Church was the formation in 1971 of the Brethren in Christ National Conference, including all of the churches in Yamaguchi-ken Prefecture, with Asao Nishimura from the Nagato Church as the first chairman. Another sign was the growing evangelistic outreach of the small community of believers, which by 1972 was considering the extension of its witness as far as Okinawa.[53]

The Brethren in Christ mission to Japan developed its own unique characteristics. Because of the advanced level of Japanese life and culture, the missionaries found no need for institutional ministries, such as schools and hospitals, which played such important roles in missions in Africa and India. They accordingly stressed small group meetings or cell evangelism, witnessing to unbelievers and nurturing believers in homes, schools, factories—wherever they were invited or could find places for small group gatherings. When church assembly rooms became necessary for additional meeting space, they were small and simple; the emphasis was upon more groups of believers rather than large groups.[54]

Another characteristic was the development of the program around lay leadership. The missionaries did not envision the use of full-time professional Japanese pastors. Instead, they concentrated on the training of lay pastors, who earned their own living in offices, banks, classrooms, or through self-employment.[55]

Fellowship meal of church leaders in Yamaguchi-ken Prefecture, Japan.

A third characteristic of the Japanese mission was its effort to avoid the impression of importing another religious system into a land which already had over 200 different denominations. As churches formed in new communities, they took the names of towns and areas rather than the denominational church name from America. When, however, these churches decided to unite in a national conference, they chose to include "Brethren in Christ" in their conference name.[56]

The path of Brethren in Christ missions in Japan had not been an easy one to travel. A complex national language, a national seven-day work week which made difficult the arrangement of group meetings, entrenched Shintoism and Buddhism, family opposition to members who converted from the ancient faiths, and an affluent society saturated with materialism and hedonism have been some of the obstacles to overcome.[57]

In the face of these obstacles, the work has grown slowly but steadily, with the main burden for the missionary phase resting upon four couples.[58] In addition to cell groups, outreach methods have included street meetings, home visitations, tent meetings, youth camps, radio evangelism, book rooms, and classes for instruction in conversational English and cookery. These classes have been especially effective in attracting Japanese interest and in creating a setting in which the missionaries found many opportunities for witnessing.

At the close of 1975 the Brethren in Christ community in Japan numbered approximately 180 members.[59] Present missionaries are strongly emphasizing its opportunities for further evangelistic outreach.[60]

New Missions Abroad: Cuba

About the time mission work began in Japan, interest also developed in a Brethren in Christ witness to Cuba. In 1952 a ministerial acquaintance in that country invited Harry Hock to serve as guest minister in a series of services. This experience gave Hock a burden for the Cuban people, and, accompanied by his wife, he returned the next year with Charlie Byers, Dale Ulery, and their wives. This group took with them a tent in which to hold services.[61]

They pitched the tent in Havana Province and found housing about a half mile away. While walking from house to tent, they played an accordion and sang Gospel songs, stopping occasionally for a few minutes to hold street meetings. In this way they gathered an audience from people who followed them to the tent.[62] Here the pews were cement blocks and boards; they had no backs, but the people did not seem to mind sitting for a couple of hours singing and listening to sermons which were quite long because they had to be preached twice, once by the minister and once by the interpreter.[63]

As a result of these services, the evangelistic party got "Cuba fever" and decided to present the need for a Cuban mission to General Conference of 1953.[64] Conference accepted the report but made no commitment to assume responsibility for the work.[65] The interested parties, however, formed the Brethren in Christ Cuban Missionary Society, which secured and renovated a former Baptist church building in Cuatro Caminos, population 5,000, about fourteen miles from Havana. This locality had no evangelical witness, and surrounding towns offered opportunities for branch Sunday schools. The church was dedicated on February 14, 1954.[66]

This progress in founding a Cuban mission led General Conference to accept responsibility for its development under the jurisdiction of the

Foreign Mission Board. Conference also assigned Dale Ulery and his wife for one year of service in Cuba to relieve Howard and Pearl Wolgemuth who, for several months, had carried responsibility for the work.[67]

In 1955 Ulery conducted the first communion and feet-washing service. Concerning the Cuban reaction to feet washing, a new experience for the approximately fifty people present, he reported:

> You should have been here to see how willingly these people wanted to do what the Word of God said. It was not done with such precision as we do it in the United States, but the blessing of the Lord fell . . . .[68]

One of the participants, a man seventy-two years of age, testified happily of his joy in sharing for the first time in communion and feet washing.

In 1955 Howard and Pearl Wolgemuth returned to Cuba under mission assignment. The work grew under their leadership, in spite of a growing climate of political unrest preceding Fidel Castro's rise to power.[69] By the close of 1958 John and Ruth Pawelski had joined the staff, and the mission had two church buildings, three additional places of worship, four Sunday schools with 180 attendants, and twenty-seven church members. The missionaries had also begun a Christian elementary day school.[70]

The victory of the revolutionary Castro forces did not immediately disrupt the main mission program. Outreach continued and was facilitated by a bus funded by the Women's Missionary Prayer Circle.[71] Within a year or two, however, the outlook for the work became increasingly uncertain. Gradually anti-American propaganda destroyed the missionary influence, and the Wolgemuths returned to the United States.[72] Since they could not return to Cuba, the future of the work was entirely in the hands of the Cuban Christians.

For a number of years, the Wolgemuths received correspondence from the Cuban church community, carefully worded as a safeguard against censorship. In 1961 the local believers were carrying on the work and operating four Sunday schools. They still held title to all of the church property.[73]

More than a decade elapsed thereafter with very little information about the state of the Cuban coverts. Then, in the mid-1970s, Judith Hamilton, daughter of Howard and Pearl Wolgemuth, received a letter from Juana Garcia de Gonzales, a Cuban woman who had lived with the Wolgemuths in Cuatro Caminos and assisted in the mission work. The openness of the letter suggested that there was some relaxation of the tension and fear which had hindered previous communication.[74]

Juana Garcia, president and pastor of the church, drew attention to the fact that some churches in Cuba were being visited by denominational representatives from Canada. She asked whether it might be possible for a Canadian member of the Board for Missions to visit the Brethren in Christ Church at Cuatro Caminos.[75]

After careful consideration and planning, Ross Nigh of Niagara Falls, Ontario, secured a Cuban visa and arrived in Havana in January 1976. He was greeted in the city by Rafael Curbelo, treasurer of the Cuban Church, thus renewing personal contact between the Cuban and American Brethren after a lapse of fifteen years.[76]

The next day, which was Sunday, Nigh arrived at the little church in Cuatro Caminos during the morning service. There he presented to Juana Garcia a Spanish pulpit Bible which she had requested. After all had examined this Bible, she took it into the pulpit, read a passage, and then wept as she prayed. Through an interpreter Nigh learned that her prayer was for the Bible to last until Jesus comes.[77]

Following the service, Nigh had a long conversation with Juana Garcia and her husband, Julio Gonzales. She recounted the trials of the early days of the revolution, and the difficulties of leading a church without a trained or ordained leadership. She said that for more than fifteen years they had not had a "Brethren in Christ baptism." With an ordained minister available, she wanted two recent women converts to be baptized by trine immersion. On Monday evening, therefore, Ross Nigh dedicated the pulpit Bible, spoke on baptism, and administered the rite to the new converts.[78]

The church has a current membership of eighteen and an annual budget equivalent to approximately $2,000 in United States currency. It is registered with the government as "The Brethren in Christ Church" and must make an annual report to the authorities about its finances, names and occupations of members, and organization. In spite of the tribulations through which it has passed, the church in Cuba wished the church in America to know that it is growing. The church services, Nigh noted, "are warm and spiritual, with 'Gracias, Senor,'" ['Thank you, Lord'] and 'Hallelujah' ringing out."[79]

New Missions Abroad: Nicaragua

When Howard and Pearl Wolgemuth were unable to return to the mission in Cuba, they worked for a time among the refugees from Castro's regime, first in Jamaica and then in Florida.[80] Interest soon developed, however, in the possibility of establishing a new Brethren in Christ witness in some other part of Latin America.

While in Miami the Wolgemuths gathered information about mission work in ten Latin American countries, with special attention to launching a work in Central America. Later, Howard Wolgemuth, together with Carl Ulery and Henry Hostetter representing the Board for Missions, went to Nicaragua to seek an appropriate mission location.[81]

The group decided that the region around Managua was promising, and by December 1964, the Wolgemuths were in Nicaragua holding Sunday schools and other gospel meetings, giving adult literacy lessons, visiting, and generally making friends as they planned for the development of the mission.[82] Soon they began meetings in a private home in the village of Esquipulas, a few miles from Managua. Later, a building was erected for mission purposes in this town which had not had a Protestant ministry for thirty-five years.[83] By 1969 Esquipulas had a congregation of nineteen baptized members, and the missionaries were conducting weekly services at four other points, two of which later became church centers.[84]

Like every mission field, Nicaragua had its own special problems. The tremendous social and economic problems of the people—poverty, illiteracy, and disease—indicated that the mission program needed social and economic components, in addition to its spiritual ministry.[85] When the missionaries first began work in Esquipulas, the people had no running water, but this need was met when the town developed its own water system.[86] The mission, however, took the initiative in providing the community with a medical clinic visited monthly by a Christian doctor from Managua.[87] Several years later this clinic also offered classes in hygiene.[88]

In 1974 the social service phase of the mission received new emphasis when Glen and Wanda Heise arrived in Nicaragua as voluntary service workers. Their specific assignment was to explore possibilities to help meet the social needs of the Nicaraguans. In addition to sharing in the spiritual ministries of the mission, the Heises developed adult literacy programs and promoted projects for community improvement. Wanda Heise, a nurse, also served in public health.[89]

Nature itself was hostile at times, for Nicaragua was earthquake prone. In 1972 twenty-three severe quakes brought devastation and death to thousands of people. Some of the mission staff, which included Bert and

Marian Sider, Charles and Cara Musser, and Walter and Lynda Kelly, were in Managua and in serious danger when much of the city was destroyed.[90] The Brethren in Christ missionary couples were among the few who remained and rendered assistance in the Managua area, despite the hardships which had to be endured during the period of recovery.[91]

Another problem which the mission faced was the antagonism of other religious groups competing for the loyalty of the people. As the Brethren in Christ work gained momentum, both the Catholic Church and Jehovah's Witnesses sought to turn the community against it.[92]

A temporary problem was the security of person and home in downtown Managua where the first missionaries located and from which they commuted to their field of service outside of the city. In this inner-city setting, houses had to be enclosed with high wire fences and strong, locked iron doors.[93]

While living in Managua, Pearl Wolgemuth had a traumatic experience with the breakdown of security. She was alone in the mission residence when a burglar posing as an inspector from the Department of Health persuaded her to unlock the door. After she had conducted him through the house, he ordered her into the bathroom, drew a knife, and threatened to kill her if she resisted or made an outcry while he robbed the house. He then selected what he wanted from the residence and departed. In recounting the incident Mrs. Wolgemuth observed that the experience of "living dangerously," although unpleasant, was more than compensated for by the joy of doing what the missionaries believed to be God's will for them.[94]

In the midst of the realities and problems of Nicaraguan life, the missionaries sought for methods to build a strong, enduring church. Some mission groups in Latin America had depended upon missionary pastors traveling preaching circuits. This created an attitude of congregational dependence upon the missionary, and the churches tend to die if deprived of his leadership. Other groups have conducted month-long evangelistic campaigns, at the close of which promising new converts are designated as pastors. Often a young Christian assuming this responsibility is unable to nurture the work and it flounders.[95]

The Brethren in Christ in Nicaragua employ a different method. They seek out potential pastors and nurture and train them until they mature enough to be assigned to churches. The missionaries thereafter continue to assist them as necessary and to provide a continuing training program.[96]

In 1973 a seminary extension course was started with three students.[97]

The next year Bishop Roy Sider and Reverend J. Earl Musser ordained to the Christian ministry the first two Brethren in Christ Nicaraguans, Antonio Moreno and Enrique Palacios.[98] Other potential pastors are developing among the lay leadership of the churches.[99]

A hurricane in Honduras gave the Nicaraguan church its first opportunity to send men out of the country to help others in a time of emergency need. Three men who went to Honduras averaged almost three weeks of service in that country. They returned "rejoicing in the Lord for the concrete ways they had been able to help the brethren in Honduras."[100]

In spite of problems, the Brethren in Christ mission work in Nicarauga is growing. By the summer of 1976, there were eight churches and 150 members.[101] Although the rural people among whom the mission began were poor, and school opportunities were inadequate, the decision to concentrate first upon a church-planting ministry has produced healthy congregations and indigenous pastors who are maturing in capacity to fill the pastoral office.[102]

A new mission ministry is developing among the lower middle class of Bello Horizonte within the city of Managua. This poses for the emerging Nicaraguan church the challenge of discerning the intent of the gospel to make brethren and sisters in Christ of converts from different social backgrounds.[103]

Financial Stewardship

Costs of church activities spiraled upward after the mid-century. Church schools and benevolent institutions sought increased maintenance and capital funds support, while church boards expanded their programs and, in some instances, added full or part-time executive offices. At the same time, more local churches employed salaried pastors and engaged in extensive building operations.

These circumstances created increasing need for systematic financial planning at both general and local church levels. This resulted in the development of a budget system which sought to stimulate increased giving and also to allocate available financial resources as equitably as possible.

In 1954 General Conference created a Finance Budgetary Commission to "review, revise, and approve" the operating and capital funds budgets of general church boards and institutions.[104] The next year this commission submitted its first budget proposals. General Conference approved them, and because the commission reported directly to Conference rather than to a board or boards, changed the name of the agency to Budget Committee.[105]

In 1957 the Budget Committee reverted to commission status under the new Board of Administration. In that same year, Conference approved a budget plan for local congregations, to encourage appropriate distribution of giving for both local and general church needs.[106]

As the Brethren budget developed, it provided opportunities to instruct and prepare the brotherhood for increased financial giving. In 1959, for example, the Budget Commission pointed out that stewardship giving across the church had fallen short of the tithe of per capita income by $93.50, and it urged the ministry to place more emphasis upon stewardship.[107]

Promotion of stewardship thereafter became an important aspect of the commission's work. In 1964 it initiated a "Stewardship Sunday" and encouraged pastors to plan the service with a special stewardship emphasis.[108] At that time the name of the agency was changed to "Budget and Stewardship Commission," and one of its members, Ross Nigh of Ontario, Canada, became the first incumbent of a new office, Director of Stewardship.[109]

Several years later Alvin Burkholder of California succeeded Nigh to become the part-time salaried Director of Stewardship with a budget to develop a stewardship program. He brought to this office his experience as a member of the Stewardship Commission of NAE. His duties were to prepare and provide stewardship literature, hold stewardship seminars, and counsel individuals in the preparation of wills and in estate planning.[110] He has also been widely used by local churches to direct building-fund campaigns. Together with the Budget and Stewardship Commission, the Director of Stewardship has sought to keep before the brotherhood the importance of continued and increased stewardship giving to the work of the church.

The Role of Women

In recent years the Brethren in Christ have been re-examining the patriarchal structures of their church life. Like many changes made by the group, those affecting the role of women reveal the potent influences of social acculturation in the modification of theological perspectives. Amid the ferment of the Women's Liberation Movement, the Brethren had to review their historic presupposition that God ordained male domination of both church and society.

As noted in various chapters of this book, the Brethren "preference for male stock" did not prevent some talented women—Sarah Bert, Rhoda Lee, Frances Davidson, and others—from attaining considerable visibility and influence in church life.[111] Scores of other women gave large segments of their lives in home and overseas missions; hundreds taught and ministered to children in Sunday and vacation Bible schools.[112]

In general, married women served the church through their husbands. General Conference of 1918 ruled that wives of church officials shared the ordination of the husbands in a "help meet" capacity.[113] A later Conference clarified this ambiguous status of wives of ordained officials by deciding that the ordination service did not confer upon the wife the actual office held by the husband; rather, her office was supportive and auxiliary to his. Thus, for example, the wife of an ordained official might preside in a worship service for which no previous arrangements had been made, provided neither a bishop, minister, nor deacon was present.[114]

Unlike married women, single women served the church in their own right. They were not, however, selected for service on the basis of merit or talent alone; often they gained service opportunities because of the unavailability of men. This is illustrated by the first missionary party to Africa in which, because only one man was available, women comprised eighty percent of the group.

Except for mission ordination, women traditionally received little official recognition from the church. The Brethren did not call them to preaching ministries nor respond sympathetically to their announcements of personal calls. In 1905 when Nancy Brillinger of Markham District expressed a personal call to the ministry, the district council promptly disposed of the matter by directing her attention to a Conference ruling that "sisters shall not preach in public meeting" and also to consideration of "the Word."[115] When the question of the right of women to preach again arose in 1919, Conference ruled that "we do not consider it the right of women to stand on equality with the man as preacher."[116]

The only woman ordained to the Brethren ministry was Anna Graybill of Oklahoma. When she made her call known in 1921, the Oklahoma Church unanimously agreed to ordain her.[117] The general church did not readily accept this ordination, however, and pointedly omitted Miss

Graybill's name from the official directory of ministers.[118] She may also have been the target of a 1933 Conference action that an ordained woman minister should be limited to preaching; she could not perform any duty requiring ecclesiastical sanction, such as marrying, baptizing, burying, presiding over councils, and serving on administrative boards.[119]

A few early twentieth-century women held the title of "evangelist." This, however, only identified them as associates of their husbands in evangelistic work.[120]

The one administrative office open to women throughout the century was that of deaconess, although few women were elected to it. As early as 1902, Conference approved the appointment of deaconesses, but the first recorded woman to hold the office was Mary J. Long, wife of Avery Long, who was chosen in 1912 by the General Executive Board to serve in Salem District, Texas.[121]

By 1938 even the memory of the office of deaconess seems to have faded, and Conference recreated it for women who, within organized districts, rendered service equivalent to home mission work.[122] The first deaconesses qualified by this action were Anna I Jefferies and Mary E. Wenger of Iowa.[123] Their election failed to set a significant precedent, for only five deaconesses held office as late as 1976.[124] Clearly the office of deaconess did little to provide official recognition for the services of women in the church.

The one area of church life reflecting a major change in the role of women is their voting representation in the general and regional conferences and the respective boards, commissions, and committees. In 1907 General Conference named three women—Alice Swalm of Ontario, Lizzie Wingert of Pennsylvania, and Anna Eshelman of Kansas—to serve on the Home Mission Board because that board needed to be made up of "the best material."[125] Although this could have set a precedent for greater involvement of women in the life of the church, it failed to do so. For reasons unknown, women ceased to be represented on the Home Mission Board after 1919.[126]

An important precedent for the involvement of women in General Conference dates from 1964 when Ruth Heisey presented herself as an elected delegate from Lancaster, Pennsylvania. Although the Conference leaders were momentarily perplexed, they found no grounds for questioning her credentials so she was officially seated.[127]

In spite of this important precedent, changes in the official role of women came slowly. Only eight of the elected delegates to the General

Conference of 1970 were women. Personnel of the Women's Missionary Prayer Circle and the Women's Missionary Sewing Auxiliary had no vote in Conference, and no woman served on any major board, commission, or committee. Similar male domination characterized the regional conferences, except for the Pacific Conference which seated a high percentage of women in 1970.[128]

The personnel of both the elected delegate body and the agencies of the 1976 General Conference reveal that the official influence of women increased significantly after 1970. More then forty women served as elected delegates, members of the Women's Missionary Prayer Circle and the Women's Missionary Sewing Auxiliary were voting members, and their respective presiding officers were ex officio members of the Board for Missions. In addition, women had representation on the Board of Christian Education and the General Conference Program Committee.[129] Minutes of the regional conferences indicated a similar increase in the involvement of women.[130] These data demonstrate that the long period of male domination of the structures and life of the Brethren in Christ is gradually coming to an end.

Divorce and Remarriage

Weakening family structures and the increasing deterioration of marriage relationships in contemporary society have forced the Brethren in Christ to review their historic position on divorce and remarriage. Prior to the mid-century they tended to perceive divorce primarily as a threat from outside of the brotherhood; members nurtured in Brethren homes rarely separated from their spouses. In more recent years, emphasis on congregational growth and the founding of extension churches have produced a growing number of converts with irregular and complex marital relationships, and divorce has begun to invade some families which have long been identified with the Brethren faith.

Faced with these realities, General Conference labored from 1963 to 1965 to find a more satisfactory approach to the problem. Finally, the brotherhood decided to offer associate membership under certain conditions to persons legally divorced and remarried.[131] One condition required consultation with the pastor so that "social relations" might be adjusted upon "the merits of the case in view of the highest good of all parties concerned." Social relations included sexual relations which, according to previous rulings, would automatically have had to cease as a qualification for membership.[132]

Divorced and remarried persons admitted to associate membership could not hold office requiring ordination or consecration. They were not eligible, furthermore, to serve on congregational church boards or in conferences at either the regional or general church level. Members who, subsequent to the taking of their church vows, became involved in divorce and remarriage faced termination of their memberships.[133]

Recently this associate membership came up for review. In 1972 General Conference authorized a church-wide study on the ministry of the church to "those persons who are party to a remarriage when one or more of the former partners are still living."[134] This study included the preparation of papers presenting various aspects of the issues involved, as well as hypothetical cases for consideration. Discussion groups met across the church, and participants shared diverse points of view with candor and in the spirit of brotherhood.[135]

Against this background of widespread concern, the question of divorce and remarriage was a major item on the agenda of the first biennial General Conference which met in 1974. After a lengthy debate conducted in an atmosphere of brotherly concern, Conference decided that congregations might receive into church membership those who "although partners in a marriage which involves a living former spouse or spouses, have received counseling from the pastor, have given evidence of acceptable repentance, and have met the [published] requirements of membership . . . ."[136] Such persons would have all membership privileges except eligibility to serve in the offices of minister and deacon. Pastors and congregations who could not conscientiously grant full membership to those involved in divorce and remarriage could continue to accept them as associate members.

Conference approved this significant departure from past policy by the two-thirds vote necessary to begin the process of amending the church bylaws involved. Such amendment required a two-thirds vote by two successive General Conferences so final disposition of the matter awaited the convening of the second biennial Conference in 1976.[137]

The brotherhood did not intend the 1974 decision to imply any degree of approval of divorce and remarriage. This was made clear in a number of strongly worded recommendations and statements such as the following:

The acceptance into the fellowship of the church of those with a history of marital irregularities is not a denial of God's will nor of the seriousness of the sin of adultery. It is rather a recognition of man's failure and sin, and the affirmation of God's forgiving grace and the good news that Christ came into the world to save sinners.[138]

In other words, the intent of the decision was to strengthen the redemptive ministry of the church to persons caught in the complexities of divorce and remarriage, while simultaneously reaffirming strong brotherhood disapproval of attitudes and actions which created such complexities.

When, in 1976, the bylaw amendments implementing the 1974 decision were presented for final Conference approval, another lengthy debate ensued. The question at issue was that part of the 1974 action which made divorced and remarried members ineligible to serve in the offices of minister and deacon. In the voting, these restrictions failed to get the two-thirds vote necessary for final approval so they were automatically eliminated from the new statement of position on this matter.[139]

Charismatic Influences

Like many other churches, the Brethren in Christ have felt the influence of the contemporary charismatic movement. One result has been some local tensions, but, by emphasizing patience and brotherhood, church leaders have sought to build bridges of understanding between members holding diverse points of view.

This was not the first experience of the Brethren with the charismatic emphasis. The Foreign Mission Board encountered it early in the century and for "the guidance and safety" of mission work, stated the position of the church.

We . . . believe in the gift of tongues, but do not place an emphasis on that gift as the only evidence of the baptism of the Spirit, or that souls should seek for that gift.

Such teaching is erroneous, and has led to much confusion and even fanaticism.[140]

The board warned all missionaries to steer clear of this error and to emphasize repentance, conversion, consecration, and sanctification on the premise that the gifts of the Spirit—"healing, prophecy, teaching or tongues, etc."—are distributed only at the discretion of the Spirit. The board also stressed that anyone who received the gift of tongues should be guided by St. Paul's admonitions in First Corinthians so that the gift would be properly used rather than abused.

A decade later charismatic influences divided the Tulare congregation in California. One of its two ministers gave leadership to those members inclined toward the charismatic position. Since the other minister sharply and publicly opposed him, the result was "chaos in the pulpit." California Bishop J. Harry Wagaman stabilized the situation for a time, but when he and Mrs. Wagaman served at the San Francisco Mission during 1922-1923, he was unable to maintain his previous close relationship with Tulare. By the time he returned, the Tulare division was so wide that reconciliation proved to be impossible, and the congregation was shattered. In 1932 only about ten members were still attending the service.[141]

The present charismatic movement among the Brethren in Christ has not produced schism. This is due, in part at least, to the deliberate efforts of leaders to encourage mutual understanding and to minimize confrontation. One panel presentation at General Conference of 1974, for example, included four participants, each of whom offered a different personal point of view about the gifts of the Spirit. This panel provided a setting in which many members of the brotherhood could weigh and evaluate the respective positions, one of which was an apology for the gift of tongues.

Thus far, the charismatic impact seems to have stimulated the Brethren to draw more heavily upon latent resources of brotherhood. Unlike some past differences between members, the present situation has not produced an increment of harsh, judgmental attitudes in any significant number of individuals.

Peace and Nonresistance

After the close of World War II, the Peace, Relief, and Service Committee continued to work in the three areas identified by its name. The 1953 appointment of one of its members, Christian Hostetter, Jr., as chairman of the Mennonite Central Committee strengthened Brethren in Christ ties with that organization which was also active in those areas.[142]

As the national optimism engendered by the defeat of Germany and Japan gave way to the "Cold War" between the United States and the Soviet Union, military conscription became a part of the United States way of life. Civilian Public Service was not revived, however, and conscientious objectors among the Brethren discharged their selective service obligation to the nation through I-W alternate work asignments under MCC.

These assignments included a variety of activities in the homeland, such as service to non-profit institutions and special agricultural projects. Conscripts could also go overseas in relief or PAX (peace) service.[143] Eventually, many draftees served in approved ways in connection with Brethren missions and institutions. Voluntary Service women and men sometimes joined in the same projects with conscientious objectors who were discharging their selective service obligation.[144] This similarity between VS and selective service assignments may have tended to blunt the edge of the issue of personal, decisive commitment to the nonresistant position.

During this period when the Peace, Relief, and Service Committee was busy with the problems of conscientious objectors, peace education continued to be a major concern. In the years 1950-1956, the committee sponsored peace conferences in Pennsylvania, Ohio, and Canada, in addition to the dissemination of peace information by other means.[145]

Statistics reported to General Conference in 1955 underlined the committee's concern for peace education. Of 430 male Brethren members in the draft age, 61.16 percent reported that they would not accept military service, 12.78 percent reported that they would accept it, and 24.04 were undecided.[146] Two years later statistics on actual Brethren draftees between 1951-1957 revealed that a substantial number had entered military service.[147]

Another significant development in this period was the selection of Henry Hostetter by the Peace Section of MCC to conduct a peace mission among the Mennonite and Brethren in Christ missions in Africa. The Peace, Relief, and Service capitalized upon Hostetter's mission to make the point that the peace testimony should be considered a "vital part of our Christian witness."[148]

By the 1960s Brethren personnel, especially men, were sharing in the activities of the Mennonite Disaster Service (MDS) which rendered assistance to people in areas devastated by natural disasters such as earthquakes and hurricanes. Three men, for example, contributed their skills to reconstruction after the Honduras hurricane which occurred during the 1960-1961 Conference year.[149] MDS activity related indirectly to the issue of nonresistance. Not only did it demonstrate positive

Christian concern for the unfortunate, but it helped to compensate for resistance of the MCC constituency to full participation in the structure of Civil Defense. In the event of a Civil Defense emergency, the organized resources of MDS would be available for reconstruction work.[150]

In 1966 the peace emphasis of the church entered a period of transition when the Peace, Relief, and Service Committee merged with the two mission boards. This merger, designed to eliminate overlapping responsibilities, provided a large Board for Missions with an executive secretary, Henry Hostetter, and four portfolios, Director of Missions, Director of Mission Churches, Director of Extension and Director of Christian Service Ministries divided between Isaac S. Kanode and J. Wilmer Heisey. These assignments related primarily to finances, personnel, and promotion, although Christian Service Ministries included responsibility for the "concerns and witness of the church in Christian social welfare and peace testimony."[151]

Promotion of peace and social concerns temporarily lapsed while General Conference was preoccupied with this major reorganization of board structures. In 1969, however, Conference gave renewed emphasis to these interests by creating a Commission on Peace and Social Concerns amenable to the Board for Missions. The new commission was to guide the church in "an effective understanding and practice of the doctrine of non-resistance" and to stimulate the conscience of the brotherhood "toward a Christ-like response to the ills of society." In addition it assumed responsibility to counsel youth concerning military conscription, to maintain liaison with the Peace Section of MCC, and to assume the duties of the former Committee on Economic and Social Relations.[152]

In its first report to General Conference, the Peace and Social Concerns Commission registered its conviction that "peace and peace-making demanded immediate priority." It accordingly called for a reaffirmation of the Brethren in Christ commitment to biblical non-resistance "including, on the one hand, the refusal to bear arms and the avoidance, when possible, of economic profit from the business of war, and on the other hand, the pursuit of all things that make for peace; . . ." Conference approved this recommendation and another providing for general church observance of a peace Sunday in May 1971.[153]

Among the later projects of the commission, one of the most important was collaboration with the Commission on Social Action of the Christian Holiness Association in sponsorship of a seminar on "Christian Holiness and the Issues of War and Peace." This seminar at Winona Lake, Indiana, in June 1973 involved approximately sixty persons from eleven holiness denominations in a discussion of whether Christians should participate in war.[154]

General Conference of 1972 assigned to the commission the task of preparing a position paper on "The Church, War, and Respect for Human Life."[155] A first draft submitted to the 1974 Conference as a study paper went beyond nonresistance to range widely over euthanasia, capital punishment, suicide, drugs, alcohol, tobacco, and highway safety. The final draft submitted for action to the 1976 Conference dealt forcefully and in considerable detail with nonresistance supported biblically on the following premises:

> Our approach to the Scriptures is to begin with Jesus Christ and the New Testament. We accept all of Scripture as the Word of God written. We interpret all Scripture through Jesus Christ. "In the past God spoke to our ancestors many times and in many ways through the prophets, but in these last days he has spoken to us through his Son . . . ." In the life and teachings of Jesus Christ, God had chosen to give the fullest and final revelation of His will.[156]

Conference adopted the position paper and authorized preparation of a short summary for widespread distribution. In this action the brotherhood strongly reaffirmed its historic peace position on basically the same presuppositions as those which had guided the group in the past. This recent shift toward renewed support for nonresistance is confirmed by a 1975 sociological study of thirty geographically representative Brethren congregations.[157]

In one significant respect, however, the 1976 commitment to nonresistance differed from the historic understanding of the Brethren. This difference was not in the doctrinal statement itself but rather in a different conception of the relationship between the doctrine and political activism. Most of the early Brethren believed that consistent adherence to nonresistance required them to stand aside from political processes. Recent evidence indicates that their spiritual descendants no longer make this assumption. A 1975 survey of ninety ministers revealed that seventy-five percent of the respondents voted in national elections and lesser numbers in provincial, state, and local elections. Slightly more than eighty percent of the United States ministers voted, while approximately thirty-eight percent of the Canadian ministers did so. In spite of their high voting record only three percent of the ninety ministers would consider running for public office, thirteen percent might do so, and about eighty-three percent would not do so.[158]

This high percentage of political activism among Brethren ministers indicates that most of them no longer perceive a conflict between commitment to nonresistance and the exercise of the franchise, although a high percentage of the group would not consider running for public office. Sociological data reveal that the laity basically agree with their ministers in both respects.[159] In spite of the more individualistic Christianity now characteristic of the brotherhood, a significant majority of members continue to have reservations about following contemporary evangelicalism into full political participation.

Awakening Concern About Racism

Throughout most of their history, the Brethren in Christ believed that they served the well-being of society primarily by actualizing the visible church and by seeking the conversion of individuals. When their mission enterprises brought them into contact with social problems such as poverty, illiteracy, and disease, they endeavored to solve these problems for the people with whom they were working. Such "social work" tended, however, to be regarded as the handmaiden of evangelism.

These presuppositions help to explain why some members have hesitated to endorse social welfare enterprises as legitimate ends in their own right. Not all Brethren feel comfortable, for example, with the MCC slogan, "In the name of Christ," when it is applied to human welfare programs which provide little opportunity for direct proclamation of a message of personal salvation. In spite of polarization of Brethren attitudes on this issue, General Conference has steadfastly adhered to identification with and participation in MCC programs. Furthermore, as the following sketch will show, the brotherhood has moved toward an enlarged concept of Christian responsibility to speak both prophetically and practically about social injustice and human need.

Except for opposition to the liquor traffic, the nineteenth-century Brethren were generally quiescent about social problems. They were more inclined to deplore the sinfulness of society than to concern themselves with social needs and social injustice.

Almost nothing is known about the Brethren reaction to slavery prior to the Civil War. The one exception is the attitude of Jacob Eisenhower who was "unalterably opposed" to the institution. Although Eisenhower believed war and violence to be wicked, he was a great admirer of Abraham Lincoln who guided the Union Government during the Civil War. When, shortly after the President's assassination, a son was born into the Eisenhower household, the father fondly named him Abraham Lincoln Eisenhower.[160]

From the Civil War until well into the twentieth century, the Brethren were northern rural people who only incidentally contacted black Americans. In 1877 a Lancaster County deacon noted that he contributed to a burial fund for "a colored man."[161] Some years later Bishop Samuel Zook of Kansas reported that he attended a black church service while visiting on the West Coast.[162]

In 1893 the first reference to blacks appeared in the *Evangelical Visitor*. This was a selected article entitled "Give the Negro a Chance," which forcefully pled the cause of the black man and asserted:

> He has reached a crisis of inhuman torture and unparalleled disgrace in the history of his freedom. He is always the man caught in the bushes to save some white Isaac, . . . He is always the scape goat [sic] to bear away the sins of some white rascals; . . .

After exploring possible causes of the Negro's condition, the article continued: "If from any of these causes this unusual assault upon the Negro has arisen, the best way is to get out of the way; for he is going and he has a just God that will help him go."[163]

Early twentieth century sources make a few brief allusions to blacks. Physician William Baker of Ohio reported that "a colored gentleman" called upon him.[164] Enos Hess was the first known member to imply the existence of racial prejudice among the Brethren. In 1904 he stressed the need for "an industrious, Spirit-filled minister, free from race prejudice" to take charge of an infant mission work in Virginia.[165] Three years later the Philadelphia Mission reported the baptism of the first known black member.[166]

Except for *Visitor* editor George Detwiler's expression of horror about the brutal lynching of a black man at Coatesville, Pennsylvania in 1911, black Americans fade out of Brethren sources until 1938.[167] At that time the United States Congress stormily debated the Patman Anti-Lynch Bill. This provided the context for Editor Vernon Stump to address an editorial to "The Race Problem." Stump was appalled by the inequities suffered by blacks.

When we think of the terrible outrages that have been perpetuated upon the
colored race by the white man, it staggers our imagination to even think of
the great and sweeping condemnation that a God of justice will have to pass
upon the white race on the great day of final reckoning.

We sincerely believe that the negro [sic] in America should be given as
great an opportunity in our educational and vocational field[s] as a white
person; that they [sic] should be given an open door to earn a livelihood on
the same footing as is granted to others; . . .[168]

The sources do not reveal how widely the brotherhood shared Stump's
sentiments, but Albert and Margie Engle were two members who shared
them. When, in 1927, they began a long term mission of service in
Kentucky, they disliked the barriers between races which extended even to
religious worship. At one of the early tent meetings in an area where
blacks were relatively numerous, Engle noticed that they stood outside of
the tent while whites occupied the pews. He accordingly went out and
invited them into the tent, which action alienated whites who ceased
attending the services. Such experiences soon taught the Engles that
community mores governing black and white relationships were so firmly
established that an integrated mission was impossible at that time.[169]

In spite of these historical glimpses of concern about racial prejudice,
the brotherhood as a whole showed little interest in the matter until the
recent Black Revolution jolted society out of its complacent attitude
toward the underprivileged black community. Then, beginning in the early
1960s, the *Evangelical Visitor* broke out in a rash of articles on race. The
main articles in an entire issue in 1968 dealt primarily with "The Urban
Crisis."[170]

These articles ranged widely over the racial issue. One reported the end
of seventy-four years of inner-city ministry in Chicago where the Brethren
were unable to cope with the changing racial composition of the
neighborhood.[171] Others recorded the beginnings of a new inner-city work
in Brooklyn, New York.[172] Several referred to the Valley Chapel
congregation near Canton, Ohio, which, according to one writer, disliked
the term "integration" because it implied "a distinction between Negro
and white which ceases to exist among friends."[173]

Meanwhile, General Conference was seeking to come to grips with
racism. In 1963 it adopted a statement on race relations. This deplored
prejudice toward black Americans who had suffered the indignities of
slavery and subsequent discrimination. It noted the determined opposition
and the "acts and methods of cruel violence" directed against the black

community as it sought to break down discriminatory barriers. Then the brotherhood declared its support of the non-violent phase of the Black Revolution.

> As the General Conference of the Brethren in Christ Church we wish to go on record as in sympathy with these aspirations of the Negro race and to extend to them an expression of our moral support in efforts for their attainment to the degree that these efforts are made in accordance with Christian principles.
>
> In this connection we have been encouraged to note the policy of non-violence which has been employed by certain Negro leaders, and we would encourage this approach as reflecting the Christian attitude, and as likely to be most successful in attaining the desired goals.[174]

Conference simultaneously called upon the Brethren membership to recognize the principle of the equality of all men and to implement this in the spirit of both human and Christian brotherhood.

Within a year after affirming support for the goals of the Black Revolution, the Brethren became uneasy about the growing tension and social activism accompanying it. Conference expressed disapproval of demonstrations, sit-ins, marches, and law violations and summoned the brotherhood to "seek to exhibit a spiritual poise, Christian dignity and a truthful calmness that . . . [would] adorn the testimony of people professing godliness." Although the Conferences of 1963 and 1970 renewed the commitment to pursue justice and equity for the racial minorities and other disadvantaged people in our world," they were vague about specific ways by which the brotherhood could implement this commitment.[175]

Coincidentally, the Conference of 1970 was able to take a practical step to challenge racism. The occasion for this was the discovery by the Allegheny Conference of a segregation clause in the bylaws of a Brethren in Christ cemetery. While blacks could be buried there, the clause required the cemetery trustees to designate a special section of the burial grounds and mark it for black burials. No attempt was made to discover how widespread such cemetery segregation was, but another example of it eventually came to light.[176]

In view of these circumstances, the Allegheny Conference took a broad action designed to eliminate racism from both the attitudes and legal documents of that part of the brotherhood. This action called upon members of the conference to seek to identify and eliminate all traces of racism from their attitudes, and it urged leaders and ministers to alert congregations to the sinfulness of racism in every form. Finally, it requested examination of official church documents, such as property deeds and cemetery bylaws, and directly that any evidences of racism be removed from them by whatever official or legal action might be necessary.[177]

Realizing that such documentary racism might have broad general church implications, the Allegheny Conference referred the preambles and recommendations of its action to General Conference. The unanimous adoption of these recommendations by the latter body placed the total brotherhood on record as opposed to racism in every form.[178]

World Hunger

The Brethren in Christ have had a long tradition of ministry to human needs, both through their own missions and institutions and through MCC. As previously noted, however, they have tended to regard social service primarily as the handmaiden of evangelism. While strongly emphasizing the doctrine of salvation, stressing the redemption of "souls," they have historically manifested little corporate concern for the stewardship of the earth and a clearly formulated concept of ministry to the "total man."

By the early 1970s, however, the Brethren were beginning to feel a greater sense of responsibility for Christian ministry to the massive material and social needs of the contemporary world. General Conference of 1974 called upon the brotherhood to reduce food consumption and expenditures during the 1974-1976 Conference biennium "as an act of discipline and sacrifice in love to make available additional monies and food for ministry to both the physical and spiritual needs of men in the name of Christ." The Commission on Peace and Social Concerns implemented planning for a "World Hunger Fund." As a meaningful way to dramatize this fund, General Conference chose as the theme for the 1974-1976 biennium, "Sharing and Conserving God's Resources."[179]

By the end of 1975 this fund had already accumulated $125,000, of which seventy-five percent was allocated for the worldwide food programs of MCC and twenty-five percent for use by the Brethren in Christ wherever they encountered major food needs, Self-help and self-development food programs were to have priority in the expenditures of these contributions.[180]

In 1976 General Conference further implemented its concern about hunger by instructing the Board for Missions to consider the selection of someone to assist the brotherhood to gain greater awareness and understanding of world poverty. This assignee would spend at least a year among the congregations during the 1976-1978 biennium stressing "the stewardship of possessions, the simple life and the underlying causes and unjust structures which contribute to widespread poverty and hunger in the world."[181]

Kenneth B. Hoover, former chairman of the Board for Missions, accepted the call to this world-hunger ministry.[182] Hoover had traveled in Latin America, Africa, and the Far East on mission and MCC assignments, thus observing Third World hunger and poverty firsthand.[183] His years of experience on the Board for Missions placed him in a position to integrate his new assignment with the total mission ministries of the church. Specifically, his commission from that board rested on the premise that "The full dimension of the Great Commission and the spiritual dynamics without which it cannot be fulfilled will be the underlying foundation of all the other issues taught."[184]

The recent concern of the Brethren with problems such as hunger, racism, and war reflects their broadening conception of the church's responsibility to speak to issues of social welfare. Their increased emphasis upon ministry to the totality of human need has not, however, caused them to develop a "social gospel" mentality. Indeed, at no time in their history have they been more self-consciously and enthusiastically evangelistic in promulgating their historic doctrine of a personal, heartfelt new birth. This is attested by membership growth in North America from approximately 7,200 in 1955 to 12,475 in 1975.[185] Since personal testimony to a pietistic conversion experience is the principal criterion for church membership, these statistics reveal that the doctrine of salvation continues to be the cornerstone of the Brethren faith.

NOTES:

[1]Single women sometimes made up the entire staff of a mission station.

[2]J. Wilmer Heisey, "Institutional Missions in Historical Perspective" (unpublished

paper, 1975), Church Archives. Heisey is Executive Secretary of the Board for Missions.

[3]*Ibid.*

[4]*General Conference Minutes,* 1958, Article 27, pp. 97-98. In 1958 the Board for Home Missions and Extension became the successor to the Home Mission Board.

[5]*Handbook of Missions,* 1965, p. 81.

[6]*General Conference Minutes,* 1965, Article 23, p. 91. It had previously been incorporated under the laws of California.

[7]*Ibid.,* 1969, Article 19, pp. 74-76. In keeping with Canadian real estate laws, the property is held in the name of the Canadian Conference of the Brethren in Christ.

[8]Heisey, "Institutional Missions."

[9]*General Conference Minutes,* 1925, Article 24, pp. 40-41; *ibid.,* 1926, Article 8, pp. 11-15; *ibid.,* 1927, Article 10, p. 12; *ibid.,* 1928, Article 7, pp. 11-12. Conference soon abolished this Church Extension Board and transferred its prerogative to enter organized districts to the Home Mission Board.

[10]*Ibid.,* 1957, Article 27, p. 91.

[11]*Ibid.,* 1959, Article 27, p. 97.

[12]Henry A. Ginder interview, April 10, 1975. Bishop Ginder, a former member of the Board for Home Missions and Extension, and successively bishop of two regional conferences, has been actively involved with the extension church movement since its beginning.

[13]Henry A. Ginder interview, April 10, 1975; Wilmer Heisey to Carlton Wittlinger, September 3, 1976.

[14]*Handbook of Missions,* 1969, pp. 56-58.

[15]As a member of the Grantham Church, the present writer personally observed the emergence of the new congregation in Dillsburg.

[16]Henry A. Ginder interview, March 12, 1974. The interviewee held many evangelistic meetings and only recently retired as the first Brethren in Christ Director of Evangelism. This section is based largely upon data provided by him and upon the present writer's personal observations.

[17]II Cor. 6:14.

[18]Henry A. Ginder interview, March 12, 1974.

[19]*General Conference Minutes,* 1967, Article 19, pp. 54. Ginder served until 1974 when he was succeeded by Bishop Roy V. Sider of the Canadian Conference.

[20]*General Conference Minutes,* 1970, Article 18, pp. 52-53.

[21]*Ibid.,* 1952, Article 18, p. 39; *ibid.,* 1953, Article 33, p. 70.

[22]*Ibid.,* 1953, Article 33, p. 70.

[23]*Ibid.,* 1952, Article 18, p. 39.

[24]*Ibid.,* 1954, Article 35, p. 79. The present writer was a member of the General Conference which heard that program tape.

[25]*Ibid.,* 1955, Article 33, p. 73.

[26]*Ibid.,* 1956, Article 27, pp. 64-65.

[27]*Ibid.,* p. 65.

[28]*Ibid.,* p. 66.

[29]Paul E. Hostetler interview, May 20, 1975. Hostetler was secretary of the Commission on Radio when Gems of Grace was produced.

[30]*General Conference Minutes,* 1957, Article 25, p. 66; *ibid.,* 1958, Article 23, p. 67.

[31]*Ibid.,* 1958, Article 23, p. 72.

[32]*Ibid.*, 1959, Article 24, pp. 75-76.

[33]*Ibid.*, p. 76.

[34]*Ibid.*, 1961, Article 22, p. 63.

[35]*Ibid.*, 1962, Article 18, pp. 58-59.

[36]*Ibid.*, 1963, Article 22, p. 71.

[37]*Ibid.*, 1964, Article 21, pp. 64-65.

[38]Charlie B. Byers to Carlton O. Wittlinger, June 3, 1975.

[39]*Ibid.*

[40]Barbara A. Lieby, "The Beginning of the Brethren in Christ Mission Work in Japan"((unpublished paper based on an extensive taped interview with Peter Willms, one of the first missionaries to Japan), p. 1, tapes in Church Archives.

[41]*Ibid.*, pp. 1-2; *General Conference Minutes,* 1952, Article 35, p. 83.

[42]Lieby, "Mission Work in Japan," p. 2.

[43]*General Conference Minutes,* 1952, Article 35, p. 89.

[44]*Ibid.*, 1953, Article 34, p. 74; Lieby, "Mission Work in Japan," pp. 2-3; The Japanese prefecture is comparable to a state or province.

[45]Lieby, "Mission Work in Japan," p. 3.

[46]*General Conference Minutes,* 1953, Article 34, p. 79.

[47]Lieby, "Mission Work in Japan," p. 4.

[48]John Graybill, "Witnessing in Japan, "1953-1973," *Visitor,* LXXXVI (October 10, 1973), p. 4. Graybill is Missionary Superintendent for Japan, and has been connected with the work since 1957.

[49]*Ibid.*, p. 5.

[50]John Graybill, "The Koganei Church," *Visitor,* LXXXVI (September 10, 1973), pp. 8-9.

[51]*Ibid.*

[52]John Graybill, "Witnessing in Japan, "1953-1973," *Visitor,* LXXXVI (October 10, 1973), p. 5.

[53]*General Conference Minutes,* 1972, Article 7, p. 16.

[54]John Graybill, "Witnessing in Japan, 1953-1973" *Visitor,* LXXXVI (October 10, 1973), p. 5.

[55]*Ibid.*

[56]*Ibid.*

[57]*General Conference Minutes,* 1954, Article 6, p. 13; *ibid.*, 1959, Article 3, p. 13; *ibid.*, 1972, Article 7, p. 16; *Handbook of Missions,* 1967, pp. 7, 40.

[58]In addition to the two couples named, these include Doyle and Thelma Book and Marlin and Ruth Zook. Other individuals have contributed periods of voluntary service.

[59]J. Wilmer Heisey interview, August 25, 1976.

[60]John Graybill, "Witnessing in Japan, "1953-1973," *Visitor,* LXXXVI (October 10, 1973), p. 5.

[61]Ruth Herr, "Cuba," (unpublished paper, Messiah College, May 27, 1954), p. 26, Church Archives. Information based upon correspondence and interviews with persons directly involved.

[62]*Ibid.*

[63]*Ibid.*, p. 27.

[64]*Ibid.*

[65]*General Conference Minutes,* 1953, Article 34, p. 75.

[66]Herr, "Cuba," pp. 27-29; *Handbook of Missions,* 1955, p. 75; *ibid.,* 1956, p. 102.

[67]*General Conference Minutes,* 1954, Article 36, p. 87; *ibid.,* 1955, Article 35, p. 87; *Handbook of Missions,* 1955, p. 75.

[68]Dale Ulery letter, *Visitor,* LXVIII (May 23, 1955), 9.

[69]*General Conference Minutes,* 1955, Article 35, p. 86; *ibid.,* 1956, Article 4, p. 13.

[70]*Ibid.,* 1958, Article 26, p. 88; *Handbook of Missions,* 1959, p. 49.

[71]*General Conference Minutes,* 1959, Article 3, p. 13; *ibid.,* Article 27, p. 86.

[72]*Ibid.,* 1961, Article 3, p. 16.

[73]*Ibid.,* 1962, Article 25, p. 97.

[74]Judith Wolgemuth Hamilton interview, August 25, 1976.

[75]*Ibid.* In the Cuban culture married women freely use their maiden names.

[76]Ross Nigh, "Tell the Church in America That We Are Growing," *Visitor,* LXXXIX. (April 25, 1976), 8.

[77]*Ibid.*; Judith Hamilton interview, August 25, 1976.

[78]Ross Nigh, "Tell the Church in America That We Are Growing," *Visitor,* LXXXIX (April 25, 1976), 8.

[79]*Ibid.*

[80]*General Conference Minutes,* 1962, Article 25, p. 97; *ibid.,* 1963, Article 29, p. 119.

[81]*Ibid.,* 1964, Article 28, p. 113; Howard Wolgemuth interview, August 27, 1976.

[82]*Handbook of Missions,* 1966, p. 91.

[83]*Ibid.,* 1967, p. 45; *ibid.,* 1968, p. 40.

[84]*General Conference Minutes,* 1969, Article 7, p. 17; *ibid.,* 1971, Article 7, p. 18; *ibid.,* 1972, Article 18, p. 75.

[85]*Handbook of Missions,* 1966, p. 91; Howard Wolgemuth interview, August 27, 1976.

[86]*Handbook of Missions,* 1969, p. 40.

[87]*Ibid.,* 1968, p. 41. A second clinic was later established at Arroyo, another church center. Brethren in Christ Missions, *Annual Reports,* 1974, p. 39.

[88]Brethren in Christ Missions, *Annual Reports,* 1972, p. 43.

[89]Brethren in Christ Missions, *Annual Reports,* 1974, p. 39; Earl Musser interview, August 27, 1976.

[90]*Ibid.,* Brethren in Christ Missions, *Annual Reports,* 1972, p. 43.

[91]*Ibid.,* 1973, p. 45.

[92]Pearl Wolgemuth Interview, August 27, 1976.

[93]*Ibid.*

[94]*Ibid.*

[95]Bert Sider, "Ten Years Old," *Visitor,* LXXXIX (February 10, 1976), pp. 3-4.

[96]*Ibid.,* p. 3.

[97]Brethren in Christ Missions, *Annual Reports,* 1973, p. 46.

[98]*Ibid.,* 1974, p. 48.

[99]*Ibid.,* 1974, p. 38.

[100]*Ibid.*

[101]"Greetings to General Conference from the Church in Nicaragua," Bert Sider, Mission Superintendent, General Conference Tapes, 1976.

[102]*Brethren in Christ Missions Yearbook,* 1975, p. 15.

[103]*Ibid.*

[104]*General Conference Minutes,* 1954, Article 29, pp. 52-54.

[105]*Ibid.,* 1955, Article 28, pp. 50-53.

[106]*Ibid.,* 1957, Article 10, p. 23; *ibid.,* 1958, Article 23, pp. 65-67.

[107]*Ibid.,* 1959, Article 24, p. 73.

[108]*Ibid.,* 1964, Article 21, p. 61.

[109]*Ibid.,* p. 74.

[110]*Ibid.,* 1967, Article 19, p. 63; *ibid.,* 1968, Article 20, pp. 52-53.

[111]The "preference for male stock" was a principle associated with hereditary monarchies which preferred a son for succession to the throne even if older daughters were better prepared to assume the crown.

[112]Conference provided for the ordination of both home and overseas missionaries, but the prerogatives of ordained women missionaries were limited to the ministry of the Word. *General Conference Minutes,* 1905, Article 33, p. 31, and Article 38, p. 37.

[113]*Ibid.,* 1918, Article 20, p. 32.

[114]*Ibid.,* 1935, Article 42, pp. 70-71.

[115]Markham District Council Minutes, February 24, 1905, Article 11, p. 175.

[116]*General Conference Minutes,* 1919, Article 24, p. 36.

[117]Oklahoma State Council Minutes, March 3, 1921, Article 12, p. 4.

[118]See the official ministerial directories in *General Conference Minutes,* 1921-1940.

[119]*Ibid.,* 1933, Article 60, p. 72.

[120]*Ibid.,* 1906, "Evangelists," p. 56.

[121]*Ibid.,* 1902, Article 53, p. 142; *ibid.,* 1912, Article 48, p. 117.

[122]*Ibid.,* 1938. Article 53, p. 89.

[123]*Ibid.,* 1938, Official Directory, p. 125.

[124]*Ibid.,* 1976, Official Directory, p. 196.

[125]*Ibid.,* 1907, Article 14, p. 10, and Article 29, p. 20.

[126]*Ibid.,* 1919, Article 1, p. 5.

[127]Henry A. Ginder interview, January 3, 1976; *General Conference Minutes,* 1964, Article 1, p. 8.

[128]Carlton O. Wittlinger, "The Role of Women in the Church," *Evangelical Visitor,* LXXXIII (December 10, 1970), p. 16.

[129]*General Conference Minutes,* 1976, Article 1, pp. 6-11, and Article 26, pp. 160-66.

[130]Based upon a survey of 1975 regional conference minutes.

[131]For the historic position of the church on divorce and remarriage, see Chapter VI, and for General Conference provision for associate membership "as a much needed step for bringing converts into the Brethren in Christ Church," see *General Conference Minutes,* 1951, Article 19, pp. 38-39.

[132]*General Conference Minutes,* 1965, Article 11, p. 35.

[133]*Ibid.*

[134]*Ibid.,* 1972, Article 17, pp. 71-73.

[135]*Ibid.,* 1974 Article 12, p. 24.

[136]*Ibid.,* p. 27.

[137]*Ibid.,* p. 28.

[138]*Ibid.,* p. 26.

[139]*Ibid.,* 1976, Article 9, p. 20.

[140]*Ibid.,* 1913, Article 16, p. 47.

[141]Paul E. Engle to Alvin C. Burkholder, June 12, 1975, original letter in C. O. Wittlinger files. Engle is the son-in-law of Bishop Wagaman.

[142]*General Conference Minutes,* 1953, Article 22, p. 38.

[143]*Ibid.,* 1951, Article 25, p. 50; *ibid.,* 1952, Article 25, p. 46; *ibid.,* 1953, Article 22, p. 37. Selective Service approved the types of work which qualified for alternate service.

[144]*Ibid.,* 1962, Article 13, pp. 36-37.

[145]*Ibid.,* Reports of Peace, Relief, and Service Committee, 1951-1957.

[146]*Ibid.,* 1955, Article 23, p. 40.

[147]For comment on these statistics, see Chapter XVI.

[148]*General Conference Minutes,* 1960, Article 17, p. 42; *ibid.,* 1961, Article 16, p. 39.

[149]*Ibid.,* 1962, Article 13, p. 37.

[150]*Ibid.,* 1957, Article 17, p. 44. At least as early as 1963, Brethren members, John Garman in Canada and Raymond Hess in the United States, were performing important administrative roles in MDS.

[151]*Ibid.,* 1964, Article 21, pp. 74-81; *ibid.,* 1966, Article 9, pp. 20-24, and Article 26, p. 95.

[152]*Ibid.,* 1969, Article 19, pp. 73-74; J. Wilmer Heisey to Carlton Wittlinger, February 20, 1977; Kenneth B. Hoover interview, March 2, 1977.

[153]*General Conference Minues,* 1970, Article 19, pp. 78-79.

[154]Paul Hostetler, ed. *Perfect Love and War:A Dialogue on Christian Holiness and Issues of War and Peace* (Nappanee, Ind.: Evangel Press, 1974).

[155]*General Conference Minutes,* 1972, Article 8, p. 88.

[156]*Ibid.,* 1976, Article 18, pp. 100-1.

[157]J. Howard Kauffman and Leland Harder, *Anabaptists Four Centuries Later: A Profile of Five Mennonite and Brethren in Christ Denominations* (Scottdale, Pa.: Herald Press, 1975), p. 133. For technical reasons, this study had to be weighted in favor of the larger Brethren in Christ congregations.

[158]Mark Charlton, "Political Activism Among Brethren in Christ Ministers" (unpublished paper, University of Western Ontario, 1975), pp. 8-9, copy in Church Archives.

[159]Kauffman and Harder, *Anabaptists Four Centuries Later,* p. 161.

[160]Sarah Ferguson, "I Remember Jacob Eisenhower, the General's Grandfather," Capper's Weekly (Topeka, Kansas) February 13, 20, 27, 1968.

[161]Abram M. Hess Diary, March 27, 1877.

[162]Samuel Zook, "A Western Mission Tour," *Visitor,* VI (February 1, 1893), 43.

[163]"Give the Negro a Chance," *Visitor,* VI (June 15, 1893), 192.

[164]William O. Baker Diary, April 30, 1903.

[165]Enos H. Hess, "The Virginia Mission Work," *Visitor,* XVIII (November 15, 1904), 6.

[166]Rhoda M. Scott, "Letters," *Visitor,* XXI (September 2, 1907), 9.

[167][George Detwiler], *Visitor,* XXV (August 21, 1911), 3.

[168][Vernon Stump], *Visitor,* LI (March 14, 1938), 87.

[169]Albert Engle interview, January 13, 1977.

[170]*Visitor,* LXXXI (June 17, 1968).

[171]"The Chicago Story," *Visitor,* LXXXI (June 17, 1968), 7.

[172]Mrs. Harold Bowers, "Brooklyn-Dedication and Open House," *Visitor,* LXXVIII (December 20, 1965), 10-11; Kathy Bowers, "Inside Brooklyn," *Visitor,* LXXX (October 23, 1967), 11.

[173]James R. Engle, "Integration is a Naughty Word at Valley Chapel, Canton, Ohio," *Visitor,* LXXXI (March 11, 1968), 5-6.

[174]*General Conference Minutes,* 1963, Article 15, pp. 45-46.

[175]*Ibid.,* 1964, Article 21, p. 73; *ibid.,* 1970, Article 19, p. 78.

[176]The present writer was a member of the Executive Committee which prepared the preambles and recommendations acted upon by the Allegheny Conference.

[177]*Allegheny Regional Conference Minutes,* 1970, Article 3, pp. 6-7.

[178]*General Conference Minutes,* 1970, Article 25, p. 110.

[179]*Ibid.,* 1974, Article 22, pp. 79, 96-97, and Article 37, p. 160.

[180]*Ibid.,* 1976, Article 18, pp. 94-95.

[181]*Ibid.,* 1976, Article 18, pp. 98-99.

[182]K. B. Hoover to J. Wilmer Heisey, September 30, 1976. K. B. Hoover files.

[183]Kenneth B. Hoover interview, March 2, 1977. In addition to his experience on the Board for Missions, Hoover had served on the former Peace, Relief, and Service Committee and, at the time of his world hunger assignment, was completing approximately a decade of service on MCC.

[184]Board for Missions Minutes, October 18-20, 1976, p. 90. K. B. Hoover files.

[185]See Appendix C.

Epilogue

The Brethren in Christ began as a small, sectarian brotherhood marked by a clear sense of self-identity distinguishing them from other religious societies. Two hundred years later they are a growing denomination characterized by diversity of thought and practice, which precludes any simple description of their self-identity.

Acculturating social forces have always impinged upon the brotherhood, but their impact increased with the growing complexities of modern life. Two major periods of transition in the late nineteenth and mid-twentieth centuries highlighted the process by which the Brethren moved closer to the mainstream of evangelical-holiness denominationalism. Always, however, their roots in Anabaptism kept them from fully accepting conservative Protestantism as it is exemplified in the United States by the National Association of Evangelicals and the Christian Holiness Association, and in Canada by ecumenical groups more compatible with a sense of Canadian nationality.

Where are the contemporary Brethren in Christ going? Historical methodology cannot answer such a question, but it can provide insights about possible directions which the brotherhood may take. Broadly conceived these are three: gradual dissolution, merger with another denomination, or indefinite continuation as a separate body.

From a historical standpoint, the first option is unrealistic. Structured institutions generally are survival-oriented. When the purposes which gave rise to them cease to be meaningful, the institutions merely generate new or modified purposes justifying their continued existence. Thus, there is little likelihood that the Brethren in Christ will gradually fade into oblivion.

History also indicates that the Brethren are unlikely to merge with another denomination in the foreseeable future. This would be feasible only if they became willing to discard significant elements of either their Pietism or their Anabaptism. Recent General Conferences and Brethren in Christ data in *Anabaptists Four Centuries Later* reveal that these respective elements continue to play vital, if sometimes discordant, roles in the life of the brotherhood.[1] Under these circumstances, the Brethren are not likely to take seriously the expressions of merger interest which surface among a few members from time to time.[2]

The foregoing considerations lead the historian to anticipate that the Brethren will continue indefinitely as a separate body, although this does not preclude the possibility of defections by dissatisfied minority groups.[3] So far, however, membership losses in the era of change which began at the mid-century have been very limited.

This unity of the brotherhood during an era of sweeping change merits further historical study, but present data make clear that the gradual transition in group attitudes and life-style was facilitated by enlarging the sphere of individual and congregational discretion. Many practices once enforced by group action through legislation or social pressure became matters of individual or local group conscience. This moved the point of tension in Brethren life to the capacity of members to accept with goodwill and brotherly love other members with whom they differed seriously about aspects of Christian faith and life.

The success of the Brethren in achieving mutual acceptance in spite of these individual differences poses another complex question of interest to the historian. For many years prior to the 1950s, the brotherhood gradually enlarged the sphere of individual and local area prerogatives. This trend, which accelerated in that decade, narrowed the scope of values common to most members. Is it now approaching to the point at which the statement "I am a Brethren in Christ" will cease to have substantive meaning?

Both historical sources and contemporary observations indicate that this point has not been reached nor is it likely to be in the foreseeable future. A recent sociological study of thirty geographically representative Brethren in Christ congregations in the United States and Canada reveals considerable congruence of belief about certain long-standing positions of the brotherhood. For example, when the respondents, a cross-section of age groups, were asked what position they would take if subject to a military draft, sixty-seven percent opted for alternate service, twelve percent for noncombatant service, and only eight percent for regular military service. One percent would refuse induction and twelve percent were uncertain of their response.[4]

This sociological study did not measure Brethren attitudes toward some of their other historic doctrines such as nonconformity to the world. That particular doctrine rested originally upon a sharply defined church-world dichotomy and resulted in a concerted effort to promote a nonconformist life-style affecting person, home, conveyance, relationships, and activities. Observation of contemporary brotherhood practices reveals that individualism and localism have replaced general consensus in the outworking of this doctrine. If, for example, there is anything inconsistent about a member driving to a feet-washing service in a luxury car, the person who does so would likely dismiss questions of consistency as indicating inappropriate concern about the exercise of his or her personal discretion.

These data lead the historian to conclude that the contemporary Brethren in Christ are more strongly attached to some of their original roots than to others. They also suggest, however, that the brotherhood has retained a greater measure of self-identity than the casual observer might expect.

The indefinite continuation of this self-identity cannot be taken for granted. Several forces which could weaken it illustrate the problem.

First, contemporary society is permeated by powerful influences of materialism, hedonism, and moral relativism. Churches must inevitably confront these influences, especially as they receive new members with little or no Christian background or previous commitment to absolute spiritual and moral values. All of these influences come to focus in a pervasive individualism which poses a serious threat to the concept of the church as a visible, disciplined community. The spirit of individualism previously received theological reinforcement among the Brethren when they endorsed second-work holiness.[5] Now, furthermore, the brotherhood confronts the contemporary climate of secularistic individualism. In today's world, increasing numbers of people assert the right to do their "own thing" without regard to any general normative standards of right and wrong.

In the second place, a single generation of Brethren adjusted to the implications of the sweeping changes made by General Conference during the 1950s and early 1960s. These members entered that period of transition with deep attachment to the brotherhood; often they supported or opposed change because of their church loyalties. Now, as the number of members from that generation declines in proportion to new members being received, the future stability of the Brethren movement will increasingly depend upon the attachment of these new members to historic values of the group.

The problem of assimilating new members from widely different backgrounds is complicated by the fact that the Brethren in Christ cannot provide their own seminary. As a result, they must rely upon the teaching of ministers prepared in a variety of theological traditions and also upon a growing number of pastors crossing over from other denominations. Furthermore, a decreasing percentage of Brethren young people enroll in the church colleges which once played a predominant role in unifying the brotherhood.[6] These circumstances create new dimensions for the task of nurturing unity and church loyalty among future generations of Brethren members.

The observer of current problems and pressures among the Brethren must also consider countervailing forces with potential to strengthen the unity of the movement. One of these is expanding memberships bringing new blood, zeal, and talents into the congregations. Among these new members are those who are genuinely interested in historic Brethren values; in some cases they were attracted to the brotherhood by those very values. Pastors who are able to speak clearly about the self-identity of the Brethren in Christ may find some of their new converts to be the most open-minded and open-hearted of their listeners.

Another factor which can help to unify the brotherhood is growing interest in the historical development of its thought and life. Any group needs to know where it has come from if it is to make intelligent decisions about where it is going. When General Conference created the Brethren in Christ Archives in 1952, the resulting accumulation of historical records provided a base for scholarly research in the history and life of the church. The fruits of this research, which are being made available through the Brethren in Christ Heritage Series and other literature, offer the membership an increasing source of insights for decision-making.[7]

A third circumstance favoring unity of the Brethren in the crucial years ahead is their increasing capacity to view less emotionally the frustrations and controversies of the mid-century. That period can thus be evaluated with more objective detachment, which facilitates a fresh approach to the quest for brotherhood self-identity.

This more relaxed psychological climate is illustrated by collaboration of the Brethren in Christ with other Historic Peace Churches in recent publication of *The Foundation Series*, a Sunday school curriculum for the lower grades. Such a project would have been unthinkable two decades ago, when the roots of the brotherhood in Anabaptism seemed to be weakening. Brethren members who have worked on this curriculum perceive it as a means to strengthen those roots without repudiating the historic linkage of the denomination to Pietism.[8]

A fourth unifying influence in contemporary Brethren life is annual regional conferences and campmeetings. While the former are business oriented and the latter accentuate piety more than obedience, they both provide important fellowship occasions where members from many congregations come to know and appreciate each other.

One of the strongest unifying forces in the life of the brotherhood is the biennial General Conference. Congregations may differ in the degree to which they are guided by the rulings of this highest legislative authority, but their representatives are present to share in debate and voting which produce denominational policy. The resulting awareness of general brotherhood sentiment cannot easily be disregarded.

Observers of recent Conferences have been impressed by the mutual respect and brotherly concern which characterize debates involving serious differences of opinion and conviction. The traditional expression "Brother Moderator," addressed to the presiding officer by any member who wishes to speak, continues to symbolize the reality that Conference is not merely a legislative body but also a visible demonstration of the spirit of brotherhood.[9]

This juxtaposition of forces threatening and sustaining their church unity is not a new experience for the Brethren in Christ. What makes the present situation unprecedented is the accelerating rate of social change and the growing complexities of contemporary life. In such a context, the price of a clear sense of self-identity for any institution or group is constant vigilance and perennial wrestling with the questions: "Who are we and where are we going?"

In recent years the Brethren have neither ignored these questions nor dealt systematically with them. Some evidence suggests a growing awareness of need to explore the historic piety-obedience synthesis to determine possible continuities and discontinuities between the two theological traditions involved. The *Evangelical Visitor*, as the voice of the whole brotherhood, is focussing some of the crucial issues. Also, in the latter part of the 1960s, leadership workshops on the Brethren concepts of

Christian experience and the church created forums for dialogue outside of the legislative context of General Conference.

During the past several years, Messiah College and Roxbury Holiness Camp have shared in efforts to help clarify the Brethren in Christ faith. The College, for example, sponsored a study conference in which a Wesleyan scholar examined the Anabaptist tradition and an Anabaptist scholar examined the Wesleyan tradition. It has also restructured its theological faculty to provide better scholarly balance between the Anabaptist and Wesleyan Holiness positions. Roxbury Holiness Camp has contributed to this balance by funding an annual Wesleyan Holiness Lectureship on the Messiah College campus.

In summary, historical studies have reconstructed the presuppositions of the founders of the Brethren in Christ and have traced the resulting society through its two-hundred-year history. These studies have also identified forces which can undermine the stability and unity of the brotherhood, as well as other forces moving the Brethren toward strength and unity.

At this point the historian must step aside. He cannot foresee which set of countervailing forces will prevail. The self-identity of the Brethren has not been lost, but it is in flux. It can be clarified and strengthened by reappraisal and reaffirmation of the longstanding commitment to the piety-obedience synthesis. If that process does not occur, or if it leads to rejection of the synthesis, some other basis for the denomination's self-identity may be found.

The Brethren have shown significant staying power through a period of two hundred years. Although they have made many important changes, they have retained a distinctiveness identifiable by the historian. If used wisely, time remains to assure substantive meaning for the statement "I am a Brethren in Christ."

NOTES:

[1]*General Conference Minutes,* 1974, 1976; Kauffman and Harder, *Anabaptists Four Centuries Later,* chs. 5-9.

[2]The United Zion Church has a broadly comparable faith, but Chapter VI records the failure of several attempts to reunite the two bodies.

[3]Several such defections occurred during the past two decades.

[4]Kauffman and Harder, *Anabaptists Four Centuries Later,* p. 133.

[5]See Chapter XI.

[6]In Canada, Niagara Christian College continues to maintain a high percentage of Brethren in Christ students. Roy V. Sider to C. O. Wittlinger July 21, 1977. In the United States, however, Messiah College enrollment of Brethren in Christ students has not been keeping pace with either the growth of the institution or the growth of the denomination.

[7]The Brethren in Christ Heritage Series is published by Evangel Press, Nappanee, Indiana. At present it includes the following: Norman A. Bert, *Adventure in Discipleship;* Martin H. Schrag and John K. Stoner, *The Ministry of Reconciliation;* Owen H. Alderfer, *Called to Obedience;* Harvey Sider, *The Church in Mission.*

[8]John Arthur Brubaker, "Foundations for Faith," *Visitor,* XC (March 10, 1977), pp. 4-5; Helmut Harder and John E. Zercher, "The Bible and the Foundation Series," *Visitor,* XC (July 10, 1977), pp. 6-7.

[9]Other unifying factors include ministers' retreats and seminars, clusters of Brethren in Christ students at the two remaining church schools, committees of the General and Regional Conferences, etc.

Appendix A

A Copy of the Confession of Faith of the Brethren*

We believe and confess a Triune, Everlasting and Almighty Being, and that a Holy, Almighty God has been from eternity, and is, and will remain, and has provided Jesus Christ as Savior of mankind before the foundation of the world; and afterward Man was created in His image; and through the devil's envy he reverted to death; thus He promised him that he was to tread upon the serpent's head; and He appeared in the fulness of time, giving for the Redemption of men favor, honor, esteem, body and blood. He reconciled God and offered a sacrifice that holds good forever, so that all who believe on Him shall not be lost, but shall have eternal life. This has all happened outside of ourselves, but to reveal this in us there appeared the healing Grace of God to convict us and to teach us that we confess that we have by nature a heart averse from God, devious and sinful. If this is confessed and acknowledged, it works a regret and sorrow and inner soul-pains; in short, the Light reveals to us the Fall into which Adam and we all have fallen; and this causes a longing, a praying, a weeping, and a calling to the promised Savior, to the World-Messiah, who died bleeding before such poor sinners. Into such an open, poor sinner's heart the Lord Jesus will and can come, holding the communion meal; that is, to bestow comfort, peace, love and trust. Then the record of sins as well as the guilt of Adam is stricken out, he receives comfort and forgiveness of sins and eternal life. A poor sinner feels and experiences that; and there the living Faith has its beginning, for Faith is a positive confidence. Here his name is written in the Book of Life, when the poor sinner offers himself obediently and subjects himself to live for the Lord Jesus and to be true from now on—to the One who has accepted him in adoption. So we confess that to be a new birth, revival of the mind, revival of the Holy Spirit. Here the Lord Jesus Christ has become a Redeemer, therefore He will be and is to be a pattern, and because children love the one who bore them, so also they love the one who is born from him; and we recognize that to be a believing community through the unity of the Spirit, which is the first and real reception in faith in the community. If this is lacking, there will be a deficiency and the Water cannot give it or make it good; and because we have said the Lord Jesus has become a pattern for us, so we believe and acknowledge from the pattern in the Written Word and through the illumination of the Good Spirit that the Lord Jesus Christ instituted and commanded, as an outer sign for such newborn children, the outer baptism of water, which He himself and His apostles and the first churches practised, thereby renouncing the devil and the world and all sinful living by means of a threefold baptism in water in the name of the Father, Son, and Holy Spirit, as a sign of the burial. We believe and confess also that basically all awakened souls, becoming believers through true repentance, who were baptized in belief on Jesus, are included in Zion, and out of this Spiritual Congregation or Church are born as new men, as the dew out of the glow of morning. We also believe that the Lord Jesus instituted the communion meal and practised it with His disciples with bread and wine in the last night of agony, when He was betrayed; this they were to commemorate and after His departure they did commemorate His broken body and His shed blood, wherein also His followers stand constantly in the teaching in the Communion, in bread-breaking, in prayer and in taking the elements with steadfast hearts, praying to God with joy. Furthermore we see, believe and acknowledge that the Lord Jesus Christ at and during His communion meal, by washing His disciples' feet, has established, practised, and ordered it to be practised, as a sign of true humility and abasement out of love and obedience to Jesus, our pattern. Herein has man entered into adoption by God, yes, inheritance of the Grace, shoots on the Vine, members in the body of Jesus Christ. We also recognize a growth according to the Holy Scriptures—cleansed, healed, and made blessed through the bath of re-birth and renewing of the Holy Spirit. To this end means are necessary, public as well as private—public assemblages where the Word is brought for penance-calling, and private where such children often gather and reveal to each other, filially, one to the other. From this love grows and faith, and confidence is strengthened, because such children are exposed to many temptations and when through filial revelation the craftiness of the devil is discovered, then one can talk openheartedly with the other so that the body of Christ is renewed, and because such children are still in flesh and blood, a Christian regulation is necessary as in the household of God, according to the Scripture, Matth. 18; and furthermore, because such children are bound through love to watch out for each other, we consider it necessary and decided that nobody in important affairs should do anything without brotherly advice, such as marry, or change his dwelling, buy land, or whatever important may occur. We also acknowledge a ban or separation of offending members, yet with a difference as above noted in Matth. 18. If a brother sins against you in small affairs and wishes to show submission, he may be addressed in filial love, not aggressively and not in childish talk. If, however, the accused brother or sister cannot understand it, let it be said to one or two and lastly to the congregation. If he is not agreeable, then consider him as a heathen and a publican. But as for such as let themselves be called brethren or sisters, according to 1 Cor. 5:11: if they, however fall into vice, there is no need of the above brotherly investigation, but they are to be given over to judgment, to which they already really have reverted. Mark the expressions of Paul: "We bid you in the name of our Lord Jesus Christ that ye withdraw yourselves from every brother who walketh disorderly 2 Thess. 3:6-14. Have nothing to do with him, so that he may become shame-red." "Now I have written to you that ye shall have nothing to do with him, not even to eat with them who are so idolatrous or have fallen into vice, to avoid them completely with hand and kiss, in eating and drinking," until the time of true repentance, sorrow and penance; "however, keep him not as an enemy, but admonish him as a brother," be help to him in need, in order to move him with love. If true repentance then follows, sorrow, penance and submission, so that they again in Jesus' blood have found forgiveness for their past sins, then also the members will again, through acquaintance with them, feel the unity of the Spirit; and they shall again be received openly to Communion, comforted and strengthened, so that they do not sink into excessive sadness. 2 Cor. 2:7. What, however, concerns other grounds, such as child baptism and unregenerate baptism, we leave to those who can satisfy themselves with them; where the teaching of the Lord Jesus and His apostles is silent, there we will also be silent. We also maintain that when believing persons, who have united themselves with God and their soul-bridegroom, are joined in matrimony, they are joined in eternity, in righteousness and uprightness, in grace and compassion. Hosea 2. Should, however, a person come to new life or to reconciliation with Christ but be not yet baptized, and yet not contrary, he also has admission to marriage, for when souls are received by God we are also willing to receive them, even children of Brethren, when the elders are obedient and follow: because children stand under the elders, the elders under the congregation, the congregation under Christ, and everything is right and proper in its order. So the congregation can join their youth in marriage with advice, and they will not be sent out into the world; and it is our heart's wish and prayer to God the All-Highest that each first should have spiritual marriage with Jesus, the soul-bridegroom, and then the outward or body marriage. We also learn from the doctrine of the Lord Jesus that swearing of pledges is forbidden, therefore it shall be forbidden to us also. Matt. 5:34. Therefore it is also completely forbidden to bear the sword for revenge or defence. Verses 39, 40. We also learn from the doctrine of the Lord Jesus and His apostles that it is forbidden to any member or follower of Jesus Christ to occupy authoritative offices, therefore it is and shall be forbidden to us. We are not to withstand authority, but be obedient in all that is right and good, paying them tax and toll and protection-money, because Paul calls it God's servant (Rom. 13); so we see that God rules all nature, and has men who rule nature, and this is for the benefit of the children of God, else it would be still more difficult to live in this world; therefore Paul commands us to pray for them, that they may perform their duty loyally, so that the children of God under them may lead a quiet and blessed life. But we shall not use them for power; for the rest, we wish in God, the All-Highest, that He might build His congregation and plant and hold it in sound growth, that we also can be green sprouts on the vine and remain in all length of Eternity in Jesus Christ. Amen.

The above is and was signed in the name of the congregation by

Johannes Meÿer
Johannes Funk
Samuel Bentzner
Jacob Engel
Stofel Hollinger
Philip Stern
Johannes Greider
Benjamin Beÿer

*Translated from the German script by William M. Meikle of Harrisburg, Pennsylvania. See Chapter II for information about this document.

Appendix B

Geographical Distribution by Counties of 864 Brethren in Christ Households in the United States and Canada in 1880*

Illinois (68)

Carroll 27
Clark 2
Edgar 4
Ogle 28
Stevenson 7

Indiana (23)

Elkhart 17
Wayne 5
Viga 1

Iowa (11)

Benton 3
Huron 1
Tama 7

Kansas (15)

Dickinson 15

Maryland (7)

Washington 7

Michigan (5)

Kent 1
St. Joseph 4

New York (8)

Erie 8

Ohio (165)

Ashland 15
Clarke 20
Darke 4
Franklin 1
Green 1
Licking 4
Miami 35
Montgomery 13
Richland 9
Starke 35
Wayne 28

Ontario (146)

Haldimand	10
Huron	8
Ontario	1
Perth	1
Simcoe	8
Victoria	1
Waterloo	32
Welland	38
York	47

Pennsylvania (415)

Bedford	9
Blair	47
Bradford	2
Bucks	7
Centre	9
Chester	2
Clinton	3
Cumberland	26
Dauphin	27
Franklin	95
Fulton	1
Lancaster	105
Lebanon	23
Lycoming	3
Montgomery	31
Perry	18
Summerset	1
York	6

Wisconsin (1)

Green	1

Compiled from the Directory of the Brethren in Christ Commonly Called River Brethren Embracing the Names & Post Office Address of the Membership So Far As Has Been Reported in the United States and Canada (West Milton, Ohio: West Milton Argus Print, 1880). This is a list of households rather than of individual members. The figures are approximate; some households were omitted, and their number could have been comparatively large. Mr. Edward Phelps, R. P. L., Regional History Librarian of The University of Western Ontario, rendered valuable assistance in fixing the county locations of a number of these families in Ontario.

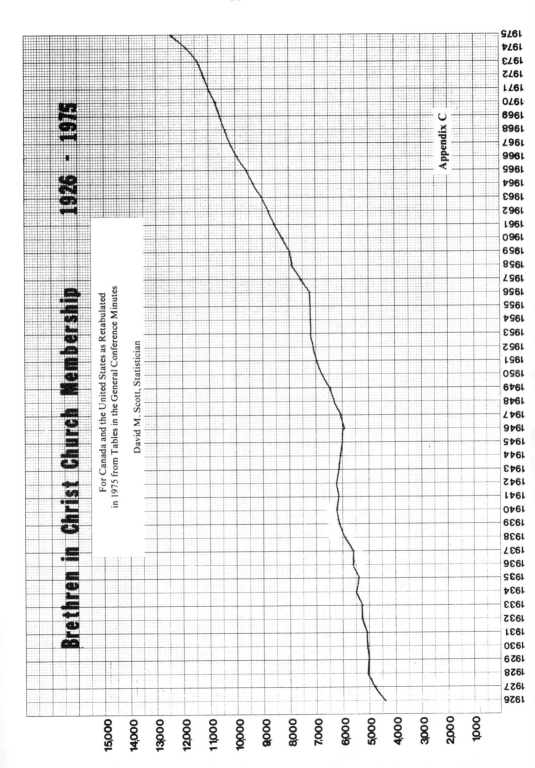

Brethren in Christ Church Membership 1926 - 1975

For Canada and the United States as Retabulated
in 1975 from Tables in the General Conference Minutes

David M. Scott, Statistician

Index

LIST OF ABBREVIATIONS

BIC	Brethren in Christ
EV	Evangelical Visitor
MC	Messiah College
MCC	Mennonite Central Committee
NAE	National Association of Evangelicals
NHA	National Holiness Association
NCC	Niagara Christian College
OORB	Old Order River Brethren